A Casebook on
Company Law

GW00726743

A Casebook on Company Law

Lyndon Mac Cann
B.A.(Mod) M.Litt, Barrister-at-Law

Butterworth (Ireland) Ltd
Dublin 1991

Republic of Ireland Butterworth (Ireland) Ltd, 16 Upper Ormond Quay. DUBLIN 7

United Kingdom Butterworth & Co (Publishers) Ltd, 88 Kingsway, LONDON WC2B 6AB
and
4 Hill Street, EDINBURGH, EH2 3JZ

Australia Butterworths Pty Ltd, SYDNEY, MELBOURNE, BRISBANE, ADELAIDE,
PERTH, CANBERRA and HOBART

Canada Butterworths Canada Ltd, TORONTO and VANCOUVER

Malaysia Malayan Law Journal Sdn Bhd, KUALA LUMPUR

New Zealand Butterworths of New Zealand Ltd, WELLINGTON and AUCKLAND

Puerto Rico Equity de Puerto Rico, Inc., HATO REY

Singapore Malayan Law Journal Pte Ltd, SINGAPORE

USA Butterworth Legal Publishers, AUSTIN, Texas; BOSTON,
Massachusetts; CLEARWATER, Florida (D & S Publishers); ORFORD,
New Hampshire (Equity Publishing); ST PAUL, Minnesota; and
SEATTLE, Washington.

All rights reserved. No part of this publication may be reproduced or transmitted in any form or
by any means, including photocopying and recording, without the written permission of the
copyright holder, application for which should be addressed to the publisher. Such written permission must also be obtained before any part of this publication is stored in a retrieval system
of any nature.

ISBN 1 85475 023 2

Published 1991

A CIP Catalogue record for this book is available from the British Library

© Butterworth (Ireland) Ltd

Typeset by Phoenix Photosetting, Chatham, Kent
Printed and bound in Great Britain by
Mackays of Chatham PLC, Chatham, Kent
Bookcover designed by Dante Design, Dublin. Ireland

To Nuala, Rebecca and Rachel

Foreword

Students entering a course of studies on Irish company law will begin by arming themselves with a copy of the Companies Act 1963. Having found that it has been amended and extended six times (twice in 1990 by two important statutes, the second of which having no less than 262 sections) aid and guidance will then be sought in an up-to-date text book on the subject. There will be found many references to a large body of case-law buried in law reports of the nineteenth and twentieth centuries of both the Irish and English courts. It is at this point that help from this volume will be welcomed. A good textbook is both a summary of, and guide to, the law with which it treats. A good casebook fulfills a different function. If well chosen and carefully edited a casebook makes readily accessible judgments and legal texts by which the knowledge and understanding of, and therefore the ability to remember, the law is greatly enhanced. This is such a volume.

The task of compiling a casebook on any legal subject is not an easy one. It becomes particularly difficult when the subject embraces so vast a volume of statute law and case law as company law does. What to select, what to omit, how to edit and summarise and paraphrase, how to present your material in an intelligible form, requires firstly a detailed knowledge of the law and its sources and secondly an informed appreciation of what is relevant to its understanding. Mr Mac Cann, as a practising lawyer and teacher of company law, has brought both to the compilation of the present volume.

The result of his labours (which I would estimate to have been immense and painstaking) will benefit practitioners as well as students. The busy practitioner may not want to read what *Blackstone* wrote about the nature of companies and corporations two centuries ago (although the serious student would do well to inquire) but he/she would certainly welcome ready access to both English and Irish judgments and may well require to know the up-to-date position on EC company directives. Mr Mac Cann has fulfilled these requirements. He has carefully and intelligently selected a number of the classical nineteenth century judgments by which the principles of company law were established or exemplified and all the important recent judgments in this country and in England by which new law has been developed or explained. His sources are not just printed sources for he has included a number of unreported judgments (including some which were only delivered a few months ago) which, notwithstanding the welcome improvements in law-reporting of recent years, have failed to find their rightful place in the printed reports. He has not reproduced any statute law (but that was not the purpose of his work), but he has given the text of a number of recent EC directives which are relevant to future developments in the law.

The Oireachtas, in recent times, has developed company law in ways carefully noted by Mr Mac Cann, partly to fulfill its EC obligations and partly as a response to a felt need to regulate more effectively the management of companies and to improve the machinery for the investigation of possible malpractice. How successful will the new legislation be? It is possible to gauge current attitudes by the frequency of references to 'shelf companies' which crops up in the course of cases touching on every part of the commercial spectrum, for this is a concept redolent of a somewhat cavalier approach to compliance with company-law obligations. If existing statutory regulation is not treated too seriously, if statutory meetings are not held and statutory returns are not made as required by long-standing laws, what chance is there that additional laws will be respected? The answer may in part depend on the efficacy on the new investigative powers and their deterrent effect on possible malefactors. But infringements of the law occur just as much from ignorance and/or indolence as from financial greed. It is here that this volume may prove helpful. There is a danger that the more the Oireachtas legislates the more arcane the subject on which it legislates becomes so that the non-specialist practitioner feels unqualified, and therefore reluctant, to advise and warn his clients of their statutory responsibilities. But company law is not a particularly difficult subject – there just happens to be a lot of it about. Now, for the first time in this country, there has been produced a volume in which have been collected a number of key judgments, a perusal of which will enable intelligent advice to be given on most problems on which most practitioners may be required to advise. Neither the busy practitioner or the concerned student will be required to master and remember all the contents of this volume – it is work of reference. But they will both find that its possession will lighten their respective labours and, dare I say it?, even make them enjoyable.

THE HIGH COURT   DECLAN COSTELLO
NOVEMBER 1991

Preface

Company Law never has been, and in all likelihood, never will be codified. It is a vast and voluminous subject, as daunting for the practitioner as for the student. For almost twenty years the only statute on the subject was the Companies Act 1963. However, in the last ten years there has been a veritable flourish of Companies Acts, often lengthy and complicated and to a large extent necessitated by our membership of the European Community. These enactments, however, provide only a partial statement of company law. In order to fully understand the subject, both at an academic and a practical level, it is necessary to have recourse to the wealth of caselaw stretching back over more than a century. This task is further complicated by the fact that much of the relevant caselaw is not Irish in origin, coming to a large extent from England and to a lesser extent, from other Commonwealth jurisdictions. One should not, however, underestimate the amount of Irish caselaw which has arisen on the subject of companies and indeed in recent years there has been a considerable boom in litigation on the subject.

Because of this growth in domestic caselaw, English company law casebooks, formerly the mainstay of Irish students, have become less and less relevant and in some respects no longer have any bearing at all in this jurisdiction. Although there are now many fine Irish company law textbooks, they should not be seen as a substitute for the reading of the judgments to which they refer. Frequently, one can only properly understand a legal principle by referring to the judgments on which that principle is based.

The purpose of this casebook is to bring together extracts from the leading cases on Irish company law. As far as possible, domestic cases have been quoted in preference to their foreign counterparts. However, in those areas where there are still no Irish authorities, English or Commonwealth decisions have been quoted instead.

Despite the constraints of space, an attempt has been made to provide some notes and comment on the more important areas as well as providing some discussion of the main provisions of the Companies Acts. This book should not, however, be regarded as a complete guide to Irish company law. For a fuller analysis of more detailed points, the reader should refer to one of the leading textbooks. In this regard, constant reference is made throughout the book to the relevant sections of the second edition of Mr Justice Keane's outstanding work, *Company Law in the Republic of Ireland*. This should hopefully be of benefit for the practitioner as well as the student.

The Acts themselves have not been reproduced since it is to be assumed that the reader will have access to his own copies.

My thanks are due to a number of people who have helped in the preparation and launch of this book. I am extremely grateful to Mr Justice Costello for agreeing to provide a foreword. Particular thanks are also due to Mr Justice Keane who read the initial drafts of the book and who made several very helpful suggestions.

I also wish to express my thanks to Jennifer Aston and the staff of the Law Library, as well as Jonathan Armstrong and Nigel Cochrane of the King's Inns Library.

Special thanks are also due to Larry Ennis, Finola O'Sullivan, Thérèse Carrick and all the staff of Butterworth (Ireland) Ltd and also to Maura Hennessey for their patience, help and support at all stages of production.

Finally, a very special word of thanks to my wife, Nuala, who has been a constant source of encouragement and assistance in the preparation of this book. She undertook the unenviable task of typing the initial drafts, as well as helping in the preparation of the Tables and Index. Responsibility for any errors is, however, solely mine.

The law is as stated as of 30 June 1991.

Lyndon Mac Cann,
Law Library,
Four Courts,
Dublin 7.

30 June 1991.

Acknowledgements

I am grateful to the following for kindly allowing the reproduction of copyright material: the Incorporated Council of Law Reporting for Ireland for the *Irish Reports*; The Round Hall Press for the *Irish Law Reports Monthly* and the *Irish Law Times Reports*; the Controller of the Stationery Office, Dublin for excerpts from statutory material and from the Report of the Company Law Committee; the Office for Official Publications of the European Communities for extracts from the EEC Treaty and from Council Directives to be found in the Official Journal of the European Communities, L 65, 14 March 1968 (68/151/EEC), L 193, 18 July 1983, (83/349/EEC), L 395, 30 December 1989 (89/666/EEC, 89/667/EEC); the President of the High Court for unreported High Court judgments; the Jurist Publishing Company for the *Irish Jurist Reports*; the Incorporated Council of Law Reporting for Northern Ireland for the *Northern Ireland Law Reports*; Butterworth Law Publishers Ltd and for the *All England Law Reports*, the *Law Times Reports* and the *Butterworths Company Law Cases*; the Incorporated Council of Law Reporting for England and Wales for the *Law Reports* and the *Weekly Law Reports*; Her Majesty's Stationery Office for English statutory material; and Butterworths of New Zealand Ltd and the New Zealand Council of Law Reporting for the *New Zealand Law Reports*.

Contents

Contents

CHAPTER 9: Capital

CHAPTER 10: Shares

CHAPTER 11: Borrowing, debentures and charges

Contents

Contents

CHAPTER 20: Winding up: part II

CHAPTER 21: Companies under protection of the court

Table of statutes

Table of statutes

Table of cases

(Paragraph references printed in **bold** type in this table indicate where the case is set out in part or in full)

Table of cases

Chapter 1

COMPANIES AND OTHER FORMS OF BUSINESS ORGANISATIONS

WHAT IS A COMPANY?

[1.01]   There is no strict legal meaning of the word 'company', although attempts have been made at a definition.[1] It is normally taken to mean an association or body of persons having some common object or objects. There are two broad categories of company. The first is the unincorporated company such as partnership, which does not itself have legal personality, although its members may be legal or natural persons. The second is the incorporated company which does have a legal personality separate from those of its constituent members.[2]

1 See generally *Keane* chapter 1.
2 Evans *What is A Company?* (1910) 26 LQR 259.

HOW IS A COMPANY CREATED?[1]

[1.02]   Corporate status may only be granted by the State. Prior to 1921 it could be conferred by Royal Charter, by special Act of Parliament or by registration under the Companies Acts. It would seem that since the establishment of the Free State only the latter two methods remain. It is possible that the royal prerogative to create companies by charter was carried over on the formation of the State and is now vested in the Government pursuant to Art 49.1 and Art 49.2. However, no attempt has ever been made to use such a prerogative. Doubts have been cast as to whether prerogatives emanating from the Crown were carried over into the Constitution at all.[2] On the other hand, s 377(4) of the Principal Act seems to indicate that there is the power to grant charters, albeit in limited circumstances. The sub-section provides that s 377 which applies certain provisions of the Act to unregistered companies, including companies incorporated by Charter 'shall not . . . restrict the power of the Government to grant a charter in lieu of or supplementary to any such charter as aforesaid . . .' Very few companies are now created by special Act of the Oireachtas and where formed, they are normally given monopolies to run undertakings of national importance or to run public utilities. Examples include Aer Rianta Teoranta and Telecom Eireann. The most common method of incorporation at the present day is by registration pursuant to the Companies Acts 1963 to 1990.[3]

Where the object is gain, then with certain exceptions, it is prohibited to form a company, association or partnership consisting of more than twenty persons unless it is registered as a company under the Companies Acts 1963 to 1990 or is formed under some other statute.[4] No unincorporated company can lawfully carry on the business of banking if its membership exceeds ten persons.[5]

[1.03] The right of free membership given to citizens under Art 40.6 of the Constitution does not include a right to incorporate that association. Corporate status is still a privilege which can only be granted by the State.

1 See *Keane*, at paras **1.01**, **1.05–1.07**, **1.10–18**.
2 See *Byrne v Ireland* [1972] IR 241; *Webb v Ireland* (Supreme Court) [1985] IR 353. See also Hogan & Morgan [1985] IR 353, *Administrative Law* (London 1986), pp 387 & 389.
3 Since the Companies Act 1963, which is the Principal Act there have been six amending statutes, one in each of 1977, 1982, 1983 and 1986 and two in 1990. In this book references to the Principal Act are to the Companies Act 1963.
4 S 376 of the Principal Act, as amended by s 13 of the 1982 Act.
5 S 372 of the Principal Act.

Private Motorists Provident Society Ltd v Attorney-General (High Court, July 15 1981)

[1.04] **Carroll J.** In my opinion the right [under Art 40.6] is a right of citizens (in the plural) to form as association or associations with each other and is not intended to include the right to form bodies with corporate existence under statute. The latter is a statutory right, given by statute and controlled by statute.

Notes
The Companies Acts do not provide a complete code. Instead one must also look to caselaw for guidance.

The legal nature of an incorporated company

See Blackstone, *Commentaries on the Laws of England*, London, 1825 (18th ed), vol 1.

[1.05] We have hitherto considered persons in their natural capacities, and have treated of their rights and duties. But, as all personal rights die with the person; and, as the necessary forms of investing a series of individuals, one after another, with the same identical rights, would be very inconvenient, if not impossible; it has been found necessary, when it is for the advantage of the public to have any particular rights kept on foot and continued, to constitute artificial persons, who may maintain a perpetual succession, and enjoy a kind of legal immortality . . .

These artificial persons are called bodies politic, bodies corporate, (corpora corporata) or corporations; of which there is a great variety subsisting, for the advancement of religion, of learning, and of commerce; in order to preserve entire and for ever those rights and immunities, which if they were granted only to those individuals of which the body corporate is composed, would upon their death be utterly lost and extinct . . .

[1.06] But when they are consolidated and united into a corporation, they and their successors are then considered as one person in law: as one person they have one will, which is collected from the sense of the majority of the individuals: this one will may establish rules and orders for the regulation of the whole, which are a sort of municipal laws of this little Republic; or rules and statutes may be prescribed to it at it's creation, which are then in the place of natural laws: the privileges and immunities, the estates and possessions of the corporation, when once vested in them, will be for ever vested, without any new conveyance to new successions; for all the individual members that have existed from the foundation to the present time, or that shall ever hereafter exist, are but one person in law, a person that never dies: in like manner as the river Thames is still the same river, though the parts which compose it are changing every instant . . .

The honour of originally inventing these political constitutions belongs to the Romans . . .

[1.07] They were afterwards much considered by the civil law, in which they were called universitates, as forming one whole out of many individuals; or collegia, from being gathered together; they were adopted also by the canon law, for the maintenance of ecclesiastical discipline: and from them our spiritual corporations are derived. But our laws have considerably refined and improved upon the invention . . .

[1.08] The first division of corporation is into aggregate and sole. Corporations aggregate consist of many persons united together into one society, and are kept up by a perpetual succession of members, so as to continue for ever: of which kind are the mayor and commonality of a city, the head and fellows of a college, the dean and chapter of a cathedral church. Corporation sole consists of one person only and his successors, in some particular station who are incorporated by law, in order to give them some legal capacities and advantages, particularly that of perpetuity, which in their natural persons they could not have had. In this sense the King is a sole corporation; so is a bishop; so are some deans and secundaries, distinct from their several chapters; and so are a parson and vicar . . .

[1.09] Lay corporations are of two sorts, civil and eleemosynary. The civil are such as are erected for a variety of temporal purposes. The King, for instance, is made a corporation to prevent in general the possibility of an interregnum, or vacancy of the throne, and to preserve the possessions of

3

the crown entire; for immediately upom the demise of one king, his successor is, as we have formerly seen, in full possession of the regal rights and dignity. Other lay corporations are erected for the good government of a town or particular district, as a mayor and commonalty, bailiff and burgesses, or the like; some for the advancement and regulation of manufactures and commerce; as the trading companies of London and other towns: and some for the better carrying on of divers special purposes . . .

[1.10] Corporations, by the civil law seem to have been erected by the mere act, and voluntary association of their members: provided such convention was not contrary to law, for then it was illicitum collegium. It does not appear that the prince's consent was necessary to be actually given to the foundation of them; but merely that the original founders of these voluntary and friendly societies (for they were little more than such) should not establish any meetings in opposition to the laws of the state . . .

But, with us in England, the King's consent is absolutely necessary to the erection of any corporation, either impliedly or expressly given . . . The methods by which the King's consent is expressly given, are either by act of parliament or charter. By act of parliament, of which the royal assent is a necessary ingredient, corporations may undoubtedly be created . . .

[1.11] When a corporation is erected, a name must be given to it; and by that name alone it must sue and be sued, and do all legal acts; though a very minute variation therein is not material. Such name is the very being of it's constitution; and, though it is the will of the King that erects the corporation, yet the name is the knot of it's combination, without which it could not perform it's corporate functions . . .

[1.12] After a corporation is so formed and named, it acquires many powers, rights, capacities and incapacities, which we are next to consider. Some of these are necessarily and inseparably incident to every corporation; which incidents, as soon as a corporation is duly erected, are tacitly annexed of course. As, (1) To have perpetual succession. This is the very end of it's incorporation; and therefore all aggregate corporations have a power necessarily implied of electing members in the room of such as go off. (2) To sue or be sued, implead or be impleaded, grant or receive, by its corporate name, and do all other acts as natural persons may. (3) To purchase lands, and hold them, for the benefit of themselves and their successors; which two are consequential to the former. (4) To have a common seal. (5) To make by-laws or private statutes for the better government of the corporation; which are binding upon themselves, unless contrary to the laws of the land, and then they are void. This is also included by law in the very act of incorporation: for as natural reason is given to the natural body for the governing of it, so by-laws or statutes are a sort of political reason to govern the body politic. And this right of making by-laws for their own government, not contrary to the law of the land, was allowed by the law of the twelve tables of Rome . . .

[1.13] There are also certain privileges and disabilities that attend an aggregate corporation. It must always appear by attorney; for it cannot appear in person, being, as Sir Edward Coke says, invisible, and existing only in intendment and consideration of law. It can neither maintain or be made defendant to, an action of battery or such like personal injuries: for a corporation can neither beat nor be beaten, in its body politic. Neither can it be committed to prison: for its existence being ideal, no man can apprehend or arrest it. And therefore also it cannot be outlawed; for outlawry always supposes a precedent right of arresting, which has been defeated by the parties absconding, and that also a corporation cannot do: for which reasons the proceedings to compel a corporation to appear to any suit by attorney are always by distress on their lands and goods. Neither can a corporation be excommunicated: for it has no soul, as is gravely observed by Sir Edward Coke . . .

In aggregate corporations also, the act of the major part is esteemed the act of the whole . . . The general duties of all bodies politic, considered in their corporate capacity, may, like those of natural persons, be reduced to this single one; that of acting up to the end or design, whatever it be, for which they were created by their founder.

Machine Watson & Co Ltd v Department of Trade and Industry and related appeals [1989] 3 All ER 523 (House of Lords)

[1.14] The International Tin Council (ITC) was created and continued in force by treaties known as International Tin Agreements. The parties to the treaties and members of the ITC were sovereign states, including the United Kingdom, Ireland and the European Economic Community. The Sixth International Agreement was concluded in 1982 and provided that the ITC 'shall have legal personality'. Each member was represented in the ITC by one delegate. Its headquarters were in London and its main objective was to regulate the world production and consumption of tin in an orderly manner, if necessary by the imposition of export controls, and to maintain a measure of stability in the world price of tin. Pursuant to Art 5 of the International Tin Council (Immunities and Privileges) Order 1972, the ITC was stated to have the 'legal capacities of a body corporate'. After the financial collapse of the ITC a number of actions were commenced in which it was claimed, inter alia, that the individual members of the ITC had either primary or secondary liability for its debts (as to which see chapter 8, *infra*). One of the grounds upon which the plaintiffs claimed that the members were personally liable for the debts of the ITC was that the ITC had no legal personality distinct from its members; that the members were an unincorporated association who traded in the name of the ITC; that the plaintiff's contracts, although made nominally with the ITC were made directly with the members, and that the members were accordingly jointly and severally liable as trading partners.

[1.15] Lord Templeman: Submission A relies on the fact that the 1972 order did not incorporate the ITC but only conferred on the ITC the legal capacities of a body corporate. Therefore it is said under the laws of the United Kingdom the ITC has no separate existence as a legal entity apart from its members; the contracts concluded in the name of the ITC were contracts by the member states.

Submission A reduces the 1972 order to impotence. The appellants argue that the 1972 order was only intended to facilitate the carrying on in the United Kingdom of the activities of 23 sovereign states and the EEC under the collective name of 'the International Tin Council'. Legislation is not necessary to enable trading to take place under a collective name. The appellants suggested that the 1972 order was intended to enable the member states to hold land in the United Kingdom in the name of a nominee. Legislation is not necessary for that purpose either. The appellants then suggested that the 1972 order was necessary to relieve the member states from a duty to register the collective name of the ITC and from complying with the other provisions of the Registration of Business Names Act 1916. This trivial suggestion was confounded when, at a late stage in the hearing, the 1916 Act (now repealed) was examined and found not to apply to an international organisation established by soverign states. The 1972 order did not confer on 23 soverign states and the EEC the rights to trade under a name and to hold land in the name of the ITC. The 1972 order conferred on the ITC the legal capacities of a body corporate. The appellants submitted that, if Parliament had intended to do more than endow 23 sovereign states and the EEC trading in this country with a collective name, then Parliament would have created the ITC a body corporate. But the government of the United Kingdom had by treaty concurred in the establishment of the ITC as an international organisation. Consistently with the treaty, the United Kingdom could not convert the ITC into a United Kingdom organisation. In order to clothe the ITC in the United Kingdom with legal personality in accordance with the treaty Parliament conferred on the ITC the legal capacities of a body corporate. The courts of the United Kingdom became bound by the 1972 order to treat the activities of the ITC as if those activities had been carried out by the ITC as a body incorporated under the laws of the United Kingdom. The 1972 order is inconsistent with any intention on the part of Parliament to oblige or allow the courts of the United Kingdom to consider the nature of an internation organisation. The 1972 order is inconsistent with any intention on the part of Parliament that creditors and courts should regard the ITC as a partnership between 23 soverign states and the EEC trading in the United Kingdom like any private partnership. The 1972 order is inconsistent with any intention on the part of Parliament that contracts made by the ITC with metal brokers, bankers, staff, landlords, suppliers of goods and services and others shall be treated by those creditors or by the court of the United Kingdom as contracts entered into by 23 sovereign states and the EEC. The 1972 order conferred on the ITC the legal capacities of a body corporate. Those capacities include the power to contract. The ITC entered into contracts with the appellants.

The appellants submitted that if there had been no 1972 order the courts would have been compelled to deal with the ITC as though it were a collective name for an unincorporated association. But the rights of the creditors of the ITC and the powers of the courts of the United Kingdom must depend upon the effect of the 1972 order and that order cannot be construed as if it did not exist. An international organisation might have been treated by the courts of the United Kingdom as an unincorporated association if the 1972 order had not been passed. But the 1972 order was passed. When the ITC exercised the capacities of a body corporate, the effects of that exercise was the same as the effect of the exercise of those capacities by a body corporate. The ITC cannot exercise the capacities of a body corporate and at the same time be treated as if it were an unincorporated association. The 1972 order brought into being an entity which must be recognised by the courts of the United Kingdom as a legal personality distinct in law from its membership and capable of entering into contracts as principal. None of the authorities cited by the appellants were of any assistance in construing the effects of the grant by Parliament of the legal capacities of a body corporate to an international organisation pursuant to a treaty obligation to confer legal personality on that organisation. In my opinion the effect is plain; the ITC is a separate legal personality distinct from its members.

The second argument of the appellants, which is known as submission B1, accepts that the ITC enjoys a separate legal existence apart from its constituent members but contends that a contract by the ITC involves a concurrent direct or guarantee liability on the members jointly and severally. This liability is said to flow from a general principle of law, that traders operating under a collective name incur a liability to third parties which can only be excluded by incorporation; the ITC has not been formally incorporated and therefore, it is said, the member states are liable concurrently. No authority was cited which supported the alleged general principle. On the contrary there is ample authority for the general proposition that in England no one is liable on a contract except the parties thereto. The only parties to the contracts between the appellants and the ITC were the appellants and the ITC. Members of a body corporate are not liable for the debts of a body corporate because the members are not parties to the corporation's contracts. The members states are not liable for the debts of the ITC because the members were not parties to the contracts of the ITC. It was said on behalf of the appellants that under the laws of Scotland, Germany, France, Puerto Rico and Jordan and elsewhere, recognition is accorded to 'mixed entities' as a description of associations which are legal entities but whose engagements, notwithstanding the separate legal personality of the associations, involve some form of liability of the members. Authorities were produced which demonstrate that by custom or by legislation the members of some corporations in some countries are not free from personal liability. But no such custom exists in the United Kingdom as a general rule and s 4 of the Partnership Act 1890, which preserves for a Scottish partnership some of the benefits of incorporation and some of the attributes of an unincorporated association, does not prove the existence of any general custom in any part of the United Kingdom, that members of a corporation or of a body analagous to corporations shall be liable for the debts of the corportion. Parliament, of course may provide that the members of a corporation shall bear liability for or shall be bound to contribute directly or indirectly to payment of the debts of the corporation to a limited or to an unlimited extent in accordance with express statutory provisions. The history of the Companies Acts illustrates the power of Parliament, if it pleases, to impose some liability on shareholders as a condition of the grant of incorporation. Parliament could have imposed some liability for the debts of the ITC on the member states. But Parliament passed the 1972 order which imposed no such liability. The 1972 order conferred on the ITC the capacities of a body corporate. Those capacities included the power to enter into contracts. In the absence of express parliamentary provision a contract entered into by the ITC does not involve any liability on any person who was not a party to the contract.'

Lord Oliver delivered a concurring judgment.

Lords Keith, Brandon and Griffiths concurred.

Notes

See also *Attorney-General v Nissan* [1969] 1 All ER 629 where Lord Pearce held that the United Nations was 'a unique legal person or corporation'. Lord Pearce was no doubt using the term 'corporation' in the loose sense; that is why he preferred it with the words 'a unique legal person'. But he clearly had no doubt that it was a legal entity.

For an extreme example of a case where legal personality was accorded to an artificial entity such that it could sue and be sued, and hold property, see Duff, *The Personality of an Idol* (1927) 3 CLJ 42.

HISTORY OF COMPANY LAW

Development to 1844[1]

[1.16]   The concept of an artificial entity having corporate status has its origins in Roman Law in the universitatas personarum.[2] This doctrine was continued by the Church in the middle ages. Under Canon Law each abbey, cloister, monastery, etc., was a legal entity having a corporate personality separate from those of its constituent members. In secular law the closest medieval comparison is the granting of corporate status to towns and cities by way of Royal Charter.

[1.17]   In the commercial sphere there was the commenda, a form of limited partnership. This was used mainly in the case of maritime travel. Commenda commonly consisted of a dormant partner and an active partner. The former, normally a financier, would put up the money for the voyage. If the enterprise failed he lost only the sum invested. If it was sucessful, he shared in the profits. The active partner, however, was a travelling merchant. It was he who made the voyage and it was he who was personally liable for all the debts of the enterprise. Similarly, he shared in the profits of the voyage, if successful.

Although the commenda was popular in medieval continental law, it never really took root in England. It was, however, adopted in Ireland by statute in 1781 (see para **1.28**), and only received statutory recognition in England more than a century later. The Limited Partnership Act 1907 forms the legislative basis for the modern limited partnership both in this jurisdiction and in England.

[1.18] Although the commenda equated more with the modern limited partnership, the Societas was the association which developed into the modern form of partnership. It was of a more permanent nature, with all the members being jointly and severally liable for all the debts of the firm. Each partner was also constituted the agent of the others in respect of acts carried out in the ordinary course of the business of the firm. The current legislative provisions regarding this type of firm are to be found in the Partnership Act 1890.

Neither the commenda nor the societas had corporate status. They were no more than collections of individuals bound together by a contract. Guilds of Merchants, on the other hand, could obtain corporate status by means of a Royal Charter. It is doubtful as to whether incorporation was really necessary in view of the fact that the members of the Guild still traded on their own account, albeit subject to the internal rules of the Guild.

However, the grant of a charter did have its advantages. The company so created was granted the privileges of a common seal and perpetual succession. In addition, it could own and deal in real property. It also had the power to make bye-laws. Such charters were commonly granted to confer on the company a monopoly in a particular sphere or market.

[1.19] The use of the charter to confer a monopoly became more widespread as colonialism developed. Companies trading abroad could be given a monopoly not only in a particular trade but also over a particular territory or market. These companies were given a quasi-governmental status having the power to set up local government and courts of law, to establish an army and to coin its own money for the area over which it was given control. The best known example of such a company is the East India Company which was granted such a charter in 1600. In return for the conferring of these extensive powers the company had to pay to the Crown fees or a share of the profits or both.

In these companies, each member could originally carry on trade privately, although there was also a joint stock to which members could, if they wished, subscribe varying amounts. This joint stock and the profits made from it were divided among the members of the company who had participated, after each voyage. However, by the middle of the seventeenth century members were prohibited from trading on their own account. All such activities had to be carried out by the company as a separate entity out of the joint stock subscribed by the members.

[1.20]   In the seventeenth century, Acts of Parliament began to replace Royal Charters as the method of incorporation for a company. Examples of companies set up by the Act during this period include the Bank of England, (1694) and the Bank of Scotland (1695). The Bank of Ireland was only incorporated by statute in 1781. (See para **1.26**).

Whether the company was set up by Charter or by Act of Parliament, it had full legal capacity. It could only act under seal. Shares in the company were generally freely transferable. Notably, the shareholders were not personally liable for the debts of the company unless the Act or Charter expressly provided for this. (See para **1.27**).

Alongside the incorporated joint stock companies, the societas was evolving along similar albeit slightly different lines. The societas had developed into a partnership in the shape of a large unincorporated joint stock company, the shares in which were freely transferable. These unincorporated joint stock companies raised capital by public subscription. They were managed by committees of directors. The company's assets were commonly settled on trustees who then administered them in accordance with the directions of the committee of directors.

Such companies commonly had a large membership which was constantly changing. In any action taken against the company it would be necessary to join all the members as parties. In many cases it would be virtually impossible to ascertain the identity of all these members thereby preventing the institution of any such action. Creditors of such companies could therefore encounter insurmountable difficulties in rendering the company itself or individual members personally liable for the company's debts.

[1.21]   During the first twenty years of the eighteenth century there was a rapid increase in the number of company flotations. Obtaining incorporation by means of an Act of Parliament or Royal Charter was a slow and expensive process. Many promoters, therefore, declined to incorporate their companies. In one case, for example, a company which intended to lend money on the security of land in Ireland acquired the Charter of the Sword Blade Company which had been formed to manufacture sword blades.

This sort of activity led to many cases of fraudulent or negligent promotion of companies. Consequently, action was needed to protect both potential investors in companies and the creditors of such companies.

Problems reached crisis point when the South Sea Company was formed to acquire almost the whole of the national debt. The company had hoped that by acquiring such an interest bearing loan where the debtor was the State, that this would provide a secure basis for raising further money to finance and extend its trade. Unfortunately for the company, it had hardly any trade to expand. In addition it had paid too much for the national debt. The company ran out of cash and ultimately collapsed. The failure of the South Sea Company had a knock-on effect, resulting in the collapse of many other companies qupted on the Stock Exchange.

[1.22] Parliament responded to the crisis by passing the Bubble Act 1720 (see para **1.25**). This Act described unincorporated joint stock companies as public nuisances and declared that they should be illegal and void. Furthermore, they were prohibited from pretending to be incorporated companies and from acting under defunct or obsolete charters. Such companies were further prohibited from raising money by public subscription and from creating transferable shares. Such unincorporated companies were not, however, prohibited by the Bubble Act if they were established prior to June 24, 1718. Although companies formed before this date were allowed to continue in business, many ultimately went bankrupt.

[1.23] Also exempted from the application of the Bubble Act were partnerships which had previously been allowed at common law. Using this exception, a number of what were known as 'deed of settlement companies' were formed. They were similar in nature to the old unincorporated joint stock companies. However, the legality of such deed of settlement companies was always in doubt. They were described by James LJ in *Smith v Anderson*[3] as '. . . a partnership which is constantly changing, a partnership today consisting of certain members, and tomorrow consisting of some only of these members along with others who have come in so that there will be a constant shifting of the partnership, a determination of the old and a creation of a new partnership, with the intention that so far as the partners can by agreement among themselves bring about such a result, the new partnership shall succeed to the assets and liabilities of the old partnership.'

Management of such companies would be delegated to a committee of directors and the property of the company would be vested in a body of trustees (some of whom might also be members of the committee of directors). The company would have a joint stock divided into a specified number of shares, to which members could subscribe.

The use of the deed of settlement company as a vehicle of commerce became quite widespread. Although companies incorporated under charter granted by the Crown or by Act of parliament continued to exist, it was only at the end of the eighteenth century, with the growth in canal building that Parliament made it less expensive and difficult to obtain a charter.

Although commonly used, the deed of settlement company had its disadvantages. An agreement between the members themselves would not suffice to relieve an outgoing member of liability for debts contracted or incurred during the period of his membership. In order to be relieved of such liability, it was necessary to obtain the consent of the creditor as well. This could prove to be a difficult if not impossible task.

[1.24] From the point of view of the creditor such companies also posed problems. Who was the creditor to sue? Only those persons who were members of the company on the day the liability was incurred, could be sued. As the membership of the company might have altered regularly (perhaps from day to day) ascertaining the identity of those members could well prove impossible. This problem might be further compounded by the absence of any record or register of members of the company. The managers or directors of the company might well be wealthy and prominent individuals. But unless they were also members on the relevant date, they could not be sued.

Even if a creditor were able to pursue one or more members to judgment (and this might be achievable in the case of more wealthy members) these members could then run into difficulties in obtaining contributions from such fellow members against whom the creditor had not proceeded. Contribution would only be possible where the identity of the company's members could be ascertained.

What was need, therefore, was a single defendant, a separate person in law, which could own and hold its own assets, and which would continue in existence despite any changes in its membership. If this were to occur, incorporation of such companies would have had to have been cheaper than by way of Royal Charter or Private Act of Parliament.

In 1825 the Bubble Act 1720 was repealed and in 1844 the Joint Stock Company Act was passed to tackle the problems connected with deed of settlement companies.

1 See generally *Keane* chapter 2. For a more detailed account see Gower' *Principles of Modern Company Law* (4th Ed 1979) (London, Chapters 2 & 3).
2 As to which see the Limmited Partnership Act 1907.
3 (1880) 15 Ch D 247.

An Act for better securing certain Powers and Privileges intended to be granted by his Majesty by two Charters for Assurance of Ships and Merchandizes at Sea, and for lending money upon bottomry; and for restraining several extrangement and unwarrantable Practices therein mentioned. 6 Geo.1.c.18

[1.25] . . . And whereas it is notorious, that several undertakings or projects of different kinds have, at some time or times since the four and twentieth day of June one thousand seven hundred and eighteen, been publically contrived and practised, or attempted to be practised, within the City of London and other parts of this kingdom, as also in Ireland and other his Majesty's dominions, which manifestly tend to the common grievance, prejudice and inconvenience of great numbers of your Majesty's subjects in their trade or commerce, and other their affairs; and the persons who contrive or attempt such damgerous and mischievous undertakings or projects, under false pretences of public good, do presume according to their own devices and schemes, to open books for public subscriptions, and draw in many unwary persons to subscribe therein towards raising great sums of money, whereupon the subscribers or claimants under them do pay small proportions thereof, and such proportions in the whole do amount to very large sums; which dangerous and mischievous undertakings or projects do relate to several fisheries and other affairs, wherein the trade, commerce and welfare of your Majesty's subjects, or great numbers of them, are concerned or interested.

. . . And whereas in many cases the said undertakers or subscribers have, since the said four and twentieth day of June one thousand seven hundred and eighteen, presumed to act as if they were corporate bodies, and have pretended to make their shares in stocks transferable or assignable, without any legal authority, either by Act of Parliament, or by any charter from the Crown for so doing; and in some cases the undertakers or subscribers, since the said four and twentieth day of June one thousand seven hundred and eighteen, have acted or pretended to act under some charter or charters formerly granted by the Crown for some particular or special purposes therein expressed, but have used or endeavoured to use the same charters for raising joint stocks, and for making transfers or assignments, or pretended transfers or assignments, for their own private lucre, which were never intended or designed by the same charters respectively; and in some cases the undertakers or subscribers, since the said four and twentieth day of June one thousand seven hundred and eighteen, have acted under some obsolete charter or charters, although the same became void or voidable by non-user or abuser, or for want of making lawful elections, which were necessary for the continuance thereof; and many other unwarrantable practises (too many to enumerate) have been, and daily are and may hereafter be contrived, set on foot, or proceeded upon, to the ruin and destruction of many of your Majesty's good subjects, if a timely remedy be not provided: And whereas it is become absolutely necessary, that all public undertakings and attempts, tending to the common grievance, prejudice and inconvenience of your Majesty's subjects in general, or great numbers of them, in their trade, commerce, or other lawful Affairs, be effectually suppressed and restrained for the future, by suitable and adequate punishments for that purpose to be ascertained and established. Now for suppressing such mischievous and dangerous undertakings and attempts, and preventing the like for the future, may it please your most excellent Majesty, at the humble suit of the said Lord's spiritual and temporal, and commons, in this present Parliament assembled that it may be enacted; and be it enacted by authority of this present Parliament, that from and after the four and twentieth day of June one thousand seven hundred and twenty, all and every the undertakings and attempts described, as aforesaid, and all other public undertakings and attempts, tending to the common grievance, prejudice and inconvenience of his Majesty's subjects or great numbers of them, in their trade, commerce, or other lawful affairs, and all public subscriptions, receipts, payments, assignments, transfers, pretended assignments and transfers, and all other matters and things whatsoever, for furthering, countenancing or proceeding

13

in any such undertaking of attempt, and more particularly the acting or presuming to act as a corporate body or bodies, the raising or pretending to raise transferable stock or stocks, the transferring or pretending to transfer or assign any share or shares in such stock or stocks, without legal authority, either by Act of Parliament, or by any charter from the Crown, to warrant such acting as a body corporate, or to raise such transferable stock or stocks, or to transfer shares therein, and all acting or pretending to act under any charter, formerly granted from the Crown, for particular or special purposes therein expressed, by persons who do or shall use or endeavour to use the same charters, for raising a capital stock, or for making transfers or assignments, or pretended transfers or assignments of such stock, not intended or designed by such charter to be raised or transferred, and all acting or pretending to act under any obsolete charter . . . shall (as to all or any such acts, matters and things, as shall be acted, done, attempted, endeavoured or proceeded upon, after the said four and twentieth day of June one thousand seven hundred and twenty) forever be deemed to be illegal and void and shall not be practised or in any way put in execution.

(19). [F]rom the said four and twentieth day of June one thousand seven hundred and twenty, all such unlawful [activities] shall be deemed to be a public nuisance and nuisances . . .

(22). Provided always . . . That this Act . . . shall not extend to any undertakings, or matters or things settled, established, or practised in point of time before the said four and twentieth day of June one thousand seven hundred and eighteen, but that the same, and every of them, shall be of such or the like force, effect or validity, and no other, as they respectively would be of, in case this Act had never been made; any thing herein contained to the contrary notwithstanding . . .

(25). Provided always, That nothing in this Act shall extend, or be construed to extend to prohibit or restrain the carrying on of any home or foreign trade in partnership, in such manner as hath been hitherto usually, and may be legally, done, according to the laws of this realm now in force, excepting only as to the insuring of ships and goods or merchandises at sea, or going to sea, and lending money upon bottomry; any thing in this act to the contrary in any wise notwithstanding . . .

(27). Provided always . . . that nothing in this Act contained shall extend, or be construed to extend to any corporation formerly created for the carrying on a trade, which they have publicly continued to exercise from the time of their establishment . . .'

*An Act for establishing A Bank, by the Name of the Governors
and Company of the Bank of Ireland 21 & 22 Geo IIIc XVI*

[1.26] (20). '. . . and in the case of . . . insolvency, that then, and in every such case, before any distribution or dividend shall be made of the said stock or the produce thereof, the said governor and company shall be obliged in the first instance, to apply the said stock and the produce thereof then in their hands, or a competent part of the same, to discharge and pay off the total sum of the debts which they shall owe to others; and in case the same shall not be suficient to pay off and discharge such debts so due to others, that then each member of the said corporation shall in his, her or their private capacity, according to the proportions of their respective interests in said capital stock, be liable to the payment of said debts, until the whole shall be discharged.'

The Commissioners of Inland Revenue v The Governor And Company of The Bank of Ireland [1925] 2 IR 90

[The facts are irrelevant]

[1.27] **Murnaghan J:** 'There is at common law no liability upon the members of a body corporate in respect of the debts and liability of the body corporate, and such liability in respect of the corporate acts must be created by statute'.

An Act to promote trade and manufacture, by regulating and encouraging partnerships. 21 & 22 Geo IIIc XLVI

[1.28] Whereas the increasing the stock of money employed in trade and manufacture, must greatly promote the commerce and prosperity of this kingdom, and many persons might be induced to subscribe sums of money to men well qualified for trade, but not of competent fortune to carry it on largely if they were allowed to abide by the profit or loss of trade for the same, and were not to be deemed traders on that account, or subject thereby to any further or other demands than the sums so subscribed; be it enacted by the King's most excellent Majesty, by and with the advice and consent of the lords spiritual and temporal, and commons in this present Parliament assembled, and by the authority of the same, That any number of persons may from and after the twenty fourth day of June, one thousand seven hundred and eighty two, by deed or instrument of partnership, under their hands and seals, executed in the presence of two or more subscribing witnesses, and to be registered as hereinafter mentioned, enter into a joint trade or co-partnership for the purpose of buying and selling in the gross or by wholesale, or for establishing or carrying on any manufacture or business for any term not exceeding fourteen years, but determinable at any shorter period, in such manner and upon such conditions as shall be agreed upon by such partnership deed; and that the said co-partners or some of them so executing the said deed, shall thereby bind themselves to pay in money towards a joint stock, such sums as they shall respectively think fit, such joint stock however not to be in any one of such companies or co-partnerships less in the whole than one thousand pounds, or more than fifty thousand pounds.

(2). [T]he said subscribers or co-partners may by such partnership deed nominate and appoint from amongst themselves one or more person or persons, to manage, conduct, or carry on said trade, business or manufacture, in whose name and names whilst living and continuing in credit, with the addition of 'and company', the business of said partnership shall be transacted and carried on, and such person or persons, so nominated and appointed, shall be called the acting partner or partners of the said co-partnership or company, and such acting partner or partners, and his or their person or persons, lands, goods and chattels, shall to all intents and purposes be as subject to the laws against bankrupts for and on account of the said partnership debts, as if such acting partner or partners had traded upon his or their own account, and without any connection in trade, with the said other partners or subscribers.

(3). The remaining subscribers or co-partners, who shall not have the actual management or conduct of said trade, business or manufacture, and whose names shall not be mentioned in the firm of said company, shall be stated anonymous partners of said company, . . . nor shall such anonymous partners, or any of them be subject to any contracts or engagements of such acting partner or partners, or to any loss or miscarriage which may happen in the said partnership business, further or otherwise than as herein after mentioned . . .

(6). Each of the said anonymous partners . . . shall and may receive and take out of said partnership after a just and fair settlement of accounts . . ., and not before, half and no more of his or their share or proportion of the net profits made by said company on the sums paid in by them severally and respectively, and the residue of the profits, and any sum or sums of money paid by a forfeiting partner, or partners as aforesaid, and the profits thereof, shall go towards increase of said capital or joint stock, until the expiration of the term of their co-partnership.

(7). Such anonymous partner or partners, having really and bona fide paid or tendered the full sum in cash by him subscribed and specified in such partnership deed, at such times as hereinbefore mentioned . . . shall not be subject to any of the laws against bankrupts, or to any greater loss, charges, or damages, for or on account of his or their having entered into such partnership, than the full sum or sums so by him or them subscribed and paid, and such proportion of the profits thereof as is herein before directed to be held over to the end of the said partnership, at the utmost or such proportion of such full sum so subscribed, and the profits thereof not received as may be necessary to make full payment and discharge of all the said partnership debts and engagements . . .

In re: Commercial Buildings Company of Dublin [1938] IR 477

[1.29]   The court held that it had jurisdiction under the Companies Acts to wind up a company incorporated by Royal charter, as an unregistered company.

[1.30]   **Johnston J:** (describing how the company came into existence). This matter comes before me on a petition for the winding up of a very ancient corporation which has been intimately associated with the history and the commercial like of Dublin for nearly a hundred and fifty years, and my principal difficulty in the case arises from the fact that the company was created as long ago as 1798 by virtue of a royal charter of George III – 'Farmer George' – and that it seemed to me almost sacrilegious to lay hands upon such a venerable institution . . .

The corporation came into existence in this way. In 1797 a number of businessmen in the City of Dublin formed themselves into a voluntary society for the purpose of 'the founding of buildings to be appropriated to the convenience of commercial dealing and intercourse within the City of Dublin.' These gentlemen bore names which are to this day well known and honoured in commercial and professional circles in this city – names such as Nathaniel Hone, Randal MacDonnell, Joshua Pim, Richard Verschoyle, George Maquay and others – and on their own application it was referred by Lord Camden, the Lord Lieutenant of the day, to the Attorney-General and Solicitor-General to inquire whether a royal charter ought to be granted. The Attorney-General of the day was none other than Arthur Wolfe, who subsequently became the ill-fated Lord Kilwarden, whilst the Solicitor-General was none other than John Toler who later was raised to the peerage as Lord Norbury, and became known to fame as 'the hanging Judge'. These gentlemen reported in favour of the scheme, and a royal charter was granted on January 1st 1798, erecting a corporation under the name of 'The Commercial Buildings Company of Dublin', with very extensive powers, including that of making bye-laws. The first of these bye-laws ordained that the common seal of the company should be 'kept in an iron repository at the office of the said company, to which there shall be three locks, each of which shall be materially different in its internal construction from the others', and the keepers of the keys should be three directors of the company, each being responsible for one key.

The commercial building, as we all know, was built on a plot of ground on the north side of Dame Street, ground granted to the company by the Commissioners of Wide Street, a statutory body which did so much in the eighteenth century to make Dublin the beautiful city that it is today . . .

. . . I am satisfied that the Act of 1908 is sufficiently general in its application to enable the present application to be granted. It cannot be suggested that a company incorporated by Act of Parliament has not a greater sanctity than a company created by royal charter, and there is no doubt that the former class of company – that is, companies incorporated by Act of Parliament – comes within the terms of the Act of 1908 . . .

. . . There will therefore be an order for the winding up of the company, as an unregistered company under and by virtue of . . . the Act of 1908 . . .

Development of Company Law from 1844 to 1958

REPORT OF THE COMMITTEE ON COMPANY LAW REFORM. (1958) Prl 4533

[1.31] 'The Joint Stock Companies Act 1844, 7 & 8 Vict c 110, was the first law which gave the privilege of incorporation by registration and without a

Royal charter or a special Act of Parliament. Under the Act, partnerships in which the capital was divided into freely transferable shares, partnerships in which there were more than 25 members and assurance companies were all required to register in a registry of companies. On registration and on filing a deed of settlement, these associations became incorporated and acquired a separate legal existence distinct from that of their members. Thus for the first time, it became possible for an enterprise to become incorporated as of right by fulfilling prescribed conditions. The deed of settlement corresponded braodly to the modern memorandum and articles of association. However, every member could be made liable for their company's debts as if it had not been incorporated; but a creditor of the company could not sue a member for a debt due by the company without first trying to levy execution against the property of the company as such.

[1.32]   In 1852 a commission, which was appointed by Parliament to consider whether any alteration should be made to partnership law so as to give limited liability to partners reported that such limited liability would not be beneficial. Nevertheless, in the following year the House of Commons passed a resolution as a result of which the Limited Liability Act, 1855, 18 & 19 Vict c 133, was passed. This Act amended the 1844 Act and made it possible for registered companies to limit the liability of all their members to the amounts due on their shares provided that certain conditions were observed.

Under the Joint Stock Companies Act, 1856, 19 & 20 Vict c 47, any seven ot more persons were entitled to register a company with limited liability. An annual return had to be filed giving information about the capital of the company and its shareholders, but filing a balance sheet with the auditor's report attached (which had been made compulsory in 1844) became no longer necessary.

[1.33]   The Companies Act, 1862, 25 & 26 Vict c 89, consolidated existing legislation regarding joint stock, banking and assurance companies, and also made provision for companies limited by guarantee. It required the objects of the company to be stated and prohibited their alteration, and thus introduced the doctrine of ultra vires. The principal features of the modern system of company law will be found in the Act of 1862.

Although the advantages of the system of companies with limited liability are considerable, in its early form it offered opportunities for fraudulent enrichment to company promoters, as numerous leading cases decided around the turn of the last century testify to. A number of Acts dealing with specific reforms in the system of company law were passed between 1862 and 1900.

[1.34]   In 1895 a committee under the chairmanship of Lord Davey recommended further legislative amendments. The collapse which had followed the over-optimism of the railway boom had caused many public companies to fail, and in some of those the promoters and the directors had made substantial illicit profits. The Companies Act 1900, made provision for a number of matters which had to be stated in every prospectus, and imposed new obligations and liabilities on directors of companies. It also re-introduced the compulsory audit of a company's accounts.

[1.35] In 1905 a committee under the chairmanship of Sir Robert Reid (subsequently Lord Loreburn, LC) was set up to enquire what additional amendments were necessary to the companies legislation. It recommended that every company should be obliged each year to file a balance sheet which would be available for inspection by every member of the public. It also made recommendations in relation to accepting the special position of 'family' companies. It had been held by the House of Lords in *Salomon v Salomon & Co* AC 22, that there was nothing in the Companies Acts which prohibited the registration of a company with seven members, six of whom held a small number of shares on behalf of the seventh, who owned the rest of the shares. The Companies Act, 1907 7 Edward VII, c 50 provided that a private company could be registered with two members only and that it should be exempt from the obligation to file a balance sheet for public inspection. A private company was defined as a company in which restrictions were imposed by the articles of association on the transfer of shares, in which the number of members of the company did not exceed fifty and in which the shares and debentures of the company had not been offered to the public. Many of the smaller limited companies previously incorporated availed of this legislation by converting themselves into private companies. Another significant development was the emergence of the 'holding company' as distinct from the operating company. The holding company was, in the main, the child of the operations of financiers interested in the development of the diamond fields in South Africa before and after the Boer War.

[1.36] All the legislation from 1862 to 1907 were consolidated by the Companies (Consolidation) Act, 1908, 8 Edward VII c 69. This Act was amended and added to in minor details by the Companies Act, 1913, 3 & 4 Geo V c 25, the Companies (Foreign Interests) Act 1917, 7 & 8 Geo V c 18, the Companies (Particulars of Directors) Act, 1917, 7 & 8 Geo V c 28, and the Companies (Reconstitution of Records) Act 1924, no 21, which was the first company law statute passed by the Oireachtas. This latter Act dealt with the reconstitution of records consequent on the destruction of the Companies Registration Office when the Customs House in Dublin was burned during the Civil War.

Development of Company Law From 1958 To The Present Day

[1.37] In 1958 the committee on Company Law Reform (The Cox Committee) presented a report (containing recommendations for the reform of Irish Company Law) and in 1962 the Jenkins Committee presented a report with a similar objective for Britain.[1] A number of the recommendations of these committees were incorporated into the Companies Act 1963 which to this date remains the legislative foundation for company law in Ireland.

The last 15 years have seen a rapid growth in the amount of domestic company legislation with Companies (Amendment) Acts in 1977, 1982, 1983, 1986 and 1990.

1 Report of the Company Law Committee (1962) Cmnd 1749.

Development of Company Law; European Community Dimension[1]

[1.38]   The objective of the European Economic Community, of which Ireland is a member, is the establishment of a common market among member states. The EEC Treaty is incorporated into domestic Irish law pursuant to Art 29.4.3 of the Constitution and the European Communities Act 1972. Where there is a conflict between ordinary domestic law and binding provisions of EEC law, the latter prevails.[2] As part of the objective of establishing a common market Art 52 of the EEC Treaty provides for freedom of establishment within the Community. Art 54 provides for the issue of Directives by the Council in order to give effect to the provisions of Art 52. There have been 11 such directives to date. The First Companies Directive (68/151/EEC) which dealt with certain disclosure requirements, was implemented by the European Communities (Companies) Regulations 1973 to the extent that the Principal Act did not already give effect to its provisions. The Second Companies Directive (77/91/EEC) which dealt with the share capital of plc's was implemented by the 1983 Act. The Third and Sixth Companies Directives (78/855/EEC and 82/891/EEC) which were concerned with the merger and division of plc's were implemented by the European Communities (Merger and Division of Companies) Regulations 1987. The Fourth Companies Directive (78/660/EEC) on the format contents and disclosure of company accounts was implemented by the 1986 Act. The Seventh Companies Directive (83/349/EEC) which deals with the consolidation of group accounts of limited liability companies and the Eighth Companies Directive (84/253/EEC) which applies to the qualifications, independence and repute of auditors have both been implemented by Part X of the Companies Act 1990. The Eleventh Companies Directive (89/666/ EEC) on the disclosure requirements for branches of foreign companies opening up in the State and the Twelfth Companies Directive (89/667/EEC) on one man companies must both be implemented by 1 January 1992. Proposals have also been put forward for a European Company Statute which would allow for the incorporation of companies at an EC level rather than purely on a domestic level, but the Regulation is still at the draft stage and awaits adoption by the Council.[3]

[1.39]   Another form of legal entity created by the EC is the European Economic Interest Grouping (EEIG). Initially established by Regulation (EEC) No 2137/85 it was implemented in this jurisdiction by the European Community (European Economic Interest Grouping) Regulations 1989.[4]

The purpose of the EEIG is to facilitate joint ventures between two or more companies registered in different Member States. The object of the EEIG which may be registered in any Member State is not to make a profit for itself, but rather for its corporate members.[5]

The European Communities (Stock Exchange) Regulations 1984 were made to give effect to the Admissions Directive (79/279/EEC), the Listing Particulars Directive (80/390/EEC) and the Interim Reports Directive (82/121/EEC).

Notes

1 See *Keane* chapter 3; Quinn, *Company Law – the European Dimension* (1989) 7 ILT (ns) November/December.
2 *Van Gend en Loos v Nederlandse Administratie der Belastingen case* 26/62 [1963] ECR 1.
3 See Quinn *The European Company, A Statute on the Scale of '92'* (1990) 8 ILT (ns) 231.
4 SI 1989/191.
5 See *Keane* paras **3.14** & **3.15**; Linnane *European Economic Interest Grouping* (1989) 7 ILT (ns) 213; *Forming an EEIG in Ireland* (1991) 9 ILT (ns) 36.

EEC Treaty Article 52

1.40 Within the framework of the provisions set out below, restrictions on the freedom of establishment of national of a Member State in the territory of another Member State shall be abolished by progressive stages in the course of the transitional period. Such progressive abolition shall also apply to restrictions on the setting up of agencies, branches or subsidiaries by national of any Member State established in the terriroty of any Member State.

Freedom of establishment shall include the right to take up and pursue activities as self-employed persons and to set up and manage undertakings, in particular companies or firms within the meaning of the second paragraph of article 58, under the conditions laid down for its own nationals by the law of the country where such establishment is effected, subject to the provisions of the chapter relating to capital.

Directives yet to be implemented

Seventh Council Directive (83/349/EEC) of 13 June 1983 based on the Article 54(3)(g) of the Treaty on consolidated accounts

Article 1
1.41 (1). A Member State shall require any undertaking governed by its national law to draw up consolidated accounts and a consolidated annual report if that undertaking (a parent undertaking):

(*a*) has a majority of the shareholders' or members' voting rights in another undertaking (a subsidiary undertaking) or
(*b*) has the right to appoint or remove a majority of the members of the administrative management or supervisory body of another undertaking (a subsidiary undertaking) and is at the same time a shareholder in or member of that undertaking; or

(*c*) has the right to exercise a dominant influence over an undertaking (a subsidiary undertaking) of which it is a shareholder or member, pursuant to a provision in its memorandum or articles of association, where the law governing that subsidiary undertaking permits its being subject to such contracts or provisions. A Member State need not prescribe that a parent undertaking must be a shareholder in or member of its subsidiary undertaking. Those Member States the laws of which do not provide for such contracts or clauses shall not be required to apply this provision; or

(*d*) is a shareholder in or member of an undertaking and:

(*aa*) a majority of the members of the administrative management or supervisory bodies of that undertaking (a subsidiary undertaking) who have held office during the financial year, during the preceding financial year and up to the time when the consolidated accounts are drawn up have been appointed solely as a result of the exercise of its voting rights; or

(*bb*) controls alone, pursuant to an agreement with other shareholders in or members of that undertaking (a subsidiary undertaking), a majority of shareholders' or members' voting rights in that undertaking. The Member States may introduce more detailed provisions concerning the form and contents of such agreements.

The Members States shall prescribe at least the arrangements referred to in (*bb*) above.

They may make the application of (*aa*) above dependent upon the holding's representing 20% or more of the shareholders' or members' voting rights.

However, (*aa*) above shall not apply where another undertaking has the rights referred to in subparagraphs (*a*), (*b*) or (*c*) above with regard to that subsidiary undertaking.

(2). Apart from the cases mentioned in paragraph 1 above and pending subsequent co-ordination, the Member States may require any undertaking governed by their national law to draw up consolidated accounts and a consolidated annual report if that undertaking (a parent undertaking) holds a participating interest as defined in Article 17 of Directive 78/660/EEC in another undertaking (a subsidiary undertaking), and:

(*a*) it actually exercises a dominant influence over it; or

(*b*) it and the subsidiary undertaking are managed on a unified basis by the parent undertaking.

Article 2

1.42 (1). For the purposes of article 1(1)(*a*), (*b*) and (*d*), the voting rights and the rights of appointment and removal of any other subsidiary undertaking as well as those of any person acting in his own name but on behalf of the Parent undertaking or of another subsidiary undertaking must be added to those of the parent undertaking.

(2). For the purposes of article 1(1)(*a*), (*b*) and (*d*) the rights mentioned in paragraph 1 above must be reduced by the rights:

22

(*a*) attaching to shares held on behalf of a person who is neither the parent undertaking nor a subsidiary thereof; or

(*b*) attaching to shares held by way of security, provided that the rights in question are exercised in accordance with the instructions received, or held in connection with the granting of loans as part of normal business activities, provided that the voting rights are exercised in the interests of the person providing the security.

(3). For the purposes of article 1(1)(*a*) and (*d*) the total of the shareholders' or members' voting rights in the subsidiary undertaking must be reduced by the voting rights attaching to the shares held by that undertaking itself by a subsidiary undertaking of that undertaking or by a person acting in his own name but on behalf of those undertakings.

Article 4
[1.43] (1). Without prejudice to articles 13, 14 and 15 a parent undertaking and all of its subsidiary undertakings shall be undertakings to be consolidated regardless of where the registered offices of such subsidiary undertakings are situated.

(2). For the purposes of paragraph 1 above any subsidiary undertaking of a subsidiary undertaking shall be considered a subsidiary undertaking of the parent undertaking which is the parent of the undertakings to be consolidated.

Article 41
[1.44] (1). For the purposes of this Directive a parent undertaking and all of its subsidiary undertakings shall be undertakings to be consolidated where either the parent undertaking or one or more subsidiary undertakings is established as one of the following types of company . . .

(*f*) In Ireland:
public companies limited by shares or by guarantee, private companies limited by shares or by guarantee;

Section (2): Preparation of consolidated accounts

Article 16
[1.45] (1). Consolidated accounts shall comprise the consolidated balance sheet, the consolidated profit and loss account and the notes on the accounts. These documents shall constitute a composite whole.

(3). Consolidated accounts shall give a true and fair view of the assets, liabilities, financial position and profit or loss of the undertakings included therein taken as a whole.

Section (3): The consolidated annual report

23

Article 36
[1.46[(1). The consolidated annual report must include at least a fair review of the development of business and the position of the undertakings included in the consolidation taken as a whole.

(2).   In respect of those undertakings the report shall also give an indication of:

(*a*)   any important events that have ocurred since the end of the financial year;
(*b*)   the likely future development of those undertakings taken as a whole;
(*c*)   the activities of those undertakings taken as a whole in the field of research and development;
(*d*)   the number and nominal value or, in the absence of a nominal value, the accounting par value of all of the parent undertakes' shares held by that undertaking itself, by subsidiary undertakings of that undertaking or by a person acting in his own name but on behalf of those undertakings. A Member State may require or permit the disclosure of these particulars in the notes on the accounts.

Section (4): The auditing of consolidated accounts

Article 37
1.47   (1). An undertaking which draws up consolidated accounts must have them audited by one or more persons authorized to audit accounts under the laws of the Member State which govern that undertaking.

(2). The person or persons responsible for auditing the consolidated accounts must also verify that the consolidated annual report is consistent with the consolidated accounts for the same financial year.

Section (5): The publication of consolidated accounts

Article 38
[1.48]   (1). Consolidated accounts, duly approved, and the consolidated annual report, together with the opinion submitted by the person responsible for auditing the consolidated accounts, shall be published for the undertaking which drew up the consolidated accounts as laid down by the laws of the Member State which govern it in accordance with article 3 of Directive 68/151/EEC.

> *Eleventh Council Directive (89/666/EEC) of 21 December 1989*
> *concerning disclosure requirements in respect of branches opened*
> *in a Member State by certain types of company governed by the*
> *law of another State*

Article 1
1.49   1. Documents and particulars relating to a branch opened in a Member State by a company which is governed by the law of another Member State and to which Directive 68/151/EEC applies shall be disclosed pursuant to the law of the Member State of the branch, in accordance with article 3 of that Directive.

(2). Where disclosure requirements in respect of the branch differ from those in respect of the company, the branch's disclosure requirements shall take precedence with regard to transactions carried out with the branch.

Article 2
[1.50] (1). The compulsory disclosure provided for in article 1 shall cover the following documents and particulars only:

(*a*) the address of the branch;
(*b*) the activities of the branch;
(*c*) the register in which the company file mentioned in article 3 of Council Directive 68/151/EEC is kept together with the registration number in that register;
(*d*) the name and legal form of the company and the name of the branch if that is different from the name of the company;
(*e*) the appointment, termination of office and particulars of the persons who are authorized to represent the company in dealings with third parties and in legal proceedings;
– as a company organ constituted pursuant to law or as members of any such organ, in accordance with the disclosure by the coompany as provided for in article 2(1)(*d*) of Directive 68/151/EEC
– as permanent representatives of the company for the activites of the branch with an indication of the extent of their powers;
(*f*) the winding up of the company, the appointment of liquidators, particulars concerning them and their powers and the termination of the liquidation in accordance with disclosure by the company as provided for in article 2(1)(*h*), (*i*) and (*k*) of Directive 68/151/EEC,
– insolvency proceedings, arrangements, compositions or any analagous proceedings to which the company is subject;
(*g*) the accounting documents in accordance with article 3;
(*h*) the closure of the branch.

(2). The Member State in which the branch has been opened may provide for the disclosure as referred to in article 1 of:

(*a*) the signature of the persons referred to in paragraph 1(*e*) and (*f*) of this article;
(*b*) the instruments of constitution and the memorandum and articles of association if they are contained in a separate instrument in accordance with article 2(1)(*a*), (*b*) and (*c*) of Directive 68/151/EEC together with amendments to those documents;
(*c*) an attestation from the register referred to in paragraph 1(*c*) of this article relating to the existence of the company;
(*d*) an indication of the securities on the company's property situated in that Member State, provided such disclosure relates to the validity of those securities.

25

Article 7

[1.51] (1). Documents and particulars concerning a branch opened in a Member State by a company which is not governed by the law of a Member State but which it of a legal form comparable with the types of company to which Directive 68/151/EEC applies shall be disclosed in accordance with the law of the Member State of the branch as laid down in article 3 of that Directive.

(2). Article 1(2) shall apply.

Article 8

[1.52] The compulsory disclosure provided for in article 7 shall cover at least the following documents and particulars:

(*a*) the address of the branch;

(*b*) the activities of the branch;

(*c*) the law of the State by which the company is governed;

(*d*) where that law so provides, the register in which the company is entered and the registration number of the company in that register;

(*e*) the instruments of constitution and memorandum and articles of association if they are contained in a separate instrument with all the amendments to these documents;

(*f*) the legal form of the company, its principal place of business and its object and at least annually, the amount of subscribed capital if these particulars are not given in the documents referred to in sub-paragraph (*e*);

(*g*) the name of the company and the name of the branch if that is different from the name of the company;

(*h*) the appointment, termination of office and particulars of the persons who are authorised to represent the company in dealings with third parties and in legal proceedings:

– as a company organ constituted pursuant to law or as members of any such organ,

– as permanent representatives of the company for the activites of the branch

The extent of the powers of the persons authorised to represent the company must be stated, together with whether they may do so alone or act jointly:

(*i*) – the winding up of the company and the appointment of liquidators, particulars concerning them and their powers and the termination of the liquidation;

– insolvency proceedings, arrangements, compositions or any analagous proceedings to which the company is subject;

(*j*) the accounting documents in accordance with article 7;

(*k*) the closure of the branch.

Twelfth Council Directive of 21 December 1989 on single-member private limited-liability companies

Article 1
[1.53]   The co-ordination measures prescribed by this Directive shall apply to the laws, regulations and administrative provisions of the Member States relating to the following types of company: – in Ireland, private company limited by shares or by guarantee.

Article 2
[1.54]   (1). A company may have a sole member when it is formed and also when all its shares come to be held by a single person (single-member company).

(2). Member States may, pending co-ordination of national laws relating to groups, lay down special provisions or sanctions for cases where:

(*a*) a natural person is the sole member of several companies,
(*b*) a single-member company or any other legal person is the sole member of a company.

Article 3
[1.55]   Where a company becomes a single-member company because all its shares come to be held by a single person, that fact, together with the identity of the sole member must either be recorded in the file or entered in the register within the meaning of article 3(1) and (2) of Directive 68/151/EEC or be entered in a register held by the company and accessible to the public.

Article 4
[1.56]   (1). The sole member shall exercise the powers of the general meeting of the company.

(2). Decisions taken by the sole member in the field referred to in paragraph 1 shall be recorded in minutes or drawn up in writing.

Article 5
[1.57]   (1). Contracts between the sole member and the company as represented by him shall be recorded in minutes or drawn up in writing.

(2). Member States need not apply paragraph 1 to current operations concluded under normal conditions.

Article 6
[1.58]   Where a Member State allows the single-member companies as defined by article 2(1) in the case of public limited companies as well, this Directive shall apply.

Article 7
[1.59]   A Member State need not allow the formation of single-member companies where its legislation provides that an individual entrepreneur may set up an undertaking the liability of which is limited to a sum devoted to

a stated activity on condition that safeguards are laid down for such under-takings which are equivalent to those imposed by this Directive or by any other Community provisions applicable to the companies referred to in Article 1.

Notes

For a discussion of the Twelfth Directive *see* MacCann *Company Law Reform: One Man Companies* (1990) 8 ILT (n.s.) 166.

Chapter 2

HOW A COMPANY IS FORMED

TYPES OF COMPANY

Various types of company may be formed under the Companies Acts:

Limited and Unlimited Companies

[2.01]   Unlimited companies can be formed with or without a share capital, although the former type is the more common. As their title suggests, in such companies the liability of their members is unlimited.[1] In the event that the company is wound up the members are potentially liable 'for the payment of its debts and liabilities, and the costs, charges and expenses of the winding up . . .'[2] Past members are also liable unless they retired at least one year before the commencement of the liquidation.[3]

In limited companies, the liability of the members is restricted to an amount stated in the memorandum of association.[4] Such companies must include the word 'limited' or 'teoranta' after their names as a warning to the public that the members liability is restricted.[5]

1 S 5(2)(*c*) of the Principal Act.
2 Ibid s 207(1). See generally, Rice *The Unlimited Company. An Anachronism or a Modern Opportunity?* (1963) 27 Conv (ns) 442.
3 S 207(1)(*a*)–(*c*).
4 S 6.
5 S 6(1)(*a*).

Companies Limited by Shares

[2.02]   The majority of registered companies in Ireland fall into this category.[1] The liability of the member is limited to the amount he has agreed to pay for his shares (to the extent that such sum remains unpaid).

1 S 5(2)(*a*) of the Principal Act.

29

Companies Limited by Guarantee

[2.03]   There are very few such companies.[1] Each member undertakes or guarantees to contribute a specified amount to the company in the event of it being wound up while he is a member or within one year of his ceasing to be a member.[2] It is also possible to create companies limited by guarantee and having a share capital.[3] These hybrid companies are rare and since 13 October 1983 may only be formed as private companies. Existing public companies limited by guarantee may continue to exist.[4]

1 S 5(2)(*b*). See Rice, *Companies Limited by Guarantees* (1964) 28 Conv (ns) 214.
2 S 6(3). *Re Premier Underwriting Association Ltd* (no 1) [1913] 2 Ch 29.
3 Table D schedule 1.
4 S 7 of the 1983 Act.

[2.04]   In a company limited by shares the share capital may be used to finance its day to day trading. The guarantee fund however can only be called up when the company is in liquidation. It cannot even be used as security for a loan.

In re Mayfair Property Company; Bartlett v Mayfair Property Company [1898] 2 Ch 28 (Court of Appeal)

[2.05]   **Lindley MR:** 'The question in this case is a very important one, and turns on the true construction of s 5 of the Companies Act 1879.[1]. . .

The contention on the part of the appellant is that a limited company can validly charge its uncalled capital if authorized so to do by its memorandum of association or by its articles; and that the capital or money which under the Act of 1879 can only be called up in the event of and for the purposes of the company being wound up is part of the capital of the company in the full and proper sense of that word; and that, there being no prohibition against creating charges upon it, the power to create such charges necessarily follows. This argument is based on *In re Pyle Works* 44 Ch 534, which finally settled that uncalled capital of a limited company governed by the Companies Act 1862, could be validly charged in favour of particular persons.

It is further contended that the payment of the secured debts of a company is as much a purpose of the company as the payment of its other debts; that there is no necessary implication requiring the court to hold reserve capital to be incapable of being charged with the payment of particular debts; and that it may be ruinous to a company to prevent it from obtaining relief from perhaps temporary pressure by raising money on the security of its most valuable asset.

Cogent as this argument is, I am convinced that it is unsound, and that to yield to it would defeat and not carry out the purpose with which the Act of 1879 was passed.

When *In re Pyle Works* 44 Ch 534 was decided I foresaw that the decision might be pressed further than I was prepared to go, and I pointed out that, in my opinion. it did not authorise mortgages of reserve capital under the Act of 1879. I adhere to that view now that I have carefully reconsidered it . . .

It appears to me plain that s 5 was framed with a double object – namely, first, to preserve for the general creditors of the company the funds which the members were liable to pay, but which the directors could not call up; and secondly, to enable the members to limit the amount of their liability on a winding-up to pay the creditors more than the amount preserved for them. Now, if the appellant's contention is right, the first of these objects will be entirely defeated, although there is not a sign of any intention on the part of the legislature to effect so great a change in the law, and although such a change would or might be ruinous to the great body of a company's creditors and be destructive of the credit which the preservation intact of reserve capital gives to those companies which avail themselves of the Act of 1879 . . . To interpret the section so as to enable a company to defeat this object by pledging or otherwise disposing of its reserve capital is, in my opinion, entirely to miss the real meaning of the Legislature as expressed in the language it has used.

1 The modern equivalent being s 6(3) of the Principal Act.

Notes

See also *Re Irish Industrial & Agricultural Fair, Cork 1932* (1933) 67 ILTR 175 and *Re Irish Club Co Ltd* [1906] WN 127. Because of the limitations on the use of the guarantee fund the company limited by guarantee is rarely used for commercial enterprises. Rather it is typically used for professional or charitable bodies, trade associations, etc., which usually rely on subscriptions, donations etc, to finance its activities.

Public and Private Companies.

[2.06]   A public company is unhelpfully defined as being 'a company which is not a private company'.[1] It is required pursuant to the provisions of the 1983 Act to have a minimum issued share capital of £30,000.[2] A private company is defined by s 33 as one which (*a*) restricts the right to transfer its shares, (*b*) limits the number of its members to 50, and (*c*) prohibits any invitation to the public to subscribe for any shares or debentures of the company.[3] A minimum of seven members are required for the formation of a public company but only two are required in the case of a private company.[4] Approximately 97% of registered companies are private.[5] A public company limited by shares, or by guarantee and having a share capital must include the words 'public limited company' or 'cuideachta phiobli theoranta' after its name. The abbreviation 'plc' or 'cpt' is also permissible.[6] Public companies limited by guarantee alone and private companies continue to use 'limited' or 'teoranta' or the abbreviations 'ltd' or 'teo'.

1 S 2 of the 1983 Act.
2 Ibid s 19.
3 S 21 of the 1983 Act makes such an invitation a criminal offence.
4 S 5(1) of the Principal Act.
5 Annual Reports of the Department of Industry and Commerce.
6 S 4(1) of the 1983 Act. See *Keane* at para **3.19**.

Registration of a company

[2.07] Incorporation of a company under the Companies Acts is achieved by delivering the prescribed documentation to the registrar of companies and payment of the registration fees and capital duty.[1] The documentation will include a memorandum and articles of association signed by the persons forming the company (and known as the subscribers), a statement containing particulars of the first secretary and directors (with their signed consent to so act) and a statutory declaration of compliance with the registration requirements. In the case of a plc the amount of the share capital stated in the memorandum to be that with which the company proposes to be registered must not be less than the 'authorised minimum' (currently £30,000).

[2.08] If satisfied that the registration requirements have been complied with and that the documentation is in order, the registrar issues a certificate of incorporation which certifies that the company is incorporated and, in the case of a limited company, that the company is limited.[2] From the date of incorporation mentioned in this certificate the subscribers become the first members of the company.[3] The persons mentioned in the statement of particulars as the first directors or secretaries of the company are also deemed to have been appointed to their respective offices from this date. Any indication in the articles specifying a person as a first director or secretary of the company will be void unless that person is specified as being appointed to that office in the statement.[4] A company registered as a plc is prohibited from doing business or exercising any borrowing powers 'even after the issue of the certificate of incorporation, until such time as he issues a 'trading certificate'.[5] If the plc does not obtain a trading certificate within one year of incorporation it runs the risk of being struck off the register of companies.[6]

[2.09] The certificate of incorporation issued by the registrar is conclusive evidence that all the requirements of the Companies Acts in respect of registration and of incidental matters and matters precedent have been complied with, and that the association is a company authorised to be registered and duly registered under the Companies Acts.[7] The according of the status of 'conclusive evidence' to the certificate of incorporation may be unconstitutional.

1 See *Keane* at paras **4.06–4.07, 9.01–9.03**.
2 S 18(1) of the Principal Act.
3 S 18(2).
4 S 3(5) of the 1982 Act.
5 Ibid s 6(1). For further details see *Keane* at paras **10.04–10.05**.
6 Ibid s 8.
7 S 19(1) of the Principal Act and s 5(4) of the 1983 Act.

Maher v Attorney General [1973] IR 146 (Supreme Court)

[The facts appear from the judgment]

[2.10]   Fitzgerald CJ: On the 22nd September 1971, the plaintiff was convicted of an offence under s 49 of the Road Traffic Act, 1961 (the principal act) as amended by s 29 of the Road Traffic Act 1968. The combined effect of those two sections is to make it an offence to drive a motor vehicle while there is present in the driver's body 'a quantity of alcohol such that, within three hours after so driving or attempting to drive, the concentration of alcohol in his blood will exceed a concentration of 125 milligrammes of alcohol per 100 millilitres of blood.' Section 48 of the Act of 1968 deals with questions of proof in the prosecution of such offences: . . . the statutory provision in section 44, sub-s 2(*a*) of the Act of 1968 provides in effect (a) that a certificate stating that it has been determined that a specimen of blood contained a specified concentration of alcohol, or that a specimen of urine contained a concentration of alcohol equivalent to a specified concentration in the blood, shall be admissible in evidence and (b) that the certificate shall be conclusive evidence in a prosecution that at the time the specimen was taken or provided the concentration of alcohol in the blood of the person from whom the specimen was obtained was the specified concentration of alcohol.

In the result it precludes the District Justice from forming any other judgment in respect of this vital ingredient of the prosecution's case: he is bound under the terms of the statutory provision to proceed and act as if this had been his own judgment on the matter. It was clearly intended by the Oireachtas that this should be the effect of the evidence because, when one compares it with the phrase 'until the contrary is shown'" in the following paragraph and the same phrase in the preceding sub-section , it is clear that the object of the statutory provision was to remove this element altogether from the area of contestable facts. In effect it means that an accused person is not free to contest the determination of the concentration of alcohol set out in the certificate . . .

The administration of justice, which in criminal matters is confined exclusively by the Constitution to the courts and judges set up under the Constitution, necessarily reserves to those courts and judges the determination of all the essential ingredients of any offence charged against an accused person. In so far as the statutory provision in question here purports to remove such determination from the judges or the courts appointed and established under the Constitution, it is an invalid infringement of the judicial power. This principle has already been clearly established by the decisions of this Court and of its predecessor in *Buckley and Others (Sinn Fein) v The Attorney General* [1950] IR 67; *Deaton v Attorney General* [1963] IR 170, and *The State (C) v The Minister for Justice* [1967] IR 106. As far as this case is concerned, the offending element of the provision is the evidential conclusiveness given to the certificate. If the word 'conclusive' had not been in the paragraph, it would not be open to the objection which has now been taken. By giving the certificate this evidential quality, the Oireachtas has invalidly impinged upon the exercise of judicial power and to that extent the statutory provision is invalid having regard to the provisions of the Constitution.

[2.11] Challenging the conclusiveness of the certificate of incorporation would not necessarily nullify the incorporation of the company.

Irish Permanent Building Society v Cauldwell [1981] ILRM 242 (High Court)

[2.12] The Irish Life Building Society (ILBS) had been registered as a building society by the Registrar of Building Societies under the Building Societies Act 1976. The plaintiffs successfully argued that the registration of the ILBS infringed various provisions of the Act of 1976. However, it was held that the registrar's mistake in registering the ILBS did not nullify its incorporation.

[2.13] **Barrington J:** The plaintiffs last submission is that the registrar has no jurisdiction to register the society. They allege that its rules violated the Act and in particular s 56 thereof. They therefore suggest that the registrar had no jurisdiction under s 11 to register the society; its registration is accordingly void and the defendant society does not exist as a corporate body . . .

The real issue in the present case is whether, because of the registrar's mistake of law, the incorporation of the building society is a nullity. It appears to me that the answer to this question is not to be found in the consideration of abstract questions of law but in ascertaining the intentions of the legislature in this particular statute.

Section 11(7) of the Act provides as follows:

'A certificate of incorporation given under this section by the registrar shall be sufficient evidence until the contrary is shown that all the requirements of this Act relating to registration of rules and matters precedent and incidental to registration of rules have been complied with and that the society is a society authorised to be incorporated and was duly incorporated under this Act.'

[I]t appears to me to be a fair conclusion that the Act contemplates that notwithstanding the vigilance of the registrar, societies with defective rules will get on to the register and also that societies may be validly incorporated notwithstanding the fact that their rules are in some particular defective.

It is clear from the wording of s 11(7) that circumstances may arise when the very incorporation of the society may be called in question. But I would be very surprised if the incorporation of a society could be invalidated by an honest mistake such as was made by the founders and the registrar in the present case. If the law were otherwise people might in good faith deal with a society for many years only to find that because of some defect in its rules the society did not exist as a corporate body. Such a society, not being a building society incorporated under the Act, could not even be wound up in accordance with the provisions of the Act. Moreover it is well known that building societies borrow short and lend long so that the problems of getting in the societies assets would be enormous. Innocent citizens might have entered into committments to build houses relying on finance from a building society which turned out not to exist. Already the defendant society has amassed assets of some £17,000,000 and has entered into many million pounds worth of mortgage committments. To hold that the society was not validly incorporated would clearly cause great damage to many innocent people and I cannot accept that the Oireachtas intended that such a catastrophic result should ensue in circumstances such as the present.

Even if the certificate of incorporation is conclusive evidence of compliance with the registration requirements and of the fact of incorporation, the Attorney General may still challenge registration by way of certiorari. Furthermore, the certificate is only conclusive to show that the company is one authorised to be registered and duly registered. Illegal objects contained in the memorandum are still open to challenge.

Bowman v Secular Society Limited [1917] AC 406 (House of Lords)

[2.14] The Secular Society Ltd had been duly registered under the Companies Acts. It was unsuccessfully alleged that the main object of the company was blasphemous and illegal. In the course of argument it was contended by the company that because of the conclusiveness of the certificate of incorporation it could not now be argued that the objects of the company were unlawful. This argument was rejected by a majority of the House of Lords.

[2.15]   Lord Parker of Waddington: The Secular Society Limited, was incorporated as a company limited by guarantee under the Companies Acts, 1862 to 1893, and a company so incorporated is by s 17 of the Act of 1862 capable of exercising all the functions of an incorporated company. Prima facie, therefore, the society is a corporate body created by virtue of a statute of the realm, with statutory power to acquire property by gift, whether inter vivos or by will. The appellants endeavour to displace this prima facie effect of the Companies Acts in the following manner. If, they say, you look at the objects for which the society was incorporated, as expressed in its memorandum of association you will find that they are either actually illegal or, at any rate, in conflict with the policy of the law. This being so, the society was not an association capable of incorporation under the Acts. It was and is an illegal association, and as such incapable of acquiring property by gift. I do not think this argument is open to the appellants, even if their major premise be correct. By the first section of the Companies Act, 1900, the society's certificate of registration is made conclusive evidence that the society was an association authorized to be registered – that is, an association of not less than seven persons associated together for a lawful purpose. The section does not mean that all or any of the objects specified in the memorandum, if otherwise illegal, would be rendered legal by the certificate. On the contrary, if the directors of the society applied its funds for an illegal object, they would be guilty of misfeasance and liable to replace the money, even if the object for which the money had been applied were expressly authorized by the memorandum. In like manner a contract entered into by the company for an unlawful object, whether authorized by the memorandum or otherwise, could not be enforced either in law or in equity. The section does, however, preclude all His Majesty's lieges from going behind the certificate or from alleging that the society is not a corporate body with the status and capacity conferred by the Acts. Even if all the objects specified in the memorandum were illegal, it does not follow that the company cannot on that account apply its funds or enter into a contract for a lawful purpose. Every company has power to wind up voluntarily, and moneys paid or contracts entered into with that object are in every respect lawfully paid or entered into. Further, the disposition provided by the company's memorandum for its surplus assets in case of winding up may be lawful though all the objects as a going concern are unlawful. If there be no lawful manner of applying such surplus assets they would on the dissolution of the company belong to the Crown as bona vacantia: *Cunnack v Edwards* [1896] 2 Ch 679.

My Lords, some stress was laid on the public danger, or at any rate the anomaly, of the courts recognizing the corporate existence of a company all of whose objects as specified in its memorandum of association, are transparently illegal. Such a case is not likely to occur, for the registrar fulfils a quasi-judicial function and his duty is to determine whether an association applying for registration is authorized to be registered under the Acts. Only by misconduct or great carelessness on the part of the Registrar could a company with objects wholly illegal obtain registration. If such a case did occur it would be open to the Court to stay its hand until an opportunity had been given for taking the appropriate steps for the cancellation of the certificate of registration. It should be observed that neither s 1 of the Companies Act 1900 nor the corresponding section of the Companies (Consolidation) Act 1908 is so expressed as to bind the Crown, and the Attorney-General, on behalf of the Crown, could institute proceedings by way of certiorari to cancel a registration which the registrar in affected discharge of his quasi-judicial duties had improperly or erroneously allowed.

Lords Dundein and Buckmaster concurred. Lord Finlay L.C. dissented.

The Registrar must refuse to register a company where one or more of its proposed objects necessarily involve a criminal offence, even if the documents delivered to the Registrar are otherwise in order.

R v Registrar of Companies, ex p Bowen [1914] 3 KB 1161 (King's Bench Divisional Court)

[2.16]   Under the Dentists Act 1878 it was made an offence for a person to use the name or title of 'dentist' or 'dental practitioner' or to imply that he was registered under that Act or that he was specially qualified to practise dentistry, unless he was in fact registered under that Act. Application was made for the registration of a company with the name of 'The United Dental Service Limited'. One of the proposed objects of the company was 'to carry on the practice, profession or business of practitioners in dentistry in all its branches'. It was intended to carry on the practice by practitioners not registered under the Dentists Act 1878. On the facts, the Court of Appeal held that no offence would be committed under the Act of 1878 by the use of the proposed name and accordingly the Registrar had no discretion to refuse to register the company.

[2.17]   Lord Reading CJ (having determined that the use of the name would not constitute an offence under the Act): The Registrar of Companies would be entitled, if the use of the proposed name would be an offence under the statute (either under this or any other statute), to refuse to register the company with that name; but having arrived at the conclusion that that would not be the effect of the use of the words 'United Dental Service', I hold that the registrar was wrong in refusing registration upon that ground.

If he came to the conclusion that the phrase used in the name of the company implied in the circumstances that an offence under the statute would be committed, he would be right in refusing registration. I am far from saying that he has no discretion at all if the association is formed for a lawful purpose. For instance, I think if the name presented to him for registration contained scandalous or obscene words he would be perfectly justified in refusing registration . . .

Avory J delivered a concurring judgment. Bankes J concurred.

R v Registrar of Joint Stock Companies ex p More [1931] 2 KB 197 (Court of Appeal)

[2.18]   Application was made for the registration in England of a company one of the objects of which was the sale there of tickets for a lottery in Ireland. The sale of the tickets would have been unlawful under s 41 of the Lotteries Act 1823. Accordingly, the registrar refused to register the company. His decision was upheld both by the trial judge and the Court of Appeal.

[2.19]   Scrutton LJ: This is a short point involving the construction of s 41 of the Lotteries Act 1832. Two gentlemen proposed to sell tickets in England in connection with an Irish lottery. For some reason they did not propose to do this themselves; they proposed to form a private company to do it. It is merely conjecture on my part that this may be due to the fact that the provisions in the Act of 1823 making offenders liable to be punished as rogues and vagabonds do not apply to a company, and so the two gentlemen intending to form this company wished in this way to avoid the risk of being prosecuted under the Act. They accordingly lodged the memorandum and articles of association of the proposed company with the Registrar of Companies, who, when he saw that the object of the company was to sell tickets in a lottery known as the Irish Free State Hospitals Sweepstake, refused to register the company. Thereupon an application was made to the court for a writ of mandamus directing the registrar to register the company. To succeed in that application the applicant must show that it is legal to sell in England tickets for the Irish Free State Hospitals Sweepstake authorised by an Act of the Irish Free State. The only Act which can be supposed to authorize the selling in England is an Irish Act, but the Irish Parliament has no jurisdiction in England, and that being so, the Irish Parliament cannot authorize lottery tickets to be sold in England. The authority to sell in any place must be given by the Parliament having jurisdiction in that place, and the Imperial Parliament has given no authority to sell lottery tickets in England.

Slesser and Greer LJJ delivered concurring judgments.

Re-Registration of Companies

[2.20] It is permissible for a corporation incorporated as one type of company to re-register as another type. For example, typically, a plc is not formed as such but will start life as a private company. For further details on the different forms of re-registration available and the appropriate procedures see *Keane* at paras **4.20–4.27**.

Companies Incorporated Outside Ireland[1]

[2.21] Companies formed outside the jurisdiction, must within one month of establishing a place of business in Ireland deliver various documents to the registrar, as set out in s 352 of the Principal Act.[2]

1 See *Keane* at para **4.28**.
2 Thereafter while the company remains within the jurisdiction other documentation as set out in ss 353–360 at the appropriate times, be delievered to the registrar.

Official Notification[1]

[2.22] Under the provisions of the European Commumities (Companies) Requlations 1973, which give effect to certain provisions of the First Companies Directive, various documents which are delivered to the registrar of companies for registration in the Companies Office must also be published in Iris Oifigiuil.

European Communities (Companies) Regulations 1973. SI No 163 of 1973

Article 4. Publication of Notices.

[2.23] (4) 1. A company shall publish in Iris Oifigiuil notice of the delivery to or the issue by the registrar of companies after the commencement of these regulations of the following documents and particulars–

(*a*) any certificate of incorporation of the company.

(*b*) the memorandum and articles of association, or the charter, statutes or other instrument constituting or defining the constitution of the company (in these regulations included in the term 'memorandum and articles of association').

(*c*) any document making or evidencing an alteration in its memorandum or articles of association.

(*d*) every amended text of its memorandum and articles of association.

(*e*) any return relating to its register of directors or notification of a change among its directors.

(*f*) any return relating to the person other than the board of directors, authorised to enter into transactions binding the company, or notification of a change among such persons.

(*g*) its annual return.

(*h*) any notice of the situation of its registered office, or of any change therein.

(*i*) any copy of a winding up order in respect of the company.

(*j*) any order for the dissolution of the company on a winding up.

(*k*) any return by a liquidator of the first meeting of the company on a winding up.

(2) A notice shall be published within six weeks of the relevant delivery or issue.

(3) In a voluntary winding up, the liquidator shall, within 14 days after his appointment publish in Iris Oifigiuil a notice of his appointment in addition to delivering notice to the registrar of companies as required by s 278 of the Act.

Article (5). Text of altered memorandum and articles.

[2.24] (5). Where any alteration is made in a company's memorandum or articles of association, notice of which the company is required to publish under regulation 4, the company shall deliver to the registrar of companies, in addition to the alterations, a copy of the text of the memorandum and articles as so altered.

Article (11). Extension of time for delivery of documents.

[2.25] (11). The court may by order at any time extend the time for delivery of documents under these regulations for such period as the court may think proper.

Note
Failure to publish the notice will not prevent the company from commencing trading.

Registered Office[2]

[2.26] Every company must have a registered office to which communications and notices may be addressed.[3] Notice thereof must be sent to the registrar of companies prior to incorporation.[4] While registration in Ireland gives a company Irish nationality and domicile, it does not determine the residence of the company.

A company resides where its 'central management and control' actually resides.[5]

John Hood & Co Ltd v Magee [1918] 2 IR 34

[2.27] Mr Hood was the sole director and manager of a company which was registered in Ireland. The company manufactured linen in Ireland which was within the jurisdiction and which was sole in the United States of America. Mr Hood resided in New York and directed the company's operations from there. He had the largest, although not a majority shareholding in the company. Most of the other shareholders also resided outside the jurisdiction. Liability to income tax depended on the company being resident in Ireland. The company argued that it was controlled from New York where Mr Hood resided and was therefore resident in America. This argument was rejected by the court. The company's general meetings were held in Ireland and at the meeting Mr Hood could technically be dismissed as director and manager. On this basis the court found that the company was controlled from Ireland and was accordingly resident in Ireland.

[2.28]   Madden J: The company was incorporated in Ireland on January 10th 1913, as a company limited by shares, having its registered office in Belfast. The object for which the company was established was to take over the business of the firm of 'John Hood & Co,' of Franklin Street, New York, who were merchants and commission agents dealing in linen, cambric, cotton, lace and articles of a similar character . . .

The memorandum of association contains this clause, 'The registered office of the company will be situated in Ireland.' It is stated that the company has been also registered in the United States of America under the same title as in Ireland. There is no further reference in the case to the American company, and I part with it, noting that as it is stated to be the company which was registered in Ireland, it is an essential part of its constitution, as defined by the memorandum of association that its registered office must be situated in Ireland. Passing on to the articles of association I find that the annual general meetings of the company are to be held at such place as the directors shall from time to time determine. The first statutory meeting of the company was held in Belfast on April 9th 1913. The first annual ordinary meeting was held at the registered offices of the company in Belfast in March 1914 and the second annual general meeting was held at the same place in April 1915. Under the articles of association it is provided that

John Hood shall be the first director of the company (article 75). Article 80 provides that the number of the directors is to be such as general meetings shall from time to time direct.

The case is a typical one of a business built up by the ability and industry of one man, and when it has attained a certain degree of success, converted into a joint stock company, registered with limited liability under the Companies Acts. In such a case it is usual to entrust the control and management of the new company in the first instance to the man by whom the business was created. But this control is in its nature temporary. The founder of the firm may from age or other reasons cease to hold the position of sole director, in which case he will ordinarily be succeeded by a board of directors appointed by the shareholders at a general meeting of the company. John Hood, in whom the powers of the directorate are vested, is at the present moment resident in New York; but his residence there does not result from anything in the constitution of the company, or necessarily follow from the nature of the business carried on by it. This business consists in the purchase in Ireland and Scotland, mainly in Ireland, of linen goods, principally damask, which are bleached and finished by firms other than the appellants', and then folded by hand in the Belfast warehouse of the company. They are sold by the sole director, Mr Hood, in America; but the remaining portion of the business is carried on in the United Kingdom. The shareholders, by re-electing Mr Hood, have acted on the belief that it is in the interest of the company that the managing director should reside where the goods in which they trade are sold, rather than where they are manufactured and bought. But this arrangement might be departed from. In my opinion, the residence of the sole director, Mr Hood, in New York is not the kind of residence of a directorate which can be relied on as determining the residence of the company for the purpose of taxation, and here lies the essential difference between the present case and the *De Beers* case [1906] AC 455.

The judgment of Lord Loreburn LC in that case is relied on by the appellant company as affording a test of residence which, when applied to the present case, leads to the conclusion that the company is resident in New York. 'In applying the conception of residence to a company', Lord Loreburn says at p 458, 'We ought, I think, to proceed as nearly as we can upon the analogy of an individual. A company cannot eat or sleep, but it can keep house and do business. We ought, therefore, to see where it really keeps house and does business.' Having referred to decisions which adopted the principle that a company resides for the purpose of income where its real business is carried on, he adds, 'I regard that as the true rule, and the real business is carried on where the central management and control actually abides.'

Applying the test supplied by Lord Loreburn I ask in the first instance where does this company keep house? Assuredly in Belfast, for here the registered office must be, under the provisions of the memorandum of association, and here the general meetings of the company are in fact held. Where does it do business? Some of the business transactions are carried on in Ireland and some in New York, and this divided business leaves unsolved the question which Lord Loreburn regards as the true test as to where the real business is carried on. This, he says, is where the central management and control actually abides.

In my opinion, the central management and control of this company abides with the general meeting of shareholders in Belfast, where the registered office of the company is situated and where the general meetings of the company are held. In the *De Beers* case [1906] AC 455 the control of the company abided, not in the general meetings, which were held in Kimberley, but in three life-governors and sixteen ordinary directors. Of the ordinary directors four necessarily resided in England. Two of the three life-governors and nine of the sixteen ordinary directors in fact resided in the United Kingdom. The House of Lords, affirming the decision of the Court of Appeal, held that the real control of the company rested with the directorate, the residence of which determined the residence of the company. The relation of this directorate to the company and the circumstances of their residence in England are widely different from those in the case of Mr Hood. If the shareholders in general meeting were to consider it more in the interests of the company that the managing director should reside where the goods in which they deal are manufactured and bought, they might refuse to re-elect him, except on the terms of his residing in Belfast. Adopting the analogy suggested by Lord Loreburn, the movement would proceed from the heart and brain of the organisation in Belfast by which the action of its organs is controlled.

1 See *Keane* **3.09**.
2 See *Keane* at paras **9.06–9.08**.
3 S 113 of the Principal Act as substituted by s 4 of the 1982 Act.
4 Ibid.
5 See Corrigan *Place of Abode Test in Establishing Tax Residence* (1988) 6 ILT (ns) 106.

Notes

This case contrasts somewhat with British authorities where it was held that central management and control 'actually abides' at the place from which the directors manage the company's affairs (*De Beers Consolidated Mines Ltd v Howe* [1906] AC 455), even if the company's constitution stipulates that they should be managed from elsewhere (*Unit Construction Ltd v Bullock* [1960] AC 351). Where the company's control is split between two or more jurisdictions, it may find itself with multiple residences (*Swedish Central Railway v Thompson* [1925] AC 495; *Egyptian Delta Land & Investment Co Ltd v Todd* [1929] AC 1). This could have the disasterous consequence of rendering the company liable to pay tax on the same profits in a number of jurisdictions.

Chapter 3

MEMORANDUM AND ARTICLES OF ASSOCIATION

[3.01] The constitution of a company is made up of two essential documents, the memorandum of association and the articles of association.[1] By registration of the memorandum the company is incorporated, whereas the articles are the company's internal regulations. Table A of the Principal Act sets out model form articles. A company limited by shares is deemed to have adopted table A if it does not itself register articles, or to have adopted so much of the regulations of table A which have not been modified or excluded by the articles actually registered.[2] The articles in part I of table A apply to public companies, the slightly modified part II applying to private companies. Depending on the type of company involved, the memorandum of association should, so far as circumstances admit, be in the form of table B, C, D or E of the Principal Act,[3] or in the case of a plc in the form prescribed by the second schedule of the 1983 Act.[4]

1 See *Keane* at paras **5.01–5.014**.
2 S 13(2).
3 S 16.
4 S .4(3) of the 1983 Act.

[3.02] The constitution of a company is not made up of the memorandum of association alone.

TJ Wilson (Inspector of Taxes) v Dunnes Stores (Cork) Limited [1982] ILRM 444

[3.03] S 47 of the Finance Act 1932 provided that a company which is prohibited by its constitution from returning profits to its members, would not be liable to corporation profits tax. The company argued that it was exempt from the tax as art 52 of its articles provided that 'no portion of the profits of the company shall be paid or transferred by way of dividend, cash bonus or capital bonus to any member of the company in respect of shares held by him.' The Appeal Commissioner upheld this contention but stated a case to the High Court as to the correctness of his decision. The appellant contended that the respondent was liable to the tax on ground that the company's constitution consisted only of its memorandum of association.

[3.04] **Kenny J.:** Counsel for the inspector contended that the taxpayer was not a corporate body which by its constitution was precluded from distributing any profits among its members because, he said, the constitution consisted of the memorandum of association only. In my opinion, the constitution referred to in s 47 of the Finance Act 1932 consists of the memorandum and articles of association. The memorandum of association cannot in my view, be the constitution of the company for it does not even contain any provision about the election of the directors or their removal from office or the holding of meetings or the rights of shareholders. I am fortified in this conclusion by the sense in which Lindley LJ, that great master of company law, used the words 'the constitution of the company' in *Re Bridgewater Navigation Company* [1891] 2 Ch 317 at 327.

It is sufficient here to say that the company was incorporated under the Companies Act 1862 and had a memorandum and articles of association. When Lindley was dealing with the effect of capitalising profits he said 'Moreover, this is a matter on which a majority cannot bind a minority unless expressly empowered to do so by the constitution of the company, wither as originally framed or as subsequently modified by some authority binding on all.' Provisions in relation to capitalising profits always appear in the articles of association and I have never seen a memorandum of association which contained any provision in relation to this. Accordingly, I reject the argument that the constitution of the tax payer does not preclude it from distributing its profits among its members because the new article 52 is in the articles and not in the memorandum of association.

[3.05] Where there is a conflict between a provision in the memorandum and a provision in the articles, the memorandum prevails.

Guinness v Land Corporation of Ireland (1883) 42 Ch D 349 (Court of Appeal)

[3.06] Under s 8 of the Companies Act 1862 (now s 6 of the Principal Act) the memorandum must state the amount of capital with which a limited liability company is proposed to be registered, divided into shares of a certain fixed amount. The memorandum of the company provided that the share capital was divided into 140,000 A shares of £5 each and 3,500 B shares of £100. However, art 8 of the articles provided, inter alia, that the class A shares should receive a preferential dividend of 5%. The court rejected the contention that the company's funds could be distributed in the manner envisaged by art 8.

[3.07] **Bowen LJ:** We have then to consider the argument that the court may turn to the articles of association to see if they do not, so to say, supplement the memorandum, and for this particular purpose admit of being read with it. I shall only say a few words as to how far, in my opinion, the articles of association may be looked at and read together with the memorandum of association . . . There is an essential difference between the memorandum and the articles. The memorandum contains the fundamental conditions upon which alone the company is allowed to be incorporated. They are conditions introduced for the benefit of the creditors, and the outside public, as well as of the shareholders. The articles of association are the internal regulations of the company. How can it be said that in all cases the fundamental conditions of the charter of incorporation, and the internal regulations of the company are to be construed together . . . In any case it is, as it seems to me, certain that for anything which the Act of Parliament says shall be in the memorandum you must look to the memorandum alone. If the legislature has said that one instrument is to be dominant, you cannot turn to another instrument and read it in order to modify the provisions of the dominant instrument.

Cotton LJ delivered a concurring judgment.

Reginald GH Roper v John Ward and Others [1981] ILRM 408 (High Court)

[The facts are irrelevant]

[3.08] **Carroll J:** In construing the articles, I am guided by the principle that they are subordinate to and controlled by the memorandum of association which is the dominant instrument. While the articles cannot alter or control the memorandum or be used to expand the objects of the company, they can be used to explain it generally or to explain an ambiguity in its terms . . .

The memorandum and articles of association of a company are commercial documents and should be construed to give them reasonable business efficacy. They are in effect a contract between the company and its members. When they are registered they bind the company and its members as if they had been sealed and signed by each member and contained covenants on the part of each member to observe all the provisions of the articles.

Notes

On the use of the articles to clarify ambiguities in the memorandum see also *Re Bansha Woollen Mill Co Ltd* (1887) 21 LR Ir 181.

In *Hennessy v National Agricultural and Industrial Development Association* [1947] IR 159 under the terms of its memorandum of association the NAIDA could only make alterations to its articles of association with the consent of the Minister for Industry and Commerce. It purported to pass two special resolutions altering the company's articles. The Minister's prior approval had not been obtained. The plaintiffs who were members of the NAIDA had objected to the alterations and sought a declaration that they were invalid, as being inconsistent with the requirements of the memorandum. Overend J., upheld their claim, holding that as a rule of law, the memorandum takes precedence over the articles.

The memorandum of association.

[3.09] S 6 of the Principal Act sets out various matters which must be stated in the memorandum.[1] It must be printed, stamped as if it were a deed, and be signed by each subscriber in the presence of at least one witness who must attest the signature.[2] A company may not alter the provisions contained in its memorandum except in the cases, in the mode and to the extent for which express provision is made in the Companies Acts.[3]

1 See generally *Keane* chapter 5.
2 S 7.
3 S 9.

The name clause

[3.10] The name of the company must be stated in the memorandum[1] and where the liability of the members is limited, this fact must be so indicated at the end of the name. Undesirable names may not be reigstered. There is a right of appeal against a refusal to register a company by a particular name. Where through inadvertance or otherwise a company is registered with a name which in the opinion of the Minister is too like the name of an existing registered company, he may, within 6 months of registration direct that the new company change its name.[2] A company may by special resolution and with the comsent of the Minister, change its name. Every company carrying on business under a name other than its corporate name must register it under the Registration of Business Names Act 1963.[3] The use of the word 'limited' or 'teoranta' may be dispensed with in the circumstances set out in s 24 as amended by s 58 of the 1983 Act.

Associated companies may be registered with similar names.

1 See Keane paras **5.03–5.10**.
2 S 21.
3 S 23(2).

IPBS v Cauldwell [1981] ILRM 240

[3.11] **Barrington J:** Under s 11(3) of the Act the registrar if satisfied that the rules of the society comply with the relevant requirements of the Act, is not to refuse to register unless he is of the opinion (inter alia) that the name of the proposed society is undesireable, or that the registration of the society would not be in accordance with the proper and orderly registration of building society business.

[3.12] The plaintiffs submit that the name Irish Life Building Society is obviously desirable because it would lead unsuspecting citizens to believe that the resources of the Irish Life Assurance Company Limited are behind the building society whereas, in fact, the building society is a separate legal entity and the Irish Life Assurance Company Limited is under no obligation in law to come to its rescue should the building society get into difficulties. The plaintiffs accept that this submission has very far reaching implications and that similar submissions could be made concerning a subsidiary company in a group of companies which bears the name of the parent company. It is usually accepted as appropriate and proper that the link between the various companies in a group should be revealed by a similarity of name. While a parent company may not be obliged in law to come to the rescue of its subsidiary, commercial considerations may make it expedient for it to do so, and this is accepted as a fact of business life

Notes
The court may grant an injunction restraining a company from registering a name which is calculated to mislead or deceive the public into thinking that the business of the new company is that of another company. See *Ewing v Buttercup Margerine Co* [1917] 2 Ch 1 and *Waring and Gillow Ltd v Gillow & Gillow Ltd* (1916) 32 TLR 389. In *Aerators Ltd v Tollitt* [1902] 2 Ch 319 the court held that in deciding whether a name is likely to deceive should consider (1) the respective businesses of the old company and the new company, and (2) the name of the old company. Furthermore, the court will not restrain the use of a word which is in ordinary use in the English or Irish language and which is descriptive only.

Company name to be used

[3.13] Under s 114 of the Principal Act the company must put its name up outside every place where it carries on business and must place its name on its seal. Its name must also appear on all letters and other documentation emanating from the company. Failure to comply with these requirements may lead to criminal penalties. If any officer or other agent of the company signs or authorises to be signed on behalf of the company any bill of exchange, promissory note, endorsement, cheque or order for money or goods wherein its name is not correctly stated that officer or agent will incur personal liability to the holder of the instrument unless it is duly paid by the company.

[3.14] Personal liability will be incurred under s 114 unless the company's name is accurately stated on the instrument. However, the holder of the instrument may be estopped from enforcing that personal liability where he has been responsible for the wrong description of the company on the instrument, or alternatively where he has expressly or impliedly represented that he will treat the incorrect description of the company as being regular and as not giving rise to personal liability.

Durham Fancy Goods Ltd v Michael Jackson (Fancy Goods) Ltd (Queen's Bench Division) [1968] 2 All ER 987

[3.15]   The plaintiff drew a bill of exchange on Michael Jackson (Fancy) Goods Ltd, but was referred to in the bill and the form of acceptance prepared by the plaintiff as 'M Jackson (Fancy Goods) Ltd'. Michael Jackson, a director and the secretary of the drawee company signed the acceptance of the bill without correcting the error in the name of the company. The drawee company went into liquidation and dishonoured the bill. The plaintiff sought to make Mr Jackson personally liable. Donaldson J. held that the misdescription of the company's name was a breach of the English equivalent of s 114 (then s 108 of the Companies Act 1948 and now s 341 of the Companies Act 1985) and accordingly Mr Jackson was prima facie personally liable. However, he went on to hold that the plaintiff was estopped from enforcing that liability, since it was responsible for the misdescription and had impliedly represented that it would treat acceptance in that form as being regular and not giving rise to personal liability.

[3.16]   Donaldson J.: Michael Jackson and Florence Jackson were the sole directors and shareholders of a Manchester company, Michael Jackson (Fancy Goods) Ltd, to whom I will refer to as 'Jacksons' . . .

Counsel for Mr Jackson submits that there was sufficient compliance with the section in the present case because (a) the bill made it clear that the acceptors were a limited company and (b) there was no confusion as to their identity . . .

Unfortunately for Mr Jackson, the second submission is unsupported by authority. Indeed it is contrary to the tenor of the decision of Denman J., and of the Court of Appeal in *Atkins v Wardle* (1898) 58 LJQB 377. There the drawer of the bill was a shareholder in 'The South Shields Salt Water Baths Company Limited' but he drew on 'Salt Water Baths Company Limited, South Shields', and the directors accepted on behalf of 'South Shields Salt Water Baths Co' which was equally incorrect. No question of confusion as to identity or as to the status of the drawers as a limited liability company could have arisen. Nevertheless the directors were held to be personally liable, Lord Esher MR, pointing out that the statute did not require the misdescription to be material.

Counsel for Mr Jackson also submitted that just as 'Ltd' was an acceptable abbreviation for 'Limited', so 'M' was an acceptable abbreviation for 'Michael'. This I do not accept. The word 'Limited' is included in a company's name by way of description and not identification. Accordingly, a generally accepted abbreviation will serve this purpose as well as the word in full. The rest of the name, by contrast, serves as a means of identification and may be compounded of or include initials or abbreviations. The use of any abbreviation of the registered name is calculated to create problems of identification which are not created by an abbreviation of 'Limited'. I should therefore be prepared to hold that no abbreviation was permissible of any part of a company's name other than 'Ltd' for 'Limited' and possibly, the ampersand for 'and'. However, it is not necessary to go as far as this. Any abbreviation must convey the full word unambiguously and the initial 'M' neither shows that it is an abbreviation nor does it convey 'Michael'.

I have therefore, no doubt that Mr Jackson committed an offence under s 108 of the Act of 1948, although a court might well decide to impose no penalty. I have also no doubt that he is liable to the plaintiffs who are admitted to be the holders of the bill of exchange since this is what the statute says; but can the plaintiffs enforce that liability? That is a different question.

This case is distinguished from all previous cases under the earlier statutory versons of the section in that here it was the holders of the bill of exchange who inscribed the words of acceptance, who chose the wrong words and who now seek to rely on their own error, coupled it is true with the defendant's failure to detect and remedy it, as entitling them to relief. Common sense and justice seem to me to dictate that they shall fail. If I am right, thus far I should be surprised if the law compelled me to find in the plaintiff's favour because, contrary to popular belief, the law, justice and common sense are not unrelated concepts.

In my judgment the principle of equity on which the promissory estoppel cases are based is applicable to and bars the plaintiff's claim.

The relevant liability is to guarantee the payment of the bill at maturity, contingent on its being accepted by Mr Jackson on Jackson's behalf without mentioning their name on the bill. Against this background, the plaintiffs did not, as one would have expected, send the bill to Jacksons without words of acceptance, but instead inscribed words of acceptance including a name which was deceptively similar to, but not the same as, that of Jacksons . . . The plaintiffs thereby implied that acceptance of the bill in that form would be, or would be accepted by them as a regular acceptence of the bill. Such an acceptance would not, of course, have involved Mr Jackson in personal liability. In these circumstances it would be inequitable that the plaintiffs whould be allowed to enforce the statutory liability of Mr Jackson without first giving him an opportunity of regularising the acceptance by inscribing the correct name of Jacksons on the bill and that it is now too late to do. Accordingly the plaintiffs are unable to enforce the statutory liability, although it continues to exist and would have been available to other holders, who were unaffected by the equitable defence.'

Notes

In *Lindholst & Co AIS v Fowler and Another* [1988] BCLC 166 the plaintiffs contracted to supply equipment to Corby Chicken Co Ltd. Payment was to be by bills of exchange, which were prepared by the plaintiffs. The bills referred to 'Corby Chicken Co', without adding 'Ltd'. The defendant signed the bills by way of acceptance on behalf of the company. The plaintiffs ultimately sued the defendant on the bills, alleging that he was personally liable thereon due to the misdescription of the company's name. The defendant was found liable. No question of estoppel arose as the words of acceptance had not been inserted by the plaintiff. According to Sir John Danaldson MR in the Court of Appeal, if the defendant had wished to avoid personal liability he should have declined to accept the bill until such time as it appeared in a proper form.

See also *Blum v OCP Repatriation SA* [1988] BCLC 170 it was held that rectification of a financial instrument will not be granted where the motivation for so doing is to avoid personal liability under s 114.

The objects clause

[3.17]   Under s 6(1)(b) of the Principal Act, a company is required to state its objects in the memorandum. The company can only pursue those stated objects and the pursuit of any other objects is deemed to be void. This is known as the ultra vires rule. The purpose behind this rule is to protect both investors in and creditors of the company. These individuals are directly or indirectly making a financial input into the company, and their money should not be risked by the company embarking on a new and unauthorised venture. For instance, the company formed to run a grocery should not embark upon the speculative and unauthorised venture of oil exploration, thereby risking investor's funds and creditor's monies. As we shall see in chapter 11, the effect of the ultra vires rules has been eroded by s 8 of the Principal Act and by reg 6 of the European Communities (Companies) Regulations 1973. Originally the objects clause was unalterable. However, now, by virtue of s 10 of the Principal Act[1] the clause can be modified by special resolution of the company, subject to the right of any dissenting minority (representing not less than 15% of the issued share capital) to apply to the court within 21 days of the passing of the resolution for relief. The court has a wide discretion as to the type of order it may make.[2] Apart from listing the objects of the company it is common to find various powers also enumerated in the objects clause. These may only be pursued as ancillary to the objects of the company.

1 S 114(2), (3), (4).
2 S 114(4).

Ashbury Rly Carriage and Iron Co v Riche (1875) LR 7 HL 653 (House of Lords)

[3.18]   **Lord Cairns LC:** [N]o object shall be pursued by the company or attempted to be attained by the company in practice, except an object which is mentioned in the memorandum of association.

Now, my lords, if that is so, if that is the condition upon which the corporation is established, if that is the purpose for which the corporation is established, it is a mode of incorporation which contains in it both that which is affirmative and that which is negative. It states affirmatively the ambit and extent of vitality and power which by law are given to the corporation, and it states, if it is necessary so to state, negatively, that nothing shall be done beyond that ambit and that no attempt shall be made to use the corporate life for any other purpose than that which is so specified.

[3.19] A company has implied power to do whatever may fairly be regarded as incidental to, or consequential upon its objects as stated in its memorandum of association.

A-G v Great Eastern Rly Co (1880) 5 App Cas 473 (House of Lords)

[3.20] **Lord Selborne LC:** I assume that your lordships will not now recede from anything that was determined in *The Ashbury Railway Company v Riche*. It appears to me to be important that the doctrine of ultra vires as it was explained in that case, should be maintained. But I agree . . . that this doctrine ought to be reasonably and not unreasonably, understood and applied and that whatever may fairly be regarded as incidental to, or consequential upon, these things which the Legislature has authorised, ought not (unless expressly prohibited) to be held, by judicial construction, to be ultra vires."

Lords Blackburn and Watson delivered concurring judgments

Martin v Irish Industrial Benefit Building Society (1960) Ir Jur Rep 42 (Circuit Court)

[3.21] The plaintiff had money on deposit with the defendant building society. She was not a member of the defendant. Members were defined as including only borrowers. The plaintiff wished to purchase a house. As a result of a discussion with the secretary of the defendant she obtained for a fee an assessors' report, printed upon the defendant's form. On the strength of the report, she subsequently borrowed money from the defendant and purchased the house, which was structurally defective. She sued the defendant in respect of the consequent loss suffered by her. The defendant pleaded that its objects expressly allowed it to prepare assessors' reports for members, but that as the objects clause was silent regarding the preparation of reports for non-members the preparation of such reports was ultra vires. Accordingly, it was argued that the contract for the preparation of the report was invalid and that the defendant was not liable to the plaintiff in damages.

[3.22] **Judge Barra O'Briain:** The defendant relies on the plea that the society have no power to enter into this contract. Counsel for the plaintiff says that the transaction was incidental to the society's objects and that the society is in fact estopped from pleading its own illegality. He refers to *Doolan v Midland Great Western Railway* but I hold that estoppel cannot be pleaded against a corporation in respect of its ultra vires acts . . . The net point is whether or not the transaction created a valid contract which is binding on the defendant society. The 'objects' of the society cover a general statement on the purpose of the society and why it was established. The society itself carries out valuations by its own assessors of property about to be purchased by members. Is there any difference where the valuation is made for a person such as the plaintiff? A case could be made on either side, depending upon whether the transaction is or is not expressly prohibited or is reasonably incidental to the objects of the society. This contract is not one expressly prohibited. Is it reasonably incidental to the objects of the society? Here we have a line ball case. If the society chooses to have valuations made for customers for a fee, business will or may result. I incline to the view that this contract here was within the powers of the society and I hold that it was not ultra vires. Subsequently, on the facts of this report, the plaintiff, I am satisfied, incurred an expense amounting to £280 of which there is a net sum of £132.19.2 directly attributable to the defective report.

Notes
See also *Northern Bank Finance Corporation Ltd v Quinn and Achates Investment Co* (8 November 1979, unreported)

[3.23] Where the objects clause consists of a series of different objects the court may try to ascertain the main objects of the company and treat all other listed objects as being merely ancillary to the 'main objects'.

Re German Date Coffee Co (1882) 20 Ch D 169 (Court of Appeal)

[The facts appear from the judgment]

[3.24] **Jessel MR:** The company is stated to be registered for several objects. The first object is to acquire a German patent granted to one Henley for manufacturing from dates a substitute for coffee. The second is to make and use the same invention or any improvement of it. That refers to the German patent. The memorandum is tautologous, an observation which need not be confined to this memorandum – it is very common as regards all memorandums of association. The third object is to adopt and carry out an agreement dated 16 February 1881. When we come to look at that, it is an agreement for the sale of the German patent. Article 4 is to manufacture and sell the preparations which are the subject of the said invention. That is pure tautology. Nobody has been able to suggest that there is anything there which is not included in articles 1 and 2. Article 5 is to grant licences. Of course, if you have no patent you cannot grant licences. Article 6 is to apply for and obtain patents for improvements or extensions of the said invention, and so on. Article 7 is to acquire and purchase, or otherwise to use, exercise and vend any other inventions for the above-mentioned or cognate subject. All those are merely ancillary provisions. Then there is article 8, which I read to be this, to import all descriptions of produce, in connection with the above-mentioned purpose or otherwise for the purposes of the company. It never can mean to import and export food produce generally. That would be making it a company for an entirely new and distinct purpose. The other reading is, in my opinion, the more grammatical reading of the two; whether it is so or not, it is I think the correct reading, and is merely ancillary. That being so, it appears to me that this memorandum, when fairly read, and notwithstanding the rather loose use of general words, is simply to buy this patent and to work it either with or without improvements. That is the substance of the whole thing.

Now what happened was this. I have no reason to doubt that the framers of the memorandum and articles believed that they would obtain the German patent, for they said 'for which a patent has or will be granted by the Empire of Germany'. But they were a little too sanguine, and they cannot complain if, like other prophets, their prophecies are sometimes not verified by the result. It turned out that the German Empire would not grant the patent. When that happened what ought they to have done? Surely they ought to have said, 'We cannot carry on business and we must wind up', and that is exactly what Mr Justice Kay ordered to be done . . . Then it turns out that the company has, quite bona fide, in anticipation of the granting of the German patent, established at Hamburg a factory for the manufacture of this substance called date coffee, and they say they have sold a good deal of it and are doing a prosperous trade. They have also entered into an agreement with the parent company, an English company called the Date Coffee Company by which that company has agreed not to compete with this company in Germany. I ought also to refer to the affidavit of Mr Gardiner, who says that he applied in September for a patent on behalf of Mr Henley, but he does not say that he obtained it, and I therefore assume that for some reason or other it was refused. This application, whatever the result may have been, appears to me no ground for varying the order which has been made. That being so, it seems to me, as the learned judge of the court below said, the whole substratum of the company is gone. Its business was not to make a substitute for coffee from dates, but to work a German patented invention in Germany; to work it under the monopoly granted by the German government to the patentee, and not to enter into any such business generally. Therefore the shareholders have a right to say, 'We did not enter into partnership on these terms' . . . It was not a general partnership to make a substitute for coffee from dates, but to work a particular patent, and as that particular patent does not exist, and cannot now exist, they are entitled to say the company ought to be wound up.

It appears to me the learned judge in the court below has arrived at the right conclusion and that this appeal ought to be dismissed. If the full effect of the general words is allowed they might carry on any business whatever.

Baggallay and Lindley LJJ delivered concurring judgments.

[3.25]   In order to get around the 'main objects' rule a sub-clause may be contained in the company's objects clause, providing that each of the stated objects is an independent and substantive object and is not to be construed as being auxiliary or subsidiary to any other stated object.

Cotman v Brougham [1918] AC 514 (House of Lords)

[The facts appear from the judgment]

[3.26] **Lord Finlay LC:** 'My Lords, the Essequibo Rubber and Tobacco Estates Limited, is a company which was registered in April 6 1910. The memorandum of association is one of a type which unfortunately has become common. The Companies (Consolidation) Act 1908, requires that the memorandum of association should set out, inter alia, "the objects of the company" (s 3). The memorandum of this company in clause 3 set out a vast variety of objects, and wound up with the following extraordinary provision: "The objects set forth in any sub-clause of this clause shall not, except when the context expressly so requires, be in any wise limited or restricted by reference to or inference from the terms of any other sub-clause, or by the name of the company. None of such sub-clauses or the objects therein specified or the powers thereby conferred shall be deemed subsidiary or auxiliary merely to the objects mentioned in the first sub-clause of this clause, but the company shall have full power to exercise all or any of the powers conferred by any part of this clause in any part of the world, and notwithstanding that the business, undertaking, property or acts proposed to be transacted, acquired, dealt with or performed do not fall within the objects of the first sub-clause of this clause.' . . .

The registrar accepted the memorandum of association and gave a certificate of incorporation and that certificate is conclusive . . . All that the courts can do is to construe the memorandum as it stands.

In the present case the question is whether it was intra vires of the Essequibo Rubber Company to enter into the transaction which has ended in the company's being put on the B list of contributories to another company, the Anglo-Cuban Oil Bitumen and Asphalt Company Limited. The Essequibo Company underwrote shares in the Anglo-Cuban Company and received an allotment of 17,200 such shares. An order was made for a compulsory liquidation of the Anglo-Cuban Company, and it was ordered that the Essequibo Company, which is already in liquidation should be placed on the B list of contributories in respect of £14,061 due upon these shares. An application was made to strike out the name of the Essequibo Company from the list of contributories on the ground that the whole transaction was ultra vires. Neville J. refused the application, and he was affirmed by the Court of Appeal.

The question depends upon the interpretation to be put upon the 3rd clause of the memorandum of association. This clause has 30 heads dealing with a multitude of objects and powers. It is only necessary to refer to the 8th and 12th heads of that clause, which I have already quoted. [His lordship then read the sub-clauses which purported to authorise the company's dealings in the shares] . . . I agree with both courts below in thinking that it is impossible to say that the acquisition of these powers was ultra vires of the Essequibo Company.'

Lord Parker Of Waddington. (Read by Lord Atkinson): The 17th section of the Act makes the certificate of incorporation conclusive evidence that (inter alia) the provisions of s 3 as to stating the objects of the company in its memorandum of association have been duly complied with. The only point, therefore, open to your Lordship's House is the true construction of such memorandum . . . My Lords, Mr Whinney in his able argument suggested that, in considering whether a particular transaction was or was not ultra vires a company, regard ought to be had to the question whether at the date of the transaction the company could have been wound up on the ground that its substratum had failed. Upon consideration I cannot accept this suggestion. The question whether or not a company can be wound up for failure of substratum is a question of equity between a company and its shareholders. The question whether or not a transaction is ultra vires is a question of law between the company and a third party. The truth is that the statement of a company's objects in its memorandum is intended to serve a double purpose. In the first place it gives protection to subscribers, who learn from it the purposes to which their money can be applied. In the second place it gives protection to persons who deal with the company, and who can infer from it the extent of the company's powers. The narrower the objects expressed in the memorandum the less is the subscriber's risk, but the wider such objects the greater is the security of those who transact business with the company. Moreover, experience soon showed that persons who transact business with companies do not like having to depend on inference when the validity of a proposed transaction is in question. Even a power to borrow money could not always be safely inferred, much less such a power as that of underwriting shares in another company. Thus arose the practice of specifying powers as objects, a practice rendered possible by the fact that there is no statutory limit on the number of objects which may be specified. But even thus, a person proposing to deal with a company could not be absolutely safe, for powers specified as objects might be read as ancillary to and exercisable only for the purpose of attaining what might be held to be the company's main or paramount object, and on this construction no one could be quite certain whether the court would not hold any proposed transaction to be ultra vires. At any rate, all the surrounding circumstances would require investigation. Fresh clauses were framed to meet this difficulty, and the result is the modern memorandum of association with its multifarious list of objects and powers specified as objects and its clauses designed to prevent any specified object being read as ancillary to some other object. For the purpose of determining whether a company's substratum be gone, it may be necessary to distinguish between power and object and to determine what is the main or paramount object of the company, but I do not think this is necessary where a transaction is impeached as ultra vires. A person who deals with a company is entitled to assume that a company can do everything which it is expressly authorised to do by its memorandum of association and need not investigate the equities between the company and its shareholders.

The only other point which I need mention is the company's name. In construing a memorandum of association the name of the company, being part of the memorandum can of course, be considered. But where the operative part of the memorandum is clear and unambiguous, I do not think its obvious meaning ought to be cut down or enlarged by reference to the name of the company. It should be remembered that the name is susceptible of alteration, and it would be impossible to hold that such alteration could diminish or enlarge a company's powers. On the other hand, the name may be very material if it be necessary to consider what is the company's main or paramount object in order to see whether its substratum is gone.

I think the appeal should be dismissed with costs.

Lord Wrenbury delivered a concurring judgment. Lord Atkinson concurred.

Notes

On the question of referring to the company's name in determining its main objects, see *Re Crown Bank* (1890) 44 Ch D 634 in which it was also stated that the objects stated in the memorandum must be specific and certain. Registration should be refused by the registrar if the company has vague objects.

[3.27]　An independent objects clause may have the effect of raising some powers contained in the objects clause to the status of independent objects. Some powers, however, by their very nature can never be objects.

Re Introductions Ltd [1970] Ch 199 (Court of Appeal)

[3.28]　**Harman LJ:** "This is an appeal from a decision of Buckley J [1968] 2 All ER 1221 on a summons in the liquidation of the plaintiff company raising the question whether the debentures held by the defendant bank are valid against the liquidator or are void as being tainted by the doctrine of ultra vires. The judge decided two questions. First, whether the activity in question was within the powers of the company. That he answered in the negative, and there is no appeal. The second question, which is the subject of the appeal, was whether in borrowing the money in question the company was acting within its powers and could give the bank a valid security.

The company started its career in 1951 in connection with the Festival of Britain and facilities to be afforded to visitors from abroad in connection with that event. It had an issued capital of £400. Subsequently for some years after 1953 it carried on business connected with deck chairs at a seaside resort. From 1958 to 1960 it carried on no business, but in the latter year there was a transfer of shares and a new board was elected which decided to make use of the company for a venture connected with pigs. It has always been the ambition apparently of the commercial community to stretch the objects clause of a memorandum of association, thus obtaining the advantage of limited liability with as little fetter on the activities of the company as possible. But still you cannot have an object to do every mortal thing you

56

want, because that is to have no object at all. There was one thing that the plaintiff company could not do and that was to breed pigs . . . Anyhow, this venture like other similar ventures, has been a disastrous failure, and the company was ordered to be wound up in 1965.

In 1960 the then new directors approached the defendant bank with a view to opening an account. This became in due course of time heavily overdrawn, and the bank, requiring security, was offered two debentures secured on the company's assets. It is common ground that before the security was given the bank was furnished with a copy of the memorandum and articles of association and also became aware, and expressly aware, that the company was carrying on as its sole business the business of pig breeding, which it has now acknowledged was ultra vires the company's powers in its memorandum. The bank has, however, relied on the fact that there is in the objects clause of the memorandum a sub-clause (n) empowering the company in general terms to borrow, in particular by the issue of debentures and to secure the loan by charge. There is also in this memorandum a form of words which is common enough, and has been for many years, the words at the end of the objects clause are these: 'It is hereby expressly declared that each of the preceding sub-clauses shall be construed independently of and shall be in no way limited by reference to any other sub-clause and that the objects set out in each sub-clause are independent objects of the company.'

Of course, the original idea of that form of words was to avoid the old difficulty, which was that there was a main objects clause and all the others were ancillary to the main objects; and many questions of ultra vires arose out of that.

It was argued therefore, that the only obligation of the bank was to satisfy itself that there was an express power to borrow money, and that this power was converted into an object by the concluding words of the objects clause which I have read. It was said that, if this was so, not only need the bank inquire no further but also that it was unaffected by the knowledge which it had that the activity on which the money was to be spent was one beyond the company's powers.

The judge rejected this view and I agree with him. He based his judgment, I think, on the view that a power or an object conferred on a company to borrow cannot mean something in the air; borrowing is not an end in itself and must be for some purpose of the company; and since this borrowing was for an ultra vires purpose, that is an end of the matter.

Mr Walton, I think, agreed that if sub-clause (n) must in truth be construed as a power, such a power must be for a purpose within the company's memorandum. He says that it is 'elevated into an object' (to use his own phrase) by the concludng words of the objects clause in the memorandum and this object being an independent object of the company, will protect the lender and that that is its purpose. I answer that by saying you cannot convert a power into an object merely by saying so. Sub-clause (n) cannot in truth stand by itself any more than certain other of the sub-clauses of the objects clause of the memorandum . . .

Russell LJ delivered a concurring judgment. Karminski LJ concurred.

Re Horsley & Weight Ltd [1982] 3 All ER 1045 (Court of Appeal)

[3.29] **Buckley LJ:** . . . It has now long been a common practice to set out in memoranda of association a great number and variety of 'objects' so called, some of which (for example, to borrow money, to promote the company's interests by advertising its products or services, or to do acts or things conducive or incidental to the company's objects) are by their very nature incapable of standing as independent objects which can be pursued in isolation as the sole activity of the company. Such 'objects' must, by reason of their very nature, be interpreted merely as powers incidental to the true objects of the company and must be so treated notwithstanding the presence of a separate objects clause: see *Re Introductions Ltd* (para **3.28** *supra*). Where there is no separate objects clause, some of the express 'objects' may on construction fall to be treated as no more than powers which are ancillary to the dominant or main objects of the company: see, for example, *Re German Date Coffee Co* (para **3.24**)

Ex hypothesi an implied power can only legitimately be used in a way which is ancillary or incidental to the pursuit of an authorised object of the company, for it is the practical need to imply the power in order to enable the company effectively to pursue its authorised objects which justifies the implication of the power. So an exercise of an implied power can only be intra vires the company if it is ancillary or incidental to the pursuit of an authorised object. So also, in the case of express 'objects' which, on construction of the memorandum or by their very nature, are ancillary to the dominant or main objects of the company, an exercise of any such power can only be intra vires if it is in fact ancillary or incidental to the pursuit of some such dominant or main object.

On the other hand, the doing of an act which is expressed to be, and is capable of being, an independent object of the company cannot be ultra vires, for it is by definition something which the company is formed to do and so must be intra vires. I shall use the term 'substantive object' to describe such an object of a company.

Notes

It would appear that the judgments in *Re Introductions Ltd* and *Re Horsley and Weight Ltd* should be read in the light of the comments of Vinelott J. in *Rolled Steel Products (Holdings) Ltd v British Steel Corporation* ([1984] BCLC 466) where he said at first instance that: "The question whether a stated 'object' is truly an independent object or purpose is always a question of construction. Even borrowing and lending money are activities capable of being pursued as independent objects – for instance, in the case of a bank or finance company; but commonly, where a sub-clause of the memorandum of association of a company states that one of the objects of the company is 'to lend or advance' or 'to borrow and raise' money it is artificial to construe the sub-clause as anything other than a power conferred for the furtherance of what are in truth its 'substantive objects' or purposes."

[3.30]   An act performed pursuant to an implied power or a power conferred expressly by the objects clause which is not a 'substantive object' does not become ultra vires by reason of the fact that the directors have exercised that power in furtherance of a purpose not permitted by the objects clause.

Rolled Steel Products (Holdings) Ltd v British Steel Corporation [1986] Ch 246, [1985] 3 All ER 52, [1984] BCLC 466 (Court of Appeal)

[3.31]   Clause 3(k) of the objects clause of RSP which conferred on it the capacity to give guarantees was drafted in such a way that despite the existence of an independent objects clause it could not become a substantive object. RSP guaranteed the debts of an associated company SSS to BSC, secured by a debenture over the property of RSP. RSP received no benefit from the guarantees. They were however, to the benefit of one of its directors, Shenkman. At first instance, Vinelott J. held that because BSC knew that the transactions were not in furtherance of RSP's objects, they were ultra vires and void. BSC appealed.

[3.32]   **Slade LJ:** For many years, the phrase 'ultra vires' has from time to time been used by company lawyers in two senses. Primarily it is used to describe acts which are beyond the capacity of a company . . . The phrase is also sometimes used to describe acts which are not beyond the capacity of the company, but simply beyond the authority of wither the board of directors or a majority of the shareholders.

In many instances the sense in which the phrase is being used is far from clear. However, I think it plain that . . . the statement of claim in this case, in alleging that each of the guarantee and the debenture were 'ultra vires and void' were intending to allege that their execution was beyond the corporate capacity of RSP, on the grounds that they were executed not for the purposes or benefit of RSP but for the purposes or benefit of Mr Shenkman.

Subject to a point relating to the true construction of the words 'as may seem expedient' in cl 3(k) of the memorandum of association, there is no doubt that these two transactions fell within the letter of cl 3(k) and (l) of the memorandum. Accordingly, two important points of principle which arise in the present context may be expressed thus. Is a transaction which falls within the letter of powers conferred on a company incorporated under the Companies Acts, but is effected for a purpose not authorised by its memorandum of association, properly to be regarded as being beyond the corporate capacity of the company . . . and, if so, in what circumstances?

The legal personality of a company incorporated under the Companies Acts exists only for the purpose of its incorporation, as defined in the objects clause, which have to be set out in its memorandum of association . . . It does not, however, follow that any act is beyond its capacity unless expressly

59

authorised by its objects clause. Any such company is treated as having implied powers to do any act which is reasonably incidental to the attainment or pursuit of any of its express objects, unless such act is expressly prohibited by the memorandum . . . Strictly, therefore, it is not essential for the memorandum to insert any reference at all to mere powers as distinct from objects.

The statutory requirement that the objects of a company shall be specified in the memorandum marks one important difference between objects and powers. In my judgment, however, whether a particular transaction, carried out in purported exercise of an express or implied power contained in a company's memorandum of association, is within the capacity of the company must still depend on the true construction of that memorandum . . .

Counsel has submitted and I agree, that there is no reason in principle why a company should not be formed for the specific purpose, inter alia, of giving guarantees, whether gratuitous or otherwise, rather unusual though such an object might be.

Attention however, has been directed to the particular wording of cl 3(k) . . . The phrase 'as may seem expedient' necessarily implies that there is some criterion by which expediency is to be tested. The only possible criterion in my opinion, can only mean 'as may seem expedient for the furtherance of the objects of the company' . . . What, then, is the position if (as I have concluded) the power to give guarantees and to become security are to be regarded as mere powers ancillary to the objects of RSP? Even on this footng, RSP, in executing the guarantee and the debenture, was performing acts of a nature which, at least seemingly, it was expressly authorised by cll 3(k) and (l) of its memorandum to perform. The particular exercises of these powers were, on the face of them, well capable of falling within the objects of RSP.

The judge, as I have read his judgment, accepted that these transactions were capable of falling within the scope of the wording of the powers conferred on RSP by its memorandum. Nevertheless, he considered that there is a general principle of company law that a transaction, which ostensibly falls within the scope of the wording of a company's memorandum but is in fact entered into for some purpose not authorised by that memorandum, will be ultra vires the company in what he called the 'wider sense', and will confer rights on another party only if he can show that he dealt with the company in good faith and did not have notice that the transaction was entered into for an unauthorised purpose. It was primarily on the basis of this principle that the judge ultimately held the defendants in the present case liable to restore the moneys which they had received.

As Lord Selborne said in *Ashbury Rly Carriage and Iron Co (Ltd) v Riche supra*) '. . . a statutory corporation created by Act of Parliament for a particular purpose is limited, as to all its powers, by the purposes of its incorporation as defined in that Act.'

Strict logic might therefore appear to require that any act purported to be done by a company in purported exercise of powers ancillary to its objects

The objects clause **3.32**

conferred on it by its memorandum of association, whether express or implied, (eg. a power to borrow) would necessarily, and in every case, be beyond its capacity and therefore wholly void if such act was in fact performed for purposes other than those of its incorporation. However, the practical difficulties resulting from such a conclusion for persons dealing with a company carrying on a business authorised by its memorandum, would be intolerable. As Buckley L. put it, in regard to a power to borrow, in *Re David Payne & Co Ltd, Young v David Payne & Co Ltd* [1904] 2 Ch 608 at 613:

> 'A corporation, every time it wants to borrow, cannot be called upon by the lender to expose all its affairs, so that the lender can say, "Before I lend you anything I must investigate how you carry on your business and I must know why you want the money, and how you apply it, and when you do have it I must see you apply it in the right way." It is perfectly impossible to work out such a principle.'

The *David Payne* decision, in my opinion, indicates the proper alternative approach. In that case, the company concerned had express power under its memorandum of association 'to borrow and raise money for the purposes of the company's business'. It borrowed money and issued a debenture to secure the loan. Its liquidator claimed that the debenture was ultra vires and void because there was evidence that the borrowing had not in fact been made for the purposes of the company's business. Buckley J in his judgment considered the force of the phrase 'for the purpose of the company's business'. He asked the question:

> '. . . is it a condition attached to the exercise of the power that the money should be borrowed for the purposes of the business, or is that a matter to be determined as between the shareholders and the directors?'

In the course of answering this question he said:

> 'A corporation cannot do anything except for the purposes of its business, borrowing or anything else; everything else is beyond its power, and is ultra vires. So that the words "for the purposes of the company's business" are a mere expression of that which would be involved if there were no such words.'

This passage has been frequently echoed in later cases, and perhaps not surprisingly, has on occasion been read as referring to the capacity of the company. However, I think that, in using the phrase 'ultra vires' in this particular context, Buckley J can only have meant 'ultra vires the directors'. This, in my opinion, is made clear by what followed. He accepted that, if the phrase 'for the purpose of the company's business' was a condition attached to the exercise of the power, a loan would be ultra vires and void if the condition had not been complied with. He did not, however, regard it as such a condition: in his view it did no more than state the obvious. In these circumstances, his conclusion was as follows:

61

'If this borrowing was made, as it appears to me at present it was made for a purpose illegitimate so far as the borrowing company was concerned, that may very well be a matter on which rights may arise as between the shareholders and directors of that company. It may have been a wrongful act on the part of the directors. But I do not think that a person who lends to the company is by any words such as these required to investigate whether the money borrowed is borrowed for a proper purpose of an improper purpose. The borrowing being effected and the money passing to the company, the subsequent application of the money is a matter in which the directors may have acted wrongly; but that does not affect the principal act, which is the borrowing of the money.'

In these circumstances, he held that the defendants 'who have paid this money and taken this debenture without notice that the money was going to be applied as it was, are not affected by anything arising in regard to that.'

The most relevant passages in the judgments of the Court of Appeal in the *David Payne* case are cited in Vinelott J's judgment and I will not repeat them. Vaughan Williams and Cozens-Hardy LJJ expressly approved the manner in which Buckley J had approached the problem. Vaughan Williams LJ expressly, and the other members of the court implicitly rejected the borrower's first argument that, since the debenture was not issued to raise money for the purposes of the company, it was ultra vires altogether 'in such a sense that nothing could make it right'.

All three members of the court considered that the plaintiff company could succeed if, but only if, it showed that, at the time of the loan, the lending company knew that the money was going to be applied by the borrowers for an improper purpose and that this had not been proved.

The one crucially important point to which Buckley J and the Court of Appeal in *Re David Payne & Co Ltd* did not expressly advert to is the basis on which the lenders would have lost their security if they had known of the improper purpose for which the moneys lent were going to be applied. The basis is, in my opinion, this. The directors of the borrowing company in fact had no authority from the company to take the loan and grant the debenture because these transactions were not effected for the purposes of the company. Nevertheless, as a general rule, a company incorporated under the Companies Acts holds out its directors as having ostensible authority to do on its behalf anything which its memorandum of association, expressly or by implication, gives the company the capacity to do. In *Re David Payne & Co Ltd* the company's memorandum gave it the capacity to borrow. As a matter of construction of the company's memorandum, the court was not prepared to construe the words 'for the purposes of the company's business' as limiting its corporate capacity, but construed them simply as limiting the authority of the directors. In the absence of notice to the contrary, the lenders would thus have been entitled to assume, on the authority of the principle in *Royal British Bank v Turquand*, and on more general principles of the law of agency, that the directors of the borrowing company were acting properly and regularly in the internal management of its affairs and were borrowing for the purposes of the company's business . . . However, a party dealing with a company cannot rely on the ostensible authority of its directors to enter into a particular transaction, if he knows they in fact have no such authority because it is being entered into for improper purposes . . . It follows that . . . the relevant transactions in the present case were beyond the corporate capacity of RSP simply because they were effected for improper purposes not authorised by its memorandum of association. Nor does this argument derive any support from the powerful judgment of Pennycuick J in *Charterbridge Corp Ltd v Lloyds Bank Ltd* [1969] 2 All ER 1185 at 1189, where one finds the following statement of principle:

> 'Apart from authority, I should feel little doubt that where a company is carrying out the purposes expressed in its memorandum, and does an act within the scope of a power expressed in its memorandum, that act is an act within the powers of the company. The memorandum of a company sets out its objects and proclaims them to persons dealing with the company and it would be contrary to the whole function of a memorandum that objects unequivocally set out in it should be subject to some implied limitation by reference to the state of mind of the parties concerned. Where directors misapply the assets of their company, that may give rise to a claim based on breach of duty. Again, a claim may arise against the other party to the transaction, if he has notice that the transaction was effected in breach of duty. Further, in a proper case, the company concerned may be entitled to have the transaction set aside. But all that results from the ordinary law of agency and has not of itself anything to do with the corporate powers of the company.'

Pennycuick J having subsequently proceeded to review the authorities cited to him apparently saw no reason to qualify this statement of the law and neither do I. I respectfully agree with it in its entirety and would regard the principles stated in *Re David Payne & Co Ltd* as giving effect to the 'ordinary law of agency'.

My conclusion from these authorities on these questions of principle may be summarised as follows. (*1*) The basic rule is that a company incorporated under the Companies Acts only has the capacity to do those acts which fall within its objects as set out in its memorandum of association and are reasonably incidental to the attainment or pursuit of those objects. Ultimately, therefore, the question whether a particular transaction is within or outside its capacity must depend on the true construction of the memorandum. (*2*) Nevertheless, if a particular act . . . is of a category which, on the true construction of the company's memorandum, is capable of being performed as reasonably incidental to the attainment or pursuit of its objects, it will not be rendered ultra vires the company merely because in a particular instance its directors, in performing the act in its name, are in truth doing so for purposes other than those set out in its memorandum. Subject to any express restrictions on the relevant power which may be contained in the memorandum, the state of mind or knowledge of the persons managing the company's affairs or of the persons dealing with it is irrelevant in considering questions of corporate capacity. (*3*) While due regard must be paid to any express conditions attached to or limitations on powers contained in a company's memorandum (eg. a power to borrow only up to a specified amount), the court will not ordinarily construe a statement in a memorandum that a particular power is exercisable 'for the purposes of the company' as a condition limiting the company's corporate capacity to exercise the power: it will regard it as simply imposing a limit on the authority of the directors . . . (*4*) At least in default of the unanimous consent of all the shareholders (as to which see below), the directors of a company will not have actual authority from the company to exercise any express or implied power other than for the purposes of the company as set out in its memorandum of association. (*5*) A company holds out its directors as having ostensible authority to bind the company to any transaction which falls within the powers expressly or impliedly conferred on it by its memorandum of association. Unless he is put on notice to the contrary, a person dealing in good faith with a company which is carrying on an intra vires business is entitled to assume that its directors are properly exercising such powers for the purposes of the company as set out in its memorandum. Correspondingly, such a person in such circumstances can hold the company to any transaction of this nature. (*6*) If, however, a person dealing with a company is on notice that the directors are exercising the relevant power for purposes other than the purposes of the company, he cannot rely on the ostensible authority of the directors and, on ordinary principles of agency, cannot hold the company to the transaction.

Notes

It is respectfully submitted that this case was incorrectly decided as it effectively purports to give the company power to do acts which are beyond its stated objects. This is surely illogical. The decision may be explained on the basis that the court was concerned to protect innocent outsiders who deal with a company, unaware that it company is pursuing an unauthorised object. Such motivation is laudable, but has resulted in the straining of logic beyond reasonable limits. In this jurisdiction the innocent outsider is adequately protected by the provisions of s 8 of the Principal Act and reg 6 of the European Communities (Companies) Regulations 1973, (discussed *supra*). Neither of these provisions validates acts beyond the company's stated objects. They merely allow the innocent outsider to enforce the invalid transaction against the company.

The objects clause may be phrased in such a way that the company may carry on such other business which can, in the opinion of the board of directors, be advantageously carried on by the company in connection with or as ancillary to its stated or main objects. These additional activities can only be carried on while the company continues to pursue its intra vires objects.

Bell Houses Ltd v City Wall Properties Ltd [1966] 2 QB 656, [1966] 2 All ER 674 (Court of Appeal)

[3.33] The business of the plaintiff company included that of property development. Clause 3(c) of the memorandum also permitted the company to 'carry on any other trade or business whatsoever which can, in the opinion of the board of directors, be advantageously carried on by the company in connection with or as ancillary to any of the above businesses or the general business of the company . . .' The plaintiff agreed to introduce the defendant company, another property developer, to a financier, in return for a commission of £20,000. Having completed its part of the bargain the plaintiff looked for payment of its commission. When this was refused the plaintiff issued proceedings claiming payment. The trial judge (Mocatta J) refusing the relief sought, held that the agreement was ultra vires the plaintiff. His decision was reversed on appeal.

[3.34] **Salmon LJ:** Sub-clause (c) is of great importance and reads as follows: 'To carry on any other trade or business whatsoever which can in the opinion of the board of directors, be advantageously carried on by the company in connection with or as ancillary to . . . the general business of the company.'

As a matter of pure construction, the meaning of these words seems to me to be obvious. An object of the plaintiff company is to carry on any business which the directors genuinely believe can be carried on advantageously in connection with or as ancillary to the general business of the company. It may be that the directors take the wrong view and in fact the business in question cannot be carried on as the directors believe. But it matters not how mistaken the directors may be. Providing they form their view honestly, the business is within the plaintiff company's objects and powers . . .

Accordingly, I come to the conclusion both on what appears to be the clear meaning of the words and on authority, that under clause 3(c) of the plaintiff company's memorandum of association the contract here sued upon was intra vires if it constituted carrying on business which in the opinion of the plaintiff's board of directors could be advantageously carried on by the plaintiffs in connection with or as ancillary to their general business . . .

Danckwerts LJ delivered a concurring judgment. Sellers LJ concurred.

The power to make gifts

[3.35] The company may have in its objects clause an express power to make gifts. Alternatively, such power may be implied. As will be seen below, in either case, the power can only be exercised for purposes 'reasonably incidental' to the company's objects. However, in the case of an express power to make gifts, where the memorandum contains an independent objects clause, the power may be elevated to the status of an independent and substantive object. See *Re Horsley & Weight Co Ltd* (para **3.17**); *Rolled Steel Products Ltd v British Steel Corporation* (para **3.18**).

[3.36] A company has the power to make gratuitous dispositions for purposes which are reasonable incidental to the company's objects.

Hutton v West Cork Railway Co (1883) 23 Ch D 654 (Court of Appeal)

[3.37] A railway company, which was in the process of being wound up, paid a gratuity of £1,050 to some of its employees for loss of employment. Although there was no provision in the articles for payming remuneration to directors, it was also resolved to pay £1,500 to the directors for their past services. The Court of Appeal by a majority and reversing the decision of Fry J, held that the payments were ultra vires.

[3.38] **Bowen LJ:** Now can a majority compel a dissentient unit in the company to give way and to submit to these payments? We must go back to the root of things. The money which is going to be spent is not the money of the majority. That is clear. It is the money of the company and the majority want to spend it. What would be the natural limit of their power to do so? They can only spend money which is not theirs but the company's, if they are spending it for the purposes which are reasonably incidental to the carrying on of the business of the company. That is the general doctrine. Bona fides cannot be the sole test, otherwise you might have a lunatic conducting the affairs of the company and paying away its money with both hands in a manner perfectly bona fide, yet perfectly irrational. The test must be what is reasonably incidental to and within the reasonable scope of carrying on the business of the company.

It seems to me you cannot say the company has only got power to spend the money which it is bound to pay according to law, otherwise the wheels of business would stop,nor can you say that directors . . . are always to be limited to the strictest possible view of what the obligations of the company are. They are not to keep their pockets buttoned up and defy the world unless they are liable in a way which could be enforced at law or in equity. Most businesses require liberal dealings. The test there again is not whether it if bona fide, but whether as well as being done bona fide, it is done within the ordinary scope of the company's business and whether it is reasonably incidental to the carrying on of the company's business for the company's benefit. Take this sort of instance. A railway company or the directors of the company, might send down all the porters at a railway station to have tea in the country at the expense of the company. Why should they not? It is for the directors to judge, provided it is a matter which is reasonably incidental to the carrying on of the business of the company and a company which always treated its employees with draconian severity and never allowed them a single inch more than the strict letter of the bond would soon find itself deserted – at all events, unless labour was very much more easy to obtain in the market than it often is. The law does not say that there are to be no cakes and ale, but there are to be no cakes and ale except such as are required for the benefit of the company.

Such is the general view of the law I should take about a company which was a going concern . . [His Lordship went on to hold that as the company was no longer a going concern the payments could not be regarded as reasonably incidental to its business; it no longer had a business. Therefore the payments were ultra vires and void.]

Cotton LJ delivered a concurring judgment. Baggallay LJ dissented.

Notes

See also *Parke v The Daily News Ltd* [1962] Ch 927. In *Re Lee Behrens & Co Ltd* [1932] Ch 46 Eve J suggested that the power to make gifts could only be used if the transaction was (a) reasonably incidental to the carrying on of the company's business (b) was bona fide; and (c) was done for the benefit and to promote the prosperity of the company. The latter two criteria have since been rejected as being irrelevant. See *Charterbridge Corporation v Lloyds Bank Ltd* [1970] Ch 62; *Re Horsley & Weight Ltd* (para **3.29**) *Rolled Steel Products v British Steel Corporation; Northern Bank Finance Corporation v Quinn* (para **3.18**); *Re Kill Inn Motel Ltd* (High Court, Murphy J (16 September 1987)) and *Re Metro Investment Trust Ltd* (para **3.39**).

Re Metro Investment Trust Ltd (High Court, 26 May 1977)

[3.39]   McWilliam J: This is an application brought by Societe Soprico Gestion SA hereinafter described as Soprico to have a claim for £30,000 admitted in the winding up of Metro Investment Trust Ltd, hereinafter described as Metro.

The claim is made on foot of a promissory note for the sum of £50,000 which was given under the following circumstances. Soprico brought proceedings against a company called Invest of Ireland Ltd, hereinafter described as Invest, for the sum of £85,563,51. Invest amd Metro were under the control of a Mr and Mrs Cawley, Mrs Cawley being a director of both companies. Apart from this, no business or other association between those two companies is alleged by Soprico and the Liquidator of Metro has put in an affidavit to the effect that he can find no record of dealings between the two companies in the books of Metro. Whatever the reason for the involvement of Metro, the proceedings against Invest were compromised on terms whereby Soprico got judgment against Invest for the full amount with a stay of execution on the basis that Invest would pay the sum of £36,563.51 forthwith and pay the balance of £50,000 by five consecutive monthly instalments of £10,000 each payable on the 12th day of each month, commencing on 12th March 1974. In consideration of this forbearance, Metro and Invest gave joint and several promissory note promising to pay the £50,000 in the manner stated. The first two instalments of £10,000 were paid, but the remaining three instalments were not, and Soprico claims the sum of £30,000 in the winding-up of Metro.

The liquidator of Metro opposes the claim on the ground that this transaction on the part of Metro was not in any way in furtherance of the objects of the company and that there is no evidence of any benefit to Metro from the transaction and that it was therefore, ultra vires and void.

On behalf of Soprico it is urged that the promissory note is expressed to be given for value, that one of the objects of the company was to make or draw negotiable instruments of all kinds that there is a presumption of value received and that Metro is estopped from denying that value was received.

I have been referred to a number of authorities . . . From these cases the principle appears to be clearly established that money can only be spent by a company for a purpose reasonably incidental to the carrying on of the company's business. Most of the cases to which I have been referred deal with claims to gratuitous payments in one shape or form which had been promised to the claimants, and the question arose in each case whether such gratuitous payments furthered the interests of the company in any way. This seems to me to be a different situation from the present in which Soprico exercised forbearance towards Invest in consideration of the guarantee by Metro; that is to say, Soprico is not claiming a gratuitous payment although, on the evidence, the assistance given by Metro to Invest appears to have been gratuitous. To this extent the *Charterbridge Corporation Ltd v Lloyd's Bank Ltd* [1970] Ch 62 most resembles the present case. There, one of a group of companies gave a somewhat similar guarantee of the debt of another member of the group. The court found that such a transaction could, under the circumstances, have been of benefit to the company giving it, but the judgment in this case reviews the authorities very fully and it seems to be clearly indicated that a third party who enters into a transaction involving a company which has power to enter into that transaction is not concerned to investigate the possibility of the transaction not being for the benefit of the company. Accordingly I am of opinion, that, however trifling the detriment to Soprico of the forbearance it agreed to exercise, Soprico is for this reason entitled to have this debt admitted. The position would be quite different were the claim being made by Invest and I express no opinion on any rights Metro may still have against Invest.

Notes

The judgment of McWilliam J appears on its face to adopt the same approach as was taken by Slade LJ in *Rolled Steel Products Ltd. v British Steel Corporation* (para **3.18**), namely that the outsider does not have to inquire whether an express power has been used by the company for an intra vires purpose. The comments of McWilliam J can however, be explained on the basis that under s 8 of the Principal Act an outsider dealing with a company can enforce a transaction against the company unless he is 'actually aware' of the ultra vires character of that transaction. S 8 does not impose any duty on the outsider to investigate whether a transaction which he proposes to enter into with the company would in fact be ultra vires.

The capital clause

[3.40]   In the case of a company having a share capital, details of the share capital must be stated in the memorandum.[1] The capital of the company is considered below. No member is bound unless he consents in writing, by an alteration of the memorandum or articles after the date on which he becomes a member, which requires him to take more shares than the number already held by him, or which increases his liability to contribute to the share capital, or otherwise to pay money to the company.

1 See *Keane* at paras **5.03–5.10**.

Alteration of other clauses

[3.41]   We have seen above, that there are special procedures which must be adopted in altering the name, objects or capital of the company. S 28 of the Principal Act states that any provision contained in the company's memorandum of association which instead could lawfully have been contained in the articles of association may be altered by special resolution. Dissenting shareholders holding between them at least 15% of the issued share capital or any class thereof may, within 21 days of the passing of the resolution apply to the court to have it cancelled. The court may grant such relief, if any, as it thinks fit. S 28 is not applicable where the memorandum itself prohibits the alteration of such provisions, or if it provides its own procedure for the making of such alterations. Neither can the section be used to vary or abrogate the special rights of any class of members.[1]

1 S 6(4).

Issue of amended memorandum

[3.42]   Where an alteration is made in the memorandum, every copy of the memorandum issued after the date of alteration, must contain that alteration. Failure to comply with these requirements, will render the company and every officer in default liable to a fine.[1] All such alterations must be notified to the Registrar of Companies and published in Iris Oifigiuil.[2]

1 S 27.
2 For variation of such class rights, see *Keane* at paras **17.10–17.14**.

The articles of association[1]

[3.43]   The articles are the 'internal regulations of the company'.[2] In addition to dealing with matters such as general meetings and the board of directors, the articles typically specify the rights attaching to various classes of shares. As mentioned previously,[3] the Acts contain model form articles which may be adopted by companies. Table A of the first schedule of the Principal Act applies to companies limited by shares and accordingly it is these model form articles which are, whether in whole or in part, most commonly adopted by Irish companies. Parts I and II of table A applies to public and private companies. If these companies decline or fail to register articles, then the appropriate part of table A will apply.[4] Further, the provisions of table A apply to the extent that they are not excluded by such articles if any, as are actually registered by the company.

1 See generally *Keane* chapter 6.
2 *Guinness v Land Corporation of Ireland* (1883) 22 Ch D 349.
3 These model form articles are to be found in tables A,C,D and E of the first schedule of the Principal Act.
4 S 13.

[3.44] No article will be considered ultra vires if its terms are the same as or substantially similar to an equivalent article in the relevant table.

New Balkis Eerstelling Limited v Randt Gold Mining Company [1940] AC 165 (Privy Council)

[The facts are irrelevant]

[3.45] Lord Davey (referring to a certificate issued pursuant to art 22 of table A of the Companies Act 1862, discharging the purchaser of shares which had been previously forfeited by the company, from calls which had been made prior to the forfeiture): The certificate follows the terms of table A, art 22. If it is in accordance with art 22, no question of ultra vires can arise, because it would be ridiculous to say that which is prescribed by an Act of Parliament, for the model articles of a company formed under that Act, could be ultra vires.

[3.46] Under s 25 of the Principal Act the memorandum and articles when registered, bind the company and its members to the same extent as if they repectively had been signed and sealed by each member, and contained covenants by each member to observe all the provisions of the memorandum and of the articles. This is known as the 'section 25 contract'. It may be enforced by and against both the company and the individual members.

Clark v Workman [1920] 1 IR 107 (Chancery Division)

[3.47] The chairman of a company, Workman, had been appointed by the general meeting when the articles required that he be appointed by the board of directors. A substantial minority of the shareholders successfully applied for an injunction restraining the board of directors from acting on resolutions which had been carried with the casting vote of the chairman.

[3.48] Ross J: We must first consider what is the position of a shareholder in this and similar companies. He does not hold his property simply at the mercy of the majority. His rights are carefully guarded and his chief protection consists in the articles of association. Now, what do the articles of association amount to in point of law? They constitute a contract between every shareholder and all the others, and between the company itself and all the shareholders. It is a contract of the most sacred character, and it is on the faith of it that each shareholder advances his money . . . see judgment of Farwell LJ in *Salmon v Quin* [1909] 1 Ch 311. Can this contract be altered or varied? It can only be varied by a special resolution . . .

The first question that arises is whether Frank Workman was lawfully chairman of the meeting of directors on the 26th November. If he were not, everything that was done was ultra vires and wholly inoperative.

The articles dealing with this matter are 91, 92 and 93. Article 91 provides that questions arising at any meeting of directors shall be decided by a majority of votes of those present, and in case of an equality of votes the chairman of the meeting shall have a casting vote. Article 92 provides that the directors may appoint a chairman and vice-chairman of their meetings and determine the period for which he or they shall hold office. There you have the precise contract with the shareholders, and it is essential that the chairman should be elected by the machinery provided by that contract and in no other way. The power of electing a chairman having a casting vote is of vital importance. The power having been delegated by the company to the directors, cannot be controlled or affected by the company, unless the contract is altered by a special resolution, but no such special resolution was passed. Article 93 provides that all meetings shall be presided over by the chairman of the directors (if any) if present . . .

The defendant, Mr Frank Workman, was never appointed by the directors a chairman of their meetings. The defendants say that the resolution passed at the general meeting of shareholders held on the 21st March 1881 was sufficient:– 'Mr John Workman and Mr Charles Workman be re-elected directors for the ensuing year, and that Mr Frank Workman be elected chairman.' This is claimed to have the effect of conferring on Mr Frank Workman the chairmanship, nor for the ensuing year only, but for life or until removal.

But the election of a chairman of directors is not the function of a general meeting. It can elect directors, but not the chairman of the directors. The minute does not state who attended. It it thirty-eight years ago since the meeting was held. But even assuming that nobody attended, it is not a meeting of directors. It is a general meeting, and all attended as shareholders and in no other capacity.

But it is contended that this is an irregularity that can be cured by acquiescence. The office of chairman becomes important in connexion with the power to give a casting vote. The question of a casting vote never became material, so far as we know, until the meeting of the 26th November 1919. I am therefore of opinion that Mr Frank Workman was not legally chairman at that meeting, and that the whole of the resolutions which were carried by his casting vote are inoperative and of no effect.

Notes

In *Lee & Company (Dublin) Limited* and *Frank Conroy v Egan (Wholesale) Limited and John Roe*, (High Court, unreported 27th April 1978) Mr Roe was the holder of 7,100 out of a total of 8,802 issued shares in the first named defendant (Egan). Roe agreed to sell the entire shareholding in Egan to the Plaintiffs. Under the articles of Egan any shareholder wishing to sell his share was required first of all, to offer them to the other shareholders who then had an option to purchase at 'fair value'. The contract of sale was entered into without complying with the pre-emption provisions in the articles. Roe subsequently refused to transfer the shares and the plaintiffs sought an order of specific performance against him. Kenny J refused to order the sale of those shares which Roe did not own. He only granted specific performance of the sale of Roe's shares subject to the other members being allowed to exercisde their pre-emption rights under the articles.

See also *A-G for Ireland v Jameson* [1904] 2 IR 644, another pre-emption rights case where Kenny J said as follows of the shareholder's rights and obligations under the s 25 contract:–

'No shareholder has a right to any specific portion of the company's property, and save by, and to the extent of, his voting power at a general meeting of the company, cannot curtail the free and proper disposition of it. He is entitled to a share of the company's capital and profits, the former . . . , being measured by a sum of money which is taken as the standard for the ascertainment of his share of the profits. If the company disposes of its assets, or if the latter be realised in a liquidation, he has a right to a proportion of the amount received after the discharge of the company's debts and liabilities. In acquiring these rights – that is, in becoming a member of the company – he is deemed to have simultaneously entered into a contract under seal to conform to the regulations contained in the articles of association . . . What ever obligations are contained in these articles, he accepts the ownership of the shares and the position of a member of the company, bound and controlled by them. He cannot divorce his money interest, whatever it may amount to, from these obligations. They are inseparable incidents attached to his rights, and the idea of a share cannot, in my judgment, be complete without their inclusion . . . The money interest and the contractual obligations form one whole, and no member could be heard to say that he had a right to retain the former and disclaim the latter.'

[3.49]   The s 25 contract can only be enforced by a member of the company and in his capacity as member.

Eley v The Positive Government Security Life Assurance Company Limited *(1876)* 1 Ex D 20 (Court of Appeal)

[3.50]   Article 118 of the company's articles provided that: 'Mr William Eley of No 27, New Broad Street, in the City of London, shall be the solicitor to the company and shall transact all the legal business of the company, including parliamentary business, for the usual and accustomed fees and charges and shall not be removed from his office unless for misconduct.' Eley was a member of the company and acted as the company solicitor for a period of time. He was never formally appointed to the post and subsequently another person was appointed solicitor. Eley brought an action against the company for breach of contract in not employing him as solicitor in accordance with the terms of the articles.

[3.51]   Lord Cairns LC: This case was first rested on the 118th article. Articles of association, as is well known, follow the memorandum, which states the objects of the company, while the articles state the arrangement between the members. They are an agreement inter socios, and in that view, if the introductory words are applied to article 118, it becomes a covenant between the parties to it that they will employ the plaintiff. Now, so far as that is concerned, it is *res inter alios acta*, the plaintiff is no party to it. No doubt he thought that by inserting it he was making his employment safe as against the company; but his relying on that view of the law does not alter the legal effect of the articles. The article is either a stipulation which would bind the members, or else a mandate to the directors. In either case it is a matter between the directors and the shareholders, and not between them and the plaintiff . . .
  Lord Coleridge and Mellish LJJ concurred.

Hickman v Kent or Romney Marsh Sheep Breeders Association [1915] 1 Ch 881 (Chancery Division)

[3.52]   Article 49 of the defendant association's articles provided for the submission of disputes between the defendant and any of its members to arbitration. Hickman, a member of the defendant association, brought the present proceedings alleging certain irregularities in the defendant's affairs. The defendant applied for a stay of the proceedings on the ground that art 49 was binding on the plaintiff and the matter should therefore be referred to arbitration instead.

[3.53]   Astbury J: An outsider to whom rights purport to be given by the articles in his capacity as such outsider, whether he is or subsequently becomes a member, cannot sue on those articles treating them as contracts between himself and the company to enforce those rights. Those rights are not part of the general regulations of the company applicable alike to all shareholders and can only exist by virtue of some contract between such person and the company, and the subsequent allotment of shares to an outsider in whose favour such an article is inserted does not enable him to sue the company on such an article to enforce rights which are *res inter alios acta* and not part of the general rights of the corporators as such . . .

The wording of s 25 is difficult to construe or understand. A company cannot in the ordinary course be bound otherwise than by statute or contract and it is in this section that its obligation must be found. As far as the members are concerned, the section does not say with whom they are to be deemed to have covenanted, but the section cannot mean that the company is not to be bound when it says it is to be bound, nor can the section mean that the members are to be under no obligation to the company under the articles in which their rights and duties as corporators are to be found. Much of the difficulty is removed if the company be regarded, as the framers of the section may very well have so regarded it, as being treated in law as a party to its own memorandum and articles.

It seems clear from other authorities that a company is entitled as against its members to enforce and restrain breaches of its regulations. See, for example, *MacDougall v Gardiner* (1875) 1 Ch D 13; *Pender v Lushington* (1877) 6 Ch D 70, and *Imperial Hydropathic Hotel Co Blackpool v Hampson* 23 Ch D 1, 13. In the last case Bowen LJ said: 'The articles of association by s 16 are to bind all the company and all the shareholders as much as if they had put all their seals to them.'

It is also clear from many authorities that shareholders as against their company can enforce and restrain breaches of its regulations . . .

I think this much is clear, first, that no articles can constitute a contract between the company and a third person, secondly, that no right merely purporting to be given by an article to a person, whether a member or not, in a capacity other than that of a member, as, for instance as solicitor, promoter, director, can be enforced against the company; and thirdly, that articles regulating the rights and obligations of the members generally as such do create rights and obligations between them and the company respectively . . .

In the present case, the plaintiff's action is, in substance, to enforce his right as a member under the articles against the association. Article 49 is a general article applying to all the members as such, and . . . it would seem reasonable that the plaintiff ought not to be allowed in the absence of any evidence filed by him to proceed with an action to enforce his rights under the articles, seeing that the action is in breach of his obligation under article 49 to submit his disputes with the association to arbitration . . .

[3.54] A contract may be made between the company and a third party based on the terms of the articles, even though that third party is not a member of the company. The contract may be inferred by the conduct of the parties. An alteration of the articles cannot retrospectively alter the terms of the contract.

Swabey v Port Darwin Gold Mining Co (1889) 1 Meg 385 (Court of Appeal)

[3.55] The company whose articles of association provided that directors' remuneration should be at a certain rate altered these articles by special resolution, which purported to make the altered rate of remuneration effective from a date prior to the special resolution. The Court of Appeal (reversing the decision of Stephen J) held that though the articles did not constitute a contract between the company and the directors, they did point out the terms upon which the directors were serving. Further these terms could be altered by a special resolution altering the articles. However, the alteration could only take effect prospectively, and the directors were entitled to remuneration at the old rate for the period prior to the alteration.

[3.56] **Lord Halsbury LC:** The articles themselves do not constitute a contract, they are merely the regulations by which provision is made for the way the business of the company is to be carried on. A person who acts as director with those articles before him enters into a contract with the company to serve as a director, the remuneration to be at the rate contemplated by the articles. The person who does this has before him, as one of the stipulations of the contract, that it shall be possible for his employer to alter the terms upon which he is to serve, in which case he would have the option of continuing to serve, if he thought proper, at the reduced rate of remuneration. Those terms, however, could be altered only as to the future. In so far as the contract on those terms had already been carried into effect, it is incapable of alteration by the company.

    Lord Esher MR: I am of the same opinion. The articles do not themselves form a contract, but from them you get the terms upon which the directors are serving. It would be absurd to hold that one of the parties to a contract could alter it as to service already performed under it. The company has power to alter the articles, but the directors would be entitled to their salary at the rate originally stated in the articles up to the time the articles were altered.

    Lindley LJ concurred.

In re Anglo Austrian Printing and Publishing Union; Isaacs' case [1892] 2 Ch 158 (Court of Appeal)

[3.57] Sir Henry Isaacs acted as a director of the company. The articles contained terms upon which directors were to be appointed. The Court of Appeal (affirming Stirling J.) was prepared to hold that Sir Henry had been appointed pursuant to a contract with the company incorporating those terms, even though he himself was not a member of the company.

[3.58] **Lindley LJ:** I do not think there is any real difficulty in this case, and we are all of the same opinion. I do not know that I can improve in any way upon the judgment of Mr Justice Stirling, which seems to me to place the matter in the right light.

    [His Lordship then read articles 71 and 72 and continued] Those are the terms upon which Sir Henry Isaac became a director, and those articles he signed. I do not think that the latter circumstance is essential, but it is not unimportant . . . Regarding the articles simply as an offer to Sir Henry

Isaacs, and other people, of terms on which they are to become directors and this is perhaps the proper view of them , still Sir Henry Isaacs accepted those terms and he became a director. He became a director, to my mind, by signing the articles . . . But any possible doubt as to any inference to be drawn from the mere signing is removed by the fact that he actually acted as a director. There is no question as to his having accepted the terms.

Bowen and Kay LJJ: delivered a concurring judgment

Alteration of articles

[3.59]   Under s 15 of the Principal Act, the articles may be altered or added to, subject to the provisions of the Companies Acts 1963–1990 and to the conditions in the memorandum. However, where the alteration involves the variation of 'class rights' (ie. the rights attaching to a particular class of shares) special considerations apply.

[3.60]   An alteration of the articles must be made in good faith and for the benefit of the company as a whole.

Clark v Workman [1920] 1 IR 107 (Chancery Division)

[3.61]   **Ross J:** When the test of bona fides comes to be applied, all these matters and the surrounding circumstances call for the most careful attention. I refer in this connection to the weighty observations of Lord Lindley when Master of the Rolls in *Allen v Gold Reefs Co of West Africa* (para **3.38**). Even the statutory powers of altering articles of association by a special resolution must be exercised subject to those general principles of law and equity which are applicable to all powers enabling majorities to bind minorities. They 'must be exercised', says the learned Master of the Rolls, 'not only in the manner required by law, but also bona fide for the benefit of the company as a whole, and must not be exceeded. These conditions are always implied, and are seldom if ever expressed.' These observations refer to the exercise of powers by shareholders. They apply with augmented force when the powers are being exercised by directors.

[3.62]   It is for the shareholders, and not for the court to say whether an alteration of the articles is for the benefit of the company, provided that there are reasonable grounds upon which the alteration could be regarded as beneficial.

Shuttleworth v Cox Brothers And Company (Maidenhead) Limited [1927] 2 KB 9 (Court of Appeal)

[3.63]   The company's articles provided that the plaintiff and four others should be the first and permanent directors, and could only be dismissed on any one of six specified grounds. The plaintiff had been guilty of misconduct in relation to the affairs of the company. A special resolution was passed amending the articles to allow for a seventh ground for dismissal of a director, namely a request in writing by all his co-directors that he should resign his office. Such a request was made to the plaintiff who brought the present action claiming that his dismissal was wrongful.

[3.64] **Atkin LJ:** The contract that they shall be permanent directors at a salary is contained in the articles only . . . In these circumstances the proper inference appears to be that there was a contract contained in articles which could be altered by a special resolution of the company in accordance with the provisions of the Companies Act; and inasmuch as the contract contemplated the permanent office being vacated in one of six contingencies, it is not inconsistent with the contract that the article should be altered so as to add a seventh contingency. In other words, it is a contract made upon the terms of an alterable article, and therefore neither of the contracting parties can complain if the article is altered. Consequently, I cannot find that there has been any breach of contract in making the alteration.

The only other question is whether the article is upon general principles objectionable as being not honestly made within the powers of the company. Here the limits to the power of a company to alter its articles have to be considered. Certain limits there are, and they have been laid down in several cases, notably by Lindley MR in *Allen v Gold Reefs of West Africa Ltd* [1900] 1 Ch 656, the case I have already referred to upon the first point. There in a reasoned and lucid judgment the Master of the Rolls uses the phrase 'bona fide for the benefit of the company.' But neither this court nor any other court should consider itself fettered by the form of words, as if it were a phrase in an Act of Parliament which must be accepted and construed as it stands. We must study what its real meaning is by the light of the principles which were being laid down by the Master of the Rolls when he used the phrase. I am satisfied that the true meaning of the words and the principle to be applied have been stated in the judgments of my brothers. The only question is whether or not the shareholders in considering whether they shall alter articles, honestly intend to exercise their powers for the benefit of the company. If they do then, subject to one or two reservations which have been explained, the alteration must stand. It is not matter of law for the court whether or not a particular alteration is for the benefit of the company; nor is it the business of a judge to review the decision of every company in the country on these questions. And even if the question were not for the shareholders themselves, but for some other body, it must be a question of fact. In this case there is a finding of fact by the jury that the alteration was for the benefit of the company; but I do not decide the case on that ground. In my view the question is solely for the shareholders acting in good faith. The circumstances may be such as to lead to one conclusion only, that the majority of the shareholders are acting so oppressively that they cannot be acting in good faith; or, to put it in another way, it may be that their decision must be one which could be taken by persons acting in good faith with a view to the benefit of the company. But these are matters outside and apart from the question, does this or that tribunal consider, in the light of events which have happened, that the alteration was or was not for the benefit of the company? With great respect to a very learned judge, I cannot agree with the judgment of Peterson J to the contrary on this point. In my view the passage which has been cited from the judgment of Lord Sterndale MR in *Sidebottom's* case [1920] 1 Ch 154, 167, makes it clear that in his view the ultimate decision is to be the decision of the majority of the shareholders.

Bankes and Scrutton LJJ delivered concurring judgments.

[3.65] 'The company as a whole' refers to the individual hypothetical member.

Greenhalgh v Arderne Cinemas Limited [1951] Ch 286 (Court of Appeal)

[3.66] The articles of the company contained pre-emption rights giving existing shareholders first option on shares being transferred by another member. By special resolution, these pre-emption rights were removed, thereby facilitating the sale of certain shares to a non-member. The plaintiff, who was a shareholder of the company claimed that alteration of the articles was invalid on the ground that the interests of the minority of shareholders had been sacrificed to those of the majority. The Court of Appeal, affirming the decision of Roxburgh J held that the alteration was for the benefit of the company as a whole.

[3.67] Evershed MR: [After stating the facts.] The burden of the case is that the resolution was not passed bona fide and in the interests of the company as a whole, and there are, as Mr Jennings has urged, two distinct approaches.

The first line of attack is this, and it is one to which, he complains, Roxburgh J, paid no regard: this is a special resolution, and, on authority, Mr Jennings says, the validity of a special resolution depends upon the fact that those who passed it did so in good faith and for the benefit of the company as a whole . . . In the first place, I think it is now plain that 'bona fide for the benefit of the company as a whole' means not two things but one thing. It means that the shareholder must proceed upon what, in his honest opinion, is for the benefit of the company as a whole. The second thing is that the phrase 'the company as a whole', does not (at any rate in such a case as the present) mean the company as a commercial entity, distinct from the corporators: it means the corporators as a general body. That is to say, the case may be taken of an individual hypothetical member and it may be asked whether what is proposed is, in the honest opinion of those who voted in its favour, for that person's benefit.

I think that the matter can, in practice, be more accurately and precisely stated by looking at the converse and by saying that a special resolution of this kind would be liable to be impeached if the effect of it were to discriminate between the majority shareholders and the minority shareholders, so as to give to the former an advantage of which the latter were deprived. When the cases are examined in which the resolution has been successfully attacked, it is on that ground. It is therefore not necessary to require that persons voting for a special resolution should, so to speak, dissociate themselves altogether from their own prospects and consider whether what is thought to be for the benefit of the company as a going concern. If, as commonly happens, an outside person makes an offer to buy all the shares, prima facie, if the corporators think it a fair offer and vote in favour of the resolution, it is no ground for impeaching the resolution that they are considering their own position as individuals.

Accepting that, as I think he did, Mr Jennings said, in effect that there are still grounds for impeaching this resolution: first, because it goes further than was necessary to give effect to the particular sale of the shares; and secondly, because it prejudiced the plaintiff and minority shareholders in that it deprived them of the right which, under the subsisting articles, they would have of buying the shares of the majority if the latter desired to dispose of them.

What Mr Jennings objects to in the resolution is that if a resolution is passed altering the articles merely for the purpose of giving effect to a particular transaction, then it is quite sufficient (and it is usually done) to limit it to that transaction. But this resolution provides that anybody who wants at any time to sell his shares can now go direct to an outsider, provided that there is an ordinary resolution of the company approving the proposed transferee. Accordingly, if it is one of the majority who is selling, he will get the necessary resolution. This change in the articles, so to speak, franks the shares for holders of majority interests but makes it more difficult for a minority shareholder, because the majority will probably look with disfavour upon his choice. But, after all, this is merely a relaxation of the very stringent restrictions on transfer in the existing article, and it is to be borne in mind that the directors, as the articles stood, could always refuse to register a transfer. A minority shareholder, therefore, who produced an outsider was always liable to be met by the directors (who presumably act according to the majority view) saying, 'We are sorry, but we will not have this man in' . . .

Although I follow the point, and it might perhaps have been possible to do it the other way, I think that this case is very far removed from the type of case in which what is proposed, as in the *Dafen* case [1920] 2 Ch 124, is to give a majority the right to expropriate a minority shareholder, whether he wanted to sell or not, merely on the ground that the majority shareholders wanted the minority man's shares.

As to the second point, I felt at one time sympathy for the plaintiff's argument, because, after all, as the articles stood he could have said: 'Before you go selling to the purchaser you have to offer your shares to the existing shareholders, and that will enable me, if I feel so disposed, to buy, in effect, the whole of the shareholding of the Arderne company.' I think that the answer is that when a man comes into a company, he is not entitled to assume that the articles will always remain in a particular form; and that, so long as the proposed alteration does not unfairly discriminate in the way which I have indicated, it is not an objection, provided that the resolution is passed bona fide, that the right to tender for the majority holding of shares would be lost by the lifting of the restriction. I do not think that it can be said that that is such a discrimination as falls within the scope of the principle which I have stated . . .

Asquith and Jenkins LJJ concurred.

Notes

Even if the alteration is made 'bona fide for the benefit of the company as a whole' it may still be open to challenge under s 205 if oppressive or in disregard of the interests of a member. See *In re Williams Group Tullamore Ltd* and *Clemens v Clemens Bros Ltd* [1976] 2 All ER 268

[3.68]   A company cannot bind itself by contract not to alter its articles.

Southern Foundries Ltd v Sherlow [1940] 2 All ER 445 (House of Lords)

[The facts are irrelevant]

[3.69]   **Lord Porter:** The general principle therefore may, I think, be thus stated. A company cannot be precluded from altering its articles thereby giving itself power to act upon the provisions of the altered articles, but so to act may nevertheless be a breach of contract if it is contrary to a stipulation in a contract validly made before the alteration.

Nor can an injunction be granted to prevent the adoption of the new articles and in that sense they are binding on all and sundry, but for the company to act upon them will nonetheless render it liable in damages if such action is contrary to the previous engagements of the contrary.

Notes

See also *Carvill v Irish Industrial Bank*; *Punt v Symons & Co Ltd* [1903] 2 Ch 506; cf *British Murac Syndicate Ltd v Alperton Rubber Co Ltd* [1915] 2 Ch 186.

Doubt has been expressed as to whether Lord Porter was correct in stating that a company cannot be restrained from acting on foot of altered articles, even though to so act would constitute a breach of contract. See *Keane* at para **6.10** and Gower's *Principles of Modern Company Law* (4th Ed) London 1979 at pp. 558/9.

[3.70]   The articles of association may lawfully be altered even though the alteration retrospectively affects the rights of members.

Allen v Gold Reefs of West Africa Ltd [1900] 1 Ch 656 (Court of Appeal)

[3.71]   Article 29 of the company's articles gave it a lien for all debts of any member to the company 'upon all shares (not being fully paid) held by such member'. The company amended article 29 by deleting the words 'not fully paid'. The only shareholder to be affected by this alteration was one Zuccani. After his death his executors challenged the validity of the company's lien on his fully paid shares. The Court of Appeal held (reversing the decision of Kekewich J) that the alteration of the articles was valid and enforceable.

[3.72]   Lindley MR: [T]he company is empowered by the statute to alter the regulations contained in its articles from time to time by special resolutions . . . and any regulation or article purporting to deprive the company of this power is invalid on the ground that it is contrary to the statute: *Walker v London Tramways Co* [1879] 12 Ch 705 (see also *Punt v Symons & Co Ltd* [1903] 2 Ch 506).

The power thus conferred on companies to alter the regulations contained in their articles is limited only be the provisions contained in the statute and the conditions contained in the company's memorandum of association. Wide, however, as the language of s 50 [ie s 15 of the Principal Act] is, the power conferred by it must, like all other powers, be exercised subject to those general principles of law and equity which are applicable to all powers conferred on majorities and enabling them to bind minorities. It must be exercised, not only in the manner required by law, but also bona fide for the benefit of the company as a whole, and it must not be exceeded. These conditions are always implied, and are seldom, if ever, expressed. But if they are complied with I can discover no ground for judicially putting any other restrictions on the power conferred by the section than those contained in it. How shares shall be transferred, and whether the company shall have any lien on them, are clearly matters of regulation properly prescribed by a company's articles of association. This is shown by table A . . . Speaking, therefore, generally, and without reference to any particular case, the section clearly authorises a limited company, formulated with articles which confer no lien on fully paid up shares, and which allow them to be transferred without any fetter, to alter those articles by special resolution, and to impose a lien and restrictions on the registry of transfers of those shares by members indebted to the company.

But then comes the question whether this can be done so as to impose a lien or restriction in respect of a debt contracted before and existing at the time when the articles are altered. Again, speaking generally, I am of opinion that the articles can be so altered, and that, if they are altered bona fide for the benefit of the company, they will be valid and binding as altered on the existing holders of paid-up shares, whether such holders are indebted or not indebted to the company when the alteration is made . .

I take it to be clear that an application for an allotment of shares on the terms of the company's articles does not exclude the power to alter them nor the application of them, when altered, to the shares so applied for and allotted. To exclude that power or the application of an altered article to particular shares, some clear and distinct agreement for that exclusion must be shown, or some circumstances must be proved conferring a legal or equitable right on the shareholders to be treated by the company differently from the other shareholders.

The fact that Zuccani's executors were the only persons practically affected at the time by the alterations made in the articles excites suspicion as to the bona fides of the company. But, although the executors were the only persons who were actually affected at the time, that was because Zuccani was the only holder of paid-up shares who at the time was in arrear of calls. The altered articles applied to all holders of fully paid shares, and made no distinction between them. The directors cannot be charged with bad faith.

After carefully considering the whole case, and endeavouring in vain to discover grounds for holding that there was some special bargain differentiating Zuccani's shares from other, I have come to the conclusion that the appeal from the decision of the learned judge, so far as it relates to the lien created by the altered articles, must be allowed . . .

Romer LJ delivered a concurring judgment. Vaughan Williams LJ dissented.

Notes

Generally, on the capacity of the company to alter its articles, see Trebilcock, *The Effect of Alterations to Articles of Association* (1967) 31 Conv (NS) 95.

Chapter 4

COMPANY FORMATION

PROMOTERS

[4.01]   A promoter is anyone who, acting as a principal, is involved in bringing about the formation of a company.[1] This definition would normally exclude persons acting solely as agents such as solicitors, accountants and financial advisers.[2] The definition however is wide and extends not only to the professional former of companies but also to the sole trader who sets up a company to take over his existing business or to run a new business.

1 See generally *Keane* chapter 9.
2 *Re Great Wheel Polgooth Ltd* (1883) 53 LJ Ch 42.

Definition of promoter

Twycross v Grant (1877) 2 CPD 469 (Common Pleas Division)

[4.02]   **Cockburn CJ:** A promoter, I apprehend, is one who undertakes to form a company with reference to a given project and to set it going, and who takes the necessary steps to accomplish that purpose. That the defendants were the promoters of the company from the beginning can admit of no doubt. They framed the scheme; they not only provisionally formed the company, but were, in fact, to the end its creators; they found the directors, and qualified them; they prepared the prospectus; they paid for printing and advertising, and the expenses incidental to bringing the undertaking before the world . . . All the things I have just referred to were done with a view to the formation of the company, and so long as the work of formation continues, those who carry on that work must, I think, retain the character of promoters. Of course, if a governing body, in the shape of directors, has once been formed, and they take . . . what remains to be done in the way of forming the company, into their own hands, the functions of the promoter are at an end. But, so long as the promoters are permitted by the directors to carry on the work of formation, the latter remaining passive, so long, I think, would a jury be warranted in finding that whay was done by them was done as promoters.

Components Tube Co v Naylor [1900] 2 IR 1 (Queen's Bench Division)

[4.03] **Palles CB** (in holding that Mr MacCabe was a promoter of the Components Tube Co): The Cycle Components Manufacturing Company had agreed to lease to Mr Hooley the business in question . . . In the following November, Mr Hooley and Dr MacCabe met; and there is evidence that, from this period, MacCabe acted as if he knew that he could acquire the property from Hooley for £50,000. He appears, shortly afterwards, to have conceived the idea of purchasing it, in the event of his being able successfully to float a company to buy it from him at an advance; and thenceforward the one governing motive which operated upon the minds of MacCabe and those acting with him, in reference to the acquisition of the property, was that they might form a company to take the property off their hands at a profit . . . Accordingly, MacCabe proceeded to take steps to promote such a company; and he did this before he had agreed, even verbally, with Hooley for the purchase; so that . . . he was during the entire of the period which we have to review, stamped with the character of a promoter.

Notes

For other examples of cases where the court had to determine whether or not a person was a promoter see: *Whaley Bridge Calico Printing Co Ltd v Green & Smith* (1879) 5 QBD 109; *Erlanger v New Sombrero Phosphate Co* (1878) 3 App Cas 1218; *Gluckstein v Barnes* [1900] AC 240; *Tracey v Mandalay Pty Ltd* (1953) CLR 215; *Lagunas Nitrate Co v Lagunas Syndicate* [1899] 2 Ch 392.

[4.04] The promoter of a company stands in a fiduciary position to that company. Disclosure of personal profit made from his position as promoter must be made either to an independent board of directors or to the company in general meeting.

Sean Hopkins v Shannon Transport Systems Ltd (High Court, unreported, 10 July 1972)

[4.05] The plaintiff with one Mr Gorman were promoters and directors of a private company formed in 1967 to provide a ferry service on the River Shannon. They were also the first shareholders of the company and the initial capital was made up of 100 £1 shares. On 22 March 1968 the company was converted into a public company and its capital was increased to £100,000. On 20 March 1968 the plaintiff and Mr Gorman had entered into an agreement with the company for the sale to the company of certain lands and other assets which they had previously purchased and which would be used by the company to commence business. In the period prior to 20 March 1968 a large number of people had subscribed for shares in the company, although shares were only allotted to them in July 1968. In order to obtain State grants for the initiation of the ferry service it was necessary that the plaintiff leave the company. The terms of the plaintiff's resignation were incorporated in an agreement dated 11 April 1968 concluded between the plaintiff and Mr Gorman (the latter acting on behalf of the company). This agreement confirmed the contract of 20 March and provided the the plaintiff was to be paid his balance of the purchase price plus an extra £1,000 by 6 September 1968. The plaintiff stood to make a large profit from the sale of these lands and other assets. Disclosure of this fact was only made to Mr Gorman who also stood to profit from the transaction. The company subsequently adopted the contract of sale, although disclosure of the profit made by the plaintiff and Mr Gorman was never made to the independent subscribers. The plaintiff issued proceedings claiming his share of the purchase price from the company. Pringle J held that the plaintiff' claim should be paid, less any sum he would otherwise have made by way of profit on the sale.

Pringle J: It is important, in considering the alleged agreement of 11th April 1968, on which the plaintiff's first claim is based, to arrive at a conclusion as to its legal effect. At the date upon which it was entered into the only directors of the company were the plaintiff and Mr Gorman, as Mr Barrett, who had been appointed a director on 19th November 1967 had then ceased to be a director owing to not having acquired his qualifying share by 19th January 1968. The plaintiff and Mr Gorman were also at this date the only shareholders in the company and at the same time, they were quite clearly the promoters of the company. The position therefore was that the promoters and sole directors of the company purported by this agreement to sell to the company certain assets belonging to them (in the case of the lands together with Mrs Hopkins) as partners. Furthermore, in regard to two of the items, the goodwill and the lands, they were being sold at a substantial profit to the promoters and directors.

Under article 8 of the company's articles where a contract is being entered into in which the directors have an interest, that interest, in order to make the contract valid, must be disclosed at the meeting of the directors at which the contract is determined on and the interested director must not vote (see also s 194(1) of the Companies Act 1963). Furthermore, it has been held that the disclosure must be to directors who are independent, and not to other directors who are equally interested in the contract in question (see *Lagunas Nitrate Co v Lagunas Syndicate* 1899 2 Ch 392; *Gluckstein v Barnes* 1900 AC 24; *Erlanger v New Sombrero Phosphate Co* 1879 3 AC 1218), nor does it avail when two or more directors are interested to split up the resolution and for each director to abstain from voting on the part in which he is interested (see *North Eastern Insurance Co* 1919 1 Ch 198). Here there is no evidence and there is no minutes, as to any meeting of directors having been held in reference to this agreement and in fact no such meeting capable of passing any resolution could have been held, because the quorum of directors was two and when a director is not entitled to vote he cannot be reckoned in estimating a quorum (see the cases referred to above). Nor is there any evidence of any general meeting having been held to approve of the contract and in any event the only registered shareholders were the

85

plaintiff and Mr Gorman who owned the entire authorised capital of the company and, while their restriction on voting as directors would not apply to their voting as shareholders at a general meeting, I do not consider that, even if there were no other persons who had subscribed for shares, this contract could have been legally ratified by a general meeting at which the two parties interested would have been the only persons entitled to vote. But I am satisfied that, as the plaintiff and Mr Gorman were not the only directors, but also promoters of the company, any contract under which they were to make a profit would be voidable by the company unless full disclosure were made to the persons who at that time had subscribed for shares, even though their shares had not yet been allotted to them . . .

It appears to be clear, therefore, that if, as here, there was no independent board of directors to whom disclosure could have been made, and as the promoters themselves were the only actual shareholders, in order to prevent the contract being voidable by the company, full disclosure would have had to be made to the subscribers for shares and this, as I have already found, was not done. It follows that, on one or more of the grounds stated, this contract . . . was voidable by the company and could have been rescinded. But in fact the company did not rescind it and eventually took over most of the assets agreed to be sold by the promoters and directors to the company and I shall have to consider later what the legal effect of this was . . .

The only other director, apart from the plaintiff, was Mr Gorman and no resolution of the directors could have been passed authorising the entering into the contract on behalf of the company on the sole vote of Mr Gorman, as the plaintiff, being an interested party, could not be counted in order to form a quorum. In fact there is no evidence, either in the minutes or otherwise, of any meeting of the directors to consider the entering into of the agreement or of any resolution purporting to have been passed in reference thereto by the board, nor was any general meeting of the company held which would be necessary in order to make valid a payment to the plaintiff as a consideration for his retirement from office in accordance with s 126 of the Companies Act 1963 upon which, although specially not pleaded, the company is entitled to rely as a matter of law. Furthermore, as there was no independent board of directors to whom the plaintiff could disclose his interest, his duty to the company as a director was to declare his interest to the subscribers who had put up money for shares in the company (see the authorities which I referred to in relation to the agreement of 20th March), and I am satisfied that this was never done . . .

My findings in regard to the alleged agreement . . . are that . . . this agreement was not binding on the company. But this is not a complete answer to the plaintiff's claim based on this alleged agreement or on the agreement of 20th March, because the company in fact eventually acted on the agreement of 20th March by taking over most of the assets thereby agreed to be sold and on the agreement of 11th April by accepting the plaintiff's resignation as a director and his renunciation of any rights he had to the allotment of shares in the company. So far from these contracts with the plaintiff being reprobated by the company, they were in fact approbated to a substantial extent. It appears to be clear that failure by a promoter or a director to make full disclosure of his contracts with the company renders the contract *voidable* by the company, but not void (see *Re Cape Breton Co* (1885) 29 ChD 795; *Burland v Earle* 1902 AC 83, 99, and *Hely-Hutchinson v Brayhead Ltd* [1967] 3 WLR 1406), where, as in the *Hely-Hutchinson* case there is no question of a profit arising to the promoter or director, if the company has adopted the benefit of the contract and recission is no longer possible, the contract can be enforced against the company, but this does not mean that the ordinary rule does not apply, that the promoter or director must account to the company for any profit which he has made on the contract.

Notes
   For a note of this judgment see *O'Dowd* (1989) 11 DULJ (ns) 120.

[4.06]   Where the promoters have obtained a secret profit as a result of their dealings with the company, the company's remedy will typically be an action for damages. It may, however, also be entitled to an order rescinding the contract in question.

Northern Bank Finance Corporation Ltd v Charlton [1979] IR 149
(Supreme Court)

[4.07]   The defendants along with two others wished to acquire control of a public company, J & G Mooney & Co Ltd ('Mooney'). They consulted the plaintiff bank who advised them to form a holding company to make the acqusition. The plaintiff agreed to act as the promoters' agent and to advance the major portion of the sum needed to buy the shares in Mooney. The holding company was to be the borrower of this sum and the shares when purchased, were to be transferred to the holding company. The plaintiff however, stipulated that £500,000 was also to be provided by the promoters for the acquisition. The sum to be provided by each promoter to make up the £500,000 was agreed upon and it was further agreed that these sums should be deposited with the plaintiff and kept at that level until the bid for the shares of Mooney either succeeded or failed. The promoters formed the holding company and its issued share capital was allotted to them. The plaintiff advanced £1.3 million to the holding company upon security provided by the promoters and the holding company. The defendants deposited their agreed contributions with the plaintiff and the purchase of the shares in Mooney began. Unknown to the defendants, the fourth promoter had only deposited three-quarters of his agreed contribution. During the course of the acquisition of Mooney the fourth promoter's shares in the holding company were purchased by the defendants with the aid of £50,000 advanced by the plaintiff. Before making this advance the plaintiff told the defendants, contrary to fact, that the fourth promoter was not indebted to the plaintiff in any substantial amount. The holding company acquired a majority of the shares in Mooney but the shares of the latter transpired to be worthless when it was refused a requotation of its shares. The defendants' failed to pay an instalment of the £50,000 loan and the plaintiff sued for the unpaid balance plus interest. The defendants pleaded that they had been induced to take the loan by the plaintiff's fraudulent misrepresentation as to the solvency of the fourth promoter. The trial judge (Finlay P) found as fact that the fraudulent misrepresentation of the plaintiff had induced the original acquisition of Mooney via the holding company and had also induced the loan for the acquisition of the fourth promoter's shares. He accordingly ordered recission of all the transactions and ordered that the plaintiff pay damages to the defendants. On appeal, the Supreme Court, by a majority refused recission on the ground that restitutio in integrum was not possible and ordered that the case be returned to the High Court for assessment of the defendants' damages.

Henchy J: Where a person has been induced by a fraudulent misrepresentation made collaterally by the other party to a contract to alter his position to his disadvantage, there are two alternative courses open to him; he may claim damages in tort for the deceit or he may sue for recission of the contract which was induced by the misrepresentation. The latter relief, which is an equitable one, will be granted when the court considers that it would be just and equitable to do so in order to restore the parties, at least substantially, to their respective positions before the fraudulent misrepresentation was acted on. That is the relief which the defendants have chosen primarily in their counterclaim, and it is the relief which the order of the High Court purported to give them. But, be it noted, the restitutio in integrum by restoring the *status quo ante* (which is the object of this form of relief) can be granted only as an adjunct to the recission of the contract between the parties. In this case the defendants sought and were granted recission of the contract between the defendants and the bank but, in an effort to restore the *status quo ante*, the court went further. By requiring the bank to take the place of the defendants in each of the many instances of the purchase of shares, the court purported to rescind and amend executed contracts which had been made between the defendants and third-party vendors of shares who were not before the court. In my opinion, that is something which the court had no jurisdiction to do.

Since the purpose of the recission of a contract on the ground of misrepresentation is the restoration of the *status quo ante* on the ground that the voidable contract is to be deemed wholly void ab initio, each side must divest itself in favour of the other of what it has received under the contract . . . Now, in the present case, the orders of recission made in the High Court cannot operate in that way. The moneys which it requires the bank to repay to the defendants are not moneys which it received, in any permanent or beneficial sense, under the contract with the defendants. Those moneys only passed through the bank's hands on their way to the vendors of the shares in question. It was those vendors who really received those moneys under the contract. So the bank cannot, by way of recission, be compelled to repay them to the defendants. But even more radically, the order of recission in requiring the bank to take up all the shares purchased by them for the defendants runs counter to the object of the restoration of the *status quo ante.*

The compulsory acquisition by the bank of those shares could not be said to be a 'taking back' since the bank had never owned those shares. If effect were to be given to the order of recission made in the High Court, the bank (which, as far as one can gather from the evidence, was never the beneficial owner of a single Mooney share) would become the unwilling owners of over 900,000 shares in that company. Clearly an order of recission with that result could not be said to restore the *status quo ante.* . . .

In my opinion, the order of recission made in the High Court, and the orders consequential and ancillary thereto, should be set aside.

In their counterclaim the defendants have pitched their claim for damages in comprehensively wide terms but . . . they are confined in this action to a claim for damages for the tort of fraud or deceit in that respect. While it is said that the measure of damages for breach of contract is the amount of money necessary to put the damnified person in the position in which he would have been if the tort had not been committed. As far as the tort of fraud or deceit is concerned, it is well settled that the measure of damages is based on the actual damage directly flowing from the fraudulent inducement, and that the award may include, in an appropriate case (of which this may not be an example), consequential damages representing what was reasonably and necessarily expended as a result of acting on the inducement . . .

In this case the defendants were induced by the deceit to purchase shares, of which the plaintiff bank was not the owner. It is well established by judicial authority that the correct measure of damages in such a case is the cost of acquiring the shares, less their actual value at the time of acquisition . . . The price paid for the shares is to be regarded only as evidence of their value and not as proof of it (per Lord Coleridge CJ in *Twycross v Grant*), so it will be for the court to make a true and fair valuation of the shares as they stood when they were transferred to the defendants or their nominees; that is the crucial time for the assessment of their value. Subsequent fluctuations in their value, from whatever cause, may be taken into reckoning for the purpose only to the extent that such movements in value may throw light on their real value at the time they were transferred to the defendants.

Because the trial judge considered that the defendants' remedy lay in recission, there was no adjudication in the High Court of the question of the measure of damages and of their assessment. Therefore, there is no judicial determination of the correct amount which each of the defendants may be said to have laid out in the purchase of the shares which were transferred to him or his nominee, nor is there any judicial finding as to the true value of those shares at the time of such transfer. Because the measure of damages will be the difference between those two figures, and because the defendants failed to adduce at the trial the evidential data which would enable those figures to be computed, it is not possible for this Court to assess the damages.

Therefore, I would remit the case to the High Court to have the defendants' damages assessed on the basis I have indicated.

Griffin and Parke JJ delivered concurring judgments. O'Higgins and Butler JJ dissented.

Notes

On recission, see also *The Component Tube Company Limited v Naylor* [1900] 2 IR 126; *Erlanger v New Sombrero Phosphate Co* (1878) 3 App Cas 1218. The problems concerning breach of fiduciary duty by promoters are not likely to be of major concern in the case of small private companies whose shareholders are also the promoters. The company may in such situations be regarded as having assented to the breach of duty by virtue of its subsequent failure to take steps against the promoters. This is a situation which is likely to arise where a sole trader forms a company to take over his existing business, as in *Salomon v Salomon & Co* [1897] AC 22. However, in the case of a plc the acts of the promoters may be the subject of independent inquiry if they are subscribers to the memorandum. Under s 32 of the 1983 Act if the company acquires non-cash assets from the subscribers for a consideration equal in value to one tenth of the nominal capital of the company within two years from the date when it is issued with a certificate that it is entitled to do business, the non-cash assets must be independently valued. A copy of the valuation report must be delivered to the company. The agreement must be approved by an ordinary resolution of the company, a copy of which must then be delivered to the registrar of companies. See *Keane* para **9.15**. Further, under the third schedule para 13 of the Principal Act where shares are being offered to the public the prospectus must disclose promoter's profits and remuneration.

Flotation of a Company[1]

[4.08] Flotation involves the offer of shares for sale to the public or the clients of an issuing house.[2] This procedure only applies to companies formed as public companies, or companies converting to public company status.[3] In floating the company the shares may be disposed of in a number of ways. There may be a sale by way of *direct offer* to the public or there may be what is known as an *offer for sale* whereby the entire issue of shares is sold to an issuing house, which in turn sells them to the public. By using the latter method it is the issuing house rather than the company that runs the risk if the issue is not fully subscribed by the public. The issuing house has in this case 'underwritten' the issue. Another possible option is for the issuing house to place large blocks of shares with its clients, often large institutional investors. The issuing house may act as agent for the company, or alternatively, it may have previously purchased the shares itself, from the company.

Rather than fix the sale price itself, the company may offer the shares by tender, setting a minimum price, and with the shares going to the highest bidder. If the company decides to issue new shares for sale to existing shareholders, rather than to the public at large, this is known as a rights issue.

1 See generally *Keane* chapter 8.
2 As to which see *Keane* para **8.01**.
3 Under s 33 of the Principal Act, private companies are prohibited from inviting the public to subscribe for its shares. See also s 21 of the 1983 Act.

Information to accompany issue of shares

[4.09] Where shares or debentures are being offered to the public for subscription or purchase, the offer must be accompanied by detailed information designed to protect and inform potential investors.

Prospectuses

[4.10] Under s 44 of the Principal Act where shares or debentures are being offered to the public, the offer must be accompanied by what is known as a 'prospectus'.[1] The definition of what constitutes an issue to the public is widely defined by s 61. Notably, a prospectus is not required in the case of a rights issue.[2] The vast array of detailed information which must be included in the prospectus is set out in ss 43 to 52 and schedule 3 of the Principal Act.

1 Defined in s 2(1) of the Principal Act as "any prospectus, notice, circular, advertisement or other invitation offering to the public for subscription or purchase any shares or debentures of a company."
2 S 44(7) of the Principal Act.

Listing particulars

[4.11] In practice, a company seeking a flotation will require a 'quotation' on the stock exchange. In addition to complying with the statutory requirements, a company must also comply with the requirements of the stock exchange. These requirements which were quite stringent did not have legislative status until the coming into force of the European Communities (Stock Exchange) Regulations 1984[1] which implemented the Admissions Directive,[2] the Listing Particulars Directive[3] and the Interim Reports Directive.[4] Briefly, where a company with a stock exchange listing seeks to issue shares to the public it must provide the stock exchange with what are known as 'listing particulars'.[5] Before publication of the particulars they must first be registered with the registrar of companies. If approved by the stock exchange, these particulars may take the place of and are deemed to be a prospectus, thereby exempting the company from the requirements of ss 43 to 52 and schedule 3 of the Principal Act. The stock exchange may require a company seeking a listing for its shares to comply with more stringent requirements than those set out in the Admissions Directive and

1984 Regulations. The Stock Exchange requirements are set out in the Yellow Book.[6] It should be noted that companies on the Unlisted Securities Market are not subject to the provisions of the 1984 Regulations. Regulation 10 of the 1984 Regulations also provide that a refusal by the Stock Exchange to grant a listing, or a withdrawal of a listing is subject to review by the High Court.

1 On 1 January 1985.
2 No 79/279/EEC.
3 No 80/390/EEC.
4 No 82/121/EEC.
5 'The information to be contained in listing particulars is contained in schedule A of the Listing Particulars Directive and is grouped under the following headings:–
Chapter 1: Information concerning those responsible for listing particulars and the auditing of accounts.
Chapter 2: Information concerning admission to official listing and the shares for the admission of which application is being made.
Chapter 3: General information about the issuer and its capital.
Chapter 4: Information concerning the issuers' activities.
Chapter 5: Information concerning the issuers' assets and liabilities, financial position and profits and losses.
Chapter 6: Information concerning administration, management and supervision.
Chapter 7: Information concerning the recent development and prospects of the issuer.
6 No 82/121/EEC. As to Directives see *Keane* at paras **8.06–8.13**.

Definition of 'public' for the purposes of issuing a prospectus

[4.12]   Under s 61 an 'offer to the public' includes an offer 'to any section of the public, whether selected as members or debenture holders of the company concerned or as clients of the person issuing the prospectus or in any other manner . . .' but does not include an offer which 'can properly be regarded, in all the circumstances, as not being calculated to result, directly or indirectly, in the shares or debentures becoming available for subscription or purchase by persons other than those receiving the offer or invitation or otherwise as being a domestic concern of the persons making and receiving it, and in particular'. However, an offer may still be regarded as having been made to the public despite a provision in a company's articles prohibiting invitations to the public to subscribe for shares or debentures.

Government Stock and Other Securities Investment Co Ltd v Christopher
[1956] 1 All ER 490 (Chancery Division)

[4.13]   The bidder company, the British and Commonwealth Shipping Co Ltd wished to take over two target companies, Union-Castle and Clan. It sent circulars to all the members of the target companies offering to acquire their shares in exchange for shares in the builder company. The exchange was implemented by the issue of non-renounceable letters of allotment to the members of the target companies. The allotment of shares in the bidder company was held not to be an issue of shares to the public.

Wynn-Parry J: I am . . . of opinion that the circular was not distributed to the public. I accept the proposition put forward by counsel for the defendants, namely, that the test is not who receives the circular, but who can accept the offer put forward. In this case it can only be persons legally or equitably interested as shareholders in the shares of Union-Castle or Clan. In the case of those who accept non-renounceable letters of allotment will be issued. In these circumstances the case appears to fall within s 55(2) of the Companies Act 1948 [ie s 61(2) of the Principal Act].

Notes

In *Corporate Affairs Commission v David James Finance Ltd* [1975] 2 NSWLR 710 an invitation restricted to the company's employees (who totalled 12,500 individuals) was held not to be an invitation to the public. In *Nash v Lynde* [1929] AC 158 Lord Hailsham LC was of the opinion that an offer to one person as a member of the public was an issue of a prospectus. However, Lord Sumner was of the view that there must be an issue to the public generally. If the latter view were correct difficulties could arise on the facts of a particular case as to what is a general issue. For an example of a case where the court found that an issue of shares to the public had taken place see *Re South of England Natural Gas and Petroleum Co* [1911] 1 Ch 573 where a promoter issued 3,000 copies of a prospectus marked 'For private circulation only' to shareholders of certain gas companies in which he had an interest. See also *Lee v Evans* (1965) ALR 614 and Heerer *Directors and Public Issues* (1967) 5 Melbourne UL Rev 429.

Civil remedies for misleading statements made in connection with flotations

[4.14]   Where misleading statements have been made to a person subscribing for shares the injured party may have a number of civil remedies open to him. Actions may lie against all or some of the following:–

(a) the company;
(b) the issuing house;
(c) those responsible for the listing particulars or prospectus.

Recission

[4.15]   The contract of allotment of shares may be rescinded by the injured party where it has been induced by a misrepresentation of a material fact. In such circumstances the contract is not void ab initio but is voidable at the instance of the injured party. Misrepresentation may occur even though the statutory disclosure requirements have been complied with.

Aaron's Reefs v Twiss [1895] 2 IR 207 (Court of Appeal)

[4.16]   A prospectus was issued by the plaintiff company offering approximately 200,000 £1 shares in a company which was to work a gold mine in Venezuala. Although the mine was described as 'rich' this was probably not in fact the case. The prospectus disclosed the existence of a contract between the promoters and the company, selling the mine to the company. At that time the statute merely required the disclosure of the existence of such a contract, but not of its terms. If the terms thereof had been disclosed it would have shown that the purchase price was £150,000 and which would swallow up virtually all of the company's funds, thereby rendering it almost impossible to work the mine. It also prevented the company from paying the 100 per cent dividend suggested in the prospectus as the probable return on investments made. The defendant, a resident of County Limerick subscribed for 100 shares. A call of four shillings per share was made a year later which the defendant refused to pay, resulting in the forfeiture of his shares. When the company sued him for unpaid calls the defendant successfully raised the defence of fraudulent misrepresentation. The contract of allotment was thereby rendered voidable and the defendant was able to obtain an order rescinding it.

   Fitzgibbon LJ: On the question of fraud, in an action by a company, under such circumstances as we have here, I do not admit any distinction between such fraudulent concealment of material facts, as took place here, and actual misrepresentation . . . If a company cannot float if the whole truth be disclosed by its prospectus, it cannot be honestly launched at all . . . Though uberrima fides, ie. the obligation to disclose everything known that could influence an intending subscriber, is not demanded of the authors of a prospectus, no case has, as yet, applied the rule *caveat emptor* to an invitation to the public to take shares . . . But I am satisfied that the very farthest limitation that has been ever suggested upon the duty of disclosure which authors of prospectuses must discharge, leaves untouched the principle that they must not conceal anything which, if stated, would contradict or even substantially alter any material representation actually made by the prospectus, as an inducement to take shares. This prospectus, in my opinion, actually represents what was false to the knowledge of those who drew it, with respects to a vital matter, namely, the destination of the money subscribed. Every prospectus is a request for money to be invested with a prospect of profit, upon the faith of the statements which it contains and every prospectus discloses the purpose to which the subscriptions which it invites are to be applied. If money is knowingly obtained upon a false pretence as to how it is to be spent, that is both a fraud and a crime . . .

   [A]ll the non-disclosure of previous dealings, of the successive failures of other companies (one of which had spent £42,500 on the mine 'already proved to be rich'), and of the partition of the concession; the omission of dates from the reports; the uncertainty about where the samples came from; in fact all the other ugly circumstances about the prospectus, whether we regard them as *suppressiones veri* or as *suggestiones falsi* are at least evidence of fraud, and we don't need to rely on them as anything more, when the prospectus starts with an actual misrepresentation upon the vital fact that none of the money applied for could be spent upon the mine.

At the same time, the loss of £42,500, which had been spent upon the mine, and the failure of the previous companies, are strangely inconsistent with the statement that it had been 'already proved to be rich.' The proof of its 'richness' is that it had beggared everybody who had undertaken the experiment . . .

The reference to the contracts of February, 1890 [i.e. the contracts of sale of the mine], is relied on as an answer to this . . . because the reference to the contracts complied in form with the statute, and that every subscriber thereby had imputed notice of the contents of those contracts. In other words, no one who subscribed, on the faith of the false and fraudulent representation that his money was to be spent on machinery, was cheated, because he had imputed knowledge that it was to go into the 'open drains', which were in fact the pockets of Larchin and Gilbert, who drew the prospectus, and their colleagues. It may be that where the statute is complied with by giving dates and names, the subscriber has imputed notice of facts consistent with the prospectus which the contracts disclose; but I entirely deny that any reference to contracts, whether in the terms of the statute or not, can make any prospectus honest which is in fact fraudulent. Further, and a *fortiori*, if a prospectus contains any material representation of fact which is fake and fraudulent, it cannot be the law that a reference in the statutory form to a document which would reveal the falsehood can place the framers of the prospectus in the same position as if they had not made the misrepresentation. It is no answer to a plea of false and fraudulent representation to say that the person who made it had supplied the person whom he defrauded with means by which he might have discovered the fraud before he acted upon it. Such a principle, as I once ventured to say in another case, would introduce the plea of contributory negligence as a defence to an action for deceit.

[Affirmed unanimously in the House of Lords [1896] AC 273.]

Notes

In *Components Tube Co v Naylor* [1900] 2 IR 1 the defendant subscribed for shares in the plaintiff company in reliance upon a prospectus issued on behalf of the plaintiff by certain promoter/directors. The prospectus fraudulently concealed the fact that the plaintiffs business had been purchased from its promoters who stood to make a considerable profit for themselves as a result. The defendant was granted an order rescinding the contract of allotment of the shares. On the duty involved in preparing a prospectus Sir P O'Brien LCJ said:–

'It appears to me to be one of the most elementary obligations of law as well as of morality that a prospectus, upon which the public are invited to buy, should be an honest and a candid one. When an invitation is held out to the public to buy on the faith of a prospectus, candour, entire candour, becomes an essential element of honesty.'

Recission of the contract of allotment will not be allowed where *restitutio in integrum* is impossible, as where the rights of third parties, such as the creditors of the company, would be adversely affected. For example in *Oakes v Turquand and Harding; Peek v Turquand and Harding* [1867] LR 2 HL 325 rescission was refused because the company had since gone into liquidation. To have permitted rescission would have resulted in the supervening rights of the company's other creditors being adversely affected. See also *Tennant v City of Glasgow Bank* (1879) 4 App Cas 615. Rescission will also be refused where the inaccuracies in the prospectus are only minor or trivial. See *Re South of England Natural Gas & Petroleum Co Ltd* [1911] 1 Ch 573.

[4.17] Where a person has been induced to take shares in a company by a fraudulent misrepresentation he may not claim damages against the company while he is still a member.[1]

1 This does not however, prejudice the shareholders right of action against promoters, directors, etc., who were responsible for the fraudulent misrepresentation.

Houldsworth v City of Glasgow Bank (1880) 5 App Cas 317

[4.18] The plaintiffs bought shares in the defendant bank, allegedly having been induced to do so by fraud. The bank, which was an unlimited company, went into liquidation, and calls were made upon the plaintiff in the sum of £29,000. He sought to claim damages from the company in respect of (i) the sum he paid for the shares, (ii) money paid on calls, and (iii) the estimated amount of future calls. The House of Lords held that the action could not be mortgaged. The company now being in liquidation recission was impossible and damages could not be claimed as against a company of which he remained a member.

Lord Selborne: This is not a case of parties at arm's length with each other, one of whom has suffered a wrong of which damages are the simple and proper measure, and which may be redressed by damages without any unjust or inconsistent consequences. For many purposes a corporator with whom his own corporation has dealings, or on whom it may by its agents inflict some wrong, is in the same position towards it as a stranger; except that he may have to contribute, rateably with others, towards the payment of his own claim. But here it is impossible to separate the matter of the pursuer's claim from his status as a corporator, unless that status can be put an end to by rescinding the contract which brought him into it. His complaint is, that by means of the fraud alleged, he was induced to take upon himself the liabilities of a shareholder. The loss from which he seeks to be indemnified by damages is really neither more nor less than the whole *aliquot* share due from him in contribution of the whole debts and liabilities of the company; and if his claim is right in principle I fail to see how the remedy founded on that principle can stop short of going this length. But it is of the essence of the contract between the shareholders (as long as it remains unrescinded) that they should all contribute equally to the payment of all the company's debts and liabilities.

Such an action of damages as the present is really not against the corporation as an aggregate body, but is against all the members of it except one, viz the pursuer; it is to throw upon them the pursuer's share of the corporate debts and liabilities. Many of those shareholders . . . may have come and probably did come into the company after the pursuer had acquired his shares. They are all as innocent of the fraud as the pursuer himself; if it were imputable to them it must, on the same principle be imputable to the pursuer himself as long as he remains a shareholder; and they are no more liable for any consequences of fraudulent or other wrongful acts of the company's agent than he is. Recission of the contract in such a case is the only remedy for which there is any precedent, and it is in my opinion the only way in which the company could justly be made answerable for a fraud of this kind. But for recission the appellant is confessedly too late . . ."

Lords Hatherley, Blackburn and Cairns LC delivered concurring opinions.

Notes

See also *Re Addlestone Linoleum Co* (para **4.27**). How are these cases to be reconciled with the principle in *Salomon v Salomon & Co* that the company has a separate legal personality from that of its members. The matter is discussed by *Hornby & Gower* (1956) 19 MLR 54,61,185.

Statutory compensation[1]

[4.19] Under s 49 of the Principal Act, where a prospectus invites persons to subscribe for shares in or debentures of a company, various persons connected with its issue[2] are liable to pay compensation to any person who subscribes for any shares or debentures on the faith of the prospectus and who suffers loss or damage as a result of any 'untrue' statement contained in that prospectus. Under art 12 of the European Communities (Stock Exchange) Regulations 1984 the application of s 49 is extended to 'untrue' statements contained in any listing particulars. It has been held that the appropriate criteria for measuring damages under s 49 are those traditionally applied in measuring damages in tort. It should be noted that the right of action lies only against those parties specified in s 49 who are connected with the issue; it does not lie against the company. Mere concealment of facts does not constitute an 'untrue statement' for the purposes of s 49.[3]

1 See *Keane* at paras **8.15–8.16**.
2 (a) every person who is a director of the company at the time of the issue of the prospectus.
  (b) every person who has authorised himself to be named and is named in the prospectus as a director or as having agreed to become a director either immediately or after an interval of time.

(c) every person being a promoter of the company.
(d) every person who has authorised the issue of the prospectus.
3 *McConnell v Wright* [1903] 1 Ch 546; *Clark v Urguhart* [1930] AC 28, [1930] NI 4.

Damages for negligent misstatement

[4.20]   It is clear since the case of *Hedley Byrne & Co v Heller & Partners Ltd* [1964] AC 465 that damages may be recovered for pure economic loss resulting from the negligent making of a statement. It would appear that the scope of the remedy available in this instance is somewhat wider than that available under s 49 of the Principal Act. In principle at least, the action could lie not only against those responsible for issuing the prospectus or listing particulars, but also against the company itself.

[4.21]   Damages for negligent misstatement are only recoverable by those to whom the prospectus is issued, and not by those who incidentally obtain sight of its contents.

Securities Trust Ltd v Hugh Moore & Alexander Ltd [1964] IR 417 (High Court)

[4.22]   **Davitt P:** The facts of this case, briefly summarised, appear to be as follows: Mr Kevin Anderson was at all material times chairman and managing director of the plaintiff company. In December 1961, the company authorised the purchase of shares in the defendant company. The authority to purchase was a continuing authority, and purchases were made thereunder from time to time. In December 1961, 200 ordinary shares were bought at twelve shillings per share and 100 preference at 13s 6d. These shares were purchased by Mr Kevin Anderson, and were transferred to him respectively on the 6th February 1962 and the 31st January 1962. They were registered in his name on the 23rd February 1961. They were of course, bought on the company's behalf.

Early in April 1962, Mr Anderson wrote to the secretary of the defendant company requesting a copy of its memorandum and articles of association and enclosing the statutory shilling. He did not attach any description to his signature and the letter did not anywhere refer to, or bear the name of, the plaintiff company. There was nothing in it to indicate that it was written on behalf of the plantiff company, or on behalf of anyone other than the writer. On the 9th April he received a reply acknowledging receipt of his shilling and enclosing a copy of the memorandum and articles. This was addressed to him personally at the address given in his letter.

Other shares in the defendant company were purchased as follows: 250 ordinary and 378 preference on the 4th January 1962 at 15s 0d in each case; 100 ordinary at 14s 6d on the 16th July 1962; 150 preference on the 25th October 1962 at 20s 0d; 450 preference at 21s 0d on the 26th October 1962; and 250 preference at 21s 0d on the 30th October 1962. These shares were registered in the name of the plaintiff company, the first such registration being made on the 4th May 1961.

By article 155 of the defendants' articles of association, as it appeared in the copy supplied to Mr Anderson, it was provided as follows:– 'If the company shall be wound up, the surplus assets distributable amongst members shall be applied first in repaying to the holders of preference shares the amount paid up on the said preference shares respectively, with the dividends thereon to date of repayment; and if such assets shall be insufficient to repay same in full, they shall be applied rateably so that the loss shall fall on the holders of preference shares in proportion to the amount called up on their shares respectively; and the balance of such surplus assets (if any) shall be applied in repaying to the holders of ordinary shares the amount paid up on their shares respectively, and if such balance shall be insufficient to repay the said amount in full it shall be applied rateably, so that the loss shall fall on the said holders of ordinary shares in proportion to the amount called up on their shares respectively. If the balance of said surplus assets shall be more than sufficient to repay to the said holders of shares the whole amount paid up on their shares, the balance shall be distributed among them in proportion to the amount actually paid up on their shares respectively'.

There had been rumours of a takeover bid for the shares of the defendant company as well as of a voluntary winding up; and on the 26th June 1962, a statement was issued by the chairman which clearly indicated that a voluntary winding up was in contemplation. These circumstances, coupled with the provision contained in the last sentence of article 155, influenced the plaintiff company to increase their holdings of preference shares; and the last three lots were purchased at par or over, and above their ordinary market value.

On the 30th October 1962, the secretary of the defendant company wrote to Mr Anderson saying that the attention of the directors had been called to the fact that in the reprint of the articles prepared in 1941 there was a serious printers' error in article 155. In the original articles as filed in 1898 the last clause in the article reads: 'If the balance of said surplus assets shall be more than sufficient to repay the said holders of ordinary shares the whole amount paid up on their shares, the balance shall be distributed among them in proportion to the amount actually paid up on their shares respectively.' In the reprint a copy of which had been supplied to Mr Anderson, the word, 'ordinary' had been omitted with the result of making it appear that the holders of preference shares were entitled to share in the surplus. On the 4th October 1962, a resolution to wind up the company had been passed. The company went into liquidation and Mr Garnet Walker was appointed liquidator. He refused to allow the claim of the plaintiff company to participate in the surplus assets in respect of their preference shares; and on the 5th February 1964, they issued their summons in the present proceedings.

In their statement of claim they aver that they applied for a copy of the memorandum and articles of association through their agent, Mr Anderson, and were supplied with the one containing the printers' error. They claim that be reason of the negligent misrepresentation of the defendant company they were induced to purchase the 850 preference shares at a price exceeding their market value and have thereby suffered damage. The substantial defences raised in the defendants' pleadings are: that the copy of the memorandum and articles supplied to Mr Anderson were not supplied to him as agent for the plaintiff company; that the defendant company owed no duty of care to the plaintiff company to supuply them with an accurate copy of the memorandum and articles; that there was no negligence on their part; and that the plaintiff company did not suffer the alleged or any damage; or, alternatively, that the damages claimed are too remote.

The law to be applied in this case is not in controversy. It would appear that the proposition that innocent (i.e. non-fraudulent) misrepresentation cannot give rise to an action for damages is somewhat too broadly stated, and is based upon a misconception of what was decided by the House of Lords in *Derry v Peek* 14 App Cas 337. Such action may be based on negligent misrepresentation which is not fraudulent. This was pointed out in *Nocton v Lord Ashburton* [1914] AC 932, particularly in the speech of Lord Haldane LC. At page 948 he says:– 'Although liability for negligence in word has in material respects been developed in our law differently from liability for negligence in act, it is none the less true that a man may come under a special duty to exercise care in giving information or advice. I should accordingly be sorry to be thought to lend countenance to the idea that recent decisions have been induced to stereotype the cases in which people can be held to have assumed such a duty. Whether such a duty has been assumed must depend on the relationship of the parties, and it is at least certain that there are a good many cases in which that relationship may be properly treated as giving rise to a special duty of care in statement'. It was apparently considered in some quarters that such a special duty could arise only from a contractual or fiduciary relationship. In *Robinson v National Bank of Scotland* (1916) SC (HL) 140, Haldane LC was at pains to dispel this idea. At page 157 he says:–

'The whole of the doctrine as to fiduciary relationships, as to the duty of care arising from other special relationships which the courts may find to exist in particular cases, still remains, and I should be very sorry if any word fell from me which would suggest that the courts are in any way hampered in recognising that the duty of care may be established when such cases really occur.'

The proposition that circumstances may create a relationship between two parties in which, if one seeks information from the other and is given it, that other is under a duty to take reasonable care to ensure that the information given is correct, has been accepted and applied in the case of *Hedley Byrne & Co Ltd v Heller and Partners Ltd* [1963] 3 WLR 101, recently decided by the House of Lords. Counsel for the defendant company did not seek to dispute the proposition. He submitted, however, that the circumstances of this case created no such special relationship.

Sect 18 sub-s 1 of the Companies (Consolidation) Act 1908, provides:– 'Every company shall send to every member, and on payment of one shilling or such less sum as the company may prescribe, a copy of the memorandum and of the articles (if any). 'At the time that Mr Anderson made his request to the secretary of the defendant company for a copy of their memorandum and articles of association he was a shareholder. The plaintiff company had not then been registered as owner of any shares. He was a member of the defendant comany; his company was not. The position was that he was entitled to receive it personally qua member; he was not entitled to receive it qua agent of the plaintiff company. In these circumstances I must, I think, conclude that the copy was requested and supplied, in accordance with the provisions of s 18 sub-s 1 of the Act, by the defendant company to Mr Anderson personally and not as agent for the plaintiff company. It seems to me that there was no relationship between the parties in this case other than such as would exist between the defendant company and any person (other than Mr Anderson) who might chance to read the copy supplied to him; or, indeed, between that company and any member of the community at large, individual or corporate, who chanced to become aware of the last sentence in article 155 of the defective reprint of the memorandum and articles. It can hardly be seriously contended that the the defendant company owed a duty of care to avoid mistakes and printers' errors in the reprint of their articles. In my opinion, counsel is correct in his submission that in this case the defendant company owed no duty to the plaintiff company to take care to ensure that the copy of the articles supplied to Mr Anderson was a correct copy. For these reasons there must, in my opinion, be judgment for the defendant company.

Damages for the tort of deceit

[4.23]   If a person has been induced to acquire shares in a company as a result of a fraudulent misrepresentation made to him, he may, instead of seeking to rescind the contract, issue proceedings seeking damages for deceit. It has been observed that an action for damages may not lie against the company without first rescinding the contract of purchase of the shares.[1] An action may, however, still lie against the individuals responsible for making the fraudulent statement. In fact deceit may occur not only as a result of statements made, but also as a result of material omissions from the prospectus or listing particulars.[2]

1 *Houldsworth v City of Glasgow Bank* (1879) 4 Ex D 216.
2 *Aaron's Reefs Ltd v Twiss*; *Derry v Peek* (1889) 14 App Cas 337.

Jury v Stoker & Jackson (1882) 9 LR Ir 385 (Chancery Division)

[4.24]   The plaintiff was induced to purchase shares in the Cork Milling Co, on the faith of a prospectus which contained a fraudulent misrepresentation that the person from whom the company had purchased its mills (Jackson) would be investing £7,500 in the company. The company subsequently went into liquidation, resulting in the loss of the entire of the plaintiff's investment. The plaintiff successfully claimed damages for the tort of deceit from the directors who had been responsible for the issue of the prospectus.

[4.25]   Sullivan MR: In my opinion, the shareholders of this company were entitled to have all the circumstances bearing on the affairs and formation of the company in the prospectus. There is no document in which it is of more consequence to state fully and fairly the real facts than the prospectus of a projected company. Some men will speculate by taking shares in a company, no matter how ridiculous it may be. But the law was not made for such persons. Thousands of persons of small property are striving to increase their income by investment in the shares of a company, and in nine cases out of ten, persons who are not lawyers act on the prospectus, which ought to be a fair *resume* of the affairs of the company . . . In my opinion, the prospectus was deliberately and fraudulently adopted to make the concern attractive. The plaintiff jury acted on the prospectus and took the shares. I have a very strong opinion that the representation was false and fraudulent, to induce men to take shares in this company, and if loss has resulted from it, the person who made the false representation should be made to answer for the loss, even if the matter rested at common law and outside any ststute. The representation was false, fraudulent and material, made to induce a man to take the shares and loss has resulted to the plaintiff. The defendant who makes such a representation cannot be heard to say, 'Oh you might have found out that it was wrong if you had gone to the office and seen the instrument yourself.' I am, therefore, clearly of opinion, on the first part of the case, that Mr Stoker is answerable to the plaintiff for the loss which he has sustained by the false statement in the prospectus as to the cash capital of £7,500.

Notes
    For a recent discussion of liability for deceit see *Northern Bank Finance Corporation v Charlton* (para **4.07**)

Claim for breach of contract

[4.26]   A person who has acquired shares in a company on the faith of inaccurate statements contained in a prospectus may have a claim in damages against the company for breach of contract, on the grounds that those statements have been incorporated as terms into the contract of purchase of the shares. However, no claim for damages will be entertained against the company for breach of contract while the plaintiff remains a member of the company.

Re Addlestone Linoleum Co (1887) 37 Ch D 191 (Court of Appeal)

[4.27]   The company had issued certain £10 preference shares at a discount of 25%. Those individuals who had acquired these shares were subsequently called upon to pay a further £2.50 per share. They in turn claimed to be entitled to prove in the winding up for the same amount as damages for breach of contract. Their claim was rejected both by the trial judge and the Court of Appeal.

[4.28]   **Cotton LJ** [Having found that the contract was to issue shares at a discount and not (as had been alleged) to issue fully paid shares]: This, I think the company had no power to do . . . But if the contract was to issue fully paid-up shares, I am of opinion that the decision in *Houldsworth v City of Glasgow Bank* precludes us from allowing this proof. A person there who had been induced to take shares by misrepresentation on the part of the company, brought an action of deceit against the bank and its liquidators, after an order had been made for winding up the company. The House of Lords in substance, said that the claim was made on the ground of misrepresentation which would have enabled the shareholder to repudiate the shares, and separate himself from the company – that he had elected to continue in the company – or, at all events, had taken no steps to repudiate his shares before the winding up after which it was too late to do so, and that having thus irrevocably fixed himself with the liabilities of a shareholder, he could not come to claim out of the assets of the company a sum not included in the debts and liabilities, to the payment of which he, as a shareholder, had agreed that those assets should be devoted. When those shareholders, supposing the contract to have been a contract to give them fully paid-up shares, got shares which in the eye of the law were not fully paid up, they had a right to say, 'You have given us something quite different from what we agreed for, take us off the register,' and when that had been done, they might have made a further claim for damages, if they had sustained any. But now they come here as shareholders, and in substance retain their shares and seek to sue the company for breach of the contract under which they took them.

Notes

This case was primarily decided on the basis that the contract was not for the issue of fully paid shares, but rather for the issue of shares at a discount, which was illegal. Accordingly, that part of the judgment which follows *Houldsworth v City of Glasgow Bank* must properly be regarded as being obiter dictum. For reasons mentioned *supra* it is respectfully submitted that the *Houldsworth* case is not good law.

Criminal liability in respect of misstatements in connection with flotations

[4.29]

(*a*) Liability under s 50 of the Principal Act, as amended by s 15 of the Act of 1982, for issuing a prospectus containing an untrue statement.[1]

(*b*) Liability under reg 6 of the European Communities (Stock Exchange) Regulations 1984 for publishing listing particulars containing false or misleading statements.

(*c*) Liability under s 44 of the Principal Act as amended by s 15 of the Act of 1982 for failing to issue a prospectus when one was required, or failing to comply with the statutory disclosure requirements.

(*d*) Liability under s 46 of the Principal Act for issuing a prospectus without the consent of a relevant expert.

(*e*) Liability under s 47 of the Principal Act for failing to register a prospectus.

(*f*) Liability under reg 13(3) of the European Communities (Stock Exchange) Regulations 1984 for publishing listing particulars before a copy has been delivered to the registrar of companies.

(*g*) Liability under s 84 of the Larceny Act 1861 for circulating or publishing, or concurring in the making, circulating or publishing of any written statement or account which the person knows to be false in any material particular, with intent to induce any person to become a shareholder of the company.[2]

1 See *Keane* at para **8.18**.
2 See *R v Kylesent* [1932] 1 KB 442, where it was held that liability under s 84 may arise even though no individual statement is untrue, provided the statements when combined constitute a false statement.

Chapter 5

APPLICATION FOR AND ALLOTMENT OF SHARES

[5.01] Allotment refers to the taking of newly issued shares in a company.[1] The first allotment is to the subscribers who sign the memorandum of association. Their shares are allotted once the company has been incorporated. Thereafter other individuals may apply for and have shares allotted to them. Under s 31 of the Principal Act the subscribers become members of the company once it is registered even though their shares have not been allotted to them.[2] Anyone else wishing to become a member of the company must not only acquire shares in the company, but also have his name entered in the register of members.[3] An enforceable contract of allotment arises when the applicant is notified that he has been allotted the shares for which he has applied. The allottee may then if necessary, obtain a decree of specific performance to enter his name on the register of members.[4]

1 See generally *Keane* chapter 9.
2 *Evan's* case (1867) 2 Ch App 427.
3 S 31 of the Principal Act. See also *Re Allied Metropole Hotel Ltd* (Gannon J, unreported, High Court, 19th December 1988), noted by *MacCann* (1989) 7 ILT 196.
4 *New Brunswick & Carody Rly Co v Muggeridge* (1860) 4 Ex D 216. However, see also *Holwell Securities v Hughes* [1947] 1 All ER 161. On the postal rule generally see Clark *Contract* (2nd Ed) (London, 1986) at pp 12–13.

The allotment

[5.02] Notification may be written, oral, or by conduct[1] and is subject to the provisions of the 'postal rule'.[2] The applicant may (subject to certain statutory exceptions,[3] revoke his application at any time before notice of the allotment is given. However, revocation must be made within a reasonable time.[4] The letter of allotment may be 'renounceable' (ie the allottee may 'renounce' or assign it to another person who then becomes entitled to have his name entered on the register of members). Under s 20 of the 1983 Act the authority of the company in general meeting or of a provision in the articles of association is required before the directors may allot shares in the company. The authority may continue in force for no more than five years and may be varied or revoked during that time or renewed for further periods of five years by the company in general meeting. The authorisation may be general or limited, conditional or unconditional. S 20 does not apply to shares taken by subscribers to the memorandum, to the allotment of shares pursuant to an employee's share scheme, nor to a right to subscribe for, or to convert any security into shares.[5]

[5.03] Under s 23 of the 1983 Act statutory rights of pre-emption are given to existing members of the company, when a fresh allotment of shares is being made. The right of pre-emption gives the shareholder the right to subscribe for the fresh issue of shares on a pro rata basis. The pre-emption right applies to the issue of 'equity securities' which excludes preference shares and shares allotted under an employee's share scheme. However, the holders of emplpoyee's shares are themselves given s 23 pre-emption rights. The section does not apply where the shares are to be paid for wholly or partly by a non-cash consideration. It may also be excluded by a provision to that effect in the memorandum or articles of association of a private company, or by the authorisation of allotment given under s 20 of the 1983 Act.[6]

1 *Gunn's* case (1867) Ch App 40.
2 Discussed in *Keane* at para **9.22**.
3 *Crawley's* case (1869) 4 Ch App 322.
4 On s 20 of the 1983 Act see *Keane* at paras **9.07–9.08**.
5 On the statutory right of pre-emption see *Keane* at paras **9.09–9.11** and Forde *The Companies (Amendment) Act 1983* (1983) Irish Jurist 289.
6 See *Keane* at paras **9.13–9.15**.
7 S 58(1)(b) of the Principal Act. See for example *McCoy v Greene* (High Court, Costello J, 19 January 1984) where the non-cash consideration was the performance of the role of mediator/director in a company split by a family dispute.
8 S 26(3) of the 1983 Act.

[5.04] The directors must exercise their power to allot shares in good faith and in the best interests of the company.

Nash v Lancegaye (Ireland) Ltd (1958) 92 ILTR 11 (High Court)

[5.05] Approximately 49% of the voting shares in the defendant company were held by Ryan and his associates, the remainder being held by the plaintiff and certain proxies which he had obtained. Differences arose between the plaintiff and Ryan. Ryan and his associates dominated the board of directors which by resolutions of 17 May and 16 June 1955 made a fresh issue of shares. The allotment was made in such a way as to give the Ryan and his associates control of over 51% of the issued voting shares. The plaintiff challenged the validity of this allotment.

[5.06] **Dixon J:** The plaintiff however does not dispute the power of the directors to deal with the unissued capital under article 6, so long as the power is properly exercised. He relies on the well established principle that the directors are trustees of the powers entrusted to them, including that of allotting shares and that the court will intervene in the case of an improper use or the abuse of any of their powers . . .

The defendant directors take up the position that the sole object of the resolution of 17th May 1955, was to avail of an offer of fresh capital made at a time when fresh capital was not only needed but needed urgently . . . I find the suggestion of urgency wholly unconvincing and quite inadequate to explain the somewhat indecent haste with which the matter was put through. No agenda or notice of any resolution was sent out beforehand and in the agenda circulated at the meeting the only heading the matter could be related to was 'capital position', which was an item appearing in the agenda and discussed at nearly every general meeting. Mr Nash's plea for adjournment and an opportunity of further consideration was rejected rather summarily . . .

The resolution of 16th June was clearly subsidiary and ancillary to that of May 17th and tainted with the same lack of good faith and the same lack of due consideration of the matters revelant to be considered by directors in exercising their discretionary and fiduciary powers and it must stand or fall with the resolution of 17th May.

For the defendants reliance was placed on *Foss v Harbottle* but I do not think the principle of that case applies to the present proceedings. It, and the cases which have followed and applied it, were concerned with wrongs alleged to be done to the company as a whole and in respect of which it was, therefore for the company as such to complain or not. See *Edwards v Haliwell* [1950] 2 All ER 1064. In the present case particular wrong has been done to individual shareholders including the plaintiff by the lack of good faith on the part of the directors in the purported exercise of their discretionary powers. In *Clark v Workman* [1920] 1 IR 107, Ross J held notwithstanding *Foss v Harbottle* having been cited, that the transfer of a controlling interest in a company is not a matter of mere internal management, it may involve a complete transformation of the company and consequently such a transfer may in a proper case be restrained. Again, the decision of Peterson J in *Piercy v S Mills & Co Ltd* [1920] 1 Ch 77 is very much in point here. He there held that directors are not entitled to use their power of issuing shares merely for the purpose of maintaining their control or the control of themselves and their friends over the affairs of the company or merely for the purpose of defeating the wishes of the existing majority of shareholders.

Part of the principle of *Foss v Harbottle*, if not the main feature of it, is that, in the case of a matter capable of being legalised or regularised by a majority of the shareholders, the person complaining of some action by the directors of the company, should await and abide by the outcome of a general meeting of the company; and, for this reason, it was contended that the present action was prematurely and unsustainable. I think in the circumstances of the present case, this argument overlooks the fundamental point that it was precisely the question whether the 15,000 votes of James Ryan could be used at the general meeting that was in issue. By the time of the commencement of the action in June 1955, the forces on each side had been mustered and it was agreed at the hearing that the respective figures were approximately 51,000 votes for the plaintiff and his supporters and nearly

53,000 for the Ryan family and their supporters. This 53,000 would include the 15,000 from the allotment to James Ryan. If he were entitled to use these votes the Ryan family and supporters would not thereby have an absolute majority of the issued capital but there is little doubt that they would have had an actual majority at the meetings. Without the 15,000 votes ranking the plaintiff would have had an absolute majority (51,000 out of a total voting strength of 96,000), but the general meeting would not have had power to undo or reverse what had been done by the directors in the exercise of the power and discretion delegated to them. On the other hand a majority at the meeting could have approved, if so minded of what had been done but this would leave the question undetermined and still outstanding whether the directors had acted in bad faith to the prejudice of individual shareholders. This position is, I think, recognised in the following portion of the passage from Buckley on the Companies Acts dealing with the principle of *Foss v Harbottle* and cited by Danckwerts J, in *Pavlides v Jenson* [1956] 2 All ER 518 at p 521 – '. . . it is idle to say that a meeting ought to be called in which the alleged wrongdoers should not vote for that would be trying the question of fraud as a preliminary step for ascertaining the form of the action in which it is to be tried'. Again if I am right in my view that the entry of James Ryan in the register of shareholders on 2nd June 1955 was invalid the plaintiff was entitled to bring the first action when he did without waiting for a general meeting to consider the matter. For these reasons I think the proceedings were not premature or unsustainable. A somewhat similar position arose in *Punt v Symons & Co Ltd* [1903] 2 Ch 506 and Byrne J there held that where shares had been issued by directors not for the general benefit of the company but for the purpose of controlling the holders of the greatest number of shares by obtaining a majority of voting power, the directors ought to be restrained from holding the meeting at which the votes of the new shareholders were to have been used. He considered and distinguished *Foss v Harbottle*. It makes no difference to my view in this respect, that in fact the number of shares issued would not have been sufficient to ensure an absolute majority. I am concerned with motive and it is irrelevant to that consideration whether the objects would have been fully achieved . . .

I have arrived at the conclusion that the resolutions of 17th May and 16th June 1955, were not an honest exercise of the directors powers in the interests of either the shareholders or the company, and cannot be allowed to take effect; and the entry of James Ryan in the share register was invalid and must be set aside.

Notes

For other cases on the requirement of good faith in allotting shares, see *Mills v Mills* (1938) 60 CLR 150; *Hogg v Cramphorn Ltd* [1966] 3 WLR 254; *Howard Smith Ltd v Ampol Petroleum Ltd* [1944] AC 821; *Clemens v Clemens Bros Ltd* [1976] 2 All ER 268; *Bamford v Bamford* [1969] 2 WLR 1107. Compare *Nash v Lancegaye Safety Glass (Ireland) Ltd* (para **5.05**) with *Re Jermyn Street Turkish Baths Ltd* [1971] 1 WLR 1042 which involved a 'package deal' aimed at rescuing the company from insolvency. In return for an allotment of shares giving her control of the company one of the directors agreed to lend the company much needed cash. The injection of cash helped to stave off liquidation and the director through her efforts she managed to restore the company to profitability. The Court of Appeal held that the allotment was valid, having been made bona fide and for the benefit and prosperity of the company as a whole.

See also *Harlowe's Nominees Property Ltd v Woodside (Lake Entrance) Oil Co* (1968) 121 CLR 483 where it was held that shares may be allotted raising of money in excess of the company's immediate needs where this is done for the financial stability of the company.

Paying for shares

[5.07] Payment for an allotment of shares may be either a cash or non-cash consideration or both. A non-cash consideration may for example, include payment by the supply of goods or services and is recognised as being a permissible by s 26 of the 1983 Act. In the case of a non-cash consideration the company must deliver to the registrar of companies within one month of the allotment a copy of the contract of allotment or particulars thereof, if the contract was made orally. A plc may not accept as the whole or part of the consideration for the issue of shares an undertaking to do work or perform services for the company or any other person nor an undertaking which is to be performed more than five years from the date of allotment. Such consideration renders the allottee liable to pay part of the consideration in cash together with interest thereon. Subsequent purchasers are similarly liable unless they took the shares for value and without notice of the contravention of the section.[1] The release of a debt due by the company to the allottee is treated as cash consideration,[2] although an allotment as part of a compromise or settlement constitutes a non-cash consideration.[3] The allottee is liable for calls made, even where he holds the shares as trustee or agent and by way of security.[4]

1 As this could give rise to a double payment for the shares ie, the cash and non-cash considerations, application may be made to the court for relief under s 34(4) of the 1983 Act.
2 S 2(3) of the Principal Act. See also *Spargos* case (1873) 8 Ch App 407; *Laroque v Beachemin* [1897] AC 358.
3 *Re Johannesburg Hotel Co* [1891] 1 Ch 119.
4 *Re Munster Bank (Dillon's Claim)* (1887–87) 17 LR Ir 341.

[5.08] Shares may not be issued at a discount.

Ooregum Gold Mining Co of India v Roper [1892] AC 125 (House of Lords)

[5.09] Preference shares with a par value of £1 each were issued on the basis that 75p should be credited as having been paid on each share. This was probably the only way in which the company would get the public to subscribe for shares, short of reducing their nominal value.[1] This was because the companys' shares were then being traded on the market at a price considerably below their par value. The allotment was, on the evidence made bona fide and in the interests of the company, which needed fresh capital at the time. The ordinary shareholders brought an action to challenge the validity of the issue of the preference shares. The House of Lords held that the company could not validly issue shares at a discount and accordingly the allottees were personally liable to pay the amount of the discount to the company.

1 As to which see chapter 15 *infra*.

[5.10]   Lord Halsbury LC: My Lords, the question in this case has been more or less in debate since 1883, when Chitty J decided that a company limited by shares was not prohibited by law from issuing its shares at a discount. That decision was overruled though in a different case by the Court of Appeal in 1888 and it has not come to your Lordships for final determination.

My Lords, the whole structure of a limited company owes its existence to the Act of Parliament and it is to the Act of Parliament one must refer to see what are its powers and within what limits it is free to act. Now, confining myself for the moment to the Act of 1862, it makes one of the conditions of the limitation of liability that the memorandum of association shall contain the amount of capital with which the company proposes to be registered, divided into shares of a certain fixed amount. It seems to me that the system thus created by which the shareholder's liability is to be limited by the amount unpaid upon his shares, renders it impossible for the company to depart from that requirement and any expedient to arrange with their shareholders that they shall not be liable for the amount unpaid on the shares, although the amount of those shares has been, in accordance with the Act of Parliament fixed at a certain sum of money. It is manifest that if the company could do so the provision in question would operate nothing.

I observe in the argument it has been sought to draw a distinction between the nominal capital and the capital which is assumed to be the real capital. I can find no authority for such a distinction. The capital is fixed and certain and every creditor of the company is entitled to look to that capital as his security. It may be that such limitations on the power of a company to manage its own affairs may occasionally be inconvenient and prevent its obtaining money or the purposes of its trading on terms so favourable as it could do if it were more free to act. But, speaking for myself, I recognise the wisdom of enforcing on a comany the disclosure of what its real capital is, and not permitting a statement of its affairs to be such as may mislead and deceive those who are either about to become its shareholders or about to give it credit.

I think . . . that the question which your Lordships have to solve is one which may be answered by reference to an inquiry: What is the nature of an agreement to take a share in a limited company? and that that question may be answered by saying, that it is an agreement to become liable to pay to the company the amount for which the share has been created. That agreement

110

is one which the company itself has no authority to alter or qualify and I am therefore, of opinion that, treating the question as unaffected by the Act of 1867, the company were prohibited by law, upon the principle laid down in *Ashbury Company v Riche* Law Rep 7 HL 653, from doing that which is compendiously described as issuing shares as a discount.

Lords Watson, Herschell, Macnaughten and Morris delivered concurring judgments.

Notes

For an example of the rigid application of the prohibition of the allotment of shares at a discount see *Re Munster Bank (Dillon's Claim)* (1886–87) 17 LR Ir 341. In *Re Newtownards Gas Co* (1885–86) 15 LR Ir 51 it was held that where shares are allotted at a discount the allottees are personally laible to pay the discount even though the company is being wound up and there are sufficient assets to pay the creditors in full.

In *Hirsche v Sims* [1894] AC 654 it was held that where shares have been issued at a discount and the company is unable to recover that discount from the allottee or subsequent holders of the shares (eg because they are bona fide purchasers for value without notice of the discount), the company recoup the amount of the discount from the responsible directors, even though they acted in good faith and in what they considered were the company's best interests.

[5.11] In the case of a private company the court cannot enquire into the adequacy or otherwise of the non-cash consideration except in the case of fraud or where there consideration is clearly inadequate or illusory.

Re Wragg Ltd [1897] 1 Ch 796 (Court of Appeal)

[5.12] Wragg and Martin formed a company to acquire a business run by them. The purchase price of £46,300 was paid partly in cash and partly by the allottment to them of fully paid shares to the value of £20,000. The company subsequently went into liquidation and the liquidator alleged that the purchase price had been over-stated by £18,000. He therefore sought to treat £18,000 worth of the alloted shares as unpaid. He also claimed in the alternative that Wragg and Martin were guilty of misfeasance in their capacity of directors with regard to the acquisition of the business. Both claims were rejected by the Court of Appeal.

[5.13] **Lindley LJ:** The liability of a shareholder to pay the company the amount of his shares is a statutory liability, and is declared to be a specialty debt . . . By our law the payment by a debtor to his creditor of a less sum than is due does not discharge the debt; and this technical doctrine has also been invoked in aid of the law which prevents the shares of a limited company from being issued at a discount. But this technical doctrine, though often sufficient to decide a particular case, will not suffice as a basis for the wider rule of principle that a company cannot effectually release a shareholder from his statutory obligation to pay in money or money's worth the amount of his shares. That share cannot be issued at a discount was finally settled in the case of the *Ooregum Gold Mining Co of India v Roper* (para **5.09**), the judgments in which are strongly relied upon by the appellant in this case. It has, however, never yet been decided that a limited company cannot buy property or pay for services at any price it thinks proper and pay for them in fully paid-up shares. Provided a limited company does so honestly and not colourably and provided that it has not been so imposed upon as to be entitled to be relieved from its bargain, it appears to be settled . . . that agreements by limited companies to pay for property or services in paid-up shares are valid and binding on the companies and their creditors . . . The legislature in 1867 appears to me to have directly recognised such to be the law, but to have required in order to make such agreements binding that they shall be registered before the shares are issued. [ie s 58 of the Principal Act]

[After a review of earlier authorities his lordship concluded that they established the following principles] (1) that . . . shares must be paid for in money or money's worth; (2) that . . . they may be paid for in money's worth; (3) that . . . payment in money's worth can only be effectually made pursuant to a properly registered contract; (4) that, even if there is such a contract, shares cannot be issued at a discount; (5) that if a company owes a person 100l the company cannot by paying him 200l in shares of that nominal amount discharge him, even by a registered contract from his obligation as a shareholder to pay up the other 100l in respect of those shares. That would be issuing shares at a discount. The difference between such a transaction and paying for property or services in shares at a price put upon them by a vendor and agreed to by the company may not always be very apparent in practice. But the two transactions are essentially different and whilst one is ultra vires the other is intra vires. It is not law that persons cannot sell property to a limited company for fully paid-up shares and make a profit by the transaction. We must not allow ourselves to be misled by talking of value. The value paid to the company is measured by the price at which the company agrees to buy what it thinks is worth its while to acquire. Whilst the transaction is unimpeached, this is the only value to be considered.

Smith and Rigby LJJ delivered concurring judgments.

Notes

In *Re Leinster Contract Corporation* [1902] 1 IR 349 the company was formed for the purpose of acquiring certain patents. The purchase price was paid by the allotment of fully paid-up shares in the company. The patents ultimately proved to be worthless. However, the court refused to enquire into the adequacy of the consideration and to set the allotment aside on the ground that there was no evidence of fraud.

Compare this case with *Mosley v Koffyfontein Mines Ltd* [1904] 2 Ch 108.

Here debentures were to be issued at a discount by the company. However, each debenture was convertible into a share in the company at par at the holder's option at a subsequent date. It was clear on the face of the transaction that at the conversion date the shares might still be below par. According to the Court of Appeal, conversion in such circumstances would patently constitute the issue of shares at a discount. It therefore granted an injunction restraining the issue of the debentures.

In the case of a plc, where shares are allotted wholly or partly for a non-cash consideration s 30 of the 1983 Act requires the consideration to be valued by an independent valuer qualified at that time to be appointed as auditor of the company. He may obtain the assistance of any expert (eg a valuer) if he thinks it reasonable to do so. Where the report has not been received by the allottee or where there has been some other breach of the section of which he knows or ought to have known, he is personally liable to pay to the company such cash sum as repesents the non-cash part of the consideration.[1] S 30 does not apply where a company allots shares to all holders of shares (or a class of shares in another company) in exchange for their shares or the cancellation of their shares or all the assets of their company. The issue of bonus shares is also excluded. There are similar requirements for an independent valuation and report under s 32 of the 1983 Act where a plc acquires non-cash assets from the subscribers for a consideration equal in value to at least one-tenth of the nominal capital within two years from the date when a certificate is issued entitling it to commence business.

Where a plc is allotting shares s 28 of the 1983 Act requires that at least 25 per cent of the nominal value of the shares be paid up, together with any premium. The section does not apply to the allotment of shares pursuant to an employee share scheme. For further statutory restrictions on allotments by a plc see *Keane* at paras **9.17–9.21**.

There must be some question as to whether these cases now represent good law. Under s 27 of the 1983 Act the common law prohibition on the issue of shares at a discount has been put on a statutory footing and if this provision is to be effectively administered by the courts, they will have to look at the adequacy or otherwise of the non-cash consideration for the allotment. Where shares have been issued at such a discount the allottee is liable to pay the amount of that discount together with interest. A similar liability attaches to a subsequent purchaser of the shares who is not a purchaser for value without notice of the contravention of s 27. Under s 59 of the Principal Act a commission of up to 10% may still be paid to any person in consideration of his agreeing to take shares or procure others to take shares. This section is intended to apply to the payment of commission for the underwriting of a share issue. However, it is drafted in wide enough terms to allow for the issue of shares at a discount. Presumably the courts will give s 59 an appropriately narrow interpretation which is in harmony with the terms of s 27 of the 1983 Act.

1 Double payment for the shares could arise here, and s 34 relief may be obtained.

Issue of shares at a premium

[5.14] While shares may not be issued below their par value, there is nothing to prevent the company from issuing it for a price above its nominal value. For example, a share with a par value of £1 may be issued for £1.50. The excess figure received by the company over the par value of the share is known as the 'premium', ie 50p in the present example. The premium may arise even though payment for the allotted shares is not in cash. A common example in Ireland is where a company is formed to take over a business and the purchase price for the acquisition is the allotment of shares to the vendor of the business. For example, 100 shares of £1 each may be issued in consideration for a business with a value of £30,000. The premium on each share is £19,999. A premium on a share is not regarded as income or profit of the company and must be transferred in the company's accounts in to a separate account known a the 'share premium account.[1] The provisions on reduction of the company's capital apply equally to the share premium account. This account may be applied for a limited number of purposes set out in s 62(2) of the Principal Act.

1 S 62(1) of the Principal Act.

[5.15] Where shares in one company are allotted in consideration for the acquisition of shares in a second company in circumstances where the nominal value of the allotted shares in the first company is less than the value of the shares in the second company, the difference in value constitutes a premium which must be transferred into a share premium account. This is so even though such difference represents profits mde by the second company prior to the acquisition of its shares. These pre-acquisition profits may not be distributed by the first company by way of dividend as to do so would constitute an unlawful reduction of capital, (i.e. of the share premium account).[1]

1 See Ussher *Doubts remain on Shearer v Bercain* (1982) 3 Company Lawyer 28.

Henry Read & Co Ltd v Ropner Holdings Ltd [1952] Ch 124

[The facts appear from the judgment]

[5.16] Harman J: The defendant company is what is popularly known as a holding company and was incorporated at the end of 1948, having as its first and paramount object the acquisition for amalgamation purposes of two shipping companies formerly carried on separately under the same management. The amalgamation was of the simplest kind. The shareholders in the two companies were willing to sell their shares in the two companies in exchange for shares in the holding company. At that point there arose a question of the rate of capitalisation. Sometimes this figure is a merely nominal figure; at other times it is designed to reflect the true value of the assets being acquired. In the present case a valuation of the assets of the two companies was procured from a firm of accountants. No doubt those calculations were based on information given by persons having a knowledge of shipping, knowledge which accountants would not have, and they merely valued the physical assets of the two companies, leaving out questions of profit-earning capacity, goodwill and so forth. They then apparently arrived at a value of the assets of each of the constituent companies and advised that the one having slightly larger assets than the other should issue by way of capital profit dividend a sufficient sum to its shareholders to reduce the value of the assets to an equality with the other company.

At that point it was possible to advise, and the advice was given, that a pound-for-pound capitalisation – that is to say, a pound of the new company's shares for a pound's worth nominal of the constituent company's shares – was a fair method of performing the amalgamation. Accordingly, there was issued in the aggregate to the shareholders in the two companies the entire authorised capital of the holding company, which was £1,719,606. That did not however, do anything more than represent the aggregate of the nominal value of the shares of the constituent companies. The real value of the shares was, if the valuation was right, approximately £5,000,000 in excess of that sum. The issuing company has therefore acquired for its shares assets worth between six and seven millions, if that valuation be, as I think I must suppose it to be for these purposes a true reflection of the value of the assets acquired at the time of their acquisition. When the balance sheet of the holding company appears for the year ended March 31, 1949, one finds on the left-hand side the issued capital set out, and below that, under the words 'Capital Reserver Share Premium Account (less formation expenses),' rather than £5,000. On the other side it is stated the value of the shares in the subsidiary companies as valued in the way I have mentioned and they are valued at rather under £7,000,000. When the consolidated balance-sheet is looked at, a rather more express statement is found, namely 'Share Premium Account, being the excess of the value of the net assets of subsidiary companies at the date of acquisition over the book value of the investments (less formation expenses)'; and that is what this £5,000,000 figure is.

The directors have been advised that they are bound to show their accounts in that way, and not only they, but the plaintiffs who are large shareholders regard that as a very undesirable thing, because it fixes an unfortunate kind of rigidity on the structure of the company, having regard to the fact that an account kept under that name, namely the Share Premium Account can only have anything paid out of it by means of a transaction analogous to a reduction of capital. It is, in effect as if the company had originally been capitalised at approximately £7,000,000 instead of £1,750,000.

The question which I have to determine is whether the defendants were obliged to keep their account in that way. That depends purely on s 56 of the Companies Act 1948 [ie s 62 of the Principal Act]. Under that section the share premium account can be distributed in the same restricted way and with the same leave of the court as if paid up share capital was being returned to the shareholders.

Counsel for the plaintiff company asks who would suppose that a common type of transaction of the sort now under consideration was the issue of shares at a premium and says that nobody in the city or in the commercial world would dream of so describing it. It is with a sense of shock at first that one hears that this transaction was the issue of shares at a premium. Everybody, I suppose, who hears those words thinks of a company which being in a strong trading position wants further capital and puts forward its shares for the subscription of the public at such a price as the market in those shares justifies, whatever it may be, 30s a £1 share, £5 a £1 share or any price obtainable and the 10s or £4 above the nominal value of a share which it acquires as a result of the transaction is no doubt a premium. That is what is ordinarily meant by the issue of shares at a premium. The first words of subsection (1) are: 'Where a company issues shares at a premium'. If the words had stopped there, one might have said that the subsection merely refers to cash transactions of that sort but it goes on to say 'whether for cash or otherwise.'

What 'otherwise' can there be? It must be a consideration other than cash, namely goods or assets of some physical sort. Continuing, the subsection contains the words 'a sum equal to the aggregate amount or value of the premiums on those shares shall be transferred to an account to be called 'the share premium account.' Apparently, if the shares are issued for a consideration other than cash and the value of the assets acquired is more than the nominal value of the shares issued, you have issued shares at a premium; and I think that counsel for the plaintiff company was constrained to admit that, in the ordinary case, that was so. This subsection at least has that much result; but he says that the line must be drawn somewhere. It cannot apply, he says, where the issuing company has not assets at all other than the assets which it will acquire as the price of the issue of shares. 'Premium' (he argues) means something resulting from the excess value of its already existing assets over the nominal value of its shares. I am much attracted by that. I have every desire to reduce the effect of this section to what I cannot help thinking would be more reasonably limits, but I do not see my way of limiting it in that way. It is not stated to be a section which only applies after the company has been in existence a year or after the company has acquired assets or when the company is a going concern, or which does not apply on the occasion of a holding company buying shares on an amalgamation. Whether that is an oversight on the part of the legislature or whether it was intended to produce the effect it seems to have produced, it is not for me to speculate. All I can say is that this transaction seems to me to come within the words of the section, and I do not see my way to holding as a matter of construction that it is outside it. If that is so, the inevitable result is that the action must fail.

Notes

See also *Shearer (Inspector of Taxes) v Bercain Ltd* [1980] 3 All ER 295. In this case the defendant company had acquired the entire issued share capital of two companies, worth a total of £96,000 in consideration for the allotment of its own shares with a nominal value of £4,100 to the members of the other two companies. A figure of £92,000 was accordingly transferred to a share premium account in the book of the defendant company. Most of the value of the shares in the other two companies represented undistributed profits earned by those companies prior to their acquisition by the defendant company. The plaintiff argued that this sum of £92,000 constituted distributable profits in the hands of the defendant and was taxable accordingly. This view was rejected by Walton J who held that such pre-acquisition profits must be capitalised by the acquiring company.

Until this judgment was delivered the accounting profession was of the opinion that such pre-acquisition profits were distributable in the hands of the acquiring company. In Britain the law was amended by the Companies Act 1981 which introduced some exceptions to the rule that such pre-acquisition profits be transferred to a share premium account. These provisions are now contained in ss 131–134 of the UK Companies Act 1985. No similar amendent has been made in this jurisdiction.

Chapter 6

SEPARATE LEGAL PERSONALITY OF THE COMPANY

[6.01] A company has its own legal personality distinct from that of its members.[1] Accordingly, it can sue and be sued, hold property, enter into contracts, have a common seal, in other words it may be the subject of legal rights and the object of legal obligations or duties. It therefore follows that the members are normally not personally liable for the acts or omissions of the company. Professor Gower[2] has referred to this concept as the drawing of 'a veil of incorporation' between the company and its shareholders. However, as can be seen below, both the legislature and the courts have provided for certain circumstances where this 'veil' may be 'lifted', resulting, for example, in the liabilities of the company being treated as those of its members.

1 See generally *Keane* chapter 11.
2 Gower's *Principles of Modern Company Law* (4th Ed, London 1979) chapter 6.

[6.02] The company is a separate legal person distinct from its members even if all the shares are beneficially owned by one individual.

Salomon v Salomon & Co Ltd [1897] AC 22

[6.03] **Lord Macnaughton:** My Lords, I cannot help thinking that the appellant, Aron Salomon, has been dealt with somewhat hardly in this case. Mr Salomon, who is not suing as a pauper, was a wealthy man in July 1892. He was a boot and shoe manufacturer trading on his own sole account under the firm of 'A Salomon & Co' in High Street, Whitechapel, where he had extensive warehouses and a large establishment. He had been in trade over thirty years . . . Beginning with little or no capital he had gradually built up a thriving business and he was undoubtedly in good credit and repute.

It is impossible to say exactly what the value of the business was. But there was a substantial surplus of assets over liabilities. And it seems to me to be pretty clear that if Mr Salomon had been minded to dispose of his business in the market as a going concern, he might fairly have counted upon retiring with at least £10,000 in his pocket.

Mr Salomon however, did not want to part with the business. He had a wife and family consisting of five sons and a daughter. Four of the sons were working with their father. The eldest, who was about thirty years of age, was practically the manager. But the sons were not partners, they were only servants. Not unnaturally, perhaps, they were dissatisfied with their position. They kept pressing their father to give them a share in the concern . . . So at length Mr Salomon did what hundreds of others have done under similar circumstances. He turned his business into a limited company . . .

All the usual formalities were gone through; all the requirements of the Companies Act 1862 were duly observed. There was a contract with a trustee in the usual form for the sale of the business to a company about to be formed. There was a memorandum of association duly signed and registered, stating that the company was formed to carry that contract into effect and fixing the capital at £40,000 in 40,000 shares of £1 each. There were articles of association providing the usual machinery for conducting the business. The first directors were to be nominated by the majority of the subscribers to the memorandum of association. The directors when appointed, were authorised to exercise all such powers of the company as were not by statute or by the articles required to be exercised in general meeting; and there was express power to borrow on debentures with the limitation that the borrowing was not to exceed £10,000 without the sanction of a general meeting.

The company was intended from the first to be a private company; it remained a private company to the end. No prospectus was issued; no invitation to take shares was ever addressed to the public.

The subscribers to the memorandum were Mr Salomon, his wife and five of his children who were grown up. The subscribers met and appointed Mr Salomon and his two elder sons directors. The directors then proceeded to carry out the proposed transfer. By an agreement dated 2 August 1892, the company adopted the preliminary contract, and in accordance with it the business was taken over by the company as from 1 June 1892. The price fixed by the contract was duly paid. The price on paper was extravagant. It amounted to over £39,000 – a sum which represented the sanguine expectations of a fond owner rather than anything that can be called a businesslike or reasonable estimate of value. That, no doubt, is a circumstance which at first sight calls for observation; but when the facts of the case and the position of the parties are considered, it is difficult to see what bearing it has on the question . . . The purchase money was paid in this way: as money came in, sums amounting in all to £30,000 were paid to Mr Salomon, and then immediately returned to the company in exchange for fully paid shares. The sum of £10,000 was paid in debentures for the like amount. The balance, with the exception of about £1,000 which Mr Salomon seems to have received and retained, went in discharge of the debts and liabilities of the business at the time of the transfer which were thus entirely wiped off. In the result, therefore, Mr Salomon received for his business about £1,000 in cash, £10,000 in debentures and half the nominal capital of the company in fully paid shares for what they were worth. No other shares were issued except the seven shares taken by the subscribers to the memorandum who, of course, knew all the circumstances and had therefore no ground for complaint on the score of overvaluation.

The company had a brief career; it fell upon evil days. Shortly after it was started there seems to have come a period of great depression in the boot and shoe trade. There were strikes of workmen too; and in view of that danger, contracts with public bodies, which were the principal source of Mr Salomon's profit were split up and divided between different firms. The attempts made to push the business on behalf of the new company crammed its warehouses with unsaleable stock. Mr Salomon seems to have done what he could; both he and his wife lent the company money and then he got his debentures cancelled and reissued to a Mr Broderip who advanced him £5,000 which he immediately handed over to the company on loan. The temporary relief only hastened ruin. Mr Broderip's interest was not paid when it became due. He took proceedings at once and got a receiver appointed. Then, of course, came liquidation and a forced sale of the company's assets. They realised enough to pay Mr Broderip, but not enough to pay the debentures in full; and the unsecured creditors were consequently left out in the cold.

In this state of things the liquidator met Mr Broderip's claim by a counterclaim, to which he made Mr Salomon a defendant. He disputed the validity of the debentures on the ground of fraud. On the same ground he claimed recision of the agreement for the transfer of the business, cancellation of the debentures and repayment by Mr Salomon of the balance of the purchase money. In the alternative, he claimed payment of £20,000 on Mr Salomon's shares alleging that nothing had been paid on them.

When the trial came on before Vaughan Williams J,[1] the validity of Mr Broderip's claim was admitted and it was not disputed that the 20,000 shares were never paid up. The case presented by the liquidator broke down completely but the learned judge suggested that the company had a right of indemnity against Mr Salomon. The signatories of the memorandum of association were, he said, mere nominees of Mr Salomon – mere dummies. The company was Mr Salomon in another form. He used the name of the company as an alias. He employed the company as his agent, so the company, he thought, was entitled to indemnify against its principal. The counterclaim was accordingly amended to raise this point; and on the amendment being made the learned judge pronounced an order in accordance with the view he had expressed.

The order of the learned judge appears to me to be founded on a misconception of the scope and effect of the Companies Act 1862. In order to form a company limited by shares, the Act requires that a memorandum of association should be signed by seven persons, who are each to take one share at least. If those conditions are complied with, what can it matter whether the signatories are relations or strangers? There is nothing in the

Act requiring that the subscribers to the memorandum should be independent or unconnected or that they or any one of them should take a substantial interest in the undertaking or that they should have a mind and will of their own, as one of the learned Lord Justices seems to think, or that there should be anything like a balance of power in the constitution of the company. In almost every company that is formed the statutory number, is eked out by clerks or friends, who sign their names at the request of the promoter or promoters without intending to take any further part or interest in the matter.

When the memorandum is duly signed and registered, though there is only seven shares taken, the subscribers are a body corporate 'capable forthwith' to use the words of the enactment, 'of exercising all the functions of an incorporated company.' Those are strong words. The company attains maturity on its birth. There is no period of minority – no interval of incapacity. I cannot understand how a body corporate thus made 'capable' by one statute can lose its individuality by issuing the bulk of its capital to one person, whether he be a subscriber to the memorandum or not. The company is at law a different person altogether from the subscribers to the memorandum, and though it may be that after incorporation the business is precisely the same as it was before, and the same persons are managers and the same hands receive the profits, the company is not in law the agent of the subscribers or trustee for them. Nor are the subscribers as members liable, in any shape or form, except to the extent and in the manner provided by the Act. That is, I think, the declared intention of the enactment. If the view of the learned judge were sound, it would follow that no common law partnership could register as a company limited by shares without remaining subject to unlimited liability.

Mr Salomon appealed; but his appeal was dismissed with costs . . .[2]

Among the principal reasons which induce persons to form private companies . . . are the desire to avoid the risk of bankruptcy, and the increased facility afforded for borrowing money. By means of a private company . . . a trade can be carried on with limited liability, and without exposing the persons interested in it in the event of failure to the harsh provisions of the bankruptcy law. A company, too can raise money on debentures which an ordinary trader cannot do. Any member of a company, acting in good faith, is as much entitled to take and hold the company's debentures as any outside creditor. Every creditor is entitled to get and to hold the best security the law allows him to take.

If, however, the declaration of the Court of Appeal means that Mr Salomon acted fraudulently or dishonestly, I must say I can find that nothing in the evidence to support such an imputation. The purpose for which Mr Salomon and the other subscribers to the memorandum were associated was 'lawful'. The fact that Mr Salomon raised £5,000 for the company on debentures that belonged to him seems to me strong evidence of his good faith and of his confidence in the company. The unsecured creditors of A Salomon & Co Ltd may be entitled to sympathy, but they have only themselves to blame for their misfortunes. They trusted the company, I suppose, because they had long dealt with Mr Salomon, and he had always paid his way; but they had full notice that they were no longer dealing with an individual, and they must be taken to have been cognisant of the memorandum and articles of association . . .

It has become the fashion to call companies of this class 'one man companies'. That is taking a nickname, but it does not help one much in the way of argument. If it is intended to convey the meaning that a company which is under the absolute control of one person is not a company legally incorporated although the requirements of the Act of 1862 may have been complied with, it is inaccurate and misleading: if it merely means that there is a predominant partner possessing an overwhelming influence and entitled practically to the whole of the profits, there is nothing in that that I can see contrary to the true intention of the Act of 1862 or against public policy or detrimental to the interests of creditors. If the shares are fully paid up, it cannot matter whether they are in the hands of one or many. If the shares are not fully paid, it is easy to gauge the solvency of an individual as to estimate the financial ability of the crowd.

Lord Halsbury LC and Lords Watson and Davey delivered concurring judgments. Lord Morris concurred.

1 See *O'Kahn-Freud* (1944) 7 MLR 54, where the case is referred to as a 'calamitous decision'.
2 Reported sub nom *Broderip v Salomon* [1895] 2 Ch 323.

Notes

In *Lee v Lee's Air Farming Ltd* [1961] AC 12 the Privy Council held that the controlling shareholder and managing director of a company, acting as agent of that company, could validly enter into a contract of employment with himself in his personal capacity. He was therefore an 'employee' for the purposes of a claim under the New Zealand Workman's Compensation Scheme.

However, the principle of the separate legal personality of the company does not always operate to the advantage of the incorporator. In *Macaura v Northern Assurance Co* [1925] AC 619 it was held that the plaintiff did not have an insurable interest in timber owned by a company of which he was the controlling shareholder. When the timber was destroyed by fire he was precluded from claiming under the insurance policy. For further examples see *Keane*, paras **11.02–11.04**.

It would seem that as the company is a separate legal person it is possible to steal from it even if one beneficially owns every issued share. See *R v Pearlberg and O'Brien* [1982] Crim LR 829; *A-G's Reference (No 2 of 1982)* [1984] 2 WLR 447. These cases are discussed by *Sullivan & Dime* [1984] Crim LR 405.

Battle v Irish Art Promotion Centre Ltd [1968] IR 252 (Supreme Court)

[6.04]   Proceedings were issued against the defendant company. Its managing director who was also the major shareholder applied to the court for leave to conduct the company's defence on its behalf. The application was refused both by the High Court and the Supreme Court.

[6.05]   O'Dalaigh CJ: The court has not got any precise information as to the number of shares which have been issued but the appellant assures the court that he is virtually the owner of the company.

The appellant says the company has not now sufficient assets to permit of solicitor and counsel being engaged to present the company's defence; he also says that the company has a good defence to the action and that if, in the absence of solicitor and counsel to conduct the defence, the company were to be decreed, it would be a reflection on the appellant's reputation and standing as a businessman. It would appear that the appellant is now managing director of another company of which he is also the major shareholder . . .

In the absence of statutory exception a limited company cannot be represented in court proceedings by its managing director or other officer or servant. This is an infirmity of the company which derives from its own very nature. The creation of the company is an act of its subscribers; the subscribers in discarding their own personae for the persona of the company doubtless did so for the advantages which incorporation offers to traders. In seeking incorporation they thereby lose the right of audience which they would have as individuals; but the choice has been their own. One sympathises with the purpose which the appellant has in mind, to wit, to safeguard his business reputation; but as the law stands, he cannot as major shareholder and managing director now substitute his persona for that of the company. The only practical course open to him would, it appear be for him personally to put the company in funds for the purpose of presenting its defence. The court in my judgment should refuse this application.

Haugh and Walsh JJ concurred.

Notes

In *Abbey Films Ltd v AG* [1981] IR 158 it was held that because of the nature of a company and its difference of capacity from that of an individual, it was not a breach of the principle of equality before the law in art 40.1 of the Constitution to require a company to be represented in court by a lawyer, unlike an individual who may represent himself.

Lifting the veil of incorporation

[6.06]   Although the rule in *Salomon's* case is still regarded as good law, it has been eroded to varying degrees over the years by both the legislature and the courts. Broadly speaking where the 'veil of incorporation' has been 'lifted' by the legislature, the statute has normally recognised and preserved the separate legal personality of the company, albeit that, for example, personal liability for the company's debts may be imposed on one or more of its members. Where however, the veil has been lifted by the courts, the separate persona of the company has not always been preserved. On occasion the acts of the company may be treated as the acts of its controller. More alarmingly, in the case of a group of companies the court may in certain circumstances be prepared to ignore the separate legal personality of each company within the group and treat the acts of one company as the acts of another. It may even go further and in effect 're-incorporate' the group of companies as one single entity.

Lifting the veil of incorporation by statute

[6.07]   Examples can be found within the Companies Acts of situations where the veil is partially lifted.[1] Under s 152 of the Principal Act a holding company is required to prepared group accounts which deal with 'the state of affairs . . . of the company and the subsidiaries dealt with thereby as a whole . . .'[2] S 36 provides for the personal liability of members for company debts in certain circumstances, where the number of shareholder falls below the statutory minimum[3] and under s 297 where the company's business has been carried on for a fraudulent purpose, those who have participated in such fraudulent activity may be made personally liable for all or any of the debts of the company.[4] Under s 138 of the Companies (no 2) Act 1990, where it is 'just and equitable' the court may order one company to contribute to the debts of a related company which is is liquidation. Further, under s 139 of that Act, where it is 'just and equitable' the court may make an order pooling the assets of two related companies, both of which are in liquidation.[5] It is important to note that in the examples cited above, although the rule in *Salomon's* case may have been somewhat modified, none of these sections purports to deny the separate legal personality of the company itself.

Another notable example of lifting the veil by statute is the Land Act 1965 as amended by the Land Act 1965 (Additional Category of Qualified Person) Regulations 1983,[6] whereby in determining the nationality of those controlling the ownership of agricultural land the Land Commission is to look in the case of companies not to the place of registration of that company, but rather at the nationality of its shareholders.

Under the Landlord and Tenant (Amendment) Act 1980 a tenant's statutory right to a renewal of his tenancy is not lost by virtue of the fact that the premises are now occupied by a private company formed by him to take over his business. Neither is it lost if the tenant company's subscribing company, holding company or fellow subsidiary company is now in occupation.[7]

1 See *Keane* at paras **11.15–11.12**.
2 Note also that under part XI of the Corporation Tax Act 1976 the losses of one company in the group may be transferred to another member of the group for the purpose of reducing the latters' taxation liability.
3 See *Keane* at para **11.07**.
4 The topic of 'fraudulent trading' is considered in more detail in chapter 18, *infra* and in *Keane* at paras **38.84–38.88**.
5 Discussed in chapter 4 *supra*.
6 SI 1983 No 144.
7 S 5(3): cf *Pegler v Craven* [1952] 2 QB 69.

Lifting the veil of incorporation by the courts

[6.08] The courts may be prepared to ignore the separate legal personality of a company where that company has been formed for some fraudulent, illegal or improper purpose or for the evasion of legal obligations.

Cummings v Stewart [1911] 1 IR 236 (Chancery Division)

[6.09] The plaintiff entered into a licence agreement with the defendant for the use of his patents. The fifth clause of the agreement provided that 'the licence may . . . transfer the said licence to any limited liability company he may form to carry on his business or the business connected with one arising out of said patents and this licence'. Subsequently, the defendant transferred the licence to a company formed for that purpose. His motivation in effecting the transfer was to rid himself of liability for the payment of royalties. It was not intended that this new company should work the patents. The plaintiff successfully claimed that the defendant should be regarded as being personally liable for all arrears of royalty payments.

[6.10] Meredith MR: In my opinion, the Companies (Consolidation) Act 1908 embodies a code framed (inter alia) for the purposes of preserving and enforcing commercial morality and it would be strange indeed, if that code could be turned into an engine for the destruction of legal obligations and the overthrow of legitimate and enforceable claims. The most casual reader of the speeches of the Law Lords in the case of *Salomon v Salomon & Co* (para **6.03**) cannot fail to observe that there is nothing in any of those speeches contrary to the view I have just expressed . . .

The case (as it now stands) is a case in which the plaintiff, who is a gentleman in America, has developed and patented a particular form of what may be called a new system of 'reinforced concrete'. The defendant is a gentleman who had and has an interest a great interest, in any such system provided it could be put into practical operation and effect. Accordingly, he managed to secure the sole and exclusive right of utilizing the patent rights of the American inventor in the United Kingdom in France and in Austria on terms which he doubtless considered and which now must be held by this court to have been accepted by him as fair and reasonable terms . . . The sole question I have to decide is whether under the 5th clause of the contract between the plaintiff and defendant, the plaintiff left open to the defendant a loophole of escape from his liability, in the event of the contract turing out to be one of an unfortunate kind for the defendant. There is no reason to think that the defendant did not do his best. It is obvious that many persons – whether corporations or individuals – might fairly say to a contractor – 'your Cummings system of reinforced concrete may be the best thing in the world, but nevertheless, it has not stood, for it has had no opportunity of standing, the test of time.' Time is the great arbiter and time alone will tell whether the Cummings system of reinforced concrete will stand the test. But Mr Stewart must have known and must be held to have faced the risks incident to the

development of a novel invention. In my judgment the proviso at the end
of clause 5 of the contract can only be construed in one way, that is to say,
that the company to which the defendant without the consent of the plaintiff, might transfer his obligations and his rights was a company formed to
carry on his business or the business 'connected with and arising out of said
patents and this licence.' Mr Wilson said the fifth clause was inserted for
the purpose of mitigating in some sense the onerous liability of the defendant. I do not think it was. If I were to give an opinion on the subject, I
should say that the proviso was inserted for the purpose of enabling the
defendant to form a company for the purpose of exploiting the invention.
Let me read the clause. [His Lordship read the clause] The defendant says
he has formed a company within the meaning of that clause and that the
intention with which the company was formed and with which the two
holder of £1 shares come into this concern, is not for me and that I have no
right to comment on it. I have no right at all except for the fact that it is
demonstration that the company was formed not to carry on the business of
the plaintiff – not, in the words of the proviso, to carry on the business
'connected with and arising out of said patents and this licence', but for the
purpose of extinguishing the patent rights or at all events – and this is
sufficient to justify the plaintiff in persisting in his claim in this case – for
the purpose of refraining from carrying on any work connected with the
reinforced concrete patents of the plaintiff.

Notes

In *Gilford Motor Co Ltd v Horne* [1933] Ch 939 the defendant's contract
of employment contained a covenant whereby he agreed not to compete
with the plaintiffs should he leave their employment. In order to evade the
terms of this agreement the defendant set up a company which competed
with his former employers. Officially he was neither a shareholder nor a
director of the company, although it acted at his bidding. The plaintiffs
succeeded in obtaining an injunction restraining this competition on the
ground that the new company 'was formed as a device, a stratagem, in
order to mask the effective carrying on of the business of Mr Horne. The
purpose of it was to try to enable him under what is a cloak or a sham to
engage in business in respect of which he had a fear that the plaintiffs might
intervene and object . . .' Per Lord Hanworth MR at p 956. It should be
noted that an injunction was also granted against the new company,
thereby indicating that the court did not ignore the separate legal personality of that company.

In *Jones v Lipman* [1962] 1 All ER 442 the defendant acquired a company
to which he transferred his house. This transfer was effected in order to avoid
having to convey the house to the plaintiff with whom he had previously
entered into an enforceable contract of sale. In granting the plaintiff a
decree of specific performance against the defendant and his company again
recognising the separate persona of the company, Russell J stated that the
company was 'the creation of the defendant, a devise and a sham, a mask

which he holds before his face in an attempt to avoid recognition by the eye of equity' at p 445. See also *Re Bugle Press Ltd* [1961] Ch 270 which is considered by *Keane* at para **11.13**.

Compare these cases with *Roundabout Ltd v Beirne* [1959] IR 423. A trade dispute existed between a company and its employees who had been dismissed. The company owned and ran a licensed premises which the employees began to picket. The dispute constituted a trade dispute within the meaning of the Trade Disputes Act 1906. The employees were therefore immune from legal suit in respect of the picket. The controllers of the company set up a new company which took a lease of the premises and began to run the public house. This new company (the plaintiff) had no employees (the barmen being non-voting directors). It therefore contended that as it was not an employer there could be no 'trade dispute' between it and the picketers. This claim was upheld by Dixon J who, although admitting that the whole scheme was nothing more than a 'subterfuge', granted an injunction restraining any further picketing of the licensed premises. The refusal to 'lift the veil' is case has been explained by *Ussher* op cit at p 30 on the basis that the company had been incorporated, not to circumvent a legal duty, but rather to circumvent the immunity of the picketers under the 1906 Act.

[6.11]   Where the controllers of the company have been guilty of nothing worse than mismanagement the court will not lift the veil of incorporation.

Dublin County Council v Elton Homes Ltd [1984] ILRM 297 (High Court)

[6.12]   The defendant company which was in liquidation had failed to comply with the conditions of a planning permission granted to it previously by the plaintiff for the construction of a housing development. The plaintiff sought an injunction under s 27 of the Local Government (Planning and Development) Act 1976 compelling both the company and its directors to carry out the conditions attaching to the planning permission relating to *inter alia* remedial works and public lighting.

[6.13]   **Barrington J:** The planning authority is naturally concerned for the plight of the residents in the new houses who are living in an unfinished estate and deprived of the amenities which were conditions of the planning permission.

They have accordingly brought this motion against the company and the directors personally in an effort to secure the compliance with the conditions of the planning permissions.

Section 27(2) of the Local Government (Planning and Development) Act 1976 provides as follows:–

'Where any development authorised by a permission granted under part IV of the principal act has been commenced but has not been or is not being carried out in conformity with the permission because of non-compliance with the requirements of a condition attached to the permission or for any other reason, the high court may, on the application of a planning authority or any other person, whether or not that person has an interest in the land, by order require any person specified in the order to do or not to do or cease to do as the case may be, anything which the court considers necessary to ensure that the development is carried out in conformity with the permission specified in the order.'

The powers conferred on the High Court by the sub-section are very wide powers. It may require 'any person' specified in the order to do or not to do or cease to do, as the case may be, anything which the court considers necessary to ensure that the development is carried out in conformity with the permission.

One must assume that the sub-section was deliberately drafted in wide terms. At the same time the powers conferred on the High Court are not arbitrary powers but must be exercised in accordance with principles which are judicially acceptable.

If, in the present case, the company were solvent there would be no problem. Clearly an injunction could be granted against the company to ensure that it carried out the conditions attaching to the planning permissions. It would also appear that, in a proper case, an order could be made against the persons in control of the company (be they the directors or a liquidator) to ensure that the company fulfilled its obligations to the planning authority. The problem is that the company is insolvent. The liquidator says that his responsibility is to the creditors of the company who, as things stand, will only receive 25p in the pound. If the court were now to make an order directing the company to complete the development in accordance with the conditions it would be penalising the creditors of the company who, presumably traded with the company in good faith and already stand to lose heavily . . . In these circumstances I do not think I would be justified in making an order against the liquidator or the company.

The question arises of whether the court can or ought to make an order aganst Mr Keogh and Mr English personally as the former directors of the company. Let me say at once that I think it may be quite proper, in certain circumstances to join the directors of a company as respondents when an application is made by a planning authority against a company pursuant to the provisions of s 27 . . . There may be many cases particularly in the case of small companies where them most effective way of ensuring that the company complies with its obligations is to make an order against the directors as well as against the company itself. But in such a case the order against the directors would be a way of ensuring that the company carried out its obligations. A body corporate can only act through its agents and the most effective way of ensuring that it does in fact carry out its obligations might be to make an order against the persons in control of it.

What is sought against the second and third named respondents in the present case is very different. They are no longer in control of the company and it is not suggested that, through them, the company can be forced to

129

carry out its obligations. What is suggested is that because they were directors of the company at the time when the company obtained planning permission that they should be ordered to complete the development at their
own expense. I am not saying that there might not be a case where the court
would be justified in making such an order. If the case were one of fraud, or
if the directors had syphoned off large sums of money out of the company, so
as to leave it unable to fulfil its obligations, the court might be justified in
lifting the veil of incorporation and fixing the directors with personal responsibility. But that is not this case. The second and third named respondents
appear to be fairly small men who having failed in this particular enterprise
are now back working for others. The worst that can be imputed against
them is mismanagement.

They gave personal guarantees to the insurance company which supplied
the bond for £10,000 and to the company's bankers. They therefore stand to
lose heavily arising out of the transaction. Moreover . . . the liquidator and
his officials entertain no suspicion that there has been any impropriety on the
part of the directors in dealing with the assets of the company.

It appears to me that Mr Keogh and Mr English traded with the benefit of
limited liability in this case and that in the absence of any evidence of
impropriety on their part, I would not be justified in attempting to make
them personally responsible for the default of the company.

Notes

This decision has been followed in two subsequent cases with almost
identical facts. In the first, *Dublin Co Co v O'Riordan* [1986] ILRM 104,
Murphy J refused to lift the veil and to grant a s 27 injunction against the
directors even though the affairs of the company had been carried on 'with
scant regard for the requirements of the Companies Acts'. Similarly, in *Dun
Laoghaire Corporation v Park Hill Developments Ltd* (High Court 13
January 1989) Hamilton P refused to grant an injunction against the directors in the absence of evidence of fraud. He held that the mere failure to
comply with ss 131 and 148 of the Principal Act (failure to hold an annual
general meeting and failure to issue financial reports to the shareholders)
was not enough to justify lifting of the veil.

[6.14]   One company may be made liable for the debts of another company
where the relationship of principal and agent exists between them.

Smith Stone & Knight Ltd v Brimingham Corporation [1939] 4 All ER 116
(King's Bench Division)

[6.15]   The plaintiff company beneficially owned all the shares in a company ('the waste company') which carried on business on land owned by the
plaintiff. The land was compulsorily acquired by the defendant corporation.
The plaintiff succeeded in claiming compensation for disturbance of business for itself, by showing that the waste company in carrying on business on
the land, had been doing so as the plaintiff's agent.

[6.16]   Atkinson J: There were five directors of the waste company and they were all directors of the claimants and they all executed a declaration of trust for the share which they held, stating they held them in trust for the claimants. At no time did the board get any remuneration from the waste company . . . A manager was appointed doubtless by the company, but there was no staff. The books and accounts were all kept by the claimants; the waste company had no books at all and the manager it is found, knew nothing at all about what was in the books and had no access to them. There is no doubt that the claimants had complete control of the operations of the waste company . . . There was no tenancy agreement of any sort with the company; they were just there is name. No rent was paid. Apart from the name, it was really as if the manager was managing a department of the company. Six months after the incorporation there was a report to the shareholders that the business was under the supervision and control of the claimants and that the profits would be credited to that company in the books, as is very often done with departments . . . At the end of each year the accounts were made up by the company and if the accounts showed a profit, the claimants allocated the profit to the different mills belonging to the company, exhausting the paper profit in that way and making the profit part of the company's own profit, because allocating this profit to their different departments or different mills would have the effect of increasing their own profit by a precisely similar sum. The waste company never declared a dividend, they never thought of such a thing and their profit was in fact treated as the claimant's profit.

Those being the facts, the corporation rest their contention on *Salomon's* case and their argument is that the waste company was a distinct legal entity. It was in occupation of the premises the business being carried on in its name and the claimants only interest in law was that of holders of the shares. It is well settled that the mere fact that a man holds all the shares in a company does not make the business carried on by that company his business, nor does it make the company his agents for the carrying on of the business. That proposition is just as true if the shareholder is itself a limited company. It is also well settled that there may be such an arrangement between the shareholders and a company as will constitute the company the shareholders' agent for the purpose of carrying on the business and make the business the business of the shareholders . . .

It seems . . . to be a question of fact . . . whether the subsidiary was carrying on the business as the company's business or as its own. I find six points which were deemed relevant for the determination of the question: Who was really carrying on the business? . . . The first point was: Were the profits treated as the profits of the company? – when I say 'the company' I mean the parent company – secondly, were the persons conducting the business appointed by the parent company? Thirdly, was the company the head and brain of the trading venture? Fourthly, did the company govern the adventure, decide what should be done and what capital should be embarked on the venture? Fifthly, did the company make the profits by its

skill and direction? Sixthly, was the company in effectual and constant control? Now . . . it seems to me that every one of those questions must be
answered in favour of the claimants. Indeed if ever one company must be
said to be the agent or employee or tool or simulation of another, I think the
waste company was in this case a legal entity because that is all it was. There
was nothing to prevent the claimants at any moment saying 'We will carry on
this business in our own name.' They had but to paint out the waste company's name on the premises, change their business paper and form and the
thing would have been done. I am satisfied that the business belonged to the
claimants; they were in my view, the real occupiers of the premises. If either
physically or technically the waste company was in occupation it was for the
purposes of the service it was rendering to the claimants . . . I think that
those facts would make that occupation in law the occupation of the
claimants. An analagous position would be where servants occupy cottages
or rooms for the purposes of their business and it is well settled that if they
have to occupy those premises for the purposes of the business their occupation is the occupation of their principal. I have no doubt the business was the
company's business and was being carried on under their direction . . .

Notes
   It is submitted that this case accurately states the law. The rule in *Salomon's* case merely states that a company is not per se the agent of its shareholders. See *Ebbw Vale UDC v South Wales Traffic Area Licencing
Authority* [1936] 2 All ER 386. However, just as one individual may enter
into an agency agreement with another so too a company may expressly or
impliedly enter into a contract of agency with another party even if that party
is its shareholder. For examples of situations where an agency relationship
was found to exist between a parent company and its subsidiary see *Firestone
Tyre & Rubber Co Ltd v Llewellin* [1957] 1 All ER 561; *Re FG Films Ltd*
[1953] 1 All ER 617; *Munton Bros Ltd v Secretary of State* [1983] NI 369.
   Similarly, in some cases the facts may indicate that the company holds its
property in trust for its members even though under the rule in *Salomon's*
case a trust relationship does not per se exist between the parties. See *Re
Parnell GAA Club Ltd* [1984] ILRM 246.

[6.17]   In the case of a group of companies the courts may be prepared to
ignore the separate legal entities of various companies within a group and to
look instead at the economic entity of the whole group.[1]

1 Concluded by Professor Gower at p 131 of his book, op cit., and subsequently quoted with
   approval by Lord Denning in *DHN Food Distributors Ltd v London Borough of Tower
   Hamlets* [1976] 3 All ER 462. See generally *Keane* at para **11.17** et seq.

***Power Supermarkets Ltd v Crumlin Investments Ltd and Dunnes Stores
(Crumlin) Ltd*** (High Court, unreported, 22 June 1981)

[6.18]   In June 1974 the plaintiffs obtained a lease of a unit in Cornelscourt
Shopping Centre for use as a supermarket from the landlord of the shopping

centre, Crumlin Investments Ltd. The lease contained a covenant prohibiting Crumlin Investments from letting any other unit in the shopping centre as a supermarket. The Dunnes Stores Group, which runs a chain of supermarkets in competition with the plaintiff, subsequently purchased Crumlin Investments. The purchasing company was Cornelscourt Shopping Centre Ltd, a wholly owned subsidiary of Dunnes Stores Ltd which in turn was a wholly owned subsidiary of Dunnes Holding Co. The Dunnes Stores Group wished to open its own supermarket in the Shopping Centre. The policy of the group was that each of its retail outlets should be operated by a separate company. So Dunnes Stores (Crumlin) Ltd was formed and it became a wholly owned subsidiary of Dunnes Stores (Georges St.) Ltd which is in turn a subsidiary of Dunnes Stores Ltd. Preparations were then made for Crumlin Investments to let a unit in the shopping centre to Dunnes Stores (Crumlin) Ltd. In the present proceedings the plaintiff sought an injunction restraining both Crumlin Investments and Dunnes Stores (Crumlin) Ltd from infringing the terms of the plaintiffs lease.

[6.19]   Costello J: I come now to the actual means and method of trading in this unit of the shopping centre. The Dunne family are actively involved in the running of the Dunnes Stores Group of companies and their wishes prevail in respect of each company in the Group, including Crumlin Investments and Dunnes Stores (Crumlin). After the initial meeting of the board of directors of Dunnes Stores (Crumlin) which is comprised of members of the Dunne family in 1978 no meeting of the board has since been held. There has been no meeting of its shareholders. Company accounts for one year only have been prepared, but have not yet been presented to any meeting. No meeting of the directors was held for the purpose of deciding to take a conveyance of the property in the centre and no meetings were ever held to make decisions on trading and commercial matters. Purchases of stock are made on the company's behalf by the purchasing panel of the Dunnes Stores Group who apportion liability for purchases to each trading company in the group to whom the good are invoiced. The company is managed and controlled not by the members of the Dunne family meeting as directors of the company and not by its shareholder but by members of the Dunne family (or their servants and agents) meeting informally to manage the affairs of the group as a whole or by individual members taking decisions on the family's behalf.

An exactly similar situation has prevailed since the purchase of the shares in Crumlin Investments. Since then there has been no meeting of the board of directors of Crumlin Investments (which also comprise members of the Dunne family and their accountant) and no shareholders meeting has taken place. It too, is managed and controlled in the same way as Dunnes Stores (Crumlin) is managed and controlled. The reality of the relationship between the two companies is highlighted by the conveyance of the fee simple interest in the unit in the shopping centre. The consideration for this conveyance was only £100 which I am satisfied notwithstanding the explanation for this figure which was advanced in the course of the evidence must

133

be regarded as a gross undervalue. It contained no covenant requiring the purchasers to carry on the business which Crumlin Investments required in order to make the shopping centre commercially viable. It contained none of the usual easements granted with a conveyance of this sort. It was never registered in the Registry of Deeds. These omissions are readily understandable when it is appreciated that the two companies are merely vehicles for carrying out the wishes of the Dunne family; they would do what the Dunne family told them to do.

The plaintiffs submit that I should pierce the corporate veil and look to the realities in this case and hold notwithstanding the fact that Crumlin Investments and Dunnes Stores (Crumlin) are two separate corporate entities, that the business in the unit is being carried on by a single entity. I was referred to *Smith Stone & Knight v Birmingham Corporation* (para **6.15**), a case in which a parent company was held entitled to compensation in respect of a business carried on by its subsidiary on the basis that the subsidiary was in reality carrying it on on behalf of the parent company and to *DHN Ltd v Tower Hamlets London Borough Council* (1976) 1 WLR 852, a case also dealing with the payment of compensation for the compulsory acquisition of property. The claimants in that case were a group of three companies associated in a wholesale grocery business. The Court of Appeal held that it should pierce the corporate veil and that it should not regard the companies as separate legal entities but treat the group as a single economic entity for the purpose of awarding compensation. I need not refer to the facts of the case, however, the reasons which prompted the court's approach are very material for the resolution of the issues in the present case. Lord Denning pointed out (page 860) that the group of companies was virtually the same as a partnership in which all three were partners; that they should not be treated separately so as to defeat the claim to compensation on a technical point; that they should not be deprived of the compensation which should be justly payable for disturbance. So, he decided that the three companies should be treated as one. Lord Shaw (at page 867) pointed out that if each member of the group of companies was to be regarded as a company in isolation that nobody at all could claim compensation 'in a case which plainly calls for it', and he said that the true relationship should not be ignored because to do so would amount to a denial of justice. He too considered that the group should be regarded as a single entity.

It seems to me to be well established . . . that a court may, if the justice of the case so requires, treat two or more related companies as a single entity so that the business notionally carried on by one will be regarded as the business of the group or another member of the group if this conforms to the economic and commercial realities of the situation. It would, in my view be very hard to find a clearer case than the present one for the application of this principle. I appreciate that Crumlin Investments is a property owning not a trading company but it is clear that the creation of the new company and the conveyance to it of the freehold interest in a unit in the shopping centre were means for carrying out the commercial plans of the Dunne family in the centre. The enterprise had a two-fold aspect (a) the creation of a new retail outlet for the Dunnes Stores Group in the shopping centre and (b) the enhancement of the rents in the centre as a whole which the creation of such an outlet would hopefully produce. To treat the two companies as a single economic entity seems to me to accord fully with the realities of the situation. Not to do so could involve considerable injustice to the plaintiffs as their rights under the covenant might be defeated by the mere technical device of the creation of a company with a £2 issued capital which had no real independent life of its own. If it is established that the covenant is breached there should in my opinion be an injunction against both defendants.

[His lordship then went on to accept as a second ground for granting an injunction against Dunnes Stores (Crumlin) that the restrictive covenant ran with the land and having notice of it they were bound by it.]

Notes

The *DHN* case cited by Costello J involved a claim for compensation for disturbance of a business similar to that in *Smith Stone & Knight v Birmingham Corporation* (para **6.15**). The parent company ran the business and the land was held by the subsidiary. On the facts, however, it was clear that the land was held by the subsidiary as trustee for the parent. The parent was therefore the true owner and would in any case have been entitled to compensation. Similarly, the *Powers Supermarkets* case could have been decided in favour of the plaintiff on the basis that the restrictive covenant ran with the land. Rather than being a clear cut examples of situations where the veil should be lifted in the interests of justice, these are cases where there was no need to lift the veil at all. For a note of the judgment see Hannigan, *Piercing the Corporate Veil* [1983] 5 DULJ (ns) 111.

Doubts have been expressed by the House of Lords in *Woolfson v Strathclyde* RC (1978) SC 90, as to the correctness of the decision to lift the veil in the DHN case. These doubts were echoed by MacPherson J in *National Dock Labour Board v Pinn & Wheeler Ltd* [1989] BCLC 647.

See also, *The Queen v Waverley Construction Ltd* (1973) DLR 3d 224 where it was held that a company is not ordinarily liable for the negligence of the servant of its subsidiary company since the subsidiary is to be treated as a distinct entity, even where the two companies have common management personnel and share common office premises. Other cases where the courts have refused to lift the veil on groups of companies include *Charterbridge Corporation v Lloyds Bank Ltd* [1970] Ch 62; *Multinational Gas & Petroleum Co v Multinational Gas & Petroleum Services Ltd* [1983] 2 All ER 563.

In the Supreme Court, however, in *Re Bray Travel Ltd and Bray Travel (Holdings) Ltd* (unreported, 13 July 1981) both the *DHN* and *Powers Supermarkets* cases were approved of and followed. There were no written judgments in this case. However, it is noted by *Keane* J in the appendix to his book. The court on the application of the liquidator of Bray Travel Ltd granted an injunction freezing the assets of a number of the company's subsidiaries. Notably, both Henchy and Kenny JJ (with whom Hederman J concurred) stated that even without treating all the companies as a single entity, the injunction would have been granted on ordinary tracing principles, the evidence indicating that there had been transfers of the company's property to its subsidiaries at a gross undervalue.

Problems may arise where the courts are prepared to lift the veil of incorporation on a group of companies in the manner suggested by Costello J. For example, company A may be financially sound whereas its related company B, is now insolvent. If the veil of incorporation is lifted A may be made liable for the debts of B. This will undoubtedly be of benefit to the creditors of B, but at what cost? A minority shareholder of A may now find his investment worthless. Furthermore, creditors of A who may have expected payment in full may now find that A is insolvent as well, so that they can expect a dividend of less that 100p in the £1. Arguably this will constitute an unjust attack on the constitutional property rights of both the minority shareholder and the creditors of A: see *PMPS Ltd and Moore v A-G* [1984] ILRM 88.

[6.20] The courts will not however, lift the veil merely because a group of companies are under common ownership or control.

Rex Pet Foods Ltd v Lamb Bros (Ireland) Ltd (High Court, Costello J 5 December 1985)

[6.21] **Costello J.** This case arises because of a claim made by the receiver and manager of the plaintiff company who was appointed on the 15th July 1982. The receiver submits that the assets of the defendant companies and the plaintiff company should be aggregated and seeks a declaration that the businesses of the plaintiff company and defendant companies are one. A separate claim exists in these proceedings arising from certain goods which were in the possession of the defendant companies at the time the receiver was appointed.

The facts of this case which I find from the evidence adduced by the plaintiff company are as follows:

The plaintiff company had an existence independent of the defendant companies up to the month of March 1981. In the month of March 1981 the first named defendant company, Lamb Bros (Dublin) Ltd, was seeking a means of entering into a new line of business and purchased 52 per cent of the shares in the plaintiff company. There is no doubt that the plaintiff company remained a separate legal entity at that time. Some members of the board of directors of the defendant group of companies went onto the board of directors of the plaintiff company but the minority shareholding in the plaintiff company existed and was represented on the board of directors of the plaintiff company. What is of equal significance is that the management of the plaintiff company remained as it had been.

The plaintiff company manufactured pet food in a factory premises near Athy. At the time the shares in the plaintiff company were purchased two agreements were entered into between the plaintiff company and the first-named defendant company, one being a distributorship agreement and the other a management agreement. The effect of these agreements was that the defendant group of companies became the sole distributors for the plaintiff's goods and supplied management services to the plaintiff company, arrangements which are by no means unique and which do not in any way affect the separate corporate entities of the companies concerned.

It is clear that the plaintiff company started to get into financial difficulties some time later that year and that these difficulties became aggravated. During this period there were meetings of the board of directors of the plaintiff company and the minutes were produced to show that it operated as a separate legal entity from the defendant group of companies.

What is of equal importance is that separate books of account were maintained and I have had the benefit of the evidence of Mr Robert Gentleman, who later became secretary of the plaintiff company and who was the accountant of the group of companies formed by the defendant companies. His evidence made it clear that at all times separate books of account were kept for the plaintiff company and their separate legal entities were at all times recognised by the defendant companies.

That situation existed up to March 1982, and the trading arrangement between the parties was governed by the two agreements to which I have referred. The distributorship agreement, it is true, was not carried out to the letter of the agreement in that prices were not fixed in writing but by mutual agreement prices were fixed otherwise than in writing.

In March 1982 the situation changed. Because of the deteriorating financial position of the plaintiff company, the defendant group of companies or, to be more precise, the first-named defendant company, took up the balance of the shares in the plaintiff company as a result of which the plaintiff company became a wholly owned subsidiary of Lamb Bros. (Dublin) Ltd. The reason for this change in the shareholding of the plaintiff company was the hope that the plaintiff company could become financially sound by a change in the management structure in Athy. A change in management was brought about and the existing members were dispensed with. Mr Middlesborough, who was a manager of the defendant group, became manager of the plaintiff company; Mr Lyons became managaing director of the plaintiff company and Mr Gentleman became secretary of the plaintiff company.

In these circumstances it seems to be clear that the change of management that occurred in March 1982 was one which was a perfectly normal commercial decision and did not effect the separate corporate entity of the plaintiff company although, of course, the relationship between the two became, as I have indicated, one in which the plaintiff company was now 100 per cent owned by Lamb Bros (Dublin) Ltd.

The case that is made on the plaintiff's behalf depends on a number of aspects of the trading of the defendant group of companies and of the plaintiff company to which I will now refer.

It is alleged that the plaintiff company should be regarded merely as a branch of the defendant group as its manufacturing arm because, firstly, the defendants discharged the creditors of the plaintiff company from time to time. The evidence establishes that this in fact occurred . . . but this to my mind did not in any way affect the separate legal entity of the plaintiff company and was a normal enough arrangement for companies trading in a group such as these companies were trading. Secondly, it is suggested that the claim is supported by the fact that invoices from suppliers of the plaintiff company were sent direct to the defendant company. Factually this is so. From time to time creditors of the plaintiff company, in particular suppliers of goods and raw materials to the plaintiff company, sent invoices to one or other of the defendant companies but this does not raise any claim or sustain any claim that the two companies should be treated as one legal entity. It does perhaps, reflect some confusion but not to the extent which would justify the claim now being made on the plaintiff's behalf. Thirdly, it is suggested that the management of the plaintiff company was such that the claim being made is justified. The management changed in the way I have indicated. The explanation for the change is a reasonable one and in my view does not of itself justify the claim that has been made. Fourthly, it was suggested that there were no regular meetings of the board of directors of the plaintiff company. There were meetings of the board of directors and meetings were held up to March 1982. Thereafter it seems that no inference such as is not being sought to be drawn arises from the fact that the board of directors comprised members of the parent company for this is a situation which is normal and is to be found where a group of companies is controlled by a parent company.

Finally, the point was raised that the defendant company was sole distributor for the plaintiff company, but this was a situation which was in no way unique or which raises the inference which the plaintiffs seek to raise.

The question arises whether all these factors taken together raise the inference sought to be raised but I cannot agree that this is so. There have been some cases which counsel have referred me to where the courts have treated companies as being one legal entity but these have been cases in which the facts are very different to those which the evidence establishes in the circumstances of this case.

So in my view the plaintiffs have failed to make out a case which would justify me in making the declaration which is sought. I should add that even if the situation were different and there were circumstances in which the court should regard these companies as being one for some reason or other, this would not justify the court making another order which, indeed, is a separate order in relation to the aggregation of assets because it seems to me there has been no evidence to suggest that any funds of the plaintiff company were siphoned off into any of the defendan companies in such circumstances as would raise an equitable claim to the assets of any of the defendant companies . . .

Notes

See also *The State (Melbarien Enterprises) Ltd v The Revenue Commissioners* [1985] IR where company A had been refused a tax clearance certificate from the defendants because an associated company B had gone into liquidation owing arrears of tax. The certificate was a necessary prerequisite for those wishing to tender for public service contracts. The tax affairs of company A were, however, fully up to date. Hamilton P held that as the two companies were separate and distinct legal entities, the defendants had erred in law in refusing to issue the certificate.

[6.22]   Although the court may be prepared to lift the veil of incorporation on a group of companies at the instance of an outsider, it will not normally do so at the instance of members of that group.

The State (Thomas McInerney & Co Ltd) v Dublin County Council [1985] ILRM 513 (High Court)

[6.23]   Thomas McInerney & Co Ltd ('the applicant') and McInerney Construction Ltd ('the registered owner') were both wholly owned subsidiaries of Thomas McInerney Properties Ltd ('the parent company'). The applicant bought certain property and transferred it to the registered owner for development. Having unsuccessfully applied for planning permission in respect of the property the applicant then served a purchase notice on the local authority under s 29 of the Local Government (Planning and Development) Act 1963. The section requires that the party serving the notice be the 'owner' of the property. The applicant contended that as both companies were members of the same group the court should lift the veil, and treat them as the same entity.

[6.24]   Carroll J: The County Council claims the notice was served by a person who is not the owner within the meaning of the section and the notice is therefore invalid. The applicant claims that because the applicant and the registered owner are subsidiaries of the parent company, the corporate veil should be lifted and the applicant should be considered to be the 'owner' within the meaning of s 29 . . .

One of the cases relied on . . . was *Smith Stone and Knight v Birmingham Corporation* (para **6.15**) . . . I do not think this advances the applicant's claim. It merely establishes that if a subsidiary acts as agent, the principal/parent company is entitled to claim compensation. This would also be allowed under s 29 since the definition of 'owner' allows the purchase notice to be served by the person who is or would be entitled to receipt of the rack rent whether as beneficiary, trustee or agent. In this case the applicant does not claim to be any of those.

Another case cited was *DHN Food Distribution Ltd v Tower Hamlets London Borough Council* [1976] 3 All ER 462; [1976] 1 WLR 852. The consideration in this case was entirely different. In my opinion the corporate veil

139

is not a device to be raised and lowered at the option of the parent company or group. The arm which lifts the veil must always be that of justice. If justice requires, as it did in the *DHN* case, the courts will not be slow to treat a group of subsidiary companies and their parent company as one. But can it be said that justice requires it in this case? We have here a parent company with 30 subsidiary companies forming the McInerney Group. According to Mr Cody, the finance director of the parent company, it is group policy, depending on circumstances to operate in the name of one of these companies on various sites throughout the country. He says that McInerney Construction Ltd (the registered owner) has no resources other than those supplied by another subsidiary. The purchase moneys were provided by the applicant, (it being the intention that such moneys be repaid in due course out of the proceeds of realisation.

When those averments are considered, it appears to me that here is a group of companies operated so as to maximise the benefits to be gained from the individual corporate identity of each subsidiary. If the purchase money was to be repaid out of the proceeds of realisation, it follows that the profits of losses remained with the registered owner. If the development was not profitable the loss would be confined within the assets of that one company . . . In my opinion this is not a case where justice demands that the corporate veil be lifted . . . It is not for a corporate group to claim that the veil should be lifted to illuminate one aspect of its business while it should be left in situ to isolate the individual actions of its subsidiaries in other respects.

Therefore I am of opinion that the purchase notice to be served under s 29 was not served by the 'owner' as required by that section and the notice dated 4 April 1984 is therefore invalid.

Notes

See also *Gresham's Industries Ltd (In Liquidation) v Cannon* (unreported, High Court, 2 July 1980) where the liquidator of the plaintiff company issued proceedings against the defendant claiming repayment of monies advanced to him by the company. The defendant who was the majority shareholder in each of a group of companies including the plaintiff argued that the affairs of the group were in effect his personal activities, that the money advanced to him was in reality an investment by the plaintiff in Paulcar Ltd another company within the group and that therefore he should be entitled to set off against the debt owed by him to the plaintiff, monies owing by the plaintiff to Paulcar Ltd. Both claims were rejected by Finlay P who stated as follows:–

> 'It seems to me . . . a fundamental principle of the law that if a person decides to obtain and use the benefit of trading through limited liability companies and if for any purposes whether the limitation of his liability, tax purposes or otherwise he transfers assets from one company to another or makes drawings from one company and invest them in his own

name in another company that he cannot subsequently be heard to ignore the existence of the legal entities consisting of the different companies and to look upon the entire transaction as a personal one . . . All these claims were put forward by the defendant upon the basis that he was the effective beneficial owner of Paulcar Ltd which he asserted was a solvent company and that therefore he must be identified with the rights and liabilities of Paulcar Ltd as if they were his own rights and liabilities and that therefore he was entitled to these as a set-off or credit against the amounts due by him to the plaintiff company in liquidation . . . I am satisfied that as a matter of law even a 100% beneficial shareholder in a company cannot for the purposes of the settling of an account between him and another individual or company be identified with the company.'

Compare this decision with *Munten Bros Ltd v Secretary of State* [1983] NI 369 where Gibson LJ stated obiter that if the 'justice' of the case so requires members of the group of companies may themselves be entitled to apply to have the veil of incorporation lifted. In this case however, his lordship had already found that an agency relationship existed between the companies.On the question of 'veil lifting' generally see McCormack *Judicial Application of Salomon's Case in Ireland* (1984) Gazette.

Chapter 7

CONTRACTS

[7.01] A company being a legal person has almost the same capacity as a human being to enter into contracts.[1] It may enter into oral or written contracts, and where the contract is required by law to be under seal, it may be executed under the common seal of the company.[2] However, it cannot enter into a contract which would be ultra vires[3] and, being an artificial entity, must act through agents.

1 See generally *Keane* chapter 12.
2 S 38 of the Principal Act. See s 39 for bills of exchange and promissory notes.
3 See s 4 *supra*.

[7.02] A company may execute deeds by attorney inside or outside the State. In the case of a company with common form articles, a person acting under such a power of attorney may not use the company's seal without the authority of the directors. He can, however, execute deeds on behalf of the company by using his own name and seal, or by writing the company's name beside his own seal, or by doing both.

Industrial Development Authority v Moran [1978] IR 159 (Supreme Court)

[7.03] A receiver was appointed over the property of a company pursuant to the terms of a floating charge, the terms of which empowered him to sell the company's property 'by deed in the name and on behalf' of the company. He was also to be the company's attorney 'to execute seal and deliver' any deed required for the purpose of such sale. The company's articles contained a clause identical to art 115 of table A permitting use of the company's seal only by the authority of the directors. Property of the company was sold and in the deed of conveyance both the company and the receiver as distinct grantors purported to convey the lands to the purchaser. The receiver affixed the company's seal to the deed without the authority of the directors. He also executed the deed on his own behalf. The Registrar of Titles referred to the High Court a question as to the validity of the conveyance. The Supreme Court, reversing the decision of the High Court, held that although the execution on behalf of the company was invalid, the execution by the receiver in his own name was effective to pass title.

[7.04]   Kenny J: When the deed was presented to the Registrar of Titles, he had some doubt about its validity and he referred the matter to the High Court under s 19(2) of the Registration of Title Act 1964. Mr Justice Butler held that the seal of the company had been irregularly affixed and that the deed of the 8th October 1976, was ineffectual to transfer to the purchasers the property described in that deed. The purchasers have appealed to this court.

I think that the judge was correct on the first point concerning the use of the seal but that he was incorrect on the second point. In my view, the deed of the 8th October 1976 was effective to transfer to the purchasers all the estate and interest of the company in the part of the lands in the folio to which the deed related.

When a receiver is appointed over the assets of a company, the articles of association continue in force and bind him. A receiver, as receiver, has no authority to use the seal of the company. Article 128 required that the seal should be used only by the authority of the directors and that every instrument to which the seal was affixed should be signed by a director and should be countersigned by the secretary or by a second director. In this case the directors did not authorise the use of the seal and none of them signed the deed of the 8th October 1976. Accordingly the first part of the testimonium was without any effect.

The judge reached the conclusion that 'a company has no power to act by attorney to execute deeds within the State' as an inference from s 40 of the Companies Act 1963, which reads:–

'(1) A company may, either by writing under its common seal empower any person either generally or in respect of any specified matters as its attorney, to execute deed on its behalf in any place outside the State.

(2) A deed signed by such attorney on behalf of the company and under his seal shall bind the company and have the same effect as if it were under its common seal.'

The inference which the judge drew from s 40 of the Act of 1963 was incorrect. A company has power to act by attorney to execute deeds within the State and s 40 of the Act of 1963 is intended to give a company the power to act by attorney outside the State . . .

As [the receiver] executed the deed of transfer in his own name, the provisions of s 46(1) of the Conveyancing Act 1881 make the deed of transfer fully effective. The sub-section reads:–

'The donee of a power of attorney may, if he thinks fit, execute or do any assurance, instrument or thing in and with his own name and signature and his own seal, where sealing is required, by the authority of the donor of the power and every assurance, instrument and thing so executed and done shall be as effectual in law, to all intents, as if it had been executed or done by the donee of the power in the name and with the signature and seal of the donor thereof.'

Accordingly, the deed of transfer of the 8th October 1976, was effectual to transfer the lands described in it to the purchasers, and the order of the 1st May 1978 should be set aside. This court should declare that the deed dated the 8th October 1976, was effective to transfer to the purchasers the property therein described as being transferred: and the Registrar of Titles should be directed to register its effect on the folio.

While the deed of transfer in this case is effective because of s 46 of the Conveyancing Act 1881, I wish to point out that the power given to the receiver by clause 10 of the charge, is 'to carry any such sale into effect by deed in the name and on behalf of the company.' When a receiver is selling under such a clause, the more usual and better practice is for him to execute the deed of transfer by writing the name of the company and underneath this to write words that indicate that the name of the company has been written by the debenture. In addition, he should execute the deed in his own name. In that way he has the best of both worlds. The writing of the name of the company by the authority of the company given when it executed the debenture brings the case within the words of the debenture itself and execution by the attorney personally gives the advantage of s 46 of the Conveyancing Act 1881.

O'Higgins CJ and Parke J concurred.

Notes

See however, *Re Hussey (a bankrupt)* (High Court, Hamilton P, 23 September 1987) where a bankrupt was estopped from raising irregularities in the sealing requirements on the ground that in various previous hearings before the court he had chosen to remain silent regarding the matter. The irregularities in question were that the seal had been used without the authority of the board. Further, in breach of s 177 of the Principal Act the same person had witnessed the affixing of the seal both qua director and qua secretary.

Pre-incorporation contracts

[7.05]   Contracts purportedly made by or on behalf of the company prior to its formation may be ratified by it after incorporation, whereupon it becomes bound by that contract.[1] Prior to ratification the purported agent is personally liable on the contract in the absence of express agreement to the contrary.[2] An 'express agreement to the contrary' will not arise merely because the party signs as 'agent for the company'.[3] A contract can purport to be made by or on behalf of a company even though that company is known by both parties not to be existent at the time.[4]

1 S 37(1) of the Principal Act.
2 Ibid s 37(2).
3 *Phonogram Ltd v Lane* [1981] 3 All ER 182, 187.
4 Ibid p 183.

[7.06] Planning permission may not be granted to an applicant company which has not yet been formed.

The State (Finglas Industrial Estates Ltd) v Dublin County Council
(Supreme Court, 17 February 1983)

[7.07] Henchy J: On top of everything, the Minister's permission was granted to developers who had no existence, for they did not become incorporated until April 1981. Were the latter point the only issue in this appeal, I fear that I would hold the Minister's permission was invalid for having been granted to a non-existent legal person. I do not think that any provisions in the Companies Act 1963 validating acts done before incorporation, can detract from the fact that it is inherent in the planning code that both the planning authority and the public shall have an opportunity of vetting the planning application in the light of, amongst other matters, the identity of a named and legally existing applicant.

Notes

The dictum of Henchy J was considered and approved by Barron J in *Inver Resources Ltd v Limerick Corporation* [1988] ILRM 47.

In the case of a public unlimited company it is prohibited to commence business until the requirements of s 115 of the Principal Act (set out in *Keane* at para **10.05**) have been complied with. Contracts made or ratified by the company before the date at which it is entitled to commence business are 'provisional only' and do not bind it until such date, (s 115(4) of the principal Act). S 6 of the 1983 Act states that in the case of a plc although it is prohibited from doing business until it is issued with a trading certificate by the registrar this does not affect the validity of any transaction entered into by it prior to that date. Where the company fails to perform its part of such transactions however, the directors may incur personal liability to the other party, (s 6(8) of the 1983 Act).

Enforceability of ultra vires contract by the outsider

[7.08] It has been seen that at common law an 'ultra vires' transaction is void and unenforceable. As Overend J stated in *Hennesy v National Agricultural and Industrial Development Assosiation* [1947] IR 159: 'Acts which are ultra vires of a company are nullities . . . and are incapable of validation; and defences such as estoppel, acquiesence, laches, internal management are quite inapplicable'. See also *Ashbury Railway Carriage and Iron Co v Riche* (1875) LR 7 HL 653, 671.

The ultra vires rule was intended to protect both investors in and creditors of the company. Curiously, therefore, it had been held that parties to an ultra vires contract were unable to enforce it even if the result was that they went unpaid. See *Re Jon Beauforte (London) Ltd* [1953] Ch 131 where an unfortunate creditor of the company was unable to enforce an ultra vires transaction despite being unaware that it was beyond the company's capacity. Creditors may now avoid the injustice of results such as this, due to the protection afforded by s 8 of the Principal Act and by reg 6 of the European Communities (Companies) Regulations 1973. For an analysis of these provisions see Ussher *Questions of Capacity: The Implementation in the Republic of Ireland and in the United Kingdom of the First EEC Companies Directive* (1975) Irish Jurist 39.

Protection under s 8 of the Principal Act

[7.09] In order to mitigate some of the effects of the ultra vires rule on those dealing with the company, s 8 of the Principal Act provides that any ultra vires act of the company will be effective (and therefore enforceable) 'in favour of persons relying on such act or thing who is not shown to have been actually aware, at the time when he so relied thereon, that such act or thing was not within the powers of the company . . .' In the case of a contract entered into with the company the outsider is therefore protected unless he was 'actually aware' at the time it was concluded that it was ultra vires the company. Although the transaction may be enforced by the innocent outsider against the company the directors are still liable to the company for any consequential loss or damage suffered.[1] Further, any member or debenture holder may also apply to the court for an order restraining the company from doing ultra vires acts.[2] Section 8 may not be pleaded to enforce a transaction which is not only ultra vires but also illegal.[3]

1 See also *Rolled Steel Products (Holdings) Ltd v British Steel Corporation Ltd* [1984] BCLC 466.
2 S 8(2) of the Principal Act.
3 *Bank of Ireland Finance Ltd v Rockfield Ltd* [1979] IR 21, 26.

[7.10] An outsider may be 'actually aware' that an act is ultra vires the company in circumstances where he has read the company's objects clause and has failed to understand its contents.

Northern Bank Finance Corporation v Quinn and Achates Investment Company (High Court, 8 November 1979)

[7.11] Quinn had borrowed money from the plaintiff bank. Achates Investment Co ('the company') guaranteed the loan. The guarantee was secured by a mortgage over certain of its property. Quinn subsequently defaulted on the loan. In proceedings brought against it by the bank, the company pleaded that the guarantee and mortgage were ultra vires and were therefore unenforceable. The evidence established that the bank's solicitor had read the company's objects clause at the time of the transaction and had consequently formed the opinion that the company had capacity to give the guarantee and mortgage.

147

[7.12]   Keane J: It was submitted on behalf of the company that the execution of the guarantee was ultra vires the memorandum of association and that, accordingly, both the guarantee and the mortgage (in so far as it comprised the company's property) were void. Counsel for the bank submitted that the guarantee was intra vires the memorandum and articles of association; but that even if it were not, the bank were protected by the modification of the ultra vires rule effected by s 8 of the Companies Act 1963. He further submitted that, since the memorandum had been subsequently altered by a resolution of 18 May 1974, so as to put beyond doubt the power of the company to execute guarantees, the guarantee of 30 November 1973 was retrospectively validated and he relied in this connection on s 10(1) of the Act. Counsel for the bank finally submitted that, in any event, the company were estopped from relying on the alleged lack of vires. [His Lordship then examined the terms of the objects clause] . . .

It follows, in my view, that the memorandum conferred neither expressly nor by implication any power on the company to execute a guarantee for the purpose of securing the payment of a bank loan to Mr Quinn. In these circumstances, it is unnecessary to express any final opinion on a further submission advanced by [Counsel for the company] that, even were the memorandum to be read as conferring an express power on the company to execute such a guarantee, the transaction would nonetheless be ultra vires since no conceivable benefit could result to the company from it. The celebrated observations of Bowen LJ in *Hutton v West Cork Railway Co* (1883) 23 Ch D 654 that 'charity cannot sit at the boardroom table', and 'there are to be no cakes and ale except for the benefit of the company' may have been extended too far in *In re Lee, Behrens & Co* [1932] 2 Ch 46; and while this latter decision might appear to afford support for counsel for the company's proposition, its authority as a persuasive precedent would require reconsideration today in the light of the decision in *Charterbridge Corporation Ltd v Lloyds Bank Ltd* [1970] Ch 62. Having regard however, to the conclusion I have arrived at it is unnecessary that I should say anything more on this aspect of the case.

Counsel for the bank submitted that even if the execution of the guarantee were ultra vires the memorandum, his clients were protected by s 8(1) of the Companies Act 1963. [His Lordship then quoted the section].

Evidence was given on behalf of the bank by Mr T F O'Connell who was in November 1973 the bank's solicitor . . . Mr O'Connell said that he did not specifically recall reading the memorandum and articles. His normal procedure before drawing up the resolution of the directors was to check the objects clause.

But I think that the probabilities are that he did read the memorandum and came to the conclusion that the execution of the guarantee and the mortgage was within the powers of the company. Had he come to any other conclusion, I have not the slightest doubt but that he would have advised his principals not to close the transaction until the necessary amendment had been effected to the memorandum. It follows that Mr O'Connell was aware of the contents of the objects clause of the memorandum, but must have mistakenly believed that they empowered the company to execute the guarantee and mortgage . . .

The question accordingly, arises as to whether in these circumstances the bank were 'actually aware' within the meaning of s 8(1) of the lack of vires. Counsel for the bank submitted that the language of s 8(1) clearly demonstrated that the onus of establishing actual knowledge within the meaning of the section is on the person who asserts that such knowledge existed and that accordingly, the onus was on the company, to establish that the bank were 'actually aware' of the lack of vires. This may well be so, but I do not think it is material to the issue which has to be resolved in the present case. There is no conflict as to the facts in the present case; Mr O'Connell was the only witness on this issue and he was called by the bank. The only question that arises is as to whether, having regard to that evidence and the inferences, which, in my view, necessarily follow from it, the bank can be said to have been 'actually aware' of the lack of vires.

Counsel for the bank submitted that actual, as distinguished from constructive notice of the lack of vires was essential if a third party was to lose the protection of s 8(1). I accept that this is so: altogether apart from authority, the language used would suggest that what the legislature had in mind was actual and not constructive notice. Moreover, to interpret the section in any other way would be to frustrate its manifest object. While there is no authority of which counsel were aware or which I have been able to discover on the section, the mischief which it was designed to avoid is clear. Prior to the enactment of the section, all persons dealing with a company were deemed to have notice of the contents of the company's public documents, including its memorandum and articles. If a transaction was ultra vires, the other party to it speaking generally, had no rights at all. The manifest injustice and inconvenience which followed from this rule is amply illustrated by the decision in *Re Beauforte (Jon) (London) Ltd* [1953] Ch 131, which was referred to in the argument.

But if constructive notice can still be relied on in answer to a party claiming the protection of this section, the protection in question would be, to a significant extent eroded. It is clear, moreover, that the doctrine of constructive notice should not normally be applied to purely commercial transactions, such as the advancing of money: see the observations of Kenny J delivering the judgment of the Supreme Court in *Bank of Ireland v Rockfield Ltd* [1979] IR 21.

But while I am satisfied that the doctrine of constructive notice does not apply to the sub-section under consideration, this does not dispose of the matter. The bank, because of the knowledge of their agent, Mr O'Connell which must be imputed to them were aware of the objects of the company. There were no further facts of which they could be put on notice. But they failed to draw the appropriate inference from those facts ie. that the transaction was ultra vires. Counsel for the bank submits that, even accepting this to be so, this is not the actual knowledge which the section contemplates.

149

A great number of transactions are entered into every day by companies, public and private, without any of the parties looking at the memorandum in order to see whether the transaction in question is in fact authorised by the memorandum. I think it probable that on the occasions when the memorandum is looked at before a transaction is entered into it is normally because the company's solicitor or solicitor for a third party wishes to satisfy himself that the proposed transaction is intra vires the memorandum. I think it is clear that the section was designed to ensure that, in the first category of cases, persons who had entered into transactions in good faith with the company without ever reading the memorandum and accordingly with no actual knowledge that the transaction was ultra vires were not to suffer. I can see no reason in logic or justice why the legislature should have intended to afford the same protection to persons who had actually read the memorandum and simply failed to appreciate the lack of vires. The maxim *ignorantia juris haud neminem excusat* may not be of universal application but this is certainly one situation where it seems fair that it should apply.

This is best illustrated by an example. The directors of a public company decide to invest the bulk of the company's resources in a disastrous property speculation as a result of which the company suffers enormous losses. The company in fact had no power to enter into any such transaction but the vendor's solicitors although furnished with the memorandum and articles failed to appreciate this. If the submission advanced on behalf of the bank in this case is well founded, it would mean that, in such circumstances, the innocent shareholder would be the victim rather than the vendors. There seems no reason why the consequences of the vendors' failure to appreciate the lack of vires should be visited on the heads of the blameless shareholders. I do not overlook the fact that the sub-section gives the company a remedy against any director or officer of the company who is responsible for the ultra vires act; but such a remedy may not necessarily enable the innocent shareholder to recoup all his losses . . .

I am satisfied that, where a party is shown to have been actually aware of the contents of the memorandum but failed to appreciate that the company were not empowered thereby to enter into the transaction in issue; s 8(1) has no application. It follows that, in the present case, the bank cannot successfully rely on s 8(1).

Counsel for the bank next submitted that the execution of the guarantee was retrospectively validated by a special resolution of the company passed on 18 May 1974. It is conceded on behalf of the company that this resolution effectively amended the memorandum so as to enable a guarantee to be executed. [Counsel for the bank] relied on s 10(1) of the Act of 1963, which provides that:

> Subject to sub-section (2) a company may, by special resolution alter the provisions of its memorandum by abandoning, restricting or amending any existing object or by adopting a new object and any alteration so made shall be as valid as if originally contained therein and be subject to alteration in like manner.

He argued that the words 'shall be as valid as if originally contained therein' meant, in a case such as the present, that a transaction entered into prior to the passing of the resolution was, as it were, retrospectively validated.

I do not think that is correct. Were it so, the consequences would be strange indeed; as pointed out by [counsel for the company], if the company in the present case originally had power to execute a guarantee and deprived itself of that power by the passing of a subsequent resolution, it could hardly be said that the execution of the guarantee prior thereto was thereby invalidated. I think that the meaning of the words in question is quite clear, if one considers the provisions of s 7 which provides that:

'the memorandum must be printed must bear the same stamp as if it were a deed and must be signed by each subscriber in the presence of at least one witness who must attest the signature.'

The words relied on by counsel for the bank were clearly designed, in my view, to relieve the company from the necessity of having the memorandum in its altered form signed again by the subscribers and attesting witnesses and then reprinted . . .

Finally counsel for the bank submitted that the company were estopped at this stage from contesting the validity of the guarantee. He concedes that the doctrine of estoppel could not enable the company validly to perform an act which was ultra vires, but submits that as the company had been empowered since 18 May 1974, to enter into the transaction they cannot now be heard to say that it is ultra vires. In particular, he relies on a letter written by the company to the bank on 31 December 1976, in which they said:

'As you are aware, this company has guaranteed the borrowings from the corporation of Mr Fursey Quinn.

Please let us have details in confidence, of the guaranteed borrowings in relation to the amount outstanding including interest, the amount and timing of repayment made and interest paid to date.'

Counsel for the bank points out that the bank had power at any time to call in the amount of the loan and that following the receipt of this letter, they acted to their detriment by failing to call it in . . .

Can it reasonably be said that, in the present case, the bank acted on the representation contained in the letter of 31 December – if representation it were – and thereby altered their position to their prejudice? There is no reason to suppose that at the date this letter was written the bank entertained the slightest doubts as to the validity of the guarantee or mortgage. Had they entertained any such doubts, they would have immediately required the re-execution of the guarantee and the mortgage before allowing any further interest to accumulate. There is nothing to suggest that this letter had any effect on the attitude of the bank towards calling in the loan. I do not think that it could be said that they in any way altered their position to their prejudice as a result of any representation that may have been

151

contained in this letter. I think it is also clear that the mere fact that the company sent to the bank its memorandum and articles of association at the time of its application for a loan could not in any sense be said to constitute a representation which was subsequently acted on to their detriment by the bank. Their action in so doing was not a representation, that the company had the power in question; it was no more than an invitation to the bank to satisfy themselves that the transaction was intra vires and there is no reason to suppose that any request to alter the memorandum would not have been immediately complied with. I am accordingly satisfied that this submission also fails.

In these circumstances, I am satisfied that the execution of the guarantee was ultra vires and that the bank cannot successfully rely on any of the grounds advanced by counsel. It is, I think accepted that the mortgage is in turn dependent for its validity upon the guarantee; the company could not validly execute a mortgage in order to secure an obligation which they had no power to accept in the first place . . . The claim of the bank against the company will accordingly be dismissed.

Notes
   This decision is noted by Ussher *Company Law – Validation of Ultra Vires Transactions* [1981] DULJ 76 who argues that the bank had *actual notice* but not actual knowledge of the ultra vires nature of the transaction was ultra vires. Ussher goes on to point out that notice and knowledge are not the same thing: *Cresta Holdings Ltd v Karlin [1959]* 1 WLR 1055.

Protection under regulation 6

[7.13]   The First EC Companies Directive had as one of its objects the co-ordination of safeguards for those dealing with companies. This included the abolition of the ultra vires rule as between the company and the outsider; at least in cases where the latter was unaware that the transaction was beyond the capacity of the company. Despite the existence of s 8(1) of the Principal Act, the European Communities (Companies) Regulations 1973[1] were issued by the Minister. Regulation 6 provides for the protection of outsiders, inter alia, in the case of ultra vires transactions. It does not apply to unlimited companies,[2] and only applies to transactions entered into by the company through its board of directors or through agents registered in the Companies Office. For a definition of what constitutes an act of the board see *TCB v Gray* (para **7.59**) below.

1 SI No 163 of 1973.
2 For this reason it had no application in *Northern Bank Finance Corporation v Quinn and Achates Investment Co* (para **7.11**).

Council Directive 68/151/EEC of 9 March 1968

[7.14]   Art 9(1): Acts done by the organs of the company shall be binding upon it even if those acts are not within the objects of the company, unless such acts exceed the powers that the law confers or allows to be conferred on those organs.

However, Member States may provide that the company shall not be bound where such acts are outside the objects of the company, if it proves that the third party knew that the act was outside these objects or could not in view of the circumstances have been unaware of it; disclosure of the statutes[1] shall not of itself be sufficient proof thereof.

1 The company's constitutional documents – the memorandum and articles of association.

European Communities (Companies) Regulations 1973; (SI 163 of 1973)

[7.15] Regulation 6.

(1) In favour of a person dealing with a company in good faith, any transaction entered into by any organ of the company, being its board of directors or any person registered under these regulations as a person authorised to bind the company, shall be deemed to be within the capacity of the company and any limitation of the powers of that board or person, whether imposed by the memorandum or articles of association or otherwise, may not be relied upon as against any person so dealing with the company.

(2) Any such person shall be presumed to have acted in good faith unless the contrary is proved.

(3) For the purpose of the regulation, the registration of a person authorised to bind the company shall be effected by delivering to the registrar of companies a notice giving the name and description of the person concerned.

[7.16] Under regulation 6 an outsider may enforce an ultra vires transaction against the company unless, at the time of entering into that transaction he was aware or could not have been unaware that it was beyond the capacity of the company.

International Factors (NI) Ltd v Streeve Construction Ltd [1984] NI 245 (Queen's Bench Division)

[7.17] Gibson LJ: The plaintiff's claim is for £21,000 alleged to be due by the defendant on foot of three cheques each for £7,000 drawn on the account of the defendant in the Bank of Ireland and signed by one Robert Noble (Noble) who at the time the cheques were drawn was the managing director of the defendant and was the sole authorised signatory of cheques drawn on the account of the defendant. The defence, while not disputing any of these facts is that the cheques were drawn to discharge the personal indebtedness of Noble and not for an unauthorised purpose of the defendant: they were therefore, drawn for an unauthorised purpose which was unwarranted by the memorandum of association, and being, ultra vires, cannot be sued upon . . .

The validity of the defence depends upon a number of considerations. First, article 129 of the Companies (Northern Ireland) Order 1978, which is in identical terms with s 9(1) of the European Communities Act 1972 [ie reg 6 of the 1973 Regulations], provides that in certain circumstances persons dealing with the directors of a company are entitled to rely on the validity of the transaction regardless of the terms of the memorandum of association of the company . . .

In order that a person dealing with a company may secure the protection of the article two conditions must be satisfied. He must deal in good faith and the transaction must have been decided upon by the directors. If these conditions have been observed then the transaction is deemed to be intra vires both of the company and of the directors. The person so dealing is not put on enquiry as to the powers of the company and of the directors and his good faith is presumed until the contrary is proved. The rule whereby a person contracting with a company is estopped from denying that he knew the limitations imposed by the memorandum and article of association is to that extent abrogated.

Thus the article impinges upon the ultra vires rule and also it would seem upon the rule in *Royal British Bank v Turquand* (para **7.40**) in that the doctrine of constructive notice is abolished as regards powers of directors in relation to dealing with a third party, though not in the relationship between the directors and shareholders.

When the article speaks of a matter decided upon by the directors that would normally mean the board of directors; but where as here, the general management powers of the board have been delegated to a managing director, namely, Noble, the plaintiff, if acting bona fide, is entitled to assume that he has the full powers of a board of directors notwithstanding any limitation in his actual powers imposed by the articles of association. Provided therefore, the plaintiff was dealing with the defendant for the issue of the cheques and acted in good faith it is protected by the article.

There is no suggestion in the evidence that the plaintiff of Mr Rooney, the general manager of operations of the plaintiff, who alone acted on its behalf in its dealings with Noble had ever any sight of the memorandum or articles of association of the defendant, or was informed of any restrictive provision in them which would put the plaintiff on notice of any infirmity in the powers of the defendant or of Noble to draw the cheques in favour of the plaintiff.

Though the dealings were between the plaintiff and Noble I am satisfied that Noble was not only acting personally but was acting as managing director of his several companies as well as on his own behalf.

Therefore, the sole question to be resolved in order to decide whether article 129 can be called in aid by the plaintiff is whether it through its agent Mr Rooney acted bona fide in the matter. This involves a consideration of the details of its relationship and dealings with Noble and the defendant.

The defendant is a private company incorporated in 1980 with a share capital of £10,000. Its primary business is that of building contractors. At all material times it was a subsidiary of another private company, Streeve

Holdings Ltd, which was the registered holder of all but one of the shares issued by the defendant. Another subsidiary company of Streeve Holdings Ltd was Streeve Haulage Ltd. The managing director of all these companies was Noble and he also had the major financial intrest in them. Another of Noble's companies was W Leslie & Company (Campsie) Ltd, (Leslie) which manufactured cement blocks and other building materials. There was a close business link between the companies. The defendant carried out building construction work, Leslie supplied some at least of the materials and Streeve haulage acted as carrier for both companies.

In 1981 Leslie found difficulty in collecting its accounts as a result of which on 18 August 1981 it entered into a factoring agreement with the plaintiff by which the plaintiff agreed to purchase certain debts due or to become due to Leslie from customers. By further agreement of the same date Noble, his wife and another of Noble's companies Roe Valley Holdings Ltd (Roe) agreed to indemnify the plaintiff against any loss to the plaintiff as a result of entering into the factoring agreement. In fact substantial losses were incurred due to difficulties in collecting the debts, and on 21 October 1982 the plaintiff demanded payment from the guarantors of over £152,000. By the end of January 1983 the loss had been reduced to about £86,000 and a further demand for payment had not been met with a satisfactory response. Accordingly, a meeting was arranged between Rooney and Noble when Rooney pointed out to Noble the avenues of recovery available to the plaintiff and the consequences both to him and to his companies if he were made bankrupt and his companies put into liquidation or at best deprived of his services as a director in the event of his bankruptcy. The business dealings between the companies were discussed as a result of which it appeared that there might be an indebtedness by the defendant to Leslie. An option which might avoid pursuing judgments against Leslie and the guarantors which was discussed was that the defendant as a debtor to Leslie, might provide some payment or security. It appeared that the defendant was engaged in substantial work for the Northern Ireland Housing Executive in consequence of which considerable payments would soon become due and Noble feared lest any proceedings against Leslie and himself would seriously prejudice the business and solvency of the defendant.

Following the meeting Noble after consideration of the options open posed to the plaintiff three cheques each for £7,000 signed by him and drawn on the bank account of the defendant. They were post-dated 31 May, 30 June and 29 July. The reason why the cheques were so dated was that Noble had explained to Rooney that the cash flow of the defendant in those months was likely to be greater during the summer months than in the winter or early spring. However, upon presentation each of the cheques was returned 'not drawn according to mandate'. The plaintiff duly served notices of dishonour on the defendant. The reason for the terms of the dishonour was that on 3 March 1983 Noble had resigned as director of the defendant and the names of the persons authorised to sign cheques on behalf of the defendant on that day changed.

In such circumstances the question which I have to determine is whether the defendant has established on balance of probabilities that the plaintiff was not acting in good faith in receiving the cheques. There is no definition of the phrase 'good faith' in article 129 nor in the Companies Order of which it is part. It is recognised that in case of ambiguity in the construction of the article one may resort for assistance to the terms of the Directive from which it had its origin. The general intention as to the scope of the article is to be found in the recitals contained in the Directive which include the following 'whereas the protection of third parties must be ensured by provisions which restrict to the greatest possible extent the grounds on which obligations entered into in the name of the company are not valid.' The specific ancestor of article 129 more specifically provided: 'Member States may provide that the company shall not be bound where such acts are outside the objects of the company if it proves that the third party knew that the act was outside those objects . . . or could not in view of the circumstances have been unaware of it'. In the light of this, I would accept as was also accepted by Lawson J in *International Sales and Agencies Ltd v Marcus* [1982] 3 All ER 551 that the test of lack of good faith depends upon proof of actual knowledge that the transaction was ultra vires of the company or that the person dealing with the company could not have been unaware that he was a party to a transaction ultra vires, which amounts to a deliberate closing of one's mind to circumstances which would have pointed towards the conclusion of ultra vires.

It is clear that at the meeting in January 1983 the whole relationship between the companies in which Noble was interested was discussed. The question of indebtedness as between Leslie and the defendant was touched upon. In the previous November Noble had shown to Mr Rooney the management accounts of Leslie which indicated that a sum of £25–26,000 was stated to be due by the defendant to Leslie and I find as a fact that Mr Leslie was not at any time informed that this indebtedness had been discharged and that the total of the cheques, namely £21,000, being within that figure did not suggest to him other than that the cheques were related to the debt due by the defendant to Leslie. The issue of the cheques was after the promise by Noble at the meeting that he would look into the indebtedness of all the companies to one another. I see no reason to doubt the evidence of Mr Rooney that on receipt of the cheques he had no suspicions as their issue which, as he put it, seemed logical. I take it that by this he meant that the payment by the cheques direct to the plaintiff by the defendant was merely a short cut to avoid the defendant discharging its debt to Leslie and Leslie transmitting £21,000, the presumed amount of the debt, to the plaintiff.

There is the further consideration that though the only principal debtor to the plaintiff was Leslie, it was appreciated by Noble in his capacity as managing director of the defendant that the successful operation of each company depended upon the continuing operation of the others and also upon Noble not becoming disqualified from managing them. He was particularly anxious to preserve the survival and business activities of the defendant which he expected would in the coming months benefit from substantial income pursuant to its contracts, and I accept that Mr Rooney felt that the issue of the cheques by the defendant was designed to secure the best interests of that company in the particular circumstances in which it found itself.

At the meeting Mr Rooney was perhaps primarily anticipating that any offer would come from Noble to meet his personal debt but the entire ramifications of all the companies was under review and any payment by Noble would give him a remedy against the principal debtor, Leslie, and any embarrassment to Leslie would have repercussions on the prospects of the defendant. I think it was recognised that the entire structure was precarious and that if any company other than the defendant fell it also would be brought down. Quite apart from the question whether the cheques were in respect of indebtedness by the defendant to Leslie, the picture I have formed from the evidence is that the defendant had a very real interest in making the payments and that, whatever may have been the motives of Noble, the plaintiff. through Mr Rooney, honestly considered that such payments might be regarded as in the best interests of the defendant.

I do not think that Mr Rooney believed that all Noble's companies formed a group in the sense of the term in the companies legislation, but he knew that they were closely linked commercially and may well have suspected that their objects clauses were sufficiently wide to enable, for instance, the defendant to provide financial assistance to Leslie. My reason for this conjecture is that it was known to Mr Rooney that one of the guarantors of the factoring agreement by Leslie was another of the companies, namely, Roe, which could only legally have been done if the objects clause of Roe was wide enough to enable it to indemnify third parties against the debts of Leslie in which it seems to have had no direct financial interest. If, to the knowledge of Mr Rooney, it was a permitted object for Roe to assume responsibility for the debts of Leslie, there was no reason for him to know or suspect that the memorandum of association of the defendant would not also authorise a similar transaction for the benefit of Leslie.

I have, therefore, come to the conclusion that the enlargement of the protection of third parties in their dealings with companies contained in article 129 is sufficient to protect the plaintiff in its acceptance of the cheques issued by the defendant in this case. This means that it is unnecessary for me to embark upon an interpretation of the various objets of the defendant set out in article 3 of its memorandum of association in order to discover whether the impugned transaction was within its powers.

Notes

It would seem that reg 6 essentially provides much the same protection for the outsider as is afforded by s 8 of the Principal Act. However, it would appear that the outsider will lose his protection where he has 'actual notice' of the ultra vires nature of the transaction. Subject to *Northern Bank Finance Corp v Quinn* (para **7.11**) the protection afforded by s 8 is somewhat wider in that the outsider may enforce the transaction unless he was 'actually aware' that it was beyond the company's capacity. Regulation 6 therefore appears to be superfluous in so far as it applies to the doctrine of ultra vires. It does however, have a major impact on the extent to which a company is bound by the unauthorised acts of its agents discussed below).

The position of the outsider who is aware that the act is ultra vires

[7.18]   As has been mentioned above, where the outsider is without the protection of s 8, the ultra vires contract is void and unenforceable. This can create great hardship for the outsiders. Accordingly the courts have developed certain exceptions to this rule, whereby monies owing from the company may be indirectly recovered.

[7.19]   The ultra vires creditor may be subrogated to the rights of an intra vires creditor.

Re Lough Neagh Ship Co ex p Workman [1895] 1 IR 533 (Chancery Division)

[7.20]   The company which had been formed to purchase and work owed the sum of £7,500 to shipbuilders in respect of the price of a ship ordered by it. The company had no money with which to pay the shipbuilders. Workman who was one of the directors of the company agreed to lend it £7,500 with interest at 7 per cent. The money was advanced by J & R Workman (a firm of which Workman was a member). The shipbuilder was paid and the company acquired the ship. The company subsequently went into liquidation. It transpired that it had been was ultra vires the company to take the loan from the firm. The liquidator therefore claimed that the firm should not be allowed to prove for its debt.

[7.21]   **Porter MR:** The fact of the advance is of course, not disputed. But the argument is that the company had no power to borrow money, or at least no power to borrow part of the purchase money of this steamer; and that the transaction is simply void the company retaining the ship . . . That this result would be a startling injustice cannot determine the question particularly when the lender is himself a director . . . In my opinion there is no express power to borrow which covers this case . . . However . . . I think the claimants are entitled to succeed upon the ground of what is now usually called subrogation (a word taken from the civil law) formerly more generally termed substitution.

   The civil law on the subject is stated in the Digest, '*Plane cum tertius creditor primum de sua pecunia dimisit, in locum ejus substituitur in ea quantitae quam superiori exsolvit.*' It is true the present is not the case of several creditors. But it is the case of a person interested in the affairs of the company, discharging, with the privity and consent of the company a liability of the latter by payment. This has the effect of placing the person making the payment in the position in which the creditor stood before he was paid off: and as the ship was finished and ready to be delivered up, Workman and Clarke were under their contract entitled to be paid and could have sued for the price averring readiness to deliver or could have maintained an action for not accepting and paying for the ship according to contract. In either case they could have sustained a petition for winding up, and come in as creditors. Or, if they had given up the vessel without being paid, they could of course have taken the same course or courses.

Now, by paying [the shipbuilders] the claimants became equitable assignees of their rights to sue the company; and on that ground are, in my opinion, entitled to sustain the present claim. There has been in the result no real borrowing by the company at all. If a liability has been created towards J and R Workman an exactly equal liability to [the shipbuilders] has disappeared. It is simply a change of creditor not a new debt . . .

A question has been raised as to whether he is entitled to claim any and what interest on his advances. On that point the argument between the claimant and the company provided for interest at 7 per cent – a rate proved to be usual and reasonable in the case of advances on mortgage of a ship in course of building. But I am not giving effect to the claim as a contract liability of the company to J and R Workman. The ground on which I decide in favour of the latter on the main question simply places them in the position of [the shipbuilders] as regards the £7,500. There is nothing before me to show that [the shipbuilders] were, by their contract with the company specifically entitled to interest. If they were, I think the claimants are equitable assignees of their rights including interest at the agreed rate. If not, I have no power to give it as incident to the contract. Indeed it may well be that the payment to [the shipbuilders] which, of course, stopped any right in them to interest, could confer no right in respect of it upon the claimants. On the materials before me, I am therefore with regret obliged to decline to say anything as to interest at 7 per cent or any other agreed rate. But in the case of *Baroness of Wenlock v River Dee Co* 19 QBD 155, the Court of Appeal gave interest – I presume at the court rate – on money advanced as this money was, and I shall follow that case allowing interest at 4 per cent . . .

Notes

See also *Re Wrexham Mold & Connah's Railway* [1899] 1 Ch 440.

[7.22] A bona fide transaction with a company which is impeachable only on the ground of being ultra vires, may be set aside on terms that both parties be restored to their original position.

Flood v Irish Provident Assurance Co and the Hibernian Bank (1912)
46 ILTR 214 (Court of Appeal)

[7.23] The Irish Provident Assurance Co was permitted by its objects clause to carry on general insurance business but was expressly prohibited from effecting policies of life assurance. Despite this prohibition, the company carried on a certain amount of life assurance business. When the company went into liquidation the holders of the life policies commenced proceedings to recover the premiums they had paid under the policies. The Court of Appeal had no hesitation in ordering the return of the monies.

[7.24]   Walker LC: Two questions seem to me to arise; [the first question is irrelevant] and the second question is whether if the policies are void, the plaintiffs are entitled to a return of the premiums which they have paid . . .

It will be observed that all a policy holder can ever get under the policies we have to deal with is a payment of some proportion, according to the circumstances of the premiums actually paid by himself, so that this company trades without any risk. For the purpose of coming to a conclusion on the second question I think we are bound to decide whether the policies within the terms of the prohibition in the memorandum which I have read, viz. – whether they are 'upon or in any way relating to human life.' I have already stated the terms of the policy in each of the six cases and the reading of them seems to me irresistibly to lead to the conclusion that they relate to human life and if they do they are plainly void policies. It is the company which is sued as the corporate body, and there can be no estoppel against it which would justify us in saying that they bind the shareholders. I cannot help thinking that this company notwithstanding the terms of the memorandum were issuing policies which they were willing to believe should be considered life policies. Their prospectuses, renewal, notices, policies, the stamp duty they pay and the very terms of the policies themselves lead me to the conclusion, but this does not affect the legal question whether the premiums paid on the void policies are recoverable as being money paid without consideration. The interest on these moneys is another question which I shall deal with later on. I am of opinion that the premiums are recoverable. The contract is not an illegal contract, which distinguishes the case from such a one as *Harse v Pearl Life Assurance Co* [1904] 1 KB 558, where it was held that as the contract was illegal and the parties were not in pari delicto the premiums could not be recovered back. In the present case the contract is not illegal, although it is void. There is considerable authority that premiums received by an insurance company, whether a marine or a life one, where the consideration has failed can be recovered back . . . In *Burges and Stock's* case *(Re Phoenix Life Assurance Co)* 2 J & H 441, Wood V-C, in a considered judgment declared that the assured were entitled to prove for the amount of premiums paid by them though they had no right to prove for losses upon marine policies which there was no power to issue. The claimants had no consideration for the premiums they paid. I have already pointed out that the defendants' only obligation under the policies is to return some proportion of the premiums actually received by them so they run no risk of loss. As to the claim for interest, I do not think it is sustainable.

Holmes LJ delivered a concurring judgment. Cherry LJ concurred.

Notes

See also *Re Irish Provident Assurance Co* [1913] 1 IR 352 which involved a second claim in the liquidation of the same company for the recovery of premiums paid under ultra vires policies. Palles CB, stating that the company could not 'approbate and reprobate', ordered the return of the premiums to the policyholders.

The court will not make an order restoring the parties to their original position if to do so would indirectly enforce the ultra vires contract. Such a situation might arise if the court ordered the repayment of monies advanced on an ultra vires contract of loan: *Sinclair v Brougham* [1914] AC 398. The court in this case did, however, indicate that the ultra vires creditors might be able to trace some of the monies advanced by them. In the case of goods sold to the company, the supplier may have an action in detinue or conversion against the company.

Enforcement of ultra vires transactions by the company.

[7.25]   An ultra vires contract, being void is unenforceable by the company

Cabaret Holdings Ltd v Meeanee Sports and Rodeo Club Inc [1982] 1 NZLR 673 (Court of Appeal)

[7.26]   Pursuant to the terms of an agreement concluded with the defendant company, the plaintiff paid expenses which had been incurred by the defendant. In a subsequent action by the plaintiff for reimbursement of the sums paid on behalf of the defendant it was successfully pleaded by way of defence that the agreement and payments made thereunder were ultra vires. Accordingly the agreement was unenforceable and the monies were irrecoverable.

[7.27]   **Somers J** (delivering the judgment of the court): The plaintiff Meeanee Sports and Rodeo Club Incorporated, a body corporate under the Incorporated Societies Act 1908 sued to recover from the defendant Cabaret Holdings Ltd two sums of $3,420 and $3,000 . . .

For the purposes of trial the defendant admitted the facts pleaded by the plaintiff. But it averred that the contract pleaded was not within the powers of the plaintiff to make and that in consequence it could not recover the two sums claimed.

The Chief Justice found that the contract was ultra vires the plaintiff society. But after a review of the authorities, he held in a considered judgment, that such a circumstance provided no defence to the claims. From that determination the defendant has appealed . . .

It was not disputed and does not seem to be in doubt that an incorporated society under the Incorporated Societies Act 1908 stands in the same position as a company incorporated under the Companies Act 1955 in relation to its powers . . . The locus classicus upon the effect of lack of power on a contract purportedly made by a company is *Ashbury Railway Carriage and Iron*

Co v Riche (1875) LR 7 HL 653. That was an action against the company on a contract that had not been fully performed. The contract was held to be void from the beginning and incapable of ratification . . . That proposition has not subsequently been questioned as far as we are aware, although the legislative provisions which give rise to it have been under siege for some time.

Such an executory contract is not enforceable by the company against the other party – the invalidity of the company's promises means that those of the other party are not supported by any consideration.

It is not difficult to see that cases may arise in which a company has fully performed its part of a contract into which it has no power to enter and that unless a remedy is afforded an injustice will result to the company. In this situation it has been suggested that resort may be had to other parts of the speeches in the *Ashbury Railway Carriage* case in which reference was made to the connection between limitation of liability of members of a company and and limitation of the company's capacity to its exressed objects. The protection of shareholders, creditors, and others doing business with the company require that its objects be openly stated in its memorandum and its capacity measured by the statements so made . . . So Lord Parker of Waddington in *Cotman v Brougham* [1918] AC 514 said:

'. . . the statement of a company's objects in its memorandum is intended to serve a double purpose. In the first place it gives protection to subscribers, who learn from it the purpose to which their money can be applied. In the second place it gives protection to persons who deal with the company and who can infer from it the extent of the company's powers' (ibid 520)

Those remarks both explain the course of the legislation and justify the approach of the court to it. But it is also claimed that to prevent a company which has fully performed its part of a contract from enforcing the promise of the other contracting party is to stand the rules about ultra vires on their head.

As a matter of abstract logic it is difficult to suppose that a contract which it is beyond the power of a company to make, which could never be enforced against the company, which the company could not (before its own performance) enforce against the other party can yet ground a cause of action because that which the company 'agreed' to do has been done by it. To interpret a precedural rule that the third party may not plead ultra vires where the contract is wholly executed by the company (itself a matter of inquiry and sometimes difficulty) can hardly give life to that which was never born. On the other hand the implication of a promise by the other party arising from that which the company has done may stand differently.

We turn to the authorities . . . In England the only case in which the point has squarely arisen is *Bell Houses Ltd v City Wall Properties Ltd* [1966] 1 QB 207. Mocatta J in a judgment in which he reviewed many of the cases refused to distinguish between executory and executed contracts and held that the other party could plead the company's lack of power. Earlier in *Anglo-Overseas Agencies Ltd v Green* [1961] 1 QB 1, Salmon J seems to have supposed that the position was as Mocatta J subsequently held it to be. But later in the appeal from Mocatta J's decision without finding it necessary to decide the point the same judge thought it difficult and arguable. As Salmon LJ's remarks are at the core of the appellant's case we set them out:

> 'It seems strange that third parties could take advantage of a doctrine, manifestly for the protection of the shareholders, in order to deprive the company of money which in justice should be paid to it by the parties.' ([1966] 2 QB 656, 694).

After referring to the remarks of Lord Parker of Waddington in *Cotman v Brougham* set out above Salmon LJ continued:

> 'What Lord Parker was contemplating was that third parties proposing to deal with the company could by looking at the memorandum have the security of knowing whether they could compel performance by the company of the contract in contemplation. I hardly think that he had in mind that third parties by looking at the memorandum should have the security of knowing that they might safely enter into a contract and promise to pay the company for services without any obligation to honour their contractual promise after they had received the services. The judge in effect came to the conclusion that the reasoning in *Ashbury Railway Carriage & Iron Co Ltd v Riche* led to this strange result.'

There is a remark along the same lines in the judgment of the Privy Council delivered by Lord Davey in *National Telephone Company v Constables of St Peter Port* [1900] AC 317,321.

Some of the cases were discussed by the appellate division of the Alberta Supreme Court in *Breckenridge Speedway Ltd v The Queen* (1967) 64 DLR (2d) 488 in the context of an action to recover moneys lent, in effect by the Province, pursuant to the terms of a statute which was ultra vires the legislative power. Three members of the court held that the borrower could not be heard to impugn the transaction as ultra vires. Two considered the transaction void but that recovery could be had on principles of restitution.

Then there is *Re K L Tractors Ltd* (1961) 106 CLR 318 upon which much reliance was placed by the appellant and which was particularly referred to by the Chief Justice. We do not read that case as one in which the Commonwealth was permitted to enforce a contract which it lacked power to enter. Fullagar J pointed to the critical feature of the case when he remarked that it is not a consequence of the void nature of a contract that a person receiving goods does not have to pay for them. This is echoed in the other judgments. We do not consider the reasons for judgments given in *Re K L Tractors* are inconsistent with the conclusion reached in *Bell Houses Ltd v City Wall Properties Ltd*. Indeed as Stephen J observed in *Kathleen Investments (Australia) Ltd v Australian Atomic Energy Commission* (1977) 139

163

CLR 117 at 147–149 what was said by Mocatta J in the *Bell Houses Ltd* case is inherent in the observations of Fullagar J in the *K L Tractors* case.

A number of cases from the United States of America were mentioned in argument. While in many relief was given to the company that relief was by way of non-contractual remedy. No case was cited in which the contract itself was enforced . . .

In the end we conclude that this action cannot succeed. It is not possible for a company or incorporated society to sue upon a contract into which it had no power to enter. To say that a corporation is not barred from recovery because a transaction is ultra vires is one thing. To say that it may sue upon a contract which never came into existence is a wholly different thing. The conclusion may occasion some regret but we regard is in the present state of the law as inevitable.

Notes

See generally Furmston *Who can plead that a contract is ultra vires?* (1961) 24 MLR 715.

As has been mentioned above, the company being an artificial entity can only enter into contracts through its agents. If the agent enters into a contract without the authority to do so the company may subsequently ratify his acts and thereby adopt the contract. The company's agents can have no actual authority to enter into contracts which are ultra vires the company. However, the Supreme Court has stated, applying the principles laid down by Wright J in *Firth v Staines* [1897] 2 QB 70, 75 in *Bank of Ireland v Rockfield Ltd* [1979] IR 21,35, that for ratification to be valid the principal must have been legally capable of doing the act himself *at the time of ratification'*. Ussher has suggested at p 131 of *Company Law in Ireland*, that where the agent enters into a contract which is ultra vires his principal, the company, it may be possible for the company to alter its objects pursuant to s 10 of the Principal Act, to permit such a contract. After this alteration has been made the company may then ratify the contract entered into by the agent. This view seems plausible and may provide a means for the company to enforce an otherwise ultra vires transaction. However, it has not found favour with all legal writers. (See generally Borrie, *Commercial Law* (6th Ed) (London 1988) chapter 1. For a fuller discussion see *Bowstead on Agency* (14th Ed)).

In any case the company will presumably, it will have the some remedies in tort (for detinue or conversion) or in tracing as are available to an outsider who is without the protection of s 8. Similarly, the court may make an order applying the principles in *Flood v Irish Provident Assurance Co* (para **7.23**) putting the parties back to their original position. In *Brougham v Dwyer* (1913) 108 LT 504 the court made an order directing the return to a company of monies lent by it on an ultra vires contract of loan. Arguably, this order indirectly enforced the ultra vires contract and may no longer be considered as good law, in the light of the House of Lords decision in *Sinclair v Brougham* [1914] AC 398.

In England the ultra vires rule may no longer be pleaded as a defence in an action for the enforcement of a contract. S 35 of the Companies Act 1985, as amended by s 108 of the Companies Act 1989 now provides that 'The validity of an act done by a company shall not be called into question on the ground of lack of capacity by reason of the fact that it is beyond the objects of the company stated in its memorandum of association'. Any member may still apply to restrain the company from engaging in ultra vires activities.

Unauthorised or irregular contracts

[7.28] Although a contract may be intra vires the company, it may not bind the company if the the agent who concluded it was not in fact authorised to do so. It is a basic principle of the law of agency that a principal is normally bound by acts within the actual, usual or apparent (ostensible) authority of his agents[1]. Actual authority is that which the agent in fact possesses. Usual authority, is that which is normally conferred on that particular class of agent. The usual authority of the company's managing director, for example, will be greater than that of its typist. The agent's actual authority may be greater or less than his usual authority. Where his usual authority is less than his actual authority, he may still have 'apparent' or ostensible authority to act on behalf of his principal. This arises as a result of a representation, express or implied by his principal to those dealing with the agent, that he in fact has authority to bind the principal. The principal is estopped in equity from subsequently denying that the agent had such authority unless he had previously notified the other party of the agents' lack of actual authority. It is possible of course, that due to the representations of the principal, the agents' ostensible authority is greater than even his usual authority.

The usual authority of a company's agent is to be ascertained by reference to the standard form articles in table A.[2] These articles are commonly adopted with or without alterations by most Irish companies. The board of directors, acting collectively, have usual authority to exercise full powers of management of the company.[3] Their actual authority may be cut down by the articles in that the exercise of some powers may be subjected to the requirement of prior approval of the general meeting. Although a managing director has no prescribed set of functions[4] his usual authority is potentially as great as that of the board of directors which appointed him.[5] An individual director only has usual authority to witness the afixing of the company's seal to a document.[6] The chairman on the other hand has virtually no usual authority. In one company he may be a mere figurehead and in another he may have the powers of a managing director. One function he does possess is to sign the minutes of previous board meetings. The minutes as signed then raise a rebuttable presumption that the board meeting was duly convened and as to what happened at the meeting.[7] The extent of the usual authority of the company secretary is greater than it was one hundred years

7.28 *Contracts*

ago.[8] He may at least bind the company to contracts relating to its administrative affairs.[9] A shareholder does not have usual authority to act on behalf of the company.[10]

1 See generally Borrie *Commercial Law* (6th Ed) (London 1988) chapter 1. For a fuller discussion see *Bowstead on Agency* (14th Ed).
2 For a discussion of the usual authority of a company's agents see *Keane* at paras **12.11–12.14**.
3 Art 80 table A.
4 *Harold Holdsworth & Co (Wakefield) Ltd v Caddies* [1955] 1 WLR 352.
5 Art 112, table A.
6 Ibid art 115.
7 S 145(3) of the Principal Act.
8 *Barnett, Hoares & Co v South London Tramways Co* [1887] 18 QBD 815.
9 *Panorama Developments (Guildford) Ltd v Fidelis Furnishing Fabric Ltd* [1971] 2 QB 711.
10 *IRC v Ufitee Group Ltd* [1977] 3 All ER 924; *Kilgoblin Mink & Stud Farms Ltd v National Credit Co Ltd* [1980] IR 175.

[7.29]   As we shall see below the ordinary rules of agency as they apply to companies are modified by the doctrine of constructive notice, which is in turn modified by the Indoor Management Rule and reg 6 of the European Communities (Companies) Regulations 1973.

[7.30]   The company may be bound by a representation that an individual was authorised to act on its behalf in relation to a particular transaction, even if it should transpire that the individual lacked such authority. The representation is only binding if made by the company principal rather than by the agent.

Freeman & Lockyer v Buckhurst Park Properties (Mangal) Ltd [1964] 2 QB 480; [1964] 1 All ER 630; (Court of Appeal)

[7.31]   The defendant company had two shareholders, Kapoor and Hoon, who with a nominee each, made up the board of directors. Although the articles provided for the appointment of a managing director, none had ever been appointed. Kapoor, however, was left by the other directors to deal with the day-to-day management of the company. He requested the plaintiff firm of architects and surveyors to do some work for the company. When the plaintiff's eventually sued for their fees they were met by the defence that Kapoor had no authority to engage them. Both the County Court judge and the Court of Appeal held that the company was bound by Kapoor's acts, having implicitly represented that he had been appointed managing director.

[7.32]   **Diplock LJ:** The county court judge made the following findings of fact: (i) that the plaintiffs intended to contract with Kapoor as agent for the defendant company, and not on his own account; (ii) that the board of the defendant company intended that Kapoor should do what he could to obtain the best possible price for the estate; (iii) that Kapoor, although never appointed as managing director, had throughout been acting as such in employing agents and taking other steps to find a purchaser; (iv) that the fact that Kapoor was so acting was well known to the board . . .

The County Court judge did not hold (although he might have done) that actual authority had been conferred on Kapoor by the board to employ agents. He proceeded on the basis of apparent authority, ie that the defendant company had so acted as to be estopped from denying Kapoor's authority. This rendered it unnecessary for the judge to inquire whether actual authority to employ agents had been conferred on Kapoor by the board to whom management of the company's business was confided by the articles of association.

I accept that such actual authority could have been conferred by the board without a formal resolution recorded in the minutes, although this would have rendered them liable to a default fine under s 145(4) of the Companies Act 1948. But to confer actual authority would have required not merely the silent acquiesence of the individual members of the board, but the communication by words or conduct of their respective consents to one another and to Kapoor. [Having reviewed the evidence his lordship continued:] I myself do not feel that there is adequate material to justify the court in reaching the conclusion of fact (which the county court judge refrained from making) that actual authority to employ agents had been conferred by the board on Kapoor.

This makes it necessary to enquire into the state of the law as to the ostensible authority of officers and servants to enter into contracts on behalf of corporations. It is a topic on which there are confusing and, it may be conflicting judgments of the Court of Appeal . . . We are concerned in the present case with the authority of an agent to create contractual rights and liabilities between his principal and a third party whom I call 'the contractor' [His lordship then proceeded to give a review the law which he summarised as follows:]

If the foregoing analysis of the law is correct, it can be summarised by stating four conditions which must be fulfilled to entitle a contractor to enforce against a company a contract entered into on behalf of the company by an agent who had no actual authority to do so. It must be shown: (*a*) that a representation that the agent had authority to enter on behalf of the company into a contract of the kind sought to be enforced was made to the contractor; (*b*) that such representation was made by a person or persons who had 'actual' authority to manage the business of the company either generally or in respect of those matters to which the contract relates; (*c*) that he (the contractor) was induced by such representation to enter into the contract i.e. that he in fact relied on it; and (*d*) that under its memorandum or articles of association the company was not deprived of the capacity either to enter into a contract of the kind sought to be enforced or to delegate authority to enter into a contract of that kind to the agent.

The confusion which, I venture to think, has sometimes crept into the cases is, in my view, due to the failure to distinguish between these four separate conditions, and in particular to keep steadfastly in mind (first) that the only 'actual' authority which is relevant is that of the persons making the representation relied on and (second) that the memorandum and articles of association of the company are always relevant (whether they are in fact known to the contractor or not) to the questions (*i*) whether condition (*b*) is fulfilled, and (*ii*) whether condition (*d*) is fulfilled and (but only if they are in fact known to the contractor) may be relevant (*c*) as part of the representation on which the contractor relied.

In each of the relevant cases the representation relied upon as creating the 'apparent' authority of the agent was by conduct in permitting the agent to act in the management and conduct of part of the business of the company. Except in *Mahony v East Holyford Mining Co Ltd* (1875) LR 7 HL 869, it was the conduct of the board of directors in so permitting the agent to act that was relied upon. As they had, in each case, by the articles of association of the company full 'actual' authority to manage its business, they had 'actual' authority to make representations as to who were agents authorised to enter into contracts on the company's behalf. The agent himself had no 'actual' authority to enter into the contract because the formalities prescribed by the articles for conferring it upon him had not been complied with . . .

In *Mahony's* case no board of directors or secretary had in fact been appointed and it was the conduct of those who, under the constitution of the company were entitled to appoint them which was relied upon as a representation that certain persons were directors and secretary. Since they had 'actual' authority to appoint these officers, they had 'actual' authority to make representations as to who the officers were. In both these cases the constitution of the company, whether it had been seen by the contractor or not, was relevant in order to determine whether the pesons whose representations by conduct were relied upon as creating the 'apparent' authority of the agent had 'actual' authority to make the representations on behalf of the company. In *Mahony's* case if the persons in question were not persons who did not in fact know the constitution of the company, it may well be that the contractor would not succeed in proving condition (3), namely that he relied upon the representations made by those persons, unless he proved that he did in fact know the constitution of the company . . .

In the present case the findings of fact by the county court judge are sufficient to satisfy the four conditions, and thus to establish that Kapoor had 'apparent' authority to enter into contracts on behalf of the defendant company for their services in connexion with the sale of the company's property, including the obtaining of development permission with respect to its use. The judge found that the board knew that Kapoor had throughout been acting as managing director in employing agents and taking other steps to find a purchaser. They permitted him to do so, and by such conduct represented that he had such authority to enter into contracts of a kind which a managing director or an executive director responsible for finding a purchaser would in the normal course be authorised to enter into on behalf of the defendant company. Condition (*a*) was thus fulfilled. The articles of association conferred full powers of management on the board. Condition (*b*) was thus fulfilled. The plaintiffs, finding Kapoor acting in relation to the defendant company's property as he was authorised by the board to act, were induced to believe that he was authorised by the defendant company to enter into contracts on behalf of the company for their services in connection with the sale of the company's property, including the obtaining of development permission with respect to its use. Condition (*c*) was thus fulfilled. The articles of association which contained powers for the board to delegate any of the functions of management to a managing director or to a single director, did not deprive the company of capacity to delegate authority to Kapoor a director to enter into contracts of that kind on behalf of the company. Condition (*d*) was thus fulfilled. I think that the judgment was right and would dismiss the appeal.

Willmer and Pearson LJJ delivered concurring judgments.

Kilgobbin Mink Ltd v National Credit Co Ltd [1980] IR 175 (High Court)

[7.33]   The plaintiff company owed arrears of rent on premises leased by it from the defendant. Ejectment proceedings were commenced by the defendants which were compromised on terms that the plaintiff would surrender the lease in consideration for the waiver of all arrears of rent and the payment to it by the defendant of £8,500. The plaintiff passed a resolution authorising its chairman Leonard to surrender the premises. The chairman owned 49,999 out of 50,000 issued shares in the plaintiff. He directed the defendant to pay the £8,500 to another company Beau Monde Ltd which was controlled by him. This was done by the defendant. The lease having been surrendered, a receiver was subsequently appointed to the company pursuant to the terms of a debenture held by the company's bankers. The receiver issued proceedings in the name of the company for the recovery of the £8,500 from the defendant.

[7.34]   Hamilton J: The questions which I have to determine are partly questions of fact and partly questions of law. So far as the facts are concerned, it is clear from the evidence of Mr Briscoe [the receiver] that Mr Leonard was the chairman of the plaintiff company which had an issued share capital of 50,000 shares; that Mr Leonard held 49,999 of these shares and that Mr McEnroe was the managing director of the plaintiff company and held the remaining issued shares; that Mr Leonard held the majority of the issued shares in Beau Monde; and that Beau Monde was trading in the demised premises though the lease was held by the plaintiff company. It is clear . . . that all the dealings between the plaintiffs and the defendants were conducted by Mr Leonard on behalf of the plaintiffs. It is true that the resolution of the plaintiff company . . . authorises Mr Leonard to surrender the lease but is silent with regard to the consideration for the surrender and the manner of its disposal . . .

169

Though there is no resolution of the plaintiff company authorising Mr Leonard to dispose of the £8,500 in the manner in which he did, I am satisfied, having regard to all of the evidence that he did have such actual authority and that this can be implied from the facts that he was the chairman of the plaintiff company and one of the two directors of the company, that he was the holder of all but one of the issued shares of the company, and that he was the person expressly authorised by the plaintiff company to surrender the lease to the defendants. I am also satisfied that Mr Leonard had ostensible authority to direct or authorise payment of the £8,500 in the manner in which he did authorise that payment, and that the defendants relied on such ostensible authority to make the payment in the manner in which they did.

While on the surface it may appear to be unusual that an amount due to the plaintiff company should be directed to be paid to the credit of another company, in the circumstances of this particular case it was not so unusual as to put the defendants on enquiry as to the extent of Mr Leonard's authority because . . . Beau Monde were trading in the premises which were being surrendered.

If a receiver had not been appointed and if the plaintiff company had sued the defendants for the sum of £8,500, I cannot see how any court would be entitled to hold in favour of the plaintiff company. The receiver is in no different or better position than the plaintiff company. Consequently, in my opinion the plaintiff company's claim fails and I must dismiss the action.

Notes

This case may perhaps, be explained by reference to the degree of control exercised by Leonard over the company. Normally, as has been mentioned supra, neither the position of chairman nor that of shareholders confer on the individual any usual authority to bind the company. For a critical analysis of the decision see *Keane* at para **12.14**.

Doctrine of constructive notice

[7.35]   The ordinary principles of the law of agency have been modified by the courts in the case of companies. The doctrine of constructive notice imputes to members of the public, knowledge of the contents of those documents required by law to be registered with the registrar of companies. These include the memorandum and articles of association, the particulars of the company's directors and secretary, and special resolutions. Normally ordinary resolutions will not require to be registered. A notable exception however, is the resolution under s 20 of the 1983 Act authorising the directors to allot shares.

The doctrine may operate so as to cut down the ostensible authority of the agent of a company. For example, the board of directors has usual power to enter into contracts on behalf of the company. However, in a particular case the articles may provide that contracts can only be concluded by the board on the authority of a special resolution of the general meeting. If no such resolution has been passed the outsider, even though he has not inspected the company's public documents, is deemed to have read the articles, to have seen the limitation on the directors' powers, to have noticed that no such special resolution has been passed and to realise that the directors have no authority to conclude the contract. The doctrine of constructive notice as it applies in such cases can at best be regarded as unjust and ridiculous. It is out of touch with the realities of commercial life. Parties to commercial contracts cannot reasonably be expected to run off to the Companies Office and make a search against a company every time it is intended to do business with that company. In other situations the courts have refused to apply the doctrine of constructive notice to commercial transactions,[1] making the doctrine even more of an oddity. Fortunately, the doctrine is largely redundant as a result of the Indoor Management Rule and reg 6 of the European Communities (Companies) Regulations 1973 (discussed below).

1 *Bank of Ireland Finance Ltd v Rockfield Ltd* (1979) IR 21, 35; *Welch v Bowmaker (Ireland) Ltd* [1980] IR 251; *Manchester Trust v Furness* [1895] 2 QB 539.

[7.36] At common law a person dealing with a company is deemed to have notice of the contents of those documents of the company required by law to be registered.

Ernest v Nicholls (1857) 6 HL Cas 401 (House of Lords)

[7.37] **Lord Wensleydale:** It is obvious that the law as to ordinary partnerships would be inapplicable to a company consisting of a great number of individuals contributing small sums to the common stock, in which case to allow each one to bind the other by any contract which he thought fit to enter into, even within the scope of the partnership business, would soon lead to the utter ruin of the contributories . . .

The legislature then devised the plan of incorporating these companies in a manner unknown to the common law, with special powers of management and liabilities, providing at the same time that all the world should have notice who were the persons authorised to bind all the shareholders, by requiring the co-partnership deed to be registered, certified by the directors and made accessible to all; and, besides, including some clauses as to the management, as in the [Joint Stock Companies Act 1844]. All persons therefore, must take notice of the deed and the provisions of the Act. If they do not choose to acquaint themselves with the powers of the directors, it is their own fault, and if they give credit to any unauthorised persons they must be contented to look to them only and not to the company at large. The stipulations of the deed, which restrict and regulate their authority, are obligatory on those who deal with the company; and the directors can make no contract so as to bind the whole body of shareholders, for whose protection the rules are made, unless they are strictly complied with . . .

Indoor management rule

[7.38] The doctrine of constructive notice has been modified by the 'Indoor Management Rule', also known as the *'Rule in Royal British Bank v Turquand*. This provides that an outsider dealing with a company is entitled to presume that all matters of internal management have been performed as are required by the articles to validate the transaction or to perfect the agent's authority. For example, if an ordinary resolution of the general meeting or a resolution of the board is required to perfect the agent's authority, the outsider is entitled to presume that such resolutions have been passed, as they are mere acts of internal management. He may not, however, presume that acts of internal management have been done, where their performance or otherwise could be discovered from an inspection of the company's registered documents. For example, if the power could only be exercised on the passing of a special resolution, the outsider could not presume that this has been passed as a copy thereof would be registered in the Companies Office. Its absence would indicate that no such resolution had been passed.[1]

1 *Irvine v Union Bank of Australia* (1870) 2 App Cas 366.

[7.39] Unless there are facts putting him on inquiry a person dealing with a company is entitled to presume that all acts of internal management have been performed as are required by the articles of association.

Royal British Bank v Turquand (1856) 6 B & E 327 (Exchequer Chamber)

[7.40] The plaintiff sued Turquand as the official manager of a deed of settlement company, the Coulbrook Steam, Coal and Swansea Railway Co, on a bond which had been given by the company to secure drawings on its overdraft account. The bond was under the company's seal and had been signed by two of its directors and its secretary. The company in its defence pleaded that borrowings by the board were only permitted by a general resolution of the company in general meeting. As no such resolution had been passed the company contended that it was not bound by the bond. This argument was rejected by the court.

[7.41] **Jervis CJ:** The deed allows the directors to borrow on bond such sum or sums of money as shall from time to time, by a resolution passed at a general meeting of the company, be authorised to be borrowed: and the replication shows a resolution, passed at a general meeting, authorising the directors to borrow on bond such sums for such periods and at such rates of interest as they might deem expedient, in accordance with the deed of settlement and the Act of Parliament; but the resolution does not otherwise define the amount to be borrowed. That seems to me enough. If that be so, the other question does not arise. But whether it be so or not we need not decide; for it seems to us that the plea, whether we consider it as a confession and avoidance or a special non est factum, does not raise any objection to

172

this advance as against the company. We may now take for granted that the dealings with these companies are not like dealings with other partnerships, and that the parties dealing with them are bound to read the statute and deed of settlement. But they are not bound to do more. And the party here, on reading the deed of settlement, would find, not a prohibition from borrowing, but a permission to do so on certain conditions. Finding that the authority might be made complete by a resolution, he would have a right to infer the fact of a resolution authorising that which on the face of the document appeared to be legitimately done.

Pollock CB, Alderson and Bramwell BB and Cresswell and Crowder JJ concurred.

Allied Irish Banks Ltd v Ardmore Studios International (1972) Ltd (High Court, 30 May 1973)

[7.42] Finlay J: This matter comes before me on an application for summary judgment by the plaintiffs in respect of their claim for £40,027.30. The claim is made up of a single payment of £37,500 made by the plaintiffs on foot of a cheque dated the 28th of February 1972, the balance of the amount claimed being for interest . . . The defendants seek to avoid judgment upon the grounds that Mr Kelly, the receiver of the property and assets of the defendants appointed on the 17th of November 1972 . . . having caused a search to be made in the books and records of the defendant company, which are all in his possession, can find no record of any meeting of directors of the 28th of February 1972 nor of any resolution being passed by the directors of the defendant company authorising the borrowing of the sum of £37,500 from the plaintiff bank.

The facts . . . are not put in issue or dispute by the defendants. Shortly speaking they are, that in the month of January 1972, Mr John E Nolan, who is a customer of the plaintiff bank, requested a loan from the bank for the purpose of acquiring through the defendant company, the Ardmore Film Studios at Bray in the County of Wicklow. He informed Mr O'Halloran [a representative of the bank] that the defendant company was incorporated on the 21st of January 1972, was known as Ardmore Studios International (1972) Ltd and that he and a Mr George O'Reilly were the sole directors and shareholders of the company. He requested on behalf of the company short-term accommodation in the sum of £37,500 so that the company could place a deposit for that amount and sign a contract for the purchase of the Ardmore property. On behalf of the plaintiffs Mr O'Halloran agreed to issue a cheque for £37,500 . . . for the deposit on the strict understanding that Mr Nolan and Mr O'Reilly were in fact acting as the company's agents and that when a print of the company's memorandum and articles of association was available the company would open its bank account at the plaintiff bank and take over the overdraft formally in its own name. I have no doubt and it is not seriously disputed that Mr O'Halloran believed in these representations and that there were no grounds for suspecting that they or any of them were untrue.

On the 28th of February 1972 a certified copy of a resolution signed by Mr Nolan as director and Mr O'Reilly as secretary and managing director of Ardmore Studios International Ltd was presented to Mr O'Halloran. This certified that a meeting of the directors of the company was held on the 28th of February 1972 and that certain resolutions were passed including a resolution instructing the plaintiff bank to pay all the cheques, drawn on behalf of the company and signed by Mr Nolan and Mr O'Reilly and providing also that the company do borrow from the bank by way of overdraft on foot of their banking account, from time to time to such extent as may be arranged with the bank. At the same time a print of the memorandum of association and articles of association of the defendant company was supplied to Mr O'Halloran. Mr O'Halloran then issued the cheque of 28th February 1972 which is the foundation of this action thus transferring the loan from the personal account of Mr Nolan and Mr O'Reilly to that of the company. Consideration of this memorandum and articles of association indicates that the representations with regard to the structure and powers of the company made to Mr O'Halloran were true and correct except in one matter, that is to say that Mr Nolan and Mr Reilly, although they were the sole subscribers to the company, were not the sole directors, a Mr John Huston being in addition a director. The provisions of part one of table A are incorporated in the articles of association of the company with certain modifications but these do not effect the provision of regulation 102 and therefore the articles of association of the company provide for the transaction of business by directors on a quorum to be fixed by them and unless so fixed to be two. There is no suggestion that any quorum was fixed by the directors. The power of the company to borrow from the bank under its memorandum and articles is not in dispute.

On this set of facts which are not being disputed Mr Farrell on behalf of the plaintiff company contends that the appropriate principle of law which must be applied is that a person or firm dealing with a limited liability company and doing so bona fides is not required to enquire into irregularities in what is described as the internal management of the company and that its transactions are valid notwithstanding the existence of such irregularities if it has acted bona fide. Mr Farrell contends that borrowing from the bank, being within the clear power of the defendant company, if there was no meeting of the directors of the defendant company as is certified by the document of the 28th of February 1972, this comes within the internal management of the company by which his clients are not bound they having manifestly acted bona fide throughout.

Mr McCracken on the other hand contends on behalf of the defendants that this is not an irregularity in the internal management of the company but it is a total gap there being an absence of the fact of a meeting and that this is not something which a person even dealing . . . bona fide with the company, can ignore. He further contends that a perusal of the memorandum and articles of association which indicated that there was a third director, though not a third subscriber to the company, should have put the bank, through its agent, Mr O'Halloran, on notice that the meeting purporting to have been held on the 28th of February 1972 had not taken place.

I am satisfied that Mr Nolan and Mr O'Reilly were on the 28th of February 1972 duly appointed as directors of this company and that they were entitled to hold a valid meeting of the directors with a quorum of two, that is to say without the attendance of the third director. A perusal of the certificate of 28th February 1972 and the memorandum and articles of association would therefore not raise any suspicion of an invalidity in the meeting. Even if one assumes on the affidavits before me that they gave no notice of the holding of such a meeting to the third director who would have been entitled to it, and that they made no record or minute of the meeting, it seems to me that these frailties or defaults in the activity of the two directors of this company are classical examples of an irregularity in the internal management of the company.

I am satisfied therefore that the plaintiffs are entitled to summary judgment.

Ulster Investment Bank Ltd v Euro Estates Ltd [1982] ILRM 57 (High Court)

[7.43]   Two mortgages had been executed by the defendant in favour of the plaintiff bank to secure advances made to it. As a condition of each loan the bank had required sight of the company's memorandum and articles and of board resolutions authorising the taking of the loan and the execution of the deeds of mortgage. The loans were given and the mortgages were executed. However, the defendant company was subsequently wound up and the liquidator sought to challenge both securities. As regards the first mortgage he claimed that it was invalid having been executed at an inquorate board meeting. The articles provided that the quorum was two directors, one appointed by the holders of the 'A' ordinary shareholders and one appointed by the 'B' ordinary shareholders. The resolution had been signed by two 'B' directors.

The second mortgage purported to charge several properties. However, the bank had received a board resolution authorising the execution of the mortgage in respect of only one of the properties. The board assured the bank that a second resolution had been passed including the other properties in the mortgage as well. In fact no such resolution had been passed. The liquidator therefore claimed that the mortgage should only extend to the single property.

Both claims were rejected by Carroll J.

[7.44]   Carroll J: According to the rule in *Royal British Bank v Turquand* (para **7.40**) while persons dealing with a company are assumed to have read the public documents of the company and to have ascertained that the proposed transaction is not inconsistent therewith, they are not required to do more. They need not inquire into the regularity of the internal proceedings and may assume that all is being done regularly.

In *County of Gloucester Bank v Rudry Merthyr Steam and House Coal Colliery Co* [1895] 1 Ch 629 the directors of the joint stock company had power under their articles to fix the number of directors which should form a quorum. By resolution they fixed three as a quorum. A meeting of directors, at which two only were present, authorised the secretary to affix the company's seal to a mortgage, which was accordingly done by the secretary in the presence of the same two directors. It was held that as between the company and the mortgagees who had no notice of the irregularity, the execution of the deed was valid. Lindley LJ says (at 636):

> 'Here the directors may make any quorum they like – it may be two, or it may be three. They did apparently appoint three. The mortgage in question is under the seal of the company, signed by two directors and countersigned by the secretary. Now what could anybody think of that? What is there to put them upon inquiry? What is there to give them notice of anything irregular, if there was anything irregular. If a person looked at the deed and looked at the articles he would not see anything irregular at all; he would be at liberty to infer, and any one in the ordinary course of business would infer, that if the directors had appointed a quorum they appointed the two who signed that deed. But supposing that three were wanted, he is not bound to go and look at the directors' minutes; he has no right to look at them except as a matter of bargain. The directors' minutes unless he knows what they are, do not affect him at all. There is nothing irregular on the face of the deed even taken with the articles – there is nothing illegal in it. As to a plea of non est factum, that could not be sustained for a moment and I have not the slightest doubt myself that that deed is as good as any deed that ever was sealed.'

This passage appears to me to be relevant. In this case both deeds . . . on the face of them have been executed in accordance with the provisions of the articles in that the affixing of the seal has been signed and countersigned by two directors.

In the ordinary way a mortgage dealing with a company is entitled to rely on the rule in the *Royal British Bank v Turquand* and is not obliged to call for copies of resolutions appointing directors or authorising the borrowing (where it is within the directors powers) or approving the form of the mortgage or authorising the affixing of the seal. All of these matters are matters of internal management.

What we are dealing with here is a question whether UIB having required as a condition precedent to the first loan the right to receive and approve copies of the various board resolutions authorising the borrowing, have in some way disentitled themselves to rely on the rule in the *Royal British Bank v Turquand* in respect of matters of internal management relating to both mortgages . . .

I am completely satisfied that UIB acted bona fide throughout. In my opinion they had no reason to believe that the resolution furnished to them as having been passed at a directors meeting on 7 June 1974, was passed at a meeting at which there was no valid quorum present. UIB were entitled to assume where there were two directors present that one was a 'A' director and one was a 'B' director . . .

In relation to the . . . mortgage dated 13 October 1975, it is my opinion that UIB are similarly entitled to rely on the rule in the *Royal British Bank v Turquand* and to assume that the mortgage prepared by it and which on its face is duly executed in accordance with the articles, is the deed of the company.

UIB were aware that a resolution was passed on 10 October 1975 agreeing to give a legal mortgage on 73 Percy Place in consideration of their advancing monies . . . This was sent to them by letter dated 10 October 1975. They also received a telex from Mr Lawlor [one of the directors] on 13 October 1975 representing that the requisite resolutions to give effect to a legal mortgage over the [other properties] would be provided . . .

UIB in drafting the mortgage also included a leasehold interest in Nos 79 and 79a Percy Place and 14 Haddington Road and a leasehold interest in No 81 Percy Place.

In my opinion UIB were entitled to assume that Euro Estates approved the form of mortgage submitted by UIB and that it authorised the affixing of the seal to that mortgage. The single resolution of which UIB had notice was followed by the telex which represented that further resolutions would be provided. In my opinion UIB were not obliged to call for production of any resolution looked after in accordance with the articles. If such resolutions were not passed by Euro Estates, that cannot operate to the detriment of UIB.

Notes

In *Cox v Dublin City Distillery (No 2)* [1915] 1 IR 345, Palles CB said in considering a similar set of facts that 'It has been decided by a long line of cases, extending back certainly for fifty years, that an outsider taking debentures . . . which are invalid merely by reason of a matter of internal management, is entitled to rely on the seal of the company as showing that everything connected with such management is right, unless he has notice to the contrary . . . of any irregularity.' See generally McCormack *The Indoor Management Rule in Ireland* (1985) 79 Gazette 17.

In *Re Irish Grain (Trading Board) Ltd* (High Court, 26 November 1984) McWilliam J stated obiter that the submission of a draft resolution by an outsider for execution by the directors would not of itself, deprive the outsider of the benefit of the *Rule in Turquand's Case*.

[7.45] The indoor management rule will not protect a person who has notice of the irregularity.

AL Underwood Ltd v Bank of Liverpool and Martin [1924] 1 KB 775
(King's Bench Division)

[7.46] Mr Underwood had a personal account with the defendant bank. He formed the plaintiff company to acquire his existing business. The bank knew of the formation of the company but was unaware that it had an account with another bank. Mr Underwood who was the major shareholder and sole director of the plaintiff lodged cheques payable to it in his personal account with the bank. The company subsequently went into receivership and successfully sued the bank for conversion of its cheques. The court held that the lodging of company cheques into the personal account of its agent was so exceptional and unusual as to put the bank on inquiry. Accordingly it could not rely on the indoor management rule by way of a defence to the action.

[7.47] **Bankes LJ:** The strangeness of [Underwood's] conduct . . . in my opinion, is material not only upon the issue of negligence, but also because it brings into operation what appears to me to be an undoubted branch of the rule of law upon which this defence of the appellants rests. In *Mahony v East Holyford Mining Co* Lord Hatherley states the whole rule thus: 'And the bankers must also be taken to have had knowledge from the articles, of the duties of the directors, and the mode in which the directors were to be appointed. But after that, when there are persons conducting the affairs of the company in a manner which appears to be perfectly consonant with the articles of association, then those so dealing with them, externally, are not to be affected by any irregularities which may take place in the internal management of the company. They are entitled to presume that that of which only they can have knowledge, namely, the external acts, are rightly done, when those external acts purport to be performed in the mode in which they ought to be performed. For instance, when a cheque is signed by three directors, they are entitled to assume that those directors are persons properly appointed for the purpose of performing that function and have properly performed the function for which they have been appointed. Of course, the case is open to any observation arising from gross negligence or fraud. I pass that by as not entering into the consideration of the question at the present time. Outside persons when they find that there is an act done by a company, will of course, be bound in the exercise of ordinary care and precaution to know whether or not that company is actually carrying on and transacting business or whether it is a company which has been stopped and wound up and which has parted with its assets and the like. All those ordinary enquiries which mercantile men would in the course of their business make, I apprehend, would have to be made on the part of the persons dealing with the company.'

Applying Lord Hatherley's language to the facts of this case I ask myself what are the ordinary enquiries which mercantile men would, in the course of their business have made on presentation of these cheques for collection. On the assumption that the appellants' cashiers were acting in entire good faith in taking in these cheques without any inquiry whatever, the conclusion seems to me almost irresistible that for some reason or another they considered that they were still dealing with Underwood, the old customer, the principal, and not with a new Underwood, an agent. As, however, the appellants are relying on a rule of law applicable only to dealings with an agent they must take the rule as they find it, and if they have omitted, as I am clearly of opinion they have omitted, to make an ordinary inquiry they must take the consequences. Now what are the facts? The cheques were plainly, on the face of them, the property of the company. They were indorsed by Underwood as sole director, a fact which, instead of absolving the cashiers from inquiry, appears to me to demand the exercise of greater caution on their part, having regard to the fact that the cheques were being paid in to Underwood's private account. Many of the cheques were marked in a way which of itself, ought to have put the cashiers on inquiry. I entirely accept the view of the learned judge with regard to the conduct of the cashiers and I think his conclusion establishes not only negligence on their part, but such an absence of ordinary inquiry as to disentitle to appellants from relying on a defence founded on the ostensible authority of Underwood. I feel satisfied that the obvious inquiry whether the company had not got its own banking account would have put a stop to the fraudulent system adopted by Underwood and I do not think that it lies in the mouth of the appellants to say that an inquiry would have been useless.

Scrutton and Atkin LJJ delivered concurring judgments.

Notes

See also *B Liggett (Liverpool) Ltd v Barclays Bank Ltd* [1928] 1 KB 48; *Rolled Steel Products (Holdings) Ltd v British Steel Corporation* [1984] BCLC 466.

[7.48] The indoor management rule has no application in the case of a forgery.

Ruben v Great Fingall Consolidated [1906] AC 439 (House of Lords)

[7.49] In return for an advance of monies the secretary of the company had affixed the company seal to the certificate without due authorisation. He also forged the signatures of the two directors which appeared on the certificate. The issue before the court was whether the company was estopped by the share certificate.

[7.50] **Lord Loreburn LC:** I cannot see upon what principle your Lordships can hold that the defendants are liable in this action. The forged certificate is a pure nullity. It is quite true that persons dealing with limited liability companies are not bound to inquire into their indoor management and will not be affected by irregularities of which they had no notice. But this doctrine which is well established, applies only to irregularities that otherwise might affect a genuine transaction. It cannot apply to a forgery . . .

Notes

This decision has been followed in *Kreditbank Cassel v Schenkers* [1927] 1 KB 826 and *S. London Greyhound Racecourses v Wake* [1931] 1 Ch 496. cf

Uxbridge Building Society v Pickard [1939] 2 KB 248 where a solicitor was held liable for the frauds of his clerk even though they involved forgery. In the *Rubens* case the outsider was on notice of the irregularity. It may be therefore, that the indoor management rule should still apply in the case of forgeries provided the agent was acting within his apparent authority and the outsider was unaware of the irregularity. See *Keane* at para **12.18**.

[7.51] The indoor management rule only protects outsiders. Those within the company such as directors are in a position to know if there has been compliance with the internal procedures. However, if a director is dealing with the company qua outsider he may still be able to claim the protection of the rule.

Hely-Hutchinson v Brayhead Ltd [1967] 2 All ER 14

[7.52] The plaintiff (who is referred to in the judgment as Lord Suirdale) had issued proceedings to enforce two letters of indemnity issued purportedly on behalf of the defendant company by its chairman, Richards. The trial judge (Roskill J) rejected an argument by the defendant, that because the plaintiff was one of the directors, he should be presumed to know that Richards had not been authorised to issue the two letters of indemnity.[1]

1 This issue did not arise in the Court of Appeal, as it was found at that stage that Richards had actual authority to act in the matter.

[7.53]   Roskill J: It seems plain on the cases that if Lord Suirdale were a 'third party' as it is sometimes called, or an outside party or a 'stranger' in relation to these transactions he would prima facie be entitled to rely on the rule in *Royal British Bank v Turquand* (para **7.40**).

I have no doubt whatever that Mr Richards represented to the plaintiff that he had authority, on behalf of Brayhead, to enter into contracts of this kind . . . What is . . . contended . . . is that the plaintiff was a director of Brayhead and as a director of Brayhead (even though there would vis-a-vis a true third party be ostensible or apparent authority) the plaintiff cannot take advantage of the rule in *Turquand's* case because he is not for the purposes of that rule, a 'stranger' or an 'outsider' or a 'third party' whichever phrase one chooses to use. Counsel for the defendants naturally based this branch of his argument on the decision of the House of Lords . . . in *Morris v Kanssen* [1946] 1 All ER 586, [1946] AC 459 . . . Suffice it to say that Mr Morris the appellant had thought the he had acquired certain shares in that company, having along with other purported directors purported to allot them to himself. He sought to rely on the rule in *Turquand's* case for the purpose of establishing rights against the respondent, Kanssen. Lord Simonds who delivered the leading speech, rejected the argument . . . After stressing that Morris had been himself acting as a director in the allotment and issue of the shares to himself and others and that he was at all times the officer and agent of the company for that purpose, Lord Simonds said:

'What then is the position of the director or acting director who claims to hold the company to a transaction which the company had not, though it might have authorised? Your lordships have not in this case to consider what the result might be if such a director had not himself purported to act on behalf of the company in the unauthorised transaction. For here Morris was himself purporting to act on behalf of the company in a transaction in which he had no authority. Can he then say that he was entitled to assume that all was in order? My lords, the old question comes into my mind, "*Quis custodiet ipsos custodes*".'

It must be observed in relation to the passages which I have just read that Morris the alleged director, in doing what he did, had been acting for and on behalf of the company. As I read Lord Simonds' speech it was the fact that he had been acting for and on behalf of the company which disentitled him later to turn round as allottee of the shares and seek to take advantage of the rule in *Turquand's* case in his own favour . . .

The plaintiff did not act on behalf of Brayhead in relation to the allegedly unauthorised transaction. But leading counsel for the defendants and in his admirable argument following his learned leader, their junior counsel said it was enough to exclude the operation of the rule in *Turquand's* case, that the plaintiff was a party to the transaction and was a director of Brayhead, even though he did not act for Brayhead. With the utmost respect to that argument and the skill with which it was advanced by both counsel for the defendants, I find nothing in these cases which compels me to go so far as they have invited me to go. In some cases – and of course *Morris's* case is one and *Howard's* case is another – a director is quite plainly anything but a 'stranger' or an 'outsider' or a 'third party', but I do not think that the mere fact that a director of a company makes a contract with that company in a capacity other than that of a director, automatically affects him in the capacity in which he is contracting with constructive knowledge of such disabilities and limitations as he might be deemed to know were he also acting for the company in the transaction in question. As counsel for the plaintiff said in the course of his reply, to extend this doctrine in the way suggested would have very far reaching ramifications on ordinary day-to-day business transactions and would or might, involve very often considerable enquiry before a contract could be signed what the respective position and authority was of a particular individual by whom it was proposed that a contract should be signed. I regard the decisions in *Morris v Kanssen* and in *Howard's* case as decisions where on the facts of those particular cases, the rights sought to be enforced by the plaintiffs concerned arose from acts done by them as directors which were so closely interwoven with their duties and acts as directors as to make it impossible for the directors involved to say that they were not for all purposes to be treated as possessed of knowledge of the limitations on their powers as directors. In the present case Brayhead's agreement with the plaintiff had nothing to do with his duties and obligations as a director of Brayhead. What he was doing was to agree to advance money to an associated company of Brayhead of which he was

181

chairman and managing director against a guarantee and indemnity from Brayhead, who were expected to become the parent company of that associated company. He was acting, as I think, otherwise than in his capacity as a director of Brayhead in making that agreement. He was acting as an individual for it was he who was going to advance the money in consideration of the agreement into which Mr Richards was purporting to enter on behalf of Brayhead. He was going to be the other contracting party. I think therefore that this argument fails.

Notes

See also the comments of Lynch J in *PMPS Ltd v Moore* (High Court, 8 November 1988). This case related to a purchase of shares by the plaintiff from the defendant. It was unsuccessfully contended that the transaction was ultra vires the company. It was however, accepted by Lynch J that the agent of the plaintiff who concluded the purchase was acting in want of authority. His lordship said that the agent did not have power or authority to bind the plaintiff to such a purchase and of course the defendant as a member of the committee of management [the equivalent of a board of directors] is not entitled to rely on s 8 of the Companies Act 1963.

It would appear that Lynch J was here confusing the authority of a company's agents with the capacity of the company itself.

European Communities (Companies) Regulations 1973

[7.54] The doctrine of constructive notice is now largely redundant as a result of the 1973 regulations. Its only application in future will be to unlimited companies.[1] Reg 10 limits the circumstances in which an outsider will have constructive notice of documents which have been delivered to the registrar.

1 ie the memorandum and articles of association.

Regulation 10: Failure to notify documents.

[7.55] The documents and particulars, notice of which is required by these regulations to be published in Iris Oifigiuil may not be relied upon by the company as against any other person until after such publication unless the company proves that such person had knowledge of them. However, with regard to transactions taking place before the sixteenth day after the date of publication, they shall not be relied upon against a person who proves that it was impossible for him to have had knowledge of them.

Regulation 6: See para 7.15.

[7.56] This regulation has been of even greater effect than reg 10 in abolishing the doctrine of constructive notice of the company's registered documents. The outsider dealing in 'good faith' with the board of directors or registered agent, may enforce the transaction even where it was beyond the authority of the board or the agents. He is no longer deemed to have inspected the company's public documents. Nor indeed is he under any duty to make such an inspection.

The agency aspect of regulation 6 is based on article 9(2) of the First Companies Directive.

Council Directive 68/151/EEC of 9 March 1968

[7.57] Art 9(2) – The limits on the powers of the organs of the company, arising under the statutes[1] or from a decision of the competent organs, may never be relied on as against third parties, even if they have been disclosed.

1 This issue did not arise in the Court of Appeal, as it was found at this stage that Richards had actual authority to act in the matter.

[7.58] Lack of good faith is not established merely by showing that the outsider is on notice of internal irregularities and that these irregularities could be discovered by inspecting the company's public documents.

TCB Ltd v Gray [1986] 1 All ER 587 (Chancery Division)

[7.59] Gray had executed a guarantee in favour of the plaintiff bank TCB, to secure the indebtedness of two companies of which he was a director, Graylaw and Link. Gray was subsequently sued on the guarantee. The debenture evidencing Link's debt had been signed by a Mr Rowan, acting as Gray's attorney. However, by way of defence it was argued that the guarantee was void as cl 113 of Link's articles required the director to sign personally.

[7.60] **Browne-Wilkinson VC:** The debenture was not signed by any director of Link, but by an attorney for a director. There is no power in the articles of Link for a director to act by an attorney. Therefore, says counsel for the defendant, on the principle *delegatus non potest delegare* the seal was not affixed in accordance with the requirements of the articles: accordingly the debenture is not the act of Link.

Apart from s 9(1) of the European Communities Act 1972 [ie reg 6 of the 1973 Regulations], there would be much force in these submissions. But in my judgment that section provides a complete answer. Under the old law, a person dealing with a corporation was required to look at the company's memorandum and articles to satisfy himself that the transaction was within the corporate capacity of the company and was to be carried through in accordance with the requirements of its articles. The rigour of those requirements was only tempered to the extent that the rule in *Royal British Bank v Turquand* (para **7.40**) allowed third parties to assume that acts of internal management had been properly carried out.

It has been generally assumed that the old law has to a large extent been swept away by s 9(1) of the 1972 Act which provides as follows:

'In favour of a person dealing with a company in good faith, any transaction decided on by the directors shall be deemed to be one which it is within the capacity of the company to enter into, and the power of the directors to bind the company shall be deemed to be free of any limitation under the memorandum or articles of association; and a party to a transaction so decided on shall not be bound to enquire as to the capacity of the company to enter into it or as to any such limitation on the powers of the directors and shall be presumed to have acted in good faith unless the contrary is proved.'

Section 9(1) was passed to bring the law of England into line with art 9 of Council Directive 68/151 of the European Economic Community. In approaching the construction of the section, it is in my judgment relevant to note that the manifest purpose of both the directive and the section is to enable people to deal with a company in good faith without being adversely affected by any limits on the company's capacity or its rule for internal management. Given good faith, a third party is able to deal with a company through its 'organs' (as the directive describes them) or directors. Section 9(1) achieves this in two ways. First it 'deems' all transactions to be authorised. Second, it 'deems' that the directors can bind the company without limitations. The second part of the section reinforces this by expressly abolishing the old doctrine of constructive notice of the contents of a company's memorandum and articles. It being the obvious purpose of the section to obviate the commercial inconvenience and frequent injustice caused by the old law, I approach the construction of the section with a great reluctance to construe it in such a way as to reintroduce, through the back door, any requirement that a third party acting in good faith must still investigate the regulating documents of a company.

Counsel for the defendant (Mr Brodie QC) whilst accepting that TCB had no actual or imputed knowledge of any irregularity in the execution of the debenture, at first submitted that TCB did not act in 'good faith' within the meaning of the section since TCB was put on inquiry by the unusual manner in which the debenture had been executed. He said that TCB should have looked at the articles and would then have discovered the irregularity. Accordingly, he submitted, they were not acting in 'good faith'. On further consideration counsel for the defendant abandoned this argument, to my mind rightly. The last words of the second part of the subsection expressly provide that good faith is to be presumed: the second part further provides that the person dealing with the company is not bound to inquire as to the limitations on the powers of the directors. In my judgment it is impossible to establish lack of 'good faith' within the meaning of the section solely by alleging that inquiries ought to have been made which the second part of the subsection says need not be made.

Counsel for the defendant's next submission was that, in order for the section to apply at all, the first requirement is that there must be a transaction by the company. Since Link never sealed the debenture in the only way authorised by the articles there was here no transaction by Link at all: the debenture was not the act of Link. If this argument is right, it drives a coach and horses through the section: in every dealing with the company the third party would have to look at its articles to ensure that the company was binding itself in an authorised manner. In my judgment the section does not have that effect. The section is dealing with purported actions by a company which, having regard to its internal documents, may be a nullity eg acts outside its corporate capacity. In such a case under the old law the purported act of the company would not be the act of the company at all. Yet the first part of s 9(1) deems it to be so. Similarly a document under seal by the company executed otherwise than in accordance with its articles was not, under the old law, the act of the company: but s 9(1) deems it to be since the powers of the directors are deemed to be free from limitations, ie as to the manner of affixing the company's seal. In my judgment, s 9(1) applies to transactions which a company purports to enter into and deems them to be validly entered into.

Counsel for the defendant also submitted that art 113 (regulating the way in which Link can seal documents) is not a 'limitation' on the powers of directors to bind the company but a mandatory direction as to the only way in which the company can bind itself. I reject this submission also. Link has either actual or (under s 9(1)) deemed capacity to enter into the debenture. Being an artificial person Link can only enter into the debenture by its agents, the directors. Any provision in the articles as to the manner in which the directors can act as agents for the company is a limitation on their power to bind the company and as such falls within the first part of s 9(1).

Finally, counsel for the defendant submitted that in order to rely on the section it has to be shown that the debenture was a transaction 'decided on by the directors'. I agree. Then, says counsel for the defendant, the evidence shows that the directors of Link never did decide to enter into this debenture. The facts as I find them are that on completion of the loan there was handed to TCB a minute of a board meeting of Link held on 25 January 1982. That minute records that there were present Mr Gray, Mr Pond, Mr Green and Mr Rowan. Paragraph 2 of the minute, after reciting the proposal to grant the debenture, continued:

'It was therefore resolved that the facility be accepted and the form of debenture in favour of TCB be executed under the common seal of the company in the presence of Messrs Rowan (as attorney for Mr Gray) and Mr Green.'

Paragraph 5 of the minute provided as follows:

'It was further resolved that Messrs Rowan and Green may be authorised to deliver the said debenture to TCB and that they may be also empowered to execute any other documents required by TCB to complete the security documentation.'

The minutes are signed by Mr Rowan 'as Attorney for V Gray'. The evidence clearly established that no such meeting of the directors of Link ever took place. But in fact all the directors of Link individually had decided to grant the debenture, although not at a meeting at which they were all present.

It has to be borne in mind on this aspect of the case that I have to determine whether a valid debenture was granted by Link. In my judgment, Link, having put forward the minutes of the meeting of 25 January as one of the completion documents on the basis of which TCB made the loan, could not be heard to challenge the validity of that minute by denying that such meeting ever took place. Therefore the minute stands as irrefutable evidence against Link that the grant of the debenture was a 'transaction decided upon by the directors'.

Accordingly the necessary basis for s 9(1) of the 1972 Act to apply as between Link and TCB exists. It follows that the debenture was valid and Mr Gray's second line of defence also fails.

Notes

This case clearly establishes that the constructive notice rule has been abolished where the transaction was 'decided upon by the directors'. On the interpretation of reg 6 in so far as it applies to the ultra vires rule see *International Sales and Agencies Ltd v Marcus* [1982] 3 All ER 551; *International Factors (NI) Ltd v Streeve Construction Ltd* [1984] NI 245.

Chapter 8

TORT AND CRIME

TORTIOUS LIABILITY

[8.01]   Most classes of torts may be commited against the company.[1] However, it cannot suffer torts such as assault, battery and false imprisonment which depend on the human characteristics of the injured party.[2]

The company may also be sued in respect of torts commited by it. As it is an artificial entity it can only act through agents. It is vicariously liable for torts of these agents acting in the course of their employment with the company. However, in certain circumstances, the tort may be considered the act of the company itself and not just the act of its agent.[3]

1 See generally *Keane* chapter 13; See Ashten Cross *Liability of Corporations for the Torts of their Servants* (1950) 10 CLJ 419.
2 McMahon & Binchy *Irish Law of Torts* (Abingdon, 1981) p 74.
3 Although presumably, because it has had to act through an agent the company could also be considered liable on the ground of vicarious liability.

[8.02]   The act of an agent may be regarded as the act of the company itself if that agent is the 'directing mind and will' of the company.

Lennard's Carrying Co Ltd v Asiatic Petroleum Co Ltd [1915] AC 705
(House of Lords)

[8.03]   The appellant company was the owner of a ship the Edward Dawson which (together with her cargo) was lost at sea due to unseaworthiness. The respondent company was the owner of the lost cargo. The appellant as owner of the ship could under s 502 of the Merchant Shipping Act 1894 limit its liability if it could show that the loss happened without its 'actual fault or privity'. The trial judge found for the respondents and this was confirmed on appeal by the Court of Appeal and on further appeal by the House of Lords.

[8.04]   **Viscount Haldane LC:** The appellants are a limited company and the ship was managed by another limited company, Messrs John M Leonard & Sons and Mr J M Lennard who seems to be the active director in J M Lennard's Carrying Company Ltd. My Lords, in that state of things what is the question of law which arises? I think that it is impossible in the face of the findings of the learned judge and of the evidence, to contend successfully that Mr J M Lennard has shown that he did not know or can excuse himself for not having known of the defects which manifested themselves in the condition of the ship, amounting to unseaworthiness. Mr Lennard is the person who is registered in the ship's register and is designated as the person to whom the management of the vessel was entrusted. He appears to have been the active spirit in the joint stock company which managed this ship for the appellants; and under the circumstances the question is whether the company can invoke the protection of s 502 of the Merchant Shipping Act to relieve it from the liability which the respondents seek to impose on it . . .

Now, my Lords, did what happened take place without the actual fault or privity of the owners of the ship who were the appellants? My lords, a corporation is an abstraction. It has no mind of its own any more than it has a body of its own; its active and directing will must consequently be sought in the person of somebody who for some purposes may be called an agent, but who is really the directing mind and will of the corporation. That person may be under the direction of the shareholders in general meeting; that person may be the board of directors itself, or it may be, and in some companies it is so, that that person has an authority co-ordinate with the board of directors given to him under the articles of association, and is appointed by the general meeting of the company and can only be removed be the general meeting of the company. My Lords, whatever is not known about Mr Lennard's position, this is known for certain, Mr Lennard took the active part in the management of this ship on behalf of the owners and Mr Lennard as I have said, was registered as the person designated for this purpose in the ship's register. Mr Lennard therefore was the natural person to come on behalf of the owners and give full evidence not only about the events of which I have spoken, and which related to the seaworthiness of the ship, but about his own position and as to whether or not he was the life and soul of the company. For if Mr Lennard was the directing mind of the company, then his action must, unless a corporation is not to be liable at all, have been an action which was the action of the company itself within the meaning of s 502. It has not been contended . . . and it could not have been successfully contended, that s 502 is so worded as to exempt a corporation altogether which happens to be the owner of a ship, merely because it happens to be a corporation. It must be upon the true construction of that section in such a case as the present one that the fault or privity is the fault or privity of somebody who is not merely a servant or agent for whom the company is liable upon the footing respondent superior, but somebody for whom the company is liable because his action is the very action of the company itself. It is not enough that the fault should be the fault of a servant in order to exonerate the owner, the fault must also be one which is not the fault of the owner, or a fault to which the owner is a privity; and I take the view that when anybody sets up that section to excuse himself from the normal consequences of the maxim respondent superior the burden lies upon him to do so.

Lord Dunedin delivered a concurring judgment. Lords Atkinson, Parker of Waddington and Parmoor concurred.

Notes
It is clear that Mr Lennard was the 'directing mind and will' of J M Lennard & Sons. The judgment does not indicate precisely the grounds upon which he became the 'directing mind and will' of the appellant. For a further case which deals with the application of s 502 of the 1894 Act to a company see *The Lady Gwendolen* [1965] P 294.

[8.05] A company may be liable in tort, even if the act in question is ultra vires.

Campbell v Paddington Corporation [1911] 1 KB 869 (King's Bench Divisional Court)

[8.06] The council of the defendant corporation passed a resolution authorising the erection of a stand in Edgware. It was subsequently held liable in damages for the consequent public nuisance. The court rejected the plea that as the erection of the stand was ultra vires the corporation, it could not be held liable in tort.

[8.07] **Avory J:** First, it is said that the defendants, the mayor, aldermen and councillors of the metropolitan borough of Paddington being a corporation are not liable because the borough had no legal right to do what they did, and therefore the corporation cannot be sued. This stand was erected in pursuance of a formal resolution of the borough council. To say that, because the borough council had no legal right to erect it, therefore the corporation cannot be sued is to say that no corporation can ever be sued for any tort or wrong. The only way in which this corporation can act is by its council and the resolution of the council is the authentic act of the corporation. If the view of the defendants were correct no company could ever be sued if the directors of the company after resolution did an act which the company by its memorandum of association had no power to do. That would be absurd. The first objection therefore fails, and the defendants are liable to be sued.

Lush J: The second contention was that the act of the defendants was illegal and that therefore the only persons to be sued in respect of it are those individuals who authorised it. In support of this contention the case of *Poulton v London and South Western Ry Co* LR 2 QB 534 was cited. In that case a stationmaster, being a servant of the defendants, without any instructions or authority from the defendants gave the plaintiff into custody for refusing to pay for the carriage of his horse. The question was whether the act of the stationmaster in giving the plaintiff into custody was within the scope of his employment. It was held that, as the defendants themselves could not lawfully have done the act, it could not be within the scope of their servant's employment to do it. That case was only an illustration of the principle that where the wrongful act is done without the express authority of the corporation, an authority from the corporation to do it cannot be implied if the act is outside the statutory powers of the corporation. That principle has no application to a case where the corporation has resolved to do and has, in the only way in which it can do any act, actually done the thing which is unlawful and which causes the damage complained of. The only matter which raised any doubt in my mind upon this part of the case was that the resolution might appear to have been passed for the personal benefit of the borough councillors themselves; but the answer is that the borough councillors in their individual capacity could have no more jurisdiction over the street in question than any other member of the public. The resolution was the resolution of the corporation and the act which caused the damage, no matter for whose benefit it was done was the act of the corporation and not of the individual councillors who resolved to do it. Therefore there are no grounds for saying that the defendants are not responsible for it.

Notes

See also *National Telephone Co Ltd v The Constables of St Peter Port* [1900] AC 317, 321. The accepted view of modern text-book writers is that the *Poulton* case cited by Lush J no longer represents the law. Agents of a company may have implied authority to commit acts which are ultra vires that company and the company may therefore be vicariously liable in tort for those acts. See *McMahon & Binchy*, op cit at p 76; generally on this topic. See Jenkins *Corporate Liability in Tort and the Doctrine of Ultra Vires* (1970) 5 Ir Jur (ns) 11.

Criminal liability

[8.08]   A company can commit crimes.[1] However, as it is an artificial entity there are certain crimes of a particularly human nature which it cannot commit, such as bigamy or incest. At common law the doctrine of vicarious liability does not apply to crimes,[2] so that, in the absence of some statutory exception, the company will not be liable for unauthorised crimes committed by its agents in the course of their employment. Normally therefore, the company will only be criminally liable where the acts of the agent can be attributed to the company itself. See *Tesco Supermarkets Ltd v Natrass* (para **8.12**). It is to this agent (or collection of agents in the case, for example, of the board of directors) that one must look in order to ascertain whether the company had the requisite mens rea.[3] The issue of mens rea will not, however, arise in the case of offences of strict liability.[4]

---

1 See *Keane* at para **13.04** et seq; Winn *The Criminal Responsibility of Corporations* (1929) 3 CLJ 398; Welsh *The Criminal Liability of Corporations* (1946) 62 LQR 345. Under s 11(*c*)(*i*) of the Interpretation Act 1937 there is a presumption that 'person' include corporate bodies.
2 *Tesco Supermarkets Ltd v Natrass* [1972] AC 153; 199 (per Lord Diplock).
3 *H L Bolton & Co Ltd v T J Graham & Sons Ltd* [1957] 1 QB 159, 173.
4 See *R (King) v The Chairman and Justices of Antrim* [1906] 2 IR 298. See also *Wedick v Osmond & Son* (Dublin) Ltd [1935] IR 820.

[8.09] A company may commit an offence, an essential ingredient of which is mens rea.

R (Cottingham) v The Justices of County Cork [1906] 2 IR 415 (King's Bench)

[8.10] **Johnston J:** A limited liability company is capable of suing and liable to be sued in almost every kind of action in the nature of tort or contract. It may be made criminally responsible for most offences which are not punishable solely by imprisonment or corporal punishment. It may be enjoined, and its property may be sequestered for payment of its debts or fines imposed for offences.

Notes

When Johnson J says that a company cannot be made criminally responsible for offences punishable solely by imprisonment or corporal punishment, he presumably means that it cannot be punished and not that it cannot commit the crime. Other punishments such as fines or sequestration of assets can be suffered by a company. The latter order may be appropriate where the company is guilty of criminal contempt of court: *Re Hibernia National Review* [1976] IR 388, 392.

[8.11] The mental intent of those who have been given control of the particular situation by the company, will be ascribed to the company itself.

Tesco Supermarkets Ltd v Natrass [1971] 2 All ER 127 (House of Lords)

[8.12] Tesco Supermarkets Ltd ran a national chain of supermarkets. It was charged under s 11(2) of the Trade Descriptions Act 1968 with selling a packet of washing powder for a higher price than was advertised. The branch in question had temporarily run out of stocks at a special reduced price. An assistant restocked the shelves with packets at the normal price. She should have informed the branch manager of this but failed to do so. He failed to notice the difference in price between the posters and the packets on the shelves. The manager was responsible for ensuring that either stocks of 'special offer' goods were on the shelves or alternatively that the 'special offer' notices were taken down. This he had failed to do. The company's board had issued to its various branches extensive instructions and guidelines designed to ensure that the Act was not infringed. Under s 24 of the Act it was a defence for the accused person to prove that the commission of the offence was due to the act or default of some other person and that the accused had taken all reasonable precautions and had exercised all due diligence to avoid the commission of the offence. The company successfully pleaded the s 24 defence. It was held that the branch manager was only a subordinate. He was not the 'directing mind and will' of the company and therefore his acts could not be attributed to the company. Additionally, in view of the extensive instructions which had been issued by the company to ensure compliance with the Act it was held that all due diligence had been taken to avoid the commission of the offence.

[8.13]   Lord Reid: Where a limited company is the employer difficult questions do arise in a wide variety of circumstances in deciding which of its officers or servants is to be identified with the company so that his guilt is the guilt of the company.

I must start by considering the nature of the personality which by a fiction the law attributes to a corporation. A living person has a mind which can have knowledge or intention or be negligent and he has hands to carry out his intentions. A corporation has none of these: it must act through living persons, though not always one or the same person. Then the person who acts is not speaking or acting for the company. He is acting as the company and his mind which directs his acts is the mind of the company. There is no question of the company being vicariously liable. He is not acting as a servant, representative, agent or delegate. He is an embodiment of the company, or, one could say, he hears and speaks through the persona of the company, within his appropriate sphere and his mind is the mind of the company. If it is a guilty mind then that guilt is the guilt of the company. It must be a question of law whether once the facts have been ascertained, a person in doing particular things is to be regarded as the company or merely as the company's servant or agent. In that case any liability of the company can only be a statutory or vicarious liability . . .

Reference is frequently made to the judgment of Denning LJ in *HL Bolton (Engineering) Co Ltd v TJ Graham & Sons Ltd* [1957] 1 QB 159. He said at p 172:

'A company may in many ways be likened to a human body. It has a brain and nerve centre which controls what it does. It also has hands which hold the tools and act in accordance with directions from the centre. Some of the people in the company are mere servants and agents who are nothing more than hands to do the work and cannot be said to represent the mind or will. Others are directors and managers who represent the directing mind and will of the company and control what it does. The state of mind of these managers is the state of mind of the company and is treated by the law as such.'

In that case the directors of the company only met once a year: they left the management of the business to others and it was the intention of those managers which was imputed to the company. I think that was right. There have been attempts to apply Lord Denning's words to all servants of a company whose work is brain work or who exercise some managerial discretion under the direction of superior officers of the company. I do not think that Lord Denning intended to refer to them. He only referred to those who 'represent the directing mind and will of the company and control what it does.'

I think that is right for this reason. Normally the board of directors, the managing director and perhaps other superior officers of a company carry out the functions of management and speak and act as the company. Their subordinates do not. They carry out orders from above and it can make no difference that they are given some measure of discretion. But the board of directors may delegate some part of their functions of management giving to their delegate full discretion to act independently of instructions from them. I see no difficulty in holding that they have thereby put such a delegate in their place so that within the scope of the delegation he can act as the company. It may not always be easy to draw the line but there are cases in which the line must be drawn.

In some cases the phrase alter ego has been used. I think it is misleading. When dealing with a company the word alter is I think misleading. The person who speaks and acts as the company is not alter. He is identified with the company. And when dealing with an individual no other individual can be his alter ego. The other individual can be a servant, agent, delegate, representative but I know of neither principle nor authority which warrants the confusion (in the literal or original sense) of two separate individuals . . .

I have already said that the phrase alter ego is misleading. In my judgment this case was wrongly decided and should be overruled. When the second statute introduced a defence if the accused proved that 'he used all due diligence' I think that it meant what it said. As a matter of construction I can see no ground for reading in 'he and all persons to whom he has delegated responsibility.' And if I look to the purpose and apparent intention of Parliament in enacting this defence I think that it was plainly intended to make a just and reasonable distinction between the employer who is wholly blameless and ought to be acquitted and the employer who was in some way at fault, leaving it to the employer to prove that he was in no way to blame . . . I have said that a board of directors can delegate part of their functions of management so as to make their delegate an embodiment of the company within the spheres of the delegation. But here the board never delegated any part of their functions. They set up a chain of command through regional and district supervisors but they remained in control. The shop managers had to obey their general directions and also take orders from their superiors. The acts or omissions of shop managers were not acts of the company itself.

Lord Diplock: My Lords, a corporation incorporated under the Companies Act 1948 owes its corporate personality and its powers to its constitution, the memorandum and articles of association. The obvious and the only place to look to discover by what natural persons its powers are exercisable, is in its constitution. The articles of association, if they follow table A, provide that the business of the company shall be managed by the directors and that they may 'exercise all such powers of the company' as are not required by the Act to be exercised in general meeting. Table A also vests in the directors the right to entrust and confer upon a managing director any of the powers of the company which are exercisable by them. So it may also be necessary to ascertain whether the directors have taken any action under this provision or any other similar provision providing for the coordinate exercise of the powers of the company by executive directors or by committees of directors and other persons, such as are frequently included in the articles of association of companies in which the regulations contained in table A are modified or excluded in whole or in part.

In my view, therefore, the question: what natural persons are to be treated in law as being the company for the purpose of acts done in the course of its business, including the taking of precautions and the exercise of due diligence to avoid the commission of a criminal offence, is to be found by identifying those natural persons who by the memorandum and articles of association or as a result of action taken by the directors, or by the company in general meeting pursuant to the articles, are entrusted with the exercise of the powers of the company.

Lord Morris of Borth-y-Gest, Viscount Dilhorne and Lord Pearson delivered concurring judgments.

Notes

For other cases involving mens rea, where criminal responsibility has been imposed upon a company see *DPP v Kent & Sussex Contractors Ltd* [1944] 1 KB 146; *R v ICR Haulage Ltd* [1944] 1 KB 551; *Moore v Bresler* [1944] 2 All ER 515.

[8.14]   The agents whose acts are attributed to the company for the purpose of convicting it of a crime, may himself be convicted of aiding and abetting the company in the commission of that crime.

McMahon v Murtagh Properties Ltd and Thomas Wright [1982] ILRM 342 (High Court)

[8.15]   An intoxicating liquor licence for a public house 'The Sheaf o' Wheat' was held by the second defendant as nominee for the first defendant. The second defendant was also the manager of the public house. In a prosecution for breach of the Licensing Acts, a case was stated by the District Justice to the High Court asking whether (1) a limited liability company could itself hold a licence without the need for a nominee? (2) whether the company could, in the present case, be regarded as the holder of the licence? (3) whether the second defendant could be convicted with aiding and abetting the company in the commission of the offence? All three questions were answered in the affirmative.

[8.16]   **Barrington J:** It was at one time thought that an incorporated company could not of itself hold an intoxicating liquor licence and that it required a nominee to hold the licence on its behalf. It is hard to find the logical basis for this theory.

On incorporation, a limited liability company becomes a body corporate capable of exercising all the functions of an incorporated company and having a perpetual successtion and a common seal . . . If the powers contained in the memorandum of association include power to carry on the business of selling intoxicating liquor by retail for consumption on or off the premises, the company has power to carry on that business on obtaining the appropriate licence and complying with other relevant legal requirements . . .

However, notwithstanding this, the practice has grown up in Ireland of appointing nominees to hold licences of limited liability companies engaged in the intoxicating liquor trade. This practice has even secured statutory recognition and it is probably too late now, to say that it is wrong . . .

It is quite clear, however, that such a nominee has himself, no beneficial interest whatsoever in the licence and that he must comply with all lawful directions of the body corporate in relation to it. While the statute acknowledges that he holds the licence, he holds it only for the body corporate which is the beneficial and indeed, the real holder of the licence, just as it is the real holder of the premises in which the business is carried on.

The present practice of companies holding their licence through nominees probably goes back to the time when the implications of incorporation were not fully understood. It has, however, the authority of a passage in O'Connor's *The Licensing Laws of Ireland* which appears at page 86 of that book and which reads as follows: 'The provisions of the licensing code go to show that a licence cannot be granted to a limited company, but the application may be made in the name of the secretary or other servant or nominee'.

However, two years after the publication of O'Connor's *Licensing Laws* the matter was fully discussed in the case of *The King (Cottingham) v Justices of County Cork* [1906] 2 IR 415.

In his judgment in that case, the Chief Baron Palles emphasised that a body corporate was a 'person' and that it could therefore have a 'character' or reputation and nailed the fallacy that a body corporate could not apply for a licence because it could not satisfy the justices that it had a 'good character' . . . At page 419 he goes so far as to say:

As I said earlier, it is probably too late now, to hold that the practice of companies holding licences through nominees is wrong. But Chief Baron Palles had no difficulty whatsoever in holding that a body corporate was a 'person' capable of applying for and obtaining an intoxicating liquor licence and that it was capable of having a good character. He goes on to say:

'I cannot see why a public company cannot have a character. No doubt it has no soul; but it can act by others; and through others do acts which in the case of a natural person would affect conscience, and be a foundation of that reputation which the law knows as "character", be it good or bad. It can be guilty of fraud, or malice and of various criminal offences, some of commission, others of omission; some punishable summarily, others by indictment. "Character" as used in the section means "reputation".

195

Reputation is acquired by conduct. The conduct of the authorised agents of a company is its conduct. Why should not that conduct give rise to a reputation as to its character, good, bad or indifferent? An unincorporated company of seven persons can acquire a reputation for fair dealing, for truth in their representations, for close supervision of their business, for carrying on their business in an orderly and peaceable manner. But this reputation is not that of an individual. It is, or may be, something different from the reputation of each. It may be a reputation acquired by the aggregation of the seven; as the reputation of an unincorporated bank for solvency. Why cannot those seven persons acquire a similar reputation by their action in aggregation, although that aggregation has assumed the more intimate form of incorporation?'

Johnson J agreed with the Chief Baron's reasoning. He said:

'The second ground raises the question whether this company is a "person within the meaning of The Beerhouses (Ireland) Acts and the Licensing Act, 1874". The contention for the prosecutor is, as I understand if, that the whole scope of these Acts as ascertained from the language of the legislature in the Acts *ex visceribus actus* (C Co Litt 381b), points to the individual and personal responsibility of the applicant for a licence or transfer of a licence, and that it is in this sense his character must be "good"; and that in as much as "Beamish & Crawford Ltd" is merely an impersonal incorporated legal entity, it cannot in the nature of things obtain from the justices a certificate of good character, and therefore cannot have a wholesale beer dealers' licence.

But though this company is of such impersonal character, it is competent to employ and act, and practically must employ and act, by and through such individuals as by its constitution it is competent to engage, and engages, for its purposes, and by whose conduct within the scope of their employment, the "company" is bound. A limited liability company is capable of suing, and liable to be sued, in almost every kind of action in the nature of tort or contract. It may be made criminally responsible for most offences which are not punishable solely by imprisonment or corporeal punishment. It may be enjoined and its property may be sequestered for payment of its debts or fines imposed for offences. Good or bad character is a matter of local or public reputation and the widest discretion is given by statute to justices in respect of their certificate. In *Leader v Yell* (16 CB) (NS) 584, where this matter is discussed, Erle CJ at 593, suggests how the words "good character" came to be introduced into the Beer Acts.

I think if the house is conducted in a disorderly way, if convictions are had for breaches of the Licensing Acts, if improper characters were allowed to resort there for improper purposes, or public feeling is outraged by lewd or improper acts knowingly committed, this "company" would, through their agent or manager, who they put in charge of, or whose omissions or acts they are liable for, have an evil reputation and a bad character; but if on the contrary, the house if conducted in an orderly and decent manner, the provisions of the Licensing Acts observed, and perhaps I may venture to add, reasonably good and wholesome beer supplied, the local and public reputation of this company, through their agent or manager whom this company placed in charge and for whom they are responsible, would be good and this company would be, as the justices have certified them to be, of good character.'

The matter came up for discussion before the modern Supreme Court in the case of *The State (John Hennessy and Chariot Inns Ltd) v Superintendent J Commons* [1976] IR 238. Again, the decision in the case turned upon a different point, but in his judgment, Kenny J went out of his way to cite with approval the judgments of Johnston J and the Chief Baron in *The King (Cottingham) v Justices of County Cork*, and referred to the 'myth' widely accepted by 'both branches of the legal profession' that a company incorporated under the Companies Acts cannot be granted a licence to sell intoxicating drink and that when it seeks to be licensed in respect of premises, or when it acquires licensed premises, the licence must be granted to its nominee.

From this discussion I drew three conclusions. First the present practice of companies holding their licences through nominees has no basis in sound logic. Second, the practice has however received statutory recognition so that is is now too late to say that it is wrong. Third, the practice, not being based on sound logic, will necessarily give rise to difficulties in administering the licencing code so that one can sympathise with the position in which the learned District Justice found himself.

Nevertheless, I drew the following practical conclusions. First, a limited liability company is entitled itself to hold its licence without resorting to the device of having a nominee.

Secondly, it is not incorrect to refer to the nominee as being the 'holder' of the licence as long as it is remembered that the company is the beneficial and as previously indicated, the real holder of the licence. The nominee must comply with all legal instructions of the company in relation to the licence and he is, in effect, no more than a peg on which the company finds it convenient to hang its licence. This being so, if the company, through its agents, breaks the law in the running of the business, it is at all times liable as the holder of the licence. The nominee, provided he does no more than hold the licence, commits no offence, but if the nominee is also the manager of the business or if he assists in the commission of an offence then he may be liable for aiding and abetting the company as holder of the licence, notwithstanding that he is a nominal 'holder' himself.

Under these circumstances, I think the learned District Justice was wrong to dismiss the summonses against the defendants, and I would send the case back to him to enter continuances.

A company may commit conspiracy with the one person who is solely responsible for its acts.

Taylor v Smyth (Supreme Court, 5 July 1990)

[8.17]   The issue of law before the Supreme Court was whether Mr Smyth could conspire with companies which were under his sole direction and control.

[8.18]   **McCarthy J:** 'The principle defined in *Salomon & Co* (1897) AC 22, which was a case of a 'one man' company, has been qualified on many occasions but, as I understand it, remains the law – that a company legally incorporated does not cease to be an independent legal entity separate and distinct from the individual members of the company, simply because it is wholly controlled by one individual. But, it is said, Mr Smyth cannot conspire with himself, which is the reality of the allegation insofar as it is said that he conspired with Kape, with Calla or with Calder all of which companies he controls; reliance is placed upon a decision on trial made by Nield J in *R v McDonnell* (1956) 1 QB 233 where a criminal charge of conspiracy was brought against the defendant and it was contended that there could be no conspiracy because there were not two persons and two minds involved. Nield J emphasized that it was not a company which was being proceeded against but an individual defendant and, of course, that it was a criminal trial. He concluded that, whilst an indictment for a common law conspiracy to defraud would lie against a limited company, 'the true position is that a company and a director cannot be convicted of conspiracy when the only human being who is said to have broken the law or intended to do so is the one director, and that is the defendant in this case.' No authority was cited in support of extending this proposition to an action for civil conspiracy. In principle, it would seem invidious for example, that the assets of a limited company should not be liable to answer for conspiracy where its assets had been augmented as a result of the action alleged to constitute the conspiracy. Essentially, it would be permitting the company to lift its corporate veil as and when it suits. The matter is not devoid of authority. In *Belmont Finance Corporation Limited v Williams Furniture Limited and Others* [1979] 1 All ER 118 Williams Furniture owned City Industrial Finance which owned Belmont, whose majority directors were the seventh and eight defendants. Four other defendants owned Maximum and wanted to purchase Belmont. They agreed to sell Maximum to Belmont for £500,000 and to purchase Belmont from City Industrial for £489,000. The Belmont directors resolved to implement this agreement and the transaction was completed. Belmont went into liquidation and its receiver sued alleging that the value of Maximum was only £60,000 but that the price of £500,000 for Maximum had been arrived at to enable those four defendants to purchase Belmont with money provided by Belmont, in contravention of the Companies Act. It was held that since Belmont was a victim of the alleged conspiracy and the essence of the agreement was to deprive it of a large part of its assets, the knowledge of its directors that the agreement was illegal was not to be imputed to Belmont merely because they were directors of Belmont. Therefore, Belmont was not a party to the conspiracy. The trial judge had held that the claim in conspiracy failed *in limine* on the ground that one party to a conspiracy to do an unlawful act cannot sue a co-conspirator in relation to that act. In the course of his judgment, Buckley LJ (at 124) said:—

> 'I shall deal first with the conspiracy claim. The plaintiff's argument is to the following effect. On the allegations in the statement of claim, the agreement was illegal and they say that an agreement between two or more persons to effect any unlawful purpose, with knowledge of all the facts which are necessary ingredients of illegality, is a conspiracy and we were referred to *Crofter Hand Woven Harris Tweed Co Ltd v Veitch* [1942] AC 435 and *Churchill v Walton* [1961] 2 AC 224. The agreement was carried out and damaged the plaintiff.
>
> In the course of the argument in this court counsel for the first and second defendants conceded that the plaintiff is entitled in this appeal to succeed on the conspiracy point, unless it is debarred from doing so on the ground that it was a party to the conspiracy, which was the ground that was relied on by the judge.
>
> The plaintiff points out that the agreement was resolved on by a board of which the seventh and eight defendants constituted the majority and that they were the two directors who countersigned the plaintiff's seal on the agreement and that they are sued as two of the conspirators. It is conceded by counsel for the plaintiff that a company may be held to be a participant in a criminal conspiracy and that the illegality attending a conspiracy cannot relieve the company on the ground that such an agreement may be ultra vires; but he says that to establish a conspiracy to which the plaintiff was a party, having as its object the doing of an illegal act, it must be shown that the company must be treated as knowing all the facts relevant to the illegality; he relied on *Churchill v Walton* to which I have already referred.
>
> The plaintiff in its reply denies being a party to the conspiracy and, says counsel for the plaintiff, it would be for the defendants to allege the necessary knowledge on the part of the plaintiff. But he further submits that even if the plaintiff should be regarded as a party to the conspiracy, this would not debar the plaintiff from relief; and he relies on *Oram v Hutt* [1914] 1 Ch 98.'

The point now under consideration in this appeal did not expressly arise in the *Balmont* case, but it must underlie the entire of the argument and judgment in it. The basis of that case was that the separate legal entity of the company may, in law, conspire with those directors who, in effect control it. In *Lennard's Carrying Company v Asiatic Petroleum Company Limited* [1915] AC 705 Viscount Haldane LC said:–

> 'a corporation is an abstraction. It has no mind of its own any more than it has a body of its own; its active and directing will must consequently be sought in the person of somebody who for some purpose may be called an

199

agent, but who is really the directing mind and will of the corporation, the very ego and centre of the personality of the corporation.'

That was in the context of the company seeking to take advantage of the limitation of liability under section 502 of the Merchant Shipping Act, 1894. It is much quoted with particular enphasis upon subsequent words 'his action must, unless a corporation is not to be liable at all, have been an action which was the action of the company itself within the meaning of section 502.' But the controlling director cannot, in law, be the only director, and all of the directors are responsible for what the company does. Apart from authority, in principle, I see no reason why the mere fact that one individual controls the company of limited liability, should give immunity from suit to both that company and that individual in the case of an established arrangement for the benefit of both company and individual to the detriment of others. If such were the case, it would follow that a like arrangement to the advantage of two companies of limited liability, both controlled by the same individual would give an equal immunity from suit to both companies, and so on. I recognise the force of the reasoning by Nield J in the *McDonnell* case; I express no view in regard to his conclusion save to point out the obvious – it was a criminal case.'

Finlay CJ and Hederman J concurred

Notes

Admittedly this case involved civil conspiracy. However, despite some caution in this regard by McCarthy J, it would seem that the decision should apply equally to criminal conspiracy.

Chapter 9

CAPITAL

[9.01] The word 'capital' may take on different meanings in different situations.[1] For instance, in the law of taxation, there is a distinction between capital or fixed assets on the one hand, and current assets on the other hand. Capital assets are of a more permanent nature (such as a factory, machinery used for production, etc). Current assets, however, are of a revolving nature, being regularly acquired and disposed of by the business. These include stock in trade and cash. Profits made from the sale of fixed assets are subject to capital gains tax, whereas profits made from current assets are subject to income tax.[2] For company law purposes, however, 'capital' refers to the 'share capital' of the company.

1 See *Keane* chapters 14, 15 and 16.
2 In the case of companies, all profits are assessable under the Corporations Tax Act 1976, although the distribution between capital gains and income profit is preserved.

[9.02] The share capital is typically divided into shares[1] of a fixed value. For example, it may consist of 100 shares of £1 each. The total value of the shares which have been allotted, is known as the issued share capital. The authorised (or nominal) share capital is the maximum capital which may potentially be allotted by the company. The issued share capital may be far less than the nominal share capital. For example, the company may have a nominal share capital of £100,000 of which only 100 £1 shares have actually been allotted.

1 As to the nature of a share, see chapter 13, *infra*.

[9.03] When shares are allotted by the company, the allottees may not have to pay for them immediately. The issued share capital therefore is divided into two categories. The paid up capital is the amount which has actually been paid on the shares. The uncalled share capital is the balance of the price of the shares which the allottees have agreed to pay, if called upon to do so by the company. It may by special resolution determine that all or part of the unpaid capital is only to be called up in the case of the company being wound up. This is known as the reserve capital of the company. In certain cases where an individual has been a director of a company has gone into insolvent liquidation, the court may order that for a period of five years he is not to be director or secretary of or to be concerned in the promotion of formation of any company unless, in the case of a plc, it has an alloted share capital of £100,000 and in the case of any other company, an allotted share capital of £20,000, fully paid up in cash.[1]

1 Ss 149 & 150 of the 1990 Act.

[9.04] As has been mentioned above, the share capital is divided into shares of a fixed value. This is known as the nominal or par value. As the company's fortunes fluctuate so the price of the shares will rise and fall, when being transferred by existing shareholders. This does not effect the par value, however. If the company has performed well, its previously issued £1 shares may be trading at £5 each. The company may decide to make a fresh issue of shares. In view of the market price of existing shares, it may decide to allot the new £1 shares at £5 each. In such a case the difference between the nominal value and the issue price (ie £4) is known as a 'premium'. The amount of the premium must be transferred in the company's accounts into what is known as a share premium account.[1]

1 Discussed previously in chapter 8.

Capital maintenance[1]

[9.05] The share capital of the company has traditionally been regarded as being of major importance, even though in practice a large amount, (and in some cases, virtually all) of the company's finances may have been raised instead by way of loan capital.[2] The share capital is regarded as a fund out of which the creditors may be paid in the event of the insolvency of the company.[3] For this reason a number of judicial and statutory rules have been developed to protect and maintain this fund. It cannot be reduced by the company, unless certain statutory procedures are followed, aimed at safeguarding the interests of the creditors.[4]

1 See *Keane* chapter 15.
2 All or part of which may be secured by a fixed or floating charge. See *Keane* at para **14.14**.
3 ie where it is unable to pay its debts as they fall due.
4 This procedure is discussed below. See also *Keane* at para **16.08** et seq.

[9.06] In practice, this 'creditors fund' may prove to be worthless. For example, in the case of a private company the share capital may be as little as 2p, divided into shares of 1p each. In the case of a plc, however, the allotted share capital must be not less than the authorised minimum[1] (currently £30,000).[2] Furthermore, even if the issued share capital of the company initially constitutes a valuable fund, it may be completely lost as a result of losses incurred by the company in the ordinary course of its business. Such a loss of capital is regarded by the courts as being quite legitimate. Of course, where the share capital has been lost in such circumstances, the creditors' fund becomes in practical terms, worthless.

1 S 19 of the 1983 Act.
2 S 6 of the 1983 Act. See also *Trevor v Whitworth* (1887) 12 App Cas 409, 423.

Re Horsley & Weight Ltd [1982] 3 All ER 1045 (Court of Appeal)

[9.07] **Buckley LJ:** It is a misapprehension to suppose that the directors of a company owe a duty to the company's creditors to keep the contributed capital of the company intact. The company's creditors are entitled to assume that the company will not in any way repay any paid-up share capital to the shareholders except by means of a duly authorised reduction of capital. They are entitled to assume that the company's directors will conduct its affairs in such a manner that no such unauthorised repayment will take place. It may be somewhat loosely said that the directors owe an indirect duty to the creditors not to permit any unlawful reduction of capital to occur, but I would regard it as more accurate to say that the directors owe a duty to the company in this respect and that, if the company is put into liquidation when paid-up capital has been improperly repaid, the liquidator owes a duty to the creditors to enforce any right to repayment which is available to the company. On the other hand, a company, and its directors acting on its behalf, can quite properly expend contributed capital for any purpose which is intra vires the company.

Capital maintenance rules

[9.08] The following rules are aimed at maintaining or protecting the share capital of the company (subject to its loss in the ordinary course of business). Many of the rules have their origin in the common law. They now find expression in the provisions of the Companies Acts.

Shares are not to be issued at a discount

[9.09] This matter has already been considered in chapter 8, *supra*.

Dividends may only be paid out of profits and not out of capital

[9.10] Under s 45 of the 1983 Act, a company may only pay a dividend out of profits.[1] In this respect profits are defined as the company's 'accumulated realised profits, so far as not previously utilised by distribution or capitalisation, less its accumulated, realised losses, so far as not previously written off in a reduction or reorganisation of capital duly made.' S 51(4) of the 1983 Act provides that the reference to 'profits and losses' is to be taken as meaning both revenue and capital profits and losses.

[9.11]   The concept of a realised revenue profit or loss is straightforward. However, the position is more complex regarding realised capital profits and losses. It certainly covers the sale of fixed assets at higher or lower prices respectively than their original purchase price. Under s 45(5) of the 1983 Act any provision for depreciation of a fixed asset is to be regarded as a realised capital loss. It is compulsory to make provision for depreciation in respect of fixed asset whose value has been permanently reduced.[2] However, where there has been a revaluation of all fixed assets, or of all fixed assets other than goodwill, any losses on fixed assets may be set off against increases in value of other fixed assets, and accordingly, are not to be treated as realised capital losses. This latter provision applies, even where there has not been a revaluation of all fixed assets (other than goodwill) provided the directors can say that those assets which have not been revalued are in aggregate at least equal to their book value. A mere revaluation of a fixed asset, showing an increase in its value, does not constitute a realised capital profit, although it may be used to fund a bonus issue to members.[3]

Dividends are to be declared by reference to 'properly prepared' accounts.[4] Accounts are 'properly prepared' if they comply with the statutory requirements and with the accepted accounting practice.[5]

In the case of a a plc it can only pay a dividend if the amount of its net assets is not less than the aggregate of its called up share capital and its undistributable reserves and provided that the dividend does not reduce the amount of the net assets below that aggregate.[6] Special rules apply regarding the payment of dividend by 'investment companies' as to which see s 47 of the 1983 Act also *Keane* para **31.19**.

Members who receive a dividend knowing or having reasonable grounds for believing that it is unlawful, must under s 50 of the 1983 Act repay it to the company.

1 See also *Keane* chapter 33.
2 Para 7(2) of the 1983 Act.
3 S 51(1), (2) of the 1983 Act.
4 S 49 of the 1983 Act.
5 *Lloyd Cheyham Ltd v Little John & Company* [1987] BCLC 303.
6 S 46 of the 1983 Act. Undistributed reserves include (a) the share premium account; (b) the capital redemption reserve fund; (c) the excess of the company's accumulated unrealised profits over its accumulated unrealised losses; (d) any other reserve which the plc is prohibited from distributing either by statute or by its memorandum or articles.

[9.12]   Directors who knowingly or negligently cause the company to pay an unlawful dividend are liable personally to compensate the company for the amount of such dividend.

Re Exchange Banking Co; Flitcrofts' Case (1882) 21 Ch D (Court of Appeal)

[9.13]   For a number of years the directors had caused certain debts to be entered in the company's accounts as assets when they were in fact bad. On the basis of these account the shareholders passed resolutions declaring dividends out of what were in reality non-existent profits. The directors then paid out these dividends. The company was subsequently wound up and the liquidator successfully sued the directors for the amount of the dividend unlawfully paid out.

[9.14] **Jessel MR:** A limited company by its memorandum of association declares that its capital is to be applied for the purposes of the business. It cannot reduce its capital except in the manner and with the safeguards provided by statute, and looking at the Act . . . it clearly is against the intention of the legislature that any portion of the capital should be returned to the shareholders without the statutory conditions being complied with. A limited company cannot in any other way make a return of capital, the sanction of a general meeting can give no validity to such a proceeding, and even the sanction of every shareholder cannot bring within the powers of the company an act which is not within its powers. If, therefore, the shareholders had all been present at the meetings and had all known the facts, and had all concurred in declaring the dividends, the payment of the dividends would not be effectually sanctioned. One reason is this – there is a statement that the capital shall be applied for the purposes of the business, and on the faith of that statement, which is sometimes said to be an implied contract with creditors, people dealing with the company give it credit. The creditor has no debtor but that impalpable thing the corporation, which has no property except the assets of the business. The creditor, therefore, I may say, gives credit to that capital, gives credit to the company on faith of the representation that the capital shall be applied only for the purposes of the business, and he has therefore a right to say that the corporation shall keep its capital and not return it to the shareholders, though it may be a right which he cannot enforce otherwise than by a winding-up order. It follows then that if directors who are quasi trustees for the company improperly pay away the assets to the shareholders they are liable to replace them. It is no answer to say that the shareholders could not compel them to do so. I am of opinion that the company could in its corporate capacity compel them to do so, even if there were no winding up . . .

Notes

See also *Re City Equitable Fire Assurance Co* [1905] Ch 207 where the directors negligently paid dividends out of false profits, cf. *Dovey v Carey* [1901] AC 401. The company's auditors may be liable in damages if through therir negligence the company paid dividends out of false profits. See *Re Thomas Gerard & Son Ltd* [1968] Ch 455.

In any case, as mentioned above, the company may be able to recover the amount of the unlawful dividend from the members under s 50 of the 1983 Act. See also *Precision Dippings Ltd v Precision Dippings Marketing Ltd* [1985] BCLC 385 where the member was held in such circumstances to be a constructive trustee of the dividend for the company.

Meeting to consider serious loss of capital

[9.15] Under s 40 of the 1983 Act, where the 'net assets'[1] of the company fall to half or less, of its issued share capital, the directors have 28 days from the date when this fact comes to their knowledge, to summon an extraordinary general meeting of the company for the 'purpose of considering whether any, and if so, what measures should be taken to deal with the situation'. If the directors fail to convene this meeting, they may incur criminal penalties.[2] Although there is a statutory obligation to convene this meeting there does not appear to be any obligation to do anything to remedy the situation. In the case of many private companies with a small share capital, business may be financed by way of loan capital. In such a case it would only take a very miniscule loss for the company's liabilities to exceed its assets. Accordingly, a meeting might have to be convened under s 40 as soon as it started business. Such a meeting would seem pointless in the circumstances.

S 40 was included in the 1983 Act to give effect to art 17 of the Second Companies Directive.[3] Notably this Directive does not apply to private companies. In England the equivalent section only applies to plc's.[4]

1 Defined by s 2(4)(*b*) as being 'the aggregate of its assets less the aggregate of its liabilities'.
2 Ibid s 40(2).
3 Council Directive 77/91 EEC.
4 S 34 of the Companies Act 1980.

Restrictions on company acquiring its own shares

[9.16] Under s 41 of the 1983 Act, which gives statutory effect to earlier judicial decisions,[1] it is provided that, subject to certain exceptions, a company cannot acquire its own shares.[2] The company and any of its officers who infringe the s 41 may incur criminal penalties. There is a number of reasons behind this rule. A company should not be entitled to deal in its own shares as this could artificially raise or lower the price of its own shares.[3] Such artificial price variations could benefit directors who are also shareholders, and could act to the detriment of other investors. Additionally, if the company were able to acquire its own shares this would enable the directors who would control the votes on such shares, to muster a sufficient majority in general meeting so as to defeat any resolution calling for their dismissal.

1 eg *Trevor v Whitworth* (1887) 12 App Cas 409; cf *Re Balgooley Distillery Co* (1886–87) 17 LR Ir 173.
2 *Keane* para **15.07**.
3 Which could be relevant in the case of a take-over bid either by or for the company.

[9.17] S 41 does not apply where the company acquires its own shares otherwise than for valuable consideration[1] unless the company is a plc. Where the shares are so acquired by a plc, they must be immediately cancelled.[2] There are four other exceptions under s 41,[3] namely:–

(*a*) the redemption of preference shares in pursuance of s 65 of the Principal Act or the redemption or purchase of shares in pursuance of the 1990 Act.[4]

(*b*) the acquisition of shares in a reduction of shares duly made.

(*c*) the purchase of any shares pursuant to an order of the court under s 15 of the 1983 Act[5] or under s 10 or under s 205 of the Principal Act.

(*d*) the forfeiture of any shares or the acceptance of any shares surrendered in lieu, in pursuance of the articles for failure to pay any sum payable in respect of those shares.[6]

S 42 of the 1983 Act contains elaborate provisions aimed at preventing the circumvention of s 41 placing the shares in a nominee of the company.[7]

1 S 41(2) of the 1983 Act.
2 Ibid s 43.
3 Ibid s 41(4).
4 See generally *Nolan* (1991) 9 ILT (ns) 9. For a discussion of redemption of shares, see chapter 10 *infra*.
5 Where shareholders have applied to restrain the conversion of a public company into a private company. See *Keane* **4.24**.
6 See chapter 13 infra.
7 See *Keane* at para **15.10**. In addition s 32 of the Principal Act prevents a subsidiary from holding shares in its parent company.

Acquisition by company of its own shares or shares in parent company

[9.18] Part XI of the 1990 Act introduced a new regime for companies limited by shares or limited by guarantee and having a share capital, whereby they can by following the prescribed procedures purchase their own shares.

Under s 211 a company may, if authorised by its articles purchase its own shares (including any redeemable shares) unless as a result of the purchase there would no longer be any member of the company holding shares other than redeemable shares. Authority for a 'market purchase' of its own shares (ie a purchase on the stock exchange) may be by way of ordinary resolution, whereas a special resolution is required to authorise an 'off market purchase'. In the latter case, the contract of purchase must be available for inspection for 21 days prior to and at the meeting where the resolution is to be passed. The resolution authorising market purchases must specify the maximum number of shares which may be acquired and the maximum prices to be paid. All market purchases must be notified to the stock exchange. An authority to purchase lasts for 18 months. The company's rights under the contract of purchase are unassignable.

[9.19] Only fully paid up shares may be purchased. The purchase price must be funded out of profits available for distribution or out of the proceeds of a fresh issue of shares or out of both. Any premium payable can normally only be met out of profits. However, it can be met out of the proceeds of a fresh issue of shares up to an amount equal to:–

(*i*) the aggregate of the premiums received by the company on the issue of the shares purchased, or

(*ii*) the current amount of the company's shares premium account (including any sum transferred to that account in respect of premiums on the new shares),

whichever is less, and in any such case the amount of the company's share premium account must be reduced by a sum corresponding to the amount of any payment made out of the proceeds of the fresh issue of shares.

[9.20] Under s 208 the shares once purchased may be cancelled in which case, a sum must be transferred to the capital redemption reserve fund, equal to the proportion of the purchase price paid out of distributable profits. After cancellation the issued shares capital must be reduced accordingly, although the company may issue new shares equivalent to the nominal value of the shares cancelled, either after or one month before cancellation without attracting liability to stamp duty.

If the shares are not cancelled they are referred to as 'treasury shares'. The maximum number of treasury shares a company may hold at any one time must not exceed 10% of the issued share capital. Voting rights may not be exercised and dividends may not be paid in respect of treasury shares. They may be cancelled or re-issued. A re-issue will not attract liability to stamp duty.

The maximum and minimum prices at which treasury shares may be issued off-market must be fixed by the company in general meeting. If they were purchased off market by the company, a special resolution authorising the purchase must also have fixed the re-issue price.

[9.21] If the company in breach of contract fails to purchase the shares, it will not be liable in damages. Specific performance will not be ordered if the company cannot pay the price out of profits. If the shares should have been purchased before the date of any commencement of the winding up, the sale may be enforced against the company. However, the purchase price is only payable after all creditors, who are not members of the company, have been paid in full together with any interest payable on their debts under the Rules of Bankruptcy.

Copies or memoranda of all contracts of purchase of a company's own shares must be open to inspection at its registered office for 10 years.

[9.22] Under s 32 of the Principal Act, a subsidiary was prohibited from holding shares in its parent company, unless the shares were held as trustee, etc., on behalf of a third party. Now, however, by s 224 of the 1990 Act a subsidiary may acquire shares in its parent company if the acquisition has been authorised in advance by both the parent and subsidiary companies. Voting rights cannot be exercised in respect of these shares which must have been paid for out of distributable profits of the subsidiary (other than profits attributable to shares held by the parent company in the subsidiary).

Under s 225 of the 1990 Act if the subsidiary is wound up within six months of having acquired shares in its parent company the directors of the subsidiary will, if it is unable to pay its debts, be jointly and severally liable to repay to the subsidiary the total amount paid for the shares.

S 226 provides that within 28 days of any purchase of shares under part XI a return in the prescribed form must be made to the registrar in respect of the purchase.

The Minister has power under s 228 to make further regulations relating to the purchase by a company of its own shares or the shares in its parent company. None have been made to date.

Where shares with a stock exchange listing have been acquired under part XI of the 1990 Act, the company whose shares have been acquired must notify the exchange. The stock exchange is under a duty to co-operate with the DPP in relation to investigation and prosecution of offences under part XI.

[9.23] A purchase by a company of its own shares otherwise that in pursuance of part XI of the Companies Act 1990, is null and void, as an unlawful reduction of capital.

Re Irish Provident Assurance Company Ltd [1913] 1 IR 352 (Court of Appeal)

[9.24] Differences had arisen between the company and its managing director, Norman. A settlement was reached whereby the company was to pay him £2,000. In return he agreed to waive his claims against the company, covenanted not to compete with the company and agreed to surrender his shares in the company to it. The whole settlement was declared void on the ground that it involved, inter alia the purchase by the company of its own shares.

[9.25] Palles CB: The ground of my judgment is that part of this agreement is for the purchase by the company from Norman, and the sale by Norman to the company, of 686 of the company's own shares. I need hardly say that, although one of the terms of this agreement is that Norman shall resign the shares without payment, this term in the agreement must be taken to be part of the consideration for which the £2,000 was paid by the company; and that the real transaction, notwithstanding the conveyancing effort to conceal its true nature, included a sale to the company of the shares, not a gift of them. 'In consideration of £2,000 I (Norman) shall release you (the company) from all my claims against you, and in addition I shall give you 686 of your own shares for nothing', involves and contains as an inseparable part an agreement for the purchase by the company of its own shares. Part of the consideration, and that an undefined part, was or the purchase of those shares –

was, in fact, the price of those shares. Therefore the agreement in its entirety was void.

Cherry LJ delivered a concurring judgment. Holmes LJ concurred.

Notes

For a less rigid application of the doctrine, see *Re General Finance Co Ltd* (1889–90) 23 LR Ir 173.

[9.26] A surrender of shares, releasing the shareholder from liability in respect of unpaid calls is equivalent to a purchase of shares by the company and is therefore null and void.

Bellerby v Rowland & Marwood's Steamship Company Limited [1902] Ch 14.

[9.27] The company had accepted a surrender of shares in respect of which £415 had not yet been called. The court declared the surrender void as an unlawful reduction of capital.

[9.28] **Cozens-Hardy LJ:** Two propositions may be asserted without doubt. First, a company may forfeit shares . . . Secondly, it is not competent to a company to purchase its own shares and any such transaction is ultra vires. I think *Trevor v Whitworth* 12 App Cas 409 also decides that, under circumstances which would entitle a company to forfeit shares for non-payment of calls, the same result may be attained by means of a voluntary surrender. In the case of forfeiture the statute treats the forfeited shares as being the property of the company, and it may well be that the acquisition of this property by the company is equally lawful, whether it is acquired by hostile proceedings in the nature of forfeiture, or by a voluntary transaction producing the same result. There is no infringement of the statutory provisions in either case. There is merely an unimportant difference in form. When, however, the transaction involves, as in the present case, the release by the comany to the shareholders, of uncalled capital on their shares, it seems to me that it is, within *Trevor v Whitworth*, a reduction of capital not sanctioned by law.

The decision of the House of Lords in the *Ooregum* case [1892] AC 125, that shares in a limited company cannot be issued as a discount, involves the principle, that the company cannot by any device relieve a shareholder from the liability to pay the full amount due on his shares. This would be the result if the shares had been retained by the plaintiffs instead of being surrendered to the company. But the fact that in consideration of the release the shares were surrendered seems to me to render the transaction no better. Uncalled capital is part of the assets of the company . . . The company therefore, parted with £415, a portion of its assets, in consideration of the acquisition of the shares. This was a purchase of the shares and is directly within the authority of *Trevor v Whitworth* . . .

The real objection to a surrender of shares does not lie in the fact that money has been paid by the company to acquire the shares. The objection is founded on a larger proposition. A company cannot be a shareholder in itself. Every surrender of shares, whether fully paid up or not, involves a reduction of capital, which is unlawful, except when sanctioned by the Court under the Companies Acts . . . Forfeiture is a statutory exception, and is the only exception. For I regard a surrender under circumstances which would justify a forfeiture as merely equivalent to a forfeiture.

Collins MR and Stirling LJ delivered concurring judgments.

Giving of financial assistance by a company for the purchase of its own shares

[9.29]   Under s 60 of the Principal Act, a company is prohibited from providing financial assistance for the acquisition of its shares and shares of its holding company. This is aimed at preventing a company from funding its own takeover. The company and every officer who infringes the section is guilty of a criminal offence. *Ussher*[1] cites as an example of the type of transaction prohibited by s 60 a situation where the bidder having acquired the shares in the company then causes the company to discharge a loan which had been incurred by him previously for the purpose of financing the takeover. It is, of course possible that the type of assistance given by the company, while being prohibited by s 60, does not actually involve the dissipation of its capital. For example, rather than discharging the bidders' loan in the above situation, the company may instead guarantee his loan. If the guarantee is called on, undoubtedly the company's capital is reduced. Nevertheless, the company may possibly never have to pay up under the guarantee, as where the bidder repays the loan himself.

1 S 60(15) as amended by s 15 of the 1982 Act.

[9.30]   S 60 is subject to one major exception. Under s 60(12) it is provided that nothing is to be taken as prohibiting the payment of a dividend properly declared by a company or the discharge of a liability lawfully incurred by it. Where the company has large amounts of undistributed profits, any successful bidder for the company may, having acquired its shares, cause it to declare a large dividend. With this dividend he may then legitimately discharge the costs of his acquisition of the company's shares.

S 60(13) provides for further exceptions:–

(*a*) the lending of money in the ordinary course of business of a company who ordinary business includes the lending of money;
(*b*) the provision of financial assistance for the purchase of shares in an employee share scheme;
(*c*) the making of loans to persons other than directors, bona fide in the employment of the company or any subsidiary of it, with a view to enabling them to purchase shares in the company.

However, s $60(15)(c)$[1] provides that such assistance may only be given by a plc if the company's net assets are not thereby reduced or to the extent that they are, the assistance is provided out of profits available for dividends.

The prohibition in s 60 on a company financing the purchase of its own shares is not absolute. A procedure is laid down in s $60(2)$–(11) whereby such assistance may be given on the authority of a special resolution of the company passed within twelve months prior to the giving of the assistance. The procedure may no longer be used by plc's.[2] The resolution must be preceded by a declaration made by two or more of the directors stating the nature and recipients of the assistance and declaring that they are of the opinion that even after the assistance has been given, the company will still be solvent.[3] Absence of reasonable grounds for the opinion is a criminal offence. Dissentients holding at least ten per cent of the nominal value of the issued share capital or any class thereof, may within 28 days of the passing of the resolution, apply to the court for its cancellation.[4]

1 Op cit p 319.
2 S $60(15a)$ of the Principal Act added by para 9 of the first schedule of the 1983 Act.
3 ie able to pay its debts as they fall due.
4 For a fuller analysis of the procedure laid down by s $60(2)$–(11) see *Keane* at para **15.12**.

[9.31] The court will treat a resolution, under s 60, authorising the financing of the purchase of shares, as being null and void, where the giving of such financial assistance would be ultra vires the company or would be in breach of the terms of its articles of association.

Securities Trust Ltd v Associated Properties Ltd and Estates Development Ltd
(High Court, 19 November 1980)

[9.32] The plaintiff successfully applied to the court for the cancellation of a resolution Associated Properties Ltd ('Associated') under s 60 authorising the giving of a loan to Estates Development Ltd ('Estates) in order to purchase shares in ('associated'). The giving of such a loan was ultra vires associated defendant and was also expressly prohibited by its articles of association.

[9.33] McWilliam J: I am of opinion that the special resolution of 15th August 1979, was one which came within the provisions of s $60(12)$ of the 1963 Act so as to avoid the prohibition contained in subsection (1) and would have been effective to authorise the loan had such a resolution been within the power of the company under its memorandum and articles of association.

I am also of opinion, however, that Associated had no power under its memorandum and articles of association to advance money by way of loan or otherwise for the purchase of its own shares. Lending money was not one of the objects in the memorandum and article 7 stated unequivocally that none of the funds of the company could be employed for the purchase of shares in the company. Section 25 of the 1963 Act provides that the articles of association and memorandum bind the company and the members. Accordingly, at the time of the resolution of 15th August 1979, Associated had no power to pass the resolution making the interest free loan of £1,800,000 to Estates. This circumstance was brought to the attention of the company and its directors at the meeting but the resolution was passed notwithstanding.

The subsequent proceedings by Association to rectify the position were also unsatisfactory. The general meeting of 21st August to alter the memorandum and articles of association was effective for that purpose but, in my opinion, this would not retrospectively validate the resolution of 15th August.

[9.34] Any transaction in breach of s 60 of the Principal Act is voidable at the instance of the company against any person (whether a party to the transaction of not) who had notice of the facts which constitute such breach.[1]

1 S 60(14) of the Principal Act.

Bank of Ireland Finance Ltd v Rockfield Ltd [1979] IR 21 (Supreme Court)

[9.35] The plaintiff bank agreed to advance £170,000 to Costello and Blackmore to purchase certain property. The property was then to be mortgaged in favour of the plaintiff by way of deposit of the certificate of title. The plaintiff believed that the property would then be conveyed to a company controlled by Costello and Blackmore and called either 'Rockville Ltd' or 'Rockfield'. In fact the property in question was already owned by Rockfield Ltd. Costello and Blackmore used the loan to purchase its share capital and then caused it to deposit the certificate of title with the plaintiff by way of mortgage. If the plaintiff had looked at the folio and certificate of title for the land it would have seen that the defendant had owned the property at all material times. However, these documents were not inspected by the plaintiff, who made no inquiries as to the ownership of the property. The plaintiff had also been shown an estimate of expenses which included provision for stamp duty at a rate appropriate not for the conveyance of land, but rather, for the transfer of shares.

The plaintiff subsequently sought to enforce the mortgage. This was opposed by the defendant who sought to set the transaction aside on the ground that it was in breach of s 60 of the Principal Act. The trial judge (McWilliam J) found for the defendant on the ground that the plaintiff had constructive notice of the breach of the section. This decision was reversed on appeal to the Supreme Court, where it was held that the defendant could not avoid the transaction as it had failed to establish that the plaintiff had actual notice of the breach of s 60.

[9.36] **Kenny J:** The action was tried by McWilliam J who held that the agreement of the 30th July 1973, had been ratified by the defendants, that the plaintiffs had not actual notice that the £150,000 was to be applied in purchasing the shares in the defendant company, that the doctrine of constructive notice did not apply, and that 'notice' in s 60(14) of the Act of 1963 means actual notice; he then went on to say:– 'I fully accept the view expressed by Lindley LJ but it seems to me that there must be some limit to the extent to which a person may fail to accept information available to him or fail to make the inquiries normal in his line of business so as to leave himself in the position that he has no notice of something anyone else in the same line of business would have appreciated.' Counsel for the plaintiffs has complained that this blurs the distinction between actual notice and constructive notice, and I confess that I find considerable difficulty in understanding what the judge meant by this passage. He went on to say that the limit he had mentioned was reached in this case 'and I hold that the plaintiff should have had notice of the purpose for which the money was being applied, namely, the purchase of the defendant's own shares.' This meant that the judge was applying the doctrine of constructive notice to s 60(14) of the Act of 1963 . . .

In 1963 this section [s 60] was new to our company law; it was entered to prevent a limited company from purchasing its own shares or giving assistance to anyone who wanted to buy shares in it. When a company buys its own shares, it is reducing its share capital without the sanction of the court and so damnifying the position of its creditors . . .

[The judge referred to the provisions of s 60(1) & (14) and continued.] Sub-sections 2, 12 and 13 of s 60 have no relevance to this case and although s 60(1) appears in the (British) Companies Act 1948, nothing corresponding to sub-s 14 appears in that Act. This is the first case, as far as I know, in which the meaning of s 60(14) has been considered by any court in this country. The onus of proving that the money was advanced for the purchase of shares in the defendant company lies on the person who alleges this. The plaintiffs do not have to prove that they had no notice of facts which constituted a breach of section 60. What has to be established is that the plaintiffs had notice when lending the money that it was to be used for the purchase of shares in the defendant company. The fact which constituted such breach in this case was the application of £150,000 to the purchase of the shares in the defendant company. As the purchase followed the loan, the defendants must establish that the plaintiffs knew at the time when they made the loan that it was to be applied for this purpose. If they got notice of this subsequently, that is irrelevant.

The notice referred to in s 60(14) is actual notice and not constructive notice. As there has been considerable confusion as to the meaning of the terms 'actual notice' and 'imputed notice' and 'constructive notice' – a confusion which has been pointed out by many judges and text-book writers – I wish to say that I use the term 'actual notice' as meaning in this case that the plaintiff bank, or any of its officials, had been informed either verbally or in writing, that part of the advance was to be applied in the purchase of shares in the defendant company, or that they knew facts from which they must have inferred that part of the advance was to be applied for this purpose . . .

There is strong authority that the doctrine of constructive notice is not to be extended to commercial transactions. In *Manchester Trust v Furness* Lindley J, a great authority upon company law, said at p 545 of the report:–

'. . . as regards the extension of the equitable doctrines of constructive notice to commercial transactions, the courts have always set their faces resolutely against it. The equitable doctrines of constructive notice are common enough in dealing with land and estates, with which the court is familiar; but there have been repeated protests against the introduction into commercial transactions of anything like an extension of those doctrines, and the protest is founded on perfect good sense. In dealing with estates in land title to everything and it can be leisurely investigated; in commercial transactions possession is everything and there is no time to investigate title; and if we were to extend the doctrine of constructive notice to commercial transactions we should be doing infinite mischief and paralysing the trade of the country.' . . .

Section 60 . . . deals with financial assistance, not with mortgages. The word 'mortgage' does not appear in the section and sub-s 14 applies to all commercial transactions. The fact that there was a mortgage involved in this transaction does not mean that the sub-section is to be read in one sense for financial assistance without security and in another sense when a mortgage is involved. That would be a ludicrous interpretation. Therefore 'notice of the facts which constitute such breach' means 'actual notice' in the sense in which I have defined those words.

In the puzzling passage in the trial judge's judgment, he refers to a person failing to accept information available to him or failing to make the inquiries normal in his line of business; but these are the criteria of constructive notice. What he seems to be saying is that constructive notice becomes actual notice at some undefined point. This is incorrect; it is blurring the distinction between actual notice and constructive notice. There is nothing in this case which indicates that the plaintiffs or any of their officials knew that any part of the advance was to be applied to the purchase of shares in the defendant company, and what they did know does not lead to a conclusion that they must have inferred that the money was to be applied for the purchase of shares in the defendant company.

The matters which were relied on fixing the plaintiffs with constructive notice were, first, the failure to inspect or get a copy of the folio; secondly, the estimate of stamp duty in the estimate of the cost of the transaction which was submitted to them early on in the discussions; thirdly, the fact that planning permission was granted to the defendants in 1972 when application was made for it by them; and fourthly, counsel's opinion which is headed 'Rockfield Limited with Wicklow County Council.' The opinion is dated the 18th January 1973. I think the failure to get a copy of or to inspect the folio would be held to be constructive notice for this was a matter that the plaintiffs ought to have investigated and, if the doctrine of constructive notice applied, that failure would certainly have fixed them with that type of notice; but as it is an omission to do something which they ought to have done, it is not actual notice. I confess that I find it incomprehensible why the plaintiffs did not ask for a copy of the folio, but then laywers tend to think that everyone will take the same precautions as they do. I think that the plaintiffs ought to have inquired as to the estimate of stamp duty, but again, the fact that the stamp duty estimate was 1% of the purchase price was not notice that the money was to be applied for the purchase of the shares in the defendant company; it indicated that the purchase of another company was contemplated but not necessarily the defendant company. Knowledge that the defendants applied in 1973 for planning permission and that it was granted to them by Wicklow County Council was not either actual or constructive notice for, as I have already pointed out, until the 30th July 1974, when this court decided otherwise it was generally assumed in the legal, architectural and engineering professions that anybody could apply for planning permission without having any interest in the land. This transaction took place long before that date.

It follows that the plaintiffs are entitled to succeed in this action. Although they had constructive notice that the defendant company was the owner of the land, the plaintiffs had not actual notice and that is the knowledge which is referred to in s 60, sub-s 14 of the Act of 1963.

Re Northside Motor Co Ltd; Eddison v Allied Irish Banks (High Court 24 July 1985)

[9.37] Mr Costello owned half of the issued shares in Northside Motor Co Ltd ('Motor'). He wished to acquire the remainder of the shares and entered into an agreement with the respondent bank, whereby it was agreed that the bank would advance a sum of money to Northside Autosale Ltd, ('Autosales'), another company owned by Mr Costello. Autosales would then acquire the remainder of the shares in Motor using this loan. Costello undertook that once the shares had been acquired Motor would guarantee payment of the loan. The shares were subsequently acquired and the guarantee was given by Motor. The bank later became aware of the fact that the required procedure set out in s 60(2)–(11) had not been implemented. It therefore requested Motor to make the relevant declaration and to pass the appropriate resolution authorising the guarantee. Motor was later wound up and the liquidator applied to recover £44,139 which had been paid to the bank under the guarantee.

[9.38] **Costello J:** No attempt to comply with the subsection (2) procedures was made for some considerable time, notwithstanding the written undertakings given by Mr Costello's solicitor and accountant in that connection. In pursuance of the June agreement Northside Motor Company executed a guarantee in writing on the 4th January 1980 and sent it on to the bank, and a year after this the bank discovered that no meeting of the company had been held and no solvency declarations filed prior to its execution. As a result of pressure from the bank a special resolution was passed by the company on the 13th March 1981 purporting to authorise the execution of a guarantee by the company of the indebtedness of Northside Autosales to the bank and a solvency declaration was made by the two directors on the same day.

Seven months later (on the 13th October, 1981) the company executed a second guarantee in favour of the bank. The bank submits that the guarantee of the 13th October 1982 was executed on the authority of the procedures laid down by subsection (2), that it is accordingly valid and that the money paid under it is irrecoverable . . .

The agreement amounted to 'financial assistance' within the meaning of subsection (1) as it involved a promise to make a pecuniary payment if Northside Autosales defaulted in its obligations. The assistance thus given to purchase its own shares could only lawfully have been given on the authority of a previously adopted enabling resolution of the company supported by a previously executed solvency declaration referable to the financial position of the company at that time. This 'financial assistance' could not be retrospectively validated by the special resolution and declarations of the 13th March 1981. Accordingly, the entire transaction by which assistance was given by the June 1979 agreement was an illegal one and is voidable under subsection (14). The guarantees of the 13th October 1981 (and of course the earlier one of the 4th January 1980) are voidable and the liquidator is entitled to the return of the sum of £44,139.02 from the bank.

Whilst this concludes the first issue in the liquidator's favour I think nonetheless I should express my view on the second point of challenge to this transaction. As an alternative claim it is said that even if the enabling resolution and solvency declaration were not required in 1979 the guarantee relied on by the bank is voidable as the resolution passed and declaration made on 13th March 1981, were materially inaccurate and so they failed to validate the later transaction.

The special resolution of the 13th March 1981 reads as follows:

'That Northside Motor Company Limited will assist Northside (Autosales Ltd.) in the purchase of 7500 ordinary £1 shares in Northside Motor Company Limited, registered in the name of Declan Cummin of 7 Beech Park, Portmarnock, Co Dublin from the said Declan Cummin.

It is proposed that such assistance shall consist of Northside Motor Company Limited providing a guarantee supported by a debenture over all the assets of Northside Motor Company Limited in the sum of £57,500 to Allied Irish Banks Ltd which bank is providing a loan to Northside (Autosales) Limited to enable it to purchase the aforesaid shares.'

The only reasonable interpretation of this resolution is that the shares in the company were at that time in the name of Declan Cummin and that their sale had not yet taken place. This was incorrect. Although the exact date of the transfer was not established I am quite satisfied it had taken place long before this resolution was adopted. The resolution was a misleading one and inaccurate. The statutory declaration of the directors was also inaccurate and misleading in that its paragraph (2) was in the same form as the resolution and its paragraph (3) declared that the company 'having carried out the transaction referred to in 2 above will be able to pay its debts in full as they fall due', thereby implying that the sale of the shares had yet to take place.

In my view if a resolution and/or statutory declaration are materially inaccurate and misleading they fail to comply with the requirements of subsection (2) and (3) of section 60. As this has happened in this case, the guarantee of the 13th October 1981, was illegal under subsection (1) and the money paid on foot of it is recoverable by the liquidator.

Lombard & Ulster Banking Ltd v Bank of Ireland (High Court, 2 June 1987)

[9.39]   A group of parents formed a trust company to acquire the shares of an unlimited company, 'Brook House School'. It was agreed that the plaintiff would advance a sum of money to the trust company, in order to acquire the shares and that Brook House School would guarantee repayment of the loan. The guarantee was to be secured by a charge over the school property. Both the guarantee and mortgage were duly executed. The plaintiff subsequently sought to enforce its security. However, it transpired that the procedure laid down by s 60(2)–(11) had not been followed in that the required statutory declaration of solvency had not been made by the directors and no special resolution had been passed to authorise the giving of the assistance.

[9.40]   **Costello J:** It was urged on the plaintiff's behalf that compliance with the requirements of s 60 was satisfied when (*a*) the shareholders had authorised their solicitor to take all necessary steps and when (*b*) by informal consent all the shareholders agreed to what actually was done by some of their members. In this connection reliance was placed on *Re Duomatic Ltd* (1969) 2 Ch 365; *Re Bailey Hay* (1971) 1 WLR 1352; *Re Gee and Co (Woolich) Ltd* (1975) Ch 52; *Cane v Jones* [1980] 1 WLR 1451. I cannot agree. The section makes illegal the granting of financial assistance (as defined) and if exemption for a transaction in breach of subsection (1) is claimed because of the adoption of the procedures laid down in subsection (2) and (3) and (4) then strict compliance with the procedures is necessary. It is not sufficient to show that all the shareholders had authorised their solicitors to take the necessary steps and that they subsequently ratified what in fact was done. If the procedural requirements were not adopted the transaction is an illegal one, if in fact it involved that granting of financial assistance contrary to subsection (1).

It is now necessary to consider the parties rights in the light of these findings of fact. [His lordship then quoted s 60(1) & (14)]. What this means is (*a*) that although a transaction in breach of the section is illegal it is only 'voidable', not void and (*b*) it is only voidable against a person who had notice of the facts which constituted the breach.

There are three issues arising on the 'notice' point in this case. Firstly, the liquidator has argued that the phrase 'transaction in breach of the section' means the carrying out of a transaction prohibited by subsection (1) and that as Lombard and Ulster knew that the transaction was prohibited by subsection (1) it had sufficient 'notice' for the purpose of subsection (14) to enable the company avoid the transaction. I do not think that that can be correct. The subsection does not permit the avoidance of a transaction which is 'in breach of subsection (1) of this section' but 'any transaction in breach of this section'. And so, if a lender knows that an attempt to validate a prohibited transaction and avoid breaching the section be adopting the procedures set out in subsection (2), (3) and (4) is to be made I do not think that he has notice of any breach within the meaning of the subsection unless it can be shown (*a*) that there was in fact non-compliance with the subsections and (*b*) that he knew of the facts which resulted in non-compliance.

Secondly, as to the onus of proof. If, as has happened in this case, a defendant puts in issue the validity of a transaction prohibited by s 60 the onus is on the plaintiff to establish his case. However, if he fails to establish the validity of a transaction it does not follow that his claim on foot of a deed which is part of the transaction and is otherwise valid fails – the transaction is merely a voidable one. And it seems to me that the onus is then on the company which seeks to avoid it to show that the plaintiff had 'notice' as required by subsection (14). This means that in this case the liquidator must establish as a matter of probability that Lombard and Ulster had 'notice' that there was non-compliance with the provisions of subsection (2), (3) and (4). If he cannot do so the deed of charge is enforceable.

Thirdly, as to the nature of the 'notice', it is not sufficient for the liquidator to show that if Lombard and Ulster had made proper inquiries that they would have ascertained that the company had failed to comply with the subsections. It must be shown that Lombard and Ulster had 'actual notice' of the facts which constituted the breach, that is (a) that they or their officials actually knew that the required procedures were not adopted or that they knew facts from which they must have inferred that the company had failed to adopt the required procedures, or (b) that an agent of theirs actually knew of the failure or knew facts from which he must have inferred that a failure had occurred (see: *Bank of Ireland v Rockfield Ltd* (para **9.35**)). 'Constructive Notice' of the failure is not sufficient for subsection (14).

With these considerations in mind I now turn to the evidence in the case. It is perfectly clear that neither Lombard and Ulster or any of its officials had any idea that the required procedures which they knew were to be adopted had not in fact been carried out; on the contrary, they were expressly told . . . that all legal formalities were complied with and it was only on that representation that they allowed the loan to the Trust Company to be effected. What remains for consideration therefore is whether any of its agents had 'actual' notice of non-compliance with the statutory procedures. [His lordship then examined the evidence and concluded that the bank did not have actual notice of non-compliance with s 60].

It follows therefore, that even though the transaction was in fact one which was rendered illegal by s 60(1) the company is not at liberty to avoid it as the plaintiffs had no notice of what had happened. The deed of charge is valid and the plaintiffs are entitled as against the company to a well-charging order in respect of the sum of £787,670.84 (the amount now due on Lombard and Ulster's loan).

Notes
For an example of a breach of s 60 which also constituted 'oppression' for the purposes of s 205 see *Re Greenore Trading Co Ltd* (Unreported, High Court, 29/3/80), noted by *Ussher* in (1981) DULJ (ns) 79.

Reduction of capital[1]

[9.41] Strict procedures must be followed should the company wish to make a formal reduction of its capital.[2] References to 'reduction of capital' apply only to the reduction of the issued share capital. The cancellation of unissued shares is referred to as a 'diminution of capital'[3] and may be simply effected by the passing an ordinary resolution. Such a resolution must be authorised by the articles.[4] The procedure for reducing the issued share capital is more complex and is designed to protect both the creditors and members of the company.

S 72(2) of the Principal Act provides that subject to confirmation by the court, a company may, if so authorised by its articles,[5] by resolution, reduce its share capital. The subsection envisages three types of reduction:–

(*a*) By extinguishing or reducing the liability on any uncalled capital; or
(*b*) Either with or without extinguishing or reducing the liability on any of its shares, by cancelling any paid up share capital which is lost or unrepresented by available assets; or
(*c*) Either with or withoutr extinguishing or reducing liability on any of its shares, by paying off any paid up share capital which is in excess of the wants of the company.

1 Noted by *Ussher* (1978) DULJ 44.
2 Under s 68 of the Principal Act, the company may, if authorised by its articles, by ordinary resolution, increase its nominal share capital, consolidate and divide its shares into shares of a larger amount, subdivide its shares into shares of a smaller amount, convert shares into stock and re-convert stock into shares. Authority for such action is to be fixed in arts 40–45 of table A. See *Keane* at paras **16.03–16.07**.
3 Ibid s 68(2).
4 Ibid s 68(1)(e). The relevant article is art 45(c) of table A.
5 See art 46 of table A.

[9.42] Method (*b*) may be used where the company has incurred trading losses.[1] As we have seen supra, dividends cannot be paid until accumulated losses have been extinguished. By writing down a sufficient amount of its paid up capital, it may be able to write off its losses.[2] This form of capital reduction involves neither a return of capital to the members nor a reduction or extinction of their liability.

1 eg *Bannantyre v Direct Spanish Telegraph Co* (1886) 34 Ch D 287.
2 This is because such paid up shares represent a liability of the company. Notionally the company is liable to return this capital to the members when it is being wound up. By extinguishing the shares, the liability is also extinguished.

[9.43] A reduction of capital must be fair and equitable. Shares of the same class should be treated equally.[1] Where there are different classes of shares, the reduction must be in accordance with the rights attaching to those shares. Money is to be repaid and losses are to be borne in the same order of priority as would apply to the different classes of shares in a winding up, as regards the return or loss of capital respectively.

1 Cf *Robert Stephen Holdings Ltd* [1968] 1 WLR 522.

Re Chatterley-Whitfield Collieries Ltd [1948] 2 All ER 593 (Court of Appeal)

[9.44] The company proposed reducing its shares capital by repaying its preference shareholders and cancelling their shares. The preference shares were entitled to a 6% dividend, and in a winding up to priority of capital and arrears of dividend but to no further participation in assets.

[9.45] Lord Greene MR: A company which satisfies its capital requirements by issuing preference shares only does so where it is satisfied that the new capital will earn at least the promised rate of dividend. A company which has issued preference shares carrying a high rate of dividend and finds its business so curtailed that it has capital surplus to its requirements and see the likelihood, or at any rate the possibility, that its preference capital will not, if I may use the expression, 'earn its keep' would be guilty of financial ineptitude if it did not take steps to reduce its capital by paying off preference capital so far as the law allowed it to do so. That is mere commonplace in company finance . . . The position of the company itself as an economic entity must be considered and nothing can be more destructive of a company's financial equilibrium than to have to carry the burden of capital which it does not need, bearing a high rate of dividend which it cannot earn. In a company so situated the ordinary shareholders will be unfairly treated vis-a-vis the preference shareholders and the company may well fall into the situation when its preference dividends will begin to fall into irretrievable arrears. It is a fallacy to suppose that because ordinary shareholders will benefit, the transaction ought to be vetoed as being unfair to the preference shareholders.

It is a clearly recognised principle that the court, in confirming a reduction by the payment off of capital surplus to a company's needs, will allow, or rather require, that the reduction shall be effected in the first instance by payment off of capital which is entitled to priority in a winding up. Apart

221

from special cases where by agreement between classes the incidence of reduction is arranged in a different manner, this is and has for years been the normal and recognised practice of the courts, accepted by the courts and by business men as the fair and equitable method of carrying out a reduction by payment off of surplus capital . . .

In the argument before us there seemed to me at times to be involved some idea that preference shareholders, so far from being entitled to be paid off first, ought to be regarded as being entitled not to be paid off first, ie, that a company, having once issued preference shares is bound either to keep them forever, irrespective of the fact that it has surplus capital sufficient to pay off or at any rate is only entitled to reduce its capital by spreading the reduction rateably over its preference and its ordinary capital, with the result that the company will always be left with a certain amount of preference capital. The theory at the bottom of this idea appears to be that a preference shareholder subscribes his capital on the basis that he is to receive a preferential dividend of an agreed amount and that it is unfair to him to oust him from the company and thus deprive him of his contractual expectation of dividend. Apart from the fact that no such principle has ever been recognised by the court, it is, in my opinion, unsound for the reason that it ignores the facts (1) that the risk of a reduction of capital taking place is as much an element in the bargain as the right to a preferential dividend, and (2) that the well known practice of the courts involves what (as I have endeavoured to point out) is really in accordance with sound business practice, and moreover, is based on the recognised analogy of priorities as to capital in a winding up, viz., that, at any rate where preference shares are not entitled to participate in surplus assets, they are to be paid off first on a reduction and references to the reasonable expectations of preference shareholders which are intended to suggest that there is something inequitable in this form of treatment, have in my judgment, no support either in practice or on principle, and are unsound . . I am of opinion that the present appeal should be allowed and the proposed reduction confirmed, the application being otherwise in order.

Asquith LJ delivered a concurring judgment. Evershed LJ dissented.

Re Credit Finance Bank plc (High Court, 19 June 1989)

[9.46]   The application before the court was for approval of a restructuring of share capital involving the repayment of the preference shares and the issue of an increased number of ordinary shares.

[9.47]   **Costello J** (having referred to the fact that the company had complied with the procedures under s 72 which precede the application to court): Mr Duggan who is a shareholder of the company, made a number of points which, of course, he is entitled to do and brought to the attention of the court a number of matters so that the court could consider whether or not it was proper for the court to exercise its powers under the section. The main reason for this somewhat elaborate procedure is the protection of the creditors of the company when a company proposes to reduce its share capital and, of course there are other considerations to be taken into account and, as has been pointed out the court has a general discretion in the matter and one of the matters it takes into account is whether it is fair and equitable to reduce the share capital particularly having regard to the rights of shareholders.

A number of submissions in opposition to the petition were, broadly speaking, relating to an allegation that it was unfair and inequitable to make the order because of the facts and procedures that were adopted.

First of all, the main consideration in an application of this kind is the position of the creditors of the company. It is clear that the ordinary members will be as well looked after as before. No contingent creditors exist or have appeared to date. No contingent creditors have appeared to date despite the fact that the matter has been adequately advertised and in the circumstances the apprehension advanced by Mr Duggan that the scheme does not take adequate care of the creditors and that in some way in future the rights of all the creditors may be affected is groundless.

As to the claim made in relation to the ordinary shareholders and the fairness of otherwise of the scheme with regard to the ordinary shareholders and the preference shareholders, it is of some significance – considerable significance, indeed – that Mr Duggan is the only ordinary shareholder to have complained in this way. I would have thought if there was a real problem in this regard that other shareholders who are similarly affected, not being part of the major block of shares held indirectly through Allied Irish Banks would have come to court to make this point. The reality is, the scheme is fair between the classes of shareholders involved – the preference shareholders and the ordinary shareholders. It is true that the preference shareholders are to be repaid but this is perfectly permissible, as the *McKenzie* [*Re MacKenzie & Co* (1916) 2 Ch 450] case sanctions, namely that where there is a class of shareholders entitled to a preferential repayment of capital on winding up, repayment of such shareholders is permitted. A scheme which recognises this fact is unfair to other shareholders who have not that right. In the circumstances, there is nothing unfair to ordinary shareholders in the scheme proposed.

A further point taken, pehaps more a procedural point than anything else related to the variation of rights. It was submitted that there is a scheme involving the variation of rights and that there should have been a special meeting of this class of ordinary shareholders and none was held. It seems to me that matter is made clear from articles 5 and 6 of the articles of association, that when there are variations of special rights then a separate meeting must be held and a class meeting directed by the directors to be held but in this case there is not variation of special rights involved and a special class meeting is not required. It was pointed out that the position of the ordinary shareholders would be diluted – a massive increase in the number of ordinary shareholders of the company. To my mind, this is not a situation which would require a meeting of the special class.

In these circumstances I think this point is not one which should end up by my refusing the application now being made.

In all circumstances it is a case in which the court's discretion should be exercised in favour of the company and I will make an order confirming the reduction which was proposed.

Notes

See also *House of Fraser plc v ACGE Investments Ltd* [1987] AC 387; *Re Saltdean Estate Co Ltd* (1968) 1 WLR 1844; *Scottish Insurance Corporation Ltd v Wilson & Clyde Coal Co Ltd* [1949] AC 462.

[9.48]   A reduction of capital which is not in accordance with the rights of a class of shareholders must either be approved at a separate meeting of that class or be proved to be fair and equitable.

In Re John Power & Son Ltd [1934] IR 412 (Supreme Court)

[9.49]   The company had an issued share capital of £800,000, consisting of 400,000 preference shares of £1 each and 400,000 ordinary shares of £1 each. The preference shareholders were entitled to a cumulative dividend of 8% and to rank pari passu with the ordinary shareholders after they too had received a 8% dividend, but up to a maximum of 10%. They also had priority in a winding up to repayment of capital, however, they had no right to participate in any surplus capital. As a result of a fall in profits the board concluded that if provision were made for depreciation[1] there would not even be enough to pay the dividend on the preference shares. For the previous eight years there had not been sufficient profits to pay any dividend to the ordinary shareholders. The directors therefore proposed that the nominal value of the ordinary shares be reduced to 50p each and that the preference shares be converted into debenture stock of £1 at 5% interest per annum. The proposals were put to the ordinary and preference shareholders at separate meetings convened under (what is now) s 201 of the Principal Act. The scheme was unanimously approved by the ordinary shareholders and by the preference shareholders in the ratio of 6–1. Application was made to the court for sanction of the proposals. The dissenting shareholders unsuccessfully argued that the circular convening the meeting was misleading and that the proposals were unfair and inequitable. The scheme was unanimously approved by the Supreme Court (reversing the decision of Meredith J).

1 As to which see chapter 13 *infra*. For example, the preference shareholders may be entitled to priority in return of capital in a winding up. Therefore, where the reduction involves paying off shares or reducing or extinguishing liability on shares, the preference shareholders are affected first. However, where the reduction involves the cancellation of shares it is the ordinary shareholders who are first to go. Where neither class has priority to a return of capital, the reduction must be made rateably between both classes of shares: *Re Harrow Haematite Steel Co* (1883) 39 Ch D 582.

[9.50] **Fitzgibbon J:** It seems to have been contended in the court of first instance and the appellants certainly adumbrated a similar contention here, that where a proposal for a reduction of capital and a scheme of arrangement have been approved by majorities considerably in excess of those prescribed by the Companies Act, the court is practically bound in the absence of bad faith, or unless there is some statement or omission likely to mislead the shareholders, to give its confirmation or sanction, as the case may be, to the proposed reduction or scheme. In my opinion, the duty of the court is not confined to these considerations.

The rule was stated by the Court of Appeal in England in *In re Alabama, New Orleans, Texas and Pacific Junction Railway Company* [1891] 1 Ch 213, by a court consisting of Lindley, Bowen and Fry LJJ, and I take the following passage from the judgment of Lindley LJ:– 'What the court has to do is to see, first of all, that the provisions of that statute [ie ss 201–203 of the Principal Act] have been complied with; and secondly, that the majority have been acting bona fide. The court also has to see that the minority is not being overridden by a majority having interests of its own clashing with those of the minority whom they seek to coerce. Further than that, the court has to look at the scheme and see whether it is one as to which persons acting honestly, and viewing the scheme laid before them in the interests of those whom they represent, take a view which can be reasonably taken by business men. The court must look at the scheme and see whether the Act has been complied with, whether the majority are acting bona fide and whether they are coercing the minority in order to promote interests adverse to those of the class they purport to represent; and then see whether the scheme is a reasonable one, or whether there is any reasonable objection to it, or such an objection to it as that any reasonable man might say that he could not approve of it.' That decision came up for consideration two years later in the very important case of *In re English, Scottish, and Australian Chartered Bank* [1893] 3 Ch 385, when Sir Horace Davey argued in support of the scheme contended that the passage I have cited meant no more than that the court should see 'whether the majority were acting bona fide.' Vaughan Williams J – a great authority not only on company law but especially on the law and practice in bankruptcy, where similar principles in the case of creditors were of daily application – corrected him and pointed out in a luminous judgment, in which they are set forth as clearly and concisely as in any judgment I have read, the principles and considerations which should govern a court in dealing with such a scheme and he put his interpretation from this decision, which was affirmed in the Court of Appeal, where Lindley LJ, expressly reaffirmed all that he had said in the *Alabama* case [1891] 1 Ch 213, and Lopes and AL Smith LJJ, agreed that the law had been mostly clearly stated there. The House of Lords in *British and American Trustee and Finance Corporation v Couper* [1894] AC 399 and in *Poole v National Bank of China Ltd* [1907] AC 229, affirmed the right of a majority to bind a minority both on the question whether there should be a reduction of capital, and on the mode by which that reduction should be carried out, provided always that it was fair and equitable as between the different classes of share-holders and in the latter case Lord Macnaughton deprecated 'a growing tendency to narrow and restrict the power conferred by the Act of 1867 on companies limited by shares.'

Murnaghan J: The compromise or arrangement which can only be made binding against the wishes of dissentient shareholders requires the sanction of the court. In my opinion the court under this section can give all due weight to the opinion of the majority of the shareholders but the court is in no way bound merely to register the opinion of this majority. The sanction to be given by the court must be a real sanction, and to my mind the meaning of the section clearly is that no majority under the section can carry an arrangement which a fair and impartial mind would not sanction. Some of the earlier cases cited during the argument used language which appears to limit the court's exercise of an independent judgment as to the fairness of the proposal which it is asked to sanction . . . The case of *Poole v National Bank of China*, in the House of Lords shows that the test of the court's sanction in an analagous matter, viz., the reduction of capital, is whether the proposal is fair. Lord Loreburn says at p 236: 'The appellants represent a very small proportion of the holders of founder's shares. But if this resolution is in fact unfair, even a few opponents will prevail.' Now that the section can be invoked at any time and without the company being in process of liquidation it is incumbent on the court before giving its sanction to see that the compromise is fair in fact and in reality.

Can the court say that the proposed arrangement is not fair and reasonable? On the one hand under the scheme the preference shareholders lose any control in the management of the company and they lose their right to the preference cumulative dividend of 8 per cent, the actual payment of which is, however, in jeopardy. On the other hand, these shareholders are secured repayment of their capital and also debenture interest at 5 per cent. In a choice between these alternatives the determining element is the probable future earnings of the company, which is a matter purely of conjecture. I cannot say that the decision of the great majority of the preference shareholders to accept a certain 5 per cent in preference to an uncertain 8 per cent in the circumstances of this case involves any injustice or unfairness towards the dissentients . . .

I am of the opinion that the circular did not mislead by any positive statement, nor should any shareholder, who understands the ordinary principles of company law, have been misled by any inference to be made from the circular.

In my opinion the appeal should be allowed and the arrangement sanctioned. This involves the sanction also of the reduction of capital which should be sanctioned as part of the arrangement.

Hanna J concurred.

Notes

In *Re Holders Investment Trust Ltd* [1971] 1 WLR 583 the company proposed to reduce its capital by cancelling its redeemable preference shares

226

and replacing them with an unsecured loan stock worth less than the cash to which the preference shareholders would otherwise be entitled. The reduction was approved by a special resolution and also that a separate meeting of the preference shareholders. At the latter meeting the proposed reduction received the approval of the holders of 90% of the votes cast. However, these shareholders also held 52% of the ordinary shares and in that capacity they stood to gain from the reduction. The court refused to confirm the reduction because the majority preference shareholders had considered their personal interests rather than the interests of the preference shareholders as a whole.

If the proposed reduction violated some understanding between the shareholders on the basis of which the company was run, it might justify the presentation of a petition under s 213(f) of the Principal Act to have the company wound up on the just and equitable ground: *Re Murphs Restaurant Ltd* [1979] ILRM 141.

Procedure on a reduction of capital[1]

[9.51] When the company has passed a resolution for reducing share capital, it then applies to the court for an order confirming the reduction.[2] The application is by way of petition.[3] The procedure is contained in ss 73–77 of the Principal Act and in O 75 RSC (1986).

Where the reduction merely involved the cancellation of paid up shares the court will normally fix a day for the hearing of the petition and direct its advertisement in *Iris Oifigiuil*. Creditors objections will not normally be entertained.[4]

If the reduction involves the repayment of capital or the diminution of liability in respect of unpaid capital, s 73(2) of the Principal Act provides that the position of the creditors must be protected. A list of creditors must be settled by the court. These creditors are entitled to object to the reduction and in the case of an objection, the court can only dispense with the consent of that creditor if the company secures the payment of the debt by appropriating the full amount thereof. In the case of a disputed, contingent or unascertained debt, the company must secure by appropriation such as the court fixes after acquiring and adjudication of the type which is held in an official liquidation.[5]

1 Affirmed by the House of Lords at [1949] 1 All ER 1094.
2 Which is compulsory under the 1986 Act.
3 See *Keane* at paras **16.12–16.13**.
4 *Re Meux Brewery Co Ltd.* [1919] 1 Ch 28.
5 S 73(1) of the Principal Act.

Order for reduction of capital

[9.52] Under s 75 of the Principal Act the order only takes effect upon registration with the registrar. It must be accompanied by a minute approved by the court detailing the company's share capital as reduced. Under s 74(2) the court may require that the words 'and reduced' be added after the company's name for a specified period of time. This is presumably intended to act as a warning to outsiders dealing with the company that the 'creditors fund' has been diminished. A further and more important protection is to be found in s 76(2) of the Principal Act. This section provides that the reduction is not effective against any creditor who would have been entitled to object to it, but failed to do so due to his ignorance of the proceedings or of their nature and effect. If the company is subsequently wound up and such a creditor is not paid in full, the members will be liable to contribute an amount not exceeding the amount which they would have been liable to contribute if the capital had not been reduced.

Chapter 10

SHARES[1]

INTRODUCTION

[10.01]   In the case of a limited liability company having a share capital, the memorandum of association must state the amount of the share capital,[2] divided into shares of a fixed amount,[3] eg, 100,000 shares of £1 each. Each share must also be numbered, although this is not required if all the issued shares (or class of shares) are fully paid up and rank pari passu (ie equally).[4] In *Re Scandinavian Bank Group plc* [1987] BCLC 220 it was held that it is permissible for the company to have its share capital denominated in a foreign currency or in a number of currencies.

1 See generally *Keane* chapters 17–20.
2 S 6(4)(a) of the Principal Act.
3 Ibid.
4 S 80 of the Principal Act.

The nature of a share[1]

A-G for Ireland v Jameson [1904] 2 IR 644 (Chancery Division)

[10.02]   **Kenny J:** No shareholder has a right to any specific portion of the company's property,[2] and save by, and to the extent of his voting power at a general meeting of the company, cannot curtail the free and proper disposition of it. He is entitled to a share of the company's capital and profits the former . . . being measured by a sum of money which is taken as the standard for the ascertainment of his share of the profits. If the company disposes of its assets, or if the latter be realised in a liquidation, he has a right to a proportion of the amount received after the discharge of the company's debts and liabilities. In acquiring these rights – that is, in becoming a member of the company – he is deemed to have simultaneously entered into a contract under seal to conform to the regulations contained in the articles of association . . . Whatever obligations are contained in the articles, he accepts the ownership of the share and the position of a member of the company, bound and controlled by them. He cannot

divorce his money interest, whatever it may amount to, from these obligations. They are inseparable incidents attached to his rights, and the idea of a
share cannot, in my judgment, be complete without their inclusion.

1 See *Keane* at para **17.01**; also Rice *The Legal Nature of a Share* (1957) 21 Conv (ns) 433.
2 See also *Short v Treasury Commissioners* [1948] 1 KB 116, 124.

Notes

See also *Provincial Bank of Ireland Ltd v O'Connor* (High Court, unreported, Kenny J, 10 October 1974). See also the comments of Farwell J in
Borland's Trustee v Steel Bros & Co Ltd [1901] 1 Ch 279, (approved by
Fitzgibbon LJ in *Casey v Bentley* [1902] 1 IR 376) where he states that 'a
share is not a sum of money which is dealt with in a particular manner by
what are called for the purpose of argument executory limitations . . . A
share is the interest of a shareholder measured by a sum of money for the
purpose of liability in the first case and of interest in the second, but also
consisting of a series of mutual covenants entered into by all the shareholders *inter se*.'

In *IRC v Crossman* [1937] AC 26 Lord Russell of Killowen defines a share
as 'the interest of a person in the company, that interest being composed of
rights and obligations which are defined by the Companies Act and by the
memorandum and articles of association of the company'.

The 'mutual covenants' and 'rights and obligations' referred to by Farwell
J and Lord Russell respectively, constitute what is known as the 's 25 contract'. This contract is based on s 25 of the Principal Act which provides that
'the memorandum and articles shall, when registered, bind the company and
the members thereof to the same extent as if they respectively had been signed and sealed respectively by each member and contained covenants by
each member to observe all the provisions of the memorandum and of the
articles.'

Under s 79 of the Principal Act shares are deemed to be personalty. They
were held in *Lee & Co (Dublin) Ltd v Egan Wholesale Ltd* (High Court, 18
December 1979) to be choses in action, and are not 'goods' within the
meaning of the Sale of Goods Acts.

[10.03] A share is more than a mere contractual interest. It is a property
right protected by the Constitution.

Private Motorist's Provident Society and Moore v Attorney General [1984]
ILRM 988 (Supreme Court)

[10.04] Under s 5(2) of the Industrial and Provident Societies (Amendment) Act 1978, industrial and provident societies, including PMPS were to
be prohibited from accepting and taking deposits. This effectively prevented
PMPS from carrying on its business. PMPS argued therefore that the provisions of s 5(2) constituted an attack on its property rights under the Constitution. Mr Moore, who was a major shareholder in PMPS also argued that

the reduction in the value of his shares which resulted from the restriction of the activities of PMPS amounted to a violation of his constitutional property rights.

[10.05]   O'Higgins CJ: In the first place it is contended that the impugned legislation and in particular s 5(2) thereof, contravenes the provisions of art 40.3 of the Constitution in that it constitutes an unjust attack on property rights.

This case has been put forward on behalf both of the Society and Mr Moore. The rights which are alleged to have been infringed are among the personal rights which the Constitution guarantees to citizens. The Society is a creature of statute law and it is argued that as such is does not enjoy that constitutional protection. However, Mr Moore as a citizen is entitled to complain if the impugned legislation interferes with any of his personal rights . . . In the circumstances it is unnecessary to decide the question of the Society's rights. The court does not therefore express any opinion on this question.

Mr Moore's complaint with regard to a violation of his property rights is based on the fact that he is a shareholder in the Society. As such he claims that any attack upon his business or profitability of the Society is directly an attack upon his shareholding therein. For this reason he claims that, to the extent that the impugned legislation unjustly limits and prohibits the business of the society and thereby affects its profitability, it damages his investment as a shareholder and constitutes an attack upon his property rights. This claim is contested by counsel for the Attorney General who . . . specifically disputes Mr Moore's claim that, as a shareholder in the Society, his property rights are affected by legislation which applies only to the Society and to its business. He submits that a shareholder in an incorporated body such as the Society, while he has various contractual rights in and against that body, arising from his investment, he has no property rights in its assets or business. In the opinion of the court, it is sufficient that as a shareholder Mr Moore, has, to the extent of his investment, an interest in the Society and contractual rights arising therefrom. This interest and these contractual rights are property rights which belong to Mr Moore and which are capable of being harmed by injury done to the Society. The court, therefore, rejects the submission made on behalf of the Attorney General that as a shareholder in the Society Mr Moore has no property rights capable of being invoked for the purposes of art 40.3 of the Constitution . . .

[The court went on to hold that although s 5(2) constituted an attack on Mr Moore's property rights, it was not an unjust attack. The regulation of banking business according to the court was 'in accordance with the public interest and with the requirements of the common good.']

Finlay P, Walsh, Henchy and McCarthy JJ concurred.

Notes

In this case Mr Moore was only looking for a declaration. What would happen in a future case if the shareholder obtained damages for a breach of constitutional rights and the company subsequently obtained damages for the wrong done to it, based on some other cause of action (eg in contract or tort) which was not founded on a constitutional right? This could lead to problems of double recovery. For possible solution see: *O'Neill v Ryan and Others* (High Court, Lynch J, November 1989) and *MacCann* (1990) 8 ILTR (ns) 68.

Although O'Higgins CJ refrained from deciding whether a company had constitutional rights, the trial judge (Carroll J) was less equivocal, stating that 'Art 43(1) 1 cannot be construed as acknowledging or conferring a constitutional right on a corporate body, itself a creature of positive law. The right protected by art 43 is the right of a human person. Therefore in so far as a claim is made by the Society that its constitutional rights under art 40(3) and art 43 have been infringed by the Act, it is unsustainable, as the Society does not have such rights. This view is in accord with the view expressed by the Supreme Court in respect of art 40(1) in *Quinn's Supermarket Ltd v AG* [1972] IR 1, 14).'

Different classes of shares

[10.06] There is a presumption that the rights of all shareholders are the same.[1] However, it is not uncommon for the shares in a company to be divided into different classes with different rights. The division may be made in the memorandum or articles or pursuant to the terms of a resolution under s 68 of the Principal Act, increasing the company's capital. Most commonly, the division is made in the articles.

The basic category of shares consists of *ordinary shares*. If there is no division into classes, all shares are ordinary shares. Where special rights are given to certain classes the remaining shares will be ordinary shares. The most common type of share to which special rights are given is the preference share. Preference shares may have a right to a fixed dividend (eg. 10%) payable in priority to ordinary shares. In addition, or alternatively, they may have a right of priority over the ordinary shares, to a return of capital in a winding up.

[10.07] Preference shares may be cumulative or non-cumulative. In the latter case they are only entitled to a dividend in respect of any year in which a dividend is declared. Cumulative preference shares, however, are entitled, not only to this dividend, but also to arrears in respect of any years in which a dividend was not declared.[2] It is presumed that preference shares are cumulative[3] in the absence of a clear indication to the contrary.[4] Arrears will normally be paid out of the company's reserves.[5]

Preference shareholders commonly have no right to vote at general meetings, or alternatively may only be entitled to vote where their dividends are in arrear.[6]

Under standard form articles, a dividend is only payable when declared in general meeting and must not exceed the amount recommended by the directors.[7] They must in any case, be paid out of profits.

1 *Birch v Cropper* (1889) 14 App Cas 525.

2 Normally both the arrears and the current dividend will be payable in priority to the ordinary shareholders.
3 *Re F de Jong & Company Ltd* [1946] Ch 211; *Webb v Earle* (1875) LR 20 Eq 556.
4 *Staples v Eastman Photographic Materials Co* [1896] 2 Ch 303.
5 See *Re Lafayette Ltd* [1950] IR 100.
6 The extent of voting rights will, of course, depend on the terms of the issue of shares.
7 Art 117 of table A.

[10.08]   If the terms of issue do not differentiate between the different classes of shareholders regarding the right (*a*) to a dividend (*b*) to a return of capital (*c*) to participate in surplus assets in a winding up, or (*d*) to voting, the presumption is that all shareholders are to rank equally. A preference regarding any one of these rights does not imply a preference regarding another right.

Birch v Cropper; In Re Bridgewater Navigation Company Ltd (1889) 14 App Cas 525 (House of Lords)

[10.09]   The company's articles provided that dividends were payable in proportion to the amounts paid up on each share. The company had issued fully paid up 5% preference shares of £10 each and ordinary shares of £10 each on which £3.50 had been paid. The articles were silent as to the rights of the different classes. The House of Lords held once the capital had been returned in the liquidation of the company, then both classes of shares were to be treated alike, so that preference and ordinary shareholders were to participate in any surplus assets.

[10.10]   **Lord Macnaghten:** Every person who becomes a member of a company limited by shares of equal amount becomes entitled to a proportionate part in the capital of the company, and, unless it be otherwise provided by the regulations of the company, entitled as a necessary consequence, to the same proportionate part in all the property of the company, including its uncalled capital. He is liable in respect of all moneys unpaid on his shares to pay up every call that is duly made upon him. But he does not by such payment acquire any further or other interest in the capital of the company. His share in the capital is just what it was before. His liability is diminished by the amount paid. His contribution is merged in the common fund. And that is all . . .
  The ordinary shareholders say that the preference shareholders are entitled to a return of their capital, with 5 per cent interest up to the day of payment and to nothing more. That is treating them as if they were debenture-holders, liable to be paid off at a moment's notice. Then they say that at the utmost the preference shareholders are only entitled to the capital value of a perpetual annuity of 5 per cent upon the amounts paid up by them. That is treating them as if they were holders of irredeemable debentures. But they are not debenture holders at all. For some reason, or other the company invited them to come in as shareholders and they must be treated

233

as having all the rights of shareholders, except so far as they renounced those rights on their admission to the company. There was an express bargain made as to their rights in respect of profits arising from the business of the company. But there was no bargain – no provision of any sort – affecting their rights as shareholders in the capital of the company.

Then the preference shareholders say to the ordinary shareholders, 'We have paid up the whole of the amount due on our shares; you have paid but a fraction of yours. The prosperity of a company results from its paid up capital; distribution must be in proportion to contribution. The surplus assets must be divided in proportion to the amounts paid up on the shares.' That seems to me to be ignoring altogether the elementary principles applicable to joint stock companies of this description. I think it rather leads to confusion to speak of the assets which are the subject of this application as 'surplus assets' as if they were an accretion or addition to the capital of the company capable of being distinguished from it and open to different considerations. They are part and parcel of the property of the company – part and parcel of the joint stock or common fund – which at the date of the winding up represented the capital of the company. It is through their shares in the capital, and through their shares alone, that members of a company limited by shares become entitled to participate in the property of the company. The shares in this company were all of the same amount. Every contributory who held a preference share at the date of the winding up must have taken that share and must have held it on the terms of paying up all calls duly made upon him in respect thereof. In paying up his share in full he has done no more than he contracted to do; why should he have more than he bargained for? Every contributory who was the holder of an ordinary share at the date of the winding up took his share and held it on similar terms. He has done all he contracted to do; why should he have less than his bargain? When the preference shareholders and the ordinary shareholders are once placed on exactly the same footing in regard to the amounts paid up upon their shares, what is there to alter rights which were the subject of express contract?

Then it is said on behalf of the preference shareholders that the provision for payment of dividends in proportion to the amounts paid up on the shares leads to an inference that the distribution of surplus assets was to be made in the same proportion. I do not think that it leads to any inference of the kind. It is a very common provision nowadays, though it is not what you find in table A. And it is a very reasonable provision, because during the continuance of the company and while it is a going concern, it prevents any sense of dissatisfaction on the part of those who have paid more on their shares than their fellow shareholders of a different issue. But when it has come to an end I cannot see how it can be used to regulate or disturb rights with which it had nothing to do even while it was in force.

Lords Herschell and Fitzgerald delivered concurring judgments.

Notes

Cf *Re Bridgewater Navigation Co* [1891] 2 Ch 17, where it was held that three reserve funds representing undistributed profits belonged to the ordinary shareholders since they could have been distributed as dividends before the liquidation. It is hard to reconcile this decision with the decision of the House of Lords in *Birch v Cropper* (which, after all, dealt with the same company).

In *Wilson (Inspector of Taxes) v Dunnes Stores (Cork) Ltd* [1982] ILRM 444 Kenny J made the point that the concept of 'profits' does not survive into the liquidation; See also *Re Imperial Hotel (Cork) Ltd* [1950] IR 115, 118.

[10.11]   If the terms of the issue give the preference shareholders a right of priority to a fixed dividend, this is deemed to be exhaustive of their dividend entitlement, unless there is an express agreement to the contrary in the memorandum or articles.

Will v United Lankat Plantations Co Ltd [1914] AC 11 (House of Lords)

[10.12]   Shares were issued on terms that gave the preference shareholders an entitlement to a 'cumulative preferential dividend of 10% per annum on the amount for the time being paid upon such shares: and that such preference shares rank, both as regard capital and dividend, in priority to' the ordinary shares. The issue before the court was whether the 10% dividend was exhaustive of the preference shareholders rights, or whether they could share rateably with the ordinary shareholders in such profits as remained after the ordinary shareholders had also received 10%. The House of Lords held that the fixed dividend entitlement was exhaustive of their rights.

[10.13]   Viscount Haldane LC: The point in dispute is one of construction, and construction must always depend on the terms of the particular instrument; it is only to a limited extent that other cases decided upon different document afford any guidance.

My Lords, the action was brought by the appellant to obtain a declaration that the preferential shares which have been issued were entitled to rank for dividend pari passu with the ordinary shares of the company as against any profits of the company available for distribution as dividend after providing for a cumulative preferential dividend of 10 per cent on the preference shares and a dividend of 10 per cent on the ordinary shares. That was the claim and that was the point of controversy between the parties.

Now my lords, to see how the question so raised ought to be answered, it is necessary to turn to the documents which constituted the company. There is nothing special in the memorandum of association, but the articles contain provisions which are very material. [His Lordship then read the articles.]

A shareholder comes to the company and says 'I wish to contract with you for a share in your capital and so to become a shareholder.' He advances his money and the terms are contained in the bargain that is made between him and the company on the issue of the share to him, and that bargain is that he

235

is to receive a cumulative preferential dividend at the rate of 10 per cent on the amount paid up on his share and that his preference share is to rank both as regards capital and dividend in priority to other shares.

My Lords, I should have thought that if we were dealing with an ordinary case of two individuals coming together and if a document were produced saying 'You are to have a cumulative preferential dividend of 10 per cent' or whatever might be the equivalent in the circumstances of the bargain, it would be naturally concluded that that was the whole of the bargain between the parties on that point. You do not look outside a document of this kind in order to see what the bargain is; you look for it as contained within the four corners of the document.

My Lords . . . when you turn to the terms on which the shares are issued you expect to find all the rights as regards dividends specified in the terms of the issue. And when you do find these things prescribed it certainly appears to me unnatural to go beyond them . . .

Earl Loreburn and Lord Atkinson delivered concurring judgments. Lord Kinnear concurred.

[10.14] If the terms of the issue give the preference shareholders priority as to a return of capital, this is not exhaustive of their rights in a winding up. They may participate rateably in any surplus assets, subject to any express provision to the contrary in the memorandum or articles.

Re Cork Electric Supply Co Ltd [1932] IR 314 (Supreme Court)

[10.15] The preference shareholders were entitled to a fixed cumulative preferential dividend of 5% per annum and they also had priority to a return of capital in any winding up. Application was made to the High Court for directions as to whether these entitlements were exhaustive of their rights, or whether they should be entitled to participate rateably with the ordinary shareholders in any surplus assets in a winding up. Johnson J was of the opinion that the rights were exhaustive. However, his decision was unanimously reversed on appeal to the Supreme Court.

[10.16] **Kennedy CJ:** A rule was, however, established by the decision of the House of Lords in England in the case of *Birch v Cropper* (para **10.09**) that on the voluntary winding up of a company whose articles contained no provision as to the distribution of assets on a winding up, the assets remaining after discharging all debts and liabilities and repaying to the ordinary and preference shareholders the capital paid on their shares, ought to be divided among all the shareholders (both preference and ordinary), not in proportion to the amounts paid on the shares, but in proportion to the shares held. The decision is very important for the elementary principles it affirmed (of which there is a tendency to lose sight in argument). Preference shareholders are holders of shares in the capital of a company in the same way as ordinary shareholders are holders of shares in its capital. Both classes of shareholders are equally members of the company. Their respective positions are differentiated only to the extent to which the rights and privileges attaching to their respective shares are qualified contractually by the memorandum and articles of association of the company.

I turn, therefore, to the memorandum and articles of association of the plaintiff company to ascertain whether the right of the preference shareholders to participate in surplus assets on a winding up of the company has been abrogated, cut down or qualified in any way. There is no such specific provision . . . We have been asked to hold with Johnston J that the articles . . . is an exhaustive statement of the rights of the preference shareholders which excludes any other right or privilege and deprives (by implication) these shareholders of their right to participate in a distribution of surplus assets on a winding up . . .

After consideration, what we derive is only this, that the right to participate in a distribution of surplus assets on a winding up will be taken from preference shareholders by a clause in the articles of association delimiting their rights exhaustively to the exclusion of any other rights, and that the question whether a particular clause does so delimit the rights attached to the preference shares exhaustively and exclusively is a question of the construction of the particular articles of association in each case, and that we cannot construe one set of articles of another company (save, of course, as to any principle of rule of construction of general application authoritatively declared for the purpose of such construction).

Upon the construction of the articles of association before us it is to be observed that, while as regards participation in profits, the words of exclusion 'but to no further dividend', were carefully inserted, no such limitation was added to the immediately following clause as to priority in payment of capital. [His lordship therefore concluded that the preference shareholders should be entitled to participate in any surplus assets]

Murnaghan J: Where a right of priority is given in express terms to repayment in the event of winding-up, it seems to me that the provision is intended to deal with a situation in which the assets available will not be sufficient to repay the capital of both classes of shares in full, as it is only in such a state of affairs that a right of priority becomes material in a winding up. I do not see why such a provision should be construed as limiting the rights of holders of preference shares when the realised assets of the company representing the original subscribed classes of preference and ordinary shares are more than sufficient to repay both classes of shareholders in full.

Fitzgibbon J delivered a concurring judgment.

Notes

A similar conclusion was reached by the Court of Appeal in *Re William Metcalf & Son Ltd* [1933] Ch 142. However, in a series of cases the English courts including the House of Lords have held that a right of priority in return of capital is exhaustive of a preference shareholders' rights in a winding up. See *Re National Telephone Co* [1914] 1 Ch 755; *Scottish Insurance*

Corpn v Wilsons and Clyde Coal Co [1949] AC 462; *Prudential Assurance Co v Chatterley-Whitfield Collieries Co Ltd* [1949] AC 512. See Rice *Capital Rights of Preference Shares* (1962) 26 Conveyancer (ns) 115; Pickering *The Problem of the Preference Share* 1963 26 MLR 499.

It is presumed in the absence of an express provision to the contrary, that the cumulative preference shareholders are not entitled to arrears of undeclared dividends in a winding up. This presumption will be readily rebutted as in *Re F de Jong & Co Ltd* [1946] Ch 211 where the company's articles provided that 'the . . . preference shares shall carry the right to a fixed cumulative preferential dividend at the rate of 6% per annum on the capital for the time being paid up thereon respectively and shall have priority as to dividend and capital over the other shares in the capital for the time being.'

See also *Re EW Savory* [1951] 2 All ER 1036 where the court was prepared to construe the articles as giving a right to arrears. cf *Re Crichton's Oil Co* [1901] 2 Ch 184.

[10.17]   Arrears of dividends which have become a liability on the company before the commencement of the winding up rank as a deferred debt in the liquidation.

Re The Imperial Hotel (Cork) Limited [1950] IR 115

[The facts appear from the judgment]

[10.18]   **Gavan Duffy P:** The company incorporated in 1889 under the Companies Acts 1862 to 1886, has a paid up capital of £10,000 in preference and £15,000 in ordinary shares. On the 16th April 1946, having agreed to sell its undertaking, a hotel business, for £32,000, it went into voluntary liquidation and the liquidator estimates that, after discharging the creditors who are not members and his costs and repaying the preference share capital only, he will have about £6,500 in hand to distribute in accordance with the company's articles of association. The claimants, the preference shareholders assert that the arrears about £4,477 of their cumulative dividend is payable out of so much of that balance in hand as represents undistributed profits, while the ordinary shareholders contend that the whole balance must be applied under the articles as surplus assets towards repayment of their capital . . .

I construe the articles to effect the following bargain: (1). the profits of each separate financial year must first pay to the preference shareholders a cumulutive 6 per cent dividend, including all arrears; (2). the right of the preference shareholders to receive that dividend is a right independent of any recommendation by the board of directors and independent of any declaration of dividend by the company in general meeting and that right cannot be overridden by the board's exercises of its general powers of management and control; (3). the annual declaration of the amount of net profits by the board binds the preference shareholders, and the profits on which they have the first claim are those net profits less any deductions necessarily made thereout, for instance, payments for debenture interest . . .

I find that the claimants are seeking to enforce payment of a debt due to them by the company: I find that that is one of the liabilities that the liquidator . . . is bound to discharge before he distributes the company's property among the members entitled . . . and I find that this liability is in the peculiar position of not being payable pari passu with the liabilities generally, because the claimant's debt is a deferred debt, not payable in competition with those of creditors who are not members of the company by virtue of [s 207(1)(*g*) of the Principal Act] . . .

As to the position of the liquidator in paying the claimants he cannot ignore any statute bar that may be applicable, whether any limitation of time is expressly raised against the claimants or not.

Re Belfast Empire Theatre of Varieties [1963] IR 41 (High Court)

[10.19]   The company had not declared any dividends from 1895 to 1942. Dividends were, however, declared from 1942 to 1961 when the company went into voluntary liquidation. Dividends had not been paid to a number of shareholders who had either changed address and could not be traced or who had died and whose personal representatives could not be traced. The liquidator applied to the court for directions regarding the treatment of the unpaid dividends.

[10.20]   Kenny J: The first matter which arises for decision is whether claims for any part of the unpaid dividends are barred by the Statute of Limitations 1957 . . . It was correctly conceded by all counsel that a company which declares dividends does not become a trustee of them for any of its shareholders. This was first decided in *Smith v Cork and Bandon Railway Co* (1870) IR 5 Eq 65 . . . The same view was taken by Romer J in *Re Severn and Wye and Severn Bridge Railway Co* [1896] 1 Ch 559 and by Sir Andrew Marshall Porter MR in *Re Drogheda Steampacket Co Ltd* [1903] 1 IR 512 . . .

The next question is:– 'What length of time bars a claim for unpaid dividends' Section 11(1) of the Statute of Limitations 1957 provides:– 'The following actions shall not be brought after the expiration of six years from the date on which the cause of action accrued . . . (*a*) actions founded on simple contract,'while sub-s 5 of the same section provides:– 'The following actions shall not be brought after the expiration of twelve years from the date on which the cause of action accrued . . . (*a*) an action upon an instrument under seal . . .' The right of a company to receive dividends is conferred by the articles of association of the company: it is a right derived from the contract which the articles create between the company and each of its members. Sect 14 of the Companies (Consolidation) Act 1908 [ie s 25 of the Principal Act] provides that the memorandum and articles of the company when registered are to bind the company and the members thereof to the same extent as if the memorandum and articles had been signed and sealed by each member and contained covenants on the part of each member to observe all the provisions of the memorandum and of the articles. The decisions in *Oakbank Oil Co v Crum* [1883] 8 App Cas 65 and *Hickman v Kent or Romney Marsh Sheep Breeder's Association [1918]* 1 Ch 881 establish that the articles of association constitute a contract between the company and each of its members and although the contract is not sealed by each member or by the company, the effect of s 14 is that the contract binds the company and the members as if it were under seal . . . The appropriate statutory period is the period of twelve years prior to the 24th July 1961, when the company went into voluntary liquidation. Therefore all claims to dividends payable before the 24th July 1949 and not paid on the 24th July 1961 are now barred by the Statute of Limitations 1957 and may be ignored by the liquidator when calculating the amounts to be distributed among the shareholders.

The next matter relates to the unclaimed dividends amounting to £2,818 which became payable within the twelve years before the 24th July 1961. The declaration of a dividend by a company creates a debt due by the company to each shareholder . . . I shall direct the liquidator to send a notice by ordinary post to each shareholder who appears to him to be therein specified for unpaid dividends requiring such shareholder to prove his claim and informing him that such claim is to be proved before a date one month from the date of posting of the notice and that, in default, the shareholder will be excluded from the benefit of any distribution made before the debt is proved: the notice is to be sent to the address appearing in the register of members. I have been informed by counsel that some of the untraced shareholders lived in Northern Ireland and some in the Republic of Ireland. I shall direct the liquidator to advertise a similar notice in the three newspapers published in Dublin and in one newspaper published in Belfast. If any claims for unpaid dividends are not proved before that date in the notice the liquidator will be at liberty to distribute the assets of the company without regard to these claims.

The next set of questions relates to the way in which the liquidator is to deal with the distributions payable to shareholders who cannot be traced. It has been argued that the liquidator cannot lodge the monies representing these distributions in court as he is not a trustee and it has also been argued that he cannot dispose of these monies in any way and must retain them until claims for them are made to him. While a liquidator may be a trustee for the company of which he is liquidator, he is not, in my opinion, a trustee in any sense of the word for its members or creditors . . . If the liquidator cannot lodge in court the surplus assets which are payable to shareholders who cannot be traced, a voluntary liquidation can never be concluded unless there is some other way by which the liquidator can get a discharge for them. I think there is. When the liquidator has paid all the debts and the expense of liquidation and has distributed the proceeds of the assets among the shareholders who have proved that they are entitled to them, he should, in my opinion, bring a petition for the winding up of the company by the court for it would be just and equitable that the company should be wound up by the court . . . If a petition for the winding up of the company is presented by the liquidator in the name of the company, a winding up order will be made and the liquidator will then be given liberty to lodge in court the monies in his hands representing unclaimed assets. He can then be discharged from his office and all further proceedings under the winding up order will be stayed.

Notes

See also *Re Lafayette Ltd* [1950] IR 100 where Kingsmill Moore J found on the particular wording of the company's articles that arrears of dividends were only payable in the liquidation out of what would have constituted 'profits' when the company was a going concern.

Normally, however, the concept of 'profits' into the liquidation, as was pointed out by Kenny J in *Re Wilson (Inspector of Taxes) v Dunnes Stores (Cork) Ltd* (High Court, 22 January 1976) where he stated as follows:–

> 'The fallacy of the inspector's argument is that while what is distributed to the members in a winding up may be identified as having been profits, it is not distributed as profits but as a distribution in the winding up of the company or (as some call it) surplus assets. In a winding up of a company there may be liabilities which are related to the amount of the profits made before the company went into liquidation or the articles may confer on some shareholders a right to a dividend related to the amount of the profits before the company goes into liquidation but these are cases of the discharge of liabilities incurred before liquidation. What remains after discharge of liabilities is distributed among the shareholder not as profits but as surplus assets or as a distribution in the winding up. All the cases are consistent with this view and on close examination they refute the contention that what is distributed in a winding up is in any sense profits of the company.'

Redeemable shares[1]

[10.21]   In many respects preference shares (which commonly have a right to a fixed dividend) are akin to debentures.[2] Being a form of quasi-loan capital they may ultimately prove to be a burden on the company's finances with dividend payments leaving nothing for the ordinary shareholders. However, under s 64 of the Principal Act[3] the company could, if authorised by its articles, issue what were known as *'redeemable preference shares'*. These shares gave the company the benefit of an initial injection of possibly much needed capital. However, if this capital were no longer required it could be 'redeemed' or 'paid off' subject to conditions set out in s 64. These conditions were designed to ensure that the overall capital of the company was maintained despite the redemption. The section therefore provided that only fully paid up shares could be redeemed. Redemption could be either out of profits which would otherwise be available for dividend or out of the proceeds of a fresh issue of shares made for the purposes of the redemption. In the former case, the company had to transfer to a 'capital redemption reserve fund'[4] out of such profits a sum equal to the nominal value of the

241

redeemed shares. Any premium paid on redemption had be provided for beforehand out of profits or out of the share premium account.

S 64 has been repealed by s 220 of the 1990 Act and instead under s 207 of that Act companies limited by shares or limited by guarantee and having a share capital may now, if authorised by the articles, issue redeemable ordinary or preference shares. The conditions for redemption are broadly the same as for the purchase by a company of its own shares under part XI of that Act (as to which see paras **9.16–9.22**). The company cannot have only redeemable shares. Redemption can only take place if the shares are fully paid. Redemption is funded in the same way as a purchase of a company of its own shares under part XI. Shares which have been redeemed may be cancelled in the same way as shares purchased under part XI, and if not cancelled, they become 'treasury shares'. The reissue price of treasury shares which are to be sold 'off-market' is fixed in advance by special resolution of the company. Subject to any statutory provisions or provisions in the articles governing the alteration of class rights (as to which, see below) shares may be converted into redeemable shares. The alteration does not affect the shares of any dissenting shareholder.

[10.22]   Under s 219 if the company, in breach of contract, fails to redeem the shares, it is not liable in damages. The shareholder's right to obtain an order of specific performance against the company, or to prove for the redemption price in the winding up of the company, is subject to the same restrictions as are imposed on the shareholder where the company fails to purchase his shares under part XI.

An advantage of the redeemable share is that redemption may take place without the need to go through the capital reduction procedure of s 72 of the Principal Act.[5] An important difference between the redemption of redeemable shares under part XI and the purchase of shares under that part is that with redeemable shares redemption can only take place at the time stated in the terms of issue and provided the shares were redeemable shares at the date of issue. On the other hand a purchase under part XI gives the company greater flexibility as to the time and price of the purchase.

1 See *Keane* at para **18.09**.
2 ie secured loan capital.
3 As amended by para 11 of the first schedule of the 1983 Act.
4 This fund may be used to finance an issue of bonus shares.
5 As to which see chapter 12 *infra*.

Variation of rights of classes of shareholders[1]

[10.23]   It has already been seen in chapter 3 that provisions contained in the articles may be altered by special resolution. Different considerations apply where the alteration is to rights attaching to a particular class of shares. Under s 78 of the Principal Act it is provided that class rights may be varied where the memorandum or articles provide for their variation subject to the consent of a specified proportion of that class or with the sanction of a special resolution passed at a separate meeting of that class.[2] However, dissentients holding at least 10% of the shares of that class may apply to the court for an order cancelling the variation. If there is no such procedure provided for in either the memorandum or articles, then under s 38(2) of the 1983 Act, class rights contained in the articles may be varied only with the consent of 75% of that class or with the sanction of a special resolution of a separate meeting of that class. This is also subject to the right of dissentients representing at least 10% of that class to apply to the court for relief.[3]

1 See *Keane* at paras **17.10–17.14**; Rice *Class Rights and their Variation in Company Law* [1958] JBL 29; Rice *Problems on the Variation of Shareholders Class Rights* [1968] 41 ALJ 490.
2 Under art 3 of table A the 'specified proportion' is 75%.
3 The procedure for the application to court is discussed by *Keane* at para **17.11**.

[10.24] S 38(4) provides that class rights contained in the memorandum may be altered either in accordance with such procedure, if any, as is set out in the memorandum or in accordance with such procedure, if any, as is set out in the articles, provided that it has been contained in the articles from the date of incorporation.

[10.25] Under s 38(5) where the class rights are contained in the memorandum and neither the memorandum nor the articles contain a procedure for their variation, then they can only be varied with the consent of all the members.

It is envisaged in s 38(3) that where there is an express procedure for varying class rights in either the memorandum or articles, then that procedure need not necessarily require the separate consent of the class whose rights are to be varied.[1] Approval might, for example, be by way of a special resolution voted on by all shareholders. This is subject to the requirement, that if the alteration of class rights involves either:–

(*a*) the giving, variation, revocation or renewal of an authority to the directors to allot shares;[2] or
(*b*) a reduction of capital under s 72 of the Principal Act then the variation must receive the approval of at least 75% of that class or the sanction of a special resolution passed at a general meeting of that class.

It should be noted that under s 38(7) the alteration of a variation of class rights clause, is itself a variation of class rights.

Finally, apart from the procedures set out in s 78 of the Principal Act and s 38 of the 1983 Act, class rights may also be varied pursuant to a court order under ss 10, 201–203 or 205 of the Principal Act or s 15 of the 1987 Act, which sections are dealt with elsewhere.

1 If separate consent is required, dissentients representing at least 10% of that class may apply to the court for relief.
2 See chapter 8 *supra* and s 20 of the 1983 Act.

[10.26] The rights of a class of shareholders are neither varied nor 'affected' by the issue of new shares ranking pari passu with existing shares of that class

White v Bristol Aeroplane Co [1953] Ch 65 (Court of Appeal)

[10.27] Under art 68 of the defendant company's articles, the rights of any class of shares could only be 'affected, modified, varied, dealt with or abrogated in any manner' with the sanction of a special resolution passed at a separate meeting of that class. The company proposed to make a bonus issue of both ordinary and preference shares to the existing ordinary shareholders. The plaintiff on behalf of the existing preference shareholders claimed that their voting rights would be 'affected' by the issue of new preference shares and that therefore they should be entitled to vote on the proposed issue at a separate class meeting. This view was rejected by the Court of Appeal.

[10.28]   **Romer LJ:** The rights attaching to the preference stockholders are those which are conferred by articles 62 and 83; and the only relevant article for present purposes is article 83. Under that article it is provided . . . that on a poll every member present in person or by proxy shall have one vote for every share held by him, or in the case of the preference stock, one vote for every £1 of preference stock held by him. It is suggested that, as a result of the proposed increase of capital that right of the preference stockholders will in some way be 'affected'; but I cannot see that it will be affected in any way whatever. The position then will be precisely the same as now – namely, that the holder of preference stock will have on a poll one vote for every £1 of preference stock held by him. It is quite true that the block vote, if one may so describe the total voting power of the class, will or may, have less force behind it, because it will pro tanto be watered down by reason of the increased total voting power of the members of the company; but no particular weight is attached to the vote, by the constitution of the company, as distinct from the right to exercise the vote, and certainly no right is conferred on the preference stockholders to preserve anything in the nature of an equilibrium between their class and the ordinary stockholders or any other class.

During the course of the discussion I asked Mr Gray whether it would not be true to say that the logical result of his argument would be that the rights of ordinary shareholders would be affected by the issue of new ordinary capital on the ground that every one of the considerations on which he was relying would be present in such a case. The votes of the existing shareholders would be diminished in power; and they would have other people with whom to share the profits and on a winding up, to share the capital assets. In answer to that he was constrained, I think rightly, to say that was so. But in my opinion it cannot be said that the rights of ordinary shareholders would be affected by the issue of further ordinary capital; their rights would remain just as they were before, and the only result would be that the class of persons entitled to exercise those rights would be enlarged; and for my part, I cannot help thinking that a certain amount of confusion has crept into this case between rights on the one hand and the result of exercising those rights on the other hand. The rights, as such, are conferred by resolution or by the articles and they cannot be affected except with the sanction of the members on whom those rights are conferred; but the results of exercising those rights are not the subject of any assurance or guarantee under the constitution of the company, and are not protected in any way. It is the rights and those alone, which are protected and for the reasons which my Lord has given and in view of what I have myself said, the rights of the preference stockholders will not, in my judgment be affected by the proposed resolutions . . .

Evershed MR delivered a concurring judgment. Denning LJ concurred.

Notes
See also *Re Schweppes Ltd* [1914] 1 Ch 322; *Re John Smith's Tadcaster Brewery Co Ltd* [1953] 2 WLR 516

[10.29]   Where the voting strength of one class of shares is diluted by the increase in voting strength of another class of shares, the rights of the first class, although possibly 'affected as a matter of business' are not 'varied as a matter of law'.

Greenhalgh v Aderne Cinemas Ltd [1946] 1 All ER 512 (Court of Appeal)

[10.30]   The company had issued ordinary shares of 10s each and other ordinary shares of 2s each. Both classes of shares had one vote per share. This gave the plaintiff, who held 2s shares 40% of the votes in general meeting thereby enabling him to block any special resolution. The holders of the 10s shares passed an ordinary resolution (under the equivalent of s 68 of the Principal Act) subdividing each 10s share into five 2s shares, each of which had one vote per share. The plaintiff unsuccessfully argued that the rights attaching to his shares had been varied as a result.

[10.31]   Lord Greene MR: Looking at the position of the original 2s ordinary shares, one asks oneself: What are the rights in respect of voting attached to that class within the meaning of art 3 of table A which are to be unalterable save with the necessary consents of the holders? The only right of voting which is attached in terms to the shares of that class is the right to have one vote per share pari passu with the other ordinary shares of the company for the time being issued. That right has not been taken away. Of course, if it had been attempted to reduce that voting right, eg. by providing or attemptng to provide that there should be one vote for every five of such shares, that would have been an interference with the voting rights attached to that class of shares. But nothing of the kind has been done; the right to

245

have one vote per share is left undisturbed . . . If an attempt had been made, without subdividing the 10s shares, to give them five votes per share, it may very well be that the rights attached to the original 2s shares would have been varied, because one of the rights attached to the original class of shares was that they should have voting powers pari passu with the other ordinary shares of the company and that right might well have been affected if in the result you had two kinds of ordinary shares, one a 10s share carrying five votes and the other a 2s share carrying one vote. But that is not what was done . . .

I now come to a point which to my mind, throws a good deal of light on the validity of the argument. It was conceded by counsel for the appellant that if the company had created a number of new ordinary shares of 2s each and had issued them, each share carrying one vote, that would not have done an interference with the rights of the original 2s shares. Had that been done, of course, it would have been just as possible to swamp the appellant's voting rights as it has turned out to be by the passing of these resolutions. I do not find anything in the answers of counsel which satisfactorily explain why it would be an interference with the 2s shares in the one case and not in the other case, because, if the 2s shares had the right to prevent the voting equilibrium being upset in the way in which it has been upset, I cannot see why they could not object to the creation of new shares which would have the same result . . . I agree, the effect of the resolution is, of course, to alter the position of the 1941 2s shareholders. Instead of Greenhalgh finding himself in a position of control, he finds himself in a position where the control has gone, and to that extent the rights of the 1941 2s shareholders are effected, as a matter of business. As a matter of law, I am quite unable to hold that, as a result of the transaction, the rights are varied; they remain what they always were – a right to have one vote per share pari passu with the ordinary shares for the time being issued which include the new 2s ordinary shares resulting from the subdivision.

Morton LJ delivered a concurring judgment. Somervell LJ concurred.

Notes

An alteration in the rights of one class of shareholders, even if effected in accordance with the appropriate statutory procedures, may in some circumstances constitute oppression or disregard of the interests of another class of shareholders, within the meaning of s 205 of the Principal Act. See *Re Williams Group Tullamore Ltd* [1985] IR 613.

Share certificates[1]

[10.32]   A share certificate is issued by the company to each of its members under the common seal and is prima facie evidence of the member's title to the shares.[2] The company is estopped from denying as against a purchaser for value without notice, that the person named in the certificate is entitled to the shares.

1 See *Keane* at paras **17.15–17.16**.
2 S 87 of the Principal Act.

Re Bahia & San Francisco Railway Co (1868) LR 3 QB 584 (Queen's
Bench)

[10.33]   Five shares in the company were owned by Trittin. Without her
knowledge Stocken and Goldner forged a transfer of the shares to themselves and lodged the transfer and Trittin's share certificate with the company for registration. They were duly registered and a new certificate was
registered in their names. Relying on the new certificate Burton and Goodburn bought the shares on the stock exchange for value and without notice
of the forgery. They were registered as the holders of the shares and were
issued with share certificates to this effect, but subsequently the company
was obliged to restore Trittin's name to the register. Burton and Goodburn
brought an action against the company for an equivalent number of shares or
damages.

[10.34]   **Cockburn CJ:** I am of opinion that our judgment must be for the
claimants . . . The company are bound to keep a register of shareholders
and have power to issue certificates certifying that each individual shareholder named therein is a registered shareholder of the particular shares
specified. This power of granting certificates is to give the shareholders the
opportunity of more easily dealing with their shares in the market and to
afford facilities to them of selling their shares by at once showing a marketable title, and the effect of this facility is to make the shares of greater value.
The power of giving certificates is, therefore, for the benefit of the company
in general; and it is a declaration by the company to all the world that the
person in whose name the certificate is made out, and to whom it is given, is a
shareholder in the company and it is given by the company with the intention
that it shall be so used by the person to whom it is given and acted upon in the
sale and transfer of shares. It is stated in this case that the claimants acted
bona fide and did all that is required of purchasers of shares; they paid the
value of the shares in money on having a transfer of the shares executed to
them, and on the production of the certificates which were handed to them.
It turned out that the transferors had in fact no shares, and that the company
ought not to have registered them as shareholders or given them certificates
the transfer to them being a forgery. That brings the case within the principle
of the decision in *Pickard v Sears* 6 Ad & E 469 as explained by the case of
Freeman v Cooke 2 Ex 654 that if you make a representation with the
intention that it shall be acted upon by another, and he does so, you are
estopped from denying the truth of what you represent to be the fact.
   The only remaining question is, what is the redress to which the claimants
are entitled. In whatever form of action they might shape their claim, and
there can be no doubt that an action is maintainable, the measure of
damages would be the same. They are entitled to be placed in the same position as if the shares, which they purchased owing to the company's representation had in fact been good shares and had been transferred to them, and
the company had refused to put them on the register and the measure of

damages would be the market price of the shares at that time; if no market price at that time; than a jury would have to say what was a reasonable compensation for the loss of the shares.

Blackburn, Mellor and Lush JJ delivered concurring judgments.

Notes

See also *Balkis Consolidated Co v Tomkinson* [1893] AC 396; cf *Simm v Anglo-American Telegraph Co* (1879) 5 QBD 188.

[10.35]   The company is not bound by a forged share certificate.

Ruben v Great Fingall Consolidated [1906] AC 439

[10.36]   The plaintiff stockbrokers, Ruben and Ladenburg had obtained a loan for the secretary of the defendant's company (Rowe) on the security of a share certificate for certain shares in that company. Rowe had affixed his signature and the company's seal to the certificate and had forged the signatures of two directors. The plaintiffs having reimbursed the mortgagees then sued the defendant company for damages for failing to register them as owners of the shares. The action failed on the ground that the company was not bound by the certificate.

[10.37]   Lord Macnaghten: Ruben and Ladenburg are the victims of a wicked fraud. No fault has been found with their conduct. But their claim against the respondent company is, I think simply absurd.

The thing put forward as the foundation of their claim is a piece of paper which purports to be a certificate of shares in the company. This paper is false and fraudulent from beginning to end. The representation of the company's seal which appears upon it though made by the impression of the real seal of the company, is counterfeit, and no better than a forgery. The signatures of the two directors which purport to authenticate the sealing are forgeries pure and simple. Every statement in the document is a lie. The only thing real about it is the signature of the secretary of the company who was the sole author and perpetrator of the fraud. No one would suggest that this fraudulent certificate could of itself give rise to any right or bind or affect the company in any way. It is not the company's deed, and there is nothing to prevent the company from saying so.

Then how can the company be bound or affected by it? The directors have never said or done anything to represent or lead to the belief that this thing was the company's deed. Without such a representation there can be no estoppel.

The fact that this fraudulent certificate was concocted in the company's office and was uttered and sent forth by its author from the place of its origin cannot give it an efficacy which it does not intrinsically possess. The secretary of the company who is a mere servant, may be the proper hand to deliver out certificates which the company issues in due course, but he can have no authority to guarantee the genuineness or validity of a document which is not the deed of the company.

I could have understood a claim on the part of the appellants if it were incumbent on the company to lock up their seal and guard it as a dangerous beast and if it were culpable carelessness on the part of the directors to commit the care of the seal to their secretary or any other official. That is a view which once commended itself to a jury, but it has been disposed of for good and all by the case of *Bank of Ireland v Trustees of Evan's Charities* 5 HLC 389 in this House.

Lord Loreburn LC and Lords Davey and James of Hereford delivered concurring judgments. Lords Robertson and Atkinson concurred.

Notes

The secretary is no longer a 'mere servant' of the company (see *Panorama Developments (Guildford) Ltd v Fidelis Furnishing Fabrics Ltd* [1971] 2 QB 711) and may now have ostensible authority to guarantee the genuineness of the share certificate. Furthermore, it is a well established principle of the law of Tort that a principal is vicariously liable for the acts of his servants, including fraud, performed in the course of his employment. See *Lloyd v Grace Smith & Co* [1912] AC 716.

In earlier cases it had been suggested that where a share certificate wrongly stated that shares were fully paid up, the company was estopped from making a call on the shareholder for the unpaid amount. See *Burkinshaw v Nicholls* (1878) 3 App Cas 1004. This would however amount to the issue of the shares at a discount and has accordingly been superseded by s 27 of the 1983 Act. This section unequivocally prohibits the issue of shares at a discount and requires the allottee to pay the amount of any discount, plus interest. However, under s 27(2) payment of the discount cannot be required from subsequent purchasers for value without notice of the discount, and those deriving title from them.

Share warrants

[10.38] Under s 88 of the Principal Act a public company may, if authorised by its articles issue share warrants, instead of share certificates. These give the bearer title to the shares. In such a case the shares may be transferred simply by delivery of the warrant. No instrument of tranfer is necessary. Share warrants are in practice, extremely rare.[1]

1 See *Keane* at para **17.17**.

Calls[1]

[10.39] When shares are allotted the company may require that they be paid for in full upon issue. Alternatively, it may stipulate that only a portion of the amount be paid up immediately, the balance to be paid up subsequently and possibly by instalments.[2] The collection of the unpaid balance is by way of calls (ie. forms of demand). The unpaid balance is therefore known as the uncalled capital. The procedure for making calls is set out in arts 15–21 of table A.[3] If a member disposes of his shares he is no longer liable for calls on them, liability falling instead on the transferee.[4] Calls should normally be made pari passu on all shareholders.

1 See *Keane* at paras **19.01–19.05**.
2 Under s 28 of the 1983 Act, at least one quarter of the 'authorised minimum' (ie. £30,000) must be paid on allotment.
3 Discussed by *Keane* at paras **19.02**.
4 *Re Discoverers Finance Corp; Linders' Case* [1910] 1 Ch 207, aff'd [1910] 1 Ch 312.

[10.40] Calls should normally be made pari passu on all shareholders. Even where permitted by the articles,[1] special grounds will be required to justify a departure from this principle.

1 As in art 20 of table A.

Galloway v Halle Concerts Society Ltd [1915] 2 Ch 233 (Chancery Division)

[10.41] The plaintiffs who were in dispute with the directors had been late in paying on several calls and had failed to pay at all in one case. Because of this the directors made a call upon them for the whole of the outstanding balance on the shares. The court held that this did not constitute sufficient cause for making such a call and accordingly held that the plaintiffs were under no liability to pay.

[10.42] **Sargant J:** The question now arises whether the society is entitled to call up the full amount uncalled in respect of the contributions of the plaintiffs, while making no similar call in respect of the contributions of the other members of the society, for the reason that these two members have given trouble to the society in the past in securing and enforcing payment of the previous calls made by the society . . . There is no doubt that prima facie, as was pointed out in the speech of Lord Macnaghten in *British and American Trustee and Finance Corporation v Couper* [1894] AC 399, 417, there is by virtue of the ordinary law of partnership an implied condition of equality between shareholders in a company, and that prima facie it is entirely improper for the directors to make a call on some members of a class of shareholders who stand in the same relation to the company as the other members of the class without making a similar call on all the other members of that class. The point was decided . . . in *Preston v Grand Collier Dock Co* 11 Sim 327 . . . Is it right to make this call on these two persons alone for this large amount merely because they have been dilatory in the payment of previous calls? It is said that expense is caused to the society by the necessity of enforcing these repeated calls against them and that less expense will be caused if the amounts can be called up in a lump sum. In my opinion, that is not a sufficient reason. So far as legal expenses are concerned those legal expenses can be recovered in the ordinary way, and I cannot think that the mere fact that letter having been written to the plaintiffs before the matter was put in the solicitor's hands for the purpose of taking proceedings is a sufficient reason for the course which has been adopted. In the present case, the result might be more unfair to the plaintiffs than in the ordinary case, because, so far as I can see, in case of a winding up of the company there is no certainty at all under the memorandum of association that the sums of £80 and £75 in question would come back to the plaintiffs in priority to the payments that would have to be made to the other members of the society. However, that may be, it seems to me that the reason given by the committee of the society for making the calls on these two persons separately from any similar calls on the other members of the society is altogether insufficient, and accordingly, I propose to make a declaration substantially to the effect claimed by the writ.

Notes

See also *Alexander v Automatic Telephone Co* [1900] 2 Ch 56.

Forfeiture of shares

[10.43]   Under common form articles[1] provision is made for the forfeiture by the company of shares in respect of which calls have not been paid.[2] Forfeiture in such a case, although constituting a reduction of the company's share capital, does not require the sanction of the court under s 72 of the Principal Act.[3] Upon forfeiture the shareholder ceases to be a member of the company as regards forfeited shares,[4] although he remains liable to the company for all moneys which, at the date of forfeiture were payable to him in respect of the shares, until they have been paid by him or any new allottee of the shares. He is also liable as a former member for all unpaid sums on his former shares, in the event of a winding up within a year of his ceasing to be a member.[5] In the case of a plc, forfeiture may result in its allotted shares falling below the 'authorised minimum'.[6] Under s 43 of the 1983 Act the plc has three years within which to sell the shares. If this is not done they must be cancelled by the plc which must then reduce the amount of its nominal share capital accordingly.[7] If this brings the plc's nominal capital below the authorised minimum, it must re-register as another type of company.[8] Forfeiture is a rare occurrence due to the infrequency with which shares are allotted as partly paid up. However, due to the drastic consequences of forfeiture the procedure set out in the articles for the forfeiture of shares must be strictly followed.

1 Arts 33–39 of table A.
2 See *Keane* at paras **19.06** et seq.
3 S 41(4)(d) of the 1983 Act.
4 Art 37 of table A.
5 S 207(1)(*a*)(*b*)(*c*)(*d*) of the Principal Act.

6 See s 19 of the Principal Act. The authorised minimum is currently £30,000.
7 Application to the court for confirmation of the reduction under s 72 et seq, of the Principal Act is not required.
8 S 43 of the 1983 Act also applies to a surrender in lieu of forfeiture.

[10.44] As an alternative to going through the formal procedure of forfeiture, the shareholders may instead surrender the shares in question, provided that this is authorised by the articles. However, as surrender could, otherwise constitute an unlawful reduction of capital,[1] the shares may only be surrendered if the company would, in the circumstances have been entitled to forfeit them anyhow.

A surrender of fully paid up shares in exchange for new shares of the same nominal value is valid, where the surrendered shares remain capable of being reissued.[2]

1 *Bellerby v Rowland Marwoods Steamship Co Ltd* [1902] 2 Ch 14.
2 See *Keane* at paras **19.13** et seq.

Lien on shares[1]

[10.45] Under common form articles the company has a lien over its own shares (other than fully paid up shares) in respect of all or any sums owing by the shareholder to the company, including any unpaid balance on the shares.[2] The articles typically confer a power to enforce the lien by way of sale.[3] S 44 of the 1983 Act prohibits a plc from creating any lien or charge over its own shares, except in respect of amounts unpaid on its shares. Permitted also are charges over its own shares, created before registration or re-registration as a plc, or in the ordinary course of the plc's business, where that business involves money lending, the provision of credit or hire purchase facilities.

1 Art 11 of table A.
2 Ibid art 12. Ussher suggests at p 318 of *Company Law in Ireland* that even if there is no power of sale in the articles, the company may still have an implied power of sale under s 19 of the Conveyancing Act 1881. This section implies a power of sale in favour of mortgages by deed. Under the Principal Act the memorandum and articles of association take effect as if they were part of contract by way of deed.
3 As to which see art 7 of table A.

[10.46] Although under s 123 of the Principal Act no notice of any trust or other equitable interest in its shares is registrable by the company in its register of members, this does not entitle the company to disregard notice of such interests when a question of priorities arises between the company and a third party.

Rearden v Provincial Bank of Ireland [1896] 1 IR 532 (Chancery Division)

[10.47] Part of the assets of a trust included shares in the defendant company. The shares were registered in the name of the trustee. The bank was at all times aware of the existence and terms of the trust. When the trustee defaulted on his personal debts to the bank, the bank claimed a lien over the shares. A question of priorities arose between the trust and the bank. It was held by Porter MR and confirmed by the Court of Appeal that the trust had priority over the lien.

[10.48] **Porter MR** (Having referred to the predecessor of s 123 proceeded as follows): It cannot be doubted that the intention was to spare the company the responsibility of attending to any trusts or equities whatever attached to their shares, so that they might safely and securely deal with the person who is registered owner, and with him alone, recognising no other person and no different right; freeing them in short, from all embarassing inquiries into conflicting claims as to shares, transfers, calls, dividends, right to vote, and the like; and enabling them to treat the registered shareholder as owner of the shares for all purposes, without regard to contract as between himself and third persons. But it could never have been the object of the legislature to enable the company, say a trading company like the Provincial Bank, to ignore for their own purposes and interests the rights of other persons of which they have actual knowledge, so as, in the words of Lord Blackburn, 'to charge what they knew was one man's property with another man's debt' . . . It is right and necessary that a company should not be mixed up with outside claims and disputes. The company is to have one person, or one set of persons alone, to deal with as shareholders; and it is to be unaffected by trusts, equities and the like, which they have no means of determining or knowing anything about. In such cases, apart from [s 123] and special articles of association, they really could not protect themselves. But this immunity can have no reason to support it when it is claimed that the company may, for it's own benefit ignore facts within its own knowledge, as by creating liens in its own favour, contrary to good faith.

Section 123 provides 'No notice of any trust expressed or implied or constructive shall be entered on the register, or be receivable by the registrar, in case of companies under this Act, and registered in England or Ireland,' and clause 8 of the articles of association provides, 'No person shall be recognised by the company as holding any share upon any trust, and the company shall not be bound by, or recognise any equitable future or partial interest in any share . . . or any other right in respect of any share except an absolute right to the entirety thereof in the registered holder.' (ie art 7 of table A). In both cases the language is, I think, intended for the protection of the company; not to enable it to commit frauds or knowingly take the benefit of them.

Notes
See also *MacKereth v Wigan Coal and Iron Co Ltd* [1916] 2 Ch 293.

Transfer of shares[1]

[10.49] A share, being a chose in action,[2] is capable of being assigned. The assignee does not, however, become a member of the company until such time as his name is entered on the register of members.[3] Assignment may be voluntary or involuntary. The former is known as transfer, the latter is transmission. Under s 79 of the Principal Act, shares are freely transferable, subject to the provisions of the articles. A private company must place restrictions on the transfer of its shares.[4] Extensive restrictions are imposed by art 3 of Table A which entitles the directors 'in their absolute discretion and without assigning any reason therefor' to decline to register the transfer of any share.[5]

1 See *Keane* at paras **20.01**.
2 See *Lee & Co (Dublin) Ltd v Egan (Wholesale) Ltd* (unreported, High Court, 18/12/79).
3 See s 31 of the Principal Act.
4 S 33 of the Principal Act.
5 The power of the directors to refuse to register a transfer is more limited in the case of a public company. They may however, refuse to register a transfer where inter alia they disapprove of the transferee or believe that the transfer would imperil and prejudicially affect the company.

[10.50] A decision of the directors to decline to register a transfer of shares may only be set aside on proof that the decision was reached in bad faith or for an improper purpose. The burden of proof is on the person alleging bad faith or improper purpose. The directors are under no obligation to give reasons for their decision. However, the court may examine the validity of such reasons, if any, as the directors choose to give.

Re Dublin North City Milling Co [1909] 1 IR 179 (Chancery Division)

[10.51] The directors, in refusing to register a transfer of shares to Spicer (an existing member of the company) simply gave as their reason for the refusal, the fact that they had concluded that the transfer would be to the 'detriment and injury' of the company. Spicer sought to challenge this decision and to have the register rectified under s 122 of the Principal Act. (This section entitles a transferee whose name is omitted from the register 'without sufficient cause' to apply to the court for rectification of the register. The section may also be used by a person whose name has not been taken off the register within 28 days of his giving to the company evidence that he has ceased to be a member of the company).

[10.52] **Meredith MR:** The question practically narrows itself to this point, does the fact that Sergeant O'Connor's client, Spicer, is already a member of the shareholders of the Dublin North City Milling Company, entitle him to call on the directors to give their reasons for refusing to transfer additional shares into his name, or does it so entitle him?

The general rule applicable to cases of refusal to register is clear. Different cases before the courts from time to time, and particular circumstances render the decisions apparently not altogether harmonious; but I think that the case of *In re Coalport China Company* [1895] 2 Ch 404 sums up in as clear a way as possible the true guiding principle on which the court should act. In that case it was held by the Court of Appeal in England that, in the absence of any evidence that the directors had not acted bona fide, their refusal to register a transfer of shares could not be questioned . . .

Each transferee who demands registration of a transfer must allege and prove some indirect motive on the part of directors in refusing his application. The fact that he is already a shareholder does not prove this. The onus lies on the applicant. Sergeant O'Connor and Mr M'Gonigal suggest that the narrow margin of time between the two events, the change of front unexplained and unaccounted for, must mean that the directors were not acting bona fide in the interests of the company in refusing to register the transfer of the second lot of shares, but were acting for some obscure reason which they decline to disclose.

I dislike mystery, but I think the law is wise in refusing to compel directors to disclose their reasons for accepting or declining a transfer. The directors have kept themselves within the rule, and the reasons operating on their minds are not disclosed and I cannot speculate or guess as to what they are. There could not have been anything dishonourable or anything approaching personal unfitness on the part of Spicer. But I am of opinion that the law allows the directors to hold their tongues. It allows them to say that everything was done honestly and bona fide in the interest of their company; and they have unanimously decided that it is not for the interest or advantage of the company that these shares should be transferred to Mr Spicer and according to my view I have no power to make them say more.

If Mr Spicer had made a clear, definite charge against the directors of corruption or conspiracy or dishonesty I should have had them examined before me; and if I came to the conclusion that they had not acted fairly and honestly, I should compel them to register the transfer.

There is no proof that these directors did not act in the way they were entitled to act under the articles.

My considered judgment is that these articles the duties of the directors as regards approval or disapproval arise on every fresh transfer of shares, and that, under these articles, the mere fact that the proposed transferee is already a shareholder does not and cannot diminish their powers, or lessen their obligations, 'on behalf of the company' in respect of 'any transfer of shares.'

Notes

See also *Re Smith and Fawcett Ltd* [1942] Ch 304 where Lord Greene MR stated as follows:–

'The principles to be applied in cases where the articles of a company confer a discretion on directors with regard to the acceptance of transfers of shares are . . . free from doubt. They must exercise their discretion bona fide in what they consider – not what a court may consider – is in the interests of the company, and not for any collateral purpose. They must have regard to those considerations and those considerations only, which the articles on their true construction permit them to take into consideration and in construing the relevant provisions in the articles it is to be borne in mind that one of the normal rights of a shareholder is the right to deal freely with his property and to transfer it to whomsoever he pleases. When it is said . . . that regard must be had to this last consideration, it means, I apprehend, nothing more than that the shareholder has such a prima facie right, and that right is not to be cut down by uncertain language or doubtful implications. The right, if it is to be cut down, must be cut down with satisfactory clarity. It certainly does not mean that articles, if appropriately framed, cannot be allowed to cut down the right of transfer to any extent which the articles on their true construction permit. Another consideration which must be borne in mind, is that this type of article is one which is for the most part confined to private companies. Private companies are in law separate entities just as much as are public companies, but from the business and personal point of view they are much more analagous to partnerships than to public corporations. Accordingly, it is to be expected that in the articles of such a company the control of the directors over the membership may be very strict indeed. There are, or may be, very good business reasons why those who bring such companies into existence should give them a constitution which confers on the directors powers of the widest description . . . There is nothing in my opinion, in principle or in authority to make it impossible to draft such a wide and comprehensive power to directors to refuse to transfer as to enable them to take into account any matter which they conceive to be in the interests of the company and thereby to admit or not to admit a particular person and to allow or not to allow a particular transfer for reasons not personal to the transferee but bearing on the general interests of the company as a whole – such matters, for instance, as whether by their passing a particular transfer the transferee would obtain too great a weight in the councils of the company or might even perhaps obtain control. The question, therefore, simply is whether on the true construction of the particular article the directors are limited by anything except their bona fide view as to the interests of the company. In the present case the article is drafted in the widest possible terms and I decline to write into that clear language any limitation other than a limitation which is implicit by law, that a fiduciary power of this kind must be exercised bona fide in the interests of the company. Subject to that qualification, an article in this form appears to me to give the directors what is says, namely an absolute and uncontrolled discretion.'

In *Re Hafner; Olhausen v Powderley* [1943] IR 426 Black J was prepared to infer from the evidence before him that the directors had acted mala fides in refusing to register a transfer of shares to the plaintiff. The refusal was motivated by a desire to prevent the plaintiff from questioning and challenging exorbitant salaries which the directors had caused the company to pay to them. The decision of Black J was unanimously upheld by the Supreme Court.

In *Tett v Phoenix Property Co* [1984] BCLC 599 Vinelott J held that although the court cannot compel the directors to disclose their reasons for refusing to register a transfer of shares, if they actually give their reasons, the court is free to consider whether these reasons would justify a decision to refuse to register the transfer.

It has also been held in a number of cases that the power of the directors to refuse to register a transfer of shares will lapse if not exercised within a reasonable time. See *Re Hackney Pavilion Ltd* [1942] 1 Ch 276; *Moodie v W & J Shepherd (Bookbinders) Ltd* [1949] 2 All ER 1044; *Re Swaledale Cleaners Ltd* [1968] 1 WLR; *Tett v Phoenix Property Co* [1984] BCLC 599. Two months is regarded by the courts as a reasonable time within which to exercise the power of veto. This view is based on s 84 of the Principal Act which provides that 'if the company refuses to register a transfer . . . the company shall within 2 months after the date on which the transfer was lodged with the company, send to the transferee notice of the refusal.' In any case, the company must be given a reasonable time within which to process the application for entry on the register of members. See *Kinsella v Alliance & Dublin Consumers Gas Co* (High Court, Barron J, 5 October 1982). Pending registration of the transfer of the shares, the transferor holds them as nominee for the transferee and the latter must indemnify him against all liability in respect of those shares: See *Casey v Bentley* [1902] 1 IR 376; *Tett v Phoenix Property Co* [1984] BCLC 599; *Hawks v McArthur* [1951] 1 All ER 22.

On the form of and certification of transfers of shares, see *Keane* at paras **20.08–20.09**.

Transmission of Shares

[10.53] Transmission refers to the automatic assignment of property by operation of law, eg. on the death of a shareholder, to his executor or personal representative, in bankruptcy to the official assignee, or in winding up, to the liquidator.[1] The directors have the same power to veto the registration of a person who acquires shares by transmission as they have to veto the registration of a transfer of shares. However, such person is entitled to any dividends on the shares pending his registration as member.[2] Notably, under s 205(6) of the Principal Act the personal representative of a deceased shareholder or any trustee of, or person beneficially interested in the shares by virtue of the shareholders' will or intestacy is entitled to petition for relief under that section where there has been oppression or disregard of his interests.[3]

If the board has not been given a power under the articles to veto registration then the person taking the shares by transmission has an unqualified right to have his name entered on the register of members.[4]

---

1   This is because the assignee has a right to have the transfer registered, subject to the power of veto of the board: s 79 of the Principal Act. Also *Tangney v Clarence Hotels Ltd* [1933] IR 51. If the directors refuse to register the transfer this constitutes the non-performance of a condition subsequent of the contract of transfer, entitling either party to treat the contract at an end: *Casey v Bentley* [1902] 1 IR 376.

2 See *Keane* at paras **20.12** et seq. See also arts 29–32 of table A.
3 Arts 31–32 of table A.
4 *Re Rey-Ger Ltd; O'Flanagan v Ray-Ger Limited* (High Court, Costello J, 28/4/83) at p 37 of the transcript.

Disclosure of interest in shares[1]

[10.54]   Part IV of the 1990 Act has introduced a new regime for the disclosure of interests in shares. Chapter 1 of part IV imposes a duty on directors and secretaries of companies to disclose the interests of themselves, their spouses and minor children in shares of the company or other associated companies.[2] Chapter 2 contains detailed provisions which impose an obligation to notify acquisitions by individuals or groups of beneficial interests in shares of a plc who already have or who as a result of the acquisition have at least five per cent of any class of voting shares in the company. Notification must also be given where an individual or group with at least five per cent of such shares disposes of any of them. Under chapter 2 a plc is also empowered to investigate the ownership of its shares either of its own motion or on the application by a sufficient proportion of members.[3] Chapter 3 applies to private companies and empowers the court to order disclosure by persons of their interests in shares or debentures of the company to persons having a financial interest in the company.[4]

1 See generally *Keane*, chapter 26.
2 See *Keane* at paras **29.44–29.51**.
3 See *Keane* at paras **26.06–26.17**.
4 See *Keane* at paras **26.17–26.21**.

Insider dealing[1]

[10.55]   Insider dealing is, essentially, the use of price sensitive information relating to a company in order to make a profit in dealings in the shares or debentures of that company. The EEC Insider Dealing Directive of 1989[2] required provisions prohibiting insider dealing to be enacted in the various Member States before 1 June 1992. The relevant Irish provisions are to be found in part V of the 1990 Act.

1 See *Keane* at chapter 36: *Irish Centre for European Law Insider Dealing (Dublin 1990);* Mac Cann (1991) 9 ILT (ns) May & June.
2 89/592/EEC.

Prohibition against insider dealing

[10.56]   S 108 states that 'It shall not be lawful for a person [the insider] who is, or at any time in the preceding 6 months has been, connected[1] with a company to deal[2] in any securities[3] of that company if by reason of his being, or having been, connected with that company he is in possession of information that is not generally available, but, if it were, would be likely materially to affect the price of those securities.' The section goes on to state that it shall also be unlawful for the insider to deal in any securities of any other company if by reason of his so being, or having been, connected with the first mentioned company he is in possession of information that–

(*a*) is not generally available but, if it were, would be likely materially to affect the price of those securities, and

(*b*) relates to any transaction (actual or contemplated) involving both those companies or involving one of them and securities of the other, (eg a takeover bid) or to the fact that any such transaction is no longer contemplated.

A person [the 'tippee'] who is in possession of such price sensitive information but is not and has not within the preceding 6 months been connected with the company, is prohibited from dealing in those securities if he has received the information, directly or indirectly, from another person and is aware, or ought reasonably to be aware that that person is an insider, himself prohibited from dealing in the securities under s 108. Furthermore it is unlawful for the tippee and the insider, if precluded from dealing in the securities, to cause or procure any other person to deal in those securities. In such circumstances, they are also precluded from communicating such price sensitive information to any other person, if they know or ought reasonably to know, that the other person will make use of the information for the purpose of dealing, or causing or procuring another person to deal, in those securities.

S 108 goes on to state that it is unlawful for a company to deal in any securities at a time when any officer of that company is precluded, either as an insider or as a tippee, from dealing in those securities. However, this does not preclude the company from entering into a transaction at any time by reason only of information in the possession of an officer of the company if–

(*a*) the decision to enter into the transaction was taken on its behalf by a person other than the officer;

(*b*) it had in operation at that time written arrangements to ensure that the information was not communicated to that person and that no advice relating to the transaction was given by a person in possession of the information; and

(*c*) the information was not so communicated and such advice was not so given.

Furthermore, a company is not precluded from dealing in securities of another company at any time by reason only of the price sensitive information in its officer's possession having been received by him in the course of his duties as such officer and provided the information consists only of the fact that the first company proposes to deal in securities of the other company.

259

Under s 108(10) a person is not precluded from dealing in securities if, while not otherwise taking advantage of his possession of price sensitive information:–

(*a*) he gives at least 21 days notice to a relevant authority[4] of the relevant stock exchange of his intention to deal in the securities of the company concerned within seven days after the publication of the company's interim or final results, as the case may be and ending 14 days after such publication, and

(*b*) he in fact deals within this period, and

(*c*) the notice given by him is published by the stock exchange immediately upon its receipt.[5]

It should be noted that the prohibition in s 108 on dealing in company securities applies is extended to dealings in securities issued by the State, by s 108(13).

1 A person is connected with a company if (*a*) he is an officer of that company or of a related company; (*b*) he occupies a position that may reasonably be expected to give him access to price sensitive information by virtue of any professional, business or other relationship existing between himself (or his employer or a company of which he is an officer) and that company or a related company or his being an officer or a substantial shareholder in that company or in a related company: s 107(10). Companies are related if they have a parent – subsidiary relationship or if they both have a common parent company: s 106.

2 'Dealing' in relation to securities means (whether as principal or agent) acquiring, disposing if, subscribing for or underwriting the securities or making or offering to make, or inducing or attempting to induce a person to make or to offer to make an agreement–

   (*a*) for or relating to acquiring, disposing of, subscribing for or underwriting the securities; or

   (*b*) the purpose or purported purpose of which is to secure a profit or gain to a person who acquires, disposes of subscribes for or undertakes the securities or to any of the parties to the agreement in relation to the securities.

3 'Securities' means–

   (*a*) shares, debentures or other debt securities issued or proposed to be issued, whether in the State or otherwise and for which dealing facilities are or are to be provided by a recognised stock exchange;

   (*b*) any right, option or obligation in respect of any such shares, debentures or other debt securities referred to in paragraph (*a*);

   (*c*) any right, option or obligation in respect of any index relating to any such shares, debentures or other debt securities referred to in paragraph (*a*); or

   (*d*) such interests as may be prescribed.

4 'Relevant authority' in relation to a recognised stock exchange means–

   (i) its board of directors, committee of management or other management body,

   (ii) its manager, however described.

5 For an explanation of this sub-section see *Mac Cann* (1991) 9 ILT (ns), (May issue).

Agents

[10.57] S 108(9) provides that the prohibition on insider dealing does not preclude a person from dealing in securities, or rights or interests, of a company if–

(*a*) he enters into the transaction concerned as agent for his principal pursuant to a specified instruction of the principal to effect the transaction; and

(*b*) he has not given advice to the principal in relation to dealing in securities of that company, or right or interests in securities of the company that are in the same class as the securities being dealt in.

However, s 113 goes on to stipulate that an agent may not deal on behalf of his principal if he has reasonable cause to believe or ought to conclude that the deal would be in breach of the prohibitions laid down in s 108. A contravention of s 113 is a criminal offence.

Exempt transactions

[10.58] S 110 lists a number of categories of transactions which are exempt from the prohibition against insider dealing in s 108. They are:–

(*a*) the acquisition of securities under a will or on the intestacy;

(*b*) the acquisition of securities in a company pursuant to an employee profit sharing scheme which has been approved by the Revenue Commisioners, the terms of which have been approved by the company in general meeting, and under which all permanent employees are offered the opportunity to participate on equal terms relative to specified objective criteria;

(*c*) the obtaining by a director of a share qualification under s 180 of the Principal Act;

(*d*) a transaction entered into by a person in accordance with his obligations under an underwriting agreement;

(*e*) a transaction entered into by a personal representative of a deceased person, a trustee, or liquidator, receiver or examiner in the performance of the functions of his office;

(*f*) a transaction by way of, or arising out of, a mortgage of or charge on securities or a mortgage, charge, pledge or lien on documents of title to securities;

(*g*) transactions entered into in pursuit of monetary, exchange rate, national debt management or foreign exchange reserve policies by any Minister of the Governemnt or the Central Bank, or any person on their behalf.

The exemptions for transactions (*c*) to (*f*) apply only where entered into by the person in good faith.

Civil liability for insider dealing

[10.59] S 109 creates civil liability for insider dealing. Where a person deals in or causes or procures another person to deal in securities in a manner declared unlawful by s 108, or communicates price sensitive information in a manner prohibited by that section, he shall, without prejudice to any other cause of action which may lie against him, be liable to compensate any other party to the transaction who was not in possession of the price sensitive information for any loss sustained by that party by reason of any difference between the price at which the securities were dealt in in that transaction and the price at which they would have been likely to have been dealt in if the price sensitive information had been generally available at the time. He is also liable to account to the company that issued or made available the securities for any profit accruing to him from dealing in those securities.

The amount of compensation payable or profit for which he is accountable is taken to be respectively, the amount of the loss suffered by the other party or the profit made by person who is guilty of insider dealing, less any amount which he has been ordered to pay by a court to any other person by reason of the same act or transaction.[1]

An action for the recovery of a loss or profit cannot be commenced after the expiration of 2 years after the date of completion of the transaction in question.

1 The onus is on the person guilty of insider dealing to prove that he has already been found liable to pay such amount: s 109(3).

Criminal liability for insider dealing

[10.60] It is an offence to deal in securities in a manner declared unlawful by s 108.[1] As mentioned at para **10.57** it is also an offence to deal on behalf of another person if one has reasonable cause to believe or ought to conclude that the deal would be in breach of s 108.[2]

A person who commits an offence under part V of the 1990 Act is liable:

(*a*) on summary conviction to imprisonment for a term not exceeding 12 months or to a fine not exceeding £1,000 or both, or
(*b*) on conviction on indictment, to imprisonment for a term not exceeding 10 years or to a fine not exceeding £200,000 or to both.[3]

Furthermore a person convicted of a breach of s 108 is prohibited to deal within the period of 12 months from the date of the conviction. It is an offence to deal when prohibited from so doing. However, if he has initiated any transaction before the date of his conviction some element of which remains to be rendered, he may complete it if a relevant authority of a recognised stock exchange[4] has indicated in writing its satisfaction that–

(*a*) the transaction was initiated but not completed before the date of the conviction, and
(*b*) if the transaction were not concluded, the rights of an innocent third party would be prejudiced, and
(*c*) the transaction would not be unlawful under any other provision of part V of the 1990 Act.[5]

1 S 111.
2 S 113.

3 S 114.
4 'Recognised stock exchange' includes in particular, any exchange prescribed by the Minister which provides facilities for the buying and selling of rights or obligations to acquire stock.
5 S 112.

Reporting and investigation of insider dealing

[10.61] Under s 115 if it appears to a relevant authority of a recognised authority that any person has committed an offence under part V, the authority must forthwith report the matter to the DPP and must furnish to him such information and give to him such access to and facilities for inspecting and taking copies of any documents relating to the matter in question and is in the authority's possession or control.

If in any proceedings it appears to the court that any person has committed such an offence and that the relevant authority has not reported to the DPP, the court may direct that such a report be made.

S 115 also imposes an obligation on members of the stock exchange to report to a relevant authority, where it appears to him that an offence has been committed under part V. The relevant authority is then under a duty to report to the DPP.

Where a breach of part V is reported or referred to the DPP and he institutes criminal proceedings, then there is an obligation on the relevant authority and on every officer of the company whose securities are concerned, and on every other person who appears to the DPP to have relevant information (other than the defendant) to give all assistance in connection with the prosecution which he or they are reasonably able to give.

If it appears to the Minister, arising from a complaint to a relevant authority concerning an alleged offence under part V, that there are circumstances suggesting that the relevant authority ought to use its powers under that part or to report to the DPP, he may request the authority to do so. In such a case the authority is obliged to communicate the results of its investigations, or a copy of its report to the Minister.

However, a relevant authority of a recognised stock exchange shall not be liable in damages in respect of anything done or omitted to be done by it in connection with the exercise by it of its functions under part V unless the act or omission complained of was done or omitted to be done in bad faith.

[10.62] In investigating possible insider dealing powers of investigation are created by s 117. This provides that in order for a relevant authority to exercise its reporting functions under s 115, an authorised person[1] may require any person whom he or the relevant authority has reasonable cause to believe to have dealt in any securities, or to have any information about such dealings, to give the authorised person any information which he may reasonably require in regard to:

(*a*) the securities concerned;
(*b*) the company which issued the securities;

(*c*) his dealings in such securities; or

(*d*) any other information the authorised person reasonably requires in relation to such securities or such dealings; and to give him such access to and facilities for inspecting and taking copies of any documents relating to the matter as he reasonably requires.

On application by the authorised person to court, it may declare whether or not the exigencies of the common good require him to investigate his investigatory powers. If the exercise of his powers is not warranted he must withdraw any request for information, etc. On the other hand, if the court declares that the exercise of his powers is warranted, any person whom he has requested to furnish him with information, is under a positive obligation to do so.

Refusal, within a reasonable time to furnish the requisite information to the authorised person is punishable as if it were contempt of court.

The Minister may, under s 121, make further regulations in relation to the powers of authorised persons, or in relation to the matters in respect of which, or the persons from whom, authorised persons may require information.

1 ie a person authorised by the Minister being the manager of a recognised stock exchange or a person nominated by a relevant authority of a recognised stock exchange.

[10.63] Under s 118 there is a duty of confidentiality in relation to information obtained by a relevant authority, authorised person or present or former employee of the stock exchange, by virtue of the exercise of the exchange of its functions under part V. It is an offence to make an unauthorised disclosure of such information. However, this does not prevent a relevant authority from disclosing information to the Minister or to a similar authority in another member State.

[10.64] S 119 requires every recognised stock exchange to present to the Minister an annual report on the exercise of relevant authorities functions under part V, including–

(*a*) the number of written complaints received suggesting possible contraventions of part V;

(*b*) the number of reports made to the DPP;

(*c*) the number of instances in which, following the exercise of powers of investigation by authorised persons, reports were not made to the DPP; and

(*d*) such other information as may be prescribed.

Co-operation with foreign stock exchanges

[10.65] Where a relevant authority receives a request for information from a similar authority in another member State of the EEC in relation to the exercise of the foreign authority's functions regarding insider dealing, the Irish authority shall, in so far as it is reasonably able to do so, and making use of its powers under part V where appropriate, obtain and provide the information requested. Once the Irish authority receives a request for such assistance, it must notify the Minister who may direct the authority to refuse to provide all or part of the information requested on the ground that–

(*a*) communication of the information requested might adversely affect the sovereignty, security or public policy of the State;

(*b*) civil or criminal proceedings in the State have already been commenced against a person in respect of any acts in relation to which the request for information has been received; or

(*c*) any person has been convicted in the State of a criminal offence in respect of such acts.[1]

1 S 116.

Chapter 11

BORROWING, DEBENTURES AND CHARGES[1]

[11.01] The company may have an express power in its objects clause, or an implied power under the rule in *AG v Great Eastern Railway*,[2] to borrow money provided such borrowing can fairly be regarded as incidental to, or consequential upon any intra vires activity of the company. In addition, there may be an express or implied[3] power to secure such borrowing by way of mortgage or charge over all or part of the company's real or personal property or both.

1 See *Keane* chapters 21, 22, 23.
2 (1875) LR 7 HL 653. See also *R v Reed* (1880) 5 QBD 483, 488 & 489. For restrictions imposed upon the commencement of the power to borrow in the case of an unlimited public company, a plc, see s 115 of the Principal Act and s 6 of the 1983 Act respectively.
3 *Australian Auxiliary Steam Clipper Co v Mounsey* (1858) 4 K & J 733.

Debentures[1]

[11.02] According to s 2(1) of the Principal Act, the term 'debenture' includes 'debenture stock, bonds, and any other securities of a company whether constituting a charge on the company or not'. It is an instrument which acknowledges the indebtedness of the company. It may, but need not be secured by way of a charge over some or all of its property.[2]

The debenture may be a single instrument between the company and a particular lender, or it can be one of a number of debentures issued by the company to members of the public. Where debentures are issued to the public, it may be by way of a series of debentures in identical terms and ranking pari passu, but for different amounts to different lenders. More commonly, however, the issue to the debenture holder may be divided into stock units of a specified amount, in the same way that shares of a fixed value are issued to shareholders, eg. £1,000 debenture stock divided into stock units of £1 each. The debenture holder gets a stock certificate and typically, all or part of the stock may be transferred[3] by registration in much the same way as a transfer of shares is registered.[4] Bearer debentures may be transferred by delivery in the same way as in the case of share warrants. The holder of debenture stock may resemble a preference shareholder to an extent, in that both will commonly be entitled to payment of a fixed sum per annum (either by way of dividend or interest as the case may be). However, the debenture holder is not a member of the company[5] and accordingly, a repayment of debentures (being a repayment of loan capital) does not constitute a reduction of capital requiring the sanction of the court under s 72 of the Principal Act.[6] Although it is a fundamental feature of a standard mortgage or charge that the borrower may redeem upon payment of all capital and interest, at any time or at a specified time in the future, the company may, under s 94 of the Principal Act, issue debentures which are unredeemable or redeemable only on the happening of a contingency, however remote, or at the expiration of a period, however long.[7] Where debentures are being issued to the public the company must comply with broadly the same requirements regarding prospectuses, etc, as are necessary for the issue of shares.[8] Indeed it is possible for the company to issue debentures which are convertible into shares.

1 See *Keane* at paras **22.01–22.13**.
2 *British India Steam Navigation Co v IRC* (1881) 7 QBD 165.
3 See s 61 of the Principal Act.
4 See chapter 13 *infra*.
5 See s 31 of the Principal Act.
6 Debenture stock is typically regulated by a trust deed. Commonly the investors advance the money to the trustee who in turn advance it to the company. The debenture stock is then issued to the trustees. The investors then subscribe to this fund in the appropriate amount.
7 *See Knightsbridge Estates Trust Ltd v Byrne* [1940] AC 613.
8 See *Keane* at para **22.09**.

[11.03]   In the case of unsecured debentures, payment can be enforced by way of an ordinary action in personam, although in the case of a debenture secured by a charge the debenture holder has the powers of enforcement of a mortgagee, including the power to appoint a receiver. Where a series of debentures has been issued, enforcement by one debenture holder is on behalf of all the debentureholders, similar to the shareholders' derivative action.

Definition of debenture

Levy v Abercorris Slate and Slab Company (1887) 37 Ch D 260

[11.04]   Chitty J: In my opinion, a debenture means a document which either creates a debt or acknowledges it, and any document which fulfills either of these conditions is a 'debenture'. I cannot find any precise legal definition of the term, it is not either in law or commerce a strictly technical term, or what is called a term of art.

Charges

[11.05]   The company, in order to secure its obligations may grant a mortgage over part or all of its property.[1] A mortgage involves the transfer of the ownership of the property by way of security by the debtor to the creditor, subject to an express or implied term that the property will be re-transferred to the debtor when he has fulfilled his obligations (usually the repayment of capital and interest). A charge on the other hand, does not necessarily involve the transfer of ownership. It constitutes an agreement between the creditor and the debtor that a particular asset or assets are to be appropriated toward the satisfaction of the debt. The creditor is entitled to look to these assets for payment in priority to the unsecured creditors, and subsequent secured creditors. This charge is an equitable interest, whereas a mortgage may be legal or equitable. It is a mere incumbrance and a bona fide purchaser for value of the legal title, without notice, takes free of the incumbrance or charge.

A mortgage being an appropriation of property towards the satisfaction, is also a charge. But it is more, as it also constitutes a transfer of ownership. However, a mere charge, not involving a transfer of ownership is not a mortgage. As Walker LC put it in *Shea v Moore*[2] 'every charge is not an equitable mortgage, though every equitable mortgage is a charge.'

1 See generally WJ Gough; *Company Charges* (London, 1978); Goode, *Legal Problems of Credit and Security* (2nd Ed) (London 1988); *Keane* at para **22.14** et seq.
2 [1894] IR 158, 163.

Fixed charge

[11.06] The security granted by the company may be fixed or floating. In the former case the company grants a mortgage or a fixed charge over a specified asset or assets, present or future,[1] in order to secure the debt in question. The secured creditor may enforce his security by the usual means of sale, possession or the appointment of a receiver.

1 *Holroyd v Marshall* (1862) 10 HLC 191; *Lyster v Burroughs* (1837) 1 Dr & Wal 149; *White v Anderson* (1850) 1 Ir Ch 419; *Creed v Carey* (1857) 7 Ir Ch R 295; *Galavin v Dunne* (1881–82) 7 LR Ir 144.

Floating charge[1]

[11.07] Unlike the fixed charge, which attaches to a specific asset or assets upon creation the floating charge, does not attach to any particular asset immediately. Rather it 'hovers' over specified assets or classes of assets until an event known as 'crystallisation' whereupon the floating charge turns into a fixed charge and attaches to the property the subject matter of the security. Due to the fact that a floating charge does not immediately attach to the assets the company is free to use and dispose of them in the ordinary course of business prior to crystallisation. This form of security is therefore appropriate when wishing to charge assets of a class which are constantly changing (such as stock in trade). Commonly, the floating charge is granted over the entire undertaking and assets of the company. The problem created by such a wide charge is that there is often nothing left for the unsecured creditors should the company become insolvent. For this reason the floating charge has been much criticised.

1 See *Keane* at para **22.14** et seq. Also *Goode*, op cit; Pennington, *The Genesis of the Floating Charge* (1960) MLR 630; Farrar *Floating Charges and Priorities* (1974) 38 Conv (ns) 315.

Characteristics of the floating charge

Re Old Bushmills Distillery Co; ex p Brett [1897] 1 IR 488 (Court of Appeal)

[11.08]   Walker LJ: The debentures here are already a 'floating security', and do not become fixed till the event happens on which they are made payable. The character of such a charge has been stated in many cases, of which I may mention *Panama v New Zealand and Australian Royal Mail Company* LR 5 Ch 322 as the earliest and *Government Stock and Other Securities Investment Company v Manila Railway Company* [1897] AC 81 as the last. I think the result may be stated as follows:–

> It is involved in such a charge that the company shall continue a going concern and the debenture holder has no power to interfere till his charge becomes payable. He can claim no account of mesne profits or challenge any authorised dealing by the company with its property or business. The directors, as masters, carry on meantime the business for which the company was incorporated according to its constitution and remain clothed with the power of doing all things necessary for carrying on that business, including the meeting of special emergencies. Assets may be withdrawn by sale and the proceeds then take their place, or other assets may be substituted or additional assets added by trading; but the floating security follows the concern, reduced or added to, through every form of its trading existence, which existence continues as if the debentures were not there till the floating charge became a fixed one. Till then to use the words of one learned judge, 'the charge is dormant.'

Re Lakeglen Construction Ltd; Kelly v Mahon Ltd [1980] IR 347 (High Court)

[11.09]   Lakeglen Construction Ltd carried on business as building contractors. The company issued a debenture called a 'fixed charge' to some of its creditors to secure the company's pre-existing liabilities. The charge extended to a number of the company's assets including its book debts. The charge did not contain any provision restricting the company from using its book debts in the ordinary course of business. The company, which was insolvent at the time of creation of the charge was wound up within the following 12 months. The issue before the court was whether the debenture was in fact a floating charge. If it was a floating charge, then it would be rendered invalid by s 288 of the Principal Act.

[11.10]   Costello J: The legislature has not attempted to define the meaning of the term 'floating charge' and the courts have preferred to indicate certain tests by which a security can be identified as a floating or a fixed charge rather than to formulate an exhaustive definition of what is a floating charge. In the particular circumstances of this case I think I can best commence the elucidation of the problem of construction involved in it by pointing to the important differences which exist between the consequences which flow when a charge on book debts is a floating one and when it is a fixed one. These have been pointed out in England in judgments of the High Court the Court of Appeal and the House of Lords: See *Houldsworth v Yorkshire Woolcombers Association Ltd* [1903] 2 Ch 284 and *Illingworth v Houldsworth* [1904] AC 355. In the *Houldsworth* case Farwell J said (at p 288) that if the security he was considering (which had been given in respect of book debts) was to be treated as a specific charge then '. . . the company had no business to receive one single book debt after the date of it' . . . On the other hand, if it was intended that the charge was to remain dormant until some future date and that the company was permitted to go on receiving the book debts and using them until then, the security would contain the true element of a floating charge. In the Court of Appeal Cozens-Hardy LJ agreed with those views and concluded (at p 298) that the security in that case was to be read as containing a licence of permission by the mortgagee to the mortgagor 'to deal with the mortgage property for a certain time as though a mortgage had not been executed' and was to be regarded as a floating one.

In the House of Lords the Lord Chancellor in agreeing with the interpretation put on the documents by the lower courts said at p 57 of the report:–

> 'In the first place you have that which in a sense I suppose must be an element in the definition of a floating security, that it is something which is to float, not to be put into immediate operation, but such that the company is to be allowed to carry on its business. It contemplates not only that it should carry with it the book debts which were then existing, but it contemplates also the possibility of those book debts being extinguished by payment into the company and that other book debts should come in and take the place of those that had disappeared. That, My Lords, seems to me to be an essential characteristic of what is properly called a floating security.'

When they executed the debenture did the parties intend that in relation to its book debts the company was free to receive them and bring new book debts into existence as if the debenture had not been created until such time as the debenture holder became entitled to intervene in the company's affairs? In answering this question the first point to bear in mind is that the company was a trading company which carried on business as building contractors. Secondly, the parties expressly agreed that the company was to be permitted to carry on that business. Thirdly, in the normal course of affairs it would obviously create difficulties for a trading company if it were required to hand over to its mortgagees its book debts as it received them from time to time. In the absence of provisions to the contrary I conclude that, when permission to trade is given in a debenture permission to receive book debts is more readily to be inferred than is an arrangement by which the company is required to hand them over to a debenture holder. Is there anything in the agreement between the parties or in the debenture which would tend to displace that inference? I do not think so.

Nowhere is there a provision or a direction which requires the company to pay over the moneys which it receives from these debtors to its major creditors. The absence of such a direction bearing in mind the provisions to which I have just referred supports rather than weakens the inference that it was intended that the company was to be permitted to retain the book debts as they were paid and to create new ones from time to time, and thus generally to deal with this particular asset in the ordinary course of its business until such time as the major creditors became entitled to intervene in the company's affairs. I have come to the conclusion that I should so construe this deed.

This does not conclude the problem of construction in this case. Counsel for all the parties have made reference to a much quoted passage from the judgment of Romer LJ in the Court of Appeal in *Houldsworth's* case and I have been invited to apply to the facts of this case the tests there formulated. The passage from p 295 of the report states:–

'I certainly do not intend to attempt to give an exact definition of the term "floating charge" nor am I prepared to say that there will not be a floating charge within the meaning of the Act, which does not contain all the three characteristics that I am about to mention, but I certainly think that if a charge has the three characteristics that I am about to mention it is a floating charge. (1) If it is a charge on a class of assets of a company present and future; (2) If that class is one which in the ordinary course of the business of the company, would be changing from time to time; and (3) If you find that by the charge it is contemplated that until some future step is taken by or on behalf of those interested in the charge, the company may carry on its business in the ordinary way as far as concerns the particular class of assets I am dealing with.'

As to the first test, I am satisfied that the charge in clause 3(*b*) of the debenture is a charge in respect of moneys due to the company from both existing and future debtors . . . As to the second test suggested by Romer LJ if the charge in clause 3(*b*) is one which embraces existing and future book debts (as I believe it does) then it is quite clear that this charge passes the second test as the charge is a charge on a class of assets which, in the ordinary course of the company's business, would be changing from time to time. The views which I have already expressed indicate my opinion on the third test.

I am satisfied that the parties intended that the company should carry on its business in the ordinary way and that for this purpose it was licensed (until some future contingency arose which would justify the intervention by the debenture holders) to receive payment from its debtors from time to time without regard to the charge created by the debenture over the book debts.

I propose to answer the question raised by holding that the debenture is invalid by virtue of the provisions of s 288 of the Companies Act 1963, to the extent to which it purported to charge the book debts of the company in favour of the creditors to whom the debenture was issued.

[11.11] A company may validly create a floating charge over its present and after acquired property.

Re The Dublin Drapery Co Ltd, ex p Cox (1884–85) 13 LR Ir 174 (Chancery Division)

[11.12] The company created a floating charge over its present and future property in favour of certain debenture holders. The company was subsequently wound up and the liquidator sought to challenge the validity of the charge, inter alia, in so far as it purported to affect after acquired property.

[11.13] **Porter MR:** The question remaining for me to decide is, whether the company had power to charge future acquired property . . . In *Holroyd v Marshall* 10 HL Cas 191 it was decided that, as in equity it is not necessary that there should be a formal deed of conveyance provided there be a valid contract for transfer, future property, contracted to be conveyed for valuable consideration provided it is so identified as to be capable of being the subject of a decree for specific performance, passes at once when realised, and the vendor becomes a trustee for the vendee. That rule applies to personal property as well as to real estate. Such a contract, if made with respect to the sale or mortgage of future-acquired property, being capable of specific performance, transfers the beneficial interest in the property as soon as it is acquired to the vendee or mortgagee, who may have an injunction to restrain its removal. That decision rests on the principle of equity that what is contracted for and ought to be done is treated as done. There is no doubt that at common law, as expressed by Pollock CB in *Belding v Read* 3 H & C 955, 'a person cannot by deed, however solemn assign that which is not in himself – in other words, there cannot be a prophetic conveyance'. But the decision of Courts of Equity as shown by *Holroyd v Marshall* rests on a different principle; and if the contract be sufficiently specific it will in equity pass the property . . .

In my opinion, therefore on every point the debenture-holders succeed, and I shall declare them entitled to be paid principal and interest, not only out of the £32,000 the produce of the real estate, but also out of the £25,000 representing general assets brought in to answer their demand, together with their costs.

I shall accordingly declare that the several debentures in the notices of motion mentioned are well charged on and ought to be paid out of the funds standing in the books of the Accountant General to the credit of the matter.

[11.14] In the absence of any express prohibition in the floating charge, the company may create fixed charges on mortgages prior to crystallisation of the floating charge and ranking in priority to that floating charge, and even though the subsequent chargees or mortgagees have notice of the existence of the floating charge.

Wheatley v Silkstone and High Moor Coal Co (1885) 29 Ch D 715
(Chancery Division)

[11.15] The company created a floating charge, described as a 'first charge' over the entire of its undertaking and assets. Subsequently it granted a mortgage to another creditor over its main piece of property, a colliery. The company went into liquidation and the court was asked to determine whether the floating charge or the subsequent mortgage over the colliery had priority.

[11.16] **North J:** In this case I find that the debenture is intended to be a general floating security over all the property of the company, as it exists at the time when it is to be put in force; but it is not intended to prevent and has not the effect of in any way preventing the carrying on of the business in all or any of the ways in which it is carried on in the ordinary course; and in as much as I find that in the ordinary course of business and for the purpose of the business this mortgage was made, it is a good mortgage upon and a good charge upon the property comprised in it, and it is not subject to the claim created by the debentures. I find also that the first charge referred to in the debentures is fully satisfied by being the first charge against the general property of the company at the time when the claim under the debentures arises and can have effect given to it. There will be a declaration therefore, that the charge of the plaintiff is prior to the debentures.'

Notes
   See also *Re Castell & Brown Ltd* [1898] 1 Ch 315. However, it would appear that a company cannot create a floating charge ranking in priority to or pari passu with an earlier floating charge, as they are securities of like degree. See *Re Benjamin Cope Ltd* [1914] 1 Ch 800 and *Re Automatic Bottle Makers Ltd* [1926] Ch 412. Further in the absence of an express provision to the contrary, the crystallisation of a second charge will not automatically crystallise the first floating charge. See *Re Woodruffes (Musical Instruments) Ltd* [1985] 1 All ER 908. However, as was held in that case, when the first charge does crystallise, it has priority over the second charge.

Negative pledge clauses[1]

[11.17] In order to protect themselves against the risk that the company may subsequently create fixed charges, or mortgages ranking in priority to their securities, charges commonly include 'negative pledge clauses' in their floating charges. These clauses typically prohibit the company from creating any charge or mortgage over its property ranking in priority to or pari passu with the floating charge.

1 See *Keane* at para **22.22**. Also Farrar *Floating Charges and Priorities* (1974) 38 Conv (ns) 315; *Farrar*, (1980) 1 Co Lawyer 83.

[11.18]   A negative pledge clause is effective against the chargor and chargee and also against subsequent secured creditors having notice of the clause.

Re Old Bushmills Distillery Co Ltd; ex p Brydon [1896] 1 IR 301 (Chancery Division)

[11.19]   The company had created a floating charge, the terms of which included a stipulation prohibiting the creation of any subsequent mortgage or charge ranking pari passu with or in precedence to the floating charge. The company entered into a transaction with Brydon which was labelled as a 'sale' of part of the stock in trade (whiskey) of the company but which the court on the evidence found to be specific charges by way of pledge. Brydon was found to have notice of the negative pledge clause and was accordingly bound by it.

[11.20]   **Chatterton VC:** But then a more difficult question arises, one of law, whether assuming this to have been a loan on a pledge of the whiskey, the security though valid against the company, can take priority to, or rank equally with, the debentures issued by the company. This depends upon the operation and effect of the debentures and the deed of trust executed to secure them. It must be taken as settled law that a debenture in the form in general use till recently, operated only as it was termed by way of 'floating charge' on the company's undertaking, regarded as a going concern. But it is also decided that debentures may be so framed as to prevent a company from pledging or mortgaging their assets so as to create specific charges, to the prejudice of debenture holders, by taking priority as to the assets so pledged or mortgaged over the debentures . . . The importance of such a restriction to persons advancing their money on the security of debentures is plain from this that without it a company could specifically mortgage or pledge any amount of their assets to subsequent lenders without notice, and thus all, or at least a large portion of their assets might be withdrawn from the security of the debentures. There is nothing to prevent, or render illegal such an express contract being made between persons advancing money on debentures and the company with which they contract . . .

It was further contended that there is not sufficient proof of notice to Messrs Brydon of the restrictive clause of the debentures and that the case therefore comes within the authority of *English and Scottish Mercantile Investment Trust v Brunton* [1892] 2 QB 1, 700. The question there was one of constructive notice arising from the fact that on the negotiation for a loan to the company, on an assignment by them of their interest in a specific

275

portion of their assets, the solicitor of the lender knew that debentures had been issued by the company but was not aware of their form and asked the managing director of the company whether the debentures were secured by any trust deed which might affect the assets proposed to be assigned and was told by him that there was nothing whatever. He made no further inquiry and the loan was carried out. The doctrine of constructive notice was much discussed and the authorities considered . . . It is not necessary to consider such cases, for in my opinion, there is proof here of express notice. I am satisfied upon the evidence of the witnesses, Messrs Boyd and Hanna who made affidavits on behalf of the Brydons that the latter then acting for Brydon & Co, of whose firm he was a member, was informed by Boyd, the managing director of the company, that Brydon's proposal to accept the bills against the whisky, which is equivalent to lending money to the company on the security of a transfer of the whisky to Brydon, could not be carried out because of the debentures, and that he thereupon proposed to Hanna to do the same thing by way of sale, to which the latter assented. Thus Brydon & Co had express notice not only of the existence of the debentures, but further that they contained a prohibition of borrowing money on the assets. Hanna made no inquiry because he was told by Boyd without inquiry, and it was assumed by both parties that the debentures precluded a loan on the security of a transfer of whisky.

I must therefore decide that Brydon & Co were not entitled to hold the whisky from the trustee and receiver of the debenture holders . . .

Notes

See also *Cox v Dublin City Distillery* [1906] 1 IR 446.

[11.21]   A person is only deemed to have constructive notice of those particulars of a charge which require registration under ss 99 and 103 of the Principal Act. Such particulars do not include the existence or otherwise of a floating charge. Therefore a chargee is not bound by a negative pledge clause unless actually aware of its existence . . .

Welch v Bowmaker (Ireland) Ltd and The Governor and Company of the Bank of Ireland [1980] IR 251 (Supreme Court)

[11.22]   The company created a fixed charge over 3 of its 4 parcels of land and premises and a floating charge over the remainder of its property in favour of the first defendant. It subsequently created an equitable mortgage by deposit of title deeds in respect of the fourth parcel of land in favour of the second defendant. At the time of the creation of the equitable mortgage the second defendant was aware of the existence of the floating charge but was unaware of its terms (which included a negative pledge clause). In the course of the winding up of the company a question of priorities arose between the defendants in respect of the fourth parcel of land.

[11.23]   Henchy J: Counsel for Bowmaker has argued that the bank should be fixed with constructive notice of the provision in the debenture precluding the company from creating a mortgage (such as the bank got) which would have priority over the debenture. Since such a prohibition is more or less common form in modern debentures, there would be much to be said for applying the doctrine of constructive notice to such a situation such as this to seek out the precise terms of the debenture . . . Actual or express notice of the prohibition must be shown before the subsequent mortgage can be said to be deprived of priority.

Whatever attractions there may be in the proposition that priority should be deemed lost because a duty to inquire further was called for but ignored, and that such inquiry would have shown that the company was debarred from entering into a mortgage which would have priority over the debenture, the fact remains that it would be unfair to single out the bank for condemnatory treatment because of their failure to ascertain the full terms of the debenture when what they did was in accord with judicially approved practice and when such a precipitate change in the law would undermine the intended validity of many other such transactions. If the proposed extension of the doctrine of constructive notice is to be made, the necessary change in the law would need to be made prospectively and therefore, more properly by statute.

I would allow the appeal and rule that . . . the bank's equitable mortgage over that property ranks in priority to Bowmaker's rights as the owners of a floating charge over that property under the debenture.

Parke J delivered a concurring judgment. Kenny J dissented.

Notes

See also *Coveney v Persse* [1910] 1 IR 194. It would seem that even if the negative pledge clause is registered in the Companies Office along with the particulars mentioned in ss 99 and 103, subsequent charges are only bound by that clause if they have actually inspected the file in the Companies Office and seen the terms of the clause.

ш

Preferential debts

[11.24]   Under s 285 of the Principal Act as amended by s 10 of the 1982 Act, when a company goes into liquidation certain liabilities known as 'preferential debts' are entitled to payment in priority to the unsecured creditors.[1] Where there are insufficient uncharged assets to pay the preferential creditors in full they are entitled under s 285(7)(b) to payment out of assets which are subject to any floating charge, in priority to the debenture holder. Similarly, under s 98 where a charge crystallises by the appointment of a receiver, or the taking possession by the debenture holder, the receiver, or the debenture holder, as the case may be, is under an obligation to pay preferential debts out of the charged assets and in priority to the debenture holder as if the company were in liquidation.[2]

1 See s 285 of the Principal Act as amended by s 10 of the 1982 Act. See also *Keane* at para **38.72**.
2 *IRC v Goldblatt* [1972] Ch 498; *Re GL Saunders Ltd* [1986] BCLC 40; *In re PMPA Oil Co* (High Court, 28/4/88) Costello J held that s 98 does not apply where the receiver is appointed pursuant to a court order.

[11.25]   S 98 of the Principal Act does not apply in the case of a fixed charge.

Re United Bars Ltd (In Receivership) and Walkinstown Inn Ltd (In Receivership) (High Court, 3 June 1988)

[11.26]   A receiver was appointed over the company's lands consisting of licensed premises pursuant to the terms of a debenture which comprised both a fixed and a floating charge. The chargee was owed £1,033,584. The lands were sold for £1,119,000, leaving a surplus of £85,417. The receiver applied to the court for a determination as to whether he should apply this surplus in payment of preferential creditors pursuant to s 98.

[11.27]   **Murphy J:** The question posed for consideration of the court in these proceedings is whether the receiver is bound, having regard to the provisions of s 98(1) of the Companies Act 1963, to use all or any part of the said sum of £85,417 in payment of the persons who are or would be preferential creditors of the company if and when those companies are wound up. Counsel on behalf of the receiver relied principally and primarily and indeed understandably on the decision of Norse J in *GL Saunders Ltd* [1986] BCLC 40. That case has, to say the least of it, considerable similarity with the facts of the present case. The company GL Saunders Ltd executed two debentures by which it created fixed and floating charges over its assets. A receiver was appointed and after paying the debts due to the bank, by whom he was appointed, the receiver was left with a surplus of £444,000 from the sale of the assets subject to the fixed charge. The question arose whether all or part of that money should be used for the payment of preferential creditors or should be paid to the mortgagor, that is to say the company. Norse J held that the money should be repaid to the company and not applied in payment of the preferential creditors. In essence, the decision of Norse J on s 94 of the United Kingdom Companies Act of 1948 (which is similar to that of the Irish s 98), was based on an oral judgment in *Re Lewis Merthyr Consolidated Collieries* [1929] 1 Ch 498. In that case Tomlin J held that s 107 of the Companies Consolidated Act 1908, which was the predecessor of the UK s 94 and the Irish s 98, applied only in respect of accounts coming to the hands of the receiver which were the subject of a floating charge and not to assets subject to a fixed charge. That decision was confirmed by the Court of Appeal in England, whose decision is contained in the same report. That effectively disposed of the matter before Norse J but he went on, having regard to the facts as he said, that the issue was considered a vexed question on which differing leading counsel had expressed different views. He went on to express further views in an analysis which I find more difficult to follow. He explained that if debenture holders' debts or the particular debt had been extinguished there was no principle or interest owing to the debenture holder and accordingly the section would have no application. As I say, I find that analysis difficult to follow. But the main part of the decision is simply the application of the long-standing decision in the *Lewis Merthyr Consolidated Collieries* case and that is the primary basis of his decision. In those circumstances counsel on behalf of the Revenue Commissioners, who are named as defendants in the proceedings, makes two points. First, of all he draws attention to the form and content of the mortgage debenture given by United Bars Ltd to the bank and points out that the charge is, in the first instance, and primarily, a charge by way of floating security and it is only in the secondary phase that the document goes on to provide for futher securing the monies aforesaid, so that there was, as counsel points out, a floating charge on all of the assets of the company, necessarily including its fixed premises and there was an additional or secondary security in the form of the fixed charge, so that it could be said in considering the rights of the bank or the nature of their security, that they did have a floating charge and did indeed have primarily the floating charge on these premises in respect of which there was also an undoubtedly fixed charge.

There are, undoubtedly, ambiguities and difficulties in the interpretation of s 98. It is clear and agreed rightly and necessarily by both parties that assets subject to a fixed charge may and can be realised by a variety of procedures under which no question of payment of preferential creditors would arise. It may even be that where a receiver is appointed that the monies representing the proceeds of sales of some assets did not reach his hands, but perhaps the strongest point is one made by counsel on behalf of the receiver in saying that if the section was to be interpreted in such a way, that the proceeds of sale of fixed assets by a receiver were to be made available in whole or in part for preferential creditors, that this would infer upon them a benefit of entitlement which they would not have in the event of a liquidation because in a liquidation their rights would be to a priority over creditors who had a floating charge, in those who had a fixed charge, and if s 98 were to be assessed as giving them priority over a fixed charge this would be an unexplicable and unwarranted additional benefit to the preferential creditors whereas the scheme of the Act was to give a particular right to preferential creditors in a winding up and that the function of s 98 and its predecessors was to prevent that right being gained either intentionally or accidentally bar the appointment where no liquidation took place and the only purpose of s 98 should be to equate the rights of preferential creditors in a receivership with those of a liquidation not to improve on those rights.

They are facts which undoubtedly have to be taken into account in considering the literal interpretation versus the teleological interpretation of the section. But at the end of the case it seems to me that predominant in the case is neither the literal interpretation or the original interpretation of the section. The fact that must influence me most is the fact that the 1929 decision has stood the test of time. That has been, although an English decision, part of the corpus of our law for nearly sixty years, and whilst it has not been referred to, so far as I am aware, in many cases it is known and existed in the authorities and I think one must presume was known to the legislature and its legal advisors at the time of the enactment of the Companies Act of 1963.

Furthermore, it seems to me of the utmost importance in dealing with commercial matters to maintain some measure of consistency and to proceed on the footing that parties to commercial transactions have organised their affairs on the basis of the law as they understand and believe it to be for many years, and any change to that law should be made preferably by the Oireachtas or at any rate by the final court of appeal in this country or any revision or correction of the law apart from any actual judge should be dealt with by the highest court in the land or preferably by the Oireachtas. In the circumstances, it seems to me that I must apply the law as it was interpreted in the 1929 decision originally and more recently in the 1986 decision, notwithstanding any reservations that I might have had on the strength of the arguments brought forward by counsel on behalf of the Revenue.

In the circumstances it seems to me that the question raised by the receiver, Mr Jackson, should be answered to the effect that the surplus monies in his hands in representing the proceeds of sales of assets, subject to the fixed charge should not be applied in payment of the preferential creditors.

Notes

Ss 98 and 285 also have no application where the floating charge has crystallised prior to the appointment of a receiver, the taking of possession by the debenture holder, or the commencement of winding up. This is because the debenture has become a fixed charge upon crystallisation. See *Re Brightlife Ltd* (para **11.32**); *Re Permanent Houses (Holdings) Ltd* [1983] BCLC 563; *Re Griffin Hotel Co* [1940] 4 All ER 324; *Re Christanette International Ltd* [1982] 3 All ER 225. In England however, under s 40 of the Insolvency Act 1986 preferential creditors are entitled to priority in respect of any charge 'which as created was a floating charge', thereby circumventing the effect of *Re Brightlife Ltd*.

Crystallisation of floating charge

[11.28] 'Crystallisation' is the process whereby the floating charge becomes a fixed charge and thereby attaches to the assets comprised in it. A floating charge will crystallise automatically upon the appointment of a receiver if the chargee goes into possession or on the winding up of the company. Crystallisation will not automatically occur, in the absence of an express provision in the debenture to the contrary, merely because the company ceases to carry on business or ceases to be a going concern.

Halpin v Cremin [1954] IR 19 (High Court)

[11.29] In 1888 the Listowel and Ballybunion Railway Co created a floating charge in favour of the plainitff over its undertaking and assets. The company ceased trading in 1925 although it was never wound up. The defendant then removed the fence between his land and the company's property and went into possession In 1928 the plaintiff obtained a well charging order in respect of the property but took no steps to enforce the order. For 25 years the defendant enjoyed uninterrupted possession of the property. The plaintiff then sought an order for possession which was resisted by the defendant on the grounds that he had acquired a prior title through adverse possession.

[11.30]   Lavery J: The Real Property Limitation Act 1837 explaining the Real Property Act 1833 provided that it should be lawful for any person claiming under any mortgage of land to make an entry or bring an action or suit to recover such land at any time within twelve years (Real Property Limitation Act 1874 s 9) after the last payment of any part of the principal money or interest secured by such mortgage although more than twelve years may have elapsed since the time at which the right to make such entry or bring such action or suit have first accrued.

It was held and is well established that this Act does not confer a new right of entry on the mortgagee where at the date of the mortgage a person is in possession adversely to the mortgagor and the statute has begun to run in his favour against the mortgagor; *Thornton v France* [1897] 2 QB 143 . . . In my opinion, the decisive consideration in this case is what is the position of a debenture holder whose charge retains the character of a floating security at the time when a person enters into possession of a particular part of the assets of the company and commences to acquire a title by possession certainly against the company . . . It is clear that if a mortgage were created by the company after 1925 when the defendant took possession both company and debenture holder would be barred . . .

It has now to be considered what is the position where a floating security having been created a person enters into possession before the holder of the security has done anything to change its character into a fixed security on specific assets and the statute runs out in his favour without question against the company which has created the security.

The nature of a floating security . . . is that it leaves the company free to dispose of its property by sale or otherwise in the ordinary course of its business. The company may mortgage or sell part or even the whole of its property – if not ultra vires – and may issue debentures: *Governments Stock and Other Securities Investment Co v Manila Railway Co* [1897] AC 81; *In re Borax Company* [1901] 1 Ch 326.

A debenture constituting a floating security over the undertaking and assets of a company does not specifically affect any particular assets until some event occurs or some act on the part of the mortgagee is done which causes the security to crystallise into a fixed security: *Evans v Rival Granite Quarries Ltd* [1910] 2 KB 979.

In the words of Buckley LJ – a great authority on this branch of law – 'the holder [of a debenture] cannot affirm that the assets are specifically mortgaged to him.'

The charge becomes specific on the appointment of a receiver or on a winding up.

In the present case it is clear that nothing was done to make the charge specific till, at the earliest, the issue of the summons on the 12th November 1928, on which the [well charging] order of the 26th November 1928 was made. At that date the defendant was in possession . . .

I therefore hold that the defendant has acquired a title by possession good against not only the Railway Company but against the plaintiff as the purchaser from the holder of the debenture.

Notes

Cf *Re Woodroffes (Musical Instruments) Ltd* [1986] 1 Ch 366 where Norse J held that cessation of business causes crystallisation. See *Gill* (1986) 4 ILT 160.

[11.31] The parties to a floating charge are free to stipulate whatever events they wish as causing the charge to crystallise.

Re Brightlife Ltd [1987] 2 WLR 197 (Chancery Division)

[11.32] The company executed a floating charge in favour of Norandex Inc over its entire undertaking and assets. Immediately prior to the company going into liquidation Norandex served a notice on the company pursuant to the terms of the debenture purporting to crystallise the charge and to turn it into a fixed charge. Norandex was by this stage owed over £200,000. Unpaid value added tax (which constituted a preferential debt) amounted to over £70,000. A question arose as to whether a floating charge could crystallise other than in the circumstances mentioned in *Halpin v Cremin*. If the charge had not crystallised prior to the liquidation, then the preferential creditors would rank in priority to Norandex in respect of the amounts realised under the charge (which totalled approximately £40,000). Hoffmann J upheld the validity of the automatic crystallisation clause and accordingly Norandex Inc took in priority to the preferential creditors.

[11.33] Hoffmann J: I come next to the alternative submission for Norandex, namely that the floating charge was converted into a fixed charge before the resolution for winding up.

Mr Sheldon relies on the notice served under cl 3(*b*) as having crystallised the floating charge over all the assets before the winding up. Alternatively, he relies on the notice under cl 13 as having done so in respect of the book debts. The uninitiated might ask why it is important to ascertain whether the

floating charge crystallised on 13 December. After all, if it did not, there can
be no doubt that it would have done so when the winding up resolution was
passed on 20 December. The importance of the dates lies in the construction
given to what is now s 614(2)(*b*) of the Companies Act 1985 [s 285(7)(*b*) of
the Principal Act] by Bennett J in *In re Griffin Hotel Co Ltd* [1914] Ch 129.
He decided in that case that the priority given by the statute to preferential
debts applied only if there was a charge still floating at the moment of the
winding up and gave the preferential creditors priority in property which at
that moment was comprised in the floating charge.

[His Lordship having referred to the English equivalents of ss 98 and 285
of the Principal Act proceeded as follows]. One imagines that they were
intended to ensure that in all cases preferential debts had priority over the
holder of a charge originally created as a floating charge. It would be difficult
to think of any reason for making distinctions according to the moment at
which the charge crystallised or the event which brought this about. But *In re
Griffin Hotel Co Ltd* reveals a defect in the drafting, it meant, for example,
that if the floating charge crystallised before winding up, but otherwise than
by the appointment of a receiver, the preferential debts would have no priority under either section . . .

Mr Mummery said that the events of crystallisation were fixed by law and
not by the agreement of the parties. Those events were (1) winding up, (2)
appointment of a receiver and (3) ceasing to carry on business. These three
events and only these three would cause crystallisation notwithstanding any
agreement to the contrary. Their common features were that in each case
the business of the company would cease or at any rate, cease to be conducted by the directors . . .

Mr Mummery said that public policy required restrictions upon what the
parties could stipulate as crystallising events. A winding up or the appointment of a receiver would have to be noted on the register. But a notice under
clause 3(*b*) need not be registered and a provision for automatic crystallisation might take effect without the knowledge of either company or the
debenture-holder. The result might be prejudicial to third parties who gave
credit to the company. Considerations of this kind impressed Berger J in the
Canadian case of *R v Consolidated Churchill Copper Corporation Ltd* [1978]
5 WWR 652 where the concept of 'self-generating crystallisation' was
rejected.

I do not think that it is open to the courts to restrict the contractual freedom of parties to a floating charge on such grounds. The floating charge was
invented by victorian lawyers to enable manufacturing and security of a
charge over the whole of the company's undertaking without inhibiting its
ability to trade. But the mirror image of these advantages was the potential
prejudice to the general body of creditors, who might know nothing of the
floating charge but find that all the company's assets, including the very
goods which they had just delivered on credit, had been swept up by the
debenture-holder. The public interest requires a balancing of money against
the possibility of injustice to unsecured creditors. These arguments for and

against the floating charge are matters for Parliament rather than the courts and have been the subject of public debate in and out of Parliament for more than a century . . . [It is] in my judgment wholly inappropriate for the courts to impose additional restrictive rules on grounds of public policy. It is certainly not for a judge of first instance to proclaim a new head of public policy which no appellate court has even hinted at before. I would therefore respectfully prefer the decision of the New Zealand Supreme Court in *In re Manurewa Transport Ltd* [1971] NZLR 909 recognising the validity of a provision for automatic crystallisation to the contrary dicta in the Canadian case I have cited. For present purposes, however, it is not necessary to decide any questions about automatic crystallisation. The notice under clauses 3(*b*) and 13 constitute intervention by the debenture-holder and there is in my judgment no conceptual reason why they should not crystallise the floating charge if the terms of the charge upon their true construction have this effect.

I therefore declare that the debt secured by the debenture ranks in priority to the preferential debts in respect of all assets in the hands of the liquidator.

Notes

See also *Stein v Saywell* (1969) 121 CLR 529. For a criticism of the automatic crystallisation clause see The Report of the Review Committee on *Insolvency Law and Practice* ('the *Cork Report*') Cmnd 8558 at paras 1575 et seq. Also *Farrar* (1980) 1 Co Lawyer 83; Wilkinson and Turner *Automatic Crystallisation of Floating Charges* (1987) 8 Co Lawyer 75.

[11.34] Crystallisation constitutes an equitable assignment to the debenture-holder of all the property comprised in the floating charge but confers on the debenture-holder no greater title than that which was enjoyed by the company itself.

Tempany v Hynes [1976] IR 101 (Supreme Court)

[11.35] The plaintiff was appointed a receiver of the undertaking and assets of the company (including certain registered lands) pursuant to the terms of a fixed and floating charge. The plaintiff in exercise of a power of sale, agreed to sell the lands to the defendant who paid the contractual deposit. Before the sale was completed two judgment mortgages were registered as burdens on the lands. The defendant contended that as a result of these judgment mortgages he would not get title to the lands. The receiver sought specific performance of the contracts claiming that his power of sale could convey the lands free from the judgment mortgages.

[11.36]   Kenny J: The plaintiff's argument was that, when the receiver was appointed, there was an equitable assignment to the debenture holders of all the property which was subject to the floating charge, and that the result of this was that the claim of the debenture holders in relation to the lands in the three folios ranked before that of the judgment mortgagees.

The two mortgage debentures created a specific charge over all the other assets present and future of the company; and the effect of the appointment of a receiver under a debenture is that there is an equitable assignment to the debenture holder of all the property which is subject to the floating charge . . . The equitable assignment effected by the appointment of the receiver was, in my opinion, an unregistered right subject to which the company held the lands . . . In my opinion the claim of the debenture holders in relation to the lands in the three folios ranks before the rights of the four judgment mortgagees and the vendor has shown a good title to all of the lands in the three folios. When the transfer from the plaintiff and the company to the defendant, the mortgage debentures and the appointment of the receiver are produced to him, it will be the duty of the registrar of titles to cancel the entries of the four judgment mortgages which appear on the folios without proof of the payment of any sum in respect of any of them.

O'Higgins CJ concurred. Henchy J delivered a concurring judgment.

Notes

See also *Hobson v Bute Investments Ltd* (High Court, Hamilton J, 14 February 1980).

In *Rother Iron Works Ltd v Canterbury Precision Engineers Ltd* [1974] QB 1 it was held that as the debenture holder obtains no greater title than that which was enjoyed by the company, he therefore takes subject to any right of set off which relates to pre-crystallisation debts.

[11.37]   A right of set-off may not be exercised by a creditor in respect of a debt becoming due by a company after crystallisation if to do so would give the creditor priority over the debenture holder.

Lynch v Ardmore Studios (Ireland) Ltd and Michael Hayes [1966] IR 133

[11.38]   In 1963 the defendant company brought an unsuccessful action against members of a trade union, seeking to restrain picketing of the company's premises. The action was dismissed with costs. Later in the same year a receiver was appointed over the entire undertaking and assets of the company pursuant to the terms of a floating charge. The receiver caused the company to issue fresh proceedings against an entirely different group of trade union members seeking to restrain picketing of the premises. The action was successful and the company was awarded costs. The defendants from the first set of proceedings assigned their award of costs to the defendants in the second action (the plaintiffs in the present proceedings). Notice of assignment was given to the company and the plaintiffs then purported to set-off the two sets of costs and to tender the balance to the company. Budd J, refused to allow set-off on the ground that the award of costs in the second set of proceedings belonged in equity to the debenture holder.

Budd J: On the actual point in issue in this action, regarding the right to set-off a debt due by a company before the appointment of a receiver against a debt becoming due to the company after the appointment of a receiver, there was cited to me a case of *NW Robbie & Co Ltd v Witney Warehouse Co Ltd* [1963] 1 WLR 1324, which has many features strikingly similar to the present case as will be seen from the following recital of the facts.

In January 1960, the plaintiff company issued a debenture to the Bank of Ireland. In July 1961, the bank appointed a receiver and manager. Prior to the appointment of the receiver and manager the plaintiff company had sold goods to the defendant company on credit for £95. After the receiver was appointed he permitted the plaintiff company to carry on business and the plaintiff company sold further goods to the value of £1,251 to the defendant company, again on credit, the goods being a portion of the stock of the company when the receiver was appointed. Between November 1960, and January 1961 that is, before the appointment of the receiver, the plaintiff company purchased goods from a company called English Spinners Ltd to the value of £852. After the appointment of the receiver, English Spinners Ltd on the 6th October 1961, assigned the benefit of their debt to the defendant company. The plaintiffs sued the defendants for the sum of £1,346 due to them. The defendant company, admitting that the balance of £494 was due, claimed to set off the sum of £852. It was held that it was not entitled to do so by a majority of the court . . The decision is founded on the following reasoning, neatly summarised in the head-note of the report of the case in [1963] 3 All ER 613 which I have paraphrased somewhat. The charge created by the debenture crystallises on assets including choses in action as they come into existence. Therefore debts as they became due became subject to the equitable charge (tantamount to an equitable assignment) to the debenture holder. Thus the debts due to the plaintiff company became assigned in equity to the debenture holder before the cross-claim arose. There was therefore no mutuality at the first moment of assertion of the set-off because the cross-claim by the defendant company did not involve the debenture holder, being against the plaintiff company alone and consequently there was no right of set off . . .

I find myself, with respect, in accord with the reasoning and decision in *NW Robbie & Co Ltd v Witney Warehouse Co Ltd* and applying the reasoning to the present case, the position is this: the first named defendants in these proceedings (being the plaintiffs in the second action) recovered a judgment for costs amounting to the sum of £1,208 0s 8d. That was a judgment debt owing to the company. The charge created by the debenture crystallised on that asset of the company when it came into existence and it became assigned in equity to the debenture holder at latest upon the taxation of the costs on the 5th August 1965. That was before the assignment of the cross-debt of the costs in the first action on the 15th October 1965. At the time of the assertion of the set-off on the 27th October 1965, there was no mutuality because the claim founded upon the judgment in the first action involved the company alone and did not involve the debenture holder. Accordingly, following the decision in *NW Robbie & Co Ltd v Witney Warehouse Co Ltd*, I am of the view that there can be no valid set off of the nature claimed by the plaintiffs . . .

Since in my view no set-off is available to the plaintiffs in these proceedings, it follows that the defendant company is entitled to levy execution on foot of its judgment against the plaintiffs and that I must refuse the relief sought and dismiss the proceedings.

Notes

See also *Re Harrex Ltd; Murphy v The Revenue Commissioners* [1976] IR 15 where the company received a large tax repayment in respect of its terminal trading loss. A receiver having previously been appointed over the company pursuant to the terms of a floating charge, the repayment was in equity assigned to the debenture holder, thereby preventing the Revenue Commissioners claiming a right to set off the repayment against the company's unpaid arrears of taxes.

[11.39] Upon crystallisation the debenture holder takes the property the subject matter of the floating charge free from any order in personam which has been previously obtained against the company although the receiver if the agent of the company is bound by such an order.

Cretanor Maritime Co Ltd v Irish Marine Management Ltd [1978] 3 All ER 164 (Court of Appeal)

[11.40] The owners of a ship (a foreign company) chartered the vessel to the defendant the charterers who in turn executed a floating charge in favour of an Irish bank charging their undertaking and property as security for money due or to become due to the bank. A dispute arose between the owner and the charterer regarding the charter party and the owners obtained a Mareva injunction against the charterers freezing their assets up to a value of US $700,000 then present in the UK. The debenture holder subsequently appointed a receiver under the debenture to get in all moneys owing by the charterers. The defendants' assets included a fund of over £70,000 deposited at a bank in the United Kingdom. The receiver applied to have the injunction discharged in relation to the fund claiming that the debenture had priority.

[11.41] **Buckley LJ:** The receiver, having been appointed to collect and get in the charterers' assets as the charterers' agent, could only get in those assets subject to any contractual rights of third parties in relation to those assets created before his appointment and in my opinion, to any limitations on the charterers' powers to deal with the assets or any of them which existed at the date of his appointment.

Counsel for the charterers has contended that the injunction did not create any right or interest capable of ranking in priority to the debenture. That may be so, but we are not for the present purpose concerned with the priorities of interests in the deposited fund; we are concerned with the capacity or incapacity of the charterers to remove that fund out of the jurisdiction. This the charterers were already restrained from doing when the receiver was appointed. In these circumstances it seems to me that the receiver as the charterers' agent is also bound by the injunction. But the debenture holder is not so bound . . .

Under such an injunction the plaintiff has no rights against the assets. He may later acquire such rights if he obtains judgment and can thereafter successfully levy execution on them, but until that event his only rights are against the defendant personally.

In the absence of evidence to the contrary I think we can properly assume that the law in the Republic of Ireland relating to floating charges and to appointment of receivers under powers contained in debentures such as we have in the present case is the same as English law. If so, the debenture created an immediate equitable charge on the assets of the charterers, wherever situated, subject to a power in the charterers, so long as the charge continued to float, to deal with their assets in the course of their business, notwithstanding such charge, as though it did not exist . . . While the charge continued to float, third parties dealing with the charterers in the course of their business could ignore it. This, however, does not mean that as between the charterers and the debenture holder the charge did not exist or had no operative effect. The appointment of the receiver merely crystallised the existing charge, that is to say, it put an end to the power under which, until that time, the charterers were able to deal with their assets in the course of their business as if no charge existed. The equitable assignment thereupon for the first time took complete and unqualified effect. In my opinion, the debenture holder then became entitled to a fixed charge on the deposited fund in this country being one of the charterers' assets at that time but subject to the necessity of getting the injunction discharged so as to enable the receiver to remove that asset from this jurisdiction . . . In my judgment it is open to the debenture holder as equitable assignee under Irish law of the deposited fund in England to apply for the discharge of the injunction.

By his summons . . . seeking to have the injunction discharged the receiver does not in terms as agent of the charterers, but I think that for reasons already indicated he must be taken to have done so in that capacity, for there is not evidence so far as I am aware, that he was ever authorised by the debenture holder to make such application on the debenture holder's behalf. For reasons which I have stated when dealing with the owners' first head of argument I do not think that the receiver in his capacity as agent of the company can obtain the dischage of the injunction, but I see no reason why the debenture holder should not apply for this.

Treating the application as made by the debenture holder, ought we to dissolve the injunction? The evidence indicates that there is no prospect of any surplus being available for unsecured creditors in the liquidation of the charterers after satisfaction of the claims of the debenture holder and of preferential creditors. Taking into account the facts that the debenture holder is now an equitable assignee of the deposited fund, that the injunction gives the owners no present rights against the deposited fund but was made merely with a view to the retention of that fund in England so as to be available in the event of the owners becoming able to levy execution on it, and that, if the owners were hereafter to attempt to levy execution on it, their rights as execution creditors would have to give way to prior rights in the fund, including the rights of the debenture holder, I think that the deposit certificate should be released to the receiver free from the injunction.

Goff LJ and Sir David Cairns concurred.

Notes

Similarly, although a judgment creditor will take priority where he has completely executed his judgment before crystallisation (*Evans v Rival Granite Quarries Ltd* [1910] 2 KB 979) the judgment is no more than a right in personam against the company and accordingly loses its priority if crystallisation precedes execution (*Re Opera* [1891] 3 Ch 260).

Avoidance of floating charges

[11.42]   As we have seen above, the scope of a floating charge is potentially wide enough to cover all the company's property, thereby leaving nothing for the unsecured creditors. The Principal Act makes some attempt to curb the effect of such charges such as by giving preferential creditors priority in certain circumstances, over the debenture holder. Further limitations are imposed by ss 288 and 289.

S 288, as substituted by s 136 of the 1990 Act provides that where a company is being wound up, a floating charge created within 12 months before the commencement of the winding up shall 'unless it is proved that the company immediately after the creation of the charge was solvent, be invalid, except as to money actually advanced or paid, or the actual price or value of goods or services sold or supplied, to the company at the time of or subsequently to the creation of and in consideration for the charge, together with interest on that amount at the rate of 5 per cent per annum'.

The 12 month period is extended to 2 years where the charge is created in favour of a connected person (ie a director or shadow director of the company, a person connected with a director, a related company, or a trustee of, or any surety or guarantor for the debt due to any of the foregoing categories of person).

The value of any goods or services sold or supplied in consideration for the charge is the amount of money which at the time they were sold or supplied could reasonably have been expected to be obtained for them in the ordinary course of business and on the same terms (apart from consideration) as those on which they were actually sold or supplied.

S 289 adds further restrictions where the company is being wound up and was within the 12 month period indebted to any of its officers. If during this period the indebtedness was discharged whether wholly or partly by the company or by any other person and during the same period the company created a floating charge in favour of the officer, then the charge will be invalid to the extent that the indebtedness was discharged unless it is proved that the company was solvent immediately after the creation of the charge. For the purposes of the section 'officer' includes the spouse or nominee of an officer. Notably, unlike s 288 this s 289 does not provide for the validation of the charge to the extent, of any cash paid in consideration for its creation.

[11.43] The term 'solvent' in ss 288 and 289 means 'an ability to pay ones debts as they fall due' and does not simply refer to a situation where the company's assets exceed its liabilities.

Re Creation Printing Co Ltd; Crowley v Northern Bank Finance Corporation Ltd and Kelso [1981] IR 353 (Supreme Court)

[11.44] On 4 June 1975 Creation Printing Co Ltd created a floating charge over its undertaking and assets in favour of the defendant bank. The consideration for the charge was the forbearance of the bank to demand immediately repayment from the parent company of Creation Printing Co Ltd of monies owing to it by the parent. At the date of execution of the charge the company's fixed and current assets exceeded its liabilities. However, its current assets, alone would have been insufficient to meet the liabilities (including the liability under the floating charge). A receiver was appointed under the charge on 26 November 1975. On 23 December 1975 the company went into liquidation. The receiver sought the directions of the courts as to whether for the purposes of s 288 the company was solvent immediately after creation of the floating charge.

[11.45] **Kenny J:** 'solvent' and 'insolvency' are ambiguous words. It has now been established by the decided cases that, for the purposes of s 288 of the Act of 1963, the test to be applied in determining this question is whether immediately after the debenture was given, the company was able to pay its debts as they became due. The question is not whether its assets exceed in estimated value its liabilities, or whether a business man would have regarded it as solvent: *Ex p Russell* (1882) 19 Ch D 588; *Re Partick and Lyon Ltd* [1933] Ch 786. The question whether a company was solvent on a specified date is one of fact and it involves many difficult inferences. If there is, or is likely to be a large deficiency of assets when the liquidation starts, the temptation to hold that the company was not solvent when the charge was given is strong. But the deficiency may have been caused by some change in economic or market conditions happening after the charge was given. So an examination of the financial history of the company both before and after the charges were given is necessary.

Although the solvency of a company is a question of fact, some guidelines as to how this question is to be approached are given by the decided cases. *Ex parte Russell* related to s 91 of the Bankruptcy Act 1869 which provided that any settlement of property made by a trader (not being made in contemplation of marriage or in favour of a purchaser or incumbrancer) should if the settlor became bankrupt at any subsequent time within 10 years after the date of such settlement, be void against the trustees in bankruptcy 'unless the parties claiming under such settlements can prove that the settlor was at the time of making the settlement able to pay all his debts without the aid of the property comprised in such settlement.' Mr Butterworth was a baker who had traded profitably and bought some houses as an investment. In 1878 he settled these in favour of his wife and children. He then purchased a grocery business in which he lost money. He filed a bankruptcy petition in 1881. He had continued to carry on his bakery business after the purchase of the grocery business. When the settlement was impeached he claimed that in deciding whether he was solvent in 1878, the property, assets and stock-in-trade of the bakery business should be taken into account. Lindley LJ, dealt with this contention in these words at p 601 of the report:–

'I also think the settlement falls within the 91st section of the Bankruptcy Act. When we look at the words of that section and have to consider whether a man is able to pay his debts, we must not merely look at the amount of his assets and liabilities, but we must consider the position which he is assuming. If, for example, this baker had been retiring from trade of course, we must have taken into account all his pots and shovels the goodwill of his business, and everything else, all those things would be the means of paying his debts. But if he is going on with his baker's business it appears to me idle that we should take such things into account as assets. He must be able to pay his debts in the way in which he proposes to pay them, that is by continuing his business.'

Those words of Lindley LJ were written in 1882 in relation to an individual. At that time floating charges by a company were rare. Their validity had been recognised only in 1870 in *In re Panama, New Zealand and Australian Royal Mail Co* (1870) 5 Ch App 318. His remarks show that when considering whether a company was solvent immediately after it had created a particular floating charge, in circumstances where its directors intended that the company would continue to carry on its business after that time, the fixed and moveable assets of the company are not to be taken into account. However, the capacity of the company immediately after the creation of the particular charge to borrow money on the security of another charge on its assets must be taken into account. This necessarily involves the court in an inquiry as to whether any creditor would advance money to the company on the security of another and later floating charge which would rank in priority after the particular debenture whose validity is in question. If a sum could be borrowed on the security of such a subsequent charge, it should be taken into the reckoning which has to be made when determining the company's solvency . . .

I have no doubt that on the 4th June, 1975 the parent company and all its subsidiaries considered as a unit were not solvent.

It was strenuously contended by counsel for the defendant bank that the question to be decided was not whether the parent company together with all its subsidiaries was solvent but whether Creation Printing was solvent . . . On the 4th June 1975 Creation Printing intended to carry on its trade. Therefore the value of the fixed assets must be excluded in deciding whether it was solvent. On that basis there was on the most optimistic view, the sum of £134,727 (the sum standing to the credit of the profit and loss account) available to meet the liability of £305,000 – for Creation Printing must be proved to have been solvent *after* the debenture of the 4th June 1975, was given.

In my opinion, the defendant bank has completely failed to prove that Creation Printing was solvent within the meaning of that term as used in s 288 of the Companies Act 1963.

O'Higgins CJ and Parke J concurred.

[11.46] For the purposes of s 288, a floating charge is validated to the extent of 'money actually advanced or paid' between the agreement to create a charge and its actual creation provided that the delay in creation and registration was not intended to deceive creditors and was not unreasonable or culpable.

Re Daniel Murphy Ltd [1964] IR 1 (High Court)

[11.47] The company had an existing overdraft of £9,759 with the bank, which was secured by an equitable mortgage of its premises. It required further accomodation up to £15,000. This was agreed upon by the bank provided the facility was security by a floating charge. There was a delay of some 55 days in execution and registering of the charge, during which time the company lodged £30,887 to its account, while drawing cheques on the account totalling £36,003. Within approximately two weeks of the execution and registration of the charge, the company went into liquidation. A question arose as to whether the money advanced by the bank prior to the execution of the charge was 'cash paid . . . at the time of . . . the creation of the charge'. A further question before the court was whether the money lodged by the company after the date of the agreement to execute the charge was to be appropriated first in reducing the pre-existing overdraft of £9,759.

[11.48] **Kenny J:** The correspondence shows that on the 8th June the company had agreed to give a floating charge on 'their stocks and debtors' and I am satisfied that the bank allowed the company to increase the amount of its overdraft because this promise to create the charge had been given. The charge was not, however, sealed by the company until the 2nd August and the company went into voluntary liquidation on the 21st August. There was thus an interval of fifty-five days between the date when the company agreed to give the charge and the date when it was sealed. The preparation, approval, engrossment and execution of a charge require some time; it has to be considered by the board of directors of the company and by their solicitors and accountants and I do not think that the delay between the agreement and the charge and its execution was unreasonable or culpable. The explanation given for the company's delay in dealing with the charge is convincing and the bank acted with all possible expedition. The delay was not intended to and did not deceive or mislead other creditors. Moreover it is desireable that lenders should be encouraged to advance money when a promise to create a charge has been given, for tht is usually the time when the money is urgently needed. It has been argued that the monies advanced to the company between the 8th June and the 2nd August were not advanced 'at the time of the charge' and that that sum secured by the charge is that advanced after the 2nd August. The Companies (Consolidation) Act 1908 shows that the words, 'at the time of the creation' of the charge do not mean 'at the date of its creation', for s 93 (which deals with registration of charges) provides that a charge of the kind described in that section is to be void unless it is registered within 21 days 'after the date of its creation', while that words in s 212 are:– 'at the time of or subsequently to the creation of'. If seems to me that monies advanced after an agreement (not registered in the Companies Registration Office) to give a charge but before its execution are advanced at the time of the charge provided that the delay in having the charge completed was not intended to deceive creditors and was not unreasonable or culpable . . . In this case, the bank did not suggest or acquiesce in the delay in giving the charge: they acted with all possible expedition. A satisfactory explanation for the delay has been given and I am of opinion that the sums advanced by the bank from the 9th June until the company went into liquidation were paid to the company at the time of or subsequently to the creation of the charge.

The next argument was that the amount secured by the charge was not £14,860 and interest but that sum less £9,760, the amount due to the bank on the 8th June 1961 and I was invited to look at the substance and reality of the transaction. It was said that the purpose of the charge was to enable the company to get more accommodation than they had already, and that the substance of the transaction was that the increased accommodation only was secured by the charge. For the bank it was said that the rule in *Clayton's* case 1 Mer 572, applied so that payments made to the credit of the no 1 account after the 8th June must be regarded as having been first appropriated to discharge the liability of £9,759 due on that date. If the rule in *Clayton's* case applies, the effect would be that the entire sum of £14,860 due on the 21st August 1961 would have been advanced after the 9th June 1961. It is not necessary for me to deal with the many authorities in which the rule in *Clayton's* case has been discussed; it is sufficient to refer to a passage in the speech of the Earl of Selborne LC in *In re Sherry London and County Banking Co v Terry* (1884) 25 Ch D 662:– 'The principle of *Clayton's* case and of the other cases which deal with the same subject is that where a creditor having a right to appropriate monies paid to him generally and not specifically appropriated by the person paying them, carries them into a

293

particular account kept in his books, he prima facie appropriates them to that account and the effect of that is that the payments are de facto appropriated according to the priority in order of the entries on the one side and on the other of that account. It is of course, absolutely necessary for the application of those authorities that there should be one unbroken account and entries made in that account by the person having a right to appropriate the payment to that account; and the way to avoid the application of *Clayton's* case where there is no other principle in question is to break the account and open a new and distinct account. When that is done and the payment is entered to that new and distinct account whatever other rule may govern the case, it certainly is not the rule of *Clayton's* case or of *Bodenham v Purchase* 2 B & Ald 39 and other authorities of that class . . .

In this case the company's no 1 account with the bank was not ruled out or closed when the promise to give the charge had been made or when the floating charge was executed and I do not see any reason why the rule in *Clayton's* case should not apply. If it does the monies due to the bank by the company on the 8th June must be regarded as having been discharged by the monies subsequently lodged and the total sum due on the 21st August is now due to the bank on the security of the floating charge.

I gave judgment in this case immediately after the arguments had concluded as I was informed that the matter was urgent. Some time afterwards the decision of Plowman J in *Re Yeovil Glove Co Ltd* [1962] 3 All ER 400 was reported. In that case Plowman J had to consider circumstances similar to those in this case and in particular the application of the rule in *Clayton's* case when at the date of the charge there is a sum due by a customer of a bank to which the charge had been given. I am glad that the conclusion which I reached was the same as that of Plowman J in the case before him.

Notes

In *Re Yeovil Glove Co Ltd* it was held that the phrase 'cash paid' includes cheques met by the bank on behalf of the company. A similar decision was reached in *Re Thomas Mortimer Ltd* [1965] Ch 186. Cash paid to the company will be ignored if that money is to be channelled through to a third party as there has in substance been no payment to the company. See *Re WG McCleave & Co Ltd* (1913) 47 ILTR 214; *Re Matthew Ellis Ltd* [1933] Ch 458.

Forbearance to sue will not constitute 'cash paid' for the purposes of s 288. See *Creation Printing Co Ltd* [1981] IR 353 and *Re Lakeglen Construction Ltd* [1980] IR 347.

[11.49]   A floating charge which has already been redeemed cannot be avoided under s 288 of the Principal Act.

Mace Builders (Glasgow) Ltd v Lunn [1987] Ch 191 (Court of Appeal)

[11.50]   The defendant was the managing director of the plaintiff company. On 21 May 1981 the plaintiff executed a floating charge to secure all pre-existing and future indebtedness to the defendant up to a sum of £100,000. In

November 1981 the plaintiff having failed to repay sums owing to the defendant he appointed himself receiver under the floating charge, sold the charged assets and applied the proceeds (£95,000) towards repayment of the monies owing to him. Subsequently on 20 May 1982 the company went into liquidation and the liquidator sought to challenge the validity of the charge under the then equivalent of s 288 (s 322 of the Companies Act 1948). It was admitted that the company was insolvent at the time of the creation of the charge and also that the defendant had advanced £20,000 by way of new money in consideration for the creation of the floating charge. The liquidator claimed repayment of £75,000 of the proceeds of sale.

[11.51] Sir John Donaldson MR: Curiously no similar situation ever appears to have been considered by the courts. The nearest approach was in *Re Parkes Garage (Swadlincote) Ltd* [1929] 1 Ch 139 where the company which was not solvent granted a debenture to a trustee for a group of its more pressing creditors, sold some assets and used the proceeds to redeem the debenture. Section 212 of the Companies (Consolidation) Act 1908 was in force in the same terms as s 322 of the 1948 Act. Thereafter the company went into liquidation and the liquidator sought a declaration that the debenture was invalid and the repayment of the moneys received by the trustee. A divisional court of the Chancery Division (Eve and Maugham JJ) held that the charge contained in the debenture was invalid, but that the covenants to pay the principal and interest therein contained were unaffected and that the money had been paid in pursuance of those covenants. It was thus not repayable. No argument was addressed to the court on whether the invalidity of the charge related back to the time of repayment, because on the facts the rights conferred by the charge had never been exercised. The company had simply repaid the debenture holders' debts in order to redeem the debenture . . .

I am thus left only with the section itself. The opening words are 'where a company is being wound up . . .' The section thus has no application unless and until the company is being wound up. I would follow that if, for example, the company had mortgaged any part of its assets otherwise than by a floating charge, in December 1981, that is to say after the creation of the floating charge and before the winding up, the defendant could have claimed and would have been granted a declaration that his rights had priority over those of the subsequent mortgagee. No question of fraudulent preference could have arisen since the six month period would have expired and there would have been no certainty that the company would be wound up before 21 May 1982 or indeed at all. The application of s 322 at that time would have been entirely speculative.

Yet if counsel's argument for the plaintiff is accepted, the result would be that in May 1982 immediately following the commencement of the winding up, the same court would have to declare that contrary to what it had previously declared, the defendant had no such priority and retrospectively had never had any such priority. I am loath to accept in the absence of much clearer words that Parliament intended so Gilbertian a situation, ie order, counter-order, disorder . . .

This view is reinforced as the judge pointed out, by a consideration of the position of a bona fide purchaser for value of the company's assets from the preferred creditor before the winding up. His position is protected in the event of invalidation of the charge under s 320 [which relates to fraudulent preferences], by the importation of s 44(2) of the Bankruptcy Act 1914: 'This section shall not affect the rights of any person making title in good faith and for valuable consideration through or under a creditor of the bankrupt'. No such protection would be available under s 322 if that section has retrospective effect. There would in addition, be the surprising anomaly that the charge would be at risk of being invalidated over a period of 12 months, whereas the more objectionable fraudulently preferential transaction would only be at risk over a period of six months.

I am therefore satisfied that the application of s 322 is confined to the winding up and that transactions effected under the authority of the charge which are completed before the commencement of the winding up are unaffected by the section. My conclusion is unaffected by the consideration much stressed by counsel for the plaintiff that this construction could lead to an unseemly race between beneficiaries under a floating charge to realise their security and other creditors to begin the winding up of the company.

Norse LJ delivered a concurring judgment. Glidewell LJ concurred.

Fixed charges on book debts[1]

[11.52] It has long been recognised that a floating charge may validly extend to a company's book debts.[2] In order to avoid the problems attaching to floating charges by virtue of ss 98, 285 and 288 of the Principal Act, bankers have sought to create fixed charges over as many of the company's assets as possible including not only its fixed assets, but also its book debts. No problem arises in charging the former class of assets as they are not of a type which in the ordinary course of business will be changing from time to time. However, if restrictions are imposed upon the company's freedom to deal with book debts (which is after all an essential characteristic of a fixed charge) it may suffer cash flow problems resulting in insolvency.

1 See *Keane* at para **22.18**.
2 *Tailby v Official Receiver* (1888) 3 App Cas 523.

[11.53] A charge over book debts will be regarded as a fixed charge if the company's freedom to deal with the book debts in the ordinary course of business is restricted by the chargee.

Re Keenan Brothers Ltd (In Liquidation) [1985] ILRM 641 (Supreme Court)

[11.54] In May 1983 the company created two charges over its present and future book debts, one in favour of Allied Irish Bank Ltd and the other in favour of Allied Irish Investment Bank Ltd. Both were expressed to be fixed charges and required the company to pay all moneys it received 'in respect of the bank and other debts' into designated bank accounts. Withdrawals from these accounts could only be made with the consent of the relevant bank. The company was subsequently wound up and the liquidator applied for directions as to whether the charges were floating charges out of which preferential debts could be paid.

[11.55]   McCarthy J: The banks appeal against the decision of the High Court (Keane J) which held that the charges which had been created by the instruments of 3 May and 5 May 1983 were floating charges rather than fixed charges over the present and future book debts of the company. The result of that decision is that monies due to the Revenue have priority over the claims of the banks on foot of the instruments of May 1983; the claim by the banks is in respect of advances made between May 1983 and November 1983 when the company went into liquidation.

The underlying basis was that the company in May 1983 was in serious financial difficulties and the banks, if they could secure the advances were prepared to lend financial assistance. Because of the Companies Act 1963, a floating charge would not secure the required priority but a fixed charge would. In *Siebe Gorman & Co Ltd v Barclays Bank Ltd* [1979] 2 Lloyd's Rep 142, Slade J had given a judicial blessing in England to a claim by way of fixed charge on book debts where this was purported to be created by an instrument with marked similarities to those the subject of this appeal; during the course of the hearing we were informed that they were in fact modelled on those in *Siebe Gorman* although it was emphasised that monies received in respect of the book debts in the instant case were paid into a special account and not as in *Siebe Gorman* into the ordinary account of the mortgagor.

In *In re Armagh Shoes Ltd* [1982] NI 59 Hutton J in the High Court of Northern Ireland identified an apparent divergence of judicial view and legal precedent in a series of decisions . . . It may well be that there are factual differences in the several cases but I think it desirable to identify some common ground so as to isolate the underlying principle and thereby resolve the two legal issues raised in this appeal that is, (*a*) can a fixed charge be validly created in respect of future book debts? and (*b*) did the relevant instruments in this case do so?

Clearly, the parties wanted to secure the bank's advances in priority to all other claims, wanted to achieve this by a fixed charge whilst enabling the company to avail of advances from the bank covered so to speak by anmounts received by the company in discharge of book debts and lodged to the special account; and wanted to achieve this result by using the *Siebe Gorman* scheme. It is not suggested that mere terminology itself – such as using the exression 'fixed charge' – achieves the purpose one must look, not within the narrow confines of such term, not to the declared intention of the parties alone but to the effect of the instruments whereby they purported to carry out that intention; did they achieve what they intended, or was the intention defeated by the ancillary requirements? . . .

In my view it is because it was described as a specific or fixed charge and was intended to be such that the requirement of a special bank account was necessary; if it were a floating charge, payment into such an account would entirely inappropriate and indeed would conflict with the ambulatory nature of the floating charge to which Lord Macnaughten refers. In *In re Yorkshire Woolcombers Association Ltd* [1903] 2 Ch 284 at p 295 Romer LJ postulated three charactertistics of a floating charge, the third being that 'if you find that by the charge it is contemplated that until some future step is taken by or on behalf of those interested in the charge, the company may carry on its business in the ordinary way as far as concerns the particular class of assets I am dealing with'. Mr Cooke SC has argued that this latter characteristic is essential to a floating charge and that the banking provision in the instrument here negatives such a characteristic; I would uphold this view. I have sought to identify from the speech of Lord Macnaughten the badge of a specific or fixed charge; that of the floating charge seem to me to be the absence of immediate effect or possibly ultimate effect – in short it may never happen; if the advances made or the debts incurred are repaid or discharged, then the cloud is dispersed never to return in that exact form . . .

The charge whatever its nature, for its validity had to be registered under the Companies Act 1963 and its existence would have been known to anyone upon casual enquiry – its existence was described as a fixed charge. Whilst acknowledging that the charge is somewhat hybrid in form because of the concession in respect of the collection of debts and lodgment to a special account, I do not recognise in it the ordinary characteristics of a floating chargre – that it may crystallise on the happening of some future event. If the borrower, the company, is driven to such financial straits that it is prepared to effect an immediate charge upon its book debts, the existence of which charge is in effect, published to the commercial and financial world, I do not accept that an elaborate system set up to enable the company to benefit by the collection of such debts detracts from its qualifying as a specific or fixed charge.

The remaining question as raised by the Revenue Commissioners is whether or not it is possible in law to create a fixed charge on future book debts. There appears to be ample authority in England in support of the contention going back to *Tailby v Official Receiver* (1888) 13 App Cas 523, and asserted in Canada in *Evans, Coleman & Evans v RA Nelson Construction Ltd* (1985) DLR 123. I am content to adopt the observations of Davey J at p 127 of the latter report and hold that there is no legal bar to there being a fixed charge on book debts.

Henchy J delivered a concurring judgment. Finlay CJ and Hederman J concurred.

Walsh J: Book debts and other debts cease to be such the moment they are discharged by the debtors irrespective of whether the payment is made directly to the creditor or on his order to some other party on his account.

From the dates of the execution of the charges until October 1983 all monies received by the company whether from book debts or other sources were lodged to the company's No 1 current account with the bank. During that period the company also had four other accounts with the bank, namely a creditors account, two wages accounts and a deposit account. During that period all these accounts were operated in the ordinary way and without any special restriction on any of them imposed by the bank.

On 4 October 1983 a new bank account was opened by the company with the bank under the name 'Keenan Brothers Ltd Allied Irish Banks Ltd Book Debts RAC', the letters RAC standing for Receivable Account. From that date until the commencement of the liquidation on 29 November 1983 all receipts of the company whether from debtors or otherwise were lodged to the receivable account. The total receipts from debtors lodged amounted to £665,948.53 and a further sum of £11,184.76 in respect of cash sales and sundries respectively were also lodged. No withdrawals or transfers or payments could be made from that account without the countersignature of the bank manager who had in fact the sole discretion to permit withdrawals or transfers from that account. Some book debts paid into the No 1 account immediately transferred into the receivable account.

The company's day to day expenses and payments due by the company to its business creditors were paid out of the No 1 account which was in effect an overdraft account and which from time to time received transfers of funds from the receivable account. These payments were of course only possible with the consent of the bank.

At all relevant times the receivable account was in credit. As the relationship between banker and customer is one of debtor and creditor all sums from time to time standing to credit in that account were owed by the bank to the company and were not book debts due to the company or debts in the contemplation of the deed of charge or the debenture even though the account was opened to receive the collected book and other debts due to the company, which of course ceased to be debts from the moment they were collected. According to the copy of the bank's statement of the receivable account exhibited in this case the highest credit balance was £46,395.97 which stood to credit on 24 November 1983. On 25 November £42,000 was transferred to the No 1 account. On 28 November the credit balance was £22,375.14. On 29 November 1983, £20,137 was transferred to the No 1 account leaving a balance of £2,238.14. 29 November was the date of the order of the High Court for the liquidation of the company. The material before the court does not disclose whether this was effected before or after the order for liquidation. If it was the latter then it is for the examiner to examine the legal effect of the transaction. No monies in that account are or ever were subject to the fixed charge . . . I do not find it necessary to identify what particular monies were or are the subject of the fixed charge beyond repeating my opinion that none of the monies in the receivable account were ever so subject after they were lodged to that account.

Notes
No other judge expressed an opinion on the matter raised by Walsh J. It may well be that Walsh J was correct. In this regard see *Re Brightlife Ltd* (para **11.57**).

In *Re AH Masser Ltd (in receivership), McCann and Long v Revenue Commissioners.* (High Court, 6 October 1986) Barron J confirmed that it is possible to create a fixed charge over book debts without having to open a separate receivables account. As in the *Siebe Gorman* case it suffices that the book debts must be paid into the company's ordinary trading account and that restrictions are placed on the company's freedom to make withdrawals from that account.

[11.56] A charge over 'book debts or other debts' will not normally be regarded as extending to a credit balance at a bank.

Re Brightlife Ltd [1987] 2 WLR 197 (Chancery Division)

[11.57] The company purported to create a 'fixed specific charge' in favour of Norandex Inc over inter alia, 'all book debts and other debts now or at anytime during the continuance of this security due or owing to Brightlife'. The company went into liquidation owing Norandex £200,000. The charged assets realised £40,000 of which £18,000 was derived from the collection of book debts and £19,000 was the amount standing in the company's bank account. The liquidator sought directions as to whether the £19,000 in the bank account constituted 'book debts or other debts' for the purposes of the charge.

[11.58] **Hoffmann J:** I must first dispose of certain questions of construction. The debenture is dated 11 April 1983. It is expressed to secure all present and future indebtedness of Brightlife to Norandex. The charging clause is 3(*a*). Sub-clause (i) creates a 'first specific equitable charge' over freehold and leasehold property. Sub-clause (ii) charges

'by way of first specific charge (*a*) all book debts and other debts now or at any time during the continuance of this security due or owing to Brightlife and the benefit of all securities and guarantees now or at any time held by Brightlife in relation thereto; (*b*) the goodwill and uncalled for capital for the time being of Brightlife; and (*c*) the benefit of any licences for the time being in Brightlife . . .

First, I do not think that the bank balance falls within the term 'book debts or other debts' as it is used in the debenture. It is true that the relationship between banker and customer is one of debtor and creditor. It would not therefore be legally inaccurate to describe a credit balance with a banker as a debt. But this would not be a natural usage for a businessman or accountant. He would ordinarily describe it as 'cash at bank' . . . If clause 3(*a*)(ii) stood alone, I might have been left in some doubt over whether 'debts' was being used in a commercial or strictly legal sense. But in my judgment the ambiguity is resolved by the use of the same words in clause 5(ii) which prohibits Brightlife from dealing with its 'book or other debts' without the prior consent in writing of Norandex 'otherwise than in the ordinary course of getting in and realising the same'. A credit balance at the bank cannot sensibly be 'got in' or 'realised' and the proviso cannot therefore apply to it. If 'book or other debts' includes the bank balance, the consequence is the Brightlife could not have dealt with its bank account without the written consent of Norandex. It would have had to obtain such consent wvery time it issued a cheque. The extreme commercial improbability of such an arrangement satisfies me that the parties used 'book debts and other debts' in a sense which excludes the credit balance at the bank.

Notes

See also *Re Ann Roulston Ltd; Northern Bank Ltd v Ross* (Court of Appeal in Northern Ireland, Unreported 1989) In *Re Permanent House (Holdings) Ltd* [1988] BCLC 563, Hoffmann J in following his decision in *Re Brightlife Ltd*, stated obiter that the latter case did not decide that a credit balance could not in any context be a 'book debt' or 'other debt'. The effectiveness of the fixed charge over book debts has now been largely negated by s 115 of the Finance Act 1986 which provides:–

'(1) Where a person holds a fixed charge (being a fixed charge which is created on or after the passing of this Act) on the book debts of a company (within the meaning of the Companies Act 1963) and the company fails to pay any relevant amount for which it is liable, then the said person shall, on being notified accordingly in writing by the Revenue Commissioners, become liable to pay such relevant amount on due demand and on neglect or refusal of payment may be proceeded against in like manner as any other defaulter:

Provided that:–

(*i*) the amount or aggregate amount which the person shall be liable to pay in relation to a company in accordance with this section shall not exceed the amount or aggregate amount which that person has while the fixed charge on book debts in relation to the said company is in existence, receiver, directly or indirectly from that company in payment or in part payment of any debts due by the company to that person, and

(*ii*) this section shall not apply to any amounts received by the holder of the fixed charge from the company before the date on which he is notified in writing by the Revenue Commissioners that he is liable by reason of this section of a relevant amount due by the company.

(2) In this section 'relevant amount' means any amount which the company is liable to remit–

(*a*) under chapter IV of the Income Tax Act 1967, and

(*b*) under the Value Added Tax Act 1972.'

Reservation of title clauses[1]

[11.59] Under the Sale of Goods Act 1893, property in goods frequently passes to the buyer when the contract is made, it being immaterial that the buyer has not yet paid for them.[2] If goods are supplied to a company on credit, as is often the case, the seller runs the risk that the company might go into liquidation or receivership between the date of delivery and the due date for payment. As the goods will have become assets of the company, they will be sold to pay off the company's creditors. The supplier will rank as an unsecured creditor. If the company has previously created a floating charge over the undertaking and assets of the company (which ironically will include the goods supplied by the creditor) then there will frequently be nothing left with which to pay the unsecured creditors. The supplier may therefore seek to protect himself by incorporating a retention (or reservation) of title clause into the contract for the sale of goods. Under such a clause the supplier attempts to retain ownership to the goods until they have been paid for so that they cannot in the meantime be charged by the buyer or sold to pay other creditors. The efficacy of such a clause has been long recognised in this jurisdiction[3], although they only really became popular when resurrected in England after the case of *Aluminium Industrie Vaasen BV v Romalpa Aluminium Ltd*[4] (hence they are popularly known as 'Romalpa Clause'. Nonetheless care must be taken in drafting such clauses to avoid creating what is in reality a charge which will be void if not registered under s 99 of the Principal Act.

1 See *Keane* at para **22.26**. See generally Pearce *Reservation of Title on the Sale of Goods in Ireland* (1985) 20 Ir Jur (n.s.) 264; Goode *Proprietory Rights and Insolvency in Sales Transactions* (1989, London) (2nd Ed).
2 S 18 of the Sale of Goods Act 1893.
3 *Bateman v King* (1868) IR 2 Cl 166.
4 [1979] 2 All ER 552.

[11.60] The Sale of Goods Act 1893 recognises the right of the parties to a contract of sale of goods to agree that title will not pass until all the agreed conditions have been fulfilled.

Sale of Goods Act 1893

[11.61] S 17(1) Where there is a contract for the sale of specific or ascertained goods the property in them is transferred to the buyer at such time as the parties to the contract intend it to be transferred.

(2) For the purpose of ascertaining the intention of the parties regard shall be had to the terms of the contract the conduct of the parties and the circumstances of each case.

S 19(1) Where there is a contract for the sale of specific goods or where goods are subsequently appropriated to the contract the seller may, by the terms of the contract or appropriation reserve the right of disposal of the goods until certain conditions are fulfilled. In such a case, notwithstanding the delivery of the goods to the buyer, or to a carrier or other bailee or custodian for the purpose of transmission to the buyer, the property in the goods does not pass to the buyer until the conditions imposed by the seller are fulfilled.

(2) Where goods are shipped and by the bill of lading the goods are deliverable to the order of the seller or his agent, the seller is prima facie deemed to reserve the right of disposal.

[11.62] A retention of title clause will be regarded as valid where the seller merely reserves the legal and beneficial[1] title to the goods in their unaltered form until they have been paid for in full. This type of clause is known as a 'simple clause'.

1 If the seller merely retains 'equitable and beneficial' ownership the court will hold that title to the goods has passed to the buyer and that a charge over the goods has been created in favour of the seller, requiring registration under s 99. *Re Bond Worth* [1979] 3 All ER 919.

Somers v James Allen (Ireland) Ltd [1984] ILRM 437 (High Court)

[11.63] The respondent had supplied goods to Charles Dougherty & Co Ltd (the company) which was in the animal feed business on terms which provided that ownership would not pass until the invoice price had been paid in full. The applicant was subsequently appointed as receiver of the company and he applied to the court for directions regarding the validity of the retention of title clause. At the time of the application to court the goods were identifiable and had not been used in the company's manufacturing process.

[11.64] **Carroll J:** At the time of the appointment of the applicant as receiver, the respondent had supplied the company with the ingredients mentioned. These goods were identifiable and had not become intermingled with other similar goods or been manufactured into feeding compound. Their value has been agreed.

The respondent supplied the goods subject to conditions of sale set out on the back of their invoice. It includes the following clause:

(9). The transfer of title to you of the goods as detailed in this contract shall not occur until the invoice covering same has been paid in full and accordingly the goods wherever situated shall be thereupon at your risk.

It is not denied that the conditions formed part of the contractual relations between the company and the respondent.

The applicant has asked for directions on the following questions:

(1). What is the effect of clause 9?
(2). What obligations are owed by the applicant to the respondent in the light of the answer to that question?

Mr Kelly has put forward four propositions on behalf of the applicant . . . The second proposition is based on a dictum of Bridge LJ in *Borden UK Ltd v Scottish Timber Products* [1979] 3 All ER 961 at p 971 to the effect that if a seller of goods to a manufacturer who knows his goods are to be used in the manufacturing process before they are paid for, wishes to reserve to himself an effective security for the payment of the price, he cannot rely on a simple reservation of title clause. Mr Kelly submits that the reservation of title clause in this case is simple, the goods were intended to be used in a manufacturing process and therefore the clause was ineffectual to reserve a security.

Thirdly, he submits that the Bills of Sale (Ireland) Act 1879 applies to the transaction because the contract confers on the company rights to manufacture, to intermix, and to sell with no requirement to segregate the goods or to keep separate accounts in relation thereto. This effectively conferred equitable ownership on the buyer leaving legal title only in the seller. The creation of any charge on the equitable ownership is registrable under the Bills of Sale (Ireland) Act 1879 and as no registration took place, the security fails for lack of registration . . .

The second proposition is based on a misinterpretation of the dictum of Bridge LJ in the *Borden* case. The learned judge was referring to an attempt to acquire rights over the manufactured article. He goes on to say in the next sentence (at p 971):

'If he (ie. the seller) wishes to acquire rights over the finished product, he can only do so by express contractual stipulation.'

In this case, I am not concerned with whether the reservation of title clause was effective to create or reserve an interest in the goods to be manufactured. I am concerned only with goods which still exist in the same state as they were supplied by the respondent. They have not been mixed with similar goods or transmitted into a manufactured product. The question therefore is whether a simple reservation of title clause is effective to reserve title in the goods in the same state as they were supplied.

In *Borden UL Ltd v Scottish Timber Products* Bridge LJ was prepared to admit to this. At page 966 while he says that he is attracted by the view that the beneficial interest in the resin passed to the buyers and the sellers retained bare legal title, he goes on to say:

'But I am quite content to assume that this is wrong and to suppose that up to the moment when the resin was used in manufacture it was held by the buyers in trust for the sellers in the same sense in which a bailee or a factor or an agent holds goods in trust for his bailor or his principal. If that was the position then there is no doubt that as soon as the resin was used in the manufacturing process it ceased to exist as resin and accordingly the title to the resin simply disappeared.'

In the same case, Templeman LJ said:

'They (the buyers) could not sell and make title to the resin because the title had been retained by the sellers. But the buyers were free to employ the resin in the manufacture of chipboard. When the resin was incorporated in the chipboard the resin ceased to exist, the sellers title to the resin became meaningless and the sellers security vanished. There was no provision in the contract for the buyers to provide substituted or additional security. The chipboard belonged to the buyers (at p 973).'

In my opinion, the simplicity of the provision in the contract does not per se prevent its being an effective reservation of title of the goods as supplied to the company and still existing in that state. Prima facie title is not to be transferred until payment in full. That title has not been extinguished in manufacture. It still exists and because payment has not been made, that title has not been transferred.

The third proposition is that s 8 of the Bills of Sale (Ireland) Act 1879 applies to the contract because an immediate beneficial interest passes to the buyer. That Act applies to bills of sale of personal chattels, whether absolute or subject to a trust, whereby the holder or grantee has power with or without notice, either immediately or at any future time, to take possession of such chattels. There must be a maker or giver of the bill of sale and a holder or grantee of the bill. The purpose of the Act was to prevent the owner of chattels defeating the claims of his creditors by making or giving a bill of sale which would entitle the holder or grantee to seize or take possession of chattels where those chattels remained in the possession or apparent possession of the giver.

In the case of a contract for sale, the goods belong initially to the seller. If he contracts to sell goods and is paid by the buyer and then becomes insolvent, not having delivered the goods within seven days, the contract for sale unless registered within seven days under the Bills of Sale Act is void against the seller's creditors.

If the goods are delivered to the buyer who has not paid for them, on terms that title remains with the seller until he is paid, the buyer's creditors cannot seize the goods. Even though the goods are in the apparent possession of the buyer, he is not the maker or giver of the bill of sale. He is the holder or grantee under the bill.

However, if a contract deals with the future title of the buyer in the goods to be manufactured from the goods supplied, then as regards that future title, the contract would be a bill of sale in which the buyer is the maker or giver and the seller is grantee . . .

In this case the clause in question is not complex enough to create a charge over future manufactured goods, the title to which cannot exist at the date of

305

the contract. The contract deals only with the present title to the goods sold and not with future title of goods to be manufactured.

The Sale of Goods Act 1893 allows the parties to decide when the property in the goods is to be transferred to the buyer. (s 17) Here, the parties have agreed by a simple condition to reserve title and risk to the seller until payment. The goods were to be used in manufacture. It follows therefore, that the unpaid seller intended to retain title as long as those goods existed, as supplied. When those goods were manufactured into another product, the seller's title disappeared.

I do not accept Mr Kelly's submission that the parties intended to split the legal and equitable title to the goods or that such split occurred as a necessary consequence of their contract. I do not see it as an impossible legal concept that the seller of goods to be used in a manufacturing process can retain title as long as the goods exist in the state they were supplied. Therefore, in my opinion, the clause is an effective reservation of title clause for the goods in that state.

Accordingly, s 8 of the Bills of Sale (Ireland) Act 1879 does not apply to this contract . . .

The answers to be given to the questions asked by the applicant are as follows:

(1). The effect of clause 9 is to reserve title to the respondent in goods supplied to the company in the state in which they were supplied and identifiable as such.

(2). The applicant must account to the respondent for the said goods.

Notes

See also *Bateman v King* (1868) IR 2 CL 166; *Sugar Distributors Ltd v Monaghan Cash & Carry Ltd* [1982] ILRM 399; *Frigoscandia (Contracting) Ltd v Continental Irish Meat Ltd* [1982] ILRM 396; *Clough Mill Ltd v Martin* [1985] BCLC 64.

Where the goods have become so affixed to land as to be in the nature of tenant's fixtures which could be removed by the tenant the supplier may still retain possession. See *Re Galway Concrete Ltd* [1983] ILRM 402. Similarly if the goods supplied have been incorporated into another product in such a way that their identity has not been lost the reservation of title clause will be valid, if the goods can be easily removed without damaging the product into which they have been incorporated. See *Hendy Lennox Ltd v Grahame Patrick Ltd* [1984] 2 All ER 152.

A retention of title clause may purport to reserve the legal and beneficial title to the goods in their unaltered form until the whole of the buyer's indebtedness to the seller no matter how arising has been discharged. This type of clause is known as a 'current account clause' or 'all monies clause'. Its validity was first recognised in the Romalpa case where the condition provided that 'ownership . . . will only be transferred to the purchaser when he has met all that is owing to AIV no matter on what grounds.' Subsequent UK cases such as *John Snow & Co Ltd v DBG Woodcroft & Co Ltd* [1985] BCLC 54; *Clough Mill Ltd v Martin* [1985] BCLC 64 and *Carron Co v Thyssen Edelstahlwerke* have also recognised the validity of this type of clause. It is merely an expression of the parties' intent pursuant to ss 17 & 19 of the Sale of Goods Act 1893 as to when property should pass.

Clear words however, must be used in order to create a current account clause and where the clause is ambiguous it will be interpreted as being a 'simple clause' only: *Re Stokes & McKiernan Ltd* [1978] ILRM 240.

[11.65] A clause which purports to claim title to goods after the original identity has been lost or which purports to claim title to any products into which the goods have been incorporated is a charge requiring registration under s 99 of the Principal Act.

Kruppstahl AG v Quitmann Products Ltd and Dermot Fitzgerald [1982] ILRM 551 (High Court)

[11.66] The plaintiff supplied steel to the Quitmann Products Ltd (Quitmann) for use in the manufacture of steel bins. The contracts of supply contained terms purporting not only to retain title in the steel until the price had been paid but also purporting to claim title to goods manufactured with the steel. Mr Fitzgerald was subsequently appointed receiver of Quitmann. The plaintiff sought a declaration that the retention of title clause was effective against the debenture holder who had appointed the Mr Fitzgerald. Quitmann claimed that the clause was a charge void for non-registration under s 99.

[11.67] **Gannon J:** As between Quitmann and other parties including a debenture holder or other creditor, the unworked steel in the possession of Quitmann at Portumna which was delivered there by Krupps pursuant to the German contract in respect of which payment was more than one month overdue is, according to Irish law not the property of Quitmann.

The next stage is to consider what are the requirements of Irish law in relation to any of the steel the property of Krupps in the possession of Quitmann at Portumna which was put to use by Quitmann with the agreement of Krupps in accordance with the German conditions and law in a manufacturing process notwithstanding Quitmann's liability for overdue payments to Krupps in respect thereof. This involves also a consideration of what effect, if any, can be given in Irish law to the agreement between Krupps and Quitmann in their conditions in relation to manufactured goods incorporating Krupps' steel (that is for which payments were overdue) which were sold by Quitmann to other parties. As paragraphs 2 to 7 inclusive of clause *a* (iii) as construed in accordance with German law, constitute an immediate assignment of future interests and an agrement for security for whatever indebtedness on the part of Quitmann to Krupps might later arise paragraph 9 gives recognition to the applicability of Irish law relative to the enforcement of the security. In so far as the steel (the subject of overdue payment account) is put to use by Quitmann in the manufacturing process although the property of Krupps, such use is with the consent of Krupps as limited by the conditions. To that extent therefore Quitmann are constituted trustee of property of Krupps for which Quitmann are accountable to Krupps in the manner prescribed by the contract. The accountability is limited to the extent only of the indebtedness and the manner of securing payment is a form of 'tracing' conforming to the equitable principles as expounded by Jessel MR in *In Re Hallet's Estate* 13 Ch D 696. As such it is in the nature of a charge upon the property as a means of security for the discharge of an indebtedness which is the primary factor in that agreement. But the agreement goes beyond the scope of mere tracing goods for their value. On the basis that German law permits the possessor of goods which are not his own property to sell and recover the value of his workmanship in converting them other marketable articles Krupps and Quitmann have agreed that the property and the interest therein so conferred by German law upon Quitmann in processed goods incorporating Krupps' steel (the subject of overdue payment account) are by this contract assigned in anticipation to Krupps. Such agreement relates in part to an existing quantity of steel delivered by Krupps but to the extent only that it may later be incorporated in a finished manufactured article not then in existence or identifiable and only if and when such article should have been manufactured. Any such assignment can be construed only as an equitable interest in the nature of a floating charge manifestly created only as a means of security for a potential indebtedness. I have arrived at this conclusion after careful consideration of the judgments of Kenny J in *In re Interview Ltd* [1975] IR 382 of Mocatta L and of the three Lord Justices of Apeal in *Aluminium Industrie Vaasen BV v Romalpa Ltd* [1976] 1 WLR 676, of Slade J in *Re Bond Worth Ltd* [1980] Ch 321 and of the Lord Justices of Appeal in *Borden (UK) Ltd v Scottish Timber Products Ltd* [1981] Ch 25 and the arguments thereon in the course of the hearing.

The realisation or enforcement of any such security granted by way of charge created by a company will not be permitted in Ireland unless the particulars of the charge have been registered with the registrar of companies pursuant to s 100 of the Companies Act 1963. Having regard to the comprehensive definitions in s 4 of the Bills of Sale (Ireland) Act, 1879 of the expressions 'bills of sale', 'personal chattels' and 'apparent possession' there cannot be any doubt that the quantities of steel delivered to and in the possession of Quitmann at Portumna the subject matter of the general conditions of sale accepted from Krupps, are 'personal chattels' to which the provisions of that Act would apply. Having regard to the interpretation in accordance with German law of clause *a* (iii) paragraphs 2 to 7 inclusive of these general conditions as shown by the evidence those clauses upon acceptance would constitute charges such that had the parties been individuals and not companies, they would have required registration as bills of sale under the 1879 Act in respect of any steel authorised to be used in the making of articles to be sold to other persons. As such they come within the class of charge referred to at s 99(2)(*c*) of the Companies Act 1963, having been created by Quitmann after 1908 and so should have been registered pursuant to s 100 of the Act. The provisions of s 99 of the Companies Act 1963, declare such charges to be void as against the claims against Quitmann of other creditors such as a debenture holder unless registered in accordance with s 100 of the 1963 Act. It has been agreed by the parties that no charge in favour of Krupps to which s 99 of the Companies Act 1963 applies has been registered with the registrar of companies. Accordingly any claims by Krupps against Quitmann in respect of overdue payments for any such steel used in manufacturing process must be deferred to the claims of the debenture holder and of the receiver although such overdue payments still remain payable to Krupps by Quitmann.

Notes

See also *Re Peachdart Ltd* [1983] 3 All ER 204; *Somers v Allen* [1984] ILRM 437 ; *Clough Mill Ltd v Martin* [1985] BCLC 64; *cf Carbery Pig Producers Co-Operative Society Ltd v Lunham Bros Ltd* (High Court, 16 May 1986) where Carroll J permitted the sellers to claim title to various types of pork product processed from pigs supplied by them.

[11.68]   A retention of title clause which purports to claim the proceeds of sale of goods until the purchase price has been paid, will be regarded as a registrable charge unless the contract expressly creates a fiduciary relationship between the supplier and the buyer, imposes a duty on the buyer to keep the proceeds separate from his other monies and requires him to account for such proceeds to the supplier.

Re WJ Hickey Ltd (In Receivership); Uniacke v Cassidy Electrical Supply Co Ltd [1988] IR 126 (High Court)

[11.69]   The applicant as receiver of the company applied to court for directions regarding the validity of a retention of title clause contained in a contract under which the respondent had supplied goods to the company. The clause stated that property in the goods was not to pass until full payment had been received. Until then the buyer was to hold the goods in trust for the respondent in a manner which enabled them to be identified and to return the goods to the respondent on demand. The company was permitted to sell the goods to third parties in the normal course of business but any proceeds of sale were to be held in trust for the respondent in a manner which enbled them to be identified as such.

[11.70]   **Barron J:** The applicant submits that the use of the words 'in trust' in this clause indicates that the legal estate in the goods passed to the buyer and that the beneficial interest retained by the respondent was an interest by way of charge only. He relies upon the judgment of Slade J in *In re Bond Worth Ltd* [1980] Ch 228. That case was one in which the seller sold fibre to the buyers for use by the buyers in the manufacture by them of carpets. The reservation of title clause in that case dealt not only with the position while the goods were in the possession of the buyer but also with that when the goods were resold or became a constituent in another product manufactured by the buyer. So far as it is material to the facts of the present case, the clause was as follows:

'The risk in the goods passes to the buyer upon delivery, but equitable and beneficial ownership shall remain with us until full payment has been received (each order being considered as a whole) or until prior resale, in which case our beneficial entitlement shall attach to the proceeds of resale or to the claim for such proceeds.'

The decision of Slade J so far as it related to the construction of this clause centred upon the meaning to be given to the words 'equitable and beneficial ownership'. He regarded this clause as one which gave to the seller rights characteristic of those of a mortgagee under a mortgage. Having referred to a passage from the judgment of Romer LJ in *In re George Inglefield Ltd* [1933] Ch 1, at pp 27–28 which summarised the three essential characteristics of a mortgage he said at p 249:

'Mutatis mutandis all these three features of a charge are present in this case. Bond Worth was entitled to redeem the charge in favour of Monsanto by paying to it the outstanding debt due under the relevant order. If Monsanto in exercise of the rights conferred on it by the retention of title clause were to compel a sale of the relevant assets for a sum more than sufficient to pay this debt, the parties' intention was surely that Bond Worth rather than Monsanto would be entitled to receive the surplus. In contrast if such last mentioned sale were to produce a sum less than the outstanding debt, they surely intended that Monsanto would remain entitled to recover the balance from Bond Worth as a simple contract debt.'

Slade J was also considerably influenced in his view that the purpose of the clause was to obtain security for a debt and rejected the argument that the clause created a trust under which the seller was the sole beneficiary. He construed the clause together with all the other relevant provisions of the contract, as effecting a sale in which the entire property in the goods passed to the buyer 'followed by a security *eo instanti*, given back by' the buyer to the seller – see p 256 of the report. The significance of *In re Bond Worth Ltd* is that the words 'equitable and beneficial ownership' in the context in which they were used led only to the conclusion that a charge was created. The existence of a trust relationship in favour of a seller was not excluded as a valid provision. *Aluminium Industrie BV v Romalpa Ltd* [1976] 1 WLR 676 in which a fiduciary relationship between the buyer and seller was accepted as valid albeit on the admission of counsel for the buyer that such was the relationship was not disapproved. It, together with *Borden (UK) Ltd v Scottish Timber Products* [1981] Ch 25, (which together with *In Re Bond Worth* and the *Romalpa* case formed for several years the English case law on the topic) was expressly distinguished in the following passage at pp 265–266:–

'It follows that the *Romalpa* and *Borden* decisions themselves provide no answer to the attack made on the validity of the retention of title clause in the present case by reference to *In re Nevill; Ex parte White* 6 Ch App 397, *Foley v Hill* 2 HL Cas 28; *South Australian Insurance Co v Randell* LR 3 PC 101 and *Henry v Hammond* [1913] 2 KB 151. In my judgment there can be no answer to this attack in so far as it relates to the particular interpretation of the retention of title clause, which Mr Sears on behalf of Monsanto has invited me to adopt. The implicit authority and freedom of Bond Worth to employ the relevant raw materials products and other monies as it pleased and for its own purposes during the subsistence of the operation of the retention of title clause were in my judgment quite incompatible with the existence of a relationship of Bond Worth as trustee and Monsanto as beneficiary solely and absolutely entitled to such assets which is the relationship asserted.'

In each of the four cases referred to, the relationship of the parties was found to be that of debtor and creditor rather than trustee and beneficiary. The distinguishing feature is set out clearly in the following passage from the judgment of Channell J in *Henry v Hammond* [1913] KB 151 cited on page 521:–

'It is clear that if the terms upon which the person receives the money are that he is bound to keep it separate either in a bank or elsewhere and to hand that money so kept as a separate fund to the person entitled to it, then he is a trustee of that money and must hand it over to the person who is his cestui que trust. If on the other hand he is not bound to keep the money separate but is entitled to mix it with his own money and deal with it as he pleases and when called upon to hand over an equivalent sum of money then in my opinion, he is not a trustee of the money but merely a debtor.'

Clearly a specific obligation to keep the goods and proceeds of sale separate and distinct might have led to a different result. There is no basic reason why a seller under a contract for sale of goods should not impose a term whereby property in the goods does not pass until the goods have been paid for. This general proposition was stated by McWilliam J in *Frigoscandia (Contracting) Ltd v Continental Irish Meat Ltd* [1982] ILRM 396. In that case McWilliam J upheld a clause in the following form:–

'Until all sums due to the seller have been fully paid to it the plant, machinery and materials supplied by the seller herein shall remain the seller's personal property and retain its character as such no matter in what manner affixed or attached to any structure.'

In that case the particular item sold was not intended to be kept in the factory of the purchaser but also was not of such a nature that its resale could have been reasonably contemplated by the parties. McWilliam J said at p 398:–

'The parties to a contract can agree to any terms they wish and amongst others they can agree that the property in the goods shall not pass to the purchaser until all the instalments of the purchase price have been paid. See *McEntire v Crossley Brothers* [1985] AC at 463 and s 17 of the Sale of Goods Act 1893.'

Reference to s 17 of the Sale of Goods Act 1893 is all important. In the sale of specific or ascertained goods the property is transferred to the buyer at such time as the parties to the contract intend it to be transferred. This section and the other sections dealing with transfer of property follow from s 1 of the Act which provides inter alia as follows. [His lordship then quoted s17]. Clearly, there is nothing foreign to the law of sale of goods in seeking to postpone the date of the passing of the property in the goods agreed to be sold. An unpaid seller is entitled to protect himself. It is not his intention which is paramount because it must always be to safeguard his own financial position. What is important is whether he passed the property or not and if he does, whether or not he takes back a charge on the goods sold. In so far as Slade J may have expressed a contrary view this has been disapproved more recently in England in *Clough Mill Ltd v Martin* [1985] 1 WLR 111.

There is nothing in the present clause to warrant a construction that it creates no more than a charge in favour of the respondent. I can find no ground for construing the clause in such a way that all the property must have passed to the company and that it assigned back an equitable interest in the goods by way of charge. The existence of such an assignment is essential to the applicant's case. Where charges have been found to exist, as in *In re Interview Ltd* [1975] IR 382 and *Kruppstahl AG v Quitmann Products Ltd* [1982] ILRM 551 there was a clear assignment of such an interest. There can be none here since the entire property never passed. The words 'no property in any goods shall pass' must be given their literal meaning.

The true construction of the clause is dependent upon an understanding of the meaning of the words 'in trust'. The retention of an equitable interest does not automatically indicate the creation of a charge as has been submitted. In *In re Bond Worth Ltd* the contest was between two situations in each of which the seller would have had an equitable interest. The expression 'trust monies' is one which is familiar to those dealing with receiverships and the winding up of companies. The expression relates not just to monies owed by one person to another, but to monies which one person has an obligation to keep separate and distinct from his own monies om behalf of another. The principle is fully illustrated in the passage from *Henry v Hammond* to which I have referred and in the other three cases which Slade J linked with *Henry v Hammond* and more recently in England in *Re Andrabell Ltd* [1984] 3 All ER 407. It is clear from the words used in the present clause that the obligation imposed on the company is one to keep the good identifiable as those of the respondent and when sold to keep the proceeds equally identifiable. To specify these obligations is largely repetitious since the words 'in trust' impose such an obligation in any event.

I am satisfied that the goods identified by the applicant as having been supplied by the respondents to the company were supplied under a conditional contract of sale. Such contract was an agreement to sell within the meaning of s 1 of the Act of 1893 since 'the transfer of the property in the goods (was) to take place at a future time.' That transfer never took place. At all material times the property in the goods has remained in the respondents.

Notes

See also *EI Pfeiffer Weinkellerei – Weineinkauf Gmb H & Co v Arbuthnot Factors Ltd* [1988] 1 WLR 150; cf *Re Stokes & McKiernan Ltd* [1978] ILRM 240; *Sugar Distributors Ltd v Monaghan Cash and Carry Ltd* [1982] ILRM 399; *SA Foundries du lion MV v International Factors (Ireland) Ltd* [1985] ILRM 66 and the *Romalpa* case [1976] 2 All ER 552 where the mere existence of a simple reservation of title clause was regarded as sufficient to entitle the supplier to claim title to the proceeds of sale. These cases may no longer be regarded as good law in the light of the *Uniacke* decision. In *Carroll Group Distributors Ltd v G & F Bourke Ltd and Bourke (Sales) Ltd* (High Court, 4 October 1989) Murphy J refused to allow the supplier to trace into the proceeds of sale of the goods supplied, when the buyer in breach of the terms of the contract failed to segregate the proceeds and to keep them in a separate account.

Where the retention of title clause purports to assign to the supplier any claims the buyer may have against sub-buyers of the goods the proper inference is that the clause is in fact a charge registrable under s 99 of the Principal Act. See *Re Interview Ltd* [1975] IR 382.

Registration of charges

[11.71]   S 99 of the Principal Act as amended by s 122 of the 1990 Act lists various charges which if created by a company must be registered with the registrar.[1] If the prescribed particulars of the charge are not delivered to or received by the registrar within 21 days of creation of the charge it[2] will be void as against the liquidator and any creditor[3] of the company.[4] The moneys secured by the charge then become immediately payable and the chargee ranks as an unsecured creditor of the company. The charges to which the s 99 applies are:[5]

'(*a*) a charge for the purpose of securing any issue of debentures;[6]
(*b*) a charge on uncalled share capital of the company;
(*c*) a charge created or evidence by an instrument which, if executed by an individual, would require registration as a bill of sale;[7]
(*d*) a charge on land, wherever situate or any interest therein but not including a charge for any rent or other periodical sum issuing out of the land;[8]
(*e*) a charge on book debts of the company;[9]

(*f*) a floating charge on the undertaking or property of the company;
(*g*) a charge on calls made but not paid;
(*h*) a charge on a ship or aircraft or any share in a ship or aircraft;[10]
(*i*) a charge on goodwill on a patent or a licence under a patent, on a trademark or on a copyright or a licence under a copyright.'[11]

The Minister may by regulation add to or reduce the list of registerable charges, and may amend the description of charges requiring registration.

The primary duty to register is placed upon the company and failure to do so may result in a fine for the company and every officer in default.[12] Because of the serious consequences of non-registration any person interested in the charge may deliver the prescribed particulars. [13] Under ss 101 and 102 the company is under a duty respectively to register charges already affecting the land when acquired by the company and judgment mortgages[14] affecting the company's lands. In both instances failure to register merely results in a fine. Registration of particulars of a charge only constitutes notice to the world at large of those provisions of the charge in respect of which registration is obligatory under s 99.[15]

1 See generally *Keane* chapter 23; *McCormack* (1984) 2 ILT (ns) 67.
2 The term 'charge' includes a mortgage; s 99(10). Registration is required even if the security is an equitable mortgage by deposit of title deeds unaccompanied by any written memorandum: *Re Wallis & Simmonds (Builders) Ltd* [1974] 1 All ER 561.
3 Seemingly an execution secured creditor: *Re Monolithic Building Co* [1915] 1 Ch 643.
4 But only if the company goes into liquidation. See *Alexander Hull & Co Ltd v O'Carroll Kent & Co Ltd* (1955) 89 ILT 70.
5 Ibid s 99(2).
6 This refers to a charge securing an issue of a series of debentures as opposed to a single debenture. See *Automatic Association (Canterbury) Inc v Australasian Secured Deposits Ltd* [1973] 1 NZLR 417.
7 ie. Under the Bills of Sale (Ireland) Acts 1879 to 1883. This legislation applies only to charges securing the payment of money. See *Re Castlemahon Poultry Products Ltd* (High Court, Barrington J, 3/5/85). See *Stoneleigh Finance Ltd v Philips* [1965] 2 QB 537. A charge registrable under s 99(2)(c) is expressly excluded from the registration requirements of the Bills of Sale Acts. See *Re Royal Marine Hotel, Kingstown, Ltd* [1895] 1 IR 368.
8 Registration of the charge should also be effected in the Land Registry or the Registry of Deeds depending on whether the land is registered or unregistered. See *Keane* at para **23.09**.
9 'Book Debts' mean all debts accruing in the ordinary course of business as are usually entered in well kept trade books. See *Paul & Frank Ltd v Discount Bank (Overseas) Ltd* [1966] 2 All ER 922; *Re Kent and Sussex Sawmills Ltd* [1947] Ch 177; *Re Kum Tang Restaurant (Dublin) Ltd*; *Re Brian Tucker Ltd*; *Farrell v Equity Bank Ltd* (High Court, Lynch J, 13/12/88). A bank account is not however a book debt. See *Re Brightlife Ltd* [1987] 2 WLR 197 and *Re Permanent House (Holdings) Ltd* [1988] BCLC 563.
10 A three tonne yacht does not constitute a ship: *Re South Coast Boatyard; Barbour v Burke* (Supreme Court, 31/5/80). Legal mortgage over ships must comply with the provisions of the Mercantile Marine Act 1955.
11 Charges over patents and registered trademarks must also be notified to the Patent's Officer.
12 S 100 of the Principal Act as amended by s 15 and sch 1 of the 1982 Act.
13 Ibid.
14 As to which see *Keane* at para **23.13**.
15 *Welch v Bowmaker (Ireland) Ltd* [1980] IR 251; *Wilson v Kellard* [1910] 2 Ch 306; *Siebe Gorman & Co Ltd v Barclays Bank Ltd* [1979] 2 Lloyds Rep 142.

[11.72] When the prescribed particulars are delivered to the registrar he issues a certificate of registration. This certificate is conclusive evidence that the registration requirements have been complied with. The decision of the registrar to issue the certificate cannot be challenged.

Lombard and Ulster Banking (Ireland) Ltd v Amurec Ltd (In Liq) (1978) 112 ILTR 1 (High Court)

[11.73] In November 1972 the defendant company granted an undated mortgage over its property in favour of the plaintiff bank. The bank subsequently inserted the date 21 March 1974 on the mortgage and within 21 days of that date delivered the prescribed particulars for registration. The registrar subsequently issued a certificate under s 104 that the statutory registration requirements had been observed. The company later went into liquidation and the property was sold. The bank claimed the proceeds of sale. The liquidator defended the action arguing that the charge was void for non-registration.

[11.74] Hamilton J: The evidence clearly establishes that the charge created by the indenture of mortgage is a charge to which the said section applies, that it was created on the 1st day of November 1972, and the prescribed particulars of the charge were not delivered to or received by the Registrar of Companies for registration as required by the act within twenty-one days after the date of its creation . . .

On behalf of the plaintiff company Mr O'Neill submitted that the Registrar's certificate is conclusive evidence that the requirements of part IV of the Companies Act 1963 as to registration had been complied with and that if the certificate is conclusive evidence that all that requires to be done for the purpose of registration under the Act has been done, that must include the time within which the particulars are to be registered.

He submitted that this is the position even if the certificate is obtained wrongfully as was done in this case . . .

On behalf of the liquidator Mr Barron submitted that by virtue of the terms of s 99(1) of the Companies Act 1963 the charge was void as against the liquidator and the creditors of the company, that it is a condition precedent to the validity of the charge that the particulars be delivered within twenty-one days of its creation, that s 104 has no application where particulars are not delivered in time, that registration where particulars had not been delivered within twenty-one days after the creation of the charge is a nullity and that it would be inequitable to allow this certificate obtained in the manner in which it was obtained in this case, to have the effect provided for in s 104 of the Companies Act 1963 . . . I have considerable sympathy with the submissions made by Mr Barron. I am however, bound by the terms of s 104 of the Companies Act 1963, which provides that:–

'The registrar shall give the certificate under his hand to the registration of any charge registered in pursuance of this part, stating the amount thereby

315

secured and the certificate shall be conclusive evidence that the requirements of this part as to registration have been complied with.'

On of the requirements of part IV of the Act is that the prescribed particulars of the charge be delivered to or received by the Registrar of Companies within twenty one days after the date of its creation. The time limit is an essential part of the requirements of the Act as to registration.

In *In re Eric Holmes (Property) Limited* [1965] Ch 1052 Pennycuick J held that the certificate was conclusive as to the delivery of particulars within the twenty-one days period after the creation of the charge, though an incorrect date had been inserted in the charge in particulars delivered as in the register, and the charge had been created more than twenty-one days before the particulars were delivered . . . I have no alternative but to reach a similar conclusion, the wording of s 104 is clear and unambiguous . . .

As stated by Mr Justice Pennycuick in the *Holmes* case at page 1072:–

> 'It is I think possible that there is some lacuna in the Act here in as much as the Act gives, apparently protection where the certificate was made upon the basis of particulars which are incorrect.

I have however, no alternative but to hold that the charge is a valid charge and is not void against the liquidator.

Notes

In *R v Registrar of Companies ex p Central Bank of India* [1986] 1 QB 1114 the Court of Appeal suggested obiter that the Companies Acts do not bind the State and that therefore the Attorney General could seek a judicial review of the Registrar's certificate. As Slade J stated at p 1177, there is 'no question of the registrar being wholly beyond the reach of the law.' See generally O'Riordan and Pearce *The Conclusiveness of Certificates of Registration of Company Charges* (1986) 80 Gazette 281. In *Bank of Ireland Finance Ltd v DJ Daly Ltd* [1978] IR 79 it was held that s 99 only applies to charges created by the company. It does not apply to charges arising by operation of law (such as unpaid vendors' and purchasers' liens). See also *Re Barrett Apartments Ltd* [1985] IR 350, 356, per Keane J.

[11.75]   S 99 of the principal act does not apply to charges over the future proceeds of sale of land.

Re Kum Tong Restaurant (Dublin) Ltd; Byrne v Allied Irish Banks Ltd
[1978] IR 446 (High Court)

[11.76]   The company contracted to sell its business premises at a time when it was in serious financial difficulties. In order to continue business pending completion of the sale the company requested the respondent bank to advance a sum of money to it. In a letter to the bank the company's solicitors stated that in consideration for the loan, they undertook to hold the documents of title in trust for the bank and to hand over sufficient moneys out of the proceeds of sale to redeem the loan as soon as the sale was closed. The company went into liquidation before completion of the sale. The sale was approved by the court and the purchase price was placed on deposit while the liquidator applied for directions regarding the banks entitlement to part of the proceeds. The liquidator contended that the solicitor's undertaking constituted a registrable charge void for non-registration under s 99.

[11.77] McWilliam J: The relevant paragraphs of the letter of the 8th April 1974 from Wm Fry & Sons on which the claim of Allied Irish Banks Ltd is based are as follows:–

> 'We now therefore undertake in consideration of your granting the company a bridging loan of £4,000 on the strength of the contract for the sale of their premises in Grafton Street to hold such documents of title to the said premises as we may have in trust for the Bank and to hand over sufficient monies out of the proceeds of the sale to redeem this bridging finance as soon as the sale is closed. It is however to be strictly understood that this firm undertakes only to hand over out of the proceeds of sale and should there be any delay in closing the sale the firm cannot be held responsible for the money until the sale has been finalised.'

Having decided that this letter was sufficient to create an equitable charge, I had this matter re-entered for argument on the question of what property was charged and if it was the purchase money which was charged, whether it was a charge that was required to be registered under s 99 of the Companies Act 1963, either as a charge on land or any interest therein or as a charge on book debts of the company.

On behalf of the bank it was argued first, that a vendor is a trustee for a purchaser after a binding contract for sale has been signed and that such vendor retains no interest in the land which can be charged: *Hillingdon Estates Co v Stonefield Estates Ltd* was cited in support of this proposition. Secondly, it was argued that this is what was intended to be charged and was charged in the present case, and that it was not a book debt within the meaning of the section. As to book debts, *Paul & Frank Ltd v Discount Bank (Overseas) Ltd* was cited.

On behalf of the liquidator it was argued that this was a mortgage by deposit of title deeds, that it was a charge on the vendor's interest in the premises, that the vendor did have an interest in the premises which could be charged and that it was not intended to charge the proceeds of sale. No argument was advanced to support the proposition that the proceeds of sale were a book debt . . .

The letter of the 8th April 1974, dealt solely with the proceeds of sale; the title deeds were stated to be held solely to secure payment out of the proceeds of sale. Although not stated in so many words, the clear intention was to charge the proceeds of sale and no argument has been advanced to me to show that the proceeds of sale cannot be charged as such and I can see no reason why they should not be so charged. Although the fact that the documents of title were to be held by the solicitors in trust would normally create a charge on the vendor's interest in the lands, and very possibly would have done so in this case had it been registered, the purchase price would only be paid on handing over the deeds so that the holding of the deeds would be equally attributable to securing the proper application of the purchase price.

I am satisfied that it was intended to charge the purchase money, that the letter was effective to do this, and that the purchase price is not a book debt within the meaning of the section. Accordingly, I will make the necessary declaration in favour of the bank.

Notes

A solicitor's undertaking to deposit their client company's title deeds with the bank as security for a loan is itself an equitable mortgage requiring registration under s 99. See *Re Farm Fresh Frozen Foods Ltd* [1980] ILRM . Notably s 99 does not apply to a charge created by a company over shares in its subsidiary company. See *Fitzgerald* (1968) VIII Irish Jurist 258; *McCormack* (1984) ILT (ns) 67. In *Nunan v Group 4 Securities (International) BV* (High Court, Blayney J, 28 July 1986) it was held that a contract between the company, a lender and a third party, that the third party would buy from the company certain property (over which the lender already had a charge) in the event of default by the company on the loan, was not a registrable charge on land under s 99.

Extension of time and rectification of errors[1]

[11.78] Under s 106 application may be made to the court to extend the time for registration of charges or to rectify any omission or mis-statement of any particulars which were delivered.[2] The court can only make an order under the s 106 if it is satisfied that the failure to register in time or the error in the particulars 'was accidental or due to inadvertence or to some other sufficient cause, or is not of a nature to prejudice the position of creditors or shareholders of the company, or that on other grounds it is just and equitable to grant relief.'

1 S 104 of the Principal Act.
2 See *Keane* at para **23.15**.

[11.79] An order extending the time for registration of a charge will be made subject to a proviso that it is to be without prejudice to the rights of secured creditors or liquidator acquired against the property prior to the registration. If the liquidation of the company is imminent an order extending time will only be made on terms, that if a liquidator is appointed within a specified time after registration of the charge he may apply to have the charge removed from the register. An extension of time will not be granted where the company is already in liquidation.

Re Telford Motors Ltd; Doody v Mercantile Credit Co of Ireland Ltd (High Court, 27 January 1978)

[11.80]   Hamilton J: In this matter the applicant as liquidator of Telford Motors Limited seeks 1. direction in relation to the matters follows:–

(*a*) whether the charge created by deed of charge dated 2nd May 1974 and made between the above named Telford Motors Ltd of the one part and Mercantile Credit Co Ltd of the other part, over certain property described in folio 1168 F of the Register County Queens is void as against the applicant and the unsecured creditors of Telford Motors Ltd ('the company')

(*b*) whether the rights of unsecured creditors of the company rank prior to the charge of Mercantile Credit Co Ltd created by the said deed of charge and in the distribution of the proceeds of sale of the said premises . . .

Though the deed of charge was registered as a burden on the said folio, the prescribed particulars of the charge were not delivered to or received by the Registrar of Companies for registration as required by the Companies Act 1963.

Prior to the 6th day of February 1976, it was decided that 'the company' was insolvent and could not continue trading and that it should be voluntarily wound up.

In accordance with the provisions of s 266 of the Companies Act 1963 a notice of the meeting of the members at which the resolution for voluntarily winding up of 'the company' was sent to the creditors and dated the 6th day of February 1976.

Such notice included a notice sent to the respondent. It seems then to have been realised by 'the respondent' that the prescribed particulars of the charge had not been delivered to the Registrar of Companies and on the 10th day of February 1976 a special summons was issued in which the plaintiff claimed an order pursuant to s 106 of the Companies Act 1963 extending the time limited by s 99 thereof for the registration in the companies office of the deed of charge.

When the matter was heard by me on the 17th day of February 1976 and being satisfied that the omission to register the charge within the time required by s 99 of the Companies Act 1963 was due to inadvertance I ordered, pursuant to s 106 of the Companies Act 1963 that the time for registration of the particulars of the said charge be extended until the 9th day of May 1976 but expressly provided that the said order was without prejudice to the rights (if any) of the parties acquired prior to the time when particulars of such charge shall be actually registered.

As a condition of obtaining the said order, the 'respondent' undertook that, in case a resolution for the winding up of 'the company' should become efective within twenty one days from the date of perfection of the said order and in the 'the company' by its liquidator should within twenty one days after the commencement of such winding up apply to the court to discharge the said order, then 'the respondent' would submit that the court might make for the rectification of the register of the company by the removal therefrom of any registration effected under this present order.

The necessary particulars and documents to secure the registration of the particulars of the said charge were lodged by the solicitor for 'the respondent' in the Office of the Registrar of Companies at approximately 10 am on the morning of the 18th day of February 1976.

The resolution of 'the company' that 'the company' be wound up voluntarily was passed on the 18th day of February 1976 at a meeting of the creditors summoned in accordance with the provisions of s 266 of the Companies Act 1963 held immediately following the meeting of the company at which the resolution to voluntarily wind up the company was passed, the applicant herein was appointed liquidator of the company. The particulars of charge was not registered by the Registrar of Companies until the 20th day of February 1976.

On the 2nd day of March 1976 the applicant, as liquidator of 'the company' caused to be issued a notice of motion which was served on 'the respondent' seeking an order discharging the order made by me on the 17th day of February 1976 and an order for the rectification of the register of the company by the removal there from of any registration effected under the said order of the 17th day of February 1976.

On the hearing of the said motion I made no order as I did not think it necessary in view of the fact that the resolution proposing the voluntary winding up of 'the company' had been passed prior to the date of registration of the particulars of the aforesaid charge made by the Registrar of Companies in pursuance of the order made by me dated the 17th day of February 1976 . . .

On the basis of the foregoing facts the liquidator seeks directions as to whether the charge created by the said deed of charge . . . is void as against him and the unsecured creditors of 'the company' and whether the rights of the unsecured creditors of the company rank prior to the charge and in the distribution of the proceeds of sale of the said premises. [His Lordship then quoted from s 99].

Despite the learned submissions made by Mr Criven on behalf of 'the respondent' the position seems to be very clear.

The order made by me on the 17th day of February 1976 extending the time for registration of the particulars of the charge was expressly stated to be without prejudice to the rights (if any) of parties acquired prior to the time when particulars of the charge shall be actually registered.

The inclusion of such a provision saving rights acquired before actual registration has as stated by Templeman J in *Watson v Duff Morgan and Vermont Ltd* 1 WLR 454 been common form since the decision in *In re Joplin Brewery Co Ltd* [1902] 1 Ch 79.

As stated in many cases the object of this provision is to save rights acquired before actual registration and as stated by Cozens Hardy LJ in *In re*

Ehrmann Brothers Limited [1906] 2 Ch 709 the rights intended to be preserved are:

'Rights acquired the property of the company or affecting the property of the company intervening between the expiration of the twenty one days and the extended time allowed by the order.'

It is also quite clear that when a company goes into liquidation the liquidator acquires the right and duty to distribute all the assets of the company between its creditors.

It was held in *In re Sparrel Globe Limited* [1902] 1 Ch 396 that:

'the rights and duties of the liquidator to distribute all the assets of the company between its creditors is a right acquired against the company's property and is protected by the proviso if before registration of the particulars of charge the company has gone into liquidation.'

[His Lordship referred to the order of 17th February 1976] [T]he proviso therein contained which is no empty formula but specifically designed to protect the rights over the property of 'the company' acquired prior to the date of actual registration and in common usage since 1902 . . . Consequently I am satisfied that the deed of charge is void against the liquidator and the creditors of the company.

Notes

In *Re International Retail Ltd* (High Court, 19 September 1974) Kenny J stated as follows:–

'The extension of time for registration of the particulars will clearly prejudice the position of the creditors of the company for the effect of such an order will be to make this charge valid and so the amount secured by it will rank before sums due to creditors. It seems to me that the court should not extend the time for registration of a charge against a company's property unless there is evidence that a petition for the winding up of the company has not been presented and that the members are not contemplating a resolution for its winding up. The purpose of s 99 of the Act of 1963 . . . was to ensure that every creditor who dealt with the company would know that he was giving credit to a company which had given security for some of its debts and so the charge, if not registered, becomes void when the company goes into liquidation . . . This view is supported by what has been the invariable practice of the courts in Ireland and England on applications such as this. This has been to require evidence that no winding up of the company is pending or contemplated and that no judgments have been recovered against it which are unpaid before extending the time for registration.'

See also *Re Farm Fresh Frozen Foods Ltd* [1980] ILRM; *Re O'Carroll Kent & Co Ltd* (1955) 89 ILTR. It has been suggested that in 'very exceptional cases' an application for extension of time will be entertained despite any intervening liquidation. See *Re J Abrahams & Sons Ltd* [1902] 1 Ch 695; *Re Mechanisations (Eaglescliffe) Ltd* [1966] Ch 20; *Re Resonoid & Mica Products Ltd* [1983] Ch 132; *Victoria Housing Estates Ltd v Ashpurton Estates Ltd* [1983] Ch 110. For an example of 'exceptional circumstances' see *Re RM Arnold & Co Ltd* [1984] BCLC 535.

[11.81] A registered charge has priority over an earlier unregistered charge even if the holder of the later charge had notice of the earlier unregistered security. However, if the later charge is expressly subordinated to the earlier charge, that earlier charge will regain priority by late registration under s 106.

Re Clarets Ltd; Spain v McCann and Stonehurst Bank (Ireland) Ltd [1978] ILRM 215

[11.82] On 17 January 1977 Clarets Ltd ('the company') created a debenture in favour of the second defendant ('the bank'). This debenture was expressed to be subject to the rights of a prior mortgagee, McCann ('the defendant'). The bank's mortgage was registered on 7 February 1977. Due to an oversight the defendant's mortgage had not yet been registered. On 29 July 1977 the court extended the time for the filing of particulars and the mortgage was duly registered on 23 August 1977. The bank appointed a receiver who sold the charged property. The bank claimed priority over the defendant in relation to the proceeds of sale.

[11.83]   Costello J: The sheet anchor of [the bank's] case is a decision of the Court of Appeal in England (*In Re Monolithic Building Co* [1915] 1 Ch 643) which has recently been referred to with approval by Kenny J (See *In Re Interview Ltd* [1975] IR 382 at 396) . . . The plaintiff had, through an error failed to register his mortgage but he had obtained an order of the court extending the time for doing so without prejudice to the rights of parties prior to the time of actual registration. The defendant held a second mortgage debtebture which had been properly registered in accordance with the provisions of the Act. The defendant when he took the second mortgage debenture, had notice of the plaintiff's mortgage (indeed he had witnessed its execution) and the issue which the court had to determine was whether the first mortgage took priority over the second mortgage debenture. The court decided that it did not – holding that the effect of the section was to avoid an unregistered mortgage as against a subsequent registered encumbrancer even though he had express notice of the prior mortgage at the time when he took his own security.

Mr Barron SC, on behalf of the defendant in the present proceedings has argued that the facts in the present case are clearly distinguishable from those in the *Monolithic Building Co* case. I agree with him. The Court of Appeal was considering a subsequent encumbrancer who had knowledge of a prior mortgage and held that this knowledge did not preclude him from insisting on his rights as a registered holder of a subsequent debenture. The second debenture did not (as the mortgage debenture did in the present case) contain any reference to the prior mortgage and did not make it in any way subject to the prior mortgage . . . In the present case, it was expressly agreed between the company and the bank that the bank's mortgage debenture was subject to the plaintiff's mortgage. Thus, the bank's rights were at all times subject to those of the prior encumbrancer and therefore the right to appoint a receiver, enforce their security by sale of the company's premises were expressly made subject to the defendant's rights under his prior mortgage. The effect of the court's order of 29 July 1977 was that the defendant's security became a valid one when registration was effected without prejudice to the bank's rights under their mortgage debenture. What were those rights? They were clearly limited and qualified ones – they were subject at all times to those of the first mortgagee. The bank, it seems to me, are bound by the words of their agreement and they cannot now obtain a priority which they expressly agree they would not have.

Chapter 12

RECEIVERS

INTRODUCTION

[12.01]   A secured creditor wishing to enforce a fixed or floating charge over the assets of a company may do so either by taking possession himself or more commonly, by appointing a receiver.[1] There are two categories of company receiverships. The first and rarer, is where the receiver is appointed by the court. The second is where he is appointed pursuant to a power contained in the terms of the debenture itself. Regardless of the method of appointment, it has the effect of automatically crystallising a floating charge.[2] A receiver appointed pursuant to the terms of a debenture is tyically appointed as manager of the company as well. The following are prohibited from being appointed receiver:–

(*a*) a body corporate; (*b*) an undischarged bankrupt; (*c*) a person who was officer or servant of the company in the 12 months prior to the commencement of the recievership; (*d*) a parent, spouse, brother, sister or child of such an officer (*e*) a partner or employee of such an officer or servant (*f*) a person who is disqualified from acting as receiver of an associated company.[3] If a receiver becomes disqualified from acting as such he must immediately vacate office, giving written notice of disqualification to the company, the registrar and to the debentureholder or court (as the case may be) which appointed him. Acting while disqualified renders him liable to imprisonment or a fine or both.

1 See *Keane* chapter 24; Kerr on *Receivers* (17th Ed) (London), Picards *The Law Relating to Receivers and Managers* (London 1984).
2 *Halpin v Cremin* [1954] IR 19. The taking of possession by a mortgagee/chargee has the same effect.
3 S 314 of the Principal Act as amended by s 15 of the 1982 Act & as substituted by s 170 of the 1990 Act.

Appointment by the court[1]

[12.02]   Application by the court is by way of petition and the appointment is made by the court in the exercise of its equitable jurisdiction. There is also a limited statutory power of appointment.[2] A receiver appointed under the courts equitable jurisdiction is an officer of the court. He is agent neither of the company nor the chargee[3] whereas the receiver appointed pursuant to the statutory power is deemed to be the agent of the mortgagor (ie the company).[4]

1 See *Keane* at para **14.10**.
2 Under s 19 of the Conveyancing Act 1889. See *Wylie* op.cit at **13.048**.
3 *Parsons v Sovereign Bank of Canada* [1913] AC 160.
4 S 24(2) of the Conveyancing Act 1881.

[12.03] A receiver may be appointed under the court's equitable jurisdiction if the debenture has failed to include a power of appointment or if the power of appointment has been drafted in terms which do not cover events which have arisen and which have placed the security in jeopardy.[1]

1 *Alexander Hull & Co Ltd v O'Carroll, Kent & Co* (1955) 89 ILTR 70.

Appointment under the terms of a debenture

[12.04] In the absence of an express provision to the contrary in the debenture, the receiver will be regarded as the agent of the debenture holder who appointed him. In practice, however, the standard form debenture will provide that the receiver is to be the agent of the company instead. In this way the debenture holder avoids the risk of any personal liability for the acts or omissions of the rceiver. The winding up of the company terminates the receivers agency.[1] Thereafter he acts as principal although should the debenture holder direct him regarding the conduct of the receivership, he may be deemed to be the debenture holder's agent. Such a finding of agency would render the debenture holder personally liable for the acts and omissions of the receiver.[2] The agency of a receiver is unusual. The company, his principal cannot dismiss him nor direct him as to how he should act. Virtually all powers of the directors are suspended while the company is in receivership, management of the company having been taken over by the receiver. However, the statutory duties of the directors continue.[3] Under s 178 of the 1990 Act, the receiver has same power to seek the return of assets which have been disposed in in defraud of creditors, as is available to a liquidator in a winding up under s 139 of that Act.

1 *Gosling v Gaskell* [1897] AC 575; *Sowman v David Samuel Trust Ltd* [1976] 1 WLR 22.
2 *Standard Chartered Bank Ltd v Walker* [1982] 1 WLR 1410.
3 Such as the duty to prepare annual accounts and to have them audited, to call statutory meetings of shareholders (such as the AGM) to maintain the share register and to lodge the various statutory returns.

[12.05] It is an implied term of a debenture charging the property of the company that the debenture holders may appoint a receiver where the security is in jeopardy.

Angelis v Algemene Bank Nederland (Ireland) Ltd (High Court, 4 July 1974) (High Court)

[12.06] Kenny J: Algemene Bank Nederland (Ireland) Ltd, ('the bank'), the first named defendants, are a banking company incorporated in the state. The second named defendant is a well known accountant who has been appointed receiver by the bank over the assets and property of the defendant Commercial Ferries Limited ('the company'). The third, fourth, fifth and sixth named defendants are shareholders in the company. The company was incorporated in the State on the 13th October 1972 and the plaintiff, the third named defendant, the fourth named defendant, the fifth named defendant and the sixth named defendant were directors of it.

On the 13th of May 1974 the company gave a debenture to the bank to secure all monies due by the company to the bank and charged all its assets and undertaking with payment of the sum due. There is a sum of at least £250,000 due by the company to the bank and this is secured by the debenture. The debenture was subject to certain conditions as to payment and the bank agreed that they would not exercise some of their powers under the debenture if £7,000 per month was paid off the amount due on the debenture. After the debenture had been given Texaco (Ireland) Limited recovered judgment against the company. It is not necessary to cite authority for the proposition that when the assets charged by a debenture are in danger of seizure a debenture holder may immediately appoint a receiver. The bank appointed the second named defendant to be the receiver and manager of all the assets and undertaking of the company. The company is also indebted to the Ulster Bank Limited for £49,800 and this is secured by guarantee given by the plaintiff.

The plaintiff began these proceedings on the 24th June 1974 in which he claimed a declaration that the appointment of the second named defendant as receiver was invalid and an order restraining him from interfering with the assets of the company . . . I am satisfied that the appointment by the bank of the receiver was valid because the assets of the company were in danger of being seized under the judgment . . .

Notes

No authorities are cited by Kenny J. The judgment has not been considered in any subsequent Irish case. If this decision is correct the debenture holder will rarely if ever need to apply to the court for the appointment of a receiver. Cf *Cryne v Barclays Bank plc* [1987] BCLC 548.

[12.07] Under s 316(2) of the Principal Act, a receiver is personally liable, subject to an indemnity out of the company's assets on any contract entered into by him in the performance of his functions (whether entered into by him in the company's name or in his own name as receiver or otherwise) unless the contract expressly excludes such personal liability. He is not personally liable on contracts entered into by the company prior to his appointment, in the absence of a novation.

Cf *Moore v Donnelly* (High Court, 17/6/85) where Carroll J, noted that the receiver, although not liable as against the landlord to pay the rent on the charged premises, was obliged under the terms of the debenture to discharge 'all outgoings affecting or payable in respect of the mortgage property'. Curiously, Carroll J made an order on the application of the guarantor of the rent who was not a party to the debenture, declaring the receiver liable to pay the rent for a period when he was in beneficial occupation and possession of the premises. Notably, counsel for the receiver had conceded during the hearing that if the receiver did enjoy the use of the property he should also discharge the rent in priority to the mortgage debt.

Ardmore Studios (Ireland) Ltd v Lynch [1965] IR 1 (High Court)

[12.08]   On 1st January 1959 the plaintiff company entered into an agreement with a trade union that the company would only hire those electricians whose names appeared on a list supplied by the trade union. The company subsequently went into receivership and the receiver hired electricians whose names did not appear on the trade union list. The union contended that the receiver was bound by the terms of the agreement.

[12.09]   **McLoughlin J:** In the course of the argument I have been referred to many cases as to the effect of the appointment of a receiver for debenture holders . . . *In re B Johnson & Co (Builders)* [1955] 1 Ch 634 is not directly in point on the issue whether or not the receiver is bound or not by the alleged seniority list agreement, but many of the views expressed by the distinguished judges who constituted the Court of Appeal in that case are certainly helpful. At page 644 Evershed MR, after stating some of the powers given to the receiver under the debenture which are similar to those in this case continued:–

'The situation of someone appointed by a mortgagee or a debenture holder to be a receiver and manager – as it is said, 'out of court' – is familiar. It has long been recognised and established that receivers and managers so appointed are, by the effect of the statute law or the terms of the debenture or both, treated while in possession of the company's assets and exercising the various powers conferred upon them, as agents of the company in order that they may be able to deal effectively with third parties. But in such a case as the present at any rate, it is quite plain that a person appointed as receiver and manager is concerned not for the benefit of the company but for the benefit of the mortgagee bank to realise the security: that is the whole purpose of his appointment and the powers which are conferred upon him and which I have to some extent recited are . . . really ancillary to the main purpose of the appointment which is the realisation by the mortgagee of the security (in this case as commonly) by the sale of the assets.

All that is perhaps elementary; but it bears upon what I shall have to say as regards the charges made against the receiver for it appears to me

328

inevitable to negative the proposition that a person appointed, as Mr Aizlewood was appointed owes some duty to the company to carry on the business of the company and to preserve its goodwill.'

Jenkins LJ in the course of his judgment says (for the sake of brevity I begin the quotation in the middle of a paragraph, at p 661):–

'. . . whereas a receiver and manager for debenture holder is a person appointed by the debenture holders to whom the company has given powers of management pursuant to the contract of loan constituted by the debenture and as a condition of obtaining the loan, to enable him to preserve and realise the assets comprised in the security for the benefit of the debenture holders. The company gets the loan on terms that the lenders shall be entitled for the purpose of making their security effective to appoint a receiver with powers of sale and of management pending sale and with full discretion as to the exercise and mode of exercising those powers. The primary duty of the receiver is to the debentureholdrs and not to the company.'

Finally, Parker LJ at p 664 says:–

'What, however in my judgment is decisive of the case is that anywork of management done by a receiver is not done as manager of the company. The powers of management are ancillary to his position as receiver and in exercising those powers he is not acting as manager of the company but as manager of the whole or part of the property of the company.'

This case of course, if not an authority binding on me, but the views expressed in it are very persuasive and deserving of respectful consideration.

Another up to date English case, *Robbie & Co v Witney Warehouse Co* [1963] 3 All ER 613 is not directly in point, but in effect seems to support the contention that a receiver appointed by debenture holders is not bound by a contract made by the company before his appointment . . .

The defendants' argument put most relevance on the clause in the debenture deed that the receiver is made the agent of the company but it should be pointed out that this does not make him the servant of the company; the same clause – number 14(*c*) of the debenture deed – also provides that the receiver shall in the exercise of the powers authorities and discretions conform to the directions from time to time given by the debenture holder. As agent for the company the company is made fully responsible for his acts but it is not a corollary to this that he is bound by all company contracts and agreements entered into by the company before the date of his appointment.

The mortgaged property of which the receiver entered into possession as defined by the deed includes also the property charged and assigned, ie. all the undertaking and assets, machinery, book debts and goodwill; the argument of the defendants amounts to this: that he also took over by operation of law, the obligations of the company under the alleged agreement by the company to employ the union's electricians on the production of films in the studio. In as much as I find that it was the union's insistence on this agreement that gave rise to the circumstances leading to the debenture holders putting in a receiver over all the company's property and assets, this would seem to lead to an absurdity.

I have no hesitation in holding that there is no legal basis for their contention that the agreement as to the seniority list, even if it existed as an agreement on the date of the appointment of the receiver became binding on him . . .

Notes

See also *Re Newdigate Colliery Co Ltd* [1912] 1 Ch 68; *Parsons v Sovereign Bank of Canada* [1913] AC 160; *Nicoll v Cutts* (1986) 1 BCLC 99. Notably however, a supplier to the company (including a public utility) may insist on payment of all arrears with an undertaking from the receiver that he be personally liable for all future supplies. See *W & L Crowe Ltd v ESB* (High Court, Costello J, 9 May 1984). This has the effect of putting the supplier in the position of a form of super-preferential creditor of the company. In England, under s 233 of the Insolvency Act 1986 public utilities can no longer demand payment of arrears by the insolvency practitioner (ie. receiver, liquidator or administrator) before undertaking to continue supplies.

If personal liability on a contract is excluded by the receiver under s 316(2) of the Principal Act creditors under such contracts may look to the company's uncharged assets for payment. Where these assets are insufficient to meet their claims, they are paid out of the charged assets as an expense of the receivership in priority to the claims of the debenture holders: *Re British Power Traction and Lighting Co* [1906] 1Ch 497; *Healy v Oliver* [1918] 1 IR 366. Where a receiver is appointed under a charge which subsequently turns out to be defective he may apply to the court under s 316(3) for an order relieving him from personal liability and transferring the personal liability to the chargee.

[12.10]   The appointment of a receiver does not divest the directors of the company of their power to pursue a right of action if it is in the company's interest, does not impinge prejudicially on the conduct of the receivership and does not imperil the charged assets.

Wymes v Crowley (High Court, 27 February 1987)

[12.11]   The plaintiffs who were directors of the company, Bula Ltd had issued proceedings against the defendant receiver seeking to restrain him from selling the charged assets on improper terms or at an improper price. The plaintiffs applied to have the name of the company added as a plaintiff in the proceedings against the receiver.

[12.12]   **Murphy J:** The defendants properly recognise that the appointment of a receiver in pursuance of the powers in that behalf contained in a mortgage debenture does not terminate the powers vested by law in the directors of the company. The combined effect of the mortgage debenture and the appointment of a receiver is to appoint the receiver as the attorney of the company to deal with and dispose of the assets charged in accordance with the terms of the contractual documents and subject to certain statutory provisions which are applicable in those circumstances. References have been made to 'the residual powers of the directors' notwithstanding the appointment of a receiver. This expression may be appropriate as in practice the security granted by a company would ordinarily extend to all of its assets present and future and impose thereon a fixed or floating charge as might be appropriate to the nature of the assets and include in addition – as is done in the present case – a power to carry on the business of the company. In such cases and with that range of powers irrevocable delegated to the receiver, the areas in which directors may lawfully and effectively exercise powers in no doubt limited but, as I say, that is the practical consequence of granting an extensive charge over the assets of the company. If the parties were to confine themselves to a specific or limited area of charge or at any rate to exempt some of the properties of the company from the mortgage debenture it would be appreciated more clearly in principle that the powers of the receiver are those conferred upon him for the purpose of realising the security over which he is appointed and that all of the other powers to manage the affairs of the company remain vested in the board of directors thereof.

I have no doubt but that the directors of Bula Ltd retain their power to institute proceedings in an appropriate case. The limitation on their powers is that they must not deprive the debenture holders of the security granted to them and the very practical difficulty that the extensive nature of the charge deprives the company of the means of financing litigation. That the directors of Bula Limited would be entitled to institute proceedings in the name of that company to sue for negligence a receiver appointed over the assets of that company could not be questioned as a matter of law.

What was urged on behalf of the first named defendant was that the intended proceedings were an abuse of the process of the court in as much as the company was seeking to restrain the receiver disposing of the assets charged in favour of the defendant banks notwithstanding the fact that no challenge had been raised to the validity of the debentures or the appointment of the receiver. It was contended that the proceedings were seeking to 'stultify or frustrate the receiver's activities' contrary to the terms of the debentures as had been held by Chapman J in *Newhart Developments Ltd v Co-Operative Commercial Bank Ltd*. That decision was reversed on appeal (1978) QB 814. At page 821 of the report Shaw LJ, explained the position in the following terms:–

> 'I see no principle of law or expediency which precludes the directors of a company, as a duly constituted board (and it is not suggested here that they were not a duly constituted board when they took the step of instituting this

action) from seeking to enforce the claim, however ill-founded it may be, provided only, of course, that nothing in the course of the proceedings which they institute is going in any way to threaten the interest of the debenture holders.'

If and insofar as it is suggested that the purpose of these proceedings is to prevent the realisation *on improper terms* of any part of the assets of the company that could not be contrary to the interest of the debenture holders and I cannot see that the allegations made in the interlocutory proceedings or the relief sought in the plenary summons, if supported by appropriate evidence, could be seen as a threat to the legitimate interests of the debenture holders.

In the circumstances . . . Bula Ltd should be joined as a co-plaintiff.

Notes

In *Hawkesbury Development Co Ltd v Landmark Finance Pty Ltd* [1969] 2 NSWLR 782 it was held that the directors of the company had power to issue proceedings in the name of the company challenging the validity of the security under which the receiver was appointed.

[12.13]   The appointment of a receiver and manager pursuant to the terms of a debenture does not automatically terminate an employee's contract of employment with the company unless his continued employment is inconsistent with the role and functions of the receiver and manager.

Griffiths v Secretary of State for Social Services [1974] QB 468 (Queen's Bench Division)

[12.14]   Griffiths was employed as managing director of DGG Lubricants Ltd. The Secretary of State determined for the purposes of the National Insurance Acts that Griffiths' employment had terminated as a matter of law on the company going into receivership. Griffiths appealed from this decision.

[12.15]   **Lawson J:** I now have to ask myself this question. What is the state of the law as to the effect of an appointment of a receiver and manager by debenture holders upon contracts of employment with the company in such a case as in the present where it is common ground that the appointment of the receiver and manager is an appointment of him as agent for the company . . .

The first case to which I was referred was *Reid v Explosives Co Ltd* (1887) 19 QB 264. In that case a receiver and manager of the defendant company had been appointed by order of the court, in fact the Chancery division, at the instance of holders of debentures of the company. The plaintiff had been in the service of the defendant company, as manager of their works. His contract provided that his employment might be determined by six months' notice. The receiver and manager was appointed by order of the Chancery division and the plaintiff by the instructions of the receiver and manager continued for more than six months and discharged his former duties at the same salary. There was, therefore a fresh arrangement after the appointment of the receiver and manager by the order of the court of the company's employee, the manager of their works. As the plaintiff under these new arrangements had for more than six months continued his old work at the same rate of pay, the business was sold to a new company and he was dismissed without notice. He brought an action for wrongful dismissal and the Court of Appeal affirming the judgment of Manisty J, held that:

'. . . the appointment of a manager and receiver operated to discharge the servants of the company and the defendant could not recover.'

In the course of that case, no reference was specifically made to the appointment of a receiver and manager otherwise than by or under the order of the court, but in the course of his judgment, Lord Esher MR, at p 267 drew a parallel between the position of the mortgagor's property assuming it would be a business property and the effect that that would have which was in his view that that action would operate as a dismissal of the mortgagor's servants. Fry LJ, however, concurring with Lord Esher MR's view as to the decision when a receiver and manager for debenture holders is appointed under order of the court said at p 269:

'I am not prepared to lay down that every entry by a mortgagee is a dismissal of the servants of the mortgagor from his employment. I think to see whether that has happened we should look to the facts in each case.'

That case has been widely cited as authority for the proposition that the appointment of receivers and managers by the order of the court for debenture holders of the company takes effect as terminating the services of the company's employees. [His lordship then reviewed the various authorities and made the following conclusions].

I therefore find the law to be this . . . that the appointment by debenture holders of a receiver and manager as agent of the company, not an appointment under order of the court, does not of itself automatically terminate contracts of employment previously made and subsisting between the relevant company and all its employees. There are three situations in which this may be qualified.

The first situation is where – and this was, of course, the position *In re Foster Clark Ltd's Indenture Trusts* [1966] 1 WLR 125 – the appointment of a receiver is operated out of court by the debenture holders and he is appointed as agent of the company and the appointment is accompanied by a sale of the business; that will operate to terminate contracts of employment not because it is the appointment of the receiver and manager, but because what is happening is that the company is selling its business and there is no longer any business for which the employees can work. That is a qualification of the general proposition which I find the law to support. That, of course, is not the present case at all.

The second situation is where it happens that, simultaneously or very soon after the appointment of a receiver and manager as agent of the company appointed by debenture holders and not by order of the court, such a receiver and manager enters into a new agreemeent with a particular employee that may be inconsistent with the continuation of his old service contract. That is the position which is not decided but whch is indicated *In re Mack Trucks (Britain) Ltd* [1967] 1 WLR 780.

The third situation and this is the situation with which I am concerned here, is where . . . the continuation of the employment of a particular employee is inconsistent with the role and functions of a receiver and manager. The mere fact that he is labelled 'managing director' does not, in my judgment indicate that because he is so labelled his employment in that capacity or office is inconsistent with the position, role and functions of a receiver and manager for two reasons. On analysis one may find – and there is a finding of fact in this case – that the person described as the managing director was, so to speak, under a fairly stringent board control which was not only theoretical but which had in practice from time to time from the facts of this case been exercised. Secondly, I think that one has to be a little realistic about what the role and functions of a receiver and manager are. The normal course one may I think say is that one finds debenture holders appointing a receiver and manager – one person – not with the intention that he should be employed full-time to conduct all the company's business but as someone who is going to exercise supervision and control of the way in which the company's business is run, particularly the financial implications of the way in which the business is run, as from the time when the receiver is appointed . . .

So my conclusion is that unless such an inconsistency of roles be found as a matter of fact, then one is not concerned with the termination of a subsisting contract of employment as of the date when the receiver and manager is appointed because it is right to assume that in the absence of a finding of inconsistency or roles, the old contract of employment continued notwithstanding the appointment of the receiver and manager. It therefore follows on that basis that as a matter of law on the facts found by the Secretary of State I hold the appellant's contract of employment as managing director with the company did not terminate upon Mr Christie being appointed as receiver and manager and agent of the company by appointment in writing made by the debenture holders. I therefore hold that on the facts as found the present is not such a case as entitled the Secretary of State so to find as he did.

Notes

As the receiver is not bound by pre-appointment contracts of employment those employees who have not been dismissed may go unpaid. See *Nicoll v Cutts* (1986) 1 BCLC 99.

Receivers duties

[12.16] It has been held that regardless of the method of the appointment of a receiver, his position is a fiduciary one.[1] His primary duty is to the debenture holder,[2] although as can be seen from the cases below, he owes a secondary duty to his principal the company, and to any guarantors of the company's debts. Where he has been appointed pursuant to the terms of a floating charge he is also under a duty where the company is not already in liquidation to pay the claims of preferential creditors, who will rank in priority to the claims of the debenture holder.[3] The receiver is under the same duty as a liquidator in a voluntary winding up, to report criminal conduct of officers and members of the company to the DPP and to assist him in the case of a prosecution.[4]

1 *Byre v McDonnell* (1864) Ir Ch R 534.
2 *Lynch v Ardmore Studios (Ireland) Ltd* (para **12.17**).
3 S 98 of the Principal Act, discussed in chapter 14 *supra*.
4 S 179 of the 1990 Act.

[12.17]   The duty of a receiver is primarily to the company.

Lynch & Others v Ardmore Studios (Ireland) Ltd and Michael Hayes [1966] IR 133 (High Court)

[For the facts of this case see para **12.08**.]

[12.18]   Budd J: The effect of the appointment of Mr Sandys under the terms of the debenture was to make his receiver and manager of the Company's business and property. As to the position of a person appointed to be a receiver and manager under a mortgage debenture of this kind there are some observations in the judgments of the Court of Appeal in England *In re Johnson & Co (Builders)* [1955] 1 Ch 634 to which I wish to refer. The applicant in that case sought an order under the Companies Act 1948 for the investigation of the conduct of the receiver and the liquidator. It was held that the receiver was not within the class of persons whose conduct could be the subject of an examination under the section proceeded on, but in the course of arriving at this conclusion the character of a receiver's managership was considered. At p 644 Lord Evershed MR said:

'The situation of someone appointed by a mortgagee or debenture holder to be a receiver and manager – as it is said, "out of court" – is familiar. It has long been recognised and established that receivers and managers so appointed are, by the effect of the statute law or of the terms of the debenture or both, treated while in possession of the company's assets and exercising the various powers conferred upon them, as agents of the company in order that they may be able to deal effectively with third parties. But, in such a case as the present at any rate, it is quite plain that a person appointed as receiver and manager is concerned not for the benefit of the company but for the benefit of the mortgagee bank, to realise the security; that is the whole purpose of his appointment; and the powers which are conferred upon him and which I have to some extent recited are (as Sir Lynn observed and I think fairly observed) really ancillary to the main purpose of the appointment which is the realisation by the mortgagee of the security (in this case, as commonly) by the sale of the assets.'

At p 661 Jenkins LJ states the position of a receiver as follows:–

'. . . receiver and manager for debenture holders is a person appointed by the debenture holders to whom the company has given powers of management pursuant to the contract of loan constituted by the debenture and as a condition of obtaining the loan, to enable him to preserve and realise the assets comprised in the security for the benefit of the debenture holders. The company gets the loan on terms that the lenders shall be entitled for the purpose of making their security effective to appoint a receiver with powers of sale and of management pending sale and with full discretion as to the exercise and mode of exercising those powers. The primary duty of the receiver is to the debenture holder and not to the company. He is receiver and manager of the property of the company for the debenture holders not manager of the company. The company is entitled to any surplus of assets remaining after the debenture debt has been discharged and is entitled to proper accounts. But the whole purposes of the receiver and manager's appointment would obviously be stultified if the company could claim that a receiver and manager owes it a duty comparable to the duty owed to a company by its own directors or managers.'

Finally at p 664 Parker LJ says:–

'What however, in my judgment is decisive of the case is that any work of management done by a receiver is not done as manager of the company. The powers of management are ancillary to his position as receiver and in exercising those powers he is not acting as manager of the company but as manager of the whole or part of the property of the company.

These observations with which I respectfully concur support the contentions made that a receiver appointed acts for the benefit of the debenture holder.

[12.19]   A receiver owes a duty to exercise the care of a reasonable man in the disposal of the charged assets to obtain the best possible price which the circumstances of the case permit. This duty of care although owed primarily to the debenture holder is also owed to the company and to guarantors of the company's debts.

Lambert Jones Estates Ltd v Donnelly (High Court, 5 November 1982)

[12.20]   The defendant had been appointed receiver of the company's property. The plaintiff's (who included the company itself, the directors, certain shareholders and unsecured creditors) sought an injunction restraining the defendant from selling the company's main asset (a piece of property) on the ground that the proposed method of sale was negligent. The court refused the plaintiffs application.

[12.21]   O'Hanlon J: The defendant claims that since his appointment as receiver he has been engaged in negotiations and transactions which will make the property more attractive to a potential purchaser – securing a clear site and getting rid of burdensome claims against the property which existed in favour of Green Group Ltd under the terms of an agreement of the 28th November 1973 and made between that company of the one part and the first named plaintiff of the other part. He now says that the property is ripe for sale and has proceeded to put it on the market for sale as a single unit, the sale being by public tender . . .

The plaintiffs bring these proceedings for the purpose of preventing the defendant from carrying through his avowed purpose of selling the entire site as a single unit by public tender in the manner adopted by him. They claim that they have expert advice to the effect that it would be much more profitable to divide up the property into smaller units; to apply for and obtain planning permission for schemes of development of such smaller units and then proceed to sell off such parcels – individually in a series of transactions . . . They claim that the receiver is only concerned with getting in sufficient funds to discharge the claims of the bank creditors, or of its shareholders, directors or unsecured creditors . . .

The defendant is a chartered accountant and sought and obtained the advice of a prominent firm of estate agents, surveyors and valuers . . . He claims to have acted on their advice at all stages and that he is still acting on their advice with regard to the proposed method of sale of the property.

The plaintiffs have consulted other experts in the property field and have been advised that a considerably enchanced purchase price could in all probability, be obtained for the site if it were sold off in several smaller lots over a period with planning permission having first been obtained for the development of such smaller units.

The defendant does not set out to dispute the claim that by adopting the method suggested by the plaintiffs a higher scale price might ultimately be obtained for the property taken as a whole. He says however, that he is advised that the apparent gain to the vendors would in all probability be illusory. They would be likely to be involved in long delays while new development schemes were prepared for the different units and planning permission was sought for same. In the meantime interest at over £1m per annum would continue to accumulate against the company as long as there was no return from the property. The costs involved in the plaintiffs alternative plan of campaign would be very heavy and there are no funds available to meet such costs. Indeed, the banks have already had to contribute some £200,000 to enable the defendant to clear the site and the title for the purposes of the sale now proposed.

There is another divergence of views between the experts in relation to one of the grants of planning permission which exists in relation to the property and which is the subject of an appeal to An Bord Pleanala. The defendant says he has been advised to let that appeal lie dormant for the time being until the sale goes through for reasons which are explained in the affidavits. The plaintiffs say with the support of their experts that the sale should be deferred until An Bord Pleanala has given its decision . . .

I am prepared to accept that a receiver owes a duty of care to the owner of property and possibly also to the creditors of the owner, when he proceeds to realise property for the primary purpose of discharging the claims of a secured creditor by whom he has been appointed. That duty of care would render it incumbent upon him to take all reasonable steps to obtain the best possible price for the property. (See *Latchford v Beirne* [1981] 2 All ER 705; and *Standard Chartered Bank Ltd v Walker* [1982] 1 WLR 1410) . . . I can see very clearly on the affidavits that the plaintiffs have radically different ideas from the defendant as to the best way of realising the assets of the company, and that they have the support of a prominent firm of chartered valuation surveyors for the opinion they have formed. It is equally clear, however, that the defendant has also taken expert advice and has acted upon it in deciding how he should proceed with the sale of the property. He is anxious to sell, if at all possible at an early date to minimise the enormous burden of interest on the bank debt which is accumulating against the company with each day and month that pass. He does not want to take a course which will involve him in new and costly and protracted planning applications for multiple units of property. He says he has no funds available to finance such transactions and the plaintiffs have not suggested that any source of finance is available to him. Finally he has stated through his counsel in the course of the hearing, that if and when he is allowed to proceed with sale by tender it is his intention to seek the approval of the court before accepting the highest or any tender.

I fail to see, on the evidence now before the court how the defendant could conceivably be said to be guilty of negligence or breach of duty and in my opinion any such finding on such evidence as is now available would be perverse . . .

Notes

See also *McGowan v Gannon* (para **12.24**); *Irish Oil and Cake Mills Ltd v Donnelly* (para **12.25**); *Amercian Express v Hurley* [1985] 3 All ER 564. It would seem that the duty of care is not owed directly to the company's unsecured creditors: *Lathie v Dronsfield Bros Ltd* [1987] BCLC 321.

Under s 316a of the Principal Act, as inserted by s 172 of the 1990 Act, the receiver is now under an express statutory duty in selling the company's property to 'exercise all reasonable care to obtain the best price reasonably obtainable for the property at the time of sale'. He is not entitled to any indemnity or compensation in respect of liablity under s 316a, notwithstanding the provisions of s 316(2) of the Principal Act. Neither shall it be a defence that the receiver was acting as agent of the company or under a power of attorney given by the company. A receiver may be under a duty to continue the company's business where failure to do so would adversely affect the price obtainable for the charged assets: *Airline Airspaces Ltd v Handley Page Ltd* [1970] 1 Ch 193. Cf *Re B Johnson & Co (Builders) Ltd* [1955] Ch 634.

It is clear from the terms of s 316a that the receiver does not have to wait for the market to rise before selling the charged assets. Even if the market rises after an earlier sale at the best price then obtainable, the receiver will not be guilty of a breach of duty. See *McGowan v Gannon* (para **12.24**).

Under s 316a a receiver may not sell by private contract a non-cash asset of the 'requisite value' to a person who is, or who, within three years prior to the date of appointment of the receiver, has been, an officer of the company unless he has given at least 14 days' notice of his intention to do so to all creditors of the company who are known to him or who have been intimated to him. A non-cash asset is of the requisite value if it is not less than £1,000 but, subject to that, exceeds £50,000 or 10% of the amount of the company's 'relevant assets', which are defined as:

(*a*) the net assets as determined by reference to the annual accounts for the last financial year; or
(*b*) where there are no such accounts, the amount of the called-up share capital.

Duty to provide information on the receivership

[**12.22**] Regardless of the method of appointment of the receiver, the debenture holder has seven days from the date of the order or of the appointment, to publish notice thereof in *Iris Oifigiuil* and in at least one daily newspaper circulating in the district where the company's registered office is situated and to deliver to the registrar a similar notice.[1] The receiver must deliver a similar notice to the registrar in the event of his ceasing to act as such.[2]

Where a receiver has been appointed over the whole or substantially the whole of the company's property on behalf of the holders of a floating charge he must immediately give notice thereof to the company.[3] Within 14 days of receipt of the notice or such longer period as may be allowed by the court or receiver, the company must submit a statement of affairs in the prescribed form[4] to the receiver.[5] The statement of affairs must be prepared by the directors and secretary although the receiver can require past and present officers of the company to prepare it instead.[6] If those persons who have been requested to prepare the statement fail to do so, they may be liable to a fine or imprisonment or both.[7] Within two months of receipt of the statement of affairs the receiver must send a copy of it and any amendments he sees fit to make thereon to the registrar, the court, the company, to any trustees for the debenture holders on whose behalf he was appointed and to the debenture holders themselves, so far as he is aware of their addresses. If

339

a statement of affairs is not submitted, in breach of ss 319 and 320, the court may on the application of the receiver or any creditor of the company, make whatever order it thinks fit, including an order compelling the preparation and submission of the statement of affairs.[8]

Every six months the receiver must send an abstract in the prescribed form[9] detailing his progress in realising the charged assets. A similar abstract must be delivered within one month of ceasing to act as director. In all receiverships every invoice, order for goods or business letter issued by or on behalf of the company or receiver must, if it contains the name of the company also state that it is in receivership.[10]

Under s 322 the court may, on application by any member or creditor of the company or by the registrar order the receiver to make good any default in filing documents required by law. On application of the liquidator the court can also order the receiver to render proper accounts of his receipts and payments and to vouch same and to pay over to the liquidator any amount properly payable to him. In *Stewart v Campbell* (High Court, 13 June 1986) Carroll J held that the liquidator may only require proper accounts of receipts and payments made by the receiver personally. He may not demand such accounts in respect of the receipts and payments of the receivers' predecessor in office who has since retired, died or otherwise vacated office. 'Proper accounts' constitute more than a mere abstract of receipts and payments. The receiver is entitled to reasonable charges for necessary work done in preparing such accounts.

1 S 102(1) of the Principal Act; Forms 53 and 57a of the Companies (Forms) Order 1964. SI No 45 of 1964.
2 S 107(2) of the Principal Act.
3 Ibid s 319(1).
4 Companies (Forms) Order, Form no 17. The prescribed contents of the statement of affairs are set out in s 320 of the Principal Act. The statement of affairs must be verified by affidavit in the case of a court appointment and otherwise by statutory declaration.
5 S 319(2) of the Principal Act.
6 Ibid s 320(6).
7 S 320 as amended by s 173 of the 1990 Act.
8 S 320A as inserted by s 174 of the 1990 Act.
9 Companies (Forms) Order 1964, Form no 57, containing details set out in s 319(2). This is without prejudice to his equitable duty to account: s 319(6).
10 S 317.

[12.23]   The receiver is under an equitable duty to account to the debenture holder and to the company, but not to any guarantor of the company's debts.

McGowan v Gannon [1983] ILRM 516 (High Court)

[The facts appear from the judgment]

[12.24]   **Carroll J:** This judgment concerns the right of a guarantor and/or creditor of a company to information from a receiver concerning the proposed purchase price of the company's assets. This was a preliminary issue which arose when the matter first came before me. The defendant is receiver of a company called Food Products (Donegal) Limited. All the plaintiffs are creditors of the company. Some of them are directors and the first named plaintiff, Patrick McGowan is also a guarantor of the company's debts.

The plaintiffs sought to restrain the sale of the company's factory premises and plant in Donegal by the receiver because they apprehended that it was being sold at an undervalue. On the initial application none of the plaintiffs knew the details. The plaintiffs applied to restrain the sale until they were sold the purchase price and then have liberty to consider whether to apply for an injunction to restrain the sale completely . . . Among the authorities cited by the plaintiffs was the case of *Chaine-ickson v The Bank of Ireland* [1976] IR 393 which held that a potential beneficiary under a discretionary trust was entitled to information about the administration of the fund. Another case cited was *Standard Chartered Bank Ltd v Walker* [1982] 3 All ER 938 which held that a guarantor could sue a receiver for negligence in disposing of the assets of a company whose debts were guaranteed as there was sufficient proximity between the receiver and guarantor for the receiver to owe a duty of care to the guarantor.

Under clause 7(*c*) of the debenture under which the receiver was appointed it is provided that the receiver should be the agent of the borrower and the borrower should be solely responsible for his acts and defaults and for his remuneration. Therefore under the ordinary law of contract the company as principal is entitled to the information from its agent, the receiver. No point arises of this issue now as the receiver has supplied the information on request.

However, I am satisfied that a guarantor is entitled to any information regarding the sale of the company's assets. The guarantor is not in the same position as a potential beneficiary under a discretionary trust. Nothing has been cited to me to show that a receiver is a trustee for a guarantor. There is no contractual relationship between a guarantor and a receiver. Therefore in my opinion there is no basis on which a guarantor can require the information. That is not to say that a receiver does not owe a duty of care to the guarantor of a company as was held in *Standard Chartered Bank Ltd v Walker*. That is a different relationship altogether.

Therefore Mr McGowan is not entitled to the information. The other plaintiffs are creditors and they are in no better position than a guarantor and are not entitled to the information either.

The company has applied to be joined as a plaintiff and seeks an injunction on the grounds that prima facie the assets of the company are being sold at an under value.

It was decided in *Casey v Irish Intercontinental Bank* [1979] IR 364 that if a mortgagee enters into a contract for sale which all the circumstances and valuations show is the best price at the time, it is a binding contract even though a higher offer is subsequently made. The company is therefore concerned that no contract be signed if there is danger of sale at an undervalue. In *Standard Chartered Bank Ltd v Walker* it is stated that the duty of a

341

receiver is to use reasonable care to obtain the best price which the circumstances of the case allow. Denning MR said it may be that the receiver can choose the time of the sale within a considerable margin but he should exercise a reasonable degree of care about it. He states as follows:

> 'If it should appear that the mortgagee or receiver have not used reasonable care to realise the assets to the best advantage, then the mortgagor, the company and the guarantor are entitled in equity to an allowance. They should be given credit for the amount which the sale should have realised if reasonable care had been used.' (at 942)

Mr Sweetman for the plaintiff says the price which they now know, is worse than they had anticipated and that it is a giveaway price. This raises the issue, whether a receiver who has tested the market and found that the market is very bad, is entitled to sell at a giveaway or knockdown price because he cannot get better. Should he be obliged to wait for any given period in the hope that there would be an upswing in the market? That point has not been argued.

There is a large difference between the price which the plaintiff's valuer has put on the premises and the price negotiated by the receiver with a potential customer. But as against that, the plaintiffs' valuer does not appear to base his valuation on any recent sales.

In all the circumstances I am of opinion that the status quo should be preserved for a short time so that the company can consider its position in the light of the information which it has only just received. I propose to grant an injunction for a further three weeks.

Irish Oil and Cake Mills Ltd and Irish Oil and Cake Mills (Manufacturing) Ltd v Donnelly (High Court, 27 March 1983)

[12.25]   On 28 October 1983 the defendant was appointed receiver and manager of the plaintiff companies by the Northern Bank under two floating charges. On 29th February 1984 the plaintiffs wrote to the defendants seeking detailed accounts and information of the receivership and when this was not forthcoming they sought a mandatory injunction directing the defendant to furnish the requested material.

[12.26]   **Costello J:** [Counsel for the plaintiff] submits that his case is in essence a simple one – as a matter of principle the defendant he says is under a duty to furnish the information sought and the court should order him to fulfill his duty. The duty he says arises because under the terms of the floating charges the defendant as receiver and manager is agent for the plaintiffs and so a contractual duty as such agent exists to supply the information. Alternatively and independent of contract there is a duty of care owed by the defendant to the plaintiffs which obliges him to furnish the information sought. In the further alternative there is an equitable duty to account which on the authority of a recent case in England (*Smith Ltd v Middleton* [1979] 3 All ER 843) obliges him to account as requested.

Before examining these submissions I should refer in greater detail to the information which the plaintiffs say the defendant is obliged to give them. The letter of the 29th February 1984 requests the following information:–

1. Financial management account for all periods from the 1st October 1983 to date.
2. Latest balance sheet analysis as to:
   (a) All debtors and stock
   (b) All creditors – showing separately pre and post receivership preferential creditors.
3. Details of all tonnages and costs of raw materials purchased since 29th October 1983.
4. Details of refinery programmes since the 29th October 1983.
5. Details of sales made, by tonnage price and commodity since the 29th October 1983.
6. The present manufacturing/sales programme.
7. Staff levels by job description to include management, administration and refinery indicating present and proposed (if different) and salary/wages levels.
8. Receiver's estimate of break-even point and how calculated.
9. Details of all sales and purchase contracts.
10. Present status of amounts due to and by foreign traders arising out of 10CM raw material purchase and sale contracts prior to the 29th October 1983.

The net question which now arises is this; Is this information which as a matter of law, a receiver and manager is after 4 months of his receivership, obliged to give the company?

The plaintiffs first submission is that the receiver is under a contractual duty to provide the requested information.

The receiver derives his appointment and his authority from the contract entered into between the parties. In this case, as is usual, the parties agreed that he is to be treated as the agent of the mortgagors, the plaintiffs herein. This provision protects the debenture holders from liability as mortgagees in possession and establishes the relationship between the receiver and the company. But the contract is silent as to the nature of his duties and the plaintiffs here submit that there is to be implied an obligation to account as claimed in the February letter. The agency here is of course very different from the ordinary agency arising every day in commercial transactions. Here the receiver has been appointed by the owner in equity of the companies' assets with the object of realising their security and for this purpose to carry on the companies business. The exceptional nature of his status is to be seen from the fact that notwithstanding his appointment as agent he is to be personally liable under contracts entered into by him (with a right of indemnity out of the assets) unless the contract otherwise provides (s 316(2) Companies Act 1963).

343

I can find no basis for implying a term into the contract in this case which would oblige the receiver to furnish the information now sought.

I think that the company has a right to an account from a receiver as I will point out later, but I think it is an equitable right and that the plaintiffs herein have not a right arising from an implied term in the debenture for the information claimed in their February letter . . .

The second basis on which the claim is put forward is that the defendant threatens to breach a duty of care which he owes to the plaintiffs. The argument proceeds as follows. It is said:

(*a*) that a duty of care lies on the receiver to take reasonable steps to get the best possible price for the company's assets and that this is a duty which he owes to the company.

(*b*) in failing to give the information sought the receiver is in breach of this duty in that (i) with its assistance the company could prepare a scheme of re-construction or arrangement which would mean that the price for the assets would be greater than that recoverable on a sale in the open market and (ii) alternatively two of the directors of the company, Mr Rabbitte and Mr Senexio are interested in purchasing the companies' assets and that if the company gets the information sought it will be available to these directors and enable them to formulate a bid for the company which would be higher than would otherwise be obtained.

The receiver does not deny that he owes a duty to the company as alleged, but he urges that he has not been nor is he in breach of it . . .

The plaintiffs claim to the information is based on the general legal principles which they claim are applicable and not on any allegation of wrong-doing on the receiver's behalf.

As to (i) (the argument based on the possibility of a scheme of re-construction) . . . Nearly five months have elapsed since the receiver was appointed and in the absence of a satisfactory explanation for (*a*) the failure to put forward a realistic scheme and (*b*) as to how the information sought could assist in ensuring that the financial backing necessary would be available and (*c*) in the absence of satisfactory evidence to show that purchase of the assets under the proposed scheme could avoid a sale of the assets or produce a better price than their sale in the ordinary way, the plaintiffs have not satisfied me that the receiver is acting in any way in breach of his duty to the company on the ground I am now considering.

The second ground is a different one. It is said that if the company got this information two of its directors would be in a position to make a bid for the company's assets. But the companies' assets have been advertised for sale since 11th November 1983 and whilst an offer was made for part of the assets of the group none has ever been made for the companies principal assets.

Again to justify the court making the entirely novel and wholly exceptional order, which is now claimed, it is not sufficient for the company to assert that the information sought would produce the result suggested. To justify the court in holding that the receiver is in breach of a duty of care to the company it should be shown that evidence in support of the assertion is available. This has not been done to my satisfaction in this case. The receiver is of course prepared to give to the directors the same information which is available to other prospective purchasers. He is entitled to make a commercial judgment in the matter and decide that it would not be conducive to procuring an enhanced price to give these directors any more information. The evidence falls short in showing that by so concluding he is in breach of duty.

The plaintiffs advanced a second argument to support the contention that the receiver is in breach of the duty of care he owes to the company. It is said that apart from the special facts of this case the general duty on receiver and manager to take reasonable steps to secure the best possible price for the companies' assets includes a duty 'to keep the company appraised of how the business of the company is going'. This is a very far-reaching proposition, unsupported by any authority and I must reject it. There may well be special circumstances in which, to ensure that the best price possible is obtained for the assets trading information since the appointment of a receiver should be given to the company's directors. But in the absence of special circumstances which might favourably affect the price a receiver/manager is not under any duty of care which involves him in reporting as suggested to the directors on his management of the business.

It cannot be said that a receiver/manager is under no duty to account to the company whose affairs he is managing nor did the defendant so urge in this case. The extent and nature of the duty and the extent and nature of the accounts he must furnish will depend on the facts of each individual case. *Smith Ltd v Middleton* illustrates this point. That was a case in which an account was ordered after a receivership had come to an end, the court holding that as agent an equitable obligation to account existed which had not been obviated by statute. But the plaintiffs (having perhaps been misled by the head-note to the report) are not correct in finding in that case a general legal proposition to support their contentions in this case. I am not required now to lay down any general principles and I gladly refrain from doing so.

Notes

In *Gomba Holdings (UK) Ltd v Homan* [1986] BCLC 331 Hoffman J held that the statutory duty to provide information is not exhaustive. The extent of a receiver's obligation to provide additional information could be deduced from the nature of the receivership and the express or implied terms of the debenture under which the receiver was appointed. The learned judge held that this duty to supply reasonable information was certainly owed to the debenture holder for whose benefit he was acting, however, he went on to say that the right of the company to such extra information would depend upon proof that the information was needed to enable the directors to exercise their residual powers or to perform their duties. Any right which a company had to obtain information from the receiver had to be qualified by the receivers' primary responsibility to the debenture holder, which entailed that the receive would be entitled to withhold information where he formed the opinion that this would be contrary to the interests of the debenture holder in realising the security. In *Re Neon Signs (Australia) Ltd* [1965] VR 123 it was held that he can however disclose secret information about company contracts in exceptional cases in order to persuade a third party to buy the company's business because this result would be beneficial to the debenture holders.

Application for directions

[12.27] Under s 316 of the Principal Act as amended by s 171 of the 1990 Act the receiver may apply to the court for directions regarding the exercise of his functions. Any officer, member, contributory or liquidator of the company, employees representing at least half in number of the full time workforce, and any creditor owed more than £10,000 may also apply to the court for directions under s 316, provided. However, if the application is not by the receiver, it must be supported by such evidence as the court may require, that the applicant is being unfairly prejudiced by any actual or proposed act or omission of the receiver.

Remuneration of a receiver[1]

[12.28] In the case of a court appointment, the receiver's remuneration is fixed by the court.[2] Otherwise it is a matter for agreement between the receiver and the debenture holder. Nonetheless, the liquidator or any creditor or member of the company may apply to court to fix the receiver's remuneration, if it is felt that the agreed remuneration is excessive.[3]

1 See *Keane* at para **24.16**.
2 O 50 r 16 of the Rules of the Supreme Court.
3 S 318 of the Principal Act.

Resignation and removal

[12.29] The debenture holder may remove the receiver at any time if expressly entitled to do so by the terms of the debenture. Under s 322A of the Principal Act as inserted by s 175 of the 1990 Act the receiver may also, on cause shown, be removed by the court. The court may then appoint a successor to fill the vacancy. In the proceedings both the receiver and his replacement are entitled to be appear and be heard. Under s 322B as inserted by s 176 of the 1990 Act, in a compulsory winding up or creditors' voluntary winding up the liquidator may apply to the court on seven days notice to the receiver for an order that the receiver (whether he was appointed before or after the commencement of the winding up) shall cease to act or act only in respect of certain specified assets. No order made under this section shall affect any charge or security over property of the company. The liquidator or receiver (but not seemingly the debenture holder)? can subsequently apply to have the order rescinded or varied.

Under s 322C as inserted by s 177 of the 1990 Act, a receiver appointed under the terms of a debenture may resign provided he gives one month's notice to the holders of any fixed or floating charges over company property and to any liquidator of the company. A receiver appointed by the court can only resign with the leave of the court and on such terms and conditions as may be laid down by the court.

Chapter 13

MEMBERSHIP AND MEETINGS

Membership

[13.01]   S 31(2) of the Principal Act provides that any person 'who agrees to become a member of a company and whose name is entered in its register of members shall be a member of the company'.(1) In the case of a company limited by shares, acquisition of such shares may be by allotment,[2] transfer,[3] or transmission.[4] Accordingly, if the shares are registered in the name of a nominee, then it is the nominee who is regarded as being the member.[5] The subscribers of the memorandum are deemed to be members of the company and their names must be entered in the register of members, even if shares have not been allotted to them.[6] However, if the total authorised share capital has been issued to parties other than the subscribers, they cannot simply by signing the memorandum be treated as members of the company. An individual who permits his name to be entered in the register of members, may be estopped from denying that he is a member, even if he is not in fact the owner of any shares in the company.

1 See generally *Keane* chapter 25.
2 See chapter 8 *supra*.
3 See chapter 13 *supra*.
4 Ibid.
5 *Re Allied Metropole Hotel Ltd* (High Court, Gannon J 1988). Noted by *MacCann* (1989) 7 ILT 195. In addition s 123 of the Principal Act provides that no notice of any trust is to be entered on the register. See also art 7 of table A. These provisions are discussed *supra* in chapter 10.
6 See also *Evans* case (1867) 2 Ch App 427.

Register of members[1]

[13.02]   Every company is obliged to keep a register of members,[2] which is to be open to inspection by the members free of charge and by the public on payment of a small fee.[3] In the case of public companies an index of members must also be maintained unless the register itself constitutes an index.[4] Both the register and index must be kept at a place within the State, normally the registered office of the company.[5] The register is prima facie evidence of matters directed or authorised to be inserted therein by the Companies Acts.[6] Under s 122 of the Principal Act the court may order that the register be rectified if:–

(*a*) the name of a person is entered therein; or omitted therefrom without sufficient cause;[7] or

(*b*) default is made in entering on the register within the prescribed 28 day period, the fact of a person having ceased to be a member.

Application may be by the person aggrieved, by any member of the company or by the company itself. The court has a power to order payment of compensation in addition to making any order of rectification.

1 See *Keane* at para **25.06**.
2 S 116 of the Principal Act as amended by s 20 of the 1982 Act.
3 S 119 of the Principal Act.
4 Ibid s 117.
5 Ibid s 116(5), (6).
6 Ibid s 124.
7 Eg. due to misrepresentation: *Stewart's* case (1866) 1 Ch App 574; The court's power is discretionary (*Trevor v Whitworth* (1887) 12 App Cas 409. 440) and rectification of a voidable registration may be refused on grounds of undue delay (*Sewell's* case): *Re Scottish Petroleum Co* (1883) 23 Ch D 413, 434 or where the company has since gone into liquidation (*Oakes v Turquand* [1867] LR 2 HL 325).

Meetings

[13.03]   Members of a company, to the extent that they participate in its affairs do so through the general meetings. There are two main types of meeting, the annual general meeting and the extra-ordinary general meeting. In addition where the rights or liabilities of a particular class of shareholders are to be affected, the company may be obliged to convene separate class meetings.

Annual general meeting

[13.04]   The annual general meeting (AGM) must be held each with not more than a fifteen month interval between each such AGM.[1] For the year of incorporation and the following year it suffices to hold one AGM within 18 months of the date of incorporation.[2] The 'ordinary business' of an AGM is set out in art 53 of table A.[3] All other business is 'special business'. The notice convening a general meeting must specify the general nature of any special business.[4]

Failure to convene the AGM may result in a fine for the company and every officer in default.[5] If default is made in holding the AGM any member may apply to the Minister to call or direct the calling of the meeting.[6] Apart from the first AGM all such subsequent meetings must be held within the State, unless a foreign venue was approved at the previous AGM or was approved of in writing by all members entitled to attend and vote, and provided the articles do not expressly require the meeting to be held within this jurisdiction.[7]

1 S 131(1) of the Principal Act.
2 Ibid s 131(2).
3 It includes the declaration of a dividend, the consideration of the accounts, balance sheets and the reports of the directors and auditors, the election of the directors in the place of those retiring, the re-appointment of the retiring directors and the fixing of the remuneration of the auditors. Art 53 is commonly amended to include the fixing of the remuneration of the directors within the ordinary business of the AGM.
4 Art 51 of table A.
5 S 131(6) of the Principal Act as amended by s 15 of the 1982 Act.
6 Ibid s 131(3).
7 Ibid s 140.

Extraordinary general meeting[1]

[13.05]   Where there are matters which the directors feel ought to be considered at a general meeting of the company, and they cannot wait for the next AGM they may instead call an extraordinary general meeting.[2] In addition, they are obliged to convene an EGM if one is requisitioned by shareholders holding between them at least one tenth of the paid up share capital carrying voting rights.[3] If the directors fail to convene the EGM[4] within 21 days of the date of deposit of the requisition the requisionists themselves may convene the meeting[5] and are entitled to recoup their expenses in so doing from the company.[6] All business transacted at an EGM is 'special business'.

1 See *Keane* at paras **16.06–26.07**.
2 S 132(1) of the Principal Act.
3 Ibid. One shareholder with at least the same amount of shares may also requisition the meeting. See *Re Elsombrero Ltd* [1958] Ch 900.
4 To be held within 2 months of the date of requisition.
5 S 132(3) of the Principal Act.
6 Ibid s 132(5).

[13.06]   A general meeting cannot exist unless at least two members of the company are present.

Re London Flats Ltd [1969] 1 WLR 711 (Chancery Division)

[13.07]   The applicant and respondent were the only two members of the company. The existing liquidator having died the respondent proposed a resolution at a general meeting appointing himself as liquidator. The applicant walked out of the meeting before a vote could be taken. The respondent then purported to vote on the resolution and to appoint himself to the office of liquidator. The applicant subsequently sought an order declaring the respondent's apppointment invalid.

Plowman J: Was the respondent ever validly appointed liquidator? Under s 286(1) of the Companies Act 1948 the vacancy caused by Mrs Oppenheim's death could be filled by the company in general meeting and the question is: Was the respondent appointed by the company in general meeting? In my judgment, he was not, for the reason that at the moment when he was in the course of proposing himself as liquidator, the applicant left the meeting and from that moment there was only one member present and therefore no meeting. It is well settled that as a general rule a single shareholder cannot constitute a meeting . . . In the present case I can find no context which enables me to say that a meeting of one member is good enough.

It is true that in *In re Hartley Baird Ltd* [1955] Ch 143 Wynn-Parry J held on the construction of the company's memorandum and articles which were, I think so far as material, similar to those in the present case, that if a quorum was present at the beginning of a meeting the subsequent departure of a member reducing the meeting below the number required for a quorum does not invalidate the proceedings of the meeting after his departure. But the quorum in that case was 10 and the departure of one member still left nine, so that the point with which I am concerned did not arise. There the question was quorum or no quorum, while here it is meeting or no meeting . . In my judgment therefore, the respondent's purported appointment of himself as liquidator was a nullity.

Notes

See also *Sharp v Dawes* (1876) 2 QBD 26. To get around this problem s 131(3) of the Principal Act provides that where an AGM is called by the Minister he may, inter alia, direct that one member present in person or by proxy is to constitute a meeting. Further under s 135 the court may convene a general meeting of the company where it is impracticable to do so otherwise. In ordering the meeting to be convened the court may give such consequential directions as it thinks fit, including a direction that the presence of one member will suffice to constitute a meeting. See *Keane* at para **26.08**.

[13.08] The court will only convene a general meeting of the company under s 135 of the Principal Act where it is otherwise impracticable to convene it.

Angelis v Algemene Bank Nederland (Ireland) Ltd & Others (High Court, 4 July 1974)

[13.09] **Kenny J:** The plaintiff began these proceedings on the 24th June 1974 in which he claimed . . . an order under s 135 of the Companies Act 1963 directing the third named defendant to hold a meeting of the company and by motion of the 21st of June he applied for an order that the . . . third, fourth and fifth named defendants be ordered to assist the plaintiff in holding a meeting of the company or directing the same to be held . . .

It seems to me to be probable that the plaintiff agreed to resign as a director of the company and therefore he cannot convene a meeting of directors.

By letter dated 14th June 1974 he purported to convene a directors meeting for the 17th June 1974. If this be read as a requisition to call a meeting of the company, then it was clearly invalid because under s 132 of the Act of 1963 the directors have a period of 21 days within which to convene a meeting. Moreover a plenary summons was issued on the 24th June 1974 and that is less than 21 days from the letter of the 14th June. Section 135 of the Act of 1963 gives the court power to call a meeting of a company if it is impracticable to do so. I am not satisfied that it is impractible to call a meeting of the company. I think that the directors could without difficulty convene a meeting of the company. The requisition served on them to convene a meeting was invalid and they were not bound to act on it. Circumstances have not arisen in which the court should order a meeting of the company to be convened. As a receiver is in possession of the assets of the company I do not see what purpose would be served by holding a meeting of the company. The directors are of course free to convene a meeting at any time they think fit and will have to hold a meeting if members of the company holding not less than one tenth of the paid up share capital of the company serve a valid requisition on them to hold such a meeting . . .

Notes
See Getz *Court Ordered Company Meetings* (1969) 83 Conv 399.

Notice of meetings[1]

[13.01] At least 21 days notice[2] must be given of an AGM.[3] At least seven days notice of an EGM must be given in the case of a private or unlimited company, and 14 days notice must be given for a plc.[4] Meetings can be called by shorter notice only with the consent of the auditors and all the members who are entitled to attend and vote.[5] At least 21 days notice must be given of a general meeting at which a special resolution is to be proposed; and the notice must specify the intention to propose the resolution as a special resolution.[6] A special resolution may, however be proposed at a meeting called by shorter notice if a majority of the members entitled to attend and vote thereat and holding at least 90% of the voting shares so consent.[7]

1 See *Keane* at paras **26.09–26.12**.
2 By 'notice' is meant 'clear notice'. See art 51 of table A. A similar conclusion will be reached where the articles are silent on the matter. See *Re Hector Whaling Ltd* [1936] Ch 208; cf *Re Neil McLeod & Sons Ltd* (1967) 5 LT 46.
3 S 133(1)(a) of the Principal Act.
4 Ibid s 133(1)(*b*).
5 Ibid s 133(3).
6 Ibid s 141(1).
7 Ibid s 141(2).

A notice of a general meeting will be invalid if it fails to specify either the entire text or the entire substance of any resolution which is intended to be proposed as a special resolution.

Re Moorgate Mercantile Holdings Ltd [1980] 1 WLR 227 (Chancery Division)

[13.11] The company proposed to reduce its share capital by cancelling the share premium account. Notice was sent convening a general meeting at which a special resolution was to be proposed 'that the share premium account of the company amounting to £1,356,900.48 be cancelled'. The amount of the share premium account had been understated by £321.17 in the notice. The error was subsequently noticed and at the meeting a special resolution was passed 'that the share premium account of the company amounting to £1,356,900.48 be reduced to £321.17'. The court however, refused to confirm the reduction of capital on the ground that the special resolution had been passed on foot of an invalid notice.

[13.12] **Slade J:** I shall now attempt to summarise what are in my judgment the relevant principles relating to notices of and the subsequent amendment of special resolutions.

(1) If a notice of the intention to propose a special resolution is to be a valid notice for the purposes of s 141(2), it must identify the intended resolution which it is intended to propose. In the case of a notice of intention to propose a special resolution, nothing is achieved by the addition of such words as 'with such amendments and alterations as shall be determined upon at such meeting.'

(2) If a special resolution is to be validly passed in accordance with s 141(2) the resolution as passed must be the same resolution as that identified in the preceding notice; the phrase 'the resolution' in s 141(2) means 'the aforesaid resolution'.

(3) A resolution as passed can properly be regarded as 'the resolution' identified in a preceding notice even though, (*a*) it departs in some respects from the text of a resolution set out in such notice – for example by correcting those grammatical or clerical errors which can be corrected as a matter of construction, or by reducing the words to more formal language – or (*b*) it is reduced into the form of a new text, which was not included in the notice provided only that in either case there is no departure from the substance.

(4) However, in deciding whether there is complete identity between the substance of a resolution as passed and the substance of an intended resolution as notified, there is no room for the court to apply the de minimis principle or a 'limit of tolerance'. The substance must be identical. Otherwise the condition precedent to the validity of a special resolution as passed which is imposed by section 141(2) namely that notice has been given 'specifyng the intention to propose the resolution as a special resolution' is not satisfied.

(5) It necessarily follows from the above propositions that an amendment to the previously circulated text of a special resolution can properly be put

to and voted on at a meeting if, but only if, the amendment involves no departure from the substance of the circulated text in the sense indicated in propositions (3) and (4) above.

(6) References to notices in the above propositions are intended to include references to circulars accompanying notices. In those cases where notices are so accompanied, the notices and circulars can and should in my judgment, ordinarily be treated as one document.

(7) All the above propositions may be subject to modification where all the members of a class of members or a company unanimously agree to waive their rights to notice . . .

I would emphasise that these propositions are directed solely to special resolutions. Very different considerations may apply in the case of ordinary resolutions . . . In relation to special resolutions however, I think that my conclusions of principle accord not only with the wording of the Act of 1948 and with the authorities but also with the following considerations of public policy . . . It may, I think fairly be said that all the situations in which special resolutions are required are special situations, where the resolutions in question are by their nature likely either to affect the company's constitution or to have an important effect on its future . . . It is therefore . . . important that each shareholder should . . . have clear and precise advance notice of the substance of any special resolution which it is intended to propose, so that he may decide whether he should attend the meeting or is content to absent himself and leave the decision to those who do; the provisions imposed by s 141(2) of the Act of 1948 must be intended as much for the protection of the members who in the event decide to absent themselves as of those who decide to attend . . . If it were open to the members who did attend to propose and vote on a special resolution differing in substance albeit slightly from the resolution of which notice had been given, there would be a risk of unfair prejudice to those members who after due consideration had deliberately absented themselves . . .

I now turn to apply the seven propositions set out above to the facts of the present case. The qualifications referred to in the last of them are not relevant here, since not all members of the company entitled to vote threat were present at the meeting of 26 April 1979. While I have no reason to doubt that the amendment to the resolution was put to the meeting in good faith and on legal advice, it was in my judgment improperly put and voted on. Miss Arden accepted and I accept, the correctness of the advice given to Mr Silman on the facts that no shareholder who had made up his mind to vote on the resolution in its original form could reasonably have adopted a different view in regard to the amended form. For this reason I have a measure of sympathy with this petition. This point however, in my judgment is irrelevant to law. In my judgment, the crucial point is that the resolution which the meeting of 16 April 1979 approved was not the same resolution either in form or in substance as that of which the text had been circulated to shareholders in the notice of 2 April 1979.

355

There is no room for the application of any de minimis principle; a resolution to reduce the share premium account of a company to £321 could not even be deemed to be the same as a resolution to reduce it to £320.

In the circumstances the resolution was not in my judgment validly passed in accordance with s 141(2) of the Act of 1948. The court therefore has no jurisdiction to confirm the reduction of the share premium account as asked by this petition.

Notes

In *Roper v Ward* [1981] ILRM 408 resolutions were declared invalid by Carroll J. The notice convening the meeting at which the resolutions were passed was defective in that it did not give adequate notice of the general nature of the special business which was transacted.

In *Jackson v Munster Bank Ltd* (1884–85) 13 LR Ir 118 it was held by Chatterton VC that a company may be restrained from holding a general meeting where the notice convening it, or any accompanying circular is inaccurate and misleading.

A deliberate failure to give notice of a meeting to a person entitled to such notice, renders that meeting invalid. See *Musselwhite v CH Musselwhite & Son Ltd* [1962] Ch 964 where the plaintiffs had executed transfers of their shareholdings in the company. However, they still remained on the company's register of members as the holders of the shares. The directors deliberately omitted to give the plaintiffs notice of a general meeting on the mistaken belief that they were no longer members of the company. The plaintiffs succeeded in obtaining a declaration that they were still technically members and that the failure to give them notice rendered the meeting invalid.

However, standard form articles of association provide that an accidental omission to give notice to a member will not invalidate the meeting. See art 52 of table A.

[13.13] A unanimous decision of the members, even if informally reached, binds the company, unless it is ultra vires or illegal.

Re SM Barker Ltd [1950] IR 123 (High Court)

[13.14] Before the company was sold the only three directors and shareholders ('the Latchmans') resolved at an improperly convened meeting that the company should release debts owing by them. The company subsequently went into liquidation and the liquidator sought payment of the debts. His claim was rejected on the ground that the release by the company was valid and effective.

[13.15] **Gavan Duffy P:** It cannot be stressed too emphatically that on the evidence the three Latchmans were in truth the owners of the entire share capital, so that they were at liberty to do virtually whatever they chose, short of acting dishonestly or ultra vires . . .

Here was a small private company owned and controlled by a family group, who acted unanimously and in concert with the incoming members about to replace them at the September and October meetings; and what they did they did in good faith and in natural reliance for the technical mechanics of their operations and of the deal upon an accountant-auditor belonging to a firm of high repute. However improvident the resolution releasing Latchmans' indebtedness and however regrettable the failures to observe the requirements and the formalities of company law, quite beyond their ken, I think the outstanding fact is that fact that the true owners of the property acting with the full assent of their prospective assignees all concurred at the two meetings and throughout in every step taken. Consequently in my view, the company cannot through its liquidator make the Latchman shareholders liable in their capacity of directors for the value of the released debt . . .

Peter Buchanan Ltd v McVey [1954] IR 89

[13.16]   The defendant had been the holder of all bar one of the shares in the plaintiff company. The remaining share was held by the cashier and book-keeper of the company as the defendant's nominee. The two shareholders informally agreed to give part of the company's property to the defendant. The object of the disposition was to defeat the tax claims of the Scottish Revenue. The company subsequently went into liquidation and the liquidator issued proceedings to recover the property from the defendant. Both the trial judge (Kingsmill J) and the Supreme Court held that the informal decision to give the property to the defendant would have been effective as an act of the company save for the fact that it had been motivated by a dishonest desire (ie. to defraud the Scottish Revenue) and was void as being a distribution to a member out of capital rather than out of profits.

[13.17]   Kingsmill Moore J: Mr Leonard opening for the defence raised two points only. First, that the defendant was not liable to account as a shareholder and that what he did was quoad the company, unexceptionable . . . [This] point seems to me to admit of a relatively short answer. Admittedly the defendant received the moneys in his capacity as a shareholder and as such would not ordinarily be liable to account to the company. But the money was paid to him by means of cheques which he signed as director, or was paid to his use in pursuance of instructions issued by him as director. A director is in a fiduciary capacity and so is liable to account for his dealings with the property of the company over which he has control. The defendant is therefore prima facie, liable to account. He may be able to account satisfactorily if he shows that he was merely obeying the lawful commands of the company, his fiduciary and Mr Leonard says that this is what has happened and that accordingly even if the defendant should be liable to account he has discharged himself.

There was no formal meeting of the company to authorise the disposal of its property to the defendant, no resolution, however informal to that effect. It is now settled law that neither meeting nor resolution is necessary. If all the corporators agree to a certain course then, however informal the manner of their agreement, it is an act of the company and binds the company subject only to two pre-requisites: *In re Express Engineering Works Ltd* [1920] 1 Ch 466; *Parker and Cooper Ltd v Reading* [1926] 1 Ch 975.

The two necessary pre-requisites are, (1) that the transaction to which the corporators agree should be intra vires the company; (2) that the transaction should be honest: *Parker and Cooper Ltd v Reading* [1920] 1 Ch 466, per Astbury J, at pp 984, 985.

Mr Leonard submits that the transaction was intra vires the company and moreover (in the eyes of a court not administering Scots law) was honest. Mr Wilson for the plaintiffs, with a wealth of argument submitted it was neither . . .

No memorandum however specific, can sanction an act which is contrary to the provisions of the companies acts or to the fundamental principles of company law as laid down by the courts. One such principle which has been recognised from the earliest period of company law is that the power of a company to pay dividends or distribute its property is not unlimited. There are the interests of the creditors to be considered. A company may not save in certain exceptional cases and subject to special procedure, reduce its capital or return capital to its members. It may not make a distribution out of borrowed money. It may only distribute what can properly and commercially be regarded as profits . . . I do not overlook the fact that the assessment of the company did not take place till March 1945, after the distribution had been made and that an assessed tax does not involve any immediate liability till after the assessment has been made . . . But where such an assessment is pending and the basis of the assessment has been fixed by statute so that it is known within very narrow limits, it is impossible to contend that in computing what are the net profits legitimately available for distribution to shareholders such contingent liability can be ignored. To do so is clearly to defraud the creditors of the company who will find all its available assets and capital swallowed up by a priority rvenue claim. Accordingly it would appear that the agreement came to between the corporators was an agreement to distribute property otherwise than out of profits and so was to do an act ultra vires the company and was inoperative for that reason.

Does the agreement satisfy the second test of honesty? Mr Leonard and the defendant when giving evidence was quite open in admitting that the whole object of the transactions was to defeat the tax claims of the Scottish Revenue and that from the point of view of Scots law it was an agreement to work a fraud upon the Revenue.

Notes

See also *Re Fletcher Hunt (Bristol) Ltd* [1989] BCLC 109; *Re Oxted Motor Co* [1921] 3 KB 32; *Re Duomatic Ltd* [1969] 2 Ch 365; *Re Horsley Weight Ltd* [1982] 3 All ER 1045; *Cane v Jones* [1981] 1 WLR 1451.

Under s 141(8)(*a*) of the Principal Act it is provided that:–

'Notwithstanding anything to the contrary in this Act, in any case in which a company is so authorised by its articles, a resolution in writing signed by all the members for the time being entitled to attend and vote on such a resolution at a general meeting (or being bodies corporate by their duly appointed representatives) shall be as valid and effective for all purposes as if the resolution had been passed at a general meeting of the company duly convened and held and if described as a special resolution shall be deemed to be a special resolution with the meaning of this Act.'

This provision implements recommendations of the Jenkins Committee's Report (*Report of the Company Law Committee*) 1962, Cmnd 1749 at paras 460, 468(*d*), that the law on informal resolutions be clarified 'and that there should be an express provision . . . that a resolution in writing signed by or on behalf of all those who would have been entitled to vote upon it at a general meeting shall be equivalent to a special or ordinary resolution (as the case may require) passed by the appropriate majority at a general meeting convened by the appropriate notice.' See art 6 of part II of table A.

Does this mean, as *Ussher* suggests (op. cit at pp 73–78) that the older cases no longer represent good law and that an informal resolution will only be valid now if it is (*a*) expressly called a resolution; (*b*) is in writing, and (*c*) is signed by all members who are entitled to vote?

In any case where the members have informally and unanimously approved a resolution they may then be estopped from asserting the irregularity of any transaction implemented on foot of that transaction; Per Keane J *Re Greenore Trading Co Ltd* [1980] ILRM 94, 100.

Proceedings at meetings[1]

[13.18] For a meeting to be valid there must first be a proper quorum.[2] The chairman is typically appointed by the directors. Voting may be by person or by proxy and may be either by a show of hands or by way of a poll. Where voting is by a show of hands members have one vote each. As this may not fairly represent their shareholding in the company, members have a statutory right subject to certain restrictions[3] to demand a poll in which case the members will typically have one vote per share. Unless the articles provide otherwise, in the absence of an express and valid demand for a poll voting is on a show of hands. In *Re Credit Finance Bank plc* (unreported High Court, 9/6/89) Costello J held that it is permissible for a resolution to be decided on by a poll without having a show of hands first.

1 See generally *Keane* at paras **26.15–26.25** and arts 53–74 of part I of table A and art 5 of part II of table A.
2 As to which see s 134(*c*) of the Principal Act; art 54 of part I of table A and art 5 of part II of table A.
3 S 137 of the Principal Act and art 50 of table A.

[13.19]   Only those persons whose names are entered on the register of members are entitled to vote at a general meeting.

Kinsella and Others v Alliance and Dublin Consumers Gas Company and Others (High Court, 5 October 1982)

[13.20]   Voting rights of members of the company were governed by the Company Clauses Consolidation Act 1845 which provided that each member had one vote for each share held by him up to ten, one additional vote for every five shares beyond the first ten up to one hundred, and an additional vote for every ten shares held by him beyond the first one hundred shares. The plaintiff shareholders requisitioned an EGM to remove the directors of the defendant company. In order to increase their voting strength the plaintiffs transferred a number of shares to nominees. However, due to the volume of transfers and even taking on extra staff, the secretary of the defendant company was not physically able to register all the transfers prior to the EGM. The votes of all unregistered nominees having been disallowed at the EGM, the plaintiffs issued proceedings claiming that the proceedings at the EGM were invalid.

[13.21]   **Barron J:** The basic question raised in these proceedings is the stage at which a transferee of shares in the company becomes entitled to exercise his or her voting rights in respect of such shares. The plaintiffs say it is when the transfer of such shares is acknowledged by the secretary of the company to have been received by him. The defendant say it is when the stockholder is actually registered as a stockholder in the register of shareholders . . .

The provisions of the 1845 Act like any other document must be construed as a whole. I am of the view that they are quite clear. Persons entitled to stock must be registered in the register of shareholders. Until they are, they are not entitled to vote. This is a well established principle and I would be wrong not to follow it . . .

It follows from my decision on the question of voting that the meeting was a valid meeting. Only the votes of those entitled to vote were accepted whether in person or by proxy. The decision of the meeting was therefore in accordance with its constitution. The plaintiffs next submission is that nevertheless the chairman of the meeting should have adjourned the meeting to enable the transfers which had not been registered to be registered. His basic argument is that the true verdict of the stockholders of the company could not otherwise have been obtained.

This argument is one with which I have considerable sympathy on in practise rather than on a legal basis. The purpose of the meeting was to test voting strength. The agreement of the board to resign, if the first resolution was determined against them, shows this. Accordingly, when it became apparent that the real purpose of the meeting was not going to be achieved, it would have been in keeping with the intention of the parties that the meeting should have been adjourned to enable the transfers to have been registered so that all the transferees could vote at the meeting.

Nevertheless, the chairman of the meeting had no obligation to adjourn the meeting, nor could he have done so if the majority was against it. The meeting was entitled to proceed on the basis of the register of shareholders as it then existed. In my view, the failure of the board to put the question of an adjournment to the meeting is a matter of comment, it does not affect the validity of the meeting or of what took place at it . . .

The meeting was properly held on the basis of the register of shareholders as it then existed. I accept that the secretary of the company has a reasonable time in which to register transfers received by him. In the present case, all reasonable efforts were made to register transfers and the failure to register them is not a ground on which the plaintiffs are entitled to rely.

In this case, the plaintiffs are not entitled to the relief they seek. This does not however mean that they are not entitled to call a further extra-ordinary general meeting with a similar order of business to that of the meeting of the 10th September 1982.

Minutes of meeting

[13.22]   Under s 145 of the Principal Act the minutes, when signed by the chairman constitute prima facie evidence of what happened at the meeting. Importantly, they also then raise a rebuttable presumption that the meeting was duly held and convened, that all proceedings of the meeting were duly conducted and that all appointments of directors or liquidator's made thereat are valid.

Chapter 14

MAJORITY AND MINORITY RIGHTS

INTRODUCTION

[14.01]   Where a wrong has been done to the company, the proper plaintiff is, subject to certain exceptions, the company itself and not individual shareholders.[1] This is known as the rule in *Foss v Harbottle*.[2] However, if the wrong has been done to a member's personal rights then it is the member as opposed to the company who may bring proceedings. Where the wrong done to the member relates to the internal management of the company he may also, in appropriate circumstances, (discussed below) seek relief under s 205 of the Principal Act.

1 See generally *Keane* chapter 28.
2 (1843) 2 Hare 461.

The rule in Foss v Harbottle[1]

[14.02]   Where a wrong has been done to the company which could validly be ratified or forgiven by a majority of the members in general meeting, the proper plaintiff is the company itself.

1 See generally MacCann *The Rule in Foss v Harbottle; Recent Developments* (1990) 8 ILTR (n.s.) 68 and *Keane* at paras **28.09** and **28.10**.

Foss v Harbottle (1843) 2 Hare 461 (Court of Chancery)

[14.03]   Two shareholders of 'The Victoria Park Company' brought proceedings against the directors (who were also shareholders in the company) claiming that the directors had fraudulently misapplied certain of the company's property. An order was sought compelling the directors to either return the property in question or alternatively to make good the losses suffered by the company as a result of their wrongdoing. It was held that the plaintiffs had no locus standi to bring the proceedings.

[14.04]   **Wigram VC:** The first objection taken in the argument for the defendants was, that the individual members of the corporation cannot in

363

any case sue in the form in which this bill is framed. During the argument I intimated an opinion, to which upon further consideration I fully adhere, that the rule was much too broadly stated on the part of the defendants. I think there are cases in which a suit might properly be so framed. Corporations like this, of a private nature are in truth little more than private partnerships; and in cases which may easily be suggested it would be too much to hold that a society of private persons associated together in undertakings which, though certainly beneficial to the public, are nevertheless matters of private property, are to be deprived of their civil rights inter se, because in order to make their common objects more attainable the crown or the legislature may have conferred upon them the benefit of a corporate character. If a case should arise of injury to a corporation by some of its members, for which no adequate remedy remained, except that of a suit by individual corporators in their private characters, and asking in such character the protection of those rights to which in their corporate character they were entitled, I cannot but think that . . . the claims of justice would be found superior to any difficulties arising out of technical rules respecting the mode in which corporations are required to sue.

But on the other hand, it must not be without reasons of a very urgent character that established rules of law and practice are to be departed from – rules which though in a technical sense are founded on general principles of justice and convenience; and the question is, whether a case is stated in this bill, entitling the plaintiffs to sue in their private characters . . .

Whilst the supreme governing body, the proprietors at a special general meeting assembled, retain the power of exercising the functions conferred upon them by the act of incorporation, it cannot be competent to individual corporators to sue in the manner proposed by the plaintiffs on the present record. This in effect purports to be a suit by cestui que trust, complaining of a fraud committed or alleged to have been committed by persons in a fiduciary character. The complaint is, that those trustee have sold lands to themselves ostensibly for the benefit of the cestui que trusts. The proposition I have advanced is, that although the act should prove to be voidable the cestui que trusts may elect to confirm it. Now, who are the cestui que trusts in this case? The corporation in a sense, is undoubtedly the cestui que trust; but the majority of the proprietors at a special general meeting assembled, independently of any general rules of law upon the subject, by the very terms of the incorporation in the present case, has power to bind the whole body and every individual corporator must be taken to have come into the corporation upon the terms of being liable to be so bound. How then can this court act in a suit constituted as this is, if it is to be assumed for the purposes of argument, that the powers of the body of the proprietors are still in existence and may lawfully be exercised for a purpose like that I have suggested? Whilst the court may be declaring the acts complained of to be void at the suit of the present plaintiffs, who in fact may be the only proprietors who disapprove of them, the governing body of proprietors may defeat the decree by lawfully resolving upon the confirmation of the very acts which are the subject of the suit. The very fact that the governing body of proprietors assembled at the special general meeting may so bind even a reluctant minority is decisive to show that the frame of this suit cannot be sustained whilst that body retains its functions.

Duggan v Bourke and Others (High Court, Costello J 30 May 1986)

[14.04] Bye-law 97 of the Bank of Ireland required directors within two months of appointment to purchase a qualifying number of shares and to have their names entered in the register of members in respect of those shares. Failure to do so would result in the directors being deemed to have automatically vacated their office. The defendants were appointed as directors of the bank in March 1978 and although they bought the requisite shares, they inadvertently failed to have their names entered in the register of members. This error was discovered in February 1983 and was immediately rectified. The plaintiff, a shareholder in the bank, issued proceedings seeking an order that the defendants account for remuneration received by them under their service contracts during the period from May 1978 to February 1983 (ie when their appointment as directors was defective).

[14.05] **Costello J:** At the end of the plaintiff's case, Mr O'Neill on behalf of the defendants applied for a non-suit. The principal basis on which this application was brought was reliance on the well known case and the principle decided in it of *Foss v Harbottle* . . . In my view, the defendants are entitled to rely on the case to which I have referred and in my view they are entitled to a non-suit . . .

I do not think this action is concerned, as the plaintiff seems to think it is, with an ultra vires act in relation to the payments. This action is concerned with the failure of the defendants the individual defendants, to repay the bank and the failure of the bank to take steps to require this repayment.

It seems to me that if the bank were not to sue the defendants, the defendants would be fully entitled to claim that, notwithstanding the invalidity of their appointment, they are entitled to be remunerated on a quantum meruit basis. The authority for this case is *Craven-Ellis v Canons Ltd* [1936] 2 KB 403 . . . It seems to me that it would be well within the powers of the stockholders to determine that a reasonable remuneration would be what was in fact paid to them and it would be well within the powers of the court of directors to determine that a reasonable remuneration payable to the four first-named defendants would be the remuneration and benefits which they in fact received.

In these circumstances it seems to me that it is unnecessary for this court now to make any findings of fact as to whether or not the payments which were made were made in respect of the defendants as holders of the office of director or as executive director. Even if they were, and not as is claimed in the defence and in the letter to which I have referred the payments could be validated in the way I have described. In my view there would be nothing ultra vires the company or the office of director in deciding if they so wished to do that the directors who had received payments during the period that a technical invalidity existed should be entitled to retain these sums.

In these circumstances it seems to me that the plaintiff has failed to establish that he has brought himself within the exception to the rule in *Foss v Harbottle*. In fact what the plaintiff is seeking to do is to get an order of the court to compel in one way or another, the defendants to refund to the company the moneys which they have been paid in the period to which I have referred. In my view that is just the sort of action which the rule in *Foss v Harbottle* expressly prohibits.

I agree with the view expressed in the case to which I was referred by both Mr O'Neill and the plaintiff, that the court must look to see that the rule in *Foss v Harbottle* is not applied so that an injustice is done . . . In my view no injustice was done in this case and there is no injustice done to the plaintiff as an individual. I cannot agree that the plaintiff has got any status as an individual who has suffered loss as a result of what has happened. There would be an injustice done to the four directors if this claim was permitted.

The irregularity that occured inadvertently. It was of a purely technical kind in that the four directors had in their beneficial ownership the requisite number of shares but had not through inadvertence got themselves on the register as registered proprietors of this stock. In these circumstances the company would be fully entitled to decide either that bye-law 97 was an effective remedy or that on the facts the sums received by the four defendants were received as salary as executive directors of the company or that the four defendants were entitled to quantum meruit and that this should be based upon the sums they received.

In these circumstances there is no case made out to justify an order directing the company to hold a meeting for the purpose that the plaintiff now suggests and no case has been made out to justify the court departing from the principle in *Foss v Harbottle* so as to make any of the other orders which the plaintiff seeks, and I will dismiss this action.

[14.06]   The rule in *Foss v Harbottle* applies only to wrongs done to the company. It has no application where the personal rights of a member have also been infringed.

Pender v Lushington (1877) 6 Ch D 70 (Court of Chancery)

[14.07]   A portion of the plaintiff's shareholding was registered in his own name, the remainder being registered in the names of certain nominees. In breach of the provisions of the articles the chairman refused to count the votes of the nominees at a general meeting. Consequently, a resolution which had been proposed by the plaintiff and which would otherwise have been carried, was lost. The plaintiff issued proceedings in his own name and in the name of the company, for an injunction to restrain the directors from acting on the basis that the nominees' votes were bad.

[14.08]   Jessel MR: In all cases of this kind, where men exercise their rights of property, they exercise their rights from some motive adequate or inadequate and I have always considered the law to be that those who have the rights of property are entitled to exercise them, whatever their motives may be for such exercise. [His Lordship then held that the nominees as registered shareholders were 'members' and accordingly their votes should have been counted. He continued:]

I now come to the subordinated question not very material in the view I take of the case, namely whether you have the right plaintiffs here. The plaintiffs may be described as three, though they are really two. There is, first, Mr Pender himself on behalf of himself; next, as the representative of the class of shareholders who voted with him, whose votes I hold to have been properly rejected; and next, there is the Direct United States Cable Company. It is said that the company ought not to have been made plaintiffs.

The reasons given were reasons of some singularity, but there is no doubt of this, that under the articles the directors are the custodians of the seal of the company, and the directors, who in fact are defendants, have certainly not given any authority to the solicitor for the plaintiffs on this record to institute this suit in the name of the company as plaintiffs. It is equally clear, if I am right in the conclusion to which I have come as to the impropriety of the decision of the chairman in rejecting these votes, that it is a case in which the company might properly sue as plaintiffs to restrain the directors from carrying out a resolution which had not been properly carried and then comes the question whether I ought or ought not to allow the company to remain as plaintiffs.

The first point to be considered is this: supposing there was no objection to the right of a general meeting to direct an action to be brought, could I even in that case allow the company to sue? I think I could. In that case the general meeting having a right to direct an action to be brought would act by the majority of the members. The majority wish their rights to be protected. A meeting could be called and if the court was satisfied that the majority would direct an action to be brought the company's name would not be taken away . . . But what is the court to do in the meantime, if it satisfied that a real majority [would decide] in favour of bringing an action? Surely, it must do something in the meantime and it follows, I think, from that portion of the judgment, that in the meantime the court ought to grant the injunction to keep things in statuo quo . . . I think I ought not on this summons to take away the name of the company, but to let the summons stand over, leaving either party to call a meeting to decide whether the company's name is to be used or not. In the meantime, whether this is an action in the name of the shareholders or in the name of the company in either case I think there should be an injunction . . .

But there is another ground on which the action may be maintained. This is an action by Mr Pender for himself. He is a member of the company and whether he votes with the majority or the minority he is entitled to have his vote recorded – and individual right in respect of which he has a right to sue. That has nothing to do with the question like that raised in *Foss v Harbottle* and that line of cases. He has a right to say, 'Whether I vote in the majority or minority, you shall record my vote, as that is a right of property belonging to my interest in this company and if you refuse to record my vote I will institute legal proceedings against you to compel you.' What is the answer to such an action? It seems to me it can be maintained as a matter of substance and that there is no technical difficulty in maintaining it . . .

Notes
   Cf *MacDougall v Gardiner* (1875) 1 Ch D 13.

Edwards v Haliwell [1950] 2 All ER 1064 (Court of Appeal)

[14.09]   A trade union's rules required that any increase in member's subscriptions be approved by a two thirds majority in a ballot of members. In breach of the rules, a decision was taken to increase subscriptions at a meeting of union delegates. The plaintiffs, as members of the union, sought a declaration that the decision to increase the subscription rule was invalid.

[14.10]   **Jenkins LJ:** The rule in *Foss v Harbottle* as I understand it, comes to no more than this. First, the proper plaintiff in an action in respect of a wrong alleged to be done to a company or association of persons is prima facie the company or the association of persons itself. Secondly, where the alleged wrong is a transaction which might be made binding on the company or association and on all its members by a simple majority of the members, no individual member of the company is allowed to maintain an action in respect of that matter for the simple reason that, if a mere majority of the members of the company or association is in favour of what has been done, then *cadit quaestio*. No wrong has been done to the company or association and there is nothing in respect of which anyone can sue. If, on the other hand, a simple majority of members of the company or association is against what has been done, then there is no valid reason why the company or association itself should not sue. In my judgment, it is implicit in the rule that the matter relied on as constituting the cause of action should be a cause of action properly belonging to the general body of corporators or members of the company or association as opposed to a cause of action which some individual member can assert in his own right.
   The cases falling within the general ambit of the rule are subject to certain exceptions. It has been noted in the course of argument that in cases where the act complained of is wholly ultra vires the company or association the rule has no application because there is no question of the transaction being confirmed by any majority. It has further been pointed out that where what has been done amounts to what is generally called in these cases a fraud on the minority and the wrongdoers are themselves in control of the company,

the rule is relaxed in favour of the aggrieved minority who are allowed to bring what is known as a minority shareholders' action on behalf of themselves and all others. The reason for this is that, if they were denied that right, their grievance could never reach the court because the wrongdoers themselves being in control would not allow the company to sue. Those exceptions are not directly in point in this case, but they show, especially the last one that the rule is not an inflexible rule and it will be relaxed where necessary in the interests of justice.

There is a further exception which seems to me to touch this case directly. That is the exception noted by Romer J in *Cotter v National Union of Seamen* [1929] 2 Ch 58. He pointed out that the rule did not prevent an individual member from suing if the matter in respect of which he was suing was one which could validly be done or sanctioned not by a simply majority of the members of the company or association, but only by a special majority as, for instance, in the case of a limited company under the Companies Act, a special resolution duly passed as such. As Romer J pointed out, the reason for that exception is clear, because otherwise, if the rule were applied in its full rigour, a company which, by its directors had broken its own regulations by doing something without a special resolution which could only be done validly by a special resolution could assert that it alone was the proper plaintiff in any subsequent action and the effect would be to allow a company acting in breach of its articles to do de facto by ordinary resolution that which according to its own regulations could only be done by special resolution. That exception exactly fits the present case inasmuch as here the act complained of is something which could only have been validly done, not by a simple majority, but by a two thirds majority obtained on a ballot vote. In my judgment, therefore, the reliance on the rule in *Foss v Harbottle* in the present case may be regarded as misconceived on that ground alone.

I would go further. In my judgment, this is a case of a kind which is not even within the general ambit of the rule. It is not a case where what is complained of is a wrong done to the union, a matter in respect of which the cause of action would primarily and properly belong to the union. It is a case in which certain members of a trade union complain that the union, acting through the delegate meeting and the executive council in breach of the rules by which the union and every member of the union are bound, has invaded the individual rights of the complainant members, who are entitled to maintain themselves in full membership will all the rights and privileges appertaining to that status so long as they pay contributions in accordance with the tables of contributions as they stood before the purported alterations of 1943, unless and until the scale of contributions is validly altered by the prescribed majority obtained on a ballot vote. Those rights, these members claim have been invaded. The gist of the case is that the personal and individual rights of membership of each of them have been invaded by a purported but invalid alteration of the tables of contributions. In those circumstances, it seems to me the rule in *Foss v Harbottle* has no application at all, for the individual members who are suing, not in the right of the union, but in their own right to protect from invasion their own individual rights as members . . .

Evershed MR and Asquith LJ delivered concuring judgments.

Notes

In *Clark v Workman* [1920] 1 IR 107 the court treated as a breach of an individual membership right, the election of a chairman by the shareholders rather than by the directors as was required by the articles. A similar classification was given in *Hennessy v National Agricultural & Industrial Development Association* [1947] IR 139 to the requirement for a quorum under the articles.

The court is not however, always willing to classify a wrong as one done to the shareholder. In *Mosley v Alston* (1847) 1 Ch 790, for example, the directors in breach of the terms of the articles failed to retire by rotation. The plaintiff shareholders sought an injunction restraining the defendants from acting or voting as members of the board. The court, applying the rule in *Foss v Harbottle* non-suited the plaintiffs on the basis that the wrong was one done to the company alone. Notably, the Supreme Court of Victoria has since disapproved of and declined to follow this decision, classifying the failure of the directors to retire as a breach of individual membership rights to have the company administered in accordance with the articles: *Kraus v JG Lloyd Pty Ltd* [1965] VR 232. See also *Breckland Group Holdings Ltd v London & Suffolk Properties Ltd* (1988) 4 BCLC 542 and Baxter *Irregular Company Meetings* [1976] JBL 323 and *The Role of the Judge in Enforcing Shareholder Rights* [1983] CLJ 96.

[14.11] Where a wrong has been done to the company, an individual shareholder cannot bring a personal action in respect of the consequent reduction in the value of his shareholding.

O'Neill v Ryan, Ryanair and Others (High Court, 24 November 1989)

[14.12] This was a motion brought by the third to sixth named defendants to have the plaintiffs action stayed on the basis that it disclosed no reasonable cause of action and in addition that if a cause of action was disclosed, it was not maintainable by the plaintiff personally. The plaintiffs claim against the first and second named defendants was for damages for breach of contract and wrongful dismissal from the second named defendant. The allegation made against the fourth to sixth named defendants was that they had been engaged in anti-competitive conduct in breach of arts 85 and 86 of the EEC Treaty and that this had resulted in damage to the second named defendants. It was claimed by the plaintiff that as a result the value of his shareholding in the second named defendant had been reduced in value and that consequently he was entitled to be compensated for this loss.

[14.13]   **Lynch J:** Counsel for the last four defendants (the moving parties) submitted that the plaintiff's claim against them was only as a shareholder in the second defendant and accordingly having regard to the rule in *Foss v Harbottle* to the effect that an individual shareholder cannot bring an action that should properly be brought if at all by the company the claim did not lie at the suit of the plaintiff. Counsel further submitted that although arts 85 and 86 of the Treaty had direct effect in Irish law and must therefore be enforced by Irish courts, nevertheless the articles should be enforced in the same manner and subject to the same limitations as would apply to an analagous claim under Irish national law. Consequently the rule in *Foss v Harbottle* should be applied to claims based on alleged breaches of arts 85 and 86 as much as to claims based on alleged tortious conspiracy . . .

Counsel for the plaintiff (the respondent in the motion) submitted that the plaintiff is entitled as a natural person to seek to enforce arts 85 and 86 of the Treaty and that the limitations of the rule in *Foss v Harbottle* did not apply to such a claim especially where as he alleges in this case, the breaches of the articles caused damage to himself. Counsel further submitted that the plaintiff was entitled to maintain his claim for damages for conspiracy causing loss and damage to himself and also for the declarations as claimed in the statement of claim. Counsel submitted that the jurisdiction to make declarations such as those sought in the statement of claim was much more widely accepted in Ireland than in the United Kingdom and that the plaintiff therefore is entitled to prosecute a claim for such declarations . . .

[T]he plaintiff's claim against the last four defendants is made solely as a shareholder in the second defendant for relief in respect of alleged wrongful conduct of the last four defendants (together with the first defendant in certain respects) causing damage to the second defendant and thereby to the plaintiff by reducing the value of the plaintiff's shareholding in the second defendant. The plaintiff's former status as chief executive of the second defendant has nothing to do with this claim: it is as shareholder only and not as a former officer of the second defendnat that the plaintiff claims against the last four defendants.

In order to test the validity of the plaintiff's claim against the last four defendants it is appropriate to consider what would necessarily follow if it is valid. A holder of 100 shares in a very large public company trading internationally throughout Europe with a capital of one hundred million shares would be entitled to maintain an action against one or more other companies large or small if he honestly believed that such other company or companies were seeking to limit his company's international trade by unfair means contrary to the competition rules of the European Community and/or by conspiring so to do. Many such actions could be brought by individual shareholders even though the directors of the allegedly wronged company for reasons that seemed to them to be commercially valid, did not consider that any such action should be brought by the company at all.

It was submitted however on behalf of the plaintiff that the rule in *Foss v Harbottle* does not apply to a cause of action based on a breach by other parties of the competition rules of the Treaty causing damage to the company in which the plaintiff is a shareholder. It cannot be doubted but that it is

371

the duty of national courts to enforce and give effect to directly applicable provisions of the Treaty such as competition rules and in particular arts 85 and 86 . . . It is therefore clear that I must give effect to arts 85 and 86 of the Treaty but it is also well settled that effect must be given by the national courts in like circumstances and subject to like limitations as would be applied by the national courts to an analagous cause of action in national law, it being clearly understood however, that no limit which would wholly or substantially negative the enforcement of articles 85 and 86 in Irish law could be applied . . . The rule in *Foss v Harbottle* does not wholly or substantially negative the effectiveness or enforceability of arts 85 and 86 in Irish law. Breaches of those articles can be challanged by the company which is the victim of the breaches. The rule merely prohibits persons who are not directly affected by the breaches from maintaining an action which is more properly to be maintained if at all, by the company in which such persons are shareholders. The desirability of avoiding a multiplicity of actions perhaps in many cases contrary to the will of the directors and/or the majority of shareholders is obviously a major factor in the thinking underlying the rule in Foss v Harbottle and demonstrates the sound sense of that thinking.

I am of the opinion that the plaintiff's present action against the last four defendants is a classic case to which the rule in *Foss v Harbottle* applies and I accordingly dismiss the plaintiff's action as against the last four defendants.

Notes

How is this case to be reconciled with *PMPS & Moore v AG* [1984] ILRM 88 which allowed a shareholder to take a personal action to protect his constitutional property rights in his shareholding? See MacCann *The Rule in Foss v Harbottle, Recent Developments* (1990) 8 ILT (ns) 68.

[14.14] A company cannot ratify an act which is illegal or ultra vires, and any attempt to do so will entitle an individual shareholder to sue on behalf of the company instead.

Cockburn v Newbridge Sanitary Steam Laundry Company [1915] 1 IR 237

[14.15] The managing director of the company, Llewelyn, had paid bribes to officials of the War Office in order to secure contracts for the company. Two of the shareholders brought an action against him for the repayment of the amount of the bribes to the company. Llewelyn contended that any proceedings should have been in the name of the company, and that as the majority of shareholders were not disposed to institute proceedings, the plaintiffs should be allowed to sue.

[14.16] O'Brien LC: The plaintiffs who hold a large number of shares in the company, but not a preponderating amount, seek to make Llewelyn account, or more simply, to pay to the company the money which he has received and which he refuses to pay.

The Master of the Rolls came to the only conclusion that a court could come to, that, as between Llewelyn and the company there could be no answer to the action if the company had been the plaintiffs, but he was pressed by and yielded to, the argument that in substance this was merely an attempt to enforce by a member of a company a claim against a director which the company might lawfully and reasonably refuse to enforce; that accordingly the question was one merely relating to the 'internal management' of the company and therefore that a shareholder could not invoke the aid of the court against the will of the company and compel Llewllyn to account to the company.

There is no doubt as to the attitude of the company, because they appeared by counsel and insisted that the action must be dismissed as this was only a matter in which the proper tribunal to decide the question was the company itself.

There is of course, no doubt if this was merely a matter of 'internal management' the decision of the court below could not be disturbed and the sole question that we have to determine is whether on the peculiar facts of this case this is a question of merely 'internal management'.

The rule of law and of good sense laid down in *Foss v Harbottle* is indisputable, but it is subject to the exception that where the acts complained of are of a fraudulent character, or beyond the powers of the company, the action may be maintained by a shareholder suing on behalf of himself and the other shareholders, the company being made a defendant in the action . . .

Illegality and ultra vires are not interchangeable terms, but it is difficult if not impossible, to conceive a case in which a company can do an illegal act, the illegality arising from public policy and act within its powers.

Dealing with a case not of this class but of ultra vires unaffected by criminality, Lord Cairns says in *Ashbury Railway Carriage & Iron Co v Riche* LR 7 HL 653 at p 672: 'But, my Lords, if the shareholders of this company could not ab ante have authorised a contract of this kind to be made, how could they subsequently sanction the contract after it had, in point of fact, been made . . . It appears to me that it would be perfectly fatal to the whole scheme of legislation to which I have referred, if you were to hold that in the first place, directors might do that which even the whole company could not do, and that then, the shareholders finding out what had been done, could sanction subsequently what they could not antecedently have authorised.'

How much stronger is the position where the whole matter is tainted with criminality. The real agreement which it is suggested the directors did make in this case would have been an agreement, if made, so tainted with crime and so subversive of public policy as to be illegal in itself. It would, accordingly have been quite beyond the powers of the company to have entered into it, nor could any memorandum or articles have given it power; it would be equally wrong for the company to ratify it and it would be idle to give them an opportunity to vote on such a question, because the carrying of the resolution would be, in my judgment, nugatory as being illegal and consequently wholly outside the powers of the company. To do a thing which would have for its main object either the commission of a crime or the aiding or abetting of a crime, or the hushing up of a crime could not be in any way within the powers of a company and a matter of 'internal management' in which the court should not interfere . . .

In the view that I take of the case it would not be within the power of the company either to make, ratify or adopt a proceeding of the scandalous character sought to be cloaked over in the present case by such a resolution.

The appearance of the company and the arguments of the counsel, are sufficient in my judgment to justify the court in holding that the plaintiffs are entitled to direct relief in the present case and that an account should be directed against the defendant Llewellyn in respect of the moneys which the company earned by these contracts and which he either received or ought to have received.

Holmes LJ delivered a concurring judgment. Moriarty LJ concurred.

Notes

See also *Buchanan Ltd v McVey* and *Russell v Wakefield Waterworks Co* (1875) LR 20 Eq 474. Under s 8(2) of the Principal Act the shareholder may apply to restrain an ultra vires act. In *Hennessy v National Agricultural and Industrial Development Association* [1947] IR 159 it was held that a shareholder also has locus standi to apply for a declaration that particular acts are ultra vires.

[14.17] Minority shareholders may bring an action on behalf of the company where the majority shareholders have perpetrated a 'fraud' on the company so as to benefit themselves. This is commonly known as a 'fraud on the minority'.

Menier v Hooper's Telegraph Works (1874) 9 Ch App 350 (Court of Appeal in Chancery)

[14.18] Hooper's Telegraph Works was the majority shareholder in the European Telegraph Co Menier, a minority shareholder, claimed that Hoopers had used its votes as majority shareholder to procure the transfer of the assets of the European Telegraph Co, (including a particular lucrative contract) to Hoopers. The Court of Appeal (affirming the decision of Bacon VC) held that Menier was entitled to bring a minority shareholder's action to set aside the transaction.

[14.19] **James LJ:** The defendants, who have a majority of shares in the company have made an arrangement by which they have dealt with matters affecting the whole company, the interest in which belongs to the minority as well as to the majority. They have dealt with them in consideration of their obtaining for themselves certain advantages. Hooper's company have obtained certain advantages by dealing with something which was the

374

property of the whole company. The minority of the shareholders say in effect that the majority has divided the assets of the company, more or less, between themselves to the exclusion of the minority. I think it would be a shocking thing if that could be done, because if so the majority might divide the whole assets of the company and pass a resolution that everything must be given to them and that the minority should have nothing to do with it. Assuming the case to be as alleged by the bill, then the majority have put something into their pockets at the expense of the minority. If so, it appears to me that the minority have a right to have their share of the benefits ascertained for them in the best way in which the court can do it and given to them.

It is said, however, that this is not the right form of suit, because according to the principles laid down in *Foss v Harbottle* and other similar cases the court ought to be very slow indeed in allowing a shareholder to file a bill where the company is the proper plaintiff. This particular case seems to be precisely one of the exceptions referred to by the Vice-Chancellor Wood in *Atwool v Merryweather* (1867) LR 5 Eq 464n, a case in which the majority were the defendants, the wrongdoers, who were alleged to have put the minority's property into their pockets. In this case it is right and proper for a bill to be filed by one shareholder on behalf of himself and all the other shareholders.

Sir G Mellish LJ delivered a concurring judgment.

Notes

See also *Cooks v Deeks* [1916] AC 554; *Alexander v Automatic Telephone Co* [1900] 2 Ch 56; and *Estmanco (Kilner House) Ltd v Greater London Council* [1982] 1 WLR 2.

[14.20] Negligence on the part of the majority shareholders constitute a 'fraud on the minority' if it has the effect of conferring a benefit on the majority at the expense of the company itself.

Daniels v Daniels [1978] Ch 406 (Chancery Division)

[14.21] Two directors, Mr and Mrs Daniels, who were also the majority shareholders of the company, caused the company to sell part of its property to Mrs Daniels at a gross undervalue. The plaintiff's who were minority shareholders, sought to have the transaction set aside. The defendants brought an application to strike out the proceedings as disclosing no cause of action. The application was dismissed by Templeman J.

[14.22] Templeman J: The authorities which deal with simple fraud on the one hand and gross negligence on the other do not cover the situation which arises where, without fraud, the directors and majority shareholders are guilty of a breach of duty which they owe to the company and that breach of duty not only harms the company but benefits the directors. In that case it

375

seems to me that different considerations apply. If minority shareholders can sue if there is fraud, I see no reason why they cannot sue where the action of the majority and the directors, though without fraud, confers some benefit on those directors and majority shareholder themselves. It would seem to be quite monstrous – particularly as fraud is so hard to plead and difficult to prove – if the confines of the exception to *Foss v Harbottle* were drawn so narrowly that directors could make a profit out of their negligence. Lord Hatherley LC in *Turquand v Marshall* LR 4 Ch App 376 opined that shareholders must put up with foolish or unwise directors. Danckwerts J in *Pavlides v Jensen* [1956] 1 Ch 565 accepted that the forbearance of shareholders extends to directors who are 'an amiable set of lunatics'. Examples ancient and modern, abound. To put up with foolish directors is one thing, to put up with directors who are so foolish that they make a profit of £115,000 odd at the expense of the company is something entirely different. The principle which may be gleaned from *Alexander v Automatic Telephone Co* [1900] 2 Ch 56 (directors benefiting themselves), from *Cook v Deeks* [1916] 1 AC 554 (directors diverting business in their own favour) and from dicta in *Pavlides v Jensen* [1956] 2 Ch 565 (directors appropriating assets of the company) is that a minority shareholder who has no other remedy may sue where directors use their powers intentionally or unintentionally fraudulently or negligently in a manner which benefits themselves at the expense of the company.

Notes

Where the negligence does not result in a benefit to the majority shareholders, the rule in *Foss v Harbottle* will apply, thus preventing an individual shareholder from suing: *Pavlides v Jensen* [1965] Ch 565.

[14.23]   In exceptional circumstances, where the justice of the case requires it, an individual may be permitted to sue on behalf of the company in respect of a ratifiable wrong which has been done to it.

Moylan v Irish Whiting Manufacturers Ltd (High Court, 14 April 1980)

[14.24]   The plaintiff had been a 'director' and 'chairman' of the defendant company. Following a disagreement with the other 'directors' a resolution was proposed at the next AGM calling for all directors to retire and seek re-election. All other 'directors' were re-elected individually. The plaintiff however, was not re-elected. It transpired during the course of evidence that none of the 'directors' had been validly appointed prior to the AGM as they had all been collectively appointed, in breach of s 181 of the Principal act. The plaintiff claimed that all proceedings at the AGM were invalid due to the fact that proper notice had not been given.

[14.25]   **Hamilton J:** While there may have been certain deficiencies in the notice convening the meeting, such as failure to comply with the requirements of clause 49 of table A and irregularities in the manner in which the meeting was conducted, it is quite clear that the majority of the shareholders gave their approval to the course adopted at the meeting and the decisions reached at the said meeting and the first question I have to consider is whether I have any jurisdiction to interfere with the conduct by 'the company' of its internal affairs.

In the course of his judgment in *MacDougall v Gardiner* [1875] 1 Ch 13, 21 Jones LJ stated:–

'I think that it is of the upmost importance in all these companies that the Rule which is well known to this court as the rule in *Mozley v Alston* and *Lord v Copper Miners Co* and *Foss v Harbottle* should be always adhered to; that is to say that nothing connected with internal disputes between the shareholders is to be made the subject of a bill by some one shareholder on behalf of himself and others unless there by something illegal, oppressive or fraudulent – unless there is something ultra vires the company qua company or on the part if the majority of the company so that they are not fit persons to determine it; but that every litigation must be in the name of the company if the company really desire it.'

In the course of his judgment in *Burland v Earle* [1902] AC 83, Lord Davey stated at page 93 that:–

'It is an elementary principle of the law relating to joint stock companies that the court will not interfere with the internal management of companies acting within their powers and in fact has no jurisdiction to do so . . . The cases in which the minority can maintain such an action are, therefore, confined to those in which the actions complained of are of a fraudulent character or beyond the powers of the company'.

In *Russell v Wakefield Watertanks Ltd* (1875) LR 20 Eq 474, Sir George Jessell MR stated:–

'But this is not a universal rule, that is, it is a rule subject to exceptions and the exceptions depend very much on the necessity of the case, that is the necessity for the court doing justice . . . the rule is not an inflexible rule and it will be relaxed where necessary in the interests of justice.'

In *Heything v Dupont* [1964] 1 WLR page 854 Court of Appeal Harmon LJ stated:–

'There are cases which suggest that the rule is not a right one and that an exception will be made where the justice of the case demands it.'

Having regard to the provisions of Bunreacht na h-Eireann I am satisfied that an exception to the rule must be made when the justice of the case demands it.

Does the justice of this case require that I abandon what has been described as 'an elementary principle of the law relating to joint stock companies that the court will not interfere with the internal management of companies acting within their powers and in fact has no jurisdiction to do so?

377

While the plaintiff may with a certain degree of justification feel he has been unfairly treated by his former co-directors the second, third and fourth named defendants, that is not to say that there has been anything illegal, oppressive or fraudulent in their actions and I so find.

Was their action and the action of the 'company' ultra vires the company? Their action could, in my opinion, only be ultra vires the company if on the 6th day of February 1975 he was duly appointed director of 'the company' and not due to retire on rotation.

It appears to me that all the resolutions appointing directors of 'the company' passed at the annual general meetings of the company held on the 9/11/1970, 15/3/1972, and the 24/1/1974 whereby directors were elected collectively were void having regard to the provisions of s 181 of the Companies Act 1963.

Consequently I am not satisfied that the plaintiff was at the date of the annual general meeting on the 6th day of February 1975 a duly appointed director of the company not due to retire on rotation. It follows that I am not satisfied that the actions of the defendants were in anyway ultra vires the company.

I do not consider that the circumstances of this case and the plaintiff's complaints with regard to the procedures adopted by the defendants before and at the annual general meeting are such as to justify the court in interfering with matters which relate to the internal management of the company.

Notes
Cf *Prudential Assurance Co v Newman Industries* (No 2) [1982] Ch 204.

The derivative action

[14.26] If the minority shareholder can bring himself within one of the exceptions to the rule in *Foss v Harbottle*, he may proceed against the wrongdoers by way of 'derivative action'. If the action is successful judgment is made in favour, not of the minority shareholder who is only a nominal plaintiff, but rather in favour of the company itself.

[14.27] The plaintiff minority shareholder may be entitled to an indemnity in respect of his costs out of the company's assets if the court is of the opinion that an independent board of directors would have authorised the issue of proceedings by the company itself.

Smith v Croft [1986] BCLC 207 (Chancery Division)

[14.28] The company's business (the provision of completion guarantees for films) was dependent on the skill and reputations of its directors. It was alleged however that the directors had paid themselves excessive remuneration and had made improper claims for expenses. An investigation by an independent firm of accountants found no evidence to substantiate these

378

allegations. Nonetheless, the plaintiffs minority shareholders commenced a derivative action against the directors in respect of the alleged breaches of duty. The directors held the majority of shares in the company. The remaining shareholders were divided as to whether the proceedings should be continued. WT Ltd, the largest shareholder independent of the directors, opposed the action. A preliminary issue came before the court as to whether the Master of the High Court was correct in ordering that the company should indemnify the plaintiffs with respect to their costs.

[14.29] **Walton J:** In these proceedings, the plaintiffs, following a procedure suggested and sanctioned by the judgment of the Court of Appeal in *Wallersteiner v Moir* (No 2) [1975] 1 All ER 849, applied ex parte to the master for an order that the company itself (on whose behalf ultimately the action is brought) should indemnify them against their own costs of the action and any costs which they might, if the action failed, be ordered to be paid by them, down to the conclusion of discovery and inspection of documents . . . It is, for course, not for me to question the correctness of the decision of the Court of Appeal in *Wallersteiner v Moir* but I may observe that the justice of an order which may throw upon a company which in the event, is proved to have no cause of action whatsoever against the other defendants, who may prove to be completely blameless, the entire costs of an action which it did not wish to be prosecuted is extremely difficult to comprehend. The real injustice of the situation lies in the encouragement which the Court of Appeal gave to the application for such an order being made at the commencement of the action, at a time when of necessity, the plaintiffs believe that they had a good case and will, with hand on heart swear that they have and before the completion of discovery and inspection which may well show that their beliefs, though honestly enough held are not in fact well founded. It is to be observed that in *Wallersteiner v Moir* the application was made at a late stage in the proceedings after Mr Moir (who was the plaintiff by counterclaim) had already substantially succeeded, but who had no power and shot left to finish the battle. The manifest justice of such an order in favour of a person in such a position is plain enough . . . Now it seems to me that in a normal case the order should most definitely not be made ex parte. This procedure can only lead to an appeal like that which has taken place before me against the making of the order, whereas it would obviously be far more satisfactory for all concerned that the application should be dealt with in one. It is, of course, tempting to compare an application of this nature to a *Re Beddoe's* application, although the analogy is far from exact . . . In a *Re Beddoe's* application, the trustee, who is typically a wholly independent person with no axe of any description to grind, who has, or thinks he has a cause of action vested in him, obtains leave from the court to bring the action at the expense of the trust estate. The beneficiaries concerned are joined and basically whether or not the action proceeds is determined by a majority vote of the beneficiaries, by which the minority are bound. Even when the proposed defendant is himself a beneficiary so that his voice is not to be counted, he is always made a party, allowed to be present and to address any arguments he may wish to the court: see *Re Moritz* [1959] 3 All ER 767. Nor ultimately, will any injustice be done to him by the fact that assets in which he is interested are used to finance an action against him if he wins all necessary and proper orders in relation to the costs can be made including in a proper case, an order that no part of the cost of bringing the action should be thrown upon his share of the assets.

In the case of a *Wallersteiner v Moir* application there is no such possibility of subsequent rectification of injustice: by how much the more then, must it be quite clear that in the normal case, (one can deal with an abnormal case, where it arises) it must be right that, as in the *Re Moritz* type of application the company should be joined and able to lay what facts it wishes to lay before the court . . .

The next question which arises then is, what part or parts of the plaintiffs evidence filed on the summons should the company be allowed to see? [His lordship proceeded to state that the company was entitled to see the affidavits and exhibits] . . . All such evidence should be disclosed to the company save to the extent that it consists of matters covered by legal professional privilege (this will always extend to counsel's opinion) or where there is some other excellent reason for this being held back. In the present case, for example, there had appeared that most repellent feature of modern society, the mole; it might well have been right for the identity of the plaintiffs' sources of information to have been kept secret, lest the leak of unauthorised documents ceased. Similarly, any evidence tending to show that the company or those in control, were taking steps to destroy documents cover their tracks or matters of a like nature.

Apart from such matters, examples of which will readily spring to mind, where withholding from discovery can be fully justified on the grounds that discovery would stultify the success of the action, it appears to me that everything ought to be disclosed. Unless it has been so disclosed how is the company to be in a position to lay facts which will have the effect of demolishing the plaintiffs' case before the court? And if the company is not in a position to lay such facts before the court, where they exist, it will be being condemned to considerable penalties unheard. This would be palpably unjust since as I repeat, the injustice could not thereafter be rectified . . .

I may also add that the procedure which I adopt is in the best interests of the minority shareholders . . . It would be unfortunate in the extreme if, in reliance of a *Wallersteiner v Moir* order, plaintiffs in a minority shareholders' action had gone all the way to judgment and then found out that there was in fact such a fatal flaw in what they had confidently expected would be a complete protection against costs . . .

That having been done the situation appears to me to become one very close to the situation in the old days when the Chancery Court was dealing with motions. Of course there is no room for a mini-trial, of course the court has no ability at this stage to decide the truth of the plaintiffs' allegations. What however, it can and should do is to look at all the facts, firstly those which are common ground then those alleged by the plaintiffs but denied by the company, and then those alleged by the company but denied by the plaintiffs and make up its mind. The standard suggested by Buckley J was that of an independent board of directors exercising the standard of care which prudent businessmen would exercise in their own affairs. Would such an independent board consider that it ought to bring the action? [His Lordship referred to the allegations which had been made against the directors and to the fact that no evidence of impropriety could be found by the investigating accountants.]

Consider what, using the criterion already established a completely independent board would have done when faced with an allegation of, putting it in its most general form, financial irregularities. It would surely, have called in the services of a completely independent firm of accountants to investigate and report. It would also, if it could have afforded to do so, as the company here clearly could do, have called in the services of an eminent firm and Peat Marwick Mitchell are clearly among the leading firms in their field. They would then have awaited the report after making it clear to that firm that they were to have the fullest possible free hand to investigate all matters which they considered relevant, as happened in this case. And when they had received that report, they would then have guided their future conduct accordingly. The report having indicated that there was nothing to pursue, they would surely not have pursued it.

It appears to me that, on this simple basis alone, although there is far more to it than the master's original order cannot possibly be justified and must be set aside . . .

There are however, certain wider considerations which might very well have motivated a genuinely independent board if the report had left the questions doubtful. Basically this turns on the fact that this is a company with no goodwill: it secures business through the contacts and personality of its executives . . . The volume of business is crucial and the great success of the present board has lain in obtaining a vastly increased volume of business for the company . . . The proof of the pudding lies in the eating: the present board has pushed up the value of the company's shares and the dividend payable quite dramatically . . . The company and all its shareholders have benefitted greatly from the efforts of the present board, even if the shareholders were to take the view that the directors had been extremely well paid for their efforts. Could it possibly be the view of an independent board of directors that this success should be jeopardised by the commencement of such an action as the present one which (*a*) in any event would have the effect of tying up an extremely large part of the time of the members of the board, when they might be required urgently elsewhere to deal with the monitoring of film production, which takes place all over the world: and (*b*) might well have the effect of causing the company to lose the services of its key executive? This would indeed, be what was accurately described in *Prudential Assurance Co Ltd v Newman Industries Ltd (No 2)* [1982] Ch 204 as killing the company by kindness.

This must be a matter of impression but it seems to me that any well advised independent board would very probably come to the conclusion that the benefits to the company of retaining the services of the relevant executives far outweighed any long term benefit to be obtained by pursuing any such action even if wholly well-founded . . .

But this is by no means the end of the matter . . . The position is that WT Ltd is the subsidiary of an extremely well-known reputable long established financial institution, which provides a range of merchant banking services, and which has over a period in excess of 25 years specialised in the provisions of loan monies, by way of loan or equity capital to unquoted companies . . . It is, I think quite clear from the evidence on this point that WT Ltd does indeed support the executive directors throughout but for the important reason that, in its view, 'without them our investment would be valueless'. That is a view which WT Ltd or its holding company has formed and as I have already indicated it appears to me an eminently reasonable and practical conclusion, obviously one taken in the best interests of WT Ltd itself.

In these circumstances I see no reason whatsoever when considering whether a *Foss v Harbottle* action has any real prospect of success not to take into account the views of by far the largest shareholder in the company. Accordingly, it appears to me quite clear that this is certainly an action which even if it is allowed to proceed at all should not be allowed to proceed against the express wish of the holders of the majority of the independently held shares at the expense of the company . . .

Notes

See also *Jaybird Group Ltd v Greenwood* [1986] BCLC 319, and *Prudential Assurance Co Ltd v Newman Industries Ltd* (No 2) [1982] Ch 204.

[14.30]   Where a majority of shareholders, independent of the defendants are opposed to the litigation, the plaintiff shareholder may be debarred from proceeding with the derivative action.

Smith v Croft (No 3) [1987] BCLC 355 (Chancery Division)

[14.31]   For the background to the case see para **14.28**. Subsequent to the decision of Walton J on the issue of the indemnity as to costs, an application was made by the defendants for an order dismissing the plaintiff's case as disclosing no reasonable cause of action or as being frivolous and vexatious. Upon a review of the facts it was found that the defendants had been guilty of conduct which was not only ultra vires but also involved the company in giving financial assistance for the purchase of its own shares, in breach of the English equivalent of s 60 of the Principal Act. The defendants held 62.5% of the issued shares. However, of the other shareholders, WT Ltd which held 19.66% and was by far the largest independent shareholder opposed to the action.

[14.32]   Knox J: The questions of law can be formulated as follows.

(1) Is a minority shareholder always entitled as of right to bring and prosecute an action for the company to recover money paid away in the course
of a transaction which was ultra vires the company or is the prosecution of
such an action susceptible of coming with the rule in *Foss v Harbottle* so
that there can be circumstances in which the court will not allow it to
continue?

(2) If the latter view is the correct one in relation to those categories of
claims based on ultra vires transactions, and also in all cases of minority
shareholders actions to recover money for the company in respect of acts
which consititute a fraud on the minority, will the court pay regard to the
views of the majority of shareholders who are independent of the defendants to the action on the question whether the action should proceed? . . .
Another way of putting the question is to ask whether if a minority has
been the victim of a fraud entitling the company in which they are shareholders to financial redress, the majority within that minority can prevent
the minority within that minority from prosecuting the action for redress.
The usual reason in practice for wanting to abandon such an action is that
there is far more to lose financially by prosecuting the right to redress than
by abandoning or not pursuing it, and that view will be reinforced in the
minds of those who wish to abandon the claim if their opinion is that it is a
bad claim anyway.

The third question which arises is whether in this case WT Ltd should be
treated as independent, if the views of an independent majority are relevant? That is a question of fact . . .

Upon the first question of law which arises, in my judgment the solution is
to be found by a correct analysis of the rights which the minority shareholder
is seeking to exercise or enforce in relation to the result of an ultra vires
transaction. There was no dispute before me but that any individual
shareholder, be he in a minority or not, has a personal right to apply to the
court to restrain a threatened action which if carried out would be ultra vires.
Neither the right to object to such an action nor the shareholder's locus
standi to bring proceedings admits of any doubt. The rule in *Foss v Harbottle*
poses no obstacle, because neither of the two bases for the rule is applicable,
that is to say the matter is not, by definition a mere question of internal management nor is the transaction capable of ratification by or on behalf of the
company . . . The difficulty arises in this case when one considers not the
restraint of an illegal or ultra vires transaction but the recovery on behalf of
the company of money or property which the company is entitled to claim as
the result of the ultra vires transaction . . . Treating the matter as a question
of principle for the moment, when a minority shareholder seeks to enforce a
right of the company to claim compensation for a past ultra vires transaction
there are two quite separate rights involved. First, there is the minority
shareholder's right to bring proceedings at all and secondly, that is the right
of recovery which belongs to the company but is permitted to be asserted on

its behalf by the minority shareholder . . . But as Lord Davey said in *Burland v Earle* the plaintiffs cannot have a larger right to relief than the company itself would have if it were plaintiff. And from that it follows in my judgment that if there is a valid reason why the company should not sue it will equally prevent the minority shareholders from suing on its behalf. He is therefore liable to be defeated on two points, first by any ground preventing him from exercising his procedural remedy, and secondly by any ground preventing the company from exercising its substantive right . . . Where ultra vires transactions are involved the number of grounds upon which the company can be debarred from suing is limited. In particular it was not argued that ratification of the ultra vires transction, by however large a majority of shareholders, could prevent the company from suing. There is however, a clear difference in principle between ratifying what has invalidly done in the past and abandoning, compromising or not pursuing rights of action arising out of a past ultra vires transaction, and I see no reason in principle why in appropriate circumstances the latter should not intervene to prevent the prosecution of a suit on behalf of the company in relation to such rights of action . . .

I turn now to the question whether it is right for the court to have regard to the views of the majority inside a minority which is, I assume for his purpose, in a position to bring an action to recover on behalf of the company in respect of breaches of duty by persons with overall control.

The fourth defendant and the company claim that it is; the plaintiffs claims that it is not. On the plaintiffs' view of the matter all that the court is concerned with, in cases where the exception to the rule in *Foss v Harbottle* based on frauds on the minority applies, is the single question whether the defendants have control. The issue is highlighted by the conflicting interpretations placed by the parties on what the Court of Appeal said in *Prudential Assurance v Newman Industries (No 2)*. Immediately after the formulation of the two matters which in the Court of Appeal's view a plaintiff ought at least to be required to show before proceeding with a minority shareholder's action there comes the following sentence ([1982] Ch 204 at 222):

'On the latter issue it may well be right for the judge trying the preliminary issue to grant a sufficient adjournment to enable a meeting of shareholders to be convened by the board, so that he can reach a conclusion in the light of the conduct of and proceedings at that meeting.'

Counsel for the plaintiffs submitted that the purpose of that adjournment was to enable the courts to discern whether the defendants had control. I reject that submission. In my judgment the concern of the Court of Appeal in making that statement was to secure for the benefit of a judge deciding whether to allow minority shareholder's action on behalf of company to go forward what was described as the commercial assessment whether the prosecution of the action was likely to do more harm than good or as it was put originally by counsel for Newman Industries, to kill the company by kindness (see [1982] Ch 204 at 221). The whole tenor of the Court of

Appeal's judgment was directed at securing that a realistic assessment of the practial desirability of the action going forward should be made and should be made by the organ that had the power and ability to take decisions on behalf of the company. Also the question of control pure and simple hardly admitted of any doubt in that particular case . . .

Ultimately the question which has to be answered in order to determine whether the rule in *Foss v Harbottle* applies to prevent a minority shareholder seeking relief as plaintiff for the benefit of the company is: 'Is the plaintiff being prevented improperly from bringing these proceedings on behalf of the company?' If it is an expression of the corporate will of the company by an appropriate independent organ that is preventing the plaintiff from prosecuting the action he is not improperly but properly prevented and so the answer to the question is No. The appropriate independent organ will vary according to the constitution of the company concerned and the identity of the defendants who will in most cases be disqualified from participating by voting in expressing the corporate will.

Finally on this aspect of the matter I remain unconvinced that a just result is achieved by a single minority shareholder having the right to involve a company in an action for recovery of compensation for the company if all the other minority shareholders are for disinterested reasons satisfied that the proceedings will be productive of more harm than good. If the argument of counsel for the plaintiffs is well founded, once control by the defendants is established the views of the rest of the minority as to the advisability of the prosecution of the suit are necessarily irrelevant. I find that hard to square with the concept of a form of pleading originally introduced on the ground of necessity alone in order to prevent wrong going without redress.

I therefore conclude that it is proper to have regard to the views of independent shareholders. In this case it is common ground that there would be no useful purpose served by adjourning to enable a general meeting to be called. For all practical purposes it is quite clear how the votes would be cast. [His Lordship having noted that WT Ltd was opposed to continuing the action, continued:]

There is no sufficient evidence that in relation to the present question whether these proceedings should continue, WT Ltd trust has reached its conclusion on any grounds other than reasons genuinely thought to advance the company's interests. It is not for me to say whether the decision itself is right or wrong. It is for me to say whether the process by which it was reached can be impugned and I hold that it cannot. Nor do I consider that in the circumstances there is shown to have been a substantial risk of WT Ltd's vote having been cast in order to support the defendants as opposed to securing the benefit of the company.

That conclusion means that I accede to the fourth defendant's and the company's motions and direct that the statement of claim be struck out. Before parting with the case I should like to say a further word about the procedure.

First, I consider there may well be a much stronger case for requiring a prospective plaintiff to have the onus of establishing that this case falls within the exceptions to the rule in *Foss v Harbottle* or outside it altogether than there is for putting the same onus on him to show that the company would be likely to succeed if it brought the action. On the latter it might well be appropriate to apply the usual test under RSC O 18, r 19 and the inherent jurisdiction which puts the onus on the defendants to show the case is effectively unarguable.

Second, I consider it would be highly desirable for applications in respect of costs under *Wallersteiner v Moir (No 2)* [1975] 1 All ER 849, procedure to be made at the same time as the plaintiff establishes whatever it is that he does have to establish. A great deal of expense has been caused in this case by the piecemeal way in which the matter has proceeded.

Third I believe that it would be helpful for there to be specific procedure laid down whether by way of rules of court or practice direction I know not, for the initiation and prosecution of actions by minority shareholders to recover on behalf of a company.

Notes

See also *Smith v Croft (No 2)* [1987] BCLC 206. Where the wrong in question is the allotment of shares to the defendants so as to give them a voting majority in general meeting and but for the allotment the plaintiff would have had a majority then it is unnecessary to convene a general meeting to consider the views of the shareholders before commencing the derivative action: *Nash v Lancegaye Safety Glass (Ireland) Ltd* (1958) 92 ILTR 11.

Alternative remedy in case of oppression

[14.33]   Under s 205 of the Principal Act, (which was broadly modelled on s 210 of the English Companies Act 1948) it is provided that 'any member of a company who complains that the affairs of the company are being concluded or that the powers of the directors of the company are being exercised in a manner oppressive to him or any of the members (including himself), or in disregard of his or their interests as members, may apply to the court' for relief.[1] Unlike s 205, relief could only be granted under s 210 of the 1948 Act where the circumstances would also justify winding up the company on the 'just and equitable ground.'[2] In England, relief is now available under s 459–461 of the Companies Act 1985 in respect of conduct which is 'unfairly prejudicial'.

1 See generally *Keane* at paras **28.11** et seq.
2 As to which see chapter 23 infra and s 213(*f*) of the Principal Act.

[14.34]   S 205 is primarily designed to protect minority shareholders who are being oppressed by the majority. It may be used in addition to or as an alternative to the derivative action. Under s 205(3) the court is given a discretion to 'make such order as it thinks fit whether directing or prohibiting any act or cancelling or varying any transaction or for regulating the conduct of the company's affairs in future, or for the purpose of the shares of any members of the company by other members of the company or by the company and in the case of a purchase by the company, for the reduction accordingly of the company's capital or otherwise'. If the order includes an alteration of the company's memorandum or articles, then any further amendment which is inconsistent therewith, cannot be made, except by leave of the court.[1] Despite the obvious width of the courts discretion under the section, the order most commonly made is for the purchase of the petitioner's shareholding by the wrongdoers at the value at which they would have stood, but for the oppressive conduct.[2]

1 S 205(4) of the Principal Act.
2 *Ussher* has advanced a more imaginative use of the section by the courts in granting relief. See (1979–80) DULJ 92.

[14.35] Although only a member of the company can petition for relief under s 205, where his complaint is of oppression, the oppression need not have been suffered qua member, but in some other capacity, such as director or creditor.

Re Murph's Restaurant Ltd [1979] ILRM 141

[14.36] There were three equal shareholders and directors in the company, Brian Suiter (the petitioner), Kevin O'Driscoll and G Murph O'Driscoll. The company had been run on an informal manner with no dividends declared. All profits of the company were distributed as various forms of director's remuneration. The O'Driscolls gave the petitioner notice of a general meeting at which his dismissal from the board was to be proposed. Although the meeting was never held, the O'Driscolls informed the petitioner that he was being relieved of his responsibilities as a working director and was being offered three months salary in lieu of notice. The petitioner applied to have the company wound up under s 213(*f*) on the just and equitable ground. The company sought to restrain the petitioner from advertising the petition on the ground that it was not presented in good faith and that proceedings under s 205 would be more appropriate. The injunction was refused on the grounds that the petition was presented in good faith and that s 205 only applied to oppression suffered qua member. The petitioner subsequently amended his petition to claim relief in addition under s 205. At the trial of the action Gannon J held that although the O'Driscoll's conduct had been undoubtedly oppressive the types of relief available under s 205 would not bring to an end the matters complained of by the petitioner. The judge therefore ordered that the company be wound up on the just and equitable ground.

[14.37] Gannon J: it is quite clear from the evidence taken as a whole and from practically every aspect of evidence relating to the different events and the conduct of the affairs of this company that Brian, Kevin and Murph were equal partners in a joint venture and that the company was no more than a vehicle to secure a limited liability for possible losses and to provide a means of earning and distributing profits to their best advantage with minimum disclosure. The company was never conducted in accordance with statutory requirements nor in accordance with normal regular business methods. The directors received no fees, the shareholders received no dividends and all three directors' shareholders received by mutual agreement exactly the same income from the earnings of the company adjusted according to profitability in the form of drawings recorded as salary, drawings from cash unrecorded, credit deposits of cash in building societies' accounts, perquisites of meals and cars and various expenses for purely personal purposes, in respect of all of which strict equality was always maintained. This was achieved and could be achieved, only by a relationship of mutual confidence and trust and active open participation in the management and conduct of the affairs of the company particularly in the irregularity or informality of its corporate quality of existence . . . So far as the company is concerned he appears to have no more than 800 shares of nominal value of £1 upon which no dividends are payable with no right to offer them to the public or to dispose of them save in accordance with the approval of one or both of the other two directors. It is said that he remains a director but without fees, and is being and will be denied any active participation in the affairs of the company. He is being and has been treated by his two co-directors as if he was an employee of theirs liable to be and purported to have been dismissed by them peremptorily and not under any colour of regular exercise by directors of their powers under the articles of association of the company. The action of Kevin and Murph was entirely irregular and no attempt has been made to take or confirm this action in a regular manner on behalf of the company. The action of Kevin and Murph . . . was not and could not be accepted in law as an action of the company. The action of Kevin and Murph . . . was a deliberate and calculated repudiation by both of them of that relationship of equality, mutuality, trust and confidence between the three of them which constituted the very essence of the existence of the company. The action of Kevin and Murph . . . deprived Brian of a livelihood and not simply of an investment which he was induced by their representations to take and in so doing to abandon to his irretrievable loss a secure means of livelihood in a career for which, judging by his progress, he must have had some considerable aptitude. The justification offered by evidence for the action of Kevin and Murph . . . was their dissatisfaction with his performance of duties allotted to him by them which they described as of a working director. But the evidence shows that the matters of exemplification are all within the normal range of duties of a manager, and related to a branch of the business from which two successive managers were replaced during the period to which their complaints related. Their own evidence also shows that during the same period the business of that branch had shown profitability beyond their expectations . . . Whatever cause of complaint Kevin or Murph may have found in Brian it did not relate to the talents or qualifications which he had shown . . .

In his petition Brian asks that the company be wound up under s 213(*f*) and (*g*) of the Companies Act 1963. In reply Kevin and Murph on behalf of the company submit that Brian has been deprived of his directorship for good reason and as a shareholder can be afforded sufficient relief under s 205 of the Act by allowing them to purchase his shares at a valuation. It is also submitted that it would not be in the best interests of the company to have it wound up, simply because, in the course of compulsorily winding up, the assets of the company would not meet the liabilities and Brian could gain nothing from it, and because his interest as a shareholder has not been affected he is not entitled to an order under s 213. As to the matter of his removal from directorship I am satisfied from the evidence that the reasons advanced are neither good nor sufficient and are wholly inadequate to justify that action. But the evidence further discloses that the purported removal was irregular and ineffective in law. Furthermore it is clear from the evidence that in the conduct of the affairs of the company the directors did not exercise their powers in a regular manner so far as the company is concerned, and the purported exclusion of Brian by Kevin and Murph in an irregular and arrogant manner is undoubtedly oppressive . . .

It is clear from the evidence that there is no form of order of the nature indicated in s 205(3) which could bring to an end the matters complained of by Brian in the proceedings or which could regulate the affairs of the company for the future. It appears to me that the circumstances in which by order under s 205 the court may direct the purchase of the shares of a member by other members or by the company are circumstances in which the court would do so with a view to bringing to an end the matters complained of by the person applying to the court. It is my opinion that in this case with the fundamental relationship between Brian, Kevin and Murph sundered that proceedings under s 205 would not in any circumstances be appropriate.

In the course of argument and submissions I was referred to the judgment of the House of Lords in England in *Ebrahimi v Westbourne Galleries Ltd* [1973] AC 360 in support of the claim of the petitioner Brian to have the company wound up on the grounds that such order would be just and equitable. It was relied upon also in answer to the contentions of the company, per Kevin and Murph, that Brian is not entitled to such an order on the grounds that there was no disregard of his interests as a member, that he had nothing to gain as a contributory, that there was no lack of probity or unfair dealing on their part, that their conduct was based on their concern for the welfare of the company and to ensure that business would prosper and that it would not be in the best interests of the company, its staff, customers or creditors that it be wound up.

The claim before the House of Lords was by one of three directors/ shareholders of a limited company for an order to have the company wound up pursuant to s 222(*f*) of the English Companies Act 1948, the wording of which corresponds exactly with s 213(*f*) of the Companies Act 1963. I find the opinions delivered in the course of his judgment in the House of Lords very helpful because of the statement of principle the application of which depends upon the facts under consideration. I have accordingly, set out first the facts in the case before me from which it can be seen where they may be distinguishable from those in the case to which the House of Lords judgments relates. But that judgment reminds us that the principles of equity which are applicable in every court of law are the same and should be given application in the like manner in cases affecting the commercial relations of companies, in which rules of law tend to be technical and rigid, as much as in cases of personal relations between private individuals.

Having regard to the contentions advanced on behalf of Kevin and Murph I think it appropriate to quote the following passage from the report of the speech of Lord Wilberforce in *Ebrahimi v Westbourne Galleries Ltd* [1973] AC 360:

'For some 50 years following a pronouncement by Lord Cottenham LC [*Spackman, ex parte* (1849) 1 Mac and G 170, 174] in 1849 the words 'just and equitable' were interpreted so as only to include matter *ejusdem generis* as the preceding clauses of the section, but there is now ample authority for discarding this limitation. There are two other restrictive interpretations which I mention to reject. First, there has been a tendency to create categories or headings under which cases must be brought if the clause is to apply. This is wrong. Illustrations may be used but general words should remain general and not be reduced to the sum of particular instances. Secondly, it has been suggested and urged upon us, that (assuming the petitioner is a shareholder and not a creditor) the words must be confined to such circumstances as to affect him in his capacity as shareholder. I see no warrant for this either. No doubt, in order to present a petition he must qualify as a shareholder, but I see no reason for preventing him from relying upon any circumstances of justice or equity which affect him in his relations with the company or in a case such as the present with the other shareholders.

One other signpost is significant. The same words 'just and equitable' appear in the Partnership Act 1892 s 25 as a ground for dissolution of a partnership and no doubt the considerations which they reflect formed part of the common law of partnership before its codification. The importance of this is to provide a bridge between cases under s 222(f) of the Act of 1948 and the principles of equity developed in relation to partnerships (at p 374).'

Before proceeding further with consideration of the speech of Lord Wilberforce it would be helpful to refer at this stage to what was said by Lord Cross of Chelsea:

'In some of the reported cases in which winding up orders have been made those who opposed the petition have been held by the court to have been guilty of a "lack of probity" in their dealings with the petitioners (at p 383).'

He then cites two examples and then goes on to say:

'but it is not a condition precedent to the making of an order under the subsection that the conduct of those who oppose its making should have been unjust or inequitable. This was made clear as early as 1905 by Lord McLaren in his judgment in *Symington v Symington's Quarries Ltd* (1905) 8F 121, 130. To the same effect is the judgment of Lord Cozens-Hardy Mr in *Yenidje Tobacco Co Ltd, In re* [1916] 2 Ch 426, 431–432. It is sometimes said that the order in that case was made on the ground of "deadlock". That is not so.'

Having explained why he takes that view he goes on to say:

'People do not become partners unless they have confidence in one another and it is of the essence of the relationship that mutual confidence is maintained. If neither has any longer confidence in the other so that they cannot work together in the way originally contemplated then the relationship should be ended – unless, indeed, the party who wishes to end it has been solely responsible for the situation which has arisen. The relationship between Mr Rothman and Mr Weinberg [the names of parties in the case under his then consideration] was not, of course, in form that of partners, they were equal shareholders in a limited company. But the court considered that it would be unduly fettered by matters of form if it did not deal with the situation as it would have dealt with it had the parties been partners in form as well as in substance.'

Turning again to the speech of Lord Wilberforce I draw attention to the nature of the submissions made to the court in that case as summarised in the speech of Lord Wilberforce and the manner in which he expressed his opinion on these matters following examination of a number of cases dealing with the partnership features of companies. He then says:

'My Lords, in my opinion, these authorities represent a sound and rational development of the law which should be endorsed. The foundation of it all lies in the words "just and equitable" and if there is any respect in which some of the cases may be open to criticism it is that the court may sometimes have been too timorous in giving them full force. The words are a recognition of the fact that a limited company is more than a mere legal entity, with a personality in law of its own; that there is room in company law for recognition of the fact the behind it or amongst it there are individuals with rights, expectations and obligations inter se which are not necessarily submerged in the company structure. That structure is defined by the Companies Act and by the articles of association by which shareholders agree to be bound. In most companies and in most contexts, this definition is sufficient and exhaustive, equally so whether the company is large or small. The "just and equitable" provision does not as the respondents suggest, entitle one party to disregard the obligation he assumes by entering a company, nor the court to dispense him from it. It

391

does as equity always does, enable the court to subject the exercise of legal rights to equitable considerations, considerations that is, of a personal character arising between one individual and another, which may make it unjust or inequitable to insist on legal rights or to exercise them in a particular way (at p 379).'

Lord Wilberforce then gives examples of circumstances in which relations of a special personal character may be essential to the members of a company with particular reference to mutual confidence. He then goes on to say:

'My Lords, this is an expulsion case, and I must briefly justify the application in such cases of the just and equitable clause. The question is, as always, whether it is equitable to allow one (or two) to make use of his legal rights to the prejudice of his associate(s). The law of companies recognises the right, in many ways, to remove a director from the board. S 184 of the Companies Act 1948 confers this right upon the company in general meeting whatever the articles may say. Some articles may prescribe other methods; for example, a governing director may have the power to remove (compare in *Wondoflex Textiles Pty Ltd, In re* [1951] VLR 458). And quite apart from removal powers, there are normally provisions for retirement of directors by rotation so that their re-election can be opposed and defeated by a majority or even by a casting vote. In all these ways a particular director-member may find himself no longer a director, through removal or non-election; this situation he must normally accept, unless he undertakes the burden of proving fraud or mala fides. The just and equitable provision nevertheless comes to his assistance if he can point to and prove some special underlying obligation of his fellow member(s) in good faith or confidence, that so long as the business continues he shall be entitled to management participation, an obligation so basic that, if broken the conclusion must be that the association must be dissolved. And the principles on which he may do so are those worked out by the courts in partnership cases where there has been exclusion from management (see *Const v Harris* (1824) Tur and Rus 496, 525) even where under the partnership agreement there is a power of expulsion (see *Blisset v Daniel* (1853) 10 Hare 493; Lindley on *Partnership* 13th ed (1971) pp 331, 595) (at p 380).'

I make one final quotation from this speech which concludes as follows:

'I must deal with one final point which was much relied on by the Court of Appeal. It was said that the removal was, according to the evidence of Mr Nazar, bona fide in the interests of the company; that Mr Ebrahami had not shown the contrary; that he ought to do so or to demonstrate that no reasonable man could think that his removal was in the company's interest. This formula 'bona fide in the interests of the company' is one that is relevant in certain contexts of company law and I do not doubt that in many cases decisions have to be left to majorities or directors to take which the courts must assume had this basis. It may, on the other hand, become little more than an alibi for a refusal to consider the merits of the case and in a situation such as this it seems to have little meaning other than "in the interests of the majority". Mr Nazar may well have persuaded himself, quite genuinely that the company would be better off without Mr Ebrahami, but if Mr Ebrahami disputed this or thought the same with reference to Mr Nazar, what prevails is simply the majority view. To confine the application of the just and equitable clause to proved cases of mala fides would be to negative the generality of the words. It is because I do not accept this that I feel myself obliged to differ from the Court of Appeal. (at p 381)'

I accept the statements of principles given in the Lords' speeches in that case as the correct guidance for my consideration of the questions before me on this petition.

Reverting now to the facts: there is only one answer to the question: Was Brian lawfully removed from the office of director of this company? Was this not a business in which all three engaged on the basis that all should participate in its direction and management? Was it an abuse of wrongfully or mistakenly arrogated power and a breach of the good faith which these three partners owed to each other to exclude him from all participation in the business of the company? To these question there can only be an affirmative answer . . . The action of Kevin and Murph was wholly unjustified as well as being irregular. But by that action and in their evidence relating to it, they made it clear that they did not regard Brian as a partner but simply as an employee. Their refusal to recognise any status of equality amounted to a repudiation of their relationship of which the existence of the company was founded. By ceasing to be a director Brian would lose not director's fees for there were none, nor dividends on his shares for there were none, but his very livelihood consisting of an equal share in all capital and profits and active participation in direction and management of the company.

I am satisfied that the petitioner has made out a case for a winding up order, and has shown that proceedings under s 205 would not be appropriate . . .

Notes

Although there appears to be a conflict between Gannon J and McWilliam J as to whether one must suffer oppression qua member it is submitted that the view of Gannon J is to be preferred. S 205(1) expressly states that one must suffer disregard of interests 'as members' but such restriction is not expressly imposed in respect of oppression. The oppression must only be 'to him or any of the members (including himself)'. In England caselaw expressly required the oppression to be suffered qua member. See *Re Lundie Bros Ltd* [1965] 1 WLR 1051; *Re Bellador Silk Ltd* [1965] 1 ALL ER 667; *Re Westbourne Galleries Ltd* [1971] 2 WLR 618 where oppression qua director did not entitle the petitioner to relief. However, the wording of s 210 of the 1948 Act was somewhat different to s 205, in that the former provision

393

required the conduct complained of to be 'oppressive to some part of the members (including himself)'. For a way around the requirement of s 210 that the oppression be suffered qua member, see *Re HR Harmer Ltd* [1959] 1 WLR 62. Here one of the directors and majority shareholder continued to manage the company in a manner which was inconsistent with decisions reached by the majority of the board. The other directors who were also shareholders petitioned for relief under s 210 of the 1948 Act. The Court of Appeal found that there had been oppression on two grounds. First, the refusal to abide by board decisions had damaged the company financially, thus affecting the value of the petitioner's shares. Secondly, there had been a violation of the petitioners' rights as shareholders to have the company at board level run in accordance with provisions of the memorandum and articles of association.

[14.38] The conduct or exercise of powers complained of in a petition under s 205 must relate to the internal management of the company. Acts may be oppressive even if done honestly and in good faith.

Re Irish Visiting Motorists' Bureau Ltd (High Court, 27 January 1972)

[14.39] For Irish motorists wishing to travel abroad with their car a 'green card' was necessary evidencing insurance cover against any claims incurred abroad. Green cards were issued by the Irish Visiting Motorists Bureau Ltd to those insurance companies which were members of the Bureau. These companies in turn issued the green cards to their policy holders. The PMPA Insurance Co Ltd (the petitioners) applied for and ultimately obtained membership of the Bureau. However, a resolution was passed by the existing members providing that all members other than founder members would have to pay a cash deposit of £10,000 per 1,000 green cards issued to it. The petitioner which was the only non-founder member applied to have the resolution cancelled as being oppressive.

[14.40]   Kenny J: Section 205 which had not been in any of the earlier Companies Acts, provides a remedy for a shareholder whose rights as a shareholder are affected by the way in which the affairs of the company are being conducted or in which the powers of the directors are being exercised. The shareholders' rights come from the Companies Act, equitable principles which have become part of company law and the memorandum and articles of association viewed as a contract created by membership of the company . . . The conduct or exercise of the powers complained of under s 205 must affect the person making the complaint in his character as a member and not as a creditor or a person having commercial dealings with the company . . .

The affairs of a company may be conducted or the powers of the directors may be exercised in a manner oppressive to any of the members although those in charge of the company are acting honestly and in good faith. If one defines oppression as harsh conduct or depriving person of rights to which he is entitled, the person whose conduct is in question may believe that he is exercising his rights in doing what he does. One of the most terrifying aspects of human history is that many of those whom we now regard as having been oppressors had a fanatical belief in the rightness of what they were doing. The question then when deciding whether the conduct of the affairs of a company or the passing of a resolution is oppressive is whether, judged by objective standards, it is.

Green cards which are issued for Britain and Northern Ireland are valid until the insurance policy in respect of which they are given has to be renewed so that the maximum period which they can cover is one year. The petitioners are not authorised to transact motor insurance business in Britain and Northern Ireland and as they have about 100,000 policy holders, it is reasonable to assume that they will require about 10,000 cards each year. The resolution passed in March would require them therefore to deposit £100,000 each year and at the end of ten years, the Irish Bureau would be holding securities worth one million pounds for the petitioner's contingent liabilities. At the meeting in March the directors intended to follow the precedent set by the British Motor Insurers Bureau but over looked the limitation that the deposit of £10,000 for each 1,000 cards was to relate to those issued with the preceding five years. The retention of the securities in respect of possible liabilities arising under cards issued ten years before is so unreasonable and involves such a large sum for security that I think it was oppressive. I accept the evidence that the omission of the reference to the five year period was a mistake and that the directors would probably have altered the resolution when this error was pointed out to them. The resolution however, as passed was oppressive.

Notes

According to *Ussher*, op cit at p 258 the comments of Kenny J that 'the conduct or exercise of the powers complained of under s 205 must affect the person making the complaint in his character as a member and not as a creditor or a person having commercial dealings with the company' must be confined to the distinction between the internal and external affairs of the company and should not be read as prohibiting a petition by a shareholder in respect of oppression suffered qua director in the internal affairs of the company.

[14.41]   Relief may be claimed under s 205 even if some other form of remedy is available to the petitioner, such as a derivative action.

Re Westwinds Holding Co Ltd (High Court, 21 May 1974)

[14.42]   There were two shareholders in the company, Dooley (the petitioner) and Hession. They were the only directors, the petitioner also being the company secretary. The articles required that the affixing of the company's seal be witnessed by one director and the secretary. Hession procured a transfer at a substantial undervalue of a piece of property owned by the company to another company County Developments Ltd in which he owned almost all the shares. He also forged the petitioners signature on the deed of transfer. In addition Hession caused the company to guarantee the liabilities of another company controlled by him called Archers Holdings Ltd. The guarantee was supported by an equitable deposit of title deeds to further property owned by the company. Hession created fake minutes of a meeting at which a resolution was purportedly passed, approving the guarantee and mortgage. He had also forged the petitioners signature on the minutes and had forged the petitioners signature on the sealed form of registration of the mortgage. Hession subsequently purported to pass a resolution dismissing the petitioner as director and secretary of the company. The petitioner who had been unaware of the above transactions petitioned for relief under s 205.

[14.43]   Kenny J: The sale of the lands at Knocknacarra by the company to Country Developments Ltd was made at a gross undervalue and was a fraud on the other member of the company. In 1968 planning permision for the erection of four houses on the front sites had been obtained and it was certain that adequate sewerage and water services would be available for the rest of the lands in a few years time. Full planning permision for the two acres was granted in 1973. If the lands in 1968 had, as the defendant contends, a value as agricultural land only, it is impossible to understand why they were sold to Country Developments Ltd of which Mr Martin Hession owned almost all the shares. The purchase price ultimately realised, £15,000, within four years after the sale in 1968, shows that the price paid (whether it was £600 or £730) was an undervalue. The sale benefitted Mr Martin Hession only at the expense of the company and the petitioner. The sale of the lands at Knocknacarra was an exercise by the directors of their powers in a manner which was fraudulent and oppressive to the petitioner and was in total disregard of his interest as a member of the company. On this ground alone the conditions for the exerise of the powers of the Court under s 205(3) have been fulfilled.

The mortgage by deposit of the 24th of May 1972 of deeds relating to the property at Whitestrand to guarantee the amount which Ardos Holdings Ltd owed Allied Irish Banks was not for the benefit of the company or the petitioner. It was done solely to benefit Ardos Holdings Ltd in which Mr Martin Hession holds almost all the shares. The forgery of the petitioner's signature to the minutes of the meeting at which this transaction was authorised and of his signature to the particulars of the charge which were filed with the Registrar of Companies, indicate that Mr Martin Hession was anxious to conceal the transaction. If it be assumed that the deposit was effective to create any security (and I cannot decide that issue without hearing the bank who will doubtless rely on the rule in *Royal British Bank v Turquand* (1855) 5 E & B 248: (1856) 6 E & B 325,) it was an exercise of the powers of the directors of the company which was oppressive to the petitioner and in total disregard of his interest as a member. At a late stage in his evidence Mr Martin Hession said that he bought the reversion in the lands at Whitestrand Road from the company at the full market price. No evidence to support this was given and while this may be relevant on the remedy to be given for the oppression, it does not alter the position that the transaction, when carried out, was both fraudulent and oppressive.

This is the first case in which the question of the appropriate order under s 205 of the Act of 1963 which made a profound change in the remedies available to a shareholder has been discussed. The petitioner asks that the transfer by the company of the lands at Knocknacarra to Country Developments Ltd and the charge given to Allied Irish Banks Ltd should be cancelled, but neither of these courses can be taken without hearing the parties to whom the transfer and charge were given. That will involve prolonged litigation. The company has ceased trading and a winding up by the court would be expensive and would involve the liquidator in litigation in connection with the transfer of the lands and the charge given to the bank. It seems to me therefore that the appropriate remedy is an order directing Martin Hession to purchase the shares of the petitioner at a price fixed by the court. This was the remedy which Mr Parke appearing for the petitioner asked for in his closing speech. When fixing the price of the shares, however, the court should do so on the basis that the lands sold to Country Developments Ltd are still the property of the company. In relation to the lands at Whitestrand Road, if these have not been purchased by Martin Hession from the company at the full market price, the price of the shares should be fixed without regard to the deposit of the 24th of May 1972 and the amount secured by it. The company is a private company and the articles contain elaborate restrictions on the power to transfer shares, but this should not effect the price to be fixed when it has been established that the directors of the company have exercised their powers in a fraudulent or oppressive fashion. The price will therefore be fixed on the basis that there are no restrictions on the transfer of the petitioner's shares in the company and that the directors would sanction a transfer.

Counsel for Mr Hession argued that s 205 did not apply solely because of the heading 'Minorities' to the section. The word 'minority' does not appear in any part of the section and the heading is merely a convenient way of describing the majority of cases in which the section will apply. In addition, Martin Hession was governing director and under article 42 had five votes on a show of hands or on a poll for each share of which he was the holder, while every other member was to have one vote for every hundred shares held by him. Although the two shareholders held an equal number of shares, the petitioner was certain to be outvoted and so was a minority.

The order to be made will be that the court being satisfied that the powers of the directors of the company have been exercised in a manner oppressive to the petitioner and that those powers have been exercised in disregard of the petitioner's interest as a member, Mr Martin Hession is to purchase all the petitioner's shares in the company at a price determined by an inquiry held before a judge. This price will be the fair price of the shares at the date of the order on the basis (*a*) that the two acres of the land at Knocknacarra, being part of the lands on folio 49061 of the register County Galway, sold to Country Developments Limited are still the property of the company, (*b*) that if the reversion in the lands at Whitestrand was not purchased by Martin Hession from the company at the full market price, then disregarding the deposit of the 24th of May 1972 and the amount secured by it and (*c*) that there are not restrictions on the transfer of the said shares and that the director would sanction the transfer of them by the petitioner.

Re Greenore Trading Co Ltd [1980] ILRM 94 (High Court)

[14.44] The company was formed in 1963 with three equal shareholders and directors Parge (the petitioner) Boyle and Venlandeghem, each of them holding 8,000 £1 shares. The petitioner was the company chairman, Boyle its manager and Vanlandeghem its major customer. The company's business involved the provision of services at Greenore port to exporters of cattle. In 1975 Vanlandeghem contributed £10,000 to meet the liabilities of the company, in return for the issue to him of a further 10,000 shares. All the shareholders consented to the issue of the shares, although it was inconsistent with a prior resolution that no one shareholding should exceed 8,000. At the same time the petitioner resigned as director and Vanlandeghem became managing director. In 1978 Boyle agreed to leave the company and to sell his shares to Vanlandeghem for £22,500. Boyle received £8,000 of the purchase price from Vanlandeghem and the balance was paid for by was of cheque drawn on the company. The petitioner applied for relief under s 205 claiming that the issue of 10,000 shares to Vanlandeghem and the payment of £14,500 to Boyle out of the company monies were invalid, oppressive and in disregard of his interests as a member.

[14.45]   **Keane J:** So far as the issue of 10,000 additional shares to Mr Vanlandeghem at the meeting of 5 February 1975 is concerned, it was submitted on behalf of the petitioner that it was invalid for the following reasons:

> (1) Although the allotment involved an increase in the capital of the company, no notice was given of any intention to propose a special resolution to that effect, nor was any such resolution passed.
> (2) The resolution of 14 January 1966 to the effect that the shareholding of individual members should not be increased beyond £8,000 was not rescinded.
> (3) Although the meeting of 5 February 1975 was an extra-ordinary general meeting of the company and not a meeting of the directors, it purported to allot the shares to Mr Vanlandeghem, whereas this should have been done at a meeting of the directors alone.

I think that it is clear that each of these grounds of objection is well founded. It is also the case, however, that the issue of shares was made to Mr Vanlandeghem in order to give him some security in respect of the £10,000 which he was prepared to advance to the company in order to get it out of its serious financial problems. The money was made available by him when it became obvious that neither the petitioner nor Mr Boyle could nor would come to the rescue of the company . . . While the procedure adopted was technically not in conformity with the Companies Act 1963, and the terms of the earlier resolution, the petitioner although not present at the meeting when the shares were allotted, by his conduct clearly indicated that he was satisfied that the additional shares should be allotted to Mr Vanlandeghem, provided he came to the aid of the company financially. This Mr Vanlandeghem did; but if the contention advanced on behalf of the petitioner is well founded it means that, should the company go into liquidation, Mr Vanlandeghem will have to prove for his £10,000 as an ordinary creditor and will be without any security whatsoever. This would be the result of his having foregone the debenture which would have made him a secured creditor and which was abandoned simply because the company's solicitor advised that it was against the company's interest. The company and the petitioner will accordingly, have had the benefit of Mr Vanlandeghem's £10,000 while he will be deprived of all security in relation to it, although he had acted in the reasonable belief which his fellow shareholders did nothing to dispel, that the transaction was not merely fully acceptable to them, but the only means available of saving the company.

It would seem to me entirely contrary to justice and to be singularly unfair and unreasonable that, in these circumstances the petitioner could successfully assert that the issue of shares was invalid. I think, however, that in these circumstances the doctrine of estoppel in pari pasu is applicable: because where a person has so conducted himself that another would, as a reasonable man, understand that a certain representation of fact is intended to be acted on and the other has acted on the representation and thereby altered his position to his prejudice, an estoppel arises against the party who made the representation and he is not allowed to aver that the fact is otherwise than he represented it to be . . . It is, of course, clear that a party cannot set up an estoppel in the face of a statute; but that principle does not seem to me to be directly applicable in a case such as the present, where the transaction in issue was not prohibited by law and its recognition or enforcement by the court would violate no principle of public policy or social policy . . . In this case the petitioner is clearly estopped in my opinion from asserting the irregularity of a transaction which he tacitly approved of when it was being implemented, which does not offend against any principle of law and which was entirely for the benefit of the company.

Different considerations entirely apply to the transfer of Mr Boyle's shares to Mr Vanlandeghem. It is immaterial whether the real price paid for the shares was £22,500 or whether the sum of £14,500 represented compensation to Mr Boyle for quitting the company as the respondent claims. If it was compensation of this nature, then the transaction was clearly unlawful having regard to the provisions of s 186 of the Companies Act 1963, since the proposed payment was not disclosed to the other member of the company (the petitioner) nor was it approved by the company in general meeting. Indeed the illegality of the transaction if this was its nature, was compounded by the fact that the sum paid in respect of compensation was not specified in the company's accounts, as required by s 191 of the Act. If, on the other hand, the sum of £14,500 did represent part of the consideration for the shares, the transaction was unlawful since it was a violation of s 60 of the Act, which prohibits a company from giving financial assistance for the purchase of its shares. On any view, accordingly this transaction was not merely irregular, but grossly irregular.

I am satisfied that this latter transaction constituted conduct of such a nature as to justify and indeed require the making of an order under s 205(3) of the Act. Prior to that transaction Mr Vanlandeghem as a result of the issue of 10,000 shares to him in 1975, was the holder of just over 50% of the issued share capital. Had the transfer of shares by Mr Boyle to him gone unchallenged, he would have become the owner of more than 75% of the company share capital. 'Oppressive' conduct for the purposes of the corresponding s 210 of the English Companies Act 1948 has been defined as meaning the exercise of the company's authority 'in a manner burdensome, harsh and wrongful.' (See *Scottish CWS Ltd v Meyer* [1959] AC 324 at p 342). The patent mis-application of the company's monies for the purpose of giving Mr Vanandeghem a dominant position in its affairs seems to me to be properly described as 'burdensome, harsh and wrongful' quoad the petitioner. It cannot be equated to the allotment of shares in *Re Jermyn Street Turkish Baths Limited* [1971] 1 WLR 1042 which was treated by the Court of Appeal as being one entered into in good faith for the benefit of the company. Nor can the actual mis-application of the funds be properly treated as an isolated act of oppression (which would not normally be sufficient to justify relief under the section: See *Re Westbourne Galleries* [1970] 1 WLR 1378). As I have already noted, not merely were the company's monies purportedly applied towards an unlawful purpose, ie. the payment of compensation to a director for loss of office without the sanction of a general meeting, the payment of that compensation was not separately dealt with in the company's account for the relevant year, as required by law.

It is true that the wording of the section envisages that the oppression complained of is operative at the time when the petition is launched. (see *Re Jermyn Street Turkish Baths Ltd.*) In this case the transfer of shares took place in March 1978. The accounts for the year were certified by the company's auditors on 9 June 1978. The petition was presented just over a year later on 15 June 1979, after protests had been made in correspondence on behalf of the petitioner at the manner in which the company's affairs were being conducted. The company had not merely failed to take any steps to deal with these gross irregularities in its affairs prior to the issuing of the petition; it had also wholly ignored letters written on behalf of the petitioner

400

which clearly called for an answer. It seems to me that in these circumstances the oppressive conduct can be properly regarded as having continued up to the date of the issuing of the petition.

It is obvious that the present circumstances would justify an order being made for the winding up of the company under s 213(*f*) and (*g*). It is agreed however, that such an order in the present circumstances would not be in the interests of the members and accordingly, the remedy for the oppressive conduct must be the alternative remedy provided by s 205. I think that the only effective method of bringing to an end the oppressive conduct of which the petitioner complains is an order for the purchase of his shares by Mr Vanlandeghem.

The shares accordingly, must be purchased by Mr Vanlandeghem at a fair price; and it remains to consider what that price should be, in all the circumstances of the case. Having regard to the findings I have made, it is clear that the petitioner's shareholding must be valued on the assumption that the purported purchase of Mr Boyle's shares had not taken place. This would leave the petitioner owning 8,000 shares, Mr Vanlandeghem 18,000 and Mr Boyle 8,000 shares. I doubt very much whether a shareholder already in control of more than 50% of the share capital would, in the particular circumstances of this company have paid more than their par value to acquire the shareholding of the petitioner. I do not think that the fact that Mr Boyle may have got £22,500 for his shareholding is of much assistance in determining the value of the petitioner's shareholding. In the first place, the purchaser was not willing to pay more than £8,000 for the shares from his own resources. In the second place, Mr Boyle was more conspiciously involved in the company's affairs – usually in contest with Mr Vanlandeghem – and accordingly, had more of a nuisance value from the point of view of Mr Vanlandeghem than the petitioner. In the third place, there remains the possibility that some at least, of the consideration was genuinely, if illegally related to compensation for the loss of office rather than the purchase price of the shares themselves. Having regard to the uncertain financial future of the company I doubt very much whether from the point of view of the majority shareholder, if it would have been worth paying more than £8,000 for the petitioner's shareholding; nor do I think that somebody buying an interest in the company who had not already any interest in it, would have been willing to pay more than that sum.

That, however does not conclude the matter, since it is clear in prescribing the basis on which the price is to be calculated, the court can in effect provide compensation for whatever injury has been inflicted by the oppressers (See *Scottish Co-operative Wholesale Society v Meyer* [1959] AC 324). The accounts in the present case show that the company had been pursuing a conservative policy in relation to the payment of dividends in the years immediately preceding the wrongful purchase of Mr Boyle's shares and this policy may well have been justified by the company's uncertain trading future. There seems to me, however, no reason why the petitioner should be deprived of the share to which he would have been entitled of the £14,500 wrongfully applied in the transaction regarding Mr Boyle's shares. It is

immaterial whether that sum comes back to the company following these or
other proceedings and is ultimately paid out by way of dividend or as a return
on capital to the contributors since the petitioner will derive no benefit from
that once the shares have been purchased by Mr Vanlandeghem. It follows
that he is entitled in my view, to be paid a sum bearing the same proportion
to that sum of £14,500 as his shareholding of £8,000 did to the total issued
share capital of £34,000 prior to the unlawful transaction in relation to Mr
Boyle's shares; and I will order that sum to be paid in addition to the sum of
£8,000 representing the par value of his shares.

[14.46]   Not every illegal act relating to the internal affairs of the company
will constitute oppression. Conversely, in appropriate circumstances relief
may be claimed under s 205 in respect of conduct which although oppressive
or in disregard of interests is not strictly illegal.

Re Clubman Shirts Ltd [1983] ILRM 323 (High Court)

[14.47]   The petitioner, who held about 20% of the share capital in the
company had previously been formerly a director and financial controller of
the company. He was removed from office by the board of directors in 1977,
who between them held most of the remaining shares in the company. The
petitioner claimed relief under s 205. In particular he claimed that since 1977
the company had failed to hold AGM's, to present audited accounts or to file
annual returns. This, he alleged prevented him from being informed as he
was entitled to be informed of the financial affairs of the company. At that
time the directors tried to get him to sell his shares at a very low figure. Such
offers to buy his shares were bound up with conditions requiring him, inter
alia, to waive his claims against the company. He claimed that consequently
he was subjected to unfair pressure by the directors to sell when they were in
a position to assess the true value of his shares and he was not. In addition
the directors refused to provide him with information to which he was
entitled to such as copies of the register of members and copies of the
accounts. His final complaint was that in 1980 when the company was in
grave financial difficulties and threatened with receivership or liquidation,
the directors without consulting the minority shareholders sold the company's entire business, undertaking and assets to a newly-formed company
called 'Clubman Ltd' as part of a deal whereby, although all of the company's debts were cleared, nothing was left for the shareholders. The directors of the company were also directors of the new company 'Clubman Ltd'.
There was no suggestion however that sale had been made other than in
good faith and in the firm belief that the deal was for the benefit of the company's shareholders.

[14.48]   **O'Hanlon J:** My conclusion is that the evidence tends to show a
series of irregularities by the directors in complying with their obligations
under the Companies Act, rather than a case of oppression in the sense of

s 205 of the Act. I would not classify as oppression the attempts made from time to time to buy out the petitioner's shareholding in the company. In my opinion the directors were entitled to make any offer they thought fit, whether realistic or unrealistic and to hedge their offers around with conditions if they thought fit to do so. The petitioner on receipt of the offers never responded by saying that he was unable to assess the true value of his shares by reason of the wrongful withholding of information by the directors, coupled with a request for such information as he need to safeguard his interests. Neither did he at any time sell or consider selling his shareholding or any part thereof on the terms offered to him. Consequently any claim for relief under s 205 which is based on these transactions cannot succeed.

Similarly, I would not classify as oppressive conduct within the meaning of the Act the omission to comply with the various provisions of the Act referable to the holding of general meetings and the furnishing of information and copy documents. These were examples of negligence, carelessness, irregularity in the conduct of the affairs of the company, but the evidence does not suggest that these defaults or any of them formed part of a deliberate scheme to deprive the petitioner of his rights or to cause him loss or damage.

There remain the events of 1980 to which fuller reference has been made already. In this case the petitioner had genuine ground for complaint although I have some reservations about putting it into the category of oppressive conduct towards a minority. I feel the petitioner has made out a case for limited relief, of a type which the majority shareholders appear to be willing to concede in his favour, and accordingly I would propose to make an order in his favour under s 205 of the Act directing the majority shareholders who are represented in these proceedings to buy out the petitioner's shareholding in the company at a valuation based on the true value of the shares as of 31 July 1980 – this being the time when he should in my opinion, have been given a fuller opportunity of concurring or not concurring in the course of action embarked upon by the majority shareholders.

Notes

In *PMPA Insurance Co Ltd v New Ireland Assurance Co Ltd* (High Court, 22 October 1975, reported in the Irish Times, 23 October 1975), Kenny J refused to grant an order under s 205 that the company disclose confidential information about its business to the petitioner. The petitioner was not only a minority shareholder in the company, but was also a major competitor.

[14.49] The alteration of the rights of one class of shareholders, although strictly valid may be objectionable as being in disregard of the interest of another class of shareholders.

Re Williams Group Tullamore Ltd [1985] IR 613

[The facts appear from the judgment].

[14.50]   Barrington J: This is a petition presented under s 205 of the Companies Act 1963. The petitioners are shareholders in the company – the bulk of their shares being ordinary shares in its share capital. Prior to the matters hereinafter complained of the authorised share capital of the company was £400,000 divided into 250,000 ordinary shares of £1 each and 150,000 eight percent preference shares of £1 each. The issued share capital of the company was £267,080 divided into 133,540 ordinary shares of £1 each and 133,540 eight per cent preference shares of £1 each, all of which shares had been paid up or credited as paid up.

The company is controlled by the Williams family which is divided into two branches one being the descendents of Daniel Williams and the other being the descendents of John Williams. At the incorporation of the company in 1966, the share capital was £250,000 divided into 250,000 shares of £1 each of which 133,540 shares were issued and paid up or credited as fully paid up.

The present company is a very substantial commercial enterprise. It was incorporated in the year 1966 but was the successor, after a series of reorganisation of what was formerly a relatively small trading company, DE Williams Ltd. The present company took over the share capital in DE Williams Ltd and also in Irish Mist Liqueur Company Ltd which became its subsidiaries.

The founder members had run the business in effect as a partnership. They apparently worked very well together and there was no necessity to define the powers of either of them. There was no formal post of managing director. A problem, however, came into existence when their children inherited their shares. Some of the children naturally had a greater interest in and aptitude for business than others. The result was some confusion which reflected adversely on the business. To counteract this Mr Edmund Williams was invited in 1965 to become the first managing director of the company and he has retained that post ever since.

A major reorganisation of the capital structure of the company took place in November 1972, when the preference shares were created. An amendment to the memorandum of association provided:–

(*a*) That the share capital of the company be increased from £250,000 divided into 250,000 ordinary shares of one pound each to £400,000 divided into 250,000 ordinary shares of one pound each by the creation of 150,000 eight per cent preference shares of one pound each, and that the existing shares in the company be and are hereby designated as ordinary shares.

(*b*) That the said preference shares shall confer the right out of the profits of the company resolved to be distributed to a fixed preferential dividend at the rate of eight per cent per annum on the capital for the time being paid up thereon, without any right in the case of deficiency to resort to subsequent or past profits, and the right in a winding up to payment off of capital and arrears of dividends declared before commencement of winding up, down to the commencement of the winding up in priority to the ordinary shares but shall not confer any further right to participate in profits or assets.'

At the same time an amendment was made to the articles of association of the company which provided as follows:–

'If and so long as any preference shares in the capital of the company is issued and outstanding the ordinary shares shall not confer upon the holders thereof the right to receive notice of or to attend or vote at any general meeting of the company.'

These amendments to the memorandum and articles of association of the company were carried by agreement of all concerned and their object was to consolidate control of the company in the hands of those members of the family who were most intimately concerned with its management. In time, Mr Edmund Williams came to own or control some 45% of the issued preference shares in the company. There can be no doubt that he acquired these shares fairly and by agreement. Neither can there be any doubt that under his stewardship the company has prospered and been exceedingly successful. By the capital reorganisation of 1972 the ordinary shareholders abandoned their right to receive notice of or to attend or to vote at general meetings of the company, so long as any preference share in the capital of the company remained issued and outstanding. Nevertheless the ordinary shareholders have received very substantial dividends over the years and have done very much better than the preference shareholders. No one question but that over the years, they have been very fairly treated.

The present dispute is confined to the proposed method of distributing a sum of £267,080 accrued profits earned from exporting Irish Mist Liqueur. The board of the company apparently took the view that over the years, the ordinary shareholders had done extremely well – at times earning dividends of over 64% on their capital. By comparison the preference shareholders who were stuck with their fixed interest of eight per cent, had done very poorly. Moreover, inflation had eaten away the value of their dividends. On this occasion apparently, management thought it fair to rectify the balance . . . The proposed scheme was that each ordinary and each preference shareholder should receive one fully paid up penny share in the share capital of the company for each ordinary and for each preference share held by him. This would involve the issue of 267,080 new 'A' shares. Each of these shares would then qualify for one single dividend of £1 each. The preference shareholders and the ordinary shareholders would each receive their usual dividends but over and above this, each of them would also receive a dividend of £1 for each 'A' share held by him.

A number of the ordinary shareholders objected to the scheme . . . The petitioners originally claimed that the creation and issue of the 'A' shares of

1p each amounted to a variation or abrogation of the rights of the ordinary shareholders but Mr O'Neill abandoned this point at the hearing and presented a case solely as a case of oppression under s 205 of the Act . . .

If one regards 'oppression' as a course of conduct which is 'burdensome, harsh and wrongful' or as conduct which involves lack of probity or fair dealing towards some members of the company . . . there is no history of such a course of conduct in the present company prior to the events giving rise to the present case. On the contrary the ordinary shareholders appear to have been treated extremely well.

Moreover, in the present case we are not dealing with a course of conduct but with an individual transaction. If appears however, that an isolated transaction can give rise to relief under the Irish section (see the judgment of Kenny J *In re Westwinds Holding Company Ltd* para **14.42**). Besides, in the present case we are dealing with a transaction which is ongoing at the date of the hearing of his petition in the sense that it is one which will be implemented if the petitioners do not obtain the relief they are seeking. It is perhaps worth noting that the Irish section offers relief not only when the affairs of the company are being conducted in an oppressive manner but also (and alternatively) where they are being conducted in disregard of the interests of some member or members.

There can be no doubt that the preference shareholders in passing the resolutions of the 13th May 1985, acted within their formal powers. There can be no doubt either that they acted honestly in the sense that they felt entitled to make the decision which they did make. Indeed, Mr Thomas P Hardiman who is chairman of the company and who chaired the meeting of the 13th May 1985, thought that the decision made was a fair one. Mr Hardiman was in the unique position to form an unbiased opinion because not only is he a businessman of wide experience and chairman of the company, but he holds no shares in the company and therefore has no special interest which would cause him to favour either the preference or the ordinary shareholders.

Mr O'Neill on behalf of the petitioners quoted a passage from the judgment of Sir Raymond Evershed MR in *Greenhalgh v Arderne Cinemas Ltd* [1950] 2 All ER 1120 where Sir Raymond having surveyed the English authorities continued (at p 1126 of the report):–

'Certain things, I think can be safely stated as emerging from those authorities. In the first place, it is now plain that "bona fide for the benefit of the company as a whole" means not two things but one thing. It means that the shareholder must proceed on what, in his honest opinion, is for the benefit of the company as a whole. Secondly, the phrase, "the company as a whole" does not (at any rate in such a case as the present) mean the company as a commercial entity as distinct from the corporators. It means the corporators as a general body.'

There is no doubt that shareholders voting at a general meeting of the company are entitled to have regard to their own interests. The problem is the degree to which they are entitled to disregard the interests of other shareholders. The structure of the present company prior to the 13th May 1985 contemplated that the share capital of the company should be divided between preference shareholders and ordinary shareholders. The preference shareholders were entitled to a fixed preferential dividend of eight per cent and to priority over the ordinary shareholder in the repayment of capital on a winding up of the company. This structure seem to contemplate that the ordinary shareholders wouldtake the greater risks and would in the event of the company being successful, reap the greater rewards.

The structure of the company was, however, peculiar in that the ordinary shares in the company's capital carried no voting rights as long as there were preference shares issued. This meant that at all times material to these proceedings the preference shareholders had control of the company. During this time two things have happened. The company has been hugely successful and the value of the preference shareholders' fixed dividends has been eroded by inflation. The result has been an unhappy one for the preference shareholders, but it is doubtful is if can properly be regarded as 'unfair'. Moreover, a large part of the preference shares are held by the managing director of the company. But the success of the company probably springs from his ability as managing director rather than from his status as a preference shareholder.

Mr O'Neill has admitted that the formal rights of the ordinary shareholders have not been affected by the resolutions of the 13th May 1985. However, he maintains that the effect of the resolution is to make available to the preference shareholders or more correctly those preference shareholders who receive the new 'A' shares a sum of £133,540 which would otherwise be available for distribution among the ordinary shareholders as individuals or on the winding up of the company. It is not an answer to this argument to say that this sum if not distributed in dividends to the preference shareholders need not necessarily be distributed to the ordinary shareholders. The board might put it to some other use such, for example as to reduce the borrowings of the company. But it appears to me that it must follow that if these monies are paid out to the preference shareholders or to such of the preference shareholders as hold 'A' shares they will not be available for distribution to the ordinary shareholders or for purposes of which the ordinary shareholders may approve. In that sense it appears to me that the payment out referred to is contrary to the interest of the ordinary shareholders.

It appears to me also that the resolutions of the 13th May 1985, were carried in disregard of the interests of the ordinary shareholders. It appears to me that the implementation of these resolutions is an ongoing matter in the company and justifies the view that the affairs of the company are being conducted in disregard of the interests of the ordinary shareholders. I fully accept that the proposal put forward in the resolutions of the 13th May 1985, was put forward in good faith. Nevertheless, it appears to me that it is in objective disregard of the interests of the ordinary shareholders and that to persist in implementing it would in the circumstances, be oppressive to the ordinary shareholders.

In these circumstances it appears to me that the petitioners have brought themselves within the section and that they are entitled to appropriate relief.

Notes

The preference shareholders could instead of altering the rights attaching to their own shares have merely allotted an equivalent amount of the unissued ordinary shares to themselves. Would this have been seen as being in disregard of the interests of the existing shareholders? See *White v Bristol Aeroplane Co Ltd*[1953] Ch 65.

In *Re Five Minute Car Wash Service Ltd* [1966] 1 WLR 745 Buckley J rejected the argument that incompetent management of the company could constitute oppression. His Lordship rejected the argument on the ground that there was 'no suggestion that he [the managing director] has acted unscrupulously, unfairly or with any lack of probity towards the petitioner or any other member of the company or that he has overborne or disregarded the wishes of the board of directors or that his conduct could be characterised as harsh or burdensome or wrongful towards any member of the company.' However, the Irish cases indicate that relief may be available under s 205 even if the acts complained of were done honestly and in the bona fide belief that they were for the benefit of the company. Further, both *Keane* (at para **28.17**) and *Ussher* (op cit at p 263) regard incompetent management as a disregard of the interests of members, entitling the petitioner to relief under s 205. Relief in respect of disregard of interests was not available under s 210 of the 1948 Act.

Section 205 proceedings in camera

[14.51]   Under s 205(7) if in the opinion of the court the hearing of the proceedings 'would involve the disclosure of information the publication of which would be seriously prejudicial to the legitimate interests of the company, the court may order that the hearing of the proceedings or any part thereof shall be in camera'.

[14.52]   S 205 proceedings will only be heard in camera if a public hearing would (*a*) involve the disclosure of information which would be seriously prejudicial to the legitimate interests of the company and (*b*) fall short of doing justice.

Re R Ltd [1989] ILRM 757 (Supreme Court)

[14.53]   The petitioner, who was a substantial shareholder in the company had been recently dismissed from the pose of chief executive. He brought a petition under s 205 alleging that the company had been run by the majority of its directors in a manner which was not only likely to be damaging of its interests in the short and long term, but which was actually intended to serve not the interests of the company but rather conflicting business interests of the founder of the company who was neither a director nor a member of it. The company and founder were respondents to the petition and they applied to the High Court under s 205(7) for an order that the proceedings be heard in camera. The respondents expressed concern that the disclosure of certain of the company's documents would be seriously prejudicial to its legitimate interests. These documents were a five year business plan for the company, details of the accounts of the company; and details of one particular transaction and the commercial terms of it. The High Court (Johnson J) ordered that the entire of the proceedings be heard in camera and Costello J ordered that none of the pleadings should be disclosed to anyone who was not a party to the proceedings. The petitioner appealed to the Supreme Court.

[14.54]   Walsh J: The issue before this court touches a fundamental principle of the administration of justice in a democratic state namely the administration of justice in public. Article 34 of the Constitution provides that justice shall be administered in courts established by law and shall be administered in public save in such special and limited cases as may be prescribed by law. The actual presence of the pubic is never necessary but the administration of justice in public does require that the doors of the court be open so that members of the general public may come and see for themselves what justice is done. It is in no way necessary that the members of the pubic to whom the courts are open should themselves have any particular interest in the cases or they should have had any business in the courts. Justice is administered in public on behalf of all the inhabitants of the State.

Prior to the enactment of the Constitution the question of whether or not particular matters should be heard in public was a matter for the discretion of the judges subject of course, always to particular statutory provisions which dealt with the subject. However, it was always clear that the judges had no discretion to prevent the public from attending hearings unless they were satisfied that either total privacy for the whole or part of any case was absolutely necessary to enable justice to be done. The primary object of the courts is to see that justice is done and it was only when the presence of the public or public knowledge of the proceedings would defeat that object that the judges had any discretion to hear cases other than in public. It had to be shown that a public hearing was likely to lead to a denial of justice before the discretion could be exercised to hear a case or part of a case other than in public.

This fundamental principle in the administration of justice was made part of the fundamental law of the State by art 34 of the Constitution in 1937. More than a decade later the same fundamental principle was incorporated in certain international instruments dealing with human rights. Article 10 of the Universal Declaration of Human Rights of 1948 and article 26 of the American Declaration of the Rights and Duties of Man also of 1948 had each required public hearings for the administration of justice. They were followed by several international Conventions incorporating the same principle among which are the articles 6(1) of the European Convention of Human Rights 1950 and the International Covenant on Civil and Political Rights 1966, art 14(1) . . .

The Constitution of 1937 removed any judicial discretion to have proceedings heard other than in public save where expressly conferred by statute . . . The statutory provision which arises for consideration in this case namely, s 205(7) of the Companies Act 1963 confers a discretionary power upon the court. But the discretion cannot be exercised unless the court is of opinion that the hearing of proceedings under the section would involve the disclosure of information the publication of which would be seriously prejudicial to the legitimate interest of the company. That is a condition precedent to the exercise of a discretion but in my view it is not the only condition regulating the exercise of the discretion.

I fully agree with the opinion expressed by the Chief Justice that proceedings include pleadings, affidavits and exhibits as well as oral testimony and indeed the judgment in the case. I also agree with his opinion that the section cannot be invoked simply to conceal from the public evidence or wrongful activities on the part of the company or any member of the company or the good name of any such persons or anybody else. In *Beamish and Crawford Ltd v Crowley* [1969] IR 142 this court refused to accept as a factor in deciding the venue of a trial consideration of the adverse pubicity which would affect the sale of the plaintiffs' goods in the area of the particular venue for the trial. The court held that apart from the exceptions permitted by law, publicity was inseparable from the administration of justice.

It is difficult to know what was the justification for the provisions of s 205(7) of the Act of 1963 when one bears in mind that in proceedings in any other form of action against the company whether by a shareholder or anyone else no information however damaging or embarassing to the company may be withheld from publication unless it involved the disclosure of a secret process. The fact that s 205 provided a special form of relief for minority shareholders alleging oppression does not on the face of it appear to be a reason for giving the procedure provided for in subs (7) a character different from any other proceedings. However, be that as it may, it has been so enacted by the Oireachtas. But in my view that does not obviate the overriding consideration of doing justice. In seeking to avail of the protection apparently offered by the subsection the party seeking it must be able to satisfy the court that not only would the disclosure of information be seriously prejudicial to the legitimate interest of the company but it must also be shown that a public hearing of the whole or of that part of the proceedings which it is sought to have heard other than in a public court would fall short of the doing of justice.

In the hearing before this court it appeared to be agreed between the parties that publication of information relating to the five-year business plan and programme of the company and the details of its accounts and the details of one particular transaction and the commercial terms of that transaction would be seriously prejudicial to the legitimate interest of the company. As

410

that is the condition precedent for any decision on the part of the trial judge to hear the proceedings other than in a public court the next question which must arise before the discretion can be exercised is a to whether publication of these matters would fall short of the doing of justice.

The first observation to be made is that unless the details of these matters are actually relevant to the issues to be tried they should not be admitted in evidence at all. Assuming they are relevant and admissible one must bear in mind that the nature of the proceedings is that it is the affairs of a juristic person created by the Companies Acts which are under review. That puts the case in a quite different category from the private affairs of a human person. It is difficult to see why the disclosure of evidence of this type must necessarily be deemed to be a failure to do justice in the case of a juristic person where it would not be such in the case of a human person or any unincorporated body of persons. The defendants as well as the petitioner are entitled to a fair and public hearing by the courts set up under the Constitution. Is the fact that the statutory condition precedent namely a serious prejudice to the legitimate interest of the company to be regarded as necessarily as being equivalent to those exceptional circumstances where public knowledge of the proceedings is likely to lead to an injustice or to defeat the object of the court in doing justice? I do not think so even though it might be thought that this appeal proceeded on the basis that it does. While in one sense the quarrels between a shareholder or shareholders in a limited company and the company itself might be regarded in the nature of a family squabble it is in no way comparable to family disputes in the true sense. A limited company is the creature of the law and by its very nature and by the provisions of law under whch it is created it is open to public scrutiny.

I do not say that there can never be circumstances where the public hearing of cases such as this would prevent justice being done. However, I am of opinion that in the present case no circumstances, so far at least have been shown which would justify the court at arriving at such a conclusion. I would therefore allow this appeal.

If I were of opinion that the three matters mentioned and agreed as being the ones the disclosure of which would be injurious to the legitimate interests of the company were also shown in the circumstances of the case to be such that their disclosure would prevent justice being done, it would be my opinion that this fact would not justify the whole of the proceedings being held other than in public unless it could be shown that not to do so would make the trial so unsatisfactory and difficult as to fall short of the proper administration of justice in that it would not be a fair hearing, I would support the view that the entire trial should be held other than in a public court. However, in the present case the evidence in so far as has been disclosed to this court, is such that the most one could say is that if part only of the proceedings are heard other than in public it would make the trial inconvenient and possibly even troublesome. That is a very long was from saying that such inconvenience or trouble would cause such trial to amount to a failure to do justice.

I am also of opinion that in either event a judgment should be pronounced in public. If part or the whole of the proceedings were to be heard other than in public I am of opinion that so much of the judgment as does not disclose the particular information which had been withheld from publication should be pronounced in public.

Griffin J delivered a concurring judgment. Hederman J concurred. Finlay CJ and Hamilton P dissented.

Notes

In many cases it would be in the interests of not only the company, but also the petitioner to have the proceedings heard in camera. The relief sought might not involve the purchase of the petitioners' shares. If he intends retaining the shares, he may find them seriously devalued as a result of adverse publicity arising from the case.

Section 213(f)

[14.55] This section allows for the winding up of the company where it is just and equitable to do so. It is typically sought as an alternative remedy in s 205 proceedings and is discussed in chapter 23.

Chapter 15

OFFICERS OF THE COMPANY

The Directors[1]

[15.01] Every company must have a minimum of two directors.[2] Undischarged bankrupts,[3] bodies corporate,[4] and the auditors[5] are prohibited from being directors of the company. Restrictions are imposed on the ability of directors of insolvent companies to take up new directorships, under ss 149 to 158 of the 1990 Act, and in addition, under ss 159 to 169 of that Act (discussed below) a person may be disqualified from being a director of a company. Under standard form articles, management of the company is delegated to them by the members.[6] The first directors are those named in the statement filed with the registrar under s 3 of the 1982 Act. Thereafter they are appointed in the manner prescribed by the articles and where the articles are silent, this is taken as vesting the power of appointment in the general meeting.[7] Typically, the directors are obliged to retire by rotation, although they may still be eligible for re-election.[8] If the articles require the directors to hold a specified share qualification they have two months (or such shorter period as may be fixed by the articles) from the date of their appointment to comply.[9] Failure to do so results in the office of the director being vacated. Having obtained a share qualification, should he thereafter cease to hold all or any or the specified number of shares, he will lose his office. Under s 181 of the Principal Act a motion for the appointment of two or more persons as directors by a single resolution shall not be made, unless the prior approval has been obtained of all members present at the meeting. A breach of the section renders the appointments in question void.[10]

1 See generally *Keane* chapter 29.
2 S 174 of the Principal Act.
3 Ibid s 183.
4 Ibid s 176.
5 Ibid s 169(5) as substituted by s 6 of the 1982 Act.
6 See art 80 of table A.
7 Under arts 98 and 100 casual vacancies may be filled by either the board or the general meeting.
8 See arts 92–97 of table A.
9 S 180 of the Principal Act.
10 See *Moylan v Irish Whiting Manufacturers Ltd* (unreported High Court, 14/4/80).

[15.02]   A director is an office holder. He holds his office under the articles of association. He is not, per se, an employee of the company. However, a contract of employment may be implied in appropriate circumstances and in particular if the director works full time for the company and receives regular remuneration for his services.

Re Dairy Lee Ltd; Stakelum v Canning [1976] IR 314 (High Court)

[The facts appear from the judgment]

[15.03]   **Kenny J:** Dairy Lee was unable to pay its debts and passed a resolution for voluntary winding up. The applicant is the liquidator and he has brought these proceedings for a decision by the court as to whether the respondent's claim for accrued holiday remuneration should be treated as a debt ranking in priority under s 285 of the Companies Act 1963.

The respondent who held 3,000 shares of £1 each in the company which had an issued capital of £6452 was a director of the company. He worked full time for it and was responsible for the day to day running of the business though he was not the managing director. He was paid £225 a month by the company but there are no entries in the minute book to show whether these payments were salary or director's fees. The respondent who did not have any service agreement with the company regarded the payments as salary. His employment was terminated by the applicant on the 23 July 1974 and he claimed accrued holiday remuneration . . .

A director holds his office under the articles of association of the company and so, as a director is not an employee or a clerk or servant of the company. Article 85 of the articles in table A which applied to this company, permits him to hold any other office or place of profit under the company in conjuncion with his office of director for such period and on such terms as to remuneration and otherwise as the directors may determine. The result is that a director may be employed by the company not as a director but as a salaried employee.

When a person who is a director claims priority under s 285 of the Act of 1963 the relevant questions are whether he was a director only or a director and a salaried employee. When deciding this it is relevant to consider whether the money's received by him were paid as director's fees or as salary. If he was a director and a salaried employee, he is entitled to priority under s 285 for salary and accrued holiday remuneration. When a person who is a director but is not a managing director is working wholetime with the company, the inference that he was a director and a salaried employee seems to me to be justified unless there is evidence that he was a whole-time director only and was paid as such . . . In this case the only reasonable inference is that the respondent was a director and a salaried employee and that the money he received was salary and nor director's fees. He was therefore an employee and servant of the company and I will declare that he is entitled to priority under s 285(2)(*d*) of the Companies Act 1963 in respect of his claim in the winding up for accrued holiday remuneration.

Notes

See also *Re Beeton & Co Ltd* [1913] 1 Ch 84; *Anderson v James Sutherland (Peterhead) Ltd* [1932] 2 Ch 46. On the distinction between an office holder and an employee, see *Glover v BLN* [1973] IR 388, 414.

Remuneration of directors

[15.04] The director has no right to remuneration unless provided for either in the articles or under a separate contract with the company.[1]

As was said in *Hutton v West Cork Rly Co*[2] 'it is not implied from the mere fact that he is a director that he is to have a right to be paid for it.' However, art 76 of table A provides that 'The remuneration of the directors shall from time to time be determined by the company in general meeting. Such remuneration shall be deemed to accrue from day to day.'[3]

1 See *Keane* at paras **29.10–29.12**.
2 (1883) 23 Ch D 654.
3 Even in the absence of an express provision that remuneration is to accrue from day to day, *Keane* suggests at para **29.10** that such a conclusion is to be implied under the Apportionment Act 1870.

[15.05] The company cannot retrospectively amend its articles so as to remove the directors entitlement to accrued remuneration. A prospective amendment will, however, be valid.

Swabey v Port Darwin Gold Mining Co (1889) 1 Meg 385 (Court of Appeal)

[15.06] The company's articles provided that the directors were to be paid at the rate of £200 per annum. The plaintiff was one of the directors and remained such down to 1888. In June and July of that year the company amended the articles by special resolution purporting to reduce the rate of remuneration to £5 per month to be effective from 31st December 1887. The plaintiff refused to accept this and resigned in protest claiming £50 in respect of fees for three months at the rate of £200 per annum. The Court of Appeal reversing the decision of Stephen J, found for the plaintiff.

Lord Halsbury LC: The argument which has been addressed to us proceeds upon the erroneous basis of treating the articles as a contract and that as there is a power given by the Act to alter the articles, the contract they contained could be put an end to and varied by the altering resolution. The articles do not themselves constitute a contract, they are merely the regulations by which provision is made for the way the business of the company is to be carried on. A person who acts as director with those articles before him enters into a contract with the company to serve as a director, the remuneration to be at the rate contemplated by the articles. The person who does this has before him as one of the stipulations of the contract, that it shall be possible for his employer to alter the terms upon which he is to serve, if he thought proper at the reduced rate of remuneration. Those terms, however,

415

could be altered only as to the future. In so far as the contract on those terms had aleady been carried into effect, it is incapable of alteration by the company.

Lord Esher MR: I am of the same opinion. The articles do not themselves form a contract, but from them you get the terms upon which the directors are serving. It would be absurd to hold that one of the parties to a contract could alter it as to service already performed under it. The company has power to alter the articles, but the directors would be entitled to their salary at the rate originally stated in the articles up to the time the article were altered.

Lindley LJ concurred.

Removal of directors

[15.07]   Under s 182 of the Principal Act, with the exception of a director holding office for life in a private company, directors may be dismissed by ordinary resolution in general meeting. The company must be given 28 days notice of the proposed resolution. A copy must be sent immediately to the director who is entitled to be heard on the resolution at the meeting. In addition he may require written representations to be sent out with the notices convening the meeting, or if it is too late to circulate to the representatives, they may be read out at the meeting. Section 182(7) provides that nothing in the section is to be taken 'as derogating from any power to remove a director which may exist apart from this section.' Accordingly, the dismissal of one of the directors by his fellow directors will be valid if expressly authorised by the articles. See *Lee v Chou Wen Hsien* [1985] BCLC 45.

[15.08]   In dismissing a director the company must comply not only with the provisions of s 182, but also with the requirements of natural justice.

Glover v BLN Ltd [1973] IR 388 (Supreme Court)

[15.09]   The plaintiff had, pursuant to the terms of a written contract been appointed technical director of group of companies including the defendant company. Clause 12(*c*) of the contract expressly provided that he could be dismissed if guilty of any serious misconduct or serious neglect in the performance of his duties which in the opinion of the board of directors affected injuriously the business or property of the group. The evidence before the court proved that the plantiff had been guilty of such misconduct. However, the board dismissed him without informing him of the complaints being made against him. The Supreme Court (affirming the decision of Kenny J) held that there had been a breach of natural justice in the manner in which the plaintiff was dismissed, that the dismissal was accordingly wrongful, and that the plaintiff was entitled to damages.

[15.10]   **Walsh J:** In my opinion, this case hinges entirely upon clause 12(*c*) of the service agreement. The defendants have relied upon this particular clause to justify their summary dismissal of the plaintiff . . . It appears to me quite clear that the operation of clause 12(*c*) would necessarily involve (*a*) the ascertainment of the facts alleged to constitute serious misconduct, (*b*) the determination that they did in fact constitute serious misconduct, and (*c*) that the members of the board present and voting should be unanimously of opinion that the serious misconduct injuriously affected the reputation, business or property of the holding company or of the subsidiary companies. The parties by their conduct explicitly set up the machinery for dismissal specified in clause 12(*c*) that machinery designated the board of directors as the tribunal and required unanimity of opinion upon the effect of such serious misconduct if it should be proved.

In my view, it was necessarily an implied term of the contract that this inquiry and determination should be fairly conducted. The arguments and submissions in this court ranged over a very wide field particularly in the field of consitituional justice . . . The constitution was relied upon; in particular article 40.3 of the constitution. This court in *Re Haughey* [1971] IR 217, held that that provision of the constitution was a guarantee of fair procedures. It is not, in my opinion, necessary to discuss the full effect of this article in the realm of private law or indeed of public law. It is sufficient to say that public policy and the dictates of constitutional justice require that statutes, regulations or agreements setting up machinery for taking decisions which may affect rights or impose liabilities should be construed as providing for fair procedures. It is unnecessary to decide to what extent the contrary can be provided for by agreement between the parties. In the present case the provisions of clause 12(*c*) do not seek expressly or by implication to exclude the right of any of the parties to a fair procedure.

The plaintiff was neither told of the charges against him nor was he given any opportunity of dealing with them before the board of directors arrived at its decision to dismiss him. In my view this procedure was a breach of the implied term of the contract that the procedure should be fair, as it cannot be disputed in the light of so much authority on the point, that failure to allow a person to meet the charges against him and to afford him an adequate opportunity of answering them is a violation of an obligation to proceed fairly.

Having regard to the evidence which was given at the trial, one could not say with any degree of certainty that the members of the board of directors would have come to the same conclusion on the facts as Mr Justice Kenny did, or that they would have arrived at a unanimity of opinion on the effect of such misconduct as they might have found proved, particularly when one has regard to the close personal relationships which existed between some members of the board and the plaintiff and their knowledge of his activities in the firm since he joined it. But even if one could say with certainty that, if he had been given a fair hearing, the result would still have been the same, in my view that does not offer any ground for validating retroactively a procedure which was clearly invalid. It is to be noted that the board acted with great haste in dismissing the plaintiff and on a report which did not contain complaints or allegations of misconduct set out with the particularity with which they were set out subsequently in the reply to the plaintiff's notice for particulars. Furthermore as was settled by this court in *Carvill v Irish Industrial Bank Ltd* [1968] IR 325, an employer in defending an action by an employee for wrongful summary dismissal, cannot rely upon misconduct which was not known by the employer at the time of the dismissal. I would add that the misconduct, if known but not in fact used as a ground for dismissal at the time, cannot be relied upon afterwards in an effort to justify the dismissal.

For the reasons I have already stated I am of opinion that the plaintiff was wrongfully dismissed in that the dismissal was a violation of the provisions of clause 12(*c*) of the service agreement because of the failure to give him an adequate opportunity of answering them.

O'Dalaigh CJ concurred. Fitzgerald J delivered a dissenting judgment.

Notes

The judgment of Walsh J, concentrates on the fact that the requirements of fair procedures had been implicitly incorporated into the plaintiff's contract of employment. However, where the director has no contract of employment and holds his office solely by virtue of the articles, the rules of natural justice will still apply: see *Garvey v Ireland* [1981] IR 25. Apart from the protection available by virtue of the rules of natural justice, the director who also has a contract of employment may have available to him the remedies under the Unfair Dismissals Act 1977.

[15.11]   Dismissal of a director under s 182 is without prejudice to any rights he may have to damages for breach of a contract of employment.

Carvill v Irish Industrial Bank Ltd [1968] IR 325 (Supreme Court)

[15.12]   The plaintiff had been a director of the defendant company. The articles provided that the company could remove a director before the expiration of the term of his office. It was further provided that the directors could appoint a director to be managing director for a fixed term or indefinitely, that all the provisions of the articles relating to the removal of directors should apply to the removal of the managing director, 'subject to the provisions of any contract between him and the company', and that the managing director should cease to hold that office upon ceasing to hold the office of director. The plaintiff, although never formally appointed as managing director had acted as such and had been treated by the company as such, paying him a salary of £2,000 per annum. He was subsequently dismissed as director and issued proceedings claiming he had been wrongfully dismissed.

O'Keeffe J: The real dispute between the plaintiff and the defendants is not as to whether the plaintiff was a managing director, but as to the terms upon which he held that office . . .

Once these words [ie. 'subject to the provisions of any contract between him and the company'] appear, it is open to the director to enter into a contrct with the managing director the effect of which may be to deprive the company in general meeting of the power to remove him from office without being liable to pay damages. The question is whether there is such a contract in the present case.

It appears to me that a person who is a director and who is appointed by the board of directors to the office of managing director must be deemed to hold that office under some contract either express or implied. The contract may be for a fixed term, in which case it cannot properly be terminated before the expiration of that term without a liability to pay damages. It may be for no fixed term and indeed, may be for so long only as the person holds office as director, in which case, if the person concerned ceases to be a director his office as managing director also comes to an end. An express contract might well provide that the office could be held without limitation as to term but with a provision for notice to determine it and in that case there would be implied a term that until the proper notice had been given, the person concerned would not be removed from the position of director so as to bring his appointment as managing director to a end.

What were the terms of the plaintiff's contract in the present case? . . . I . . . find a situation in which the plaintiff is appointed managing director and his salary is fixed on a yearly basis and while the figure is altered by increasing it first to £2,000 and then to £2,000 with a percentage of profits it remains fixed on a yearly basis. I think that the plaintiff must be regarded as being employed under a contract from year to year as managing director and that it must be implied also that such contract could not be determined without such notice as is appropriate to an engagement of the kind mentioned. The trial judge considered that a year's notice (or salary in lieu of notice) was appropriate and the defendants have not submitted that such length of notice was excessive although they have contended that no notice at all was required. In the circumstances I see no reason for disturbing the finding of the trial judge that the appropriate period of notice was a year although I might not myself have fixed so long a period. I think however, that the salary payable during the period of notice would be £2,000 pa not £2,500 pa. If the plaintiff is entitled to damages this is the figure which I would award.

O'Dalaigh CJ, Lavery, Haugh and Walsh JJ concurred.

Notes

See also *Nelson v James Nelson & Sons Ltd* [1914] 2 KB 770; *Southern Foundries (1926) Ltd v Shirlaw* [1940] AC 701; *Shindler v Northern Raincoat Co Ltd* [1960] 1 WLR 1038; cf *Read v Astoria Garage (Streatham) Ltd* [1952] Ch 637.

Under s 182(7) it is expressly provided that nothing in the section 'shall be taken as depriving a person removed thereunder of compensation or damages payable to him in respect of the determination of his appointment as director or compensation or damages payable to him in respect of the determination of any appointment terminating with that as director.' A similar provision is contained in art 99 of table A. Apart from the question of damages for breach of contract, it is possible that the director, if also a shareholder may in appropriate circumstances also be able to claim relief under s 205 and s 213(*f*) of the Principal Act (see *Re Murph's Restaurant Ltd infra*).

[15.13]   Under s 28 of the 1990 Act limits are placed on the director's ability to enter into service contracts which would entitle him to damages in the event of dismissal. The section applies to any term in the director's service contract by which his employment with the company of which he is the director, or where he is the director of a holding company, his employment within the group is to be continued, or may be continued, otherwise than at the instance of the company (whether under the original agreement or under a new agreement entered into in pursuance of the original agreement) for a period exceeding five years during which time he cannot be dismissed, or can only be dismissed in specified circumstances. Such a term is void unless approved by a resolution of the company in general meeting. A written memorandum setting out the terms of the proposed resolution, must be available for inspection by the members, at the registered office for not less than 15 days before, and at the meeting at which it is passed. If the term in question is not approved, the service contract may be terminated on giving reasonable notice.

S 28 also applies to situations where a *person* and not necessarily a director, is or is to be employed with a company under an agreement which cannot be terminated by the company or can only be terminated in specified circumstances, and more than six months before the expiration of the agreement, the company enters into a further agreement (otherwise than in pursuance of a right conferred by the original agreement) under which the person is to be employed with the company or, where he is a director of as holding company, within the group. If by adding the unexpired period of the first agreement to the second agreement, the period of employemnt exceeds five years, then approval of the general meeting must be obtained.

While s 28 may pose an obstacle to directors of public companies who wish to secure their positions by way of lengthy fixed term contracts, directors of smaller private companies, if also the controlling shareholders, should have little difficulty in obtaining the requisite shareholders approval.

Under s 50 of the 1990 Act must keep at its registered office, at the place where its register of members is kept (if other than the registered office) or at its principal place of business, copies of directors' service contract or 'where it is an oral contract' a memorandum setting out the terms of the contract. Copies or memoranda (as the case may be) must also be kept of directors' service contracts with any subsidiary. Variations of such contracts are also registrable. The contract or variation is only registrable if under the terms of the contract or variation there are still at least three years to run, or where for at least three years the director cannot be dismissed without the company being liable to compensate him. The company must send a notice to the company in the prescribed form of the place where the contracts or memoranda are registered and the register must be open to inspection by members during business hours. The rules regarding registration are modified where the director's obligations under the contract are to be performed outside the State. Failure to comply with s 50 renders the company and every officer in default liable to a fine and for continued contravention, to a daily default fine.

Powers and duties of directors[1]

[15.14]   Under standard form articles, the power to manage the company is delegated by the general meeting to the board of directors. Prior to 1963 the relevant article delegating powers of management was to be found in art 71 of table A of the Companies Act 1908 (subsequently incorporated into table A of the UK 1948 Act). Cases interpreting the article held that the general meeting could never interfere with the director's powers of management by way of an ordinary resolution. A special resolution was required instead.[2] However, the wording of the art 71 was different in certain respect from art 80 of table A of the Principal Act and accordingly these cases would no longer seem to represent good law in Ireland. Article 80 is understood[3] to mean that the members may by ordinary resolution validly interfere with the directors' general powers of management. In the case of other powers which have been expressly reserved to the directors by statute or by the articles themselves, the members can only interfere by special resolution.[4]

1 See *Keane* at paras **29.13–29.20**; Mac Cann *Directors' Duties: To Whom Are They Owed?* (1991) 9 ILT (ns) 3, 30; *Directors' Duties of Care, Skill and Diligence* (1991) 9 ILT (ns) 56; *Directors' Fiduciary Duties* (1991) 9 ILT (ns) 80, 104.
2 *John Shaw & Sons (Salford) v Shaw* [1935] 2 KB 133; *Salmon v Quin & Axtes Ltd* [1909] 1 Ch 311; *Breckland Group Holding Ltd v London & Suffolk Property Ltd* [1989] BCLC 100.
3 *Ussher* (1975) Gazette. For a wider interpretation of the shareholders' right to interfere with management decisions see *J. Temple Lang* (1973) Gazette 241.
4 Eg. the power to refuse to register a transfer of shares under art 3 of part II of table A or the power to elect a chairman under art 53. See *Clark v Workman* (para 15.28); *Kehoe v Waterford & Limerick Rly* (1888–89) 21 LR Ir 221.

[15.15]   The directors although in a fiduciary position towards the company, do not normlly owe such a duty directly to the members.

Percival v Wright [1902] 2 Ch 421 (Chancery Division)

[15.16]   The plaintiffs offered to sell their shares in the company. The defendants, members of the board of directors, agreed to purchase the shares at £12.50 each. After the transfer of shares had been completed the plaintiffs found out that when the defendants had been negotiating to buy their shares, the board had also been negotiating to sell the entire undertaking of the company to a third party for a price which represented well in excess of £12.50 per share. The defendants had not disclosed this fact to the plaintiffs'. Ultimately, the takeover never materialised. However, the plaintiffs claimed that the defendants as members of the board, owed a fiduciary duty to the shareholders and accordingly sought to set aside the transfer of shares on the ground of non-disclosure of material information.

[15.17]   **Swinfen Eady J:** It is urged that the directors hold a fiduciary position as trustees for the individual shareholders and that, where negotiations for sale of the undertaking are on foot, they are in the position of trustees for sale. The plaintiffs admitted that this fiduciary position did not stand in the way of any dealing between a director and a shareholder before the question of sale of the undertaking had arisen, but contended that as soon as that question arose the position was altered. No authority was cited for that proposition and I am unable to adopt the view that any line should be drawn at that point. It is contended that a shareholder knows that the directors are managing the business of the company in the ordinary course of management and impliedly releases them from any obligation to disclose any information so acquired. That is to say, a director purchasing shares need not disclose a large casual profit, the discovery of a new vein or the prospect of a good dividend in the immediate future and similarly a director selling shares need not disclose losses, these being merely incidents in the ordinary course of management. But it is urged that, as soon as negotiations for the sale of the undertaking are on foot, the position is altered. Why? The true rule is that a shareholder is fixed with knowledge of all the directors' powers and has no more reason to assume that they are not negotiating a sale of the undertaking than to assume that they are not exercising any other power. It was strenuously urged that, though incorporation affected the relations of the shareholders to the external world, the company thereby becoming a distinct entity, the position of the shareholders inter se was not affected and was the same as that of partners or shareholders in an unincorporated company. I am unable to adopt that view. I am therefore of opinion that the purchasing directors were under no obligation to disclose to their vendor shareholders the negotitions which ultimately proved abortive. The contrary view would place directors in a most invidious position, as they could not buy or sell shares without disclosing negotiations, a premature disclosure of which might well be against the best interests of the company. I am of opinion that directors are not in that position.

There is no question of unfair dealing in this case. The directors did not approach the shareholders with the view of obtaining their shares. The shareholders approached the directors and named the price at which they were desirous of selling. The plaintiffs' case wholly fails and must be dismissed with costs.

Notes
   In *Smith v Cork & Bandon Rly Co* (1870) 5 IR Eq 65 Christian LJ stated:

'I am aware that there have been cases in which, for some purposes, directors of joint stock companies have been assimulated to trustees as for example, in the not permitting them to make their office a source of private profit – but that they are actually trustees for each individual shareholder, is a proposition which presents itself to my mind with all the effect of novelty . . .'

[15.18] In some exceptional circumstances the directors may owe a fiduciary duty directly to the shareholders.

Coleman v Myers [1977] 2 NZLR 225 (Court of Appeal, Wellington)

[15.19] The defendants (Sir Kenneth and Douglas Myers) were directors and shareholders of a small private family company, C & E. The first defendant made a takeover bid for C & E, and having gained the requisite number of acceptances, sought to compulsorily acquire the shares of the remaining members, the plaintiffs, under the New Zealand equivalent of s 204 of the Principal Act. The plaintiffs only reluctantly agreed to sell. They had consistently looked to the defendants as fellow family members, for business advice. However, the defendants had withheld information from the plaintiffs affecting the true value of the shares. Mahon J at first instance held that *Percival v Wright* had been wrongly decided. The Court of Appeal, while holding that on its own facts *Percival v Wright* had been correctly decided, went on to hold that on the facts of the present case the defendants owed a fiduciary duty to the plaintiffs and were accordingly liable to compensate them for loss suffered as a result of the non-disclosure.

[15.20] **Woodhouse J:** The claim is that the directors were in breach of that duty by allowing a conflict of interest to arise in relation to the take-over bid and then failing to ensure that the shareholders were equipped to make an informed decision. It is a complaint that despite the reponse and acceptance of confidence the directors failed to disclose material facts which in a takeover situation affected the worth of the shares when considered from the point of view not only of vendors but the purchaser as well. There is, of course, the added complaint that in certain respects the shareholders were actually given wrong advice or information.

In advancing their case the appellants did not rely upon the mere status of the first and second respondents as directors of the company. They asserted that the fiduciary relationship had arisen because those respondents were executive directors in a private company with a shareholding largely spread over a few associated family groups each one of which had come to rely upon Sir Kenneth Myers and later his son, not simply for the development of policy within the company and the good management of its affairs, but for the protection and cultivation of their own particular interests as shareholders. Associated with those general considerations are a number of particular matters referable to the takeover offer itself. They include the recommendations the directors made that the offer should be accepted by the shareholders; the dimensions of the capital gain that was at stake; and the wholesale use of C & E funds which alone could make the total achievement possible. In a sentence, the complaint is that Mr Douglas Myers by the use of inside knowledge got himself into a position where he could literally name his own price for the shares and get it accepted because the shareholders were uninformed or had been positively misled . . .

In this area of the case a good deal of attention was focussed on a decision of Swinfen Eady J in *Percival v Wright* (para **15.16**). It involved a purchase of shares by the directors of a company at a time when they had knowledge of a likely and favourable sale of the whole undertaking. The vendor shareholders later brought proceedings against the directors claiming that the latter were in a fiduciary position towards them at the time of the sale. The judge disagreed and some textbook writers have regarded the decision as authority for the proposition that a company director, while owing a fiduciary duty to his company, will never have such a duty in respect of the shareholders. Not unnaturally the respondents have sought to rely upon the case which they submit should be regarded as having decided the law upon the point in New Zealand. I do not think it does.

The restricted nature of the argument addressed to the court in *Percival v Wright* and the surprising nature of a concession deliberately associated with it needs to be appreciated in order to understand the true implications of the decision. It was submitted that the directors held a fiduciary position for the shareholders where negotiations for a sale of the whole undertaking of the company were on foot; but not otherwise. The argument was that in such circumstances the directors were in the position of trustees for sale. And there was a further concession: it was accepted that there had been no unfair dealing by the directors or a purchase of the shares at an undervalue. So the very limited point put to the court was simply that fortuitous negotiations for the sale of the undertaking altered the whole position. That, in my view, could not possibly be the test and with respect, the decision of the judge in that particular case restricted as I think it was to that one point, was inevitable.

In my opinion, it is not the law that anybody holding the office of director of a limited liability company is for that reason alone to be released from what otherwise would be regarded as a fiduciary responsibility owed to those in the position of shareholders of the same company. Certainly their status as directors did not protect the defendants in a Canadian case which finally made its way to the Privy Council: see *Allen v Hyatt* (1914) 30 TLR 444. The decision in that case turned upon the point that the directors of the company had put themselves in a fiduciary relationship with some of their shareholders because they had undertaken to sell shares of the shareholders in an agency capacity. But there is nothing in the decision to suggest that in the case of a director the fiduciary relationship can arise only in an agency situation. On the other hand, the mere status of company director should not produce that sort of responsibility to a shareholder and in my opinion it does not do so. The existence of such a relationship must depend, in my opinion upon all the facts of the particular case.

When dealing with this part of the present case Mahon J himself came to the conclusion that *Percival v Wright* had been wrongly decided. Then he expressed his opinion generally upon the point in the following way:

'The essential basis of breach of fiduciary duty is the improper advantage taken by the defendant of a confidence reposed in him either by or for the benefit of the plaintiff. When one considers the legal relationship between the shareholder in a limited liability company and the directors entrusted with the management of that company, it appears to me that in any transaction involving the sale of shares between director and shareholder, the director is the respository of confidence and trust necessarily vested in him by the shareholder or by his legal status in relation to the existence of information affecting the true value of those shares.'

He then qualified that conclusion by restricting it to those holding office as directors in private companies. It may be that he intended some qualification beyond that but if he did then with respect, I think myself that conclusion is too broadly stated . . . The standard of conduct required from a director in relation to dealings with a shareholder will differ depending upon all the surrounding circumstances and the nature of the responsibility which in a real and practical sense the director has assumed towards the shareholder. In the one case there may be a need to provide an explicit warning and a great deal of information concerning the proposed transaction. In another there may be no need to speak at all. There will be intermediate situations. It is, however, an area of the law where the courts can and should find some practical means of giving effect to sensible and fair principles of commercial morality in the cases that come before them; and while it may not be possible to lay down any general test as to when the fiduciary duty will arise for a company director or to prescribe the exact conduct which will always discharge it when it does, there are nevertheless some factors that will usually have an influence upon a decision one way or the other. They include I think, dependence upon information and advice, the existence of a relationship of confidence, the significance of some particular transaction for the parties and of course, the extent of any positive action taken by or on behalf of the director or directors to promote it. In the present case each one of those matters had more than ordinary significance and when they are taken together they leave me in no doubt that each of the two directors did owe a fiduciary duty to the individual shareholders. The reasons are implicit in the account I have given of the C & E company and those associated with it together with the depth of knowledge and experience on the one side when contrasted with the relative lack of it on the other and the careful development of the takeover proposals.

Cooke and Casey JJ delivered concurring judgments.

Notes

A similar view was taken in *Securities Trust Ltd v Associated Properties Ltd* (unreported, High Court, 19/11/80) which involved an attempt to compulsorily acquire the shares of minority shareholders under s 204 of the

Principal Act, as part of a takeover bid. The minority shareholders had not been informed by the bidder that the takeover was to be financed by the company itself. McWilliam J felt that such information should then have been disclosed by the directors of the company. He said as follows:–

'I have not been addressed on the duty of directors towards their own members or their position as agents or otherwise vis a vis the shareholders on such a transaction but, although a director is not a trustee for the shareholders, directors are to some extent in a fiduciary position and I am of opinion that, on a transaction such as this, the shareholders are entitled to be given reasonably full particulars by their directors . . .'

See also *Heron International Ltd v Lord Grade* [1983] BCLC 244. Cf *Re a Co* [1986] BCLC 383; *Dawson International plc v Coats Paton plc* [1989] BCLC 233.

[15.21]   Where the company is insolvent or threatened with insolvency, the directors in administering the affairs of the company, are under a duty to have regard to the interests of the creditors.

Re Frederick Inns Ltd (High Court, 29 May 1990)

[15.22]   Frederick Inns Ltd, The Rendezvous Ltd and The Graduate Ltd, together with six other companies were all wholly owned subsidiaries of Motels Ltd. The total arrears of tax owing by the various companies in the group amounted to £2.8 million. The Revenue Commissioners were aware that each company in the group had a distinct trading identity and separate assets and creditors. They were also aware that each company was insolvent. The directors of Frederick Inns, The Rendezvous and The Graduate agreed under threat of winding up proceedings from the Revenue Commissioners, to realise the assets of these three companies and to apply the proceeds of sale in discharging the arrears of tax of all the companies in the group. The assets were duly sold and the proceeds were paid over to the Revenue. The three companies were subsequently placed in liquidation and the liquidator issued proceedings seeking recovery of the proceeds of sale of each respective company in so far as they had been appropriated in discharge of the indebtedness of any other company.

[15.23]   **Blayney J:** A fundamental attribute of a company in Irish Law is that of corporate personality. A company is a legal entity distinct from its members, capable of enjoying rights and of being subject to duties which are not the same as those enjoyed or borne by its members. This was finally established in *Salomon v Salomon & Co* and the principle has been recognised and applied in many decisions of the Irish Courts. Generally speaking this principle and the statutory rules of company law in which the principle is implicit apply to the relationship between holding companies and subsidiaries and to transactions between them and third parties. The assets of such companies are treated as owned by them legally and beneficially as distinct legal entities. And except where circumstances enable a court to discover an agency or trustee relationship between them, a holding company is not treated as the owner of its subsidiaries' assets. And the liabilities of companies which are members of the same group are those of the individual companies which incur them. There is no common group liability for the obligations of individual members of the group imposed by law. The principle is reflected in many aspects of company law; for example, in s 147 of the Companies Act 1963 every company (whether a holding company or a subsidiary) is required to keep proper books of account which must include accounts of all sums of money received and expended by the company. Such accounts must disclose with reasonable accuracy the financial position of the company and enable a balance sheet and profit and loss account to be prepared in accordance with the requirements of statute. Public companies are required to send copies of their accounts to the Registrar of Companies with the annual returns. Clearly these accounts are a record of and source of information about the company and its business for its shareholders and its creditors. The requirement that copies of accounts should be sent to the registrar did not apply to private companies which were subsidiaries of public companies. Section 150 of the Company Act 1963 required holding companies to incorporate in their public accounts the financial position and results of its subsidiaries. These group accounts normally will take the form of consolidated accounts showing the state of affairs of the entire group comprising the holding company and all its subsidiaries. This is for the purpose of informing shareholders and it is one of comparatively few instances when the legislature has to a limited extent and for a specific purpose modified the consequences of the rule in *Salomon's* case.

Taxing statutes also recognise the principle that each company is a separate legal entity, to the extent that they do not tax a holding company and its subsidiaries as if they were one. Thus, in respect of Corporation tax, companies in a group make separate tax returns and receive separate assessments on their profits and this happened in the present case in respect of each of the companies involved. This general proposition remains true despite the fact that taxing statutes in particular cases and for particular purposes (which are not relevant to the present case) have provided for the piercing of the corporate veil and for looking through the company to its shareholders.

I have referred to the principles of the *Salomon* case and to its consequences for a group of companies because they are fundamental to the decision in the present case. The submission made on behalf of the liquidator is that when any company is insolvent it is beyond its powers gratuitously to alienate its property or to make a gift to a third party out of its assets. Reliance for this proposition was placed upon *Hutton v West Cork Railway*(1883) 23 Ch D 654; *Parke v Daily News* [1962] 2 All ER 929; *Charterbridge Corporation v Lloyds Bank* [1969] 2 All ER.

I think there are two aspects to the payments made in the present case and the allocations subsequently made out of these payments by the Revenue.

427

The first, is whether irrespective of the insolvency of the company out of whose assets the payments were made, these payments to the Revenue were ultra vires. In my view they were. Insofar as payments to the Revenue were made by companies out of their assets, which exceeds their liabilities for tax, and were intended to be applied in reduction of the tax liabilities of other companies in the group, they can only be regarded as voluntary payments made without consideration for the benefit of third parties and as such in the absence of any evidence that such excess payments were for the benefit of the paying companies they are clearly ultra vires. It is common case that these payments were made as a result of the threats in the letters dated the 12th of June from the Revenue solicitor to each of the companies and after the negotiations with representatives of the Revenue Commissioners to which I have referred. They were made to stave off winding up proceedings threatened by the Revenue Commissioners which would have affected the group. The Revenue Commissioners in my view committed a serious error in dealing with the separate tax claims against the several companies as if they were a group and the claim was against the group. They insisted and brought pressure to bear on the applicants to make a settlement of the several separate liabilities as a group liability and were insufficiently concerned with the companies as separate entities.

In *Trevor v Whitworth* (1887) 23 AC 414 Lord Herschell said:

'It cannot be questioned, since the case of *Ashbury Railway Carriage and Iron Company v Riche*, that a company cannot enjoy its funds for the purpose of any transactions which do not come within the objects specified in the memorandum . . . The capital may, no doubt, be diminished by expenditure upon and reasonably incidental to all the objects specified. A part of it may be lost in carrying on the business operations authorised. Of this all persons trusting the company are aware and take the risk. But I think they have a right to rely and were intended by the legislature to have a right to rely, on the capital remaining undiminished by any expenditure outside these limits, or by the return of any part of it to the shareholders.'

This view has been adhered to in many cases where there was no insolvency. An example is *Hutton v The West Cork Railway Co Ltd* (1883) 23 Ch D 654 and a recent one by Carroll J in *Roper v Ward* [1981] ILRM 408.

The second aspect which is material is that at the time when these gratuitous payments to the Revenue were made out of the proceeds of the sale of their assets, these companies were insolvent. Does insolvency considered by itself affect a company's power or right to make a payment of this kind? The Companies Acts do not directly provide that an insolvent company shall not be entitled to continue trading or alienate its property gratuitously, assuming cases where the gratuitous alienation is authorised by the memorandum. However, there is a provision that directors may incur civil or criminal liability or be subject to disqualification if a company carries on business with intent to defraud creditors. There is also a statutory application of the rule against granting a fraudulent preference to a particular creditor. In the present case it has not been contended that the payments to the Revenue were fraudulent preferences, I think for the sufficient reason that the necessary proof of dominant purpose to prefer the Revenue may be difficult to establish. And then the payments in question cannot be said to be trading so as to be fraudulent trading. Nonetheless in my judgment, the payments to the Revenue which are in question were made by the authority of the directors of the respective companies in breach of the duty which the company and the directors owed to the general creditors of these insolvent companies. Counsel for the liquidator has referred me to a statement of law by Street CJ in *Kinsella v Russell Kinsella Property Ltd* 4 NSWLR 722 at 730 where he said:

'In a solvent company the proprietory interests of the shareholders entitle them as a general body to be regarded as the company when questions of the duty of directors arise. If, as a general body, they authorise or ratify a particular action of the directors, there can be no challenge to the validity of what the directors have done. But where a company is insolvent the interests of the creditors intrude. They become prospectively entitled, through the mechanism of liquidation to displace the power of the shareholders and directors to deal with the company's assets. It is in a practical sense their assets and not the shareholders' assets that, through the medium of the company are under the management of the directors pending either liquidation, return to solvency or the imposition of some alternative administration.'

This statement was made in relation to the law of New South Wales. It was approved by Dillon LJ in *West Mercia Safetywear Ltd (In Liquidation) v Dodd* [1988] BCLC 250. It seems to me to be consonant with the intent of Irish company legislation and to be appropriate and applicable to insolvent companies in Irish law. In my judgment therefore the payments to the Revenue which are in question were also misapplications of the respective companies' assets because they were made when the companies were insolvent and the payments were in disregard of the rights and interest of the general creditors . . .

It was also submitted that the Revenue Commissioners were entitled to rely on s 8 of the Companies Act 1963 . . . [His Lordship then quoted s 8.] By its terms this section refers to acts or things done which, if the company had been empowered to do the same, would have been lawfully and effectively done. I do not find the section capable of assisting the Revenue Commissioners in relation to companies which were insolvent, to their knowledge, even if one supposes that in the present case these companies had been empowered by their memoranda and articles to make gratuitous payments to or for the benefit of third parties out of their assets (and it is a supposition which in this case is so inconsistent with some of the basic principles of company law as to be hardly made.) For insolvent companies such payments consitute a misapplication of the companies' assets and could not have been lawful or effective as against the general unsecured creditors, since they would effectively defraud them of assets to which the creditors were entitled to have recourse.

I come therefore to the conclusion that payment to the Revenue Commissioners by any of the companies of any sum in excess of its particular tax liability was ultra vires the paying company insofar

(*a*) as it effected a gratutious reduction or alienation of its assets and

(*b*) it was done when the company was insolvent.

I am satisfied from the evidence that the payments in respect of which the liquidator brings these motions were made as part of the arrangement made with the Revenue Commissioners for a settlement of the group's tax liability. It is not clear whether that arrangement included any agreement or understanding as to how these moneys were to be appropriated in reduction of the several companies' liabilities. It is possible that it did. But at least it was implicit in the arrangement that the Revenue Commissioners would determine what appropriation would be made. And that seems to be what in fact occurred as is evidenced by the averments in the affidavits filed on behalf of the liquidator and of the Revenue Commissioners. The result was undoubtedly that the assets of some of the companies in the group were applied in reduction of the tax liabilities of the other companies. At the time when this was done the Revenue Commissioners, having regard to their status and functions must be presumed to have known that in law one company in a group cannot gratuitously alienate or permit its assets to be appropriated for the benefit of another company. Further, I am satisfied the Revenue Commissioners must be considered as having notice that the four companies involved in these motions were insolvent. Throughout it seems to me the Revenue Commissioners failed to address or take into account these considerations. Finally the effect of these ultra vires payments was to defraud the company's general unsecured creditors of assets to which they were entitled and unjustly to enrich the companies which benefitted from the appropriations and the Revenue Commissioners who received the payments.

In these circumstances the Revenue Commissioners received and held such payments in a fiduciary capacity, in my judgment as trustees upon a constructive trust for the payor companies and the purported appropriation of such payments or any part thereof, in reduction of the tax liabilities of any other company in the group constituted a breach of trust.

Notes

See also *Re John C Parkes & Sons Ltd* (High Court, Blayney J, 7 February 1990) and *MacCann* (1990) 8 ILT (n.s.) 111.

In *Byrne v Shelbourne FC Ltd* (High Court, 8 February 1984) which related to the sale of an insolvent company's assets and undertaking, the plaintiff, a creditor of the company claimed that the sale was at an undervalue and was made with intent to defraud the company's creditors. In rejecting the claim, O'Hanlon J stated that 'before any limited company can dispose of all its assets, it must do the best it can for the creditors and explore all reasonable possibilities of obtaining a better offer before selling out to a particular bidder . . . Once it comes to the knowledge of the directors of a company that another and possibly higher bidder is in the background, they cannot ignore that situation or they do so at their peril if they proceed to rush through an agreement which they already have in contemplation and which leaves the creditors unsatisfied at the end of the day.'

The first case to suggest that the directors may owe a duty to consider the interests of creditors was *Walker v Wimborne* (1976) 50 ALJR 446, noted by *Barrett* in (1977) 40 MLR 226. Here Mason J said that 'the directors of a company in discharging their duty to the company must take account of the interests of its shareholders and its creditors. Any failure by the directors to take into account the interests of creditors will have adverse consequences for the company as well as for them. The creditor of a company . . . must look to that company for payment. His interests may be prejudiced by the movement of fund between companies in the event that the companies become insolvent.'

This case involved a successful misfeasance summons by the liquidator of Asiatic against the company's directors. The respondents were also directors of Australian Sound and Communications Pty Ltd and Estoril Pty Ltd. The two transactions which gave rise to the breach of duty were concluded on the same day. The respondents caused Asiatic to pay $10,000 to Sound with security and without an express undertaking to repay. The second transaction involved a secured loan by Estoril to Asiatic thereby putting Estoril. The transactions constituted misfeasance on the part of the directors according to Mason J as they 'exposed Asiatic to the probable prospect of substantial loss, and thereby seriously prejudiced the unsecured creditors of Asiatic. It was more than an improvident transaction reflecting an error of judgment. It was undertaken in accordance with a policy adopted by the directors in total disregard of the interests of the company and its creditors.'

In *Nicholson v Permakraft (NZ) Ltd* [1985] 1 NZLR 242 Cooke J made the following remarks:–

'The duties of directors are owed to the company. On the facts of particular cases this may require the directors to consider inter alia the interests of creditors. For instance creditors are entitled to consideration, in my opinion, if the company is insolvent or nearly-insolvent or of doubtful solvency or if a contemplated payment or other course of action would jeopardise its solvency.

The criterion should not be simply whether the step will leave a state of ultimate solvency according to the balance sheet, in that total assets will exceed total liabilities. Nor should it be decisive that on the balance sheet the subscribed capital will remain intact, so that a capital dividend can be paid without returning capital to shareholders.

Balance sheet solvency and the ability to pay a capital dividend are certainly important factors tending to justify proposed action. But as a matter of business ethics it is appropriate for directors to consider also whether what they do will prejudice their company's practical ability to discharge promptly debts owed to current and likely continuing trade creditors.

To translate this into legal obligation accords with the now persuasive concepts of duty to a neighbour and the linking of power with obligation . . . In a situation of marginal commercial solvency such creditors may fairly be seen as beneficially interested in the company or contingently so.

On the other hand, to make out a duty to future new creditors would be much more difficult. Those minded to commence trading with and give credit to a limited liability company do so on the footing that its subscribed capital has not been returned to the shareholders, but otherwise they must normally take the company as it is when they elect to do business wit it. Short of fraud they must be the guardians of their own interest.

In the case of a supplier who already has an established trade relationship with a company, there is of course, a distinction between current and future debts. It seems to me neither necessary nor desirable, however, to use that distinction so as to limit the duties of the directors of the debtor company to considering whether debts already incurred can be paid. If the company's financial position is precarious the fortunes of such suppliers may be so linked with those of the company as to bring them within the reasonable scope of the dirctor's duties. They may continue to give credit in ignorance of a change damaging to their prosects of payment.

The recognition of duties to creditors restricted as already outlined, is justified by the concept that limited liability is a privilege. It is a privilege healthy as tending to the expansion of opportunities and commerce; but it is open to abuse. Irresponsible structural engineering – involving the creating, dissolving or transforming of incorporated companies to the prejudice of creditors – is a mischief to which the courts should be alive. But a balance has to be struck. There is no good reason for cultivating a paternal concern to protect business people perfectly able to look after themselves.

For those reasons, among the many authorities cited to us I would respectfully adopt the approach of Cumming-Bruce and Templeman LJJ in *Re Horsley & Weight Ltd* [1982] Ch 442, 445–456. Both Lord Justices favoured an objective test: whether at the time of the payment in question the directors "should have appreciated" or "ought to have known" that it was likely to cause loss to creditors or threatened the continued existence of the company. In my opinion, a payment made to the prejudice of current or continuing creditors when a likelihood of loss to them ought to have been known is capable of constituting misfeasance by the directors . . . I also share the view to which Cumming-Bruce and Templeman LJJ evidently incline their obiter observations that in such cases the unanimous assent of the shareholders is not enough to justify the breach of duty to the creditors. The situation is really one where those conducting the affairs of the company owe a duty to creditors. Concurrence by the shareholders prevents any complaint by them but compounds rather than excuses the breach as against the creditors.

The foregoing principles relate to actions by the company against directors, whether or not in truth brought by the liquidator. It does not exclude the possibility of an action by a particular creditor against the directors or the company for breach of a particular duty of care arising on ordinary negligence principles. For example, directors might obtain credit for the company when they ought to know that the creditor incorrectly understood a valuable asset to belong to the company. But that is territory which need not be explored in the present case. No attempt has been made to construct the action on that footing. Nor is it suggested for instance, that Odlins gave the manufacturing company credit on the understanding that it owned an equity in the factory land and buildings.'

See also *Kinsela v Russell Pty Ltd* (1986) 10 ACLR 395. Here the company which was faced with imminent collapse granted a lease of premises at substantially below the market rent with no provision for rent review during the term of the lease. The lessees were two of the directors and it was they who had caused the company to grant the lease in the first place. They were also given the option to purchase the premises at any time during the term of the lease at a price substantially below the market value. Shortly after the execution of the lease the company went into liquidation. The court found on the evidence, that the purpose of the lease (which had been approved) by all the shareholders was to put the company's assets beyond the reach of creditors. The liquidator obtained an order avoiding the transaction as having been made by the directors in breach of duty. Street CJ said:–

'It is, to my mind, legally and logically acceptable to recognise that, where directors are involved in a breach of their duty to the company affecting the interests of shareholders, then shareholders can either authorise that breach in prospect or ratify it in retrospect. Where, however, the interest at risk are those of creditors I see no reason in law or in logic to recognise that the sharheolders can authorise the reach. Once it is accepted, as in my view it must be, that the director's duty to a company as a whole extents in an insolvency context to not prejudicing the interests of creditors . . . the shareholders do not have the power or authority to absolve the directors from that breach.'

In *Grove v Flavel* (1986) 4 ACLC 564 Jacobs J held that the directors' duty to consider creditors' interests arose only in a situation where the company was insolvent or financially unstable and not otherwise. See also *David Neil & Co Ltd v Neil (1986) 3 NZCLC 99; Re Lake Tekapo Motor Inn Ltd* (1987) 3 NZCLC 100. English courts have only gradually come to accept that directors owe a duty to consider the interests of creditors. In *Lonrho v Shell Petroleum Ltd* [1980] 1 WLR 627, 634 Lord Diplock said obiter, that 'the best interests of the company are not necessarily those of the shareholders but may include those of the creditors.' More recently in the House of Lords in *Winkworth v Edward Baron Development Ltd* [1987] BCLC 193, 197 also said, albeit obiter that

'a company owes a duty to its creditors, present and future. The company is not bound to pay off every debt as soon as it is incurred and the company is not obliged to avoid all ventures which involve an element of risk, but the company owes a duty to its creditors to keep its property inviolate and available for the repayment of its debts. The conscience of the company, as well as its management is confided to its directors. A duty is owed by the directors to the company and to the creditors to ensure that the affairs of the company are properly administered and that its property is not dissipated or exploited for the benefit of the directors themselves to the prejudice of the creditors.'

The breaches of duty in this case, were the withdrawal of large sums of money from the company by the two directors (who were also the sole shareholders). The effect of the withdrawals was that the company was not able to maintain its solvency. Subsequently the company went into liquidation.

See also *West Mercia Safetywear Ltd v Dodd* [1988] BCLC 250. The facts were that the company ('West Mercia') was a wholly owned subsidiary of AJ Dodd & Co Ltd. The defendant was a director of the two companies, both of which banked with the same bank. The overdraft of AJ Dodd & Co Ltd was personally guaranteed by the defendant. In May 1984 West Mercia owed AJ Dodd & Co Ltd approximately £30,000. Both companies were in financial difficulties at the time and an accountant had told the defendant that both accounts were not to be operated. On 21 May 1984 the defendant transferred £4,000 from the West Mercia account to the account of AJ Dodd & Co Ltd. In June both companies went into liquidation and the liquidator of West Mercia brought proceedings seeking a declaration that the respondent had been guilty of misfeasance and breach of trust and that he be ordered to repay the £4,000 transferred from West Mercia to AJ Dodd & Co Ltd. Dillon LJ held, applying *Kinsela v Russell Kinsela Pty Ltd* that the defendant had been in breach of duty and made an award of damages against him.

Under s 52 of the 1990 Act the directors are also under a statutory duty to the company to have regard to the interests of the company's employees, thus reversing *Parke v The Daily News* [1961] 1 All ER 695.

[15.24] The powers conferred on the directors by the articles must be exercised bona fide for the purposes for which they are conferred.

Howard Smith Ltd v Ampol Petroleum Ltd [1974] AC 821 (Privy Council)

[15.25] Two companies, Ampol Petroleum Ltd ('Ampol') and Bulkships Ltd held 35% of the issued shares in RW Miller (Holdings) Ltd ('Miller'). Miller required more capital at the time. The litigation arose out of the struggle for the takeover and control of Miller. Ampol and Bulkships were seeking to acquire the remaining shares in Miller. Howard Smith Ltd then announced its intention to make a higher bid for the shares. The directors of Miller indicated that they were going to recommend that the Ampol/ Bulkships offer be rejected as too low. The directors then entered into an agreement with Howard Smith Ltd whereby sufficient shares were allotted so as to give it control of Miller. This had the effect of providing Miller with much needed capital. It also reduced the holding of Ampol and Bulkships to 36%. As a result of the allotment Howard Smith Ltd was now in a position to make an effective takeover offer. Ampol then issued proceedings challenging the validity of the allotment. The trial judge (Street J) found that Miller's directors had not been motivated by any purpose of personal gain or by a desire to retain their position on the board. He also found that Miller needed the capital raised by the allotment but that the primary purpose of the allotment was to reduce the proportionate shareholding of Ampol and Bulkships so that Howard Smith Ltd could proceed with its takeover bid. The allotment was therefore held to have been made for an improper purpose, it was declared invalid and an order was made to rectify the share register accordingly. The Privy Council upheld his decision.

[15.26] **Lord Wilberforce** (delivering the judgment of the court): The directors in deciding to issue shares, forming part of Millers' unissued capital to Howard Smith acted under clause 8 of the company's articles of association. This provides subject to certain qualifications which have not been invoked, that the shares shall be under the control of the directors, who may allot or otherwise dispose of the same to such persons on such terms and conditions and either at a premium or otherwise and at such time as the directors may think fit. Thus and this is not disputed, the issue was clearly intra vires the directors. But, intra vires though the issue may have been, the directors' power under this article is a fiduciary power; and it remains the case that an exercise of such a power though formally valid, may be attacked on the ground that it was not exercised for the purpose for which it was granted. It is at this point that the contentions of the parties diverge. The extreme argument on one side is that, for validity, what is required is bona fide exercise of the power in the interests of the company; that once it is found that the directors were not motivated by self-interest ie. by a desire to retain their control of the company or their positions on the board – the matter is concluded in their favour and that the court will not inquire into the validity of the reasons for making the issue. All decided cases, it was submitted, where an exercise of such a power as this has been found invalid, are cases where directors are found to have acted through self-interest of this kind.

On the other side, the main argument is that the purpose for which the power is conferred is to enable capital to be raised for the company and that once it is found that the issue was not made for that purpose, invalidity follows.

It is fair to say that under the pressure of argument intermediate positions were taken by both sides, but in the main the arguments followed the polarisation which has been stated.

In their Lordship's opinion neither of the extreme positions can be maintained. It can be accepted as one would only expect, that the majority of cases in which issues of shares are challenged in the courts are cases in which the vitiating element is the self-interest of the directors or at least the purpose of the directors to preserve their own control of the management . . . Further, it is correct to say that where the self interest of the directors is involved, they will not be permitted to assert that their action was bona fide thought to be, or was, in the interest of the company; pleas to this effect have invariably been rejected . . . just as trustees who buy trust property are not permitted to assert that they paid a good price.

But it does not follow from this, as the appellants assert, that the absence of any element of self-interest is enough to make an issue valid. Self interest is only one, though no doubt the commonest instance of improper motive; and before one can say that a fiduciary power has been exercised for the purpose for which it was conferred a wider investigation may have to be made . . .

On the other hand, taking the respondent's contention it is, in their Lordships' opinion too narrow an approach to say that the only valid purpose for which shares may be issued is to raise capital for the company. The discretion is not in terms limited in this way; the law should not impose such a limitation on directors' powers. To define in advance exact limits beyond which directors must not pass is, in their Lordships' view impossible. This clearly cannot be done by enumeration, since the variety of situations facing directors of different types of companies in different situations cannot be anticipated. No more, in their Lordships' view can this be done by the use of a phrase – such as 'bona fide in the interest of the company as a whole,' for some corporate principle applicable to fiduciary powers at best serve negatively to exclude from the area of validity cases where the directors are acting sectionally or partially ie. improperly favouring one section of the shareholders against another . . .

In their Lordships' opinion it is necessary to start with a consideration of the power whose exercise is in question, in this case a power to issue shares. Having ascertained, on a fair view, the nature of this power, and having defined as can best be done in the light of modern conditions the, or some limits within which it may be exercised, it is then necessary for the court if a particular exercise of it is challenged, to examine the substantial purpose for which it was exercised and to reach a conclusion whether that purpose was proper or not. In doing so, it will necessarily give credit to the bona fide opinion of the directors if such is found to exist and will respect their judgment as to matters of management; having done this, the ultimate conclusion has to be as to the side of a fairly broad line on which the case falls.

The main stream of authority in their Lordships' opinion, supports this approach. In *Punt v Symons & Co Ltd* [1903] 2 CH 506 Byrne J expressly accepts that there may be reasons other than to raise capital for which shares may be issued. In the High Court case of *Harlowe's Nominees Pty Ltd v Woodside (Lakes Eatrance) Oil Co NL* (1968) 121 CLR 483 an issue of shares was made to a large oil company in order, as was found, to secure the financial stability of the company. This was upheld as being within the power although it had the effect of defeating the attempt of the plaintiff to secure control by buying up the company's shares . . .

Their Lordships' were referred to the recent judgment of Berger J in the Supreme Court of British Columbia in *Teck Corporation Ltd v Millar* (1972) 33 DLR (3d) 288. This was concerned with the affairs of Afton Mines Ltd in which Teck Corporation Ltd a resource conglomerate had acquired a majority shareholding. Teck was indicating an intention to replace the board of directors or Afton with its own nominees with a view to causing Afton to enter into an agreement (called an 'ultimate deal') with itself for the exploitation by Teck of valuable mineral rights owned by Afton. Before this could be done, and in order to prevent if, the directors of Afton concluded an exploitation agreement with another company 'Canex'. One of its provisions as is apparently common in this type of agreement in Canada provided for the issue to Canex of a large number of shares in Afton thus displacing Teck's majority. Berger J, found at p 328: 'their [the directors'] purpose was to obtain the best agreement they could while . . . still in control. Their purpose was in that sense to defeat Teck. But, not to defeat Teck's attempt to obtain control rather it was to foreclose Teck's opportunity of obtaining for itself the ultimate deal. That was . . . no improper purpose.' His decision upholding the agreement with Canex on this basis appears to be in line with the English and Australian authorities to which reference has been made . . .

By contrast to the cases of *Harlows* and *Teck* the present case, on the evidence does not, on the findings of the trial judge, involve any considerations of management within the proper sphere of the directors. The purpose found by the judge is simply and solely to dilute the majority voting power held by Ampol and Bulkships so as to enable a then minority of shareholders to sell their shares more advantageously. So far as authority goes, an issue of shares purely for the purpose of creating voting power has repeatedly been condemned . . . And though the reported decisions, naturally enough are expressed in terms of their own facts, there are clear considerations of principle which support the trend they establish. The constitution of a limited company normally provides for directors with powers of management, and shareholders, with defined voting powers having power to appoint the directors and to take in general meeting, by majority vote, decisions on matters not reserved for management. Just as it is established that directors within their management powers, may take decisions against the wishes of the majority of shareholders and indeed that the majority of shareholders cannot control them in the exercise of these powers while they remain in office . . . so it must be unconstitutional for directors to use their fiduciary powers over the shares in the company purely for the purpose of destroying an existing majority, or creating a new majority which did not previously exist. To do so is to interfere with that element of the company's constitution which is separate from and set against their powers. If there is added moreover, to this

437

immediate purpose an ulterior purpose to enable an offer for shares to proceed which the existing majority was in a position to block, the departure from the legitimate use of the fiduciary power become not less but all the greater. The right to dispose of shares at a given price is essentially an individual right to be exercised on individual decision and on which a majority in the absence of oppression of similar impropriety is entitled to prevail. Directors are of course, entitled to offer advice and bound to supply information relevant to the making of such a decision but to use their fiduciary power solely for the purpose of shifting the power to decide to whom and at what price shares are to be sold cannot be related to any purpose for which the power over the share capital was conferred upon them. That this is the position in law was in effect recognised by the majority directors themselves when they attempted to justify the issue as made primarily in order to obtain much needed capital for the company. And once this primary purpose was rejected, as it was by Street J there is nothing legitimate left as a basis for their action except honest behaviour. That is not, in itself enough.

Their Lordships therefore agree entirely with the conclusion of Street J that the power to issue and allot shares was improperly exercised by the issue of shares to Howard Smith . . .

Notes

See also *Hogg v Cramphorn Ltd* [1967] Ch 254; *Piercy v S Mills & Co Ltd* [1920] 1 Ch 77; *Nash v Lancegaye Safety Glass (Ireland) Ltd* (1958) 92 ILTR 11; *Afric Sive Ltd v Oil & Gas Exploration Ltd* (High Court, Carroll J, 30 January 1989). In all these cases, the exercise of powers by directors to be valid must have been in good faith. In the recent case of *Dawson International plc v Coats Paton plc* [1989] BCLC 233, the plaintiff company entered into a contract with the directors of Coats Paton plc that they would recommend the plaintiffs takeover bid to the shareholders. Lord Cullen held that the contract was enforceable. He said in rejecting the contention that the contract as a breach of the directors' duty:–

'At the outset I do not accept as a general proposition that a company can have no interest in the change of identity of its shareholders on a takeover. It appears to me that there will be cases in which its agents, the directors will see the takeover of its shares by a particular bidder as beneficial to the company . . . Accordingly, I do not accept that . . . a company could not enter into a contract of the nature alleged by the pursuers.'

Does this mean that, despite the decision in *Howard Smith v Ampol Petroleum Ltd* (para **15.25**) the directors could allot shares to fend off a takeover bid if they bona fide believed that the takeover would be detrimental to the company? See *Teck Corporation Ltd v Millar* (1973) 33 DLR (3d) 288.

On the other hand see *Clemens v Clemens Bros Ltd* [1976] 2 All ER 268 where the plaintiff had 45% of the issued shares in the company, her aunt having the remaining 55%. The aunt, who was a director of the company issued shares to her fellow directors and to a trust for the employees, in order primarily to dilute the plaintiffs voting strength to less than 25%. This was held to be oppressive of the plaintiff entitling her to relief under the UK equivalent of s 205.

Where the execise of powers relates to the allotment of shares, it should be remembered that this power is subject to statutory restrictions imposed by ss 20 and 23 of the 1983 Act.

[15.27] A director may not fetter his discretion by a contract with an outsider.

Clark v Workman [1920] 1 IR 107 (Chancery Division)

[15.28] The chairman of the board of directors (Workman) gave an undertaking to the proposed transferee of a controlling shareholding in the company, that his interests would be 'looked after' and that he would therefore do his utmost to ensure that the board registered the transfer of the shareholding. The registration of the transfer which had been approved by the casting vote of Workman, as chairman, was declared invalid by Ross J.

[15.29] **Ross J:** [The directors] were bound to consider the interests of all the shareholders, unfettered by any undertaking or promise to any intending purchaser. They were bound to consider all offers, by whomsoever made and they were bound to weigh and consider the desirability of admitting the persons or companies who proposed to come into their concern. If they failed in any of these matters, they disabled themselves from performing their duty to the shareholders and nothing that they did would in the eye of the law be held to have been done in good faith . . .

I must now consider the action of the defendant directors their motives, and intentions and ascertain whether what they proposed and supported was, in the circumstances inconsistent with a right performance of their fiduciary duty to the company . . . I now refer to two uncontradicted statements in the affidavits para 14 of RW Smith's affidavit: 'In my presence Frank Workman stated that he had promised the chairman of the Northumberland Shipbuilding Company Ltd, that he would use his best endeavours to get the controlling interest in the defendant company into the hands of the chairman of the Northumberland Company and that he would not attempt to get any better offer from anyone else.' We must take it that this represented the motives and intentions of Mr Frank Workman and those associated with him. By acting thus he had fettered himself by a promise to the English syndicate and had disqualified himself from acting bona fide in the interests of the company he was leaving. Again, take the affidavit of Sir George Clark, para 10: 'I consider the offer of Robert Clark more beneficial to the shareholders who desire to sell than the offer of the Northumberland Shipbuilding Company or the Doxford Company and I believe the defendant directors refused to consider it, because they had entered into an agreement with the Northumberland Shipbuilding Company and the Doxford Company to force the sale of

439

the control of the defendant company to them, even at the expense to the shareholders of the defendant company.' Sir George Clark swears that he believes the defendant directors are acting in the interest of the English syndicate and not in the interest of the defendant company or its shareholders and he states his belief that if the control is transferred to the syndicate the liquid assets of the company may be used for the purpose of buying debentures in the Northumberland Shipbuilding Company instead of for the benefit of the defendant company. Although this is not quite a statement as to facts, it is declared to be the belief of Sir George Clark. It was a challenge that required some answer and no answer has been given. I desire it to be known that although I hold the defendant's action to have been wrongful and inconsistent with their duty as trustees, I do not in any way impute to them dishonourable conduct or anything in the nature of a fraud. What they have done is analagous to cases we are all familiar with, where the donee of a power executes it in pursuance of an arrangement or bargain which he thinks erroneously he is entitled to make.

Directors' duties of care, skill and diligence[1]

Re City Equitable Fire Insurance Co Ltd [1925] Ch 407 (Court of Appeal)

[15.30] The company which was in liquidation, had collapsed partly due to the failure of certain investments and partly due to the fraudulent misapplication of other investments by the chairman of the board, Bevan. The liquidator sought to make the other directors liable for the losses on the ground of negligence. The action was unsuccessful as the articles contained a provision exempting the directors from liability except for losses caused by 'their own wilful neglect or default'. However, the decision of Romer J gives a detailed analysis of the directors' duties of care, skill and diligence.

[15.31] Romer J: It has sometimes been said that directors are trustees. If this means no more than that directors in the performance of their duties stand in a fiduciary relationship to the company, the statement is true enough. But if the statement is meant to be an indication by way of analogy of what those duties are, it appears to me to be wholly misleading. I can see but little resemblance between the duties of director and the duties of a trustee of a will or of a marriage settlement. It is indeed impossible to describe the duty of directors in general terms, whether by way of analogy or otherwise. The position of a director of a company carrying on a small retail business is very different from that of a director of a railway company. The duties of a bank director may differ widely from those of an insurance director, and the duties of a director of another. In one company for instance, matters may normally be attended to by the manager or other members of the staff that in another company are attended to by the directors themselves. The larger the business carried on by the company the more numerous and the more important the matters that must of necessity be left to the managers, the accountants and the rest of the staff. The manner in which the work of the company is to be distributed between the board of directors and the staff is in truth a business matter to be decided on business lines . . .

In order, therefore, to ascertain the duties that a person appointed to the board of an established company undertakes to perform, it is necessary to consider not only the nature of the company's business, but also the manner in which the work of the company is in fact distributed between the directors and the other officials of the company, provided always that this distribution is a reasonable one in the circumstances and is not inconsistent with any express provisions of the articles of association. In discharging the duties of his position thus ascertained a director must, of course, act honestly; but he must also exercise some degree of both skill and diligence. To the question of what is the particular degree of skill and diligence required of him, the authorities do not, I think give any very clear answer. It has been laid down that so long as a director acts honestly he cannot be made responsible in damages unless guilty of gross or culpable negligence in a business sense. But as pointed out by Neville J *In re Brazilian Rubber Plantations and Estates Ltd* [1911] 1 Ch 437, one cannot say whether a man has been guilty of negligence, gross or otherwise unless one can determine what is the extent of the duty which he is alleged to have neglected. For myself, I confess to feeling some difficulty in understanding the difference between negligence and gross negligence, except in so far as the expressions are used for the purpose of drawing a distinction between the duty that is owed in one case and the duty that is owed in another. If two men owe the same duty to a third person and neglect to perform that duty, they are both guilty of negligence and it is not altogether easy to understand how one can be guilty of gross negligence and the other of negligence only. But if it be said that of two men one is only liable to a third person, for gross negligence and the other is liable for mere negligence, this, I think means no more than that the duties of the two men are different. The one owes a duty to take a greater degree of care than does the other . . . If therefore, a director is only liable for gross or culpable negligence this means that he does not owe a duty to his company, to take all possible care. It is some degree of care less than that. The care that he is bound to take has been described by Neville J, in the case referred to above as 'reasonable care' to be measured by the care an ordinary man might be expected to take in the circumstances on his own behalf. In saying this Neville J, was only following what was laid down in *Overend & Guerney Co v Gibb* LR 5 HL 480, 486 as being the proper test to apply namely:

'Whether or not the directors exceeded the powers entrusted to them or whether if they did not so exceed their powers they were cognisant of circumstances of such a character, so plain, so manifest and so simple of appreciation that no men with any ordinary degree of prudence, acting on their own behalf, would have entered into such a transaction as they entered into?'.

There are, in addition one or two other general propositions that seems to be warranted by the reported cases: (1) A director need not exhibit in the performance of his duties a greater degree of skill than may reasonably be expected from a person of his knowledge and experience. A director of a life insurance company, for instance, does not guarantee that he has the skill of an actuary or of a physician. In the words of Lindley MR: 'If directors act within their powers, if they act with such care as is reasonably to be expected from them, having regard to their knowledge and experience, and if they act honestly for the benefit of the company they represent, they discharge both their equitable as well as their legal duty to the company': See *Lagunas Nitrate Co v Lagunas Syndicate* [1899] 2 CH 392, 435. It is perhaps only another way of stating the same proposition to say that directors are not liable for mere errors of judgment. (2) A director is not bound to give continuous attention to the affairs of his company. His duties are of an intermittent nature to be performed at periodical board meetings and at meetings of any committee of the board upon which he happens to be placed. He is not, however, bound to attend all such meetings, though he ought to attend whenever in the circumstances, he is reasonably able to do so. (3) In respect of all duties that, having regard to the exigencies of business, and the articles of association, may properly be left to some other official, a director is, in the absence of grounds for suspicion, justified in trusting that official to perform such duties honestly. In the judgment of the Court of Appeal in *In re National Bank of Wales Ltd* [1899] 2 Ch 629, 673, the following passage occurs in relation to a director who had been deceived by the manager and managing director as to matters within their own particular sphere of activity: 'Was it his duty to test the accuracy or completeness of what he was told by the general manager and the managing director? This is a question on which opinions may differ, but we are not prepared to say that he failed in his legal duty. Business cannot be carried on upon principles of distrust. Men in responsible positions must be trusted by those above them, as well as by those below them, until there is reason to distrust them. We agree that care and prudence do not involve distrust; but for a director acting honestly himself to be held legally liable for negligence, in trusting the officers under him not to conceal from him what they ought to report to him, appears to us to be laying too heavy a burden on honest business men.' That case went to the House of Lords and is reported there under the name of *Dovey v Cory* [1901] AC 477 . . .

1 See generally *Keane* at para **29.20**; *Mac Cann* (1991) 9 ILT (ns) 56.

Jackson v Munster Bank Ltd, ex p Dease (1885) 15 LR Ir 356

[15.32] The company ran banking operations in both Cork and Dublin. Board meetings were held in both cities. Dease was appointed a director on 11 February 1881 and with another director had joint control of the Dublin business. He attended the weekly board meetings in Dublin which related to the Dublin operations. However, he had only attended one or two Cork board meetings. The Cork meetings related to Cork operations. Nothing improper ever happened when he attended Cork meetings. However, when he was absent the Cork directors caused the company, contrary to the articles, to make loans to themselves. In January 1883 Dease was shown a letter which put him on notice of the irregularities in Cork but took no action. Many of the loans to Cork directors ultimately proved to be irrecoverable. Dease was sued for breach of duty. It was claimed that if he had acted with greater diligence the loss could have been prevented.

[15.33]   Chatterton VC: In this case the only doubt present to my mind is where the point of liability commences. There is much to be said in excuse for Mr Dease's inaction with reference to the transactions that occurred previously to the 11th of January 1883. It was expected of him that he would remain in Dublin and there certainly was plenty of business to occupy him there. That enables a reasonable excuse to be urged for his not having taken a more active part in the business of Cork. I agree with the contention of the plaintiffs that he was bound to perform the duties of his post no matter how arduous; but the fact of his having been actively engaged in the business of the company in Dublin may be an excuse for his non-intervention in the business in Cork, where no other would avail him. There can, however be no reason for exempting him from liability from an early period in the year 1883.

On the 11th January 1883 the following letter was written by Mr Thomas Fitzgerald one of the plaintiffs, to Mr La Touche and this letter was shown to Mr Dease. [His Lordship here read the letter]. Here was a statement which, if Mr Dease had been hitherto ignorant of the affairs of the company should have startled him very much. It is strange that he should have been ignorant of them before; but at any rate, after the receipt of that letter, he was bound at once to set about investigating all this misfeasance. If he had then gone down to Cork and done his duty and examined the accounts he would have found that there had been a systematic fraudulent misappropriation of the property of the bank and the money of the customers of the bank extending over a period of years, conducted principally by the chairman of the bank with the assistance of one who had been a manager and was afterwards appointed a director of it, and with the concurrence of several other directors who formed the local board in Cork. A firm man going down in the exercise of his duty mastering the facts, and remonstrating with his brother directors could have put a stop to his nefarious system and the bank could from that time out, have been protected against the fraudulent misconduct of its directors. Mr Dease did not do so. He attended at the general meeting and was silent. He sat by and heard as false a statement as ever was made by a person in the same situation which he knew to be false and for his own benefit put forward. That was the statement made by the chairman of the company to the meeting that all these statements about overdrafts to the directors were utterly without foundation, the account of that gentleman being actually overdrawn nearly £100,000 at the time the statement was made. Subsequently to this meeting Mr Dease was appointed to make an examination of the accounts of the directors with the company, but he did not go down to Cork for this purpose for some months afterwards. It was his bounden duty to have gone at once into an investigation of these transactions an to have put a stop to them and I can listen to no excuse for his not having done so. If no better course was open to him, he was in my opinion bound to institute a suit in Chancery to put a stop to these proceedings. He did nothing of the kind. I am clear that Mr Dease is liable from February 1883.

Dorchester Finance Company Ltd v Stebbing [1989] BCLC 489

[15.34]   Stebbing, Parsons and Hamilton were of the plaintiff company which carried on a moneylending business and held a moneylender's licence under the Moneylenders Act 1900. Both Stebbing and Parsons were chartered accountants and Hamilton had considerable accounting experience. Parson and Hamilton who were non-executive directors of the plaintiff and left the management of the company's affairs to Stebbing. Because they infrequently visited the company's premises they often signed cheques in blank to be filled in by Stebbing subsequently. Stebbing used certain of these blank cheques to make loans which because of non-compliance with the provisions of the Moneylenders Act 1900 were irrecoverable. The company issued proceedings against the three directors alleging that they had been negligent in the management of the company's affairs and claiming damages for the loss suffered under the irrecoverable loans.

[15.35]   **Foster J:** For the plaintiffs three submissions were made in regard to the duties of the directors. (*a*) A director is required to exhibit in performance of his duties such a degree of skill as may reasonably be expected from a person with his knowledge and experience. (*b*) A director is required to take in the performance of his duties such care as an ordinary man might be expected to take on his own behalf. (*c*) A director must exercise any power vested in him as such honestly, in good faith and in the interests of the company and reliance was placed on *Re City Equitable Fire Insurance Co Ltd* [1905] Ch 407, *Re Sharpe* [1892] 1 Ch 154 and *Re Smith & Fawcett Ltd* [1942] 1 All ER 542.

For the first defendant it was submitted that mere negligence was insufficient and the court had to be satisfied that there had been *crassa neglentia* or gross negligence and reliance for this submission was placed on *Turquand v Marshall* (1869) LR 4 Ch App 376; *Overend & Guerney Co v Gibb* (1872) LR 5 HL 480; *Sheffield and South Yorkshire Permanent Building Society v Aizlewood* (1889) 44 Ch D 412, *Re New Mashonland Exploration Co* [1892] 3 Ch 577 and *Lagunas Nitrate Co v Lagunas Syndicate* [1899] 2 Ch 392. In none of those cases was there a suggestion of dishonesty or recklessness on the part of the directors. In those cases the directors were charged with what might be called errors of judgment. In the *New Mashonland* case [1892] 3 Ch 577 at 586 Vaughan Williams J said:

'If I had arrived at the conclusion that that was done, I should have said that the director who advanced money on a security without waiting for the security, could not have used any discretion or judgment at all. For to advance money on security without waiting for the security is so unbusinesslike an act that it cannot be called a mere error of judgment or an imprudent act.'

I find myself in agreement with Romer J in the *City Equitable* case [1925] Ch 407 at 427–428 where he says:

'For myself, I confess to feeling some difficulty in understanding the difference between negligence and gross negligence except in so far as the expressions are used for the purpose of drawing a distinction between the duty that is owed in one case and the duty that is owed in another.'

I accept the plaintiffs' three submissions as accurately stating the law applicable and counsel for the first defendant conceded that I could take into account the fact that of the three directors two are chartered accountants and the third has considerable experience of accountancy.

For a chartered accountant and an experienced accountant to put forward the proposition that a non-executive director has no duties to perform I find quite alarming. It would be an argument which, if put forward by a director with no accounting experience would involve total disregard of many sections of the Companies Act 1948 . . . The signing of blank cheques by Hamilton and Parsons was in my judgment negligent, as it allowed Stebbing to do as he pleased. Apart from that they not only failed to exhibit the necessary skill and care in the performance of their duties as directors, but also failed to perform any duty at all as directors of Dorchester. In the Companies Act 1948 the duties of a director whether executive or not are the same.

In the absence of any oral evidence by Stebbing the documents must speak for themselves. They show clearly that Stebbing as a director of Dorchester failed to exercise any skill or care in the performance of his duty as a director and that he knowingly and recklessly misapplied the assets of Dorchester to the extent of nearly £400,000. His negligence can only be described as gross negligence and he also is liable for damages.

Notes

See also *Re Brazilian Rubber Plantations and Estates Ltd* [1911] 1 Ch 425 where Neville J said that a director is 'not bound to bring any special qualifications to his office. He may undertake the management of a rubber company in complete ignorance of everything connected with rubber, without incurring responsibility for the mistakes which may result from such ignorance; while if he is acquainted with the rubber business he must give the company the advantage of his knowledge when transacting the company's business.'

See also *Land Credit Co of Ireland v Lord Fermoy* (1869–70) LR 5 Ch App 763. *Ussher* also suggests op cit at p 234 that a director who holds himself out as possessing a particular skill is liable for a failure to exercise that skill, even if not in fact possessed by him – such is reasonably to be expected from him.

The only recent Irish case to consider the directors' duty of care is *Re Mont Clare Hotels Ltd* (High Court, 2 December 1986) where Costello J stated that: 'It is not every error of judgment that amounts to misfeasance in law and it is not every act of negligence that amounts to misfeasance in law. It seems to me that something more than mere carelessness is required, some act that, perhaps may amount to gross negligence in failing to carry out a duty owed by a director to his company.'

A similar view was taken by Kenny J in *PMPA Insurance Co Ltd v New Ireland Assurance Co Ltd* (ex parte judgment, 22 October 1975, reported in the Irish Times, 23 October 1975) where he said that once the management of a company had been delegated to the directors, the court would not interfere with the management 'unless it was in breach of the articles of association or was dishonest or grossly incompetent.'

See also *Re B Johnson & Co (Builders) Ltd* [1955] Ch 634. Also generally Trebilock, *The Liability of Company Directors' Obligations for Negligence* (1969) 32 MLR 499; MacKenzie *A Company Directors' Obligations of Care and Skill* [1982] JBL 460.

What constitutes reasonably regular attendance at board meetings depends on the circumstances. In the *Marquis of Bute's* case [1892] 2 Ch 100 the Marquis had been appointed a director of a bank at the age of 6 months. There were 5 other directors appointed in similar circumstances. The Marquis attended one meeting only, just after his twenty first birthday. Twenty years later the company went into liquidation. It was found that the manager had embezzled large amounts of company money. The liquidator sought to make the Marquis personally liable for the loss on the basis that he could have prevented it by more frequent attendance at board meetings. The court rejected the claim holding that in the circumstances of the appointment of the Marquis, and the 35 other such directors, indicated that their attendance was not reasonably to be expected at board meetings. He had received regular notices of board meetings. If they had stopped being sent he might then have been on notice of irregularities (ie. that board meetings were perhaps not being held) in which case he might have been under a duty to make enquiries. Compare this case with *Dorchester Finance Co Ltd v Stebbing* (para **15.34**).

Contracts between the company and the directors

[15.36] As will be seen below in *Aberdeen Rly Co v Blaikie Bros* (para **15.41**) the director as a fiduciary is liable to account for any profit he makes from a contract with the company, unless he has made proper disclosure and to the company of his interest in the contract.

As a result of part III of the 1990 Act stringent conditions have recently been imposed on the ability of directors and shadow directors to enter into various types of transactions with the company. A shadow director is defined as 'a person in accordance with whose directions the directors of a company are accustomed to act . . . unless the directors are accustomed to so act by reason only that they do so on advice given by him in a professional capacity.'[1]

Under s 26 a person is connected with a director if he is a spouse, parent, brother sister, child, partner, a body corporate controlled by the director[2] or a trustee of a trust the principal beneficiaries of which are the director, his spouse or any of his children or any body corporate which he controls.

1 S 27 of the 1990 Act.
2 For a definition of 'control' see s 26(3), (4), (5).

[15.37] Under s 29 of the 1990 Act a company must not enter into an arrangement with a director of the company or its holding company or a person connected with such director for the acquisition by or from the company of one or more non-cash assets of the 'requisite value' (or of an interest therein) unless the arrangement is first approved by a resolution of the company in general meeting. If the other party to the transaction is a director of or a person connected with a director of the holding company a resolution of the holding company is also necessary. A non-cash asset is of the 'requisite value' if, when the arrangement is entered into its value exceeds (*a*) £50,000; or (*b*) 10% of the company's 'relevant assets' which are defined as:

(*a*) the net assets as valued in the last financial year's accounts, or
(*b*) where there are no such accounts, the called-up share capital.

Any arrangement entered into in contravention of s 29 and any transaction entered into in pursuance of such arrangement is voidable at the instance of the company unless (*a*) restitution of the non-cash asset is no longer possible or the company has been indemnified in respect of any loss or damage suffered by it; or (*b*) rights acquired bona fide for value and without notice of the breach of s 29 would be affected; or (*c*) the arrangement is, within a reasonable time, affirmed by the company in general meeting and (as the case may be) by the holding company.

Where there has been a breach of s 29, the director or person connected to him, and any other director who authorised the arrangement shall (whether or not it is avoided) be liable to account for any profit made directly or indirectly as a result and will be liable to indemnify the company in respect of any consequential loss. If the arrangement is with a person connected with the director, that director will be neither liable to indemnify to the company or to account for any profit made, if he can show that he took all reasonable steps to secure the company's compliance with s 29. The connected person himself and any director who authorised the transaction will also escape liability if they can show that at the time they entered into the arrangement they did not know the relevant circumstances constituting the contravention.

S 29 does not apply to the transfer of non-cash assets between a holding subsidiary and its wholly owned subsidiary or vice versa, or between two wholly owned subsidiaries of a third company. It is also excluded in the case of an arrangement by a company in an insolvent winding up or by a company with a member in his capacity as member.

[15.38] S 30 makes it an offence for a director, or someone acting on his behalf or at his instigation to deal in options to buy or sell certain classes of shares in, or debentures of the company, and certain associated companies, where those shares are traded on the stock exchange.[1]

1 See *Keane* at para **29.20**; *Mac Cann* (1991) 9 ILT (ns).

[15.39] S 31 provides that except in the circumstances set out below the company shall not make loans or 'quasi-loans' to, or enter into 'credit transactions' with a director of the company or its holding company, or with a person connected with such a director. Neither shall it guarantee or provide any security in connection with such arrangements.

A quasi-loan is defined by s 25 as being a transaction under which one party ('the creditor') pays or reimburses expenditure incurred by another party for another ('the borrower') on terms that the borrower reimburses the creditor.

A 'credit-transaction' is one under which one party ('the creditor')–

(*a*) supplies goods or sells land under a hire-purchase agreement or conditional sale agreement;
(*b*) leases or licenses the use of land or hires goods in return for periodical payments; or
(*c*) otherwises disposes of land or supplies goods or services on the understanding that payment (whether in a lump-sum or instalments or by way of periodical payments or otherwise) is to be deferred.

The prohibition on such arrangements does not apply to:–

(*a*) loans and quasi-loans by one member of a group of companies to another member, or the gaining of a guarantee or provision of any security in connection with a loan or quasi-loan by any person to another member of the group;
(*b*) arrangements with the company's holding company, or the provision of a guarantee or security in connection with arrangements between the holding company and a third party;
(*c*) the reimbursement of the directors' proper business expenses;
(*d*) any arrangement where its value, and the total outstanding under any other similar arrangements entered into by the company with any director of the company or any person connected with a director, together is less than 10% of the company's 'relevant assets' (defined at para **15.37**);
(*e*) any arrangement entered into by the company in the ordinary course of its business if its value is no greater and its terms no more favourable than those which the company normally offers or could reasonably be expected to have offered to another person of the same financial standing but unconnected with the company.

Breaches of s 31 incur the similar civil consequences to a breach of s 29, except that the arrangement cannot be ratified by the company.

Furthermore, persons responsible for causing the company to contravene these provisions are also guilty of a criminal offence. Most importantly, however, if the company goes into insolvent liquidation and the court considers that any the arrangement contributed materially to the company's inability to pay its debts or has substantially impeded the orderly winding up of the company, it may if it thinks it proper to do so, impose personal liability for the whole or part of the company's indebtedness, on any person for whose benefit the arrangement was made. In deciding whether to impose personal liability the court shall have particular regard to whether, and to what extent, any outstanding liabilities arising under the arrangement were discharged before the commencement of the winding up.

[15.40]   Because a director is in a fiduciary position towards the company, a contract made by the company with one of its directors or with a company or firm in which he has an interest is voidable at the instance of the company. The director may also be liable to account to the company for profits earned on such a contract.

Aberdeen Railway Co v Blaikie Bros (1854) 1 Macq 461 (House of Lords)

[15.41]   The appellant company had entered into a contract with the respondent firm whereby the latter agreed to manufacture iron chairs at £8.50 per ton. The respondents sued to enforce the contract and the appellant pleaded that it was not bound by the contract because, when it was concluded, the chairman of the board of directors was also the managing partner of the respondent.

[15.42]   **Lord Cranworth LC:** This, therefore, brings us to the general question, whether a director of a railway company is or is not precluded from dealing on behalf of the company with himself or with a firm in which he is a partner. The directors are a body to whom is delegated the duty of managing the general affairs of the company.

A corporate body can only act by agents, and it is of course the duty of those agents so to act as best to promote the interests of the corporation whose affairs they are conducting. Such agents have duties to discharge of a fiduciary nature towards their principal. And it is a rule of universal application that no one, having such duties to discharge, shall be allowed to enter into engagements in which he has or can have a personal interest conflicting or which possibly may conflict with the interests of those whom he is bound to protect. So strictly is this principle adhered to that no question is allowed to be raised as to the fairness or unfairness of a contract so entered into.

It obviously is, or may be impossible to have been the best for the interest of the cestui que trust, which it was possible to obtain.

449

It may sometimes happen that the terms on which a trustee has dealt or attempted to deal with the estate or interests of those for whom he is a trustee have been as good as could have been obtained from any other person – they may even at the time have been better. But still so inflexible is the rule that no inquiry on that subject is permitted . . . It is true that the question have generally arisen on agreements for purchases or leases of land and not as here, on a contract of a mercantile character. But this can make no difference in principle. The inability to contract depends not on the subject matter of the agreement but on the fiduciary character of the contracting party, and I cannot entertain a doubt of its being applicable to the case of a party who is acting as manager of a mercantile or trading business for the benefit of others, no less than to that of an agent or trustee employed in selling or letting land.

Was then Mr Blaikie so acting in the case now before us? – if he was, did he while so acting contract on behalf of those for whom he was acting with himself?

Both these questions must obviously be answered in the affirmative. Mr Blaikie was not only a director, but (if that was necessary) the chairman of the directors. In that character it was his bounden duty to make the best bargains he could for the benefit of the company.

While he filled that character, namely, on 6 February 1846, he entered into a contract on behalf of the company with his own firm, for the purchase of a large quantity of iron chairs at a certain stipulated price. His duty to the company imposed on him the obligation of obtaining these chairs at the lowest possible price.

His personal interest would lead him to an entirely opposite direction, would induce him to fix the price as high as possible. This is the very evil against which the rule in question is directed and here I see nothing whatever to prevent its application . . . It was Mr Blaikie's duty to give his co-directors and through them to the company, the full benefit of all the knowledge and skill which he could bring to bear on the subject. He was bound to assist them in getting the articles contracted for at the cheapest possible rate. As far as related to the advice he should give them, he put his interest in conflict with his duty and whether he was the sole director or only one of many can make no difference in principle.

The same observation applies to the fact that he was not the sole person contracting with the company; he was one of the firm of Blaikie Brothers, with whom the contract was made and so interested in driving as hard a bargain with the company as he could induce them to make . . .'

Lord Brougham delivered a concurring judgment.

Notes

Where such a contract is voidable, it may be ratified in general meeting. The director, in his capacity as shareholder, may vote in favour of the contract at the general meeting. See *Northwest Transportation Co Ltd v Beatty* (1887) 12 App Cas 589.

In the absence of a provision to the contrary in th articles, a director is not permitted to vote at board meetings on contracts in respect of which he is interested, nor may he be counted in the quorum for such a vote. *Cox v Dublin City Distillery Ltd (No 2* [1915] 1 IR 345.

In practice the strict fiduciary duty of the director is modified by allowing him to enter into contracts with the company and to retain the profits: art 85 of table A. In the case of a contract in which the director is interested, subject to certain exceptions, he may not vote thereon at any board meeting nor will he be counted in the quorum: arts 84 & 86. In the case of private companies the director may vote on such contracts and may be counted in the quorum: art 7 of part II of table A.

Section 194 disclosure

[15.43]   Under s 194 of the Principal Act as amended by ss 27 and 47 of the 1990 Act any director who is in any way whether directly or indirectly, interested in a contract or proposed contract with the company must declare the nature of his interest at a meeting of the directors of the company. Shadow directors must declare their interests by a notice in writing to the board. For the purposes of s 194 a 'contract' includes any loan, quasi-loan, credit transaction or guarantee of a loan, quasi-loan or credit-transaction (whether or not constituting a contract) and whether made by the company for the director himself or for a person connected with him.

For the purposes of the section a general notice by a director to the effect that

(*a*) he is a member of a specified company or firm and is to be regarded as interested in any contract which may, after the date of the notice, be made with that company or firm; or
(*b*) he is to be regarded as interested in any contract which may after the date of the notice be made with a specified person connected with him;

shall be deemed to be a sufficient declaration of interest in ralation to any such contract.

[15.44]   When a director fails to disclose his interest in a contract under s 194 the contract is rendered voidable and the director becomes accountable for any profit which he has made. Disclosure, to be effective under s 194 must be to the full board duly convened and not merely to a subcommittee of the directors.

Guinness plc v Saunders [1988] 2 All ER 940 (Court of Appeal)

[15.45]   Ward was a director of Guinness when it launched a takeover bid for Distillers plc. Ward and two other directors of Guinness formed a committee of the board to conduct the takeover bid. Marketing and Acquisition Consultants Ltd (MAC), a Jersey Company controlled by Ward submitted

451

an invoice to Guinness for £5.2m for services rendered in connection with
the takeover bid. Ward had disclosed his interest in MAC to the committee
of directors formed to conduct the takeover bid, but did not make a disclosure to the full board. Guinness subsequently issued proceedings seeking
repayment of the £5.2m from Ward on the ground that he held it as constructive trustee for Guinness. The Court of Appeal affirming the decision of
the trial judge (Sir Nicholas Browne-Wilkinson VC) held that Ward was liable to account.

[15.46]   **Fox LJ:** Are Guinness entitled to judgment? In relation to this
question it is necessary first of all to consider the effect of s 317 of the 1985
Act [ie s 194 of the Principal Act].

In my opinion, it imposes an obligation to make a disclosure to a meeting
of the full board of directors duly convened. Section 317(1) requires a disclosure to 'a meeting of the directors'. These words it seems to me, cannot be
satisifed by a disclosure to a subcommittee of the directors. It is simply not
what the subsection says. Nothing in the articles can alter that. Section
317(1) is a statutory requirement and its provisions are mandatory. In fact,
in my view, nothing in the articles seeks to alter it. The definition in art 2 is a
definition of the expression 'the board' for the purposes of the articles. It has
no bearing on the construction as a matter of the ordinary use of English of
the words 'a meeting of the directors' in s 317(1). Further, art 100(a)
repeats in effect, the provisions of s 317(1) and requires disclosure at 'a
meeting of the directors in accordance with the statutes'. The statutes in
view of the definition in art 2 include the 1985 Act. The words 'a meeting of
the directors in art 100 have the same meaning in my view, as that which I
have indicated in relation to the same words in s 317(1) and must have been
intended to have the same meaning.

It is said as I understand it, on behalf of Mr Ward that disclosure to the full
board would be an absurdity because the board or at any rate the executive
committee of the board for the purposes of the bid, knew about the
payment. Assuming it were true that all the members of the board knew
about the payment, that does not alter the fact that the requirement of the
statute that there be a disclosure to 'a meeting of the directors of the company' (which is a wholly different thing from knowledge by individuals and
involves the opportunity for positive consideration of the matter by the
board as a body' was not complied with.

I conclude therefore, that the statute required disclosure to a duly convened meeting of the full board of Guinness. There was, it is admitted, no
such disclosure. Mr Ward therefore acted in breach of duty in receiving the
£5.2m.

The next question is what are the consequences of the breach of duty.

A director is in a fiduciary position. A person in a fiduciary position is not
permitted to obtain a profit from his position except with the consent of his
beneficiaries or other persons to whom he owes the duty. In the case of a
director the consent required is that of the members in general meeting.

That is inconvenient in relation to the day to day running of a business. It has, therefore become the practice to relax the general rule by special provisions in the articles. The purpose of s 317(1) is not to destroy the power to relax the general rule by the articles but to impose a binding safeguard on that power.

In my opinion a provision such as art 100(d) must be read in the light of s 317(1) to which it is always subject and for that matter to art 100(a) which gives effect or perhaps more accurately draws attention to the statute. The interest of a director under any contract to which art 100(d) applies must be disclosed in accordance with s 317(1).

Accordingly I conclude that Mr Ward plainly acted in breach of duty in failing to disclose his interest in the agreement to a meeting of the directors. The consequence in my opinion, is that stated by Lord Denning MR in *Hely-Hutchinson v Brayhead Ltd* [1967] 3 All ER 98 at p 103 (which was concerned with a breach by a director of the statutory predecessor of s 317 namely s 199 of the Companies Act 1948) where he said:

'It seems to me that when a director fails to disclose his interest the effect is the same as non-disclosure in contracts uberrimae fidei, or non-disclosure by a promotor who sells to the company property in which he is interested (See *Re Cape Breton Co* (1887) 12 App Cas 652, [1886–90] All ER 333); *Burland v Earle* [1902] AC 83 at 99). Non-disclosure does not render the contract void or a nullity. It renders the contract voidable at the instance of the company and makes the director accountable for any secret profit which he has made.'

Lord Wilberforce and Lord Pearson also accepted that such a contract is voidable at the instance of the company (see [1967] 3 All ER 98 at p 109). It seems to me that consistently with these views s 317(1) must be regarded as imposing a duty which has consequences in the civil law in addition to the penalty of a fine. In addition a civil law duty arises, it seems to me under art 100(a).

It is not in doubt that, if the agreement ever existed, Guinness has exercised its right to avoid it (at the latest by the initiation of the present proceedings) and did so within due time, there is no issue as to delay. Prima facie, therefore, it seems to me that Guinness is entitled to judgment for the £5.2m.

Glidewell LJ and Sir Frederick Lawton concurred.

[Affirmed on other grounds by the House of Lords [1990] BCLC 402].

Notes

See also *Hopkins v Shannon Transport Ltd* (unreported, High Court, 10/7/72) where Pringle J held that disclosure under s 194 must be to an independent board of directors and not to directors who are equally interested in the contract.

Where the articles do not contain a provision similar to art 85 of table A, modifying the director's fiduciary duty to account, it would seem on normal principles of equity that if the director wishes to retain the benefit of the contract he must not only make disclosure to the board under s 194 of the Principal Act, but he must also obtain the consent of his principal, the company in general meeting. See *Regal Hastings Ltd v Gulliver* para **15.48** *infra* and s 194(7) which provides that 'Nothing in this section shall be taken to prejudice the operation of any rule of law restricting directors of a company from having any interest in contracts with the company.'

[15.47]   Directors, being in a fiduciary position towards the company, are accountable to the company for any profit or benefit which they derive from their office.

Regal (Hastings) Ltd v Gulliver [1942] 1 All ER 378

[15.48]   The company ('Regal') owned a cinema in Hastings. The directors decided that Regal should acquire two further cinemas in the locality and sell all three as a going concern. A subsidiary company, Hastings Amalgamated Cinemas Ltd ('Amalgamated') was formed to acquire a lease of the two cinemas. The lessor was only willing to let the cinemas if the directors of Regal were willing to personally guarantee the rent or alternatively if the paid up share capital of Amalgamated was at least £5,000. The directors were unwilling to give personal guarantees so the latter course was chosen instead. However, Regal could only pay for 2,000 £1 shares. The balance of 3,000 shares was to be taken up by the directors. Ultimately four directors took 500 shares each, the chairman, Gulliver found subscribers for a further 500 shares and the balance was taken by the Regal's solicitor Garton. The method of sale of the three cinemas which was finally decided upon involved not the sale of the properties themselves, but rather a sale of the shares in Regal and Amalgamated. This sale resulted in a profit of £2 16s 1d on each share in Amalgamated. The new shareholders in Regal (ie. the purchasers) issued proceedings against the four directors, Gulliver, and Garton seeking an order for them to account for the profit made on the sale of their shareholding in Amalgamated. There was no suggestion that the defendants had acted in bad faith or that they had acted other then for the benefit of the company. On this ground the claim failed both at first instance and in the Court of Appeal. However, the claim against the four directors succeeded in the House of Lords.

[15.49]   Lord Russell of Killowen: We have to consider the question of the respondents' liability on the footing that in taking up these shares in Amalgamated, they acted with bona fides intending to act in the interest of Regal . . . They may be liable to account for the profits which they have made if, while standing in a fiduciary relationship to Regal, they have by reason and in course of that fiduciary relationship made a profit. This aspect of the case was undoubtedly raised before the trial judge but in so far as he deals with it in his judgment, he deals with it on the wrong basis. Having stated at the outset quite truly what he calls 'this stroke of fortune' only came the way of the respondents because they were the directors and solicitors of the Regal, he continues thus: 'But in order to succeed the plaintiff company must show that the defendants both ought to have caused and should have caused the plaintiff company to subscribe for these shares and that the neglect to do so caused a loss to the plaintiff company. Short of this if the plaintiffs can establish that, though no loss was made by the company, yet a profit was corruptly made by the directors and the solicitor, then the company can claim to have that profit handed over to the company, framing the action in such a case for money had and received by the defendants for the plaintiffs' use.' Other passages in his judgment indicate that in addition to this 'corrupt' action by the directors or perhaps alternatively, the plaintiffs in order to succeed must prove that the defendants acted mala fide and not bona fide in the interests of the company or that there was a plot or arrangement between them to divert from the company to themselves a valuable investment. However relevant such considerations may be in regard to a claim for damages resulting from misconduct, they are irrelevant to a claim against a person occupying a fiduciary relationship towards the plaintiff for an account of the profits made by that person by reason and in course of that relationship.

In the Court of Appeal, upon this claim to profits the view was taken that in order to succeed the plaintiff had to establish that there was a duty on the Regal directors to obtain the shares for Regal. Two extracts from the judgment of Lord Greene MR, shows this. After mentioning the claim for damages he says:

'The case is put on an alternative ground. It is said that, in the circumstances of the case, the directors must be taken to have been acting in the matter of their office when they took those shares and that accordingly they are accountable for the profits which they have made . . . There is one matter which is common to both these claims which, unless it is established, appears to me to be fatal. It must be shown that in the circumstances of the case it was the duty of the directors to obtain these shares for their company.'

Later in his judgment he uses the language: 'But it is said that the profit realised by the directors on the sale of the shares must be accounted for by them. That proposition involves that on 2 October, when it was decided to acquire these shares and at the moment when they were acquired by the directors, the directors were taking to themselves something which properly belonged to the company.'

Other portions of the judgment appear to indicate that upon this claim to profits, it is a good defence to show bona fides or absence of fraud on the part of the directors in the action which they took or that their action was beneficial to the company and the judgment ends thus: 'That being so, the only way in which these directors could secure that benefit for the company was by putting up the money themselves. Once that decision is held to be a bona fide one and fraud drops out of the case, it seems to me there is only one conclusion, namely that the appeal must be dismissed with costs.'

My Lords, with all respect, I think there is a misapprehension here. The rule of equity which insists on those, who by use of a fiduciary position make a profit, being liable to account for that profit, in no way depends on fraud or absence of bona fides or upon such questions or considerations as whether the profiteer was under a duty to obtain the source of the profit for the plaintiff or whether he took a risk or acted as he did for the benefit of the plaintiff, or whether the plaintiff has in fact been damaged or benefitted by his action. The liability arises from the mere fact of a profit having in the stated circumstances been made. The profiteer however honest and well-intentioned cannot escape the risk of being called upon to account.

The leading case of *Keech v Sandford* (1726) Sel Cas Ch 61 is an illustration of the strictness of this rule of equity in this regard and of how far the rule is independent of these outside considerations. A lease of the profits of a market had been devised to a trustee for the benefit of an infant. A renewal on behalf of the infant was refused. It was absolutely unobtainable. The trustee, finding that it was impossible to get a renewal for the benefit of the infant, took a lease for his own benefit. Though his duty to obtain it for the infant was incapable of performance, nevertheless he was ordered to assign the lease to the infant, upon the bare ground that if a trustee on the refusal to renew might have a lease for himself, few renewals would be made for the benefit of cestuis que trust. Lord King LC said at p 62: 'This may seem hard, that the trustee is the only person of all mankind who might not have the lease, but it is very proper that the rule should be strictly pursued and not in the lease relaxed . . .'

One other case in equity may be referred to in this connection viz., *Ex p James* (1803) 8 Ves 337, decided by Lord Eldon LC. This was a case of a purchase of a bankrupt's estate by the solicitor to the commission and Lord Eldon LC refers to the doctrine thus at p 345: 'This doctrine as to purchases by trustees, assignees, and persons having a confidential character stands much more upon general principles than upon the circumstances of any individual case. It rests upon this: that the purchase is not permitted in any case however honest the circumstances; the general interests of justice requiring it to be destroyed in every instance as no court is equal to the examination and ascertainment of the truth in much the greater number of cases.'

Let me now consider whether the essential matter which the plaintiff must prove have been established in the present case. As to the profit being in fact made there can be no doubt. The shares were acquired at par and were sold three weeks later at a profit of £2 16s 1d per share. Did such of the first five respondents as acquired these very profitable shares acquire them by reason and in course of their office of directors of Regal? In my opinion, when the facts are examined and appreciated the answer can only be that they did.

It now remains to consider whether in acting as directors of Regal they stood in a fiduciary relationship to that company. Directors of a limited company are the creatures of statute and occupy a position peculiar to themselves. In some respects they resemble trustees, in others they do not. In some respects they resemble agents, in others they do not. In some respects they resemble managing partners, in others they did not. [Having considered a number of the authorities his lordship concluded.]

In the result I am of opinion that the directors standing in a fiduciary relationship to Regal in regard to the exercise of their powers as directors and having obtained these shares by reason and only by reason of the fact that they were directors of Regal and in the course of the execution of that office are accountable for the profits which they have made out of them. The equitable rule laid down in *Keech v Sandford* and *Ex p James* and similar authorities applies to them in full force. It was contended that these cases were distinguishable by reason of the fact that it was impossible for Regal to get the shares owing to lack of funds and that the directors in taking the shares were really acting as members of the public. I cannot accept this argument. It was impossible for the cestui que trust in *Keech v Sandford* to obtain the lease, nevertheless the trustee was accountable. The suggestion that the directors were applying simply as members of the public is a travesty of the facts. They could had they wished, have protected themselves by a resolution (either antecedent or subsequent) of the Regal shareholders in general meeting. In default of such approval the liability to account must remain. The result is that in my opinion, each of the respondents Bobby, Griffiths, Bassett and Bentley is liable to account for the profit which he made on the sale of his 500 shares in Amalgamated.

The case of the respondent Gulliver however, requires some further consideration, for he has raised a separate and distinct answer to the claim. He says: 'I never promised to subscribe for shares in Amalgamated. I never did so subscribe. I only promised to find others who would be willing to subscribe. I only found others who did subscribe. The shares were theirs. They were never mine. They received the profit. I received none of it.' If these are the facts, his answer seem complete. The evidence in my opinion establishes his contention. As regards Gulliver this appeal should in my opinion be dismissed . . .

There remains to consider the case of Garton. He stands on a different footing from the other respondents in that he was not a director of Regal. He was Regal's legal adviser, but in my opinion, he has a short but effective answer to the plaintiffs' claim. He was requested by the Regal directors to apply for 500 shares. They arranged that they themselves should each be responsible for £500 of the Amalgamated capital and they appealed by their chairman to Garton to subscribe the balance of £500 which was required to make up the £3,000. In law, his action which has resulted in a profit was taken at the request of Regal and I know of no principle or authority which would justify a decision that a solicitor must account for profit resulting from a transaction which he has entered into on his own behalf not merely with the consent but at the request of his client.

My Lords in my opinion the right way in which to deal with this appeal if (*i*) to dismiss the appeal as against the respondents Gulliver and Garton with costs, (*ii*) to allow it with costs as against the other four respondents and (*iii*) to enter judgment as against each of these four respondents for a sum of £1,402 1s 8d with interest at 4% . . .

Viscount Sankey and Lords Wright, Porter and MacMillan delivered concurring judgments.

Notes

This decision may seem harsh, particularly in view of the fact that the directors acted in the best interests of the company and the company did not as such, suffer loss. However, sympathy for the directors lessens when it is considered that either before taking their shares in Amlgamated or alternatively after taking the shares and before their subsequent sale the directors could have sought a release at a general meeting of Regal from their liability to account for any profit made on the transaction. See *New Zealand Netherlands Society 'Oranje' Inc v Kuys* [1973] 1 WLR 1126.

[15.50] A director who diverts to himself a business opportunity for which his company had been negotiating will be liable to account to the company for any profits made by him on the opportunity or alternatively may be liable in damages.

Canadian Aero Service v O'Malley (1974) 40 DLR (3d) 371

[15.51] The defendants, who were the president and vice-president of the plaintiff company ('Canaero') had been negotiating on behalf of Canaero for a major aerial surveying and mapping contract with the Government of Guyana. The project was to be financed by the Canadian Governments' Aid Programme. The Canadian Government later invited Canaero and other parties to put in formal tenders for the project. The defendants resigned their posts with Canaero and set up their own company 'Tera' Canaero to tender for the project. The contract was awarded to Tera. The defendants' were subsequently successfully sued by Canaero for damages for breach of duty.

[15.52] **Laskin J:** O'Malley and Zarzycki stand in a fiduciary relationship to Canaero which in its generality betokens loyalty, good faith and avoidance of a conflict of duty and self-interest. Descending from the generality the fiduciary relationship goes at least this far: a director or a senior officer like O'Malley or Zarzycki is precluded from obtaining for himself either secretly or without the approval of the company 'which would have to be properly manifested upon full disclosure of the facts), any property or business advantage either belonging to the company or for which it has been negotiating and especially is this so where the director or officer is a participant in the negotiations on behalf of the company.

An examination of the case law in this court and in the courts of other like jurisdictions on the fiduciary duties of directors and senior oficers shows the pervasiveness of a strict ethic in this area of the law. In my opinion, this ethic disqualifies a director or senior officer from usurping for himself or diverting to another person or company with whom or with which he is associated a maturing business opportunity which his company is actively pursuing; he is also precluded from so acting even after his resignation where the resignation may fairly be said to have been prompted or influenced by a wish to acquire for himself the opportunity sought by the company or where it was his position with the company rather than a fresh initiative that led him to the opportunity which he later acquired. [After citing from *Regal (Hastings) Ltd v Gulliver* Laskin J continued]:

I need not pause to consider whether on the facts in *Regal (Hastings) Ltd v Gulliver* the equitable principle was overzealously applied. What I would observe is that the principle or indeed, principles as stated, grew out of older cases concerned with fiduciaries other than directors or managing officers of a modern corporation and I do not therefore regard them as providing a rigid measure whose literal terms must be met in assessing succeeding cases. In my opinion, neither the conflict test, referred to by Viscount Sankey nor the test of accountability for profits acquired by reason only of being directors and in the course of execution of the office reflected in the passage quoted from Lord Russell of Killowen should be considered as the exclusive touchstones of liability. In this as in other branches of the law, new fact situations may require a reformulation of existing principle to maintain its vigour in the new setting.

The reaping of a profit by a person at a company's expense while a director thereof, is of course, an adequate ground upon which to hold the director accountable. Yet there may be situations where a profit must be disgorged, although not gained at the expense of the company, on the ground that a director must not be allowed to use his position as such to make a profit even if it was not open to the company, as for example, by reason of legal disability to participate in the transaction. An analagous situation, albeit not involving a director existed for all practical purposes in the case of *Boardman v Phipps* [1967] 2 AC 46 which also supports the view that liability to account does not depend on proof of an actual conflict of duty and self-interest. Another quite recent, illustration of a liability to account where the company itself had failed to obtain a business contract and hence could not be regarded as having been deprived of a business opportunity is *Industrial Development Consultants Ltd v Cooley*, [1972] 2 All ER 162, a judgment of a court of first instance.

What these decisions indicate is an updating of the equitable principle whose roots lie in the general standards that I have already mentioned, namely, loyalty, good faith and avoidance of a conflict of duty and self-interest. Strict application against directors and senior management officials is simply recognition of the degree of control which their positions give them in corporate operations, a control which rises above day accountability to owning shareholders and which comes under some scrutiny only at annual general or at special meetings. It is a necessary supplement, in the public

459

interest, of statutory regulation and accountability which themselves are, at one and the same time, an acknowledgement of the importance of the corporation in the life of the community and of the need to compel obedience by it and by its promoters, directors and managers to norms of exemplary behaviour.

Counsel for O'Malley and Zarzycki relied upon the judgment of this court in *Peso Silver Mines Ltd (NPL) v Cropper* (1966) 58 DLR (2d) 1 as representing an affirmation of what was said in *Regal (Hastings) Ltd v Gulliver* respecting the circumscription of liability to circumstances where the directors or senior officers had obtained the challenged benefit by reason only of the fact that they held those positions and in the course of execution of those offices. In urging this, he did not deny that leaving to capitalise on their positions would not necessarily immunise them, but he submitted that in the present case there was no special knowledge or information obtained from Canaero during their service with that company upon which O'Malley and Zarzycki had relied in reaching for the Guyana project on behalf of Tera.

There is a considerable gulf between the *Peso* case and the present one on the facts as found in each and on the issues that they respectively raise. In *Peso* there was a finding of good faith in the rejection by its directors of an offer of mining claims because of its strained finances. The subsequent acquisition of those claims by the managing director and his associates, albeit without seeking shareholder approval, was held to be proper because the company's interest in them ceased. What is before this court is not a situation where various opportunities were offered to a company which was open to all of them, but rather a case where it had devoted itself to originating and bringing to fruition a particular business deal which was ultimately captured by former senior officers who had been in charge of the matter for the company. Since Canaero had been invited to make a proposal on the Guyana project there is no basis for contending that it could not, in any event, have obtained the contract or that there was any unwillingness to deal with it.

It is a mistake, in my opinion, to seek to encase the principle stated and applied in *Peso*, by adoption from *Regal (Hastings) Ltd v Gulliver* in the straight-jacket of special knowledge acquired while acting as directors or senior officers, let alone limiting to to benefits acquired by reason of and during the holding of those offices. As in other cases in this developing branch of the law, the particular facts determine the shape of the priciple of decision without setting fixed limits to it. So it is in the present case. Accepting the facts found by the trial Judge, I find no obstructing considerations to the conclusion that O'Malley and Zarzycki continued, after their resignations to be under a fiduciary duty to respect Canaero's priority as against them and their instrument Tera, in seeking to capture the contract for the Guyana project. They entered the lists in the heat of the maturation of the project known to them to be under active government consideration when they resigned from Canaero and when the proposed to bid on behalf of Tera.

In holding that on the facts found by the trial judge, there was a breach of fiduciary duty by O'Malley and Zarzycki which survived their resignations I am not to be taken as laying down any rule of liability to be read as if it were a statute. The general standards of loyalty, good faith and avoidance of a conflict of duty and self-interest to which the conduct of a director or senior officer must conform must be tested in each case by many factors which it would be reckless to attempt to enumerate exhaustively. Among them are the factor of position of office held, the nature of the corporate opportunity, its ripeness, its specificness and the director's or managerial officer's relation to it, the amount of knowledge possessed, the circumstances in which it was obtained and whether it was special or indeed even private, the factor of time in the continuation of fiduciary duty where the alleged breach occurs after termination of the relationship with the company and the circumstances under which the relationship was terminated that is whether by retirement of resignation or discharge . . .

Liability of O'Malley and Zarzycki for breach of fiduciary duty does not depend upon proof by Canaero that, but for their intervention it would have obtained the Guyana contract; nor is it a condition of recovery of damages that Canaero establish what its profits would have been or what it has lost by failing to realise the corporate opportunity in question. It is entitled to compel the faithless fiduciaries to answer for their default according to their gain . . .

Notes

Compare this decision with *Island Export Finance Ltd v Umunna* [1986] BCLC 460 where a director who resigned his office was not held liable to account for profits earned on contracts made by him after his resignation. Even though the contracts were of the same nature and made with the same person as an earlier contract concluded by the company. The company had not been negotiating for such contracts at the time of his resignation, nor when he obtained the contracts. Further he had not resigned to obtain the contracts nor had he made improper use of confidential company information.

It is not per se a breach of his fiduciary duty to the company for a director to compete with the company or to become a director of a competing company. However, the director walks a fine line in such a sitaution and must be careful not to overstep the mark. He must not act in such a way that he benefits one company at the expense of the other: *Moore v McGlynn* [1894] 1 IR 74; *Bell v Lever Bros Ltd* [1932] AC 161. For an example of a case where the director overstepped the mark, see *Irish Microforms Ltd v Browne* (High Court, Murphy J, 3 April 1987). Here the defendant had been a director and the general manager of the plaintiff company. He was also director of a competing company and conducted its business on the plaintiff's premises and using the plaintiff's staff. Its debts were also paid by him out of the plaintiff's monies. Predictably the defendant was found to have been in breach of his duty to the plaintiff.

Remedies against directors[1]

[15.53] A breach of duty by a director, being a wrong to the company, thereby invokes the rule in *Foss v Harbottle*.[2] While the company is carrying on business it may pursue the director in the ordinary way. Once winding up commences, the liquidator has available to him under s 298 of the Principal Act, the 'misfeasance summons' considered infra. Under s 200 of the Principal Act, the company may not by its articles or in any contract exempt any director, auditor or other officer from liability for 'negligence, default, breach of duty or breach of trust. Any provision in breach of s 200 will be void. However, it is permissible for the company to draft its articles in such a way that, by modifying the directors' duties, the possibility of liability for breach of duty does not arise in the first place: *Movitex Ltd v Bulfield*.[3] Modification of the directors' strict fiduciary duties can be found in table A.[4] Under s 391 of the Principal Act where a director, auditor or other officer 'has reason to apprehend that any claim will or might be made against him in respect of any negligence, default, breach of duty of breach of trust' he may apply to court for relief, which may be granted if he 'has acted honestly and reasonably and . . . having regard to all the circumstances of the case . . . ought fairly to be excused therefor. Furthermore, in *Multinational Gas & Petrochemical Co v Multinational Gas and Petrochemical Services Ltd* [1983] Ch 258 it was held that the shareholders can by resolution forgive or ratify a breach of duty thereby precluding a liquidator who is subsequently appointed from pursuing the directors in respect of that breach of duty.

1 See *Keane* at paras **29.24–29.27**.
2 See chapter 17 *supra*.
3 [1988] BCLC 104, 120.
4 Eg. art 85.

Meetings of directors

[15.54] For standard form articles regulating proceedings of board meetings, see arts 101–109 of table A.

1 See *Keane* at paras **29.28–29.33**.

[15.55] Where a director has been wrongfully excluded by his fellow directors from proceedings at board meetings, he may enforce his right to participate by way of injunction, at least where he has a proprietory interest in the company.

Couborough v James Paton Ltd [1965] IR 272 (High Court)

[15.56] The plaintiff who was a director and substantial shareholder in the company was wrongfully excluded by his fellow directors from participating at board meetings. He sought an injunction restraining the directors from excluding him from further board meetings. The directors conceded that the plaintiff was a director but nevertheless they argued that in view of the opposition to his acting as such, an injunction should be refused.

[15.57] **Budd J:** On the question as to whether directors of a company may exclude one of their fellow directors several cases were cited and a question of some difficulty arises. The first case cited was *Pulbrook v Richmond Consolidated Mining Co* 9 Ch D 610. The relevant portion of the head-note reads:– 'A director of a company can, if qualified, sustain an action in his own name against the other directors on the ground of an individual injury to himself for an injunction to restrain them from wrongfully excluding him from acting as a director'. The matter came before Jessel MR, who at the beginning of his judgment stated the issue in the following words:– 'The first question is, whether a director who is improperly and without cause excluded by his brother directors from the board from which they claim the right to exclude him, is entitled to an order restraining his brother directors from so excluding him.' He then continued:– 'In this case a man is necessarily a shareholder in order to be a director and as a director he is entitled to fees and remuneration for his services and it might be a question whether he would be entitled to the fees if he did not attend meetings of the board. He has been excluded. Now, it appears to me that this is an individual wrong, a wrong that has been done to an individual. It is a deprivation of his legal rights for which the directors are personally and individually liable. He has a right by the constitution of the company to take a part in its management, to be present and to vote at the meetings of the board of directors. He has a perfect right to know what is going on at these meetings. It may affect his individual interest as a shareholder as well as his liability as a director because it has been sometimes held that even a director who does not attend board meetings is bound to know what is done in his absence. Besides that, he is in the position of a shareholder of a managing partner in the affairs of the company and he has a right to remain managing partner and to receiver remuneration for his services. It appears to me that for the injury or wrong done to him by preventing him from attending board meetings by force, he has a right to sue. He has what is commonly called a right of action . . .' And finally at page 616 he said:– 'It appears to me that Mr Pulbrook is a director lawfully elected and that he has not vacated his office. Therefore I think he is entitled to an injunction to restrain the directors as asked.' The facts in that case are similar to the present in as much as the plaintiff was a shareholder and entitled to remuneration and by the action of the other directors was excluded from meetings which he had a right to attend under the constitution of the company.

The second report that I wish to refer to is *Hayes v Bristol Plant Hire Ltd* [1957] 1 All ER 685. The head note sets out the facts. By resolution of the board of the defendant company passed by certain defendant directors in the absence of the plaintiff who was also a director, the exclusion of the plaintiff from the board for his absence from board meetings was confirmed. The consequences of the resolution, if it were valid, was that the plaintiff's office as a director of the company would be vacated. The articles of association did not require a director to hold a share qualification and did not confer on directors the right to any specified remuneration but provided that subject to the terms of any agreement between a director and the company, the directors should be paid, by way of remuneration for their services such sums as the company in general meeting might prescribe. The plaintiff had no service agreement with the company. He was a shareholder in the company. In an action for a declaration among other declarations, that the resolution confirming the exclusion of the plaintiff was invalid and for consequential relief by injunction, the defendants objected as a preliminary point that the plaintiff had no proprietary interest as entitled him to equitable relief by declaration and injunction. It was held that the action would not be stopped on the preliminary objection because, although the articles of association of the company did not require a director to hold a share qualification and although they did not confer on directors a right to specified remuneration, yet the plaintiff had a sufficient proprietary interest to enable him to pursue an action for relief by way of declaration and injunction against his exclusion from the board.

That decision follows *Pulbrook's* case and it was decided as recently as 1957. It will be helpful to read a few of the observations of Wynn-Parry J, which are relevant to the facts of this case. He first deals with the facts stating that it was the fact that the articles of association did not require a director to be a shareholder, nor did they provide any direct right to a stipulated amount for remuneration they merely provided for the payment of such amount a the company in general meeting might prescribe. Then (at the bottom of page 686) he says:–

'On those facts counsel for the defendant contend that there is no or not sufficient proprietary interest vested in the plaintiff as director. He cited to me a number of cases the principles underlying which I wholly accept. It is perfectly clear that in the case of any relationship which involves a personal relationship this court will not intervene by way of injunction to enforce on a person or on a limited company in the position of an employer a person whom the employer or the company expressing its view through the shareholders, does not want; and it is perfectly true also to say that the cases establish that the basis of the court's interference is the existence of some right of property in the person seeking the relief.'

Then he goes on to deal with *Pulbrook's* case and points out that the Master of the Rolls did not base his decision on the fact that in that case a director was necessarily a shareholder, but that his reasoning applied equally where the articles did not require a director to be a shareholder. He also took the view that the reasoning of the Master of the Rolls in *Pulbrook's* case applied equally well to cases where the articles of association of a company did not give an express right to specified remuneration but merely provides for a director being paid such remuneration as the company may prescribe. He therefore held the plaintiff entitled to proceed. It is right to add that the learned judge made it clear that he was not dealing with the case on the basis that the majority of the company did not wish the plaintiff to continue as a director. The case was really decided on the basis of a sufficient proprietory interest to maintain an action. Reading the two cases together they go this far in my view – that the plaintiff in the present proceedings has a sufficient proprietory right to maintain this action. However, the question still remains whether the court should grant the relief claimed in the circumstances existing.

In my view being a large shareholder and a director the plaintiff is in fairness entitled to know what is happening and to vote at meetings. There is the further consideration that resolution of the board may possibly be ineffectual and invalid if a person entitled to be present is excluded from meetings at which the resolutions are passed. So I have come to the conclusion on the basis of the cases of *Pulbrook v Richmond Consolidated Mining Co* and *Hayes v Bristol Plant Hire Ltd* that in the proper circumstances a director has a right to attend board meetings which may be enforced against the other directors.

So the plaintiff is in the position of being a director not validly excluded from meetings. And he is also a large shareholder. He is in consequence deprived of information on the affairs of the company and important decisions are made in his absence. In all the circumstances I feel I should exercise my discretion in favour of the plaintiff and grant him the relief claimed relevant to that part of the action that I am dealing with.

Register of information relating to directors

[15.58]   Every company is obliged to keep a register of directors and secretaries.[1] The register contains personal details of the directors and secretary including name, age, address, business occupation of any directors, and details of other directorships held by the directors. The company must within 14 days of any change in the directors, secretary or particulars thereof, send notice of same to the registrar. The directors and secretary are under a duty to assist the company in compiling the information regarding changes, for delivery to the registrar. The register is to be open for inspection for at least two hours each day, free of charge to any member, and at a fee of no more than £1 to any other person. If inspection is refused a court order may be obtained compelling inspection.

The company must also keep a register of directors shareholdings.[2] Under ss 53–66 of the 1990 Act, detailed requirements are laid down for the disclosure by directors and secretaries of interests or dealings in shares or debentures of the company by them, their spouses and minor children. The company must keep a register of such interests, details of which must also be included in the directors' report or the notes to the company's accounts.

Where the company has a stock exchange listing, it must immediately on being informed of the directors' or secretary's interests in dealings in the shares, pass on this information to the stock exchange. The stock exchange can then in turn publish the information in such manner as it may determine.

The Minister is empowered to appoint an inspector to investigate breaches of the directors' or secretary's duty to notify interests or dealings in the company's affairs.

In addition certain particulars of the directors must be stated on the company's business letters.[3] These matters are discussed in detail by *Keane* at paras **27.34–27.38**.

1 S 195 of the Principal Act as substituted by s 52 of the 1990 Act.
2 Ibid ss 190–193 & s 59 of the 1990 Act.
3 Ibid s 196.

The secretary

[15.59] Every company must have a secretary.[1] Although the secretary may also be a director of the company, where an act is required to be done by a director and the secretary[2] it cannot be done by one person acting in both capacities. The first secretary is the person (or body corporate) named as such in the statement required to be delivered to the registrar under s 3 of the 1982 Act, upon formation of the company. Thereafter, his appointment is governed by the articles.[3] S 236 of the 1990 Act requires the directors of a plc to take all reasonable steps to secure that the secretary has the requisite knowledge and experience to discharge his functions and:–

(*a*) on the commencement of s 236 held the office of secretary; or
(*b*) for at least three of the five years immediately preceding his appointment as secretary held the office of secretary of a company; or
(*c*) is a member of a recognised body;[4] or
(*d*) is a person who, by virtue of his holding or having held any other position or his being a member of any other body, appears to the directors to be capable of discharging those functions.

1 S 175.
2 Eg. the witnessing of the affixing of the seal.
3 See art 113 where the power of appointment is vested in the board of directors.
4 Regulations have yet to be made by the Minister.

[15.60] The secretary of a company has usual authority to bind the company in matters of an administrative nature.

Panorama Developments (Guildford) Ltd v Fidelis Furnishing Fabrics Ltd
[1971] 3 All ER 16 (Court of Appeal)

[15.61] The secretary of the defendant company, Bayne, hired cars from the plaintiff without having actual authority to do so and stating falsely that they were wanted by the defendant for business purposes. The cars were fraudulently used by Bayne for his personal purposes. The plaintiff sued the

466

defendant for the amount of the hire charges. The defendant denied liability on the basis that the cars had been hired by Bayne without due authorisation.

[15.62]   **Lord Denning MR:** Counsel for the defendant says that the company is not bound by the letters which were signed by Mr Bayne as 'company secretary'. He says that on the authorities a company secretary fulfils a very humble role; and that he has no authority to make any contracts or representations on behalf of the company. He refers to *Barnett, Hoares & Co v South London Tramways Co* (1887) 18 QBD 815 at 817 where Lord Esher MR said:

> 'A secretary is a mere servant; his position is that he is to do what he is told and no person can assume that he has any authority to represent anything at all . . .'

These words were approved by Lord Macnaughten in *George Whitechurch Ltd v Cavanagh* [1902] AC 117 at 124. They were supported by the decision in *Ruben v Great Fingall Consolidated* [1906] AC 439; they are referred to in some of the textbooks as authoritative. But times have changed. A company secretary is a much more important person nowadays than he was in 1887. He is an officer of the company with extensive duties and responsibilities. This appears not only in the modern Companies Acts but also by the role which he plays in the day to day business of companies. He is no longer a mere clerk. He regularly makes representations on behalf of the company and enters into contracts on its behalf which come within the day to day running of the company's business. So much so that he may be regarded as being held out as having authority to do such things on behalf of the company. He is certainly entitled to sign contracts connected with the administrative side of a companys' affairs such as employing staff and ordering cars and so forth. All such matters now come within the ostensible authority of a company's secretary. Accordingly I agree with the judge that Mr R L Bayne as company secretary had ostensible authority to enter into contracts for the hire of these cars and therefore the company must pay for them. Mr Bayne was a fraud. But it was the company which put him in the position in which he, as company secretary was able to commit the frauds. So the defendants are liable.

Disqualification and restriction of directors and other officers

[15.63]   Under s 184 of the Principal Act the court could make an order disqualifying a person from being a director of any company where he had been convicted of fraud related offences or where in the course of a winding up it appeared that he had been guilty of fraudulent conduct in relation to the affairs of the company. S 184 has been repealed by s 6 of the 1990 Act and has been replaced by the much wider provisions of part VII of that Act.

Restrictions on directors

[15.64] Ss 149–158 of the 1990 Act apply to any person who was a director or shadow director of a company at the date of or within 12 months prior to the commencement of its winding up or receivership and at any time during the course of the winding-up or receivership the liquidator or receiver, as the case may be, certifies, or it is otherwise proved to the court that the company is unable to pay its debts within the meaning of s 214 of the Principal Act.

Under s 150(1), the court must, unless satisfied as to any of the matters set out in para **15.65**, declare that any such director 'shall not, for a period of five years, be appointed or act in any way, whether directly or indirectly, as a director or secretary or be concerned or take part in the promotion or formation of any company' unless:–

(1). It has an allotted share capital of at least £100,000 in the case of a plc or at least £20,000 in the case of any other company; and
(2). The shares and any premium thereon have been fully paid up in cash;

If the company issues a share which is not fully paid up, s 156 provides that the share is treated as if the nominal value together with any premium had been received, but the allottee becomes immediately liable to pay any unpaid balance together with interest.

S 156 goes on to state that if the company allots a share in whole or in part for a non-cash consideration the allottee, together with any other holder of the share (other than a holder in good faith for value without notice of the contravention of the section) is also liable to pay the company in cash an amount equal to the nominal value together with any premium, as well as interest. This effectively means that the share is paid for twice, although s 157 allows the person affected to apply to the court for relief which may be granted on whatever terms and conditions the court thinks fit.

The provisions of s 156 does not apply to the issue of shares by the company in pursuance of an employee share scheme. Nor does the section apply to the allotment of a bonus share which is not fully paid up, unless the allottee knew or ought to have known that the share was so allotted.

[15.65] Under s 150(2) the court is not to impose restrictions on the person if it is satisfied:–

(*a*) that the director acted honestly and responsibly in relation to the conduct of the affairs of the company and there is no other reason why it would be just and equitable to impose such restrictions on him; or
(*b*) subject to paragraph (*a*), that the person was a director of the company solely by reason of his nomination as such by a financial institution in connection with the giving of credit facilities to, or the purchase of shares in, the company by such institution, provided that the institution did not obtain from any of the directors a personal guarantee of repayment of the credit advanced to the company; or

(*c*) subject to paragraph (*a*), that the person was a director of the company solely by reason of his nomination as such by a venture capital company in connection with the purchase of, or subscription for, shares by it in the first company.

[15.66] If the court makes an order under s 150 it must notify the registrar of companies who is obliged by s 153 to keep a register of restricted persons. If the court subsequently makes an order granting full or partial relief from the restrictions (as to which see para **15.68**) the registrar must be similarly notified. In the case of partial relief he must enter details thereof in the register. However, if full relief is granted, or once five years have elapsed from the date of the imposition of the restrictions, the registrar must remove the persons name from the register.

[15.67] Under s 151 where it appears to the liquidator or receiver of a company that the interests of any other company or its creditors may be placed in jeopardy because a person to who s 150 applies is appointed or is acting in any way, whether directly or indirectly, as a director or is concerned or is taking part in the promotion or formation of that other company, he must, on pain of a fine, report this matter to the court which may make whatever order it sees fit.

[15.68] Even if restrictions imposed on a director under s 150, he is entitled by virtue of s 152, within one year of the imposition of the restrictions to apply to the court for relief in whole or in part from the restrictions or from any order made in relation to him under s 151. At least 14 days notice must be given to the receiver or liquidator as the case may be, who must in turn notify the creditors and contributories. They together with the liquidator or receiver, may be heard at the application. The court may grant relief if it deems it just and equitable to do so and on such terms and conditions as it sees fit.

[15.69] S 155(6) provides that where a person is subject to restrictions under s 150 he shall not accept appointment to a position or act as a director, etc in relation to any other company unless, within the preceding 14 days, he has sent to the registered office of the company, a notification that he is subject to such restrictions.

In addition to having to meet the requirements regarding the possession of a minimum capital paid up in cash, s 155 imposes further fetters upon any company, in respect of which a restricted person acts, namely that:–

(1). It cannot provide financial assistance for the purchase of its own shares under the procedure provided by s 60(2)–(11) of the Principal Act.

(2). Non-cash assets acquired from any subscriber to the memorandum, any director or any person involved in the promotion or formation of the company be independently valued.

(3). All loans, quasi-loans and credit transactions to directors, directors of the holding company and persons connected with such directors are prohibited as well.

The court, if it deems it just and equitable to do so, grant relief under s 157 to a company which contravenes these restrictions. It may also grant relief to any person adversely affected by the restrictions (such as a person who as a result cannot obtain financial assistance from the company for the purchase of its shares). Relief is granted on such terms as the court thinks fit, but will be refused to the company where the person had given it the requisite notice that he was subject to s 150 restrictions.

Disqualification of officers generally

[15.70] Under ss 159–169 of the 1990 Act new provisions have been enacted for the disqualification of officers generally. Under s 160 where a person is convicted on indictment of an offence in relation to the company, or convicted of any offence involving fraud or dishonesty, he is automatically made subject to a disqualification order for the period of five years from the date of his conviction or such other period as the court, on the application of the prosecutor and having regard to all the circumstances of the case, may order. Once disqualified he cannot be appointed or act as an auditor, director, officer, liquidator, receiver or examiner of any company, or be in any way, whether directly or indirectly, concerned or take part in the promotion, formation or management of, inter alia, any company.

The court may also, if satisfied in any proceedings or on application, disqualify for such period as it sees fit, any person who:–

(*a*) has been guilty while a promoter, officer, auditor, receiver, liquidator or examiner, of fraud in relation to the company, its members or creditors; or

(*b*) has been guilty while a promoter, officer, auditor, receiver, liquidator or examiner, of any breach of duty in that capacity; or

(*c*) has been made personally liable for fraudulent or reckless trading; or

(*d*) has been guilty of conduct as promoter, officer, auditor, receiver, liquidator or examiner of a company which makes him unfit to be concerned in the management of a company; or

(*e*) in consequence of a report of inspectors appointed by the court or the Minister under part II of the 1990 Act (as to which see chapter 18 (*infra*), his conduct makes him unfit to be concerned in the management of a company

(*f*) has been consistently in default in relation to the filing of returns, accounts and other documents with the registrar, as required by the Companies Acts. Persistent default is conclusively proved by showing that in the five years ending with the date of the application for his disqualification he has been convicted (whether or not on the same occasion) of three or more defaults.

Of assistance to the court in this regard, the director or shadow director is obliged by s 166 in any civil or criminal proceedings against him for fraud or dishonesty in relation to the company to give the court details of all directorships currently held by him or held by him within the last 12 months, of any previous disqualification orders made against him and if so, when and for how long.

The application for disqualification on grounds (*a*)–(*d*) may be made by the DPP or any member, contributory, officer, receiver, liquidator, examiner or creditor of any company in relation to which the person has acted. Only the DPP can apply on ground (*e*) and both he and the registrar can apply on ground (*f*).

[15.71] A person disqualified under s 160 may, unless convicted of an offence under s 161 (below) apply to the court for relief from disqualification, which may be granted in whole or part, and on such conditions as are thought fit, provided it is just and equitable to do so.

[15.72] Under s 161 it is an offence to act in breach of restrictions imposed under s 150 or to act in breach of a disqualification order, and upon conviction the defaulter is subject to a disqualification order of five years duration (or such other period as the court on the application of the prosecutor may order). If, upon conviction, he was already subject to a disqualification order, its duration will be extended by 10 further years (or such other further period as the court on the application of the prosecutor may determine).

If a person who is subject to s 150 restrictions becomes a director of a company which goes into liquidation within five years after the date of the commencement of the earlier liquidation, and it appears to the liquidator of the later company, at any stage in the liquidation, that it is unable to pay its debts, he must report this matter to the court, which may, if it thinks proper, make a disqualification order of five years duration (or such other period as it thinks fit).

[15.73] S 160 provides that if a company pays a person for services performed in breach of any s 150 restrictions or in breach of a disqualification order, that money can be recovered by the company as a simple contract debt. If the company goes into insolvent liquidation while he is so acting or goes into insolvent liquidation within 12 months thereafter, the court on the application of the liquidator or any creditor, may declare such person personally liable for all or any of the debts incurred by the company while he was so acting.

Similarly, if a company has been given notice by the liquidator or receiver, that a person acting as director, etc is subject to s 150 restrictions, and the company fails to comply with the requirements regarding minimum paid up share capital, etc within a reasonable period, should that company subsequently go into insolvent liquidation, the court may on the application of its liquidator or any creditor or contributory, declare that any person who was an officer of the company while the company carried on business in breach of these requirements shall be personally liable for all or any of the company's debts. The person can, however, only be made personally liable, if he knew or ought to have known that the company had been notified that the person was subject to the s 148 restrictions.

Furthermore the court may grant relief in whole or in part from personal liability, if it considers it just and equitable to do so, and subject to such conditions as it sees fit.

[15.74] Under ss 164 and 165 a director or other officer or a member of a committee of management or trustee of any company can incur civil and criminal liability for acting in accordance with the directions or instructions of another person whom he knows to be subject to s 150 restrictions or a disqualification order. If convicted of so acting, the person becomes personally liable for the debts of the company incurred while he was so acting. In any proceedings to recover the debt from him, he may apply to the court for relief, which may be granted in whole or in part, if it is just and equitable in the circumstances.

[15.75] Under s 183 of the Principal Act as substituted by s 169 of the 1990 Act it is an offence for an undischarged bankrupt to act as officer, auditor, liquidator or examiner of, or directly or indirectly to take part in or be concerned in the promotion, formation or management of any company, except with the leave of the court. If convicted of so acting the person becomes subject to a disqualification order, if not already subject to one.

Notice to the registrar

[15.76] Under s 167 a prescribed officer of the court must give the registrar particulars of the making of any disqualification order, the granting of relief from such an order, of convictions which render a person subject to a disqualification order, of convictions for acting in breach of s 150 restrictions or in breach of a disqualification order and of convictions for acting under the directions of a person who is subject to s 150 restrictions or a disqualification order.

S 168 requires the registrar to maintain a register of disqualified persons similar to that which he must maintain in respect of persons subject to s 150 restrictions.

Chapter 16

THE ANNUAL RETURN, ACCOUNTS AND AUDIT[1]

THE ANNUAL RETURN

[16.01] Every company must make an annual return to the Registrar of Companies setting out the matters prescribed by the Principal Act.[2] In the case of a company limited by shares the return must be in the form set out in part II of the fifth schedule. The annual return must, in the case of all limited liability companies be accompanied by the documentation prescribed by the 1986 Act.[3] The documentation to be annexed to the return of an unlimited company is specified in the Principal Act.[4] The purpose of the annual return is primarily to provide information and in particular, financial details of the company, to members of the public dealing with the company (ie. creditors and potential investors). If the company fails to make its annual return, both it and every officer in default are liable to a fine.[5] More importantly, a failure to make a return for two consecutive years may result in the registrar striking the name of the company off the register, in consequence of which the company is dissolved.[6] Where the company is so struck off, the company and any creditor or member who feels aggrieved thereby may, within 20 years, apply to the court have the company's name restored to the register. If restored to the register it is deemed to have continued in existence as if it had been never struck off.[7] Alternatively the application may, if made within one year of the striking off, be made to the registrar himself, in which case the name of the company will be restored to the register on condition that the appropriate fee is paid and all outstanding returns have been filed.[8]

Under ss 248 and 249 of the 1990 Act documents required by the Companies Acts to be delivered to the registrar (including any periodic account, abstract statement or return) must be in the prescribed form. They may be delivered in legible or non-legible form (eg by electronic means). If the documents are not received in the prescribed form, the registrar can send a notice of this fact to any person who originally delivered them. If the documents are not delivered in the prescribed form within 14 days of receipt of the registrar's notice, they are then deemed not to have been delivered at all.

---

1 See generally *Keane* chapters 31 and 32.
2 S 125–129 and part I of the fifth schedule.

3 S 7, 9 and 10 of the 1986 Act.
4 S 128.
5 S 127 of the Principal Act as amended by s 15 of the 1982 Act and s 245 of the 1991 Act.
6 S 12 of the 1982 Act as amended by s 268 of the 1991 Act. Under s 361 of the Principal Act, the registrar may also strike defunct companies off the register. See generally *MacCann* (1990) Gazette 125.
7 See generally *Keane* at para **31.13**.
8 S 311a of the Principal Act as inserted by s 246 of the 1990 Act.

Contents of annual return[1]

[16.02]   The returns of all companies must include the address of the registered office, the addresses where the registers of members and debenture holders are kept (if not kept at the registered office), a statement of the company's secured liabilities and particulars relating to the directors and secretary.[2] The return of a company having a share capital must also contain details of the share capital, a list of members and those who have ceased to be members since the last return, details of the number of shares held by each member and details of the number of shares transferred by each member since the last return.

1 See *Keane* at para **31.02**.
2 S 125(1) and part I of the fifth schedule.

Documents to be annexed to annual return[1]

[16.03]   S 128 of the Principal Act, which formerly applied to all companies now only applies to unlimited companies.[2] It requires public unlimited companies to annex copies of the balance sheet, auditor's report and director's report to the return.

As regards limited liability companies,[3] s 7 of the 1986 Act requires every such company to annex to the annual return copies of the balance sheet and profit and loss account signed by the directors,[4] the directors' report and the auditors' report. These obligations are modified in respect of small and medium sized private companies.[5]

[16.04]   To qualify as a small company it must satisfy all of the following conditions:–[6]

(*a*) its balance sheet total for the year must not exceed £1,250,000;
(*b*) its turnover for the year must not exceed £2,500.000; and
(*c*) the average number of persons employed by the company in the year must not exceed 50.

To qualify as a medium sized company, it must satisfy all of the following conditions[7]:–

(*a*) its balance sheet total for the year must not exceed £5,000,000;
(*b*) its turnover for the year must not exceed £10,000,000; and
(*c*) the average number of persons employed by the company for the year must not exceed 250.

In the case of a 'small company' it need only annex to the annual return an abridged balance sheet and the auditor's report.[8] Medium sized companies may file a less abridged balance sheet, an abridged profit and loss account, the auditor's report and the directors' report.[9]

1 See *Keane* at paras **31.03–31.11**.
2 S 7(3) and s 1(1) of the 1986 Act.
3 Other than charitable and non-profit making companies: see s 2(1) of the 1986 Act.
4 S 18 of the 1986 Act.
5 S 10 of the 1986 Act.
6 S 8(2) of the 1986 Act.
7 S 8(3) of the 1986 Act.
8 Ibid s 10.
9 Ibid s 11.

[16.05]   Under s 16 of the 1986 Act, where the company has a subsidiary company or is beneficially entitled to more than 20% of the voting shares of a company, details of such companies must be included in a note to the accounts which are annexed to the annual return. In particular details must be given of the name, registered office shares, capital reserves and profit or loss of such companies. If the material is too lengthy to include by way of a note to the accounts, it may instead be included in a statement amended to the annual return. Under s 17 of the 1986 Act any private company which is a subsidiary of a company formed and registered in a Member State of the EEC, is exempt from attaching the balance sheet, profit and loss account, auditor's report and directors' report to the annual return provided:–

(*a*) all shareholders of the subsidiary[1] consent thereto;
(*b*) the holding company has given an irrevocable guarantee to the subsidiary in respect of its debts and the shareholders of the subsidiary have been informed thereof;
(*c*) the annual accounts of the subsidiary are consolidated into the group accounts and the exemption is disclosed in the accounts;
(*d*) the group accounts are prepared in accordance with the Fourth EEC Companies Directive;
(*e*) the group accounts are annexed to the annual return.

1 In the case of a wholly owned subsidiary this will refer only to the holding company.

[16.06]   All private companies must annex to the annual return certificates signed by a director to subscribe for shares or debentures of the company and also stating that the number of members, if in excess of 50, consists wholly of employees and former employees.[1] This provision is presumably designated so as to enable the registrar decide that the company still qualifies as a private company.

1 S 129 of the Principal Act.

Accounts

[16.07]   Unless it enjoys the benefit of a specific statutory exemption, a company is obliged to keep two sets of accounts.[1] These are:–

(*a*) the basic records;
(*b*) the accounts that are presented to the members annually in general meeting. Such accounts may also have to be annexed to the annual return.[2]

1 See generally *Keane* chapter 32.
2 Discussed *supra* and in *Keane* chapter 32.

Basic records[1]

[16.08]   Under s 202 of the 1990 Act every company must keep at its registered office, or at such other place as the directors think fit, 'proper books of account' that:–

(*a*) correctly record and explain the transactions of the company,
(*b*) will at any time enable the financial position of the company to be determined with reasonable accuracy,
(*c*) will enable the directors to ensure that any balance sheet, profit and loss account or income and expenditure account of the company complies with the requirements of the Companies Acts, and
(*d*) will enable the accounts of the company to be readily and properly audited.

They must contain:

(*a*) entries from day to day of all sums of money received and expended by the company and the matters in respect of which the receipt and expenditure takes place;
(*b*) a record of the assets and liabilities of the company;
(*c*) if the company's business involves dealing in goods–
  (i) a record of all goods purchased, and of all goods sold (except those sold for cash by way of ordinary retail trade), showing the goods and the sellers and buyers in sufficient detail to enable the goods and the seller and buyers to be identified and a record of all the invoices relating to such purchases and sales,
  (ii) statements of stock held by the company at the end of each financial year and all records of stocktakings from which any such statement of stock has been, or is to be, prepared, and
(*d*) if the company's business involves the provision of services, a record of the services provided and of all the invoices relating thereto.

The books of account are deemed 'proper' if they give a 'true and fair view of the state of the company's affairs and to explain its transactions.' They must be kept on a continuous and consistent basis (ie. entries must be made in a timely manner and must be consistent from one year to the next) and must be kept for at least six years from the latest date to which they relate. A director who fails to comply with the requirements of s 202 may be liable to imprisonment or a fine or both, unless he believed on reasonable grounds that a competent and reliable person was charged with the duty of seeing that the section was complied with and that such person was in a position to discharge that duty.[2] Imprisonment is only available as a punishment for wilful default. Under ss 203 and 204 of the 1990 Act, if the company goes into insolvent liquidation and the court considers that the failure to keep proper books of account has contributed to the company's inability to pay all of its debts or has resulted in substantial uncertainty as to the assets and liabilities of the company or has substantially impeded an orderly winding up every officer in default is liable to a fine or imprisonment or to both, and may on the application of the liquidator or any creditor or contributory of the company be made personally liable for all or any of the company's debts. It is a defence to both a conviction and imposition of personal liability to show that the officer believed on reasonable grounds that a competent and reliable person acting under the supervision and control of a director, was charged with the duty of seeing that proper books of account were kept and was in a position to discharge that duty.

Under s 243 of the 1990 Act any officer who destroys, mutilates or falsifies any book or document affecting or relating to the company's property or affairs, or who is privy to such conduct, shall, unless he proves that he had no intention to defeat the law, be guilty of an offence. It is also an offence for any person to fraudulently part with, alter or make an omission from any such book or document, or to be privy to such conduct.

1 See *Keane* at paras **32.04–32.07**.
2 S 147(1), (2) of the 1990 Act.

[16.09]   Every director of the company has a statutory right under s 202(6) to inspect the books of account at all reasonable times. In exercising this right he may be accompanied by an accountant and may make copies of such documents. An accountant may inspect alone the books of account on behalf of a director if so authorised by the latter in writing, provided he gives a written undertaking to use the information acquired by him from such inspection only for the purpose of advising the director.

Healy v Healy Homes Ltd [1973] IR 309 (High Court)

[The facts appear from the judgment]

[16.10]   **Kenny J:** The plaintiff and the second defendant are directors of the defendant company. The plaintiff, who complains that he has been excluded from the management of the company, sought an inspection of the register of members, the minute book and the books of account of the company and wished to have an accountant with him when he was doing this. The defendants refused to allow anyone except the plaintiff to see the books

477

of account. The right of the plaintiff and his accountant to inspect the register of members and the minute book of general meetings was not disputed and the debate was limited to the question whether the right of inspection of the books of account is personal to a director or whether he may be accompanied by an accountant when exercising it. [His Lordship then quoted s 147].

The purpose of the section is to compel companies to keep proper books of account: one of the ways in which this important object is achieved is by imposing an obligation on each director to make sure that this is being done. But a director who has not had a training in accountancy cannot decide whether proper books of account are being kept unless an accountant is allowed to inspect them; the phrase 'proper books of account' means books which give a true and fair view of the state of the company's affairs and which explain its transactions. It follows that a director's right to inspect books of account necessarily involves that an accountant nominated by him may do this. The accountant may do this when he is accompanied by the director or when the accountant has been given a written authority to do so, and he may be required to give a written undertaking that the knowledge which he gets will not be used for any purpose except in relation to the matter in connection with which he has been retained . . . The right of a director to inspect the books of a company when he has an obligation imposed on him the breach of which may involve him in criminal liability, necessarily implies that he has the right to employ a qualified agent to advise him. The question whether proper books are being kept is one on which an accountant is the only person qualified to advise as most directors would not be able to form a correct judgment on the matter. The director and his accountant are also entitled to make copies of the books of account or any part of them . . . In this case the plaintiff is prepared to have his accountant with him when he is making the inspection.

The annual accounts[1]

[16.11]   Every company must, not later than 18 months after incorporation and thereafter annually lay before the AGM of the company, a profit and loss account and a balance sheet.[2] The directors' report is to be attached to the balance sheet,[3] along with the auditor's report.[4] These items must be sent out to the members and debenture holders at least 21 days before the AGM[5]. The overriding requirement in relation to both the balance sheet and the profit and loss account is that they present a 'true and fair view' respectively of 'the state of affairs of the company as at the end of the financial year' and of the 'profit or loss of the company for the financial year'.[6]

1 See *Keane* at paras **32.08** et seq.
2 S 148((1), (2) of the Principal Act.
3 S 158 as amended by ss 13 & 14 of the 1986 Act.
4 S 157 & 163 of the Principal Act.
5 S 159.
6 S 149(1) as amended by s 3(1)(b) of the 1986 Act.

478

Contents and form of annual accounts[1]

[16.12]   In the case of unlimited companies, the form and content of the balance sheet and of the profit and loss account are governed by s 149 and the sixth schedule of the Principal Act.

As regards limited liability companies, the relevant provisions are ss 3–6, 8–12 and the schedule of the 1986 Act. Where strict compliance with the statutory provisions would not present a 'true and fair view' of the company's financial position, the directors may remedy this by including additional information in the balance sheet or profit and loss account or in the notes to the accounts or alternatively by departing, in so far as is necessary, from the requirements of the schedule to the 1986 Act, whichever is more appropriate.[2] Where either course of action is taken, a note thereof must be attached to the accounts giving the reason therefor and explaining the effect of such departure.[3] Both small and medium sized companies[4] may prepare abridged profit and loss accounts.[5] Small companies may also prepare an abridged balance sheet[6] and need attach much fewer notes to their accounts. Medium sized companies must prepare a complete balance sheet and are given very little relief regarding notes to their accounts.[7] The accounting principles to be applied in preparing the accounts are set out in s 5 of the 1986 Act and may only be departed from for 'special reasons'.[8] Such a departure must be stated in a note to the accounts. Regardless of the type of company, both its balance sheet and its profit and loss account must be signed by two directors.[9] Where loans, quasi-loans and credit transactions (or guarantees of such arrangements) have been entered into with any director of the company, any director of the holding company or any person connected with such a director, particulars thereof must be contained in the accounts, including any group accounts. Similarly, details must be given of any transactions with the company or any subsidiary in which any director of the company or of the holding company had a material interest. Details need not be given of certain small arrangements and transactions. If the required particulars are omitted the auditors must, so far as they are reasonably able, include them in their report instead.[10] Particulars of any payments to directors by way of salaries, expenses, pensions or compensation for loss of office must also be contained in the accounts or in a statement annexed thereto.[11] The directors must give the company written notice of such matters as are necessary for the company to particularise their loans and other payments in the accounts.[12]

1 See *Keane* at para **32.10**.
2 S 3(1)(*c*), (*d*) of the 1986 Act.
3 S 3(1)(*e*).
4 As to which see para **16.04**.
5 S 11(1) of the 1986 Act.
6 Ibid s 10(1).
7 Ibid s 12(1).
8 Ibid s 12(2).
9 Ibid s 6.
10 S 156 of the Principal Act.

11 Ibid s 192 as amended by ss 41–45 of the 1990 Act. Special provisions apply to licensed banks.
12 Ibid ss 191, 193. On ss 191–193 see *Keane* at paras **32.19–32.23**.

Director's report[1]

[16.13] The directors report must report on 'the state of the company's affairs and if the company is a holding company, on the state of affairs of the . . . group.'[2] It is to be signed on behalf of the board by two of the directors.[3] The matters which must be contained in it are set out in s 158 of the Principal Act and ss 13 and 14 of the 1986 Act.

1 See *Keane* at para **32.15**.
2 S 138(1) of the Principal Act. In the case of limited liability holding companies, the details regarding their subsidiary and associated companies mentioned in ss 158(4) & (5) are no longer to be included in the directors' report but are instead to be set out in notes to the accounts. See s 16(5) of the 1986 Act.
3 Ibid s 158(3).

Group accounts[1]

[16.14] In the case of a holding company it may be obliged to prepare not only accounts relating to its own affairs, but also a set of accounts in respect of the affairs of the holding company and its subsidiaries as a whole ('group accounts').[2] One company is a subsidiary of another if it

'(*i*) is a member of it and controls the composition of its board of directors, or
(*ii*) holds more than half in nominal value of its equity share capital,[3] or
(*iii*) holds more than half in value of its shares carrying voting rights . . .'[4].

A subsidiary is also a subsidiary of its holding company's holding company.[5]

1 See *Keane* at paras **32.24–32.32**.
2 S 150 of the Principal Act.
3 The ordinary shares. See s 155(5).
4 S 155(1)(*a*).
5 S 155(2).

[16.15] The group accounts must be prepared in the form of a consolidated balance sheet and consolidated profit and loss account, unless the directors are of the opinion that some other format will be more informative.[1] Whatever format is chosen it must include the same or equivalent information to that contained in consolidated accounts.[2] The contents and format of group accounts are set out in s 152 of the Principal Act and part V of the schedule of the 1986 Act. Group accounts are aimed at giving a 'true and fair view' of the group as a whole.

Subject to the overriding requirement that a 'true and fair view is presented', group accounts will not be required where the company is a wholly owned subsidiary of another company incorporated in the State.[3]

In addition, group accounts need not deal with a subsidiary of the company if the directors are of opinion that:–

'(*i*) it is unprofitable or would be of no real value to members of the company, in view of the insignificant amounts involved or would involve expense or delay out of proportion to the value to members of the company, or (*ii*) the result would be misleading; and if the directors are of such an opinion about each of the company's subsidiaries, group accounts shall not be required.'[4]

Where group accounts do not deal with a subsidiary, every member of the company is entitled to copies of the latest balance sheet, profit and loss account, director's and auditor's reports of the subsidiary.[5]

The holding company's directors are obliged to ensure that, except where there are good reasons against it, the financial year of each of its subsidiaries coincides with the holding company's own financial year.[6]

A private company which is a holding company is not obliged to prepare group accounts, but if it does not do so, the members are entitled to demand the last ten years accounts of any of its subsidiaries.[7]

1 Ibid s 151(1)(2).
2 Para 53 of the schedule of the 1986 Act.
3 Ibid s 150(2)(*a*) of the Principal Act.
4 Ibid s 151(2)(*b*). The group accounts must instead set out the matters contained in paragraph 54 of the schedule of the 1986 Act.
5 Ibid s 150(3).
6 Ibid s 153(1). See also s 153(2) for the Minister's powers in this regard, where the financial year ends of the various members of the group do not coincide, the directors should, by way of a note in the accounts explain why they consider that financial years should not so coincide.
7 S 154 of the Principal Act. See *Keane* at para **32.31**.

[16.16] Compliance with the recognised practices and standards of the accountancy profession in preparing the company's accounts is strong (but not conclusive) evidence that those accounts present a 'true and fair view' of the company.

Lloyd Cheyham & Co Ltd v Littlejohn & Co [1987] BCLC 303 (Queen's Bench Division)

[The facts are immaterial]

[16.17] Woolf J: In contending that the view of the defendants is not a proper view, the plaintiffs and Mr Cade rely heavily on statements of standard accounting practice issued by the Institute and in particular Statements of Standard Accounting Practice No 2. As to the proper treatment of such statements, the approach of both counsel was the same and I accept this approach. While they are not conclusive, so that a departure from their terms necessarily involves a breach of the duty of care, and they are not as the explanatory foreward makes clear, rigid rules, they are very strong evidence as to what is the proper standard which should be adopted and unless there is some justification, a departure from this will be regarded as constituting a breach of duty. It appears to me important that this should be the position because third parties in reading the accounts are entitled to assume that they have been drawn up in accordance with the approved practice unless there is some indication in the accounts which clearly state that this is not the case. SSAP No 2, the relevant practice, is so far as material in these terms.

Notes
See also *Dolan v AB Ltd* [1969] IR 282.

Appointment and dismissal of auditors

[16.18] Every company must have an auditor or auditors,[1] who is appointed at the AGM.[2] He holds office until the next AGM at which he is automatically re-appointed without the need for a resolution, unless he is not qualified for re-appointment or a resolution has been passed appointing someone else instead or which provides that he is not to be re-appointed or he has given notice of his unwillingness to be re-appointed.[3] The members may, however, dismiss him by ordinary resolution, before the next AGM and appoint a replacement to fill the vacancy thereby created.[4] Where at an AGM no auditor is appointed or re-appointed the Minister may appoint someone to fill the vacancy.[5] Casual vacancies may be filled by the board of directors[6] who also have power to appoint the first auditor.[7] If the directors fail to appoint the first auditor the vacancy may be filled by the members in general meeting, which also have power to replace the directors' appointee.[8] Where an existing auditor is not to be re-appointed at the next AGM or is dismissed during his term in office, the procedure to be followed is set out in s 161 of the Principal Act as amended by s 184 of the 1990 Act, and is substantially the same as the procedure for the dismissal of directors.[9] If dismissed during his term in office he is entitled to receive all notices and communications relating to the EGM at which he is to be dismissed and to attend the next AGM. He has a right to be heard at such meetings in relation to any part of the business thereof which concerns him as auditor.

1 See generally *Keane* at para **32.35**.
2 S 160(1) of the Principal Act.
3 Ibid s 160(2).
4 S 190(5) as substituted by s 183 of the 1990 Act.
5 Ibid s 160(4). Under s 160(5A) as inserted by s 183 of the 1990 Act, the Minister must be informed within 7 days if an auditor has not been appointed or re-appointed at the AGM, or if he has been removed by resolution of the members.
6 Ibid s 160(7).

7 Ibid s 160(6).
8 Ibid.
9 See para **15.07** et seq.

Resignation of auditors

[16.19] Under s 185 of the 1990 Act the auditor may resign by serving a notice in writing on the company. Within 14 days of service on the company, he must also send a copy of the notice to the registrar. (A similar notice must be served where the auditor indicates his unwillingness to be re-appointed at the next AGM). The notice must state either whether or not there are any circumstances connected with the resignation that the auditor considers should be brought to the notice of the members or creditors, detailing such circumstances if they exist. Any statement detailing such circumstances must be circulated to the members. Under s 186 of that Act the auditor may also requisition the directors to convene an EGM to consider such account and explanation of these circumstances as the auditor may wish to give. The directors must within 14 days of service of the notice convene the meeting for a date not more than 28 days after such service. The auditor can also require the company to circulate to the members before the meeting or before the next AGM at which his term would otherwise have expired, any further written statement of the circumstances connected with his resignation. He is also entitled to receive notice of, to attend and be heard at both the EGM called to fill the vacancy caused by his resignation and the AGM at which his term in office would otherwise have expired, at least in so far as the business concerns him as former auditor.

Remuneration of auditors

[16.20] Where the auditor has been appointed by the directors or by the Minister his remuneration is fixed by the directors or Minister as the case may be. Otherwise it is fixed by the company in AGM or in such manner as the company in AGM may determine.[1]

1 Ibid s 160(8).

Qualifications of auditors

[16.21] The auditor is required to have the qualifications set out in ss 187–192 of the 1990 Act. These sections implement the provisions of the Eighth Companies Directive. Under s 201 the Minister may make such supplemental regulations as are necessary to effectively implement the Directive. Basically, the auditor must be a member of a recognised professional body of accountants or hold an accountancy qualification which in the opinion of the Minister, is of an equivalent standard. There are transitional arrangements for persons who were qualified to act as or were in the process of studying for a qualification which would have entitled them to act as auditors under s 160 of the Principal Act as amended by s 6 of the 1982 Act (now repealed). The Minister also has power under s 189 to recognise equivalent foreign qualifications.

Undischarged bankrupts, bodies corporate and officers or servants of the company (or persons who were officers or servants in the year to which the accounts being audited relate) shall be disqualified to act as auditor of the company. Similar prohibitions apply to the parent, brother, spouse, child partner or employee of an officer of the company. A person is also disqualified from acting as auditor of the company, if he is disqualified from acting as auditor of the company's holding or subsidiary company, or of another subsidiary of its holding company. Persons who are subject to disqualification orders under s 160 of the 1990 Act are also prohibited from acting as auditors. In addition, under s 195 of the 1990 Act any person who is subject to a disqualification order commits an offence if he becomes or remains a partner in a firm of auditors, gives instructions or directions in relation to any part of an audit or works in any capacity on an audit. Acting in breach of s 195 will result in the period of disqualification being extended by up to 10 more years or for such other period as the court may determine. If a person becomes disqualified to act as auditor he must immediately vacate office, giving written notice thereof to the company. It is an offence to act as auditor while disqualified rendering the person liable on conviction to imprisonment or a fine or to both.

[16.22]   In granting recognition to professional bodies, the Minister may consult with them first and must ensure that the standard of their training, qualifications and repute are at least as high as those required by the Directive. If also satisfied as to the standards the body applies to ethics, codes of conduct and practice, independence, professional integrity, technical standards and disciplinary procedures, he must grant that body recognition. The Minister may withdraw recognition from the body if it fails to maintain its standards. Recognition may be given subject to such terms and conditions as the Minister thinks fit. He may vary these terms and conditions from time to time. He can also require the body to prepare a code of professional conduct, to be submitted to him for approval.

[16.23]   Under ss 198–200 of the 1990 Act the registrar of companies must maintain a register of all persons qualified to act as auditors. There is a duty on recognised bodies and persons otherwise qualified to provide the registrar with the requisite information to enable him to maintain the register.

[16.24]   A lien cannot be acquired by an auditor over book debts and documents which under the articles of association ought to be kept at the registered office of the company.

Re JJ Hopkins & Co (1959) 93 ILTR 32 (High Court)

[16.25] The official liquidator of the company applied for an order that the former auditors were not entitled to a lien on certain books and documents in their possession which belonged to the company. These included the petty cash book, the sales book, the debtor's ledger, the cash book, the cheques journal, two creditors ledgers, four wages books, the nominal ledger, the share register, the certificate of incorporation and the share counterfoils. Under the articles, the books of account were to be kept at the company's office.

[16.26] **Dixon J:** Counsel for the official liquidator concedes that there may be a lien upon books similar to the lien which a factor or artificer has on goods upon which he has worked. I would not regard the lien of an auditor as being similar to the lien of a factor or artificer as the work done by an auditor is not done on books but is done with books. I accept the proposition that the auditor may have a lien on books and papers which have come into his possession for the purpose of making up the accounts of a client.

None of the cases cited by Mr McGivern deals with the point raised by the two cases cited by Mr Kenny. In both of these cases (*In Re Capital Fire Insurance Association* (1883) 24 Ch D 408 and *In Re Anglo Maltese Hydrolic Dock Co Ltd* 33 WR 652) it was held that the lien of a solicitor could not extend to books which were required by the articles of association of a company to be kept at the registered office of the company.

The principle illustrated by the two cases is that a lien is a matter of contract and if by reason of a prohibition in the articles of association the directors of a company have no power to create a lien, there cannot be an implied contract. It has been said that the auditors are not bound by the articles of association, but even if that is correct, it seems to me to be irrelevant. The articles of association restrict the power of the company to enter into an implied contract which is necessary to create a lien. It was submitted that a valid lien had been created because the books had been left with the auditors for a valid purpose. The purpose for which the books had been left with the auditors was a temporary purpose and it seems clear that the books would have to be returned to the company as soon as the purpose for which they had been left with the auditors was completed. There is no distinction in principle between books of account which come into the hands of the auditors for legitimate purposes and books of account which come into the possession of a solicitor. I think that the position is the same for solicitors and auditors. In either case, if the books are in the hands of an agent for a legitimate purpose a lien may exist but it cannot arise when the books are of a type that are required by the articles of association of the company to be kept at the registered office of the company or are books like the register of members which are incapable of being the subject of a lien.

The two cases cited in support of the argument advanced by counsel for the official liquidator are based on a sound principle and are very much in point and I think that the official liquidator is entitled to an order for the return to him of the books of account of the company.

Notes

See also *Re Darion Fashions Ltd* [1981] 2 NZLR 47

Duties of auditors

[16.27] The auditors are obliged to report to the members on the accounts examined by them and on every balance sheet, profit and loss account and all group accounts laid before the company in general meeting during their tenure in office.[1] In carrying out the audit, the auditor is under an express statutory duty 'to carry out such audit with professional integrity'. The report must be read at the AGM and be open to inspection by the members. It must state whether the auditors have obtained all the information and explanations which, to the best of their knowledge and belief, are necessary for the purposes of the audit; whether in their opinion, proper books of account have been kept; whether, in their opinion, proper returns adequate for their audit have been received from branches of the company not visited by them; whether the accounts presented to the AGM are in agreement with the basic records of the company; whether such accounts present a true and fair view of the company and in the case of group accounts whether they present a true and fair view of the group; and whether the circumstances require an EGM to be convened under s 40 of the 1983 Act. It should also state whether in the auditors opinion the director's report is consistent with the contents of the annual accounts.[2] If the accounts fail to disclose details of loans, and quasi-loans, to and credit-transactions for the benefit of any director of the company or holding company or any person connected with such a director, then particulars of same should be included in the auditor's report.[3]

1 S 193 of the 1990 Act.
2 S 15 of the 1986 Act.
3 S 46 of the 1990 Act.

[16.28] Under s 194 of the 1990 Act, if at any time the auditors form the opinion that proper books of account are not being or have not been kept, they must, as soon as may be, serve a notice of their opinion on the company and within 7 days after serving the company, give notice in the prescribed form to the registrar as well. Notice need not be given in respect of minor or immaterial contraventions. Neither need it be given in respect of any contravention that occurred in the past where the directors have subsequently taken such steps as are necessary to ensure that proper books are kept. Failure to comply with s 220 is an offence. In addition, if the company goes into insolvent liquidation, the auditor if convicted under s 194, may be made personally liable under s 204 for all or any of the company's debts.

486

[16.29] The auditor has a right of access at all reasonable times to the books, accounts and vouchers of the company and may require from its officers, subsidiaries and the auditors of such subsidiaries such information and explanations that are within their knowledge or procurement as he thinks necessary for the performance of his duties. The company itself is under a duty to take such steps as are reasonably open to it to obtain such information and explanations from a subsidiary, when requested by the auditors.

[16.30] Under s 197 of the 1990 Act it is an offence for any officer or employee of the company to knowingly or recklessly make misleading, false or deceptive statement to the auditors. It is also an offence for the officer or employee to fail to provide to the auditors of the company or of the holding company within two days of being required to do, any information or explanation within his knowledge or procurement which has been requested by the auditors of the company or of the holding company. It is a defence, however, to show that the information could not be provided within the two days, but that it was furnished as soon as was reasonably practicable. Conviction under s 197 may result in personal liability for all or part of the company's debts under s 204.

[16.31] The auditor is entitled to attend any general meeting of the company and has the same right as the members to receive notices of and other communications relating to such meetings. He may also be heard at such meetings on any part of the business of the meeting which concerns him as auditor.

Status of auditors

[16.32] An auditor is not normally an agent for the company so that his certification of the accounts will not amount to an acknowledgement on behalf of the company of a statute barred debt referred to in the accounts.

Re Transplanters (Holding Co) Ltd [1958] 2 All ER 711

[16.33] The applicant who was one of two directors of the company sought to prove in the winding up of the company for money lent by him. The liquidator rejected his proof on the ground that the debt was statute barred. The applicant then relied upon two balance sheets of the company (which referred to the debt) as constituting an acknowledgement of the debt for the purposes of the Limitation Act. The balance sheets had been signed by the applicant and the other director and they had been certified by the auditor.

[16.34] **Wynn-Parry J:** In my view an auditor of a company is not (apart from any special contract and there is none in this case) an agent of the company at any rate for the purpose of being able to bind the company be merely signing the normal certificate at the foot of the balance sheet. To hold otherwise would, I think be contrary to the Companies Act 1948. No doubt for certain purposes the auditors may be regarded as servants of the company so that the court will not by mandatory injunction force on the company auditors whom the shareholders do not desire to act: see *Cuff v London & County Land & Building Co Ltd* [1912] 1 Ch 440. Apart however, from any special contract, the relations between the company and its auditors are governed by the provisions of the Companies Act 1948 and their duty as expressed by s 162(1) is to make a report to the members on the accounts examined by them and on every balance sheet and every profit and loss account and their report is to contain statements as to the various matters mentioned in sch 9 to that Act. That scheme seems to me designed to produce the result that a skilled professional man or a firm of skilled professional men is or are appointed in order that there shall be before the company all the requisite information indicated in the Companies Act 1948 and by his certificate the auditor pledges himself that he has properly performed his statutory duty. But I cannot spell out of the certificate anything which would amount to an acknowledgement within s 23(4) and s 24(2) of the Limitation Act 1939, because I cannot spell out of his relations with the company as to be extracted from the Companies Act 1948, any authority to do anything in the nature of giving an acknowledgement within the Limitation Act 1939 or any authority to do more than to perform the duties laid on him as auditor by the Companies Act 1948.

Notes
   Cf *Jones v Bellgrove Properties* [1949] 2 All ER 198.

[16.35]   Although an auditor is not per se an officer of the company, where he has been guilty of fraud or default in relation to the company's books and accounts, he will be treated as an 'officer' of the company for the purposes of both criminal and civil proceedings.

R v Shacter [1960] 1 All ER 61 (Court of Criminal Appeal)

[16.36]   The appellant who was auditor of the company was charged with one of its directors, with various offences under the Larceny Acts and under the UK Companies Acts. The various offences applied only to 'officers' of the company. The trial judge directed the jury that in law if the appellant had been appointed auditor and was exercising the office of auditor, he was an 'officer' of the company. The appellant was convicted and appealed on the ground that the trial judge had misdirected the jury.

[16.37]   **Lord Parker CJ** (delivering the judgment of the court): The first and main question which arises in this appeal is whether the appellant was at the material time an officer of the company . . . The authorities concerned are all under the misfeasance section in earlier Acts dealing with civil liability, but they clearly show this, that an auditor appointed to fill an office is an officer, whereas an auditor appointed ad hoc for a limited purpose is not. The first case to which we were referred was *Re London & General Bank* [1895] 2 Ch 166. In that case an auditor had been appointed by a banking company pursuant to s 7 of the Companies Act 1879 . . . The court consisting of Lindsey, Lopes and Kay LJJ, were of the opinion that the auditor was an officer of the company within the relevant misfeasance section. It is true that in that case the articles of the bank in fact defined auditors and the secretary as meaning those respective 'officers' from time to time of the company. In other words the articles, unlike the present case, were treating auditors as officers, but if one examines the judgments it is quite clear that in all three cases they are based on the appointment although the opinions expressed were confirmed or fortified by a reference to the articles. Again, in *Re Kingston Cotton Mill Co* [1896] 1 Ch 6, the court, again the Court of Appeal, followed *Re London & General Bank* and they did that despite the fact that there was nothing in the articles in that case corresponding to the articles in *Re London & General Bank*. Finally, in *Re Western Counties Steam Bakeries & Milling Co* [1897] 1 Ch 617, the same distinction was drawn, namely a distinction between somebody appointed to an office who would be an officer of the company and an auditor who was merely appointed ad hoc for some limited purpose.

It is true as I have said, that those cases were all dealing with questions of civil liability, but this court sees no reason to draw any distinction in a criminal case. Section 333, which is the present misfeasance section, must be taken to have been passed in virtually the same words as in earlier Acts with full knowledge of the decisions in those cases to which I have referred. It is a section which follows closely on the sections creating criminal offences and this court sees no reason to give any different interpretation to the word 'officer' in the penal sections to that given to it in s 333.

[16.38] An auditor must exercise reasonable care and skill in the performance of his duties. He must not certify what he does not believe to be true and he must take reasonable care and skill before he believes that what he certifies is true. Failure to exercise due care and skill may render the auditor liable to the company in damages for any consequent loss.

Irish Woollen Co Ltd v Tyson (1900) 26 The Accountant LR 13

[16.39] The directors and accountant of the plaintiff company had been guilty of supressing invoices for goods purchased or of 'carrying over' invoices for goods purchased (ie. not putting them into the ledger until a later date) with a view to creating a falsely profitable picture of the company. On foot of these false profits dividends of £4,649 were wrongfully declared and paid. The defendant auditor Kevans had been asked to carry out a monthly audit of the company in return for a higher audit fee. The company went into liquidation and sued Kevans for failing to discover the fraud.

[16.40] **Fitzgibbon LJ:** As regards the measure of the duty of a gentleman employed as Mr Kevans was in this case, the result is the same, as it occurs to me, in all cases in which professional skill is employed except one, the peculiar instance of a barrister. The measure of duty is the bringing of reasonable care and skill to the performance of the business directed to be done, having regard first to the contract of employment, then to the character of the business itself, to the remuneration of the defendant and to all the other circumstances of the case. In strict rule, however, the measure of the duty is to be ascertained by applying to all the circumstances of the case the best consideration so as to ascertain what ought to have been done under the circumstances . . .

I think the fairest way to deal with Mr Kevans in this case is to treat him as being charged with having failed to find just cause of suspicion on the face of these books, which if found, would have imposed on him the duty of pursuing his suspicion until he found whether it was or was not well founded . . . The English cases have established that the auditor is entitled in the absence of the elements of suspicion to assume that the books are honestly kept, and that therefore, unless on the fact of a presumably honest book something appears to excite his suspicion he is not guilty of negligence whatever other people might be in their departments, if he does not discover that something was wrong. [His Lordship then took by way of example, a particular creditor in whose account large sums appeared for a two month period after the trial balance had been struck.]

I cannot conceive any more clear or glaring grounds of suspicion than to discover in the account of a single customer items amounting to such a sum having got into the books after the trial balance is struck, under dates going back two months prior to the period of the ascertaining of the trial balance. There appears to be a further thing – a monthly check was to be adopted and that would have put an auditor on inquiry. It appears to me that the moment I come to the conclusion that that was on the face of it a suspicious mode of dealing with [the creditor's] figures I am bound to show how it would be corrected . . . It would then have been necessary to call for the creditors' statements of account and at that moment they would have disclosed on the face of them not merely those post-dated items but the suppressed invoices also; and at the instant that this discovery was made there is an absolute conviction of something wrong forced upon the mind of an auditor. It therefore occurs to me that . . . all that is required, both to show negligence, to arouse suspicion, and to supply the means to putting a stop to the frauds, is to be found on the face of the book . . .

Holmes LJ delivered a concurring judgment. Ashbourne LJ concurred.

Notes

See also *Leech v Stokes* [1937] IR 787 where Hanna J, in a judgment unanimously affirmed by the Supreme Court, stated that 'the duty upon an auditor is, under the circumstances of the particular case and of his employment, to exercise such skill and care as a diligent, skilled and cautious auditor would exercise according to the practice of the profession'.

[16.41] An auditor who has been or ought to have been put on inquiry by irregularities is under a duty to make an exhaustive investigation of the matter. He is not entitled to simply accept the explanation from the company's officers, but may be required to make inquiries of the customers, suppliers and other third parties who have dealings with or knowledge of the company.

Re Thomas Gerrard & Son Ltd [1967] 2 All ER 525 (Chancery Division)

[16.42] The managing director of the company, Croston, had falsified the company's books by (*a*) altering the half-yearly stock-taking figures so as to include non-existent stock; (*b*) altering invoices for purchases of stock to make it look as if the due dates for payment were just after rather than just before the half-yearly 'cut-off' date; and (*c*) altering other monies to make it look as if the due date for payment was just before rather than just after the half yearly 'cut off' date. The auditors, Kevans, had accepted the explanations given by Croston and his brother in law, Hayes regarding the altered invoices. The court held that Kevans had been negligent in simply accepting this explanation and were held liable to the company's liquidator for the amount of the dividends and tax which had consequently been paid out of false profits.

[16.43] **Pennycuick J:** It has always been the law that an auditor must exercise reasonable care and skill and it could hardly be suggested that the effect of the present statutory provisions is to diminish this obligation.

I was referred to such judicial decisions on the duties of auditors as are to be found in the books. The most important for the present purpose is the decision of the Court of Appeal in *Re Kingston Cotton Mill Co (No 2)* [1896] 2 Ch 279, in which it was held (affirming the judgment of Vaughan Williams J) that where an officer of a company had committed a breach of his duty to the company, the direct consequence of which had been a misapplication of its assets, for which he could be made responsible in an action, such breach of duty was a 'misfeasance' for which he might be summarily proceeded against . . . In that case, for some years before the company was wound up, balance sheets signed by the auditors were published by the directors to the shareholders in which the value of the company's stock-in-trade at the end of each year was grossly overstated. The auditors relied on certificates, wilfully false, given by J, one of the directors who was also manager as to the value of the stock-in-trade. Dividends were paid for some years on the footing that the balance sheets were correct; but if the stock-in-trade had been stated at its true value it would have appeared that there were no profits out of which a dividend could be declared. If the auditors had compared the different books and added to the stock-in-trade at the beginning of the year the amounts purchased during the year and deducted the amounts sold, they would have seen that the statement of the stock-in-trade at the end of the year was so large as to call for explanation; but they did not do so. It was held (reversing the decision of Vaughan Williams J,) that it being no part of the duty of the auditors to take stock, they were justified in relying on the certificates of the manager, a person of acknowledged competence and high reputation and were not bound to check his certificates in the absence of anything to raise suspicion and that they were not liable for the dividends wrongfully paid. An auditor was not bound to be suspicious where there were no circumstances to arouse suspicion; he was only bound to exercise a reasonable amount of care and skill. [His lordship then quoted several passages from the judgments in that case, including a passage in which Lopes LJ referred to the auditor as 'a watch dog but not a blood hound'].

This case appears at any rate at first sight to be conclusive in favour of Kevans as regards the falsification of the stock taken in isolation. Counsel for the liquidator pointed out that before 1900 there was no statutory provision corresponding to s 162 of the Companies Act 1948. That is so, but I am not clear that the quality of the auditor's duty has changed in any relevant respect since 1896. Basically that duty has always been to audit the company's accounts with reasonable care and skill. The real ground on which *Re Kingston Cotton Mill Co (No 2)* is I think, capable of being distinguished is that the standards of reasonable care and skill are on the expert evidence more exacting today than those which prevailed in 1896. I see considerable force in this contention. It must, I think be that it is open even in this court, to make a finding that in all the particular circumstances the auditors have been in breach of their duty in relation to stock. On the other hand if this breach of duty stood alone and the facts were more or less the same as those in *Re Kingston Cotton Mill Co (No 2)* this court would I think, be very chary indeed of reaching a conclusion different from that reached by the Court of Appeal in *Re Kingston Cotton Mill Co (No 2)* . . .

I find it impossible to acquit Kevans of negligence as regards purchases of stock before the end of each current period of account and the attribution of the price to the succeeding period of account. I will assume in their favour that Mr Nightingale was entitled to rely on the assurances of Mr Heyes and Mr Croston until he first came on the altered invoices, but once these were discovered he was clearly put on inquiry and I do not think that he was then entitled to rest content with the assurances of Mr Croston and Mr Heyes, however implicitly he may have trusted Mr Croston. I find the conclusion inescapable alike on the expert evidence and as a matter of business common sense, that at this stage he ought to have taken steps on the lines indicated by Mr MacNamara, that is to say he should have examined the suppliers' statements and where necessary have communicated with the suppliers. having ascertained the precise facts so far as it was possible for him to do so, he should then have informed the board. It may be that the board would then have taken some action; whatever the board did he should in each subsequent audit have made such checks and such inquiries as would have ensured that any mis-attribution in the cut-off procedure was detected. He did not take any of these steps. I am bound to conclude that he failed in his duty. It is important in this connexion to remember that this is not a case of some isolated failure in detection. The fraud was repeated half-yearly on a large scale for many years. The words which I have quoted from the judgment of Lindley LJ in *Re Kingston Cotton Mill Co (No 2)* are I think, precisely in point: '. . . what in any particular case is a reasonable amount of care and skill depends on the circumstances of that case; that if there is nothing which ought to excite suspicion, less care may properly be considered reasonable than can be so considered if suspicion was or ought to have been aroused.' Here suspicion ought emphatically to have been aroused and the auditors ought to have taken the steps which I have indicated.

Notes

In *Irish Woollen Co Ltd v Tyson* (para **16.39**) Holmes LJ and Fitzgibbon LJ took different approaches as to the standard of care expected from an auditor. Holmes LJ stated that he 'is entitled to see the company's books and the materials for the books, and also to ask for explanations. But he is not called to seek for knowledge outside the company or to communicate with customers or creditors. He is not an insurer against fraud or error'. Fitzgibbon LJ, on the other hand, having referred to the statement of Lopes LJ in *Re Kingston Cotton Mil Co (No 2)* that the auditor is a 'watchdog not a bloodhound', went on to say that this was 'very unfair to the bloodhound who is just as, little likely to have his sense of suspicion aroused as the watchdog. Applying this instance of the dogs to the present case, was not the watchdog bound to bark? and if, when sniffing around, you hit upon a trail of something wrong, surely you must follow it up, and there is just as much obligation on the auditor who is bound to keep his eyes open and his nose, too. As in the case of the hound, the auditor will follow up this trail to the end.' It would seem that the comments of Fitzgibbon LJ are more in keeping with the approach of Pennycuick J in *Re Thomas Gerrard & Son Ltd* (para **16.42**).

Reasonable auditing practice is to be ascertained by reference to the Companies Acts and to the extent that the Acts are silent, by reference to the Statement of Standard Accounting Practice and Auditing Guidelines. See *Lloyd Cheyham & Co Ltd v Little John & Co* (para **16.17**) *supra*; *Fomento Ltd v Selsden Fountain Pen Co Ltd* [1958] 1 WLR 45.

Under s 200 of the Principal Act any provision in the company's articles or the auditor's contract with the company indemnifying him against or exempting him from any liabiity for any negligence, breach of duty or breach of trust shall be void. However, as can be seen below, in *John Sisk & Son Ltd v Flinn* (para **16.45**) liability may be avoided by an appropriate qualification of the accounts.

[16.44] Where the auditors fail to exercise reasonable care and skill they may be liable for any loss suffered by persons who have relied on the audited accounts provided (a) such reliance was reasonable in the circumstances and (b) the auditor knew or ought reasonably to have known that the person would rely on the audited accounts.

John Sisk & Son Ltd v Flinn (High Court, 18 July 1984)

[16.45] The plaintiffs wished to purchase 75% of the shares in Irish Industrial Fabricators Ltd ('the company'). The defendants were the company's auditors. It was agreed that the shares would be purchased at a price based on the company's audited accounts. At no stage prior to the purchase was the plaintiff permitted to inspect the company's books and records to verify the accuracy of the audited accounts. The defendants knew, when auditing the accounts that they were being relied upon by the plaintiffs. After the purchase had been completed it was discovered that the work in progress had been overvalued in the audited accounts and as a result the plaintiffs suffered loss and damage. The defendants however, put the following qualification in the accounts.

> 'We have obtained all the information and explanations which to the best of our knowledge and belief were necessary for the purpose of our audit except that stock and work in progress at the beginning and end of the financial period are as certified by the management and have not been physically observed.'

Expert evidence from a leading accountant (Mr Blanc) indicated that the qualification constituted a disclaimer of liability. Finlay P (as he then was) found that if it had not been for the disclaimer the defendants would have been liable to the plaintiff in negligence.

[16.46] **Finlay P:** I am prepared to accept as correct the statement of principle contained in the decision of Reid LJ in *Hedley Byrne & Co Ltd v Heller and Partners Ltd* [1964] AC 465 where at page 486 speaking of the decision of Haldane LJ in *Derry v Peek* he stated as follows:–

> 'He speaks of other special relationships and I can see no logical stopping place short of all those relationships where it is plain that the parties seeking information or advice was trusting the other to exercise such a degree of care as the circumstances required, where it was reasonable for him to do that, and where the other gave the information or advice when he knew or ought to have known that the enquirer was relying on him.'

Applying this statement of principle to the facts of this case as I have found them, I have no doubt that it was in this case plain that the plaintiff who was the party seeking information from the defendants was trusting the defendants to exercise such a degree of case as the circumstances required. Furthermore, though the matter was contended, I have no doubt that in those circumstances it was reasonable for the plaintiff being the prospective purchasers of shares in the company to trust the auditors and accountants appointed to the company who had also a function in granting financial advice to the company and were taking an active part in the negotiation for the purchase of shares in it to exercise such care. I cannot see how it would be possible in this case to avoid the further consequential conclusion that the defendants ought to have known that the plaintiff as the enquirer was relying on them to exercise that care. This last conclusion in my view, necessarily flows from the finding which I have made on the facts that the plaintiff did not prior to the execution of the agreement on the 4th May 1978 have any opportunity of examining the books or accounts of the company except in so far as the abortive investigations in 1977 by Mr O'Flynn, their building surveyor, involved some access to those books.

The next issue of law which must necessarily arise is as to the standard of care which was required in the circumstances of the facts as I have found them from the defendants in this case.

Hedley Byrne v Heller was of course, a case of a simple enquiry as to the financial stability of a company from the bankers to the company and the facts are significantly different from the facts in this case.

Notwithstanding this difference, however, I would adopt with approval the general principle stated by Reid LJ in his judgment at page 486 as follows: 'a reasonable man knowing that he was being trusted or that his skill and judgment were being relied on, would I think, have three courses open to him. He could keep silent or decline to give the information or advice sought; or he could give an answer with a clear qualification that he accepted no responsibility for it or that it was given without that reflection or enquiry which a careful answer would require; or he could simply answer without such qualification. If he chooses to adopt the last course, he must I think be held to have accepted some responsibility for his answer being given carefully or to have accepted a relationship with the enquirer which requires him to exercise such care as the circumstances require.'

I am satisfied on the evidence in this case that no case has been made against the defendants of negligence, material to the losses which the plaintiff has suffered other than in respect of the work in progress figure. Certain evidence was given critical of the method of the audit and critical of some of the information contained in the working papers leading to the audit which were discovered. None of this, in my view amounted however to even prima facie evidence of negligence except in respect of the work in progress figure.

The evidence of Mr Blanc to which I have already referred as to the true interpretation of the qualification contained in the auditor's report on the accounts to the 30th November 1977 to the effect that it means that the auditors have no responsibiity for that item which I accept and which is the evidence on this topic adduced on behalf of the plaintiff seems to me clearly to put the defendants in the position of having adopted the second course which in the passage which I have quoted Reid LJ states 'is open to a person knowing that he is being trusted or his skill and judgment is being relied on with regard to an enquiry' . . .

In these circumstances I am satisfied that the plaintiff's action fails and that the claim must be dismissed.

Kelly v Haughey Boland & Co (High Court, 30 July 1985)

[16.47]   The plaintiffs who were directors of Cavan Crystal Ltd, wished to purchase the assets and undertaking of Royal Tara China Ltd ('the company'). The defendants were the company's auditors. Prior to the completion of the purchase of the company in 1977 the plaintiffs were given copies of the audited accounts for the years ending 1973 to 1976 inclusive. The plaintiffs had a number of meetings with the defendants prior to the sale, during which the company's stock figures in the audited accounts were explained. After the purchase had been completed the plaintiffs issued proceedings against the defendants claiming that the stock figures in the audited accounts were inaccurate as a result of which the plaintiffs had suffered loss and damage. In evidence it transpired that none of the defendants' staff had been physically present at the stocktakings. Lardner J, accepted that the defendants' owed the plaintiffs' a duty of care in respect of the audited accounts for the years ended 1975 and 1976 as they knew when performing these audits that a sale of the company's business to someone was possible. Further, it was held that the defendants had been negligent in not physically attending the stocktaking. However, on the facts the plaintiffs failed to prove that the stock figures were inaccurate.

[16.48]   Lardner J: Counsel for the defendants submitted that in cases of negligent statement or misrepresentation the issue fell to be considered within the formulation or principle expressed in *Hedley Byrne & Co Ltd v Heller & Partners Ltd* [1964] AC 465. Lord Morris said at p 502:

> 'I consider that it follows and that it should now be regarded as settled that if someone possessed of a special skill undertakes quite irrespective of contract, to apply that skill for the assistance of another person who relies upon such skill, a duty of care will arise. The fact that the service is to be given by means of or by the instrumentality of words can make no difference. Furthermore, if in a sphere in which a person is so placed that others could reasonably rely upon his judgment or his skill or upon his ability to make careful inquiry, a person takes it upon himself to give information or advice to or allows his information or advice to be passed on to another person who as he knows or should know, will place reliance upon it, then a duty of care will arise.'

This latter test, if applied, would require reliance by the plaintiffs on the skill and care of the auditor of the accounts as part of the test of liability as well a part of the chain of causation. Both counsel referred me to and relied upon a recent English decision, *JEB Fasteners v Marks, Bloom & Co* [1981] 3 All ER 289, a case in which issues very similar to those in this case arose and which contains a helpful review of the English decisions and a certain New Zealand decision, *Scott Group Ltd v McFarlane* [1978] 1 NZLR. At p 296 Woolf said:

'without laying down any principle which is intended to be of general application on the basis of the authorities which I have cited, the appropriate test for establishing whether a duty of care exists appears in this case to be whether the defendants knew or reasonably should have foreseen at the time the accounts were audited that a person might rely on those accounts for the purpose of deciding whether or not to take over the company and therefore could suffer loss if the accounts were inaccurate. Such an approach does place a limitation on those entitled to contend that there has been a breach of duty owed to them. First of all, they must have relied on the account and second, they must have done so in circumstances where the auditors either knew that they would or ought to have known that they might. If the situation is one where it would not be reasonable for the accounts to be relied on, then in the absence of express knowledge, the auditor would be under no duty. This places a limit on the circumstances in which the audited accounts can be relied on and the period for which they can be relied on, the longer the period which elapses prior to the accounts being relied on from the date on which the auditor gave his certificate, the more difficult it will be to establish that the auditor ought to have foreseen that his certificate would in those circumstances be relied on.'

I respectfully adopt that as a statement of the appropriate test of liability to apply in this case.

Applying this test to the accounts for the year ended 31 December 1976 I have no doubt that the defendants did owe such a duty of care and indeed counsel for the defendants . . . conceded as much during the course of the trial. The audit for that year appears to have occurred during the months of April and May 1977, and the accounts were certified in the month of June 1977. The first approach by Mr Murphy and Mr Murray [of Cavan Crystal] to the O'Sullivans [of the company] occurred in March and the O'Sullivans were actively considering a sale of the business from April 1977. Mr Stan McHugh [of the defendants] was made aware of this at the time the audit was being done and subsequently became aware that there were a number of potential purchasers of whom the plaintiffs were one prior to certification of the accounts.

In regard to the accounts for the year ended 31 December 1975 the defendants do not admit that they owe any duty of care to the plaintiffs. The auditor's certificate on these accounts is dated 28 October 1976 and the audit was presumably conducted in the preceding months. During 1976 Mr Kerry O'Sullivan was in declining health and this was affecting the management and performance of the business. Mr McHugh says, and I accept his evidence that in this year he was not aware that a sale was being considered by the O'Sullivans and there has been no evidence that it was, but that it was a possibility at this time. There is, however, the further factor relied on by the plaintiffs in regard to the 1975 accounts, namely that the figures in the balance sheet and the profit and loss account for that year appeared by way of comparison in the 1976 accounts which were certified and put forward by the defendants in the course of the negotiations for sale in 1977 to the plaintiffs and to other interested parties. In my view the auditors in auditing the 1975 accounts should reasonably foreseen and considered that there might be a sale of the business and the persons interested in purchasing it might rely on the 1975 accounts. As to the accounts for the year ending 31 December 1974 and 31 December 1973 there has been no evidence that these accounts were put forward by the defendants as auditors in the course of 1977 for the purposes of negotiations with the intending purchaser. The evidence has been that so far as the present plaintiffs are concerned, these accounts were delivered to them by Mrs O'Sullivan without the intervention of any of the defendants. At the times they were prepared I am not satisfied from any evidence which I have heard, that any sale of the business was in contemplation by the defendants as auditors. And in the circumstances of this case I do not think it has been established that any duty of care lay upon the defendants in the preparation of the accounts for these years in regard to the plaintiffs as intending purchasers or in regard to intending purchasers in general.

It will be convenient at this point if I refer generally to the professional duty of an auditor in regard to accounts. Evidence for the plaintiffs, which I accept and which was not really contested, was given by Mr Alan Mooney an independent chartered accountant who qualified and has been in practice since 1963 and has worked for Messrs Craig Gardner since 1965 and has for some years lectured in accountancy in University College Dublin.

He described the essential features of an audit as 'making an independent report for the shareholders on accounts prepared by the directors.' In order to do this an auditor would begin by trying to obtain a general idea of the existing business by examining the accounts of two or three previous years. He would then ascertain what arrangements the company had made that would result in reliable accounts being prepared and he would make whatever examination and tests of those arrangements he considered appropriate to determine their reliability.

He would then compare the actual draft accounts prepared by the directors with the arrangements leading to them, that is the company's accounting records. And finally, having established (*a*) that the company has made adequate arrangements leading to proper accounts, (*b*) that the system is reliable by testing and (*c*) having compared the accounts with the output of that system, he would make an overall review of the draft accounts to see whether they give a true and fair view in relation to the profit and loss account and the balance sheet.

It is clear that an auditor cannot conduct an examination of all the company's transactions during the particular accounting period. He is concerned to see that there is an adequate and proper system for recording transactions that such transactions are properly authorised and that the assets of the company are properly looked after and safeguarded.

Passing from these general considerations to the particular matter of stocktaking, Mr Moloney said that stocktaking was a physical count and was

498

recorded as a list. He described the auditor's duty and concern as firstly to ascertain what arrangements the company had made for accurate stocktaking and secondly, to test those arrangements. Evidently it was not part of the auditor's duty to conduct the stocktaking. That was a matter for the company to carry out. The auditor's duty was to see whether the client was operating and carrying out adequate arrangements for the proper counting of stock with a view subsequently to valuing that stock. One way for the auditor to carry out this duty was to attend at the stocktaking and to observe while the stock was being taken.

Mr Moloney then described the kind of arrangements which would constitute stocktaking. They would include, he said, one and one only count of all stock ensuring that everything that was stock had also been recorded as a purchase in the company's books. An important feature of this was also to identify stock of poor quality which would affect its value. After stocktaking the next step was to ensure that counted stock was translated into value by applying prices. This also was a function of the company. The auditor's duty was simply to check that stocks were valued in accordance with an acceptable principle for valuation, usually at the lower of cost or market value.

At the end of stocktaking the auditor's duty was to judge whether he could reasonably rely on the client's stocktaking or not and whether the stock appeared to be of an amount which was material in relation to the balance sheet and the turnover of the company. If he decided for some reason that he could not rely on the stocktaking he might try to reach a satisfactory appraisal of the position by some other means such as taking stock at a date shortly after the end of the financial year and working back through sales records to the years end, try to verify the client's stock figures. If however, he was unable to satisfy himself of the reliability of the figures resulting from the client's stocktaking then he must qualify the auditor's report.

Mr Moloney was asked during the course of his evidence about the case where an auditor was unable to attend at stocktaking. His reply was that there was no professional standard or statement of practice that the auditor must attend at stocktaking. He had an option to attend or not to attend. It was considered in the profession and recommended in the statement of principles that attendance at stocktaking was the best way of checking the adequacy of the stocktaking. But the auditor as a professional person might make up his own mind what he would do in the circumstances of the particular case.

Having decided that a duty of care existed in regard to the accounts for the years ended 1975 and 1976, the next question I have to consider is whether Mr McHugh as auditor of the company was guilty of negligence in auditing the company's accounts for these years . . .

There was really no dispute between the parties about the duties of an accountant in relation to stocktaking. Both accepted the statements of professional standard of the Institute of Chartered Accountants. These require that the auditor should ascertain what arrangements a company has made for accurate stocktaking and that he should test them. One way in which the auditor might fulfil this duty and which was recommended was to attend at the stocktaking and to observe the procedures being followed. Mr Alan Moloney said there was no professional standard or practice which required that an auditor must attend. He has an option to attend or not to attend. It was considered in the profession and recommended that the attendance at stocktaking was the best way of testing or checking the adequacy of the procedures of the company's servants. But the auditor as a professional man, might make up his own mind what he would do in the circumstances of each particular case. At the end of the stocktaking the auditor's duty was to judge whether he could reasonably rely on the company's stocktaking which was material in relation to the balance sheet and the turnover of the company.

In the present case at the stocktaking and audit for the 1975 and 1976 accounts, Mr McHugh had been auditing the company's accounts for over 20 years. He knew Mr Kerry O'Sullivan well and had discussed the accounts and matters such as stocktaking on many occasions with him. He was familiar with Mr O'Sullivan's way of managing the business and knew that he personally took stock. He had long experience of the company's accounting arrangements and of the books of account which were kept. He had a good opinion of them and of Mr Keane, the company's secretary. He said that in his judgment he thought he could rely on Mr O'Sullivan's stocktaking and on Mr Keane's books of account. But he admitted that neither in 1975 nor in 1976 or any previous year back to 1954 had he ever attended at stocktaking and observed the procedure followed by Mr O'Sullivan.

In regard to the accounts for the year 1976 he said he did not know whether or not Mr O'Sullivan had taken stock or who had done it. Mr O'Sullivan was not able at this time and might not have taken stock. When he went to do the audit he was given a stocksheet which had figures with the word 'estimated' written opposite them. But he said this referred to the values and he was satisfied stock had been taken. He made checks in the books of account of purchases and sales for the following weeks and he was satisfied that the figures in the stocksheets were consistent and that the figures for stock in the audited accounts were correct. Considering all the evidence on this aspect, did Mr McHugh fail to exercise reasonable care in regard to the stocktaking – in particular by failing to attend the stocktaking in either 1975 or 1976?

If these two years were exceptional and if in some previous years he had attended, observed and been satisifed I should have been slow for reason only of non-attendance in these two years to conclude that there was any want of care. But 1975 and 1976 followed on 20 years earlier in which he never attended at stocktaking. I am aware from the evidence that, over the past 40 or 50 years the standards in the profession have tended to become more exacting. In 1975 and 1976 Mr McHugh was drawing close to the end of his professional career and to retirement and it may be that his conduct in regard to stocktaking would in earlier years have been regarded as acceptable. But I have come to the conclusion that having regard to the professional standards which were recognised in 1975 and 1976 there was a failure

500

by Mr McHugh in not attending at and observing the stocktaking to exercise reasonable care.

Notes

See also *Golden Vale Co-Operative Creameries Ltd v Barrett* (High Court O'Hanlon J, 16 March 1987).

[16.49] An auditor of a public company owes no duty of care to either potential investors or existing shareholders when auditing the company's accounts.

Caparo Industries plc v Dickman [1990] 1 All ER 568 (House of Lords)

[16.50] The plaintiff bought shares in Fidelity plc. The defendants were the auditors of Fidelity. As a result of their negligence in auditing Fidelity's accounts the company was significantly overvalued. The plaintiffs mounted a successful takeover bid for the company on the basis of the audited accounts. However, once they had acquired control of the company they discovered its true worth and issued proceedings against the defendants on the grounds that they owed the plaintiffs a duty of care in auditing the accounts. The trial judge held that no such duty of care was owed. The plaintiffs appealed and the Court of Appeal held that the defendants owed them a duty of care as shareholders but not as potential investors. The defendants appealed to the House of Lords and the plaintiffs cross-appealed against the decision that they could not claim as potential investors.

[16.51] **Lord Bridge of Harwich:** In determining the existence and scope of the duty of care which one person may owe to another in the infinitely varied circumstances of human relationships there has for long been a tension between two different approaches. Traditionally the law finds the existence of the duty in different specific situations each exhibiting its own particular characteristics. In this way the law has identified a wide variety of duty situations all falling within the ambit of the tort of negligence, but sufficiently distinct to require separate definition of the essential ingredients by which the existence of the duty is to be recognised . . . The most comprehensive attempt to articulate a single general principle is reached in the well-known passage from the speech of Lord Wilberforce in *Anns v Merton London Borough* [1977] 2 All ER 492 at 198:

'Through the trilogy of cases in this House *Donoghue v Stevenson* [1932] AC 562; *Hedley Byrne & Co Ltd v Heller & Partners Ltd* [1964] AC 465 and *Home Office v Dorset Yacht Co Ltd* [1970] AC 1004, the position has now been reached that in order to establish that a duty of care arises in a particular situation, it is not necessary to bring the facts of that situation within those of previous situations in which a duty of care has been held to exist. Rather the question has to be approached in two stages. First, one has to ask whether, as between the alleged wrongdoer and the person who

501

has suffered damage there is a sufficient relationship of proximity or neighbourhood such that in the reasonable contemplation of the former, carelessness on his part may be likely to cause damage to the latter, in which case a prima facie duty of care arises. Secondly, if the first question is answered affirmatively, it is necessary to consider whether there are any considerations which ought to negative, or to reduce or limit the scope of the duty or the class of person to whom it is owed or the damages to which a breach of it may give rise (see the *Dorset Yacht* case at 1027 per Lord Reid).'

But since *Ann's* case a series of decisions of the Privy Council and of your Lordship's House notably in judgment and speeches delivered by Lord Keith have emphasised the inability of any single general principle to provide a practical test which can be applied to every situation to determine whether a duty of care is owed and if so, what is its scope . . . What emerges is that, in addition to the foreseeability of damage, necessary ingredients in any situation giving rise to a duty of care are that there should exist between the party owing the duty and the party to whom it is owed a relationship characterised by the law as one of 'proximity' or 'neighbourhood' and that the situation should be one in which the court considers it fair, just and reasonable that the law should impose a duty of the given scope on the one party for the benefit of the other. But it implicit in the passages referred to that the concepts of proximity and fairness embodied in these additional ingredients are not susceptible of any such precise definition as would be necessary to give them utility as practical tests, but amount in effect to little more than convenient labels to attach to the features of different specific situations which, on a detailed examination of all the circumstances the law recognises pragmatically as giving rise to a duty of care of a given scope. Whilst recognising of course, the importance of the underlying general principles common to the whole field of negligence, I think the law has not moved in the direction of attaching greater significance to the more traditional categorisation of distinct and recognisable situations as guides to the existence, the scope and the limits of the varied duties of care which the law imposes . . . One of the most important distinctions always to be observed lies in the law's essentially different approach to the different kinds of damage which one party may have suffered in consequence of the acts or omissions of another. It is one thing to owe a duty of care to avoid causing injury to the person or property of others. It is quite another to avoid causing others to suffer purely economic loss . . .

The damage which may be caused by the negligently spoken or written word will normally be confined to economic loss sustained by those who rely on the accuracy of the information of advice they receive as a basis for action. The question what, if any duty is owed by the maker of a statement to exercise due care to ensure its accuracy arises typically in relation to statements made by a person in the exercise of his calling of profession. In advising the client who employs him the professional man owes a duty to exercise that standard of skill and care appropriate to his professional status and will be liable both in contract and in tort for all losses which his client may suffer by reason of any breach of that duty. But the possibility of any duty of care being owed to third parties with whom the professional man was in no contractual relationship was for long denied because of the wrong turning taken by the law in *Le Lievre v Gould* [1893] 1 QB 491, in overruling *Cann v Wilson* (1888) 39 Ch D 39. In *Candler v Crane Christmas & Co* [1951] 1 All ER 426 Denning LJ, in his dissenting judgment made a valiant effort to correct the error. But it was not until the decision of the House of Lords in *Hedley Byrne & Co Ltd v Heller & Partners Ltd* that the law was once more set on the right path.

In *Candler v Crane Christmas & Co Ltd* the plaintiff invested money in a limited company in reliance on accounts of the company prepared by the company's accountant at the request of the managing director, which were shown to the plaintiff and discussed with him by the accountants in the knowledge that he was interested as a potential investor in the company. The accounts were inaccurate and misleading and the plaintiff, having invested in the company in reliance on them, lost him money. Denning LJ in his dissenting judgment held the plaintiff entitled to recover damages for the accountants' negligence.

In the *Hedley Byrne* case bankers were asked about the financial stability of a customer of the bank. They gave a favourable reference, albeit with a disclaimer of responsibility. The circumstances of the inquiry made it clear to the bankers that the party on whose behalf the inquiry was made wanted to know if they could safely extend credit to the bank's customer in a substantial sum. Acting on the reference given, the plaintiffs extended credit to the bank's customer who in due course defaulted. Although the House held that the bankers were protected by the disclaimer of responsibility, the case provided the opportunity to review the law, which led to the reinstatement of *Cann v Wilson* the overruling of the majority decision in the *Candler* case and the approbation of the dissenting judgment of Denning LJ in that case . . .

The salient feature of all these cases is that the defendant giving advice or information was fully aware of the nature of the transaction which the plaintiff had in contemplation knew that the advice of information would be communicated to him directly or indirectly and knew that it was very likely that the plaintiff would rely on that advice or information in deciding whether or not to engage in the transaction in contemplation. In these circumstances the defendant could clearly be expected subject always to the effect of any disclaimer of responsibility specifically to anticipate that the plaintiff would rely on the advice or information given by the defendant for the very purpose for which he did in the event rely on it. So also the plaintiff, subject again to the effect of any disclaimer would in that situation reasonably suppose that he was entitled to rely on the advice or information communicated to him for the very purpose for which he required it. The situation is entirely different where a statement is put into more or less general circulation and may foreseeably be relied on by strangers to the maker of the statement for any one of a variety of different purposes which the maker of the statement for any one of a variety of different purposes which the maker of the statement has no specific reason to anticipate. To hold the maker of the statement to be under a duty of care in respect of the accuracy of the statement to all and sundry for any purpose for which they may choose to rely on it is not only to subject him in the classic words of Cardozo CJ to 'liability in an indeterminate amount for an indeterminate time to an indeterminate class' . . . it is also to confer on the world at large a quite unwarranted entitlement to appropriate for their own purposes the benefit of the expert knowledge or professional expertise attributed to the maker of the statement. Hence, looking only at the circumstances of these decided cases where a duty of care in respect of negligent statements has been held to exist, I should expect to find that the 'limit to control mechanism . . . imposed on the liability of a wrongdoer towards those who have suffered economic damage in consequence of his negligence' . . . rested on the necessity to prove, in this category of the tort of negligence, as an essential ingredient of the 'proximity' between the plaintiff and the defendant, that the defendant knew that his statement would be communicated to the plaintiff, with a particular transaction or transactions of a particular kind (eg. in a prospectus inviting investment) and that the plaintiff would be very likely to rely on it for the purpose of deciding whether or not to enter on that transaction or on a transaction of that kind.

I find this expectation fully supported by the dissenting judgment of Denning LJ in *Candler v Crane Christmas & Co* [1951] 1 All ER 426 at 433–436 in the following passages:–

'Let me now be constructive and suggest the circumstances in which I say that a duty to use care in making a statement does exist apart from a contract in that behalf. First, what persons are under such a duty? My answer is those persons such as accountants, surveyors, valuers and analysts whose profession and occupation it is to examine books, accounts and other things and to make reports on which other people – other than their clients – rely in the ordinary course of business . . . Secondly, to whom do these professional people owe this duty? I will take accountants, but the same reasoning applies to the others. They owe the duty, of course, to their employer or client; and also I think to any third person to whom they themselves show the accounts, or to whom they know their employer is going to show the accounts so as to induce him to invest money or take some other action on them. I do not think, however, the duty can be extended still further so as to include strangers of whom they have heard nothing and to whom their employer without their knowledge may choose to show their accounts. Once the accountants have handed their accounts to their employer, they are not, as a rule responsible for what he does with them without their knowledge or consent . . . The test of proximity in these cases is: did the accountants know that the accounts were required for submission to the plaintiff and use by him? . . . Thirdly, to what transactions does the duty of care extend? It extends, I think only to those transactions for which the accountants knew their accounts were required. For instance, in the present case it extends to the original investment of £2,000 which the plaintiff made in reliance on the accounts, because [the accountants] knew that the accounts were required for his guidance in making that investment; but it does not extend to the subsequent £200 which he invested after he had been two months with the company. This distinction that the duty only extends to the very transaction in mind at the time in implicit in the decided cases . . . It will be noticed that I have confined the duty to cases where the accountant prepares his accounts and makes his report for the guidance of the very person in the very transaction in question. That is sufficient for the decision of this case. I can well understand that it would be going too far to make an accountant liable to any person in the land who chooses to rely on the accounts in matters of business, for that would expose him in the words of Cardozo CJ in *Ultramares Corpn v Touche* (1931) 255 NY 170 at 179 to "liability in an indeterminate amount for an indeterminate time to an indeterminate class". Whether he would be liable if he prepared his accounts for the guidance of a specific class of persons in a specific class of transaction I do not say. I should have thought he might be, just as the analyst and lift inspector would be liable in the instance I have given earlier. It is perhaps, worth mentioning that parliament has intervened to make the professional man liable for negligent reports given for the purposes of a prospectus: see s 40 and s 43 of the Companies Act 1948. That is an instance of liability for reports made for the guidance of a specific class of persons – investors in a specific class of transaction – applying for shares. That enactment does not help one way of the other to show what result the common law would have reached in the absence of such provisions, but it does show what result it ought to reach. My conclusion is that a duty to use care in statement is recognised by English law and that its recognition does not create any dangerous precedent when it is remembered that it is limited in respect of the persons by whom and to whom it is owed and the transactions to which it applies.'

It seems to me that this masterly analysis, if I may say so with respect, requires little if any amplification or modification in the light of later authority and is particularly apt to point the way to the right conclusion in the present appeal . . . these considerations amply justify the conclusion that auditors of a public company's accounts owe no duty of care to members of the public at large who rely on the accounts in deciding to buy shares in the company. If a duty of care were owed so widely, it is difficult to see any reason why it should not equally extend to all who rely on the accounts in relation to other dealings with a company as lenders or merchants extending credit to the company. A claim that such a duty was owed by auditors to a bank lending to a company was emphatically and convincingly rejected by Millett J in *Al Saudi Banque v Clark Pixley (a firm)* [1989] 3 All ER 361 . . .

The main submissions for Caparo are that the necessary nexus of proximity between it and the auditors giving rise to a duty of care stems from (1)
the pleaded circumstances indicating the vulnerability of Fidelity to a takeover bid and from the consequent probabiity that another company such as
Caparo would rely on the audited accounts in deciding to launch a take-over
bid or (2) the circumstances that Caparo was already a shareholder in Fidelity when it decided to launch its take-over bid in reliance on the accounts. In
relation to the first of these two submissions, Caparo applied, in the course
of the hearing, for leave to amend para 16(2) of the statement of claim by
adding the words 'or alternatively that it was highly probable that such persons would rely on the accounts for that purpose.'

The case which gives most assistance to Caparo in support of this submission is *Scott Group Ltd v Mc Farlane* [1978] 1 NZLR 553. The audited
consolidated accounts of a New Zealand public company and its subsidiaries
overstated the assets of the group because of an admitted accounting error.
Under the relevant New Zealand legislation its accounts were, as in England,
accessible to the public. The circumstances of the group's affairs were such as
to make it highly probable that it would attract a take-over bid. The plaintiffs
made such a bid successfully and when the accounting error was discovered
claimed from the auditors in respect of the shortfall of the assets. Quillan J
held that the auditors owed the plaintiffs no duty of care . . . The majority of
the New Zealand court of appeal (Woodhouse and Cooke JJ) held that the
duty of care arose from the probability that the company would attract a
take-over bid and the bidder would rely on the audited accounts, although
Cooke J held that the shortfall in the assets below that erroneously shown in
the accounts did not amount to a loss recoverable in tort. Richmond P held
that no duty of care was owed. He said ([1978] 1 NZLR 553 at 566):

'All the speeches in *Hedley Byrne* seem to me to recognise the need for a
"special" relationship; a relationship which can properly be treated as
giving rise to a special duty to use care in statement. The question in any
given case is whether the nature of the relationship is such that one party
can fairly be held to have assumed a responsibility to the other as regards
the reliability of the advice or information. I do not think that such a
relationship should be found to exist unless, at least, the maker of the
statement was or ought to have been, aware that his advice or information
would in fact be made available to and be relied on by a particular person
or class of persons for the purposes of a particular transaction or type of
transaction. I would especially emphasise that to my mind it does not seem
reasonable to attribute as assumption of responsibility unless the maker of
the statement ought in all the circumstances both in preparing himself for
what he said and in saying it, to have directed his mind and to have been
able to direct his mind to some particular and specific purpose for which he
was aware that his advice or information would be relied on. In many
situations that purpose will be obvious. But the annual accounts of a company can be relied on in all sorts of ways and for many purposes.'

I agree with this reasoning, which seems to me to be entirely in line with the principles to be derived from the authorities to which I have earlier referred . . . I should in any event be extremely reluctant to hold that the question whether or not an auditor owes a duty of care to an investor buying shares in a public company depends on the degree of probability that the shares will prove attractice either en bloc to a take-over bidder or piecemeal to individual investors. It would be equally wrong, in my opinion, to hold an auditor under a duty of care to anyone who might lend money to a company by reason only that it was forseeable as highly probable that the company would borrow money at some time in the year following publication of its audited accounts and that lenders might rely on those accounts in deciding to lend. I am content to assume the high probability of a takeover bid in reliance on the accounts which the proposed amendment of the statement of claim would assert but I do not think it assists Caparo's case.

The only other English authority to which I need refer in this context is *JEB Fasteners Ltd v Marks Bloom & Co (a firm)* [1981] 3 All ER 289 a decision at first instance of Woolf J. This was another case where the plaintiffs who had made a successful take-over bid for a company in reliance on audited accounts which had been negligently prepared, sued the accountants for damages. Woolf J held that the auditors owed the plaintiffs a duty of care in the preparation of the accounts. He relied on both *Ann's* case and *Scott Group Ltd v McFarlane* in reaching the conclusion that the duty could be derived from foreseeability alone. For the reasons already indicated I do not agree with this. It may well be however, that the particular facts in the JEB case were sufficient to establish a basis on which the necessary ingredient of proximity to found a duty of care could be derived from the actual knowledge on the part of the auditors of the specific purpose for which the plaintiffs intended to use the accounts.

The position of auditors in relation to the shareholders of a public limited liability company arising from the relevant provisions of the Companies Act 1985 is accurately summarised in the judgment of Bingham LJ in the Court of Appeal ([1989] 1 All ER 798 at 804):

'The members or shareholders of the company are its owners. But they are too numerous and in most cases too unskilled to undertake the day to day management of that which they own. So responsibility for day to day management of the company is delegated to directors. The shareholders despite their overall powers of control are in most companies for most of the time investors and little more. But it would of course, be unsatisfactory and open to abuse if the shareholders received no report on the financial stewardship of their investment save from those to whom the stewardship had been entrusted. So provision is made for the company in general meeting to appoint an auditor (Companies Act 1985 s 284) whose duty is to investigate and form an opinion on the adequacy of the company's accounting records and returns and the correspondence between the company's accounting records and returns and its accounts (s 237).

The auditor has then to report to the company's members (among other things) whether in his opinion the company's accounts give a true and fair view of the company's financial position (s 236). In carrying out his investigation and in forming his opinion the auditor necessarily works very closely with the directors and officers of the company. He receives his remuneration from the company. He naturally and rightly, regards the company as his client. But he is employed by the company to exercise his professional skill and judgment for the purpose of giving the shareholders an independent report on the reliability of the company's accounts and thus on their investment. Vaughan Williams J said in *Re Kingston Cotton Mill Co* [1896] 1 Ch 6 at 11: "No doubt he is acting antagonistically to the directors in the sense that he is appointed by the shareholders to be a check upon them." The auditor's report must be read before the company in general meeting and must be open to inspection by any member of the company (s 241). It is attached to and forms part of the company's accounts (ss 238(3) and 239). A copy of the company's accounts (including the auditor's report) must be sent to every member (s 240). Any member of the company even if not entitled to have a copy of the accounts sent to him is entitled to be furnished with a copy of the company's last accounts on demand and without charge (s 246).'

No doubt these provisions establish a relationship between the auditors and the shareholders of a company on which the shareholder is entitled to rely for the protection of his interest. But the crucial question concerns the extent of the shareholder's interest which the auditor had a duty to protect. The shareholders of a company have a collective interest in the company's proper management and in so far as a negligent failure of the auditor to report accurately on the state of the company's finances deprives the shareholders of the opportunity to exercise their powers in general meeting to call the directors to book and to ensure that errors in management are corrected, the shareholders ought to be entitled to a remedy. But in practice no problem arises in this regard since the interests of the shareholders in the proper management of the company's affairs is indistinguishable from the interest of the company itself and any loss suffered by the shareholders, eg. by the negligent failure auditor to discover and expose a misappropriation of funds by a director of the company, will be recouped by a claim against the auditor in the name of the company, not by individual shareholders.

I find it difficult to visualise a situation arising in the real world in which the individual shareholder could claim to have sustained a loss in respect of his existing shareholding referable to the negligence of the auditor which could not be recouped by the company. But on this part of the case your Lordships were much pressed with the argument that such a loss might occur by a negligent undervaluation of the company's assets in the auditor's report relied on by the individual shareholder in deciding to sell his shares at an undervalue. The argument runs thus. The shareholder, qua shareholder, is entitled to rely on the auditors report as the basis of his investment decision to sell his existing shareholding. If he sells at an undervalue he is entitled to recover the loss from the auditor. There can be no distinction in law between the shareholder's investment decision to sell the shares he has or to buy additional shares. It follows, therefore that the scope of the duty of care owed to him by the auditor extends to cover any loss sustained consequent on the purchase of additional shares in reliance on the auditor's negligent report.

I believe this argument to be fallacious. Assuming without deciding that a claim by a shareholder to recover a loss suffered by selling his shares at an undervalue attributable to an undervaluation of the company's assets in the auditor's report could be sustainable at all, it would not be by reason of any reliance by the shareholder on the auditor's report in deciding to sell; the loss would be referable to the depreciatory effect of the report on the market value of the shares before ever the decision of the shareholder to sell was taken. A claim to recoup a loss alleged to flow from the purchase of over-valued shares on the other hand, can only be sustained on the basis of the purchaser's reliance on the report. The specious equation of 'investment decisions' to sell or to buy as giving rise to parallel claims thus appears to me to be untenable. Moreover the loss in the case of the sale would be of a loss of part of the value of the shareholder's existing holding, which assuming a duty of care owed to individual shareholders, it might sensibly lie within the scope of the auditor's duty to protect. A loss, on the other hand, resulting from the purchase of additional shares would result from a wholly indepen-dent transaction having no connection with the existing shareholding.

I believe it is this last distinction which is of critical importance and which demonstrates the unsoundness of the conclusion reached by the majority of the Court of Appeal. It is never sufficient to ask simply whether A owes B a duty of care. It is always necessary to determine the scope of the duty by reference to the kind of damage from which A must take care to save B from harm:

'The question is always whether the defendant was under a duty to avoid or prevent that damage, but the actual nature of the damage suffered is relevant to the existence and extent of any duty to avoid or prevent it.'

Assuming for the purpose of the argument that the relationship between the auditor of a company and individual shareholders is of sufficient prox-imity to give rise to a duty of care. I do not understand how the scope of that duty can possibly extend beyond the protection of any individual sharehol-der from losses in the value of the shares which he holds. As a purchaser of additional shares in reliance on the auditor's report, he stands in no different position from any other investing member of the public to whom the auditor owes no duty.

I would allow the appeal and dismiss the cross-appeal.

Notes

It seems difficult to reconcile the reasoning of the House of Lords in this case with the decisions of Irish judges in *John Sisk & Son Ltd v Flinn* (para **16.45**) and *Kelly v Haughey Boland & Co*. One possible means of distinguishing them might be that in the *Sisk* case the purchaser was already identified before the accounts were audited. Also in the *Kelly* case (as in the *Sisk* case) the companies were private companies. Because of the limitations imposed by s 33 of the Principal Act, the range of potential investors is to an extent limited. In a plc on the other hand, the range of potential investors is limitless (ie. the world at large). However, in *James McNaughton Papers Group Ltd v Hicks Anderson & Co* [1991] 1 All ER 134 it was held that the accountants of a target company in a friendly takeover bid, owed no duty of care to the bidder company when preparing draft accounts for the target company, even though they knew that those draft accounts would be used in the takeover negotiations. Notably, the target company was a private company and the accountants knew the identity of the bidder. Furthermore, the court held that it would not be reasonable to expect that draft accounts would be treated by a person reading them as having the same degree of accuracy as final accounts of the company. See also *Ali Saudi Banque v Clark Pixley* [1989] 3 All ER 361, which was approved by the House of Lords and where it was held that the auditors of a private company did not owe a duty of care to banks who lent money to the company on foot of the audited accounts, even though it was reasonably foreseeable that the accounts would be relied upon by the banks in deciding whether to lend or continue lending money to the company.

Chapter 17

MERGERS, ARRANGEMENTS, RECONSTRUCTIONS AND TAKEOVERS[1]

[17.01] In a takeover company A purchases all the issued shares in company B or a sufficient number to gain control of B. In a merger, however, A purchases the assets and undertaking of B and in return allots shares in A to the members of B. In this way, the businesses of A and B merge or amalgamate. Alternatively, the merger could be effected by setting up a new company C which then acquires the assets and undertaking of A and B, in return allotting shares in C to the members of A and B.

The relevant provisions of the Principal Act which apply to takeovers and mergers are ss 204 and 260. Also of relevance is the procedure for schemes of arrangement under ss 201 to 203. Where the company is a plc, the European Communities (Mergers and Divisions of Companies) Regulations 1987[2] apply. These regulations implement the Third and Sixth EEC Companies Directives.[3] Public companies whether quoted on the stock exchange or on the unlisted securities market must also comply with the *City Code on Takeovers and Mergers* even though it does not have the force of law.[4]

At a domestic level the Minister has power under the Mergers, Takeovers and Monopolies (Control) Act 1978 as amended by the Restrictive Practices (Amendment) Act 1987 to prohibit or to allow subject to conditions, certain mergers or takeovers which would have an anti-competitive effect.[5] This Act applies to mergers or monopolies where the gross assets of each company involved is at least £5,000,000 or the turnover of each is at least £10,000,000.[6] The Minister also has power to break up existing anti-competitive monopolies. The Act only applies if annual sales or purchase of the monopoly are at least £6,000,000.

At a European level, the EC Commission has power to control or prohibit takeovers or mergers which would constitute an 'abuse . . . of a . . . dominant position within the Common Market or in a substantial part of it', under Art 86 of the EEC Treaty.[7]

---

1 See generally *Keane* at chapter 34.
2 SI No 133 of 1987.
3 78/855/EEC and 82/891/EEC.
4 However, the panel may be subject to judicial review: *R v Panel on Takeovers and Mergers; ex parte Datafin* [1987] 2 WLR 699.

5 See *Keane* at paras **34.18–34.24** and *Doing Business in Ireland* (2nd Ed, 1989, New York) ed. Ussher and Occoner, chapter 15.
6 S 2(7) of the 1978 Act as amended by the Mergers, Takeovers and Monopolies (Control) Act 1978 (s 2) Order 1985 (SI No 230 of 1985).
7 See McMahon & Murphy *European Community Law in Ireland* (Dublin 1989) chapter 21.

Directors' duties in a takeover or merger

[17.02]   The general fiduciary principle that a director must not make a secret profit from his office applies with equal force in the case of a takeover or merger. This is reflected in ss 187 to 189 of the Principal Act.[1] S 187 applies to a merger situation and renders unlawful payments in compensation for loss of office or in consideration for retirement from office, unless disclosed to and approved by the company in general meeting. Non-disclosure results in the payment being impressed with a trust in favour of the company.[2] S 188 on the other hand, applies to takeovers and prohibits the same type of payment. Non-disclosure, however results in the payment being impressed with a trust in favour of these shareholders who accepted the takeover bid and sold their shares. A 'payment' for the purposes of ss 187 and 188 includes the excess price which a director receiver for his shares over that paid to other shareholders.[3] The sections apply to payments to both past and present directors[4] and the reference to 'office' includes an office in not only the company itself, but also in any subsidiary.[5] They do not, however, apply to 'bona fide payment by way of damages for breach of contract or by way of pension in respect of past services' nor do they apply to payments to the director qua employee of the company.[6]

1 See *Keane* at para **34.17**.
2 S 187(2) of the Principal Act.
3 Ibid s 189(2).
4 Ibid s 189(5).
5 Ibid s 189(3).
6 Ibid. See *Taupo Totaro Timber Co Ltd v Rowe* [1977] 3 All ER 123.

[17.03]   A company may legitimately have an interest in the identity of its shareholders on a takeover. The directors may, therefore, be entitled to enter into a contract on behalf of the company not to co-operate with a rival bidder. When a takeover bid is made the directors' fiduciary duties are owed to the company and not to individual shareholders. However, if the directors take it upon themselves to advise shareholders they must do so in good faith and not mislead, whether deliberate or carelessly the shareholders.

Dawson International plc v Coats Paton plc [1989] BCLC 233 (Court of Sessions)

[17.04]   The pursuer company made a takeover bid for the defender company. The two companies agreed, through their respective boards of directors, that the directors of the defender would recommend the pursuer's bid and that the defender would not co-operate with any rival bidder, should one emerge. Subsequently, Vantonna Viyella plc ('Viyella') entered into negotiations with the defender with a view to a takeover. An agreed takeover of the defender by Viyella was later announced. The pursuer claimed that the defender's co-operation with Viyella in the takeover was in breach of the earlier agreement between the pursuer and the defender. The defender argued that the agreement was unenforceable because it was ultra vires or alternatively in breach of the directors fiduciary duty to advise the shareholders on the merits of the takeover bid. The court found for the pursuer.

[17.05]   **Lord Cullen** (delivering the judgment of the court): At the outset I do not accept as a general proposition that a company can have no interest in the change of identity of its shareholders on a takeover. It appears to me that there will be cases in which its agents, the directors will seek the takeover of its shares by a particular bidder as beneficial to the company. For example, it may provide the opportunity for integrating operations or obtaining additional resources. In other cases the directors will see a particular bid as not in the best interests of the company . . . Accordingly I do not accept that by reason of lack of any interest in the matter a company could not enter into a contract of the nature alleged by the pursuers.

I next consider the proposition that in regard to the disposal of their shares on a take-over the directors were under a fiduciary duty to the shareholders and accordingly obliged to act in such a way as to further their best interests. It is well recognised that directors owe fiduciary duties to the company. Thus the directors have the duty of fiduciaries with respect to the property and funds of the company . . . These fiduciary duties spring from the relationship of the directors to the company of which they are its agents . . . I see no good reason why it should be supposed that directors are, in general, under a fiduciary duty to shareholders and in particular current shareholders with respect to the disposal of their shares in the most advantageous way. The directors are not normally the agents of the current shareholders. They are not normally entrusted with the management of their shares . . . The absence of such a duty is demonstrated by the remarkable case of *Percival v Wright* [1902] 2 Ch 421. I think it is important to emphasise that what I am being asked to consider is the alleged fiduciary duty of directors to current shareholders as sellers of their shares. This must not be confused with their duty to consider the interests of shareholders in the discharge of their duty to the company. The creation of parallel duties could lead to conflict. Directors have but one master, the company. Further, it does not seem to me to be relevant to the present question to build an argument on the rights, some of them very important rights, which shareholders have to take steps with a view to seeing that directors act in acordance with the constitution of the company and that their own interests are not unfairly prejudiced.

If on the other hand, directors take it on themselves to give advice to current shareholders . . . they have a duty to advise in good faith and not fraudulently and not to mislead whether deliberately or carelessly. If they fail to do so the affected shareholders may have a remedy including the recovery of what is truly the personal loss sustained by them as a result. However, these cases do not, in my view demonstrate a pre-existing fiduciary duty to the shareholders but a potential liability arising out of their words or actions which can be based on ordinary principles of law. This, I may say appears to be a more satisfactory way of expressing the position of directors in this context than by talking of a so-called secondary fiduciary duty to the shareholders . . .

I have considered the passages in the city code to which my attention was drawn. On the assumption that it is proper for me to take the code into account in a debate on relevancy, its terms do not affect the conclusion at which I have come.

For these reasons I reject the view that directors are under a fiduciary duty to current shareholders in regard to the disposal of their shares in a takeover. Accordingly, I reject the arguments presented in support of the contention that the first defenders could not have entered into a contract in the terms indicated by the pursuers' averments.

Notes

In *Re a Company* [1986] BCLC 382 Hoffmann J said that, where there are several takeover bids and the directors decide to advise the shareholders regarding the various bids, he could not 'accept the proposition that the board must inevitably be under a positive duty to recommend and take all steps within their power to facilitate whichever is the highest offer'. His Lordship went on to say that he did not think 'that fairness can require more of the directors than to give the shareholders sufficient information and advice to enable them to reach a properly informed decision and to refrain from giving misleading advice or exercising their fiduciary powers in a way which would prevent or inhibit shareholders from choosing to take the better price.'

Cf *Coleman v Myers* [1977] 2 NZ LR 225 where the directors who were purchasing the company's shares were held to owe a fiduciary duty to the shareholders; also *Securities Trust Ltd v Associated Properties Ltd* (para **17.13**) where McWilliam J held that in a s 204 takeover (discussed *infra*) the directors owed a duty to provide information regarding the takeover to the existing shareholders. In the same vein see also *Heron International Ltd v Lord Grade* [1983] BCLC 244.

Where a takeover bid has been made, the directors will be in breach of duty if they make a fresh issue of shares with the dominant intention of frustrating the takeover bid. See *Howard Smith Ltd v Ampol Petroleum Ltd* [1944] AC 821. Must this case be considered in the light of *Dawson International plc v Coats Paton plc*?

Section 204 takeover

[17.06] Under s 204 of the Principal Act where company A ('the transferee') has made a takeover bid for company B ('the transferor') it may be possible to compulsorily acquire the shares of those members who rejected the bid.[1] The compulsory purchase can only take place if certain requirements have been complied with. First, the bid must have been for the 'shares affected', ie, all the shares or all of a particular class of shares in the transferor, other than those already beneficially owned by the transferee or any of its subsidiaries. Further the transferee must have received four fifths acceptance in respect of the 'shares affected'.[2] If the transferee and its subsidiaries already beneficially own at least one fifth of the shares or of the particular class of shares as the case may be, in the transferor, the compulsory purchase can only proceed if the transferee receives not only four fifths acceptance of the shares affected, but also such acceptance must represent at least three quarters in number of the holders of such shares.

Providing these requirements are complied with, the transferee may serve a notice on the dissenting shareholders requiring them to sell their shares. The notice must be sent out within 6 months from the date of the publication of the takeover bid, the bid must have received the requisite approval or acceptance within four months of its publication.[3] Further, the notice must be sent out not later then one month after the transferee has acquired the shares of the assenting members.[4] Where the bid contained two or more sets of terms upon which it could be accepted, the notice must set out these terms and state which set of terms will apply to the acquisition of the dissenting shareholders shares, should he fail to make an election within 14 days.[5] The notice having been duly served on the dissenting shareholder, he then has one month to transfer his shares to the transferee, who in turn pays over the consideration to the transferor on trust for the shareholder. However, within the one month period the dissenting shareholder may instead apply to the court for relief. The court may, if it thinks fit, prohibit the compulsory purchase.

1 See *Keane* at paras **34.11–34.16**.
2 S 204(1)(3)(11) of the Principal Act.
3 Ibid s 204(1).
4 Ibid s 204(4).
5 Ibid s 204(10).

[17.07] S 204 may not be used by existing majority shareholders as a means of compulsorily acquiring the minority shareholders shares.

Re Bugle Press Ltd [1960] 3 All ER 791 (Court of Appeal)

[17.08] There were three shareholders in the company, Shaw, Jackson and Treby. Shaw and Jackson, who each held 45% of the issued share capital wanted rid of Treby who held the remaining 10%. They therefore formed a company, Jackson and Shaw (Holdings) Ltd with a share capital of £100 which made a bid for all the shares in Bugle Press Ltd. Shaw and Jackson accepted the offer and then Jackson and Shaw (Holdings) Ltd served a notice on Treby under the equivalent of s 204 of the Principal Act requiring him to sell his shares. Treby applied to the court for relief under the section. The Court of Appeal, affirming Buckley J, held that in the circumstances the bidder company could not rely on s 204 to compel the dissenting shareholder to sell his shares.

[17.09]   **Harman LJ:** In my judgment this is a barefaced attempt to evade that fundamental rule of company law which forbids the majority of share-holders, unless the articles so provide, to expropriate a minority. It would be all too simple if all one had to do was to form a £2 company and sell it to one's shares and then force the outsider to comply. If the point had been taken earlier, I for one, should have been prepared to hold that this case never came within the section at all. Indeed, no serious attempt to comply with the section has ever been made here, that can be seen from the summons which refers to the scheme and contract made on 14 July 1959. There is no sign anywhere of any scheme or contract made on 14 July 1959 and therefore, the section does not begin to operate. The applicant might have ignored this notice altogether but he had not the courage to do that, and I am not sur-prised, and so he makes this application and he does thereby, I suppose admit that there was a scheme and a contract of 14 July 1959 though every-body must have perfectly well known that there was none. Apart from that these two individuals or their advisers did not even trouble to comply with the next part of s 209, *viz*, the length of delay and the notice that they had to give. They were in a hurry and they just ignored that part of it. The appli-cant's advisers waived that objection also, and he having applied to the court under the section must, like any other applicant prove his case, ie, set up a case which the respondents have to answer. He does that, it seems to me . . . quite simply by showing that the transferee company is nothing but a little hut built round his two co-shareholders and that the so-called scheme was made by themselves as directors of the company with themselves as share-holders and the whole thing, therefore is seen to be a hollow sham. It is then for the company to show that nevertheless there is some good reason why the scheme should be allowed to go on. The company, whether because they do not wish to go into the witness-box and be cross examined or for some other reason do not file any evidence at all . . . There is in my judgment no case to answer. The applicant has only to shout and the walls of this Jericho fall flat. I am surprised that it was thought that so elementary a device would receive the court's approval . . .

Lord Evershed MR delivered a concurring judgment. Donovan LJ concurred.

Notes

See also *Esso Standard (Inter-America) Inc v JW Enterprises* (1963) 37 DLR 2(d) 598 where 96% of the shares in the transferor were held by the transferees' holding company. The holding company had, not surprisingly, accepted the takeover bid. Nonetheless the court granted relief under the

equivalent of s 204, holding that for the section to operate, the 80% acceptance must be from shareholders who are truly independent of the transferee.

[17.10] The court will not grant relief against the compulsory purchase of
dissenting members' shares under s 204 if the procedural requirements of
the section have been complied with and the takeover bid is fair.

McCormick v Cameo Investments Ltd [1978] ILRM 191 (High Court)

[The facts appear from the judgment]

[17.11] McWilliam J: This matter comes before me on a special summons
issued by the applicants, claiming that the respondent is neither entitled nor
bound to acquire the shares of the appicants in Dublin & Central Properties
Limited (hereinafter called the transferor company) upon the terms of a
scheme or contract dated 18 November 1977, notwithstanding that it has
been approved by 9/10ths of the shareholders of the transferor company.

The scheme or contract comes within the terms of s 204 of the Companies
Act 1963. [His Lordship then quoted s 204] . . . It is accepted that the
requirements of this section have been satisfied by the respondent.

The transferor company was incorporated in 1901 as the Central Hotel
Ltd and was principally concerned with the operation of the Central Hotel in
Exchequer Street, Dublin. What might be described as a complete reorganisation of the transferor company took place in 1972 and 1973. A new issue of
shares was made in November 1972 which gave a company called
Charterhouse (Ireland) Ltd through its subsidiaries a controlling interest in
the transferor company, the hotel was closed at the end of 1973, the name of
the transferor company was changed to Dublin & Central Properties Ltd
and it became part of a property investment and development group. No
attempt has been made to explain what was the purpose or what is the result
of the involved inter-company transactions. Sufficient to say that the
respondent, one of the subsidiaries of Charterhouse (Ireland) Ltd owned a
substantial majority of the shares in the transferor company at the relevant
date, and the transferor company had three wholly-owned subsidiaries one
of which, Waterloo Holdings Ltd owned a valuable site for development in
Baggot Street.

It appears from the accounts for 1973 that Charterhouse (Ireland) Ltd
made a loan of £473,849 to the transferor company. Presumably this was
repaid as it does not appear in the subsequent accounts.

It also appears that, subsequently a loan of £600,000 or thereabouts was
made by the transferor company to the respondent in a transaction which
has variously been described as money with which property was to be purchased on behalf of the transferor company, money advanced to or deposited with the resondent and repayable with interest and money to be
invested by the respondent which was to be re-sold at cost to the transferor
company when a suitable group of sites had been assembled, presumably to

517

add to the site held by Waterloo Holdings Ltd. It is accepted that this money, then increased to £800,000 or thereabouts, was due by the respondent to the transferor company at the time of the offer under s 204. The circumstances of this transaction are relied upon strongly by the applicants in their opposition to the acquisition of their shares.

The object of a multiplicity of associated companies is to save tax, to conceal the operations of the effective owners, to conceal the actual ownership of property, to conceal the control of businesses and by means of the foregoing to increase the profits of the enterprise with particular regard to the interests of the people in effective control.

Such arrangements are (though some may think unfortunately) perfectly lawful under the provisions of the Companies Act and it has to be borne in mind that a series of transactions designed primarily to benefit the people and the company in effective control may also be to the advantage of the people and companies associated in subsidiary capacities. I emphasise this aspect of the matter because the applicants' case is, essentially that the scheme is not fair to them and they claim that the circumstances of the loan of £800,000 have not been adequately explained and that this makes it impossible for them to form an accurate opinion about the scheme and confirms their view that they are incurring a substantial loss under it.

I consider it unsatisfactory that they and I do not understand the full implications of the scheme and that a full and simple statement, elucidating the ramifications of the group or groups of companies involved and for the purpose and effect of this scheme, has not been made, but I am only concerned with the scheme as it stands and the provisions of the statute enabling it to be put through and the statutory provisions being complied with, the onus is on the applicants to establish that it is unfair to them . . .

The applicants are the personal representatives of Frederick Brian McCormick and as such, hold 4,000 shares of a nominal value of 25p . . . They say that, in the present state of the property and commercial world, this is a most unsatisfactory time for them to sell their shares and that they will become much more valuable in the future. This is denied by the accountants for the respondent and by a director of Ulster Investment Bank Ltd who was brought in in an independent advisory capacity before the scheme was submitted to the shareholders. His view was that the offer was a good one and that it is unlikely that the value of the shares will go above the price being offered although it is possible that it could do so.

The applicants further allege that there was oppression in that they were being expropriated by a company which has a majority shareholding. I was referred to the case of *In re Bugle Press Ltd* (para **17.08**) although it is not suggested that the position here is as clear as it was in that case. Not only is the position not so clear, but it seems to me that there is very little resemblance between the two cases, the main difference being that here there were several active and fairly substantial shareholders well-informed in business matters who have accepted the scheme, to whose views I should pay the greatest attention . . .

The applicants also allege that there was oppression in that the loan of £800,000 being payable on demand should have been called in by the transferor company and suggest that it was due to the controlling interest of the respondent that it was not called in and no interest was paid in respect of it during the past three years. As this policy was not queried by the applicants at general meetings or otherwise until the scheme was propounded I cannot accept that there is any evidence of oppression in this regard. It is not oppression for the directors to make an unsatisfactory decision in the conduct of the business of a company.

Finally, it is alleged that the scheme is, in effect, a breach of the provisions of s 60 of the Act in that the respondent owed the transferor company a great deal more than is being paid for the shares and therefore, it was the money of the transferor company which was being used to purchase its own shares. There is something to be said for this view of the scheme but I have the sworn testimony of Mr Crowley that he and another person were putting up the money by way of advance to the respondent for the purchase of the shares and that the respondent had not the money either to repay the loan or purchase the shares. I have no information as to the terms of this advance to the respondent but Mr Crowley stated that he and the other person were the main shareholders in the respondent, and they obviously thought it was to their advantage to make the advance. I am not satisfied that he is correct in saying that the major motivation was to see that the shareholders of the transferor company should receive the full price for their shares but this does not alter the fact that the money for the purchase has been financed by another loan. Accordingly I hold that there has not been any breach of the provisions of s 60.

Notes

See also *Re Hoare & Co* (1934) 150 LT 374; *Re Grierson, Oldham & Adams Ltd* [1968] 1 Ch 17.

[17.12] In a s 204 takeover the dissenting members whose shares are to be compulsorily acquired are entitled to be furnished with reasonably full particulars of the takeover. If such details are not provided by the transferee, then they must be furnished by the directors of the transferor.

Securities Trust Ltd v Associated Properties Ltd (High Court, 19 November 1980)

[17.13] The second named defendant ('Estates') had made a takeover bid for the first named defendant ('Associated') and began to compulsorily acquire the shares of dissenting members under s 204. The plaintiff's shares in Associated having been compulsorily acquired by Estates, a special resolution was subsequently passed by Associated under s 60 of the Principal Act, authorising the giving of a loan to Estates in implementing the takeover. The plaintiff had not been informed prior to the compulsory acquisition of his shares that the takeover was to be financed by way of a loan from Associated. If his shares had not been compulsorily acquired the plaintiff would have been able to block the special resolution under s 60. McWilliam J also considered the right of dissenting shareholders to information about the takeover where their shares were to be compulsorily acquired.

McWilliam J: The people whose shares are being compulsorily purchased are entitled to be given full particulars of the transaction, its purpose, the method of carrying it out and its consequences . . . I have not been addressed on the duty of directors towards their own members or their position as agents or otherwise *vis* a *vis* the shareholders on such a transaction but, although a director is not a trustee for the shareholders directors are to some extent in a fiduciary position and I am of opinion that, on transaction such as this, the shareholders are entitled to be given reasonably full particulars by their directors about the matters I have just mentioned. Certainly, in the offer documents in this case there was no indication that the money for the purchase of the shares was to be provided by Associated itself.

Notes
Cf *Evertite Locknuts* [1945] Ch 220.

Although the transferee may have acquired sufficient of the 'shares affected' to force the dissenting shareholders to sell their shares, it may decline to exercise its power of compulsory purchase. However, if the requisite number of 'shares affected' have been acquired the dissenting shareholders are under s 204(4)(*b*) entitled within three months to serve a notice on the transferee requiring it to purchase their shares.

Reconstruction by voluntary liquidation

[17.14]   Under s 260 of the Principal Act it may be possible to effect a merger by placing the transferor in members voluntary winding up.[1] With the sanction of a special resolution of the company in general meeting the liquidator may then sell the transferor's assets and undertaking to the transferee in consideration for the issue of shares policies or other interests in the transferee. These shares etc, are then distributed to the members of the transferor in lieu of a cash distribution.[2] The distribution is to take place in accordance with the members' class rights in a winding up.[3] Within seven days of the passing of the special resolution authorising the reconstruction any dissenting shareholder may serve notice on the liquidator requiring him 'either to abstain from carrying the resolution into effect or to purchase' the dissenting member's shares at a price to be agreed or to be determined by arbitration.[4] If there is a sufficiently large degree of dissent the liquidator may not have sufficient funds to buy out the shares of the objecting members and he may therefore be obliged to abandon the scheme. A company cannot, by a provision in its memorandum or articles, deprive dissenting shareholders of their rights under s 260.[5]

If an order is made for the winding up of the transferor within a year of the passing of the special resolution, that resolution is invalid unless sanctioned by the court.[6] This provision protects creditors whose claims have not been paid before or who are otherwise prejudiced by the reconstruction. The liquidator, in order to protect the creditors should either pay their claims in full or alternatively, obtain an adequate indemnity for such claims from the transferee. Failure to take either of these courses of action will render him personally liable to any creditor whose claim is not paid in full.[7] In a creditors voluntary winding up[8] the provisions of s 260 may be applied, 'with the modifications that the powers of the liquidator under that section shall not be exercised except with the sanction either of the court or of the committee of inspection'.[9]

1 See *Keane* at paras **34.08–34.10**.
2 S 260(1) of the Principal Act. The reconstruction cannot require shareholders to pay further cash, such as by accepting shares in the transferee as being partly paid up, unless they expressly so agree: see *Re Imperial Mercantile Credit Association* (1871) LR 12 Eq 504.
3 *Griffith v Paget* (1877) 5 Ch D 894.
4 Ibid s 260(3). The notice served on the liquidation must give him an option as to which course he wishes to pursue: see *Re Demerara Rubber Co Ltd* [1913] 1 Ch 331.
5 *Bisgood v Henderson's Transvaal Estates Ltd* [1908] 1 Ch 743.
6 Ibid s 260(5). If the scheme is unfair the court will decline to sanction the resolution for reconstruction: see *Re Consolidated South Rand Mines Deep Ltd* [1900] 1 Ch 491.
7 *Pulsford v Devenish* [1903] 2 Ch 625.
8 Where unlike a members voluntary winding up, the company is unable to meet all its debts in full.
9 S 271 of the Principal Act.

Schemes of arrangement

[17.15] If there is a sufficiently large number of dissenting creditors, it may prove extremely difficult to implement a s 260 reconstruction. It may instead be more appropriate to proceed by way of scheme of arrangement under ss 201 to 203 of the Princial Act.[1] This procedure can be used, not only for mergers and amalgamations but also for compromises with creditors or for the alteration of class rights of shareholders. Dissenters may be bound, if the appropriate majority approve the scheme and it is subsequently sanctioned by the court. Under s 201 where a compromise or arrangement is proposed between a company and its members or creditors (or any class of members or creditors) the court may order meetings of the affected parties to be summoned.[2] In summoning such meetings the court may stay or restrain all further proceedings against the company for such period as it thinks fit.[3] The parties to be affected by the scheme must be divided into meetings of their respective classes. If a majority of three quarters in value of those present and voting either in person or by proxy, is obtained at each meeting the scheme will, if sanctioned by the court become binding on the dissenting members or creditors as the case may be.[4] The court order only takes effect upon delivery to the registrar of companies.[5]

The notice convening the various meetings must explain the effect of the proposed scheme. In particular, it must state any material interests of the directors whether qua director or otherwise and the extent to which the effect of the scheme on the directors' interests differs from the effect on the like interests of other persons.[6]

Under s 203 where the scheme involves a reconstruction or amalgamation of two or more companies whereby the whole or part of the undertaking and property of the transferor is to be transferred to the transferee, the court may in sanctioning the scheme or by subsequent order, make provision for, inter alia; (*a*) the transfer to the transferee of all or part of the undertaking, property or liabilities of the transfer; (*b*) the continuation by or against the transferee of any legal proceedings pending by or against the transferor; (*c*) provision to be made for dissenting shareholders or creditors.

1 See *Keane* at paras **34.04–34.07**.
2 S 201(1) of the Principal Act.
3 Ibid s 201(2).
4 Ibid s 201(3).
5 Ibid s 201(5). Thereafter a copy of the order must be attached to every memorandum of association which is issued.
6 Ibid s 202(1). If the meetings are convened by advertisements, they must either include this statement or specify a place where creditors or members can obtain copies thereof free of charge. See s 202(1)(*b*), (3).

[17.16] The court will not summon meetings under s 201 if (*a*) the terms of the scheme do not require the approval of the company as a legal personality separate from its members, or (*b*) the scheme does not require anything to be done by the company itself.

Re Savoy Hotel Ltd [1981] 3 All ER 646 (Chancery Division)

[17.17] The issued share capital was divided into A shares representing 97.7% of the equity and B shares representing the balance of 2.3%. The B shares, however, carried 40 times as many votes per share as A shares. A shares, therefore had 51.4% of the votes while the B shares who controlled the board had 48.55%. THF who held certain A shares wished to take over the company and proposed to do so by way of a scheme of arrangement. The shares in the company were to be acquired in consideration for the issue of shares in THF. The terms of the proposed scheme required the company to register the transfers of shares but did not require the separate consent of the company either through the board or a resolution in general meeting. THF applied to the court under the UK equivalent of s 201 for an order convening separate meetings of the A and B shareholders. The purpose of convening separate meetings was to obtain the requisite 75% majority at a meeting of the A shareholders and thereby make the scheme binding on the whole company. The application was opposed by the company, through its board, on the grounds that (*a*) the scheme was not one 'between' the company and its members or any class of them since it did not sufficiently materially affect the rights and obligations between them and (*b*) if it was a scheme within the meaning of the Act, there was no jurisdiction to sanction it in the absence of the separate approval of the company.

[17.18] **Norse J:** I now consider the first argument of counsel for the Savoy. He accepts that the proposed scheme constitutes an arrangement but he says that it is not one 'between' the Savoy and its members or any class of them. Although this does not seem to have been the view universally held during the period immediately following the enactment of s 38 of the 1907 Act . . . there can be no doubt that the word 'arrangement' in s 206 [ie s 201 of the Principal Act] has for many years been treated as being one of very wide import. Statements to that effect can be found in the judgment of Plowman J in *Re National Bank Ltd* [1966] 1 All ER 1006 at 1012, and of Megarry J in *Re Calgary and Edmonton Land Co Ltd* [1975] 1 All ER 1046 at 1054. That is indeed, a proposition for which any judge who has sat in this court in recent years would not require authority and its validity is by no means diminished by what was said by Brightman J in *Re NFU Development Trust Ltd* [1973] 1 All ER 135. All that that case shows is that there must be some element of give and take. Beyond that it is neither necessary nor desireable to attempt a definition of 'arrangement'.

Counsel for the Savoy professes not to quarrel with that proposition. He says that in order for an arrangement to be one 'between' the company and its members it must materially affect the rights and obligations exising between the two . . .

I was referred to a number of authorities on this question, but the only one whch is directly in point is the Scottish case of *Singer Manufacturing Co v Robinow* (1971) SC 11, where the same point was taken on another transfer scheme of the same general mature as the present. In that case, the scheme was proposed by the company. It was argued on behalf of an opposing shareholder that the scheme was not one between the company and its members but a sale between two members in which the company had no interest. With regard to that argument the Lord President (Clyde) in delivering the opinion of the court said (at 13–14):

'This contention however is unwarranted. The petitioning company is in fact the first party to the scheme of arrangement. Moreover, the company had a very direct interest in the arrangement. If the arrangement were sanctioned by the court, they came under obligation (see clause 5 of the arrangement) on being satisfied that the consideration of 85s per share had been paid by the Morgan Guaranty Trust Co of New York to the 145,670 shareholders forthwith to register, in place of the existing shareholders, the Singer Company of New York as holder of the shares in respect of which the consideration had been paid. The courts have always interpreted s 206 and its statutory predecessors broadly, so as to enable a wide variety of different types of arrangement to be put forward and it seems to us clear that the present scheme falls within that is competent to achieve under that section. The arrangement is an arrangement between the petitioning company and 'its members or any class of them' within the meaning of s 206.'

That shows, I think, that there were three grounds for the decision. It also appears that cl 5 of the arrangement in that case was to much the same effect as cl 1(*b*) of the present scheme . . .

Counsel for THF also relied on the judgments in the Court of Appeal in *Re Guardian Assurance Co* [1917] 1 Ch 431, and in particular on a passage in the judgment of Warrington LJ. The same passage appears to have been referred to in the argument for the opposing shareholder in the *Singer* case. The part of the transaction in the *Guardian* case which required the sanction of the court under s 120 of the 1908 Act was the transfer of a proportionate part of the shares in the Guardian to another company with which it had entered into a conditional contract. With regard to that transfer Warrington LJ. said (at 449–450):

'Now, if it were possible in a large undertaking to obtain the consent of each shareholder to such a proposal there is no doubt it could be carried out, because there would be nothing to prevent any shareholder, if he pleased, transferring his shares, or a certain number of his shares, to anybody to whom he chooses to transfer them: but of course it is difficult to obtain in a large undertaking like this the actual consent of the individual shareholders. But assume that such an agreement has been made between all the shareholders in the company, it seems to me to be quite obvious that that would be an arrangement made between the shareholders and the company. I fail to see how it could be otherwise; and that is exactly what is done, because although the arrangement is not made with the individual shareholders the arrangement is one which, when sanctioned by the court under s 120 will bind all the shareholders concerned. In my view this is an arrangement between the members of the company and the company and as such is capable of being sanctioned under the 120th section.'

I think that, although the particular point was not argued and did not need to be argued (it not having been taken by Younger J at first instance) that passage does support the argument of counsel for THF on this question and I infer that the Court of Session may well have taken the same view.

I do not think that it would be right for me to decide this question without expressing a view of my own. I can do so quite shortly. In my judgment the arguments of counsel for the THF supported by the two authorities on which he has relied are correct. In spite of counsel for the Savoy's professions to the contrary, it seems to me that his argument could well have a restrictive effect on the meaning of 'arrangement'. I do not think that it is necessary that the rights and obligations existing between the company and its members should be materially affected, if by that it is meant that there should be something more material or more substantial than there is in the present case. In my judgment the decision of the Court of Session in the *Singer* case was correct and there is therefore no question but that I should follow and apply it. That means that the first argument of counsel for the Savoy fails.

I now turn to the second argument of counsel for the Savoy. It . . . raises the question whether the court has jurisdiction to sanction an arrangement which does not have the approval of the company. That is an interesting and difficult question on which there is not much authority . . . The position on this question can, as it seems to me be summarised as follows. There is one decision, *Re International Contract Co* (1872) 26 LT 358 which is in point. That decision is in favour of the view that there is no jurisdiction to sanction any arrangement with creditors of a company in the course of being wound up which does not have the approval of the liquidator. The decision is one which I ought normally to follow. The legislative history is such that there is no ground for saying that a different view is to be taken of the position of a going company in relation to a members' scheme. There has sometimes been an assumption to the same effect that having been most clearly expressed by Simonds J in *Re Oceanic Steam Navigation Co Ltd* [1938] 3 All ER 740.

In my judgment both the decision and the assumption are correct. The question turns in the end on the true construction of s 2 of the 1870 Act. Everything else follows from that. If you were to find an Act of Parliament which referred to an arrangement 'proposed between' a person who was adult and sui juris and his creditors, you would assume, first that that person would have to be a party to the arrangement and second, that he would have to consent to it. And you would not think that there was any the less need to obtain his consent if you found that it was expressly provided that the arrangement should be binding on the creditors and also on that person. You might think that they were not really necessary. But, whatever you thought you would not think that they could disturb the assumptions which had been forced on you by the words 'proposed between' and the fact that the person concerned was adult and sui juris. Nor would you think that those assumptions were any the less valid because there was no express provision for the consent to be obtained. Next, one of the essential features of the 1862 Act, without which its cardinal objective of limited liability could not have been achieved was that a company should have a legal personality distinct from that of its members and for most purposes capable of acting on its own . . . In the result I conclude that the court has no jurisdiction to sanction an arrangement under s 206 which does not have the approval of the company either through the board or if appropriate, by means of a simple majority of the members in general meeting.

Notes

See also *Re NFU Development Trust Ltd* [1973] 1 All ER 135 where the proposals merely required members to give up all their rights and to cease being members. This required nothing from the company itself and therefore did not constitute an arrangement within the meaning of s 201.

[17.19] Where the court orders meetings to be summoned under s 201 to consider proposals for a scheme of arrangement, the company must segregate the affected parties into separate classes. Separate meetings must be convened for each class of creditors or members as the case may be. The court will not give directions as to which classes of creditors or members should be summoned to the meetings nor will it give directions regarding the proper class to which an affected party belongs.

Re Pye (Ireland) Ltd (High Court, 11 March 1985)

[The facts appear from the judgment.]

[17.20]   Costello J: By order of the 30th July 1984, it was ordered that Pye (Ireland) Ltd should convene meetings of certain specified classes of creditors and members for the purpose of considering a scheme of arrangement and compromise. The order was made pursuant to the provisions of s 201 of the Companies Act, 1963. The meetings were held on the 19th September but due to the opposition of the Collector General of Revenue who was both a preferential and unsecured creditor the statutory majorities required for approval were not obtained. A new scheme of arrangement and compromise was devised and a second application was brought to this Court under s 201(1) for an order summoning meetings of different classes of creditors and members for the purpose of considering the new scheme. The summons was served on the Collector General. I considered the objections raised on his behalf were valid and I declined to make the order sought. On appeal the Supreme Court on the 22nd November 1984, having been given an undertaking by the applicants to pay a preferential debt of £52,665 due to the Collector General, made an order that meetings of three different classes of shareholders be held and that meetings of three different classes of creditors be held, namely meetings of secured, preferential and 'unsecured trade and sundry creditors' in the manner specified in the order. The preferential debt of the Collector General was paid, the meetings were duly held and the scheme obtained the necessary majorities at each of the meetings. The meeting of the unsecured creditors was, however, a close run thing. The total valid poll was, £1,690, 266.2. The amount or value voting in favour was £1,313,920.40 or 77.73%. The amount or value voting against was £377,345.82 or 22.32%. The number of votes in favour (including proxies) was 34 whilst there was only one vote against. But this vote was that of the Collector General and his unsecured debt of £377,435.82 was nearly sufficient to defeat the scheme. The applicants have now petitioned the court under s 201(3) for an order sanctioning it.

Mr Cooke on behalf of the Collector General has submitted that, apart from any view he would urge that the court in the exercise of its discretion should not sanction the scheme, there are legal objections to the making of the order now being sought. These arise, it is urged, from the failure of the company to hold meetings of different classes of unsecured creditors. Both he and Mr McCracken (on behalf of the applicants) accepted as a correct statement of the law applicable on s 201 applications the views expressed in Palmer's *Company Law* (23rd Ed. paragraph 79–10). The author points out that:–

'The court does not itself consider at this point (ie. when an application to convene meetings is brought) what classes of creditors or members should be made parties to the scheme. This is for the company to decide . . . If there are different groups within a class the interests of which are different from the rest of the class, or which are to be treated differently under the scheme, such groups must be treated as separate classes for the purpose of the scheme'; and:–
'Great care must be taken in considering what for the purpose of the scheme constitutes a class. If meetings of the proper class have not been held, the court may not sanction the scheme.'

Indeed it would seem that a failure to hold proper class meetings will generally speaking be fatal to a s 201(3) petition. This was illustrated recently in England in *Re Hellenic Trust Ltd* [1975] 3 All ER 382.

Palmer, like other text book writers quotes Bowen LJ in *Sovereign Life Assurance Co v Dodd* (1892) 2 QB 573 at 583:

'It seems plain that we must give such a meaning to the term "class" as will prevent the section being so worked as to result in confiscation and injustice and that it must be confined to those persons whose rights are not so dissimilar as to make it impossible for them to consult together with a view to their common interest.'

And the author points out (paragraph 79–11) all unsecured creditors will normally form a single class, 'except where some of them are to be treated in a manner different from the rest and have different interests which might conflict. In such cases fresh classes will be carved out.'

Three points are made about the classifications made by the applicants herein:

(*i*) Attention is drawn to the fact that the scheme provides that a number of unsecured creditors are to be paid their claims in full. (See paragraph b (*iii*)). These are creditors with claims under £25,000 and are mainly small trade creditors. The total of their claims is £132,554.00 and it is urged that these form a distinctive class from the other unsecured creditors. I agree. The paragraph b (*iii*) creditors are getting very special treatment under the scheme. As they are to be paid in full within one month of its sanction it is impossible to see how they would vote against it and obviously their interests are different to the less favoured general body of unsecured creditors amongst whom is the Collector General. If the scheme is successful the Revenue debt is to be partially paid over a three year period and part of it (the interest component) is not provided for in the scheme at all. But I do not think that this is a justification for refusal of sanction as I am not satisfied that if a separate class for the favoured creditors had been created that this would have meant that the scheme would have been defeated. The report of the meeting of the unsecured creditors shows that only 36 votes (including proxy votes) were cast at the poll and it seems that the paragraph b (*iii*) unsecured creditors did not tip the balance (admittedly a fine one) to create the requisite majority.

(*ii*) Secondly, it is pointed out that the explanatory memorandum circulated with the scheme on the direction of the Supreme Court reveals that the chairman of the company (and one of the present applicants) is a director of a firm called 'Monkstown Consultants', an unsecured creditor for £12,600 whose debt is to be paid in full. The report of the meeting of unsecured creditors discloses that this firm voted by proxy infavour of the scheme. For reasons just given at (*i*) I agree that this firm should have been placed in a separate class with other favoured creditors but I do not think the fact the company chairman is also a director of this company is an added reason for creating a further separate class. In my view this company's special relationship to Pye (Ireland) Ltd is not a reason for refusing sanction.

(*iii*) Thirdly attention is drawn to a reference in the explanatory memorandum to an unsecured creditor, Philips Electrical (Ireland) Ltd which is also a substantial shareholder in the company. This company owns 229,425 ordinary 25p shares in Pye (Ireland) Ltd., a significant and substantial proportion of the entire issued ordinary capital of the company. It is owed as an unsecured creditor a sum of £379,000 (excluding interest) and it voted at the meeting by proxy in support of the scheme. Without its vote the statutory majority would not have been obtained. There is no doubt that if the scheme is successful that the prospect for the ordinary shareholders is very much better than in a liquidation (which is the alternative if the scheme is not adopted) in which it would appear the ordinary shareholders are likely to do very badly. So it seems to me that the interests of a substantial unsecured creditor who is also a substantial shareholder are very different to those of the general body of unsecured non-shareholding creditors and that there is in reality no common interest between them – the creditor/shareholder is almost certain to support the scheme, whilst the ordinary unsecured shareholder may have (as has happened in the case of the Collector General) what is considered as valid reasons for opposing it. I think therefore that there should have been a separate class created comprising unsecured creditors who are also shareholders in the company.

It was pointed out by Mr McCracken on behalf of the applicants that the different meetings were held in this case pursuant to order of the Supreme Court. That is true, but it has not been suggested that the point I am now considering was raised at the hearing of the s 201(1) summons and adjudicated upon. Normally a s 201(1) summons would not be served on anyone and objectors to the scheme would not have any opportunity to raise a point like this until the hearing of a s 201(3) petition. In this case the

Collector General was served with the summons and was represented at the hearings. But it is by no means clear that that time the information which was contained in the explanatory memorandum (and on which the present objection is based) was known to him. And even if it was and the point now taken somehow overlooked, this is not a reason for granting sanction if the objection is a valid one. If the applicants are not in any way mislaid and if nothing in the nature of an estoppel arises it seems to me that on the present petition the court should carefully consider the validity of the procedures which have been adopted. In this case had the proper classes been constituted the views of a major creditor (the Revenue) would not have been defeated. In all the circumstances, then, I think I should exercise my discretion by refusing sanction under the section. Even had I jurisdiction to do so, the summoning of fresh meetings of the correct classes of unsecured creditors would be an otiose exercise.

Notes

In *Re John Power & Sons Ltd* it was held that the court will only confirm a scheme of arrangement if it is fair and equitable, the statutory procedures have been followed, the notice convening the meeting was not misleading and the majority at each class meeting acted bona fide. See also *Re National Bank Ltd* [1966] 1 WLR 819 and *Jackson v Munster Bank Ltd* (1884–5) 13 LR Ir 118 where it was held that the notice convening the meetings should not be misleading.

On the requirement of bona fides in voting on proposals, see also *Re Dorman Long & Co Ltd* [1934] Ch 65; *Carruth v Imperial Chemical Industries Ltd* [1937] 2 ALL ER 422; *British America Nickel Corpn Ltd v MJ O'Brien Ltd* [1927] AC 369; *Re Wedgewood Coal and Iron Co* (1877) 6 Ch D 627.

[17.21] The court can only sanction the scheme if it is intra vires the company.

Re Oceanic Steam Navigation Company Ltd [1939] Ch 41

[The facts are irrelevant]

[17.22] **Simonds J:** The question then is whether, under s 201 the company can make and the court can sanction an arrangement which is in excess of the corporate powers as defined by the memorandum. There is nothing in the language of s 201 which even remotely suggests such a conclusion. It contemplates a compromise or arrangement between a company and its creditors or any class of them or its members or any class of them, and provides machinery whereby such a compromise or arrangement may be made binding on dissentient persons by an order of the court. I find nothing here which would indicate that the company can effect an arrangement which would be otherwise ultra vires if the court will give its sanction under s 201.

Notes

S 201 cannot be used to transfer an assignable contract. See *Nokes v Doncaster Amalgamated Collieries Ltd* [1940] AC 1014.

[17.23] The court may sanction a scheme of arrangement despite the dissent of a class of members if the court is satisfied that the value of the company's assets is such that the class of members can have no interest in them.

Re Tea Corporation Ltd; Sorsbie v Tea Corporation Ltd [1904] 1 Ch 12
(Court of Appeal)

[The facts appear from the judgment]

[17.24]   Vaughan Williams LJ: Buckley J has found as a fact that the value of the company's assets is such as to negative the notion that the ordinary shareholders have any financial interest whatever in them and it is not denied that on the evidence before him the learned judge was right in coming to that conclusion . . .

It is, I think quite plain that by this section [ie s 201] the legislature intended that the contributories should have a right to vote in a manner similar to that in which the creditors were to vote under the Act of 1870, and that they should be bound in the same way. Under the Act of 1870 the creditors were to be divided into classes and each class was to vote separately and under s 24 [ie s 201] the contributories are to be dealt with in the same way. In the present case the contributories were divided into two classes, preference shareholders and ordinary shareholders and they voted in those classes and the majority of the preference shareholders voted in favour of the scheme. It is said however, that the scheme is rendered defective because the ordinary shareholders did not vote in favour of it. I think the right answer to this was given by Buckley J. You are to divide the shareholders into classes and when you have done that you find that the preference shareholders have an interest in the assets. But when you come to the ordinary shareholders you find that they have no interest whatever in the assets, and Buckley J was of opinion that having regard to this fact, their dissent from the scheme was immaterial. I think that the learned judge was right in so holding. I seems to me that by the very terms of s 24 you are to divide the contributories into classes and to call meetings of each class and if you have the assent to the scheme of all those classes who have an interest in the matter, you ought not to consider the votes of those classes who have really no interest at all. It would be very unfortunate if a different view had to be taken, for if there were ordinary shareholders who had really no interest in the company's assets and a scheme had been approved by the creditors, and all those were really interested in the assets, the ordinary shareholders would be able to say that it should not be carried into effect unless some terms were made with them.

Romer and Stirling LJJ delivered concurring judgments.

[17.25]   Where the scheme of arrangement involves a reconstruction which could have been effected under s 260, it will only be sanctioned if dissenting shareholders are given the same protection as they would enjoy under s 260

Re Anglo-Continental Supply Co Ltd [1922] 2 Ch 723 (Chancery Division)

[The facts are irrelevant]

[17.26]   **Astbury J:** 1. When a so-called scheme is really and truly a sale, etc., under s 192 simpliciter [ie s 260], that section must be complied with and cannot be evaded by calling it a scheme of arrangement under s 120 [ie s 201] . . . 2. Where a scheme of arrangement cannot be carried through under s 192, though it involves (inter alia) a sale to a company within that section for 'shares, policies and other like interests,' and for liquidation and distribution of the proceeds, the court can sanction it under s 120 if it is fair and reasonable in accordance with the principles upon which the court acts in these cases and it may, but only if it thinks fit, insist as a term of its sanction on the dissentient shareholders being protected in manner similar to that provided for in s 192. Where a scheme of arrangement is one outside s 192 entirely, the court can also and a fortiori act as in proposition 2, subject to the conditions therein mentioned . . .

In exercising its power of sanction under s 120 the court will see: first, that the provisions of the statute have been complied with. Secondly, that the class was fairly represented by those who attended the meeting and that the statutory majority are acting bona fide and are not coercing the minority in order to promote interests adverse to those of the class whom they purport to represent, and thirdly, that the arrangement is such as a man of business would reasonably approve.

[17.27]   The court will not sanction a scheme of arrangement which provides for a compulsory purchase of the shares of dissenting members in circumstances where they could not be compulsorily purchased under s 204.

Re Hellenic & General Trust Ltd [1975] 3 All ER 382 (Chancery Division)

[17.28]   A subsidiary of Hambros Ltd (referred to as 'MIT') held 53% of the ordinary shares in Hellenic & General Trust Ltd ('the company'). Under the proposed scheme of arrangement Hambros was to purchase all the ordinary shares in the company. At the meeting of ordinary shareholder the proposals received over 80% approval. The National Bank of Greece which held 14% of the ordinary shares opposed the scheme as it would result in the bank incurring a tax liability under Greek law. Templeman J refused to sanction the scheme on the grounds (*a*) that the ordinary shareholders other than MIT should have constituted a separate class; and (*b*) the scheme of arrangement procedure should not be used to compulsorily acquire shares of dissenting members in circumstances where they could not be compulsorily acquired under s 204. (The English equivalent of s 204 required approval of 90% of the 'shares affected' before the dissenting members' shares could be compulsorily purchased).

[17.29] **Templeman J:** The first objection put forward is that the necessary agreement by the appropriate class of members has not been obtained. The shareholders who were summoned to the meeting consisted, it is submitted, of two classes. First, there were the outside shareholders, that is to say, the shareholders other than MIT; and secondly MIT a subsidiary of Hambros. MIT was a separate class and should have been excluded from the meeting of outside shareholders. Although s 206 of the 1948 Act provides that the court may order meetings, it is the responsibility of the applicants to see that the class meetings are properly constituted, and if they fail then the necessary agreement is not obtained and the court has no jursidiction to sanction the arrangement. Thus in *Re United Provident Assurance Co Ltd* [1910] 2 Ch 477 the court held that holders of partly paid shares formed a different class from holders of fully paid shares. The objection was taken that there should have been separate meetings of the two classes, and Swinfen Eady J upheld the objection saying: . . .' the objection that there have not been proper class meetings is fatal and I cannot sanction the scheme.'

Similarly Eve J issued a practice direction in which he reminded the profession in dealing with the predecessor of s 206, that the responsibility for determining what creditors are to be summoned to any meeting constituting a class rests with the applicant, and if the meetings are incorrectly convened or constituted or an objection is taken to the presence of any particular creditors as having interests competing with the others, the objection must be taken on the hearing of the petition for sanction and the applicant must take the risk of having the petition dismissed. That direction applies equally to meetings of shareholders.

The question therefore is whether MIT a wholly owned subsidiary of Hambros formed part of the same class as the other ordinary shareholders. What is an appropriate class must depend on the circumstances but some general principles are to be found in the authorities. In *Sovereign Life Assurance Co v Dodd* [1892] 2 QB 573 the Court of Appeal held that for the purposes of an arrangement affecting the policy-holders of an assurance company the holders of policies which had matured were creditors and were a different class from policy-holders whose policies had not matured. Lord Esher MR said: '. . . they must be divided into different classes . . . because the creditors composing the different classes have different interests; and therefore if we find a different state of facts existing among different creditors which may differently affect their minds and their judgment they must be divided into different classes.'

Bowen LJ said: 'It seems plain that we must give such a meaning to the term "class" as will prevent the section being so worked as to result in confiscation and injustice, and that it must be confined to those persons whose rights are not so dissimilar as to make it impossible for them to consult together with a view to their common interest.'

Vendors consulting together with a view to their common interest in an offer made by a purchaser would look askance at the presence among them of a wholly owned subsidiary of the purchaser.

In the present case on analysis Hambros are acquiring the outside shares for 48p. So far as the MIT shares are concerned it does not matter very much to Hambros whether they are acquired or not. If the shares are acquired a sum of money moves from parent to wholly owned subsidiary and shares move from the subsidiary to the parent. The overall financial position of the parent and the subsidiary remains the same. The shares and the money could remain or be moved to suit Hambros before or after the arrangement. From the point of MIT provided MIT is solvent, the directors of MIT do not have to question whether the price is exactly right. Before and after the arrangement the directors of the parent company and the subsidiary could have been the same persons with the same outlook and the same judgment. Counsel for the company submitted that since the parent and the subsidiary were separate corporations with separate directors and since MIT were ordinary shareholders in the company, it followed that MIT had the same interests as the other shareholders. The directors of MIT were under a duty to consider whether the arrangement was beneficial to the whole class of ordinary shareholders and they were capable of forming an independent and unbiased judgment irrespective of the interests of the parent company. This seems to me to be unreal. Hambros are purchasers making an offer. When the vendors meet to discuss and vote whether or not to accept the offer, it is incongruous that the loudest voice in theory and the most significant in practice should come from the wholly owned subsidiary of the purchaser. No one can be both a vendor and a purchaser and in my judgment for the purpose of the class meetings in the present case, MIT were in the camp of the purchaser. Of course this does not mean that MIT should not have considered at a separate class meeting whether to accept the arrangement. But their consideration will be different from the considerations given to the matter by the other shareholders. Only MIT could say, within limits, that what was good for Hambros must be good for MIT.

Counsel for the company submitted that difficulties will arise in practice if every subsidiary or associated company may constitute a separate class. So far as a wholly owned subsidiary is concerned there is no difficulty at all, and in most cases it will be sufficient to judge the class composition by reference to the shareholding. In most cases if the parent controls 50 per cent or more of the shares of the subsidiary company it can be assumed that they have a community of interest for the purposes of s 206 of the 1948 Act and in most cases of different interests from that of other shareholders . . . Accordingly I uphold the first objection, which is fatal to the arrangement. But in view of the careful arguments put forward by both sides I will consider the other objections which are raised by counsel for the bank and which are material if the class meeting in the present case contrary to my view, was properly constituted.

The second objection is founded on the analysis of the arrangement as an offer by Hambros to acquire the ordinary shares for 48p. Section 209 of the

1948 Act [ie s 204 of the Principal Act] provides safeguards for minority shareholders in the event of a takeover bid and in a proper case provides machinery for a small minority of shareholders to be obliged to accept a takeover against their wishes. Thus s 209 provides that where a scheme or contract involving the transfer of shares in a company to another company has been approved by the holders of not less than nine-tenths in value of the shares whose transfer is involved, (other than shares already held at the date of the offer, or by a nominee for, the transferee company or its subsidiary) the transferee company may give notice to any dissenting shareholder; and then unless on an application made by the dissenting holder the court thinks fit to order other wise shall be entitled and bound to acquire those shares on the terms of the takeover bid. If the present arrangement had been carried out under s 209, MIT as a subsidiary of Hambros would have been expressly forbidden to join in any approval for the purposes of s 209 and in any event the National Bank could not have been obliged to sell because they hold ten per cent of the ordinary shares of the company.

The fact that an arrangement under s 209 produces a result which is the same as a takeover under s 209 is not necessarily fatal. It is not always so unfair as to preclude the court from exercising its discretion in favour of the scheme . . . Accepting that, the present proposals nevertheless seem to me to place the company in an inescapable dilemma. It cannot succeed under s 209 because of the express provisions of that section and the size of the shareholding of the objectors. It can only succeed under s 206 by using the votes of Hambros' subsidiary company MIT, to secure the necessary majority. In these circumstances I agree with counsel for the National Bank that the court should not in the exercise of its discretion authorise the acquisition of the shares of the National Bank against the wishes of the bank. The company cannot succeed at all under s 209 and in my judgment they cannot fairly succeed under s 206 . . .

Notes

Cf *Re National Bank Ltd* [1966] 1 WLR 819.

The court will not refuse to sanction a scheme merely because, as a matter of business judgment it might have reached a contrary decision regarding the proposals. See *Re London Chartered Bank of Australia* [1893] 3 Ch 540, where Vaughan Williams stated as follows:

'The court does not simply register the resolution come to by the creditors or the shareholders as the case may be. If the creditors are acting on sufficient information and with time to consider what they are about and are acting honestly, they are, I apprehend much better judges of what is to their commercial advantage than the court can be. I do not say that it is conclusive, because there might be some blot in a scheme which had passed that had been unobserved and which was pointed out later. While, therefore, I protest that we are not to register their decisions, but to see that they have been properly convened and have been properly consulted and have considered the matter from a proper point of view, that is with a view to the interests of the class to which they belong and are empowered to bind, the court ought to be slow to differ from them. It should do so without hesitation if there is anything wrong; but it ought not to do so in my judgment, unless something is brought to the attention of the court to show that there has been some material oversight or miscarriage.'

It may, however, sanction the scheme subject to certain conditions or subject to modification: *Re Canning Jarrah Timber Co (Western Australia) Ltd* [1900] 1 Ch 708.

Once a scheme has been sanctioned it becomes binding and can only be altered by order of the court: *Srimata Premila Devi v Peoples Bank of Northern India Ltd* [1938] 4 ALL ER 337.

Although many of the cases mentioned above related to reconstructions, takeovers or mergers, s 201 can also be used to effect a compromise or arrangement between the company and its creditors. See *Re Empire Mining Co* (1890) 44 Ch D 402 where trade creditors were paid and debenture-holders' security was converted into share capital; also *Re Dorman Long & Co* [1934] Ch 635 where some trade creditors were paid and others were given security; *Shaw v Royce Ltd* [1911] 1 Ch 138 where the scheme was used to release a guarantee; also *Re Dominion of Canada Freehold Estate and Timber Co* (1886) 55 LT 347.

European Communities (Mergers & Divisions of Companies) Regulations

[17.30] These regulations give effect to the Third and Sixth EEC Companies Directives[1] and apply only to plcs and to certain unregistered companies covered by s 377(1) of the Principal Act.

Part II of the regulations governs 'mergers by acquisition' and 'merger by formation of a new company', defined by reg 5(1) as follows:–

'(*a*) "merger by acquisition" means an operation whereby an existing company ("the acquiring company") acquires all the assets and liabilities of another company or companies in exchange for the issue to the shareholders of the company or companies being acquired of shares in the acquiring company, with or without any cash payment and with a view to the dissolution of the company or companies being acquired; and
(*b*) "merger by formation of a new company" means a similar operation where the acquiring company has been formed for the purpose of such acquisition.'

1 78/855/EEC and 82/89/EEC.

[17.31] Part II of the regulations governs 'division by acquisition' and 'division by formation of new companies' which are defined by reg 25(1) as follows:–

'(*a*) "division by acquisition" means an operation whereby two or more companies ("the acquiring companies") of which one or more but not all may be a new company acquire between them all the assets and liabilities of another company in exchange for the issue to the shareholders of that company of shares in one or more of the acquiring companies with or without any cash payment and with a view to the dissolution of the company being acquired; and
(*b*) "division by formation of new companies" means a similar operation whereby the acquiring companies have been formed for the purposes of such acquisition.'

In the case of a company being wound up it may be a party to a merger or division governed by the regulations provided that the distribution of assets to its shareholders has not begun at that date of the draft terms of merger or division as the case may be. Alternatively, it may opt for a merger or division using the existing procedures in ss 201–204, 260 and 271 of the Principal Act.[1]

The regulations require the directors of the companies which are parties to the proposed merger or division to draw up, draft terms in writing of the merger or division as the case may be.[2] The directors of each such company must also draw up a written explanatory report, explaining the draft terms, including the reasons for and implications of the proposed merger or division as the case may be.[3] The explanatory report must be signed and dated on behalf of each company by two directors of each such company. Each company is also required to appoint an independent person to examine the draft terms and prepare a written report on them to the shareholders of the company, indicating, inter alia, whether the proposed merger or division is fair and reasonable.[4] The independent person is entitled to require from the various companies who are parties to the proposed merger or division and from their officers such information and explanations as he thinks necessary to prepare his report. It is an offence for an officer to fail to supply such details or knowingly or recklessly to make false or misleading statements to the independent person.

1 Regs 5(2) and 25(2) of SI No 137 of 1987.
2 Ibid regs 6 & 26.
3 Ibid regs 7 & 27.
4 Ibid regs 8 & 28. Under reg 10, ss 30 & 31 of the 1983 Act (which relate to the independent valuation of non-cash consideration in the allotment of shares) do not apply to the issue of shares by a company formed for the purposes of a merger by formation of a new company.

[17.32] The following persons are disqualified from acting as an independent person:

(*a*) a person who is or within 12 months of the date of the draft terms has been an officer or servant of the company;

(*b*) except with the leave of the Minister, a parent, spouse, brother, sister or child of an officer of the company;
(*c*) a person who is a partner or in the employment of an officer or servant of the company.[1]

It is an offence to act as an independent person while disqualified. Where the latest annual accounts of any of the companies which are parties to the proposed merger or division relate to a financial year ended more than six months before the date of the draft terms, that company must prepare an accounting statement in the format of the last annual balance sheet and as at a date not earlier than the first day of the third month preceding the date of the draft terms. An auditors report must also be prepared.[2]

The next step then is for each company to deliver a copy of the draft terms to the registrar and to publish notice of such delivery in *Iris Oifigiuil* and two daily newspapers. This must be done at least one month before the general meeting is convened to consider the draft terms.[3] For one month before such general meeting the members are to be entitled to inspect free of charge the draft terms, the annual accounts for the last three years for each company, the explanatory reports and independent persons' reports for each company and any accounting statements as referred to above.[4]

1 Ibid regs 8(4) and 28(4).
2 Ibid regs 9 and 29.
3 Ibid regs 12 and 31.
4 Ibid regs 13 and 32. The notice convening the meeting must inform them of this right.

[17.33] The draft terms must be approved by a special resolution passed as a general meeting or class meetings of each company except that an acquiring company holding at least 90% of the shares in a company to be acquired need not hold such a meeting unless requisitioned by the holders of at least 5% of the shares. If the proposed scheme involves the formation of a new company or companies, the memorandum and articles thereof must be approved by special resolution of each of the companies being acquired.[1]

Shareholders who voted against the merger or division as the case may be, may within 15 days after the date of the last general meeting of a company which is a party to the scheme, serve a written notice on the acquiring company or companies to purchase his shares. The court also has power to make any order necessary for the protection of the interests of dissenting shareholders.[2]

1 Ibid regs 13, 14 and 32 and 33.
2 Ibid regs 14 and 34.

[17.34] Having obtained the requisite shareholder approval application is then made to the court by all companies which are party to the division or merger as the case may be for an order of confirmation of the draft terms. The application must be accompanied by a statement of the size of the shareholding of any shareholder who has requested that his shares be purchased by the acquiring company or companies; and of the measures which are proposed to comply with such request.[1] Creditors may object to the making of an order confirming the draft terms. If it orders it necessary the court may order a list of creditors to be settled and may dispose with the consent of any objecting creditor on condition that the company pays the debt or if the debt is not admitted, is contingent or not ascertained, an amount fixed by the court after the same type of inquiry and adjudication that would take place if the company were in official liquidation.[2] The holders of any securities other than shares, in the companies being acquired are to be given equivalent rights in the acquiring company or companies.[3] The court, on being satisfied that the procedural requirements and other of the regulations have been complied with may make an order confirming the proposed merger or division from such date as it appoints provided proper provision has been made for dissenting shareholders and creditors and for the safeguarding of the holders of securities in the companies being acquired. From the appointed date the assets and liabilities of the companies being acquired are transferred to the acquiring company or companies, shareholders in the acquired companies become shareholders in the acquiring companies, the companies being acquired are dissolved and any proceedings by or against them are continued by or against the acquiring company or companies. The court may also as part of the confirming order, and notwithstanding s 41 of the 1983 Act[4] order the acquiring company or companies to purchase the shares of dissenting shareholders at a price fixed by the court (being not less than their market value on the appointed date) and order that the company's capital be reduced accordingly.[5] If the merger or division comes within the ambit of the Mergers, Take-overs and Monopolies (Control) Act 1978 a confirming order cannot be made until:

(*a*) the Minister has stated that he has decided not to make a prohibition order; or

(*b*) the Minister has made a conditional order; or(c) a period of three months has elapsed from the date of notification of the proposed merger or division without the Minister having made a prohibition order.[6]

A copy of the confirming order must be sent immediately to the registrar and notice of such delivery must be published in *Iris Oifigiuil* within 14 days thereafter.[7]

---

1 Ibid regs 16 and 35.
2 Ibid regs 17 and 36. Under regs 17(3) if having regard to the special circumstances of the case it thinks proper to do so the court may dispense with the consent of any class of creditors even if unpaid.
3 Ibid regs 18 and 37.
4 Which prohibits a company from purchasing its own shares.
5 Regs 19 and 38 of SI No 137 of 1987.
6 See *Keane* at para **34.22** et seq. Ibid regs 20 and 39.
7 Ibid regs 21 and 40.

[17.35] The directors and independent persons may be personally liable for any loss or damage suffered by shareholders as a result of misconduct in the preparation or implementation of the merger or division as the case may be, or for loss or damage suffered as result of untrue statements in the draft terms, explanatory report or independent persons report as the case may be.[1] Such individuals may similarly incur criminal liability.[2]

1 Ibid regs 22 and 41. In order to escape personal liability the director and independent person must comply with the requirements of regs 22(3) and 41(3) and regs 22(4) and 41(4) respectively.
2 Ibid regs 23 and 42.

Chapter 18

INVESTIGATION OF A COMPANY'S AFFAIRS

[18.01] Under ss 165–173 of the Principal Act the Minister had power, albeit rarely used,[1] to appoint inspectors to investigate the affairs of a company.[2] These powers are now transferred to the court by part II of the 1990 Act. The court may appoint one or more inspectors if:–

(*a*) in the case of a company having a share capital on the application of not less than 100 members or by members holding at least one tenth of the paid up share capital;

(*b*) in the case of a company not having a share capital, on the application of not less than one fifth of the members;

(*c*) on the application of the company itself;

(*d*) on the application of a director of the company; or

(*e*) on the application of a creditor of the company.[3]

The court may also on the application of the Minister appoint an inspector if it is satisfied that there are 'circumstances suggesting':[4]

(*a*) that the company's affairs 'are being or have been conducted with intent to defraud its creditors or the creditors of any other person or otherwise for fraudulent or unlawful purposes or in a manner which is unfairly prejudicial[5] to some part of its members,[6] or that any actual or proposed act or omission of the company (including an act or omission on its behalf) is or would be so prejudicial, or that it was formed for any fraudulent or unlawful purpose; or

(*b*) that persons connected with its formation or the management of its affairs have in connection therewith been guilty of fraud, misfeasance or other misconduct towards it or towards its members; or

(*c*) that its members have not been given all the information relating to its affairs which they might reasonably expect.'[7]

Where an application is made to the court for the appointment of an inspector the court may require the applicant to give security of not less than £500 and not exceeding £100,000, for payment of the costs of the investigation.[8] If the court appoints an inspector it may, from time to time, give such directions as it thinks fit, whether to the inspector or otherwise, with a view to ensuring that the investigation is carried out as quickly and as inexpensively as possible.[9]

1 Having only exercised the power twice.
2 See generally *Keane*, chapter 37; Fraser *Administrative Powers of Investigation into Companies*. [1971] 34 MLR 260.
3 S 7. This section also applies to all bodies corporate incorporated outside the state which are carrying on or have at any time carried on business in the state.
4 S 8.
5 Or persons to whom shares have been transferred or transmitted by operation of law s 8(2)(*b*).
6 The concept of 'unfair prejudice' was introduced in the UK to replace the relief for members on grounds of oppression or disregard of interests ss 459–461 UK. Companies Act 1985. In view of the fact that such an amendment has not been made in this jurisdiction, the reference to 'unfair prejudice' is to say the least surprising.
7 The Minister may apply for an investigation on any one of these grounds even though the company is in voluntary liquidation.
8 S 7(3).
9 S 7(4).

The investigation

[18.02]   The inspector in conducting his investigation of the company,[1] may if he thinks it necessary in performing his duties, also investigate any related body corporate. He must however, obtain the approval of the court to so extend his investigation, in which case he will also be required to report on all the affairs of the related companies.[2] The officers and agents[3] of the company itself and of any related company under investigation, are obliged to produce to the inspectors all books and documents of or relating to their respective companies, which are in their custody or power. They must also give the inspectors all assistance which they are reasonably able to give. The inspectors can impose similar obligations on any other person whom they consider to be or might be in possession of any information concerning the company or any such related company.[4]

1 See *Keane* at paras **37.02** et seq.
2 S 9.
3 Defined in s 10(6) as including past as well as present officers or agents as the case may be, as well as the bankers, solicitors, employees and auditors of the company or related company.
4 S 10(1) & (2).

[18.03]   If an inspector has reasonable grounds for believing that a past or present director or shadow director of the company or of any related company under investigation, or any person connected with such a director, maintains or has maintained a bank account whether alone or jointly with another person and whether within this State or elsewhere, into or out of which certain classes of payments have been made, the inspector can require that person to produce to him all documents in the director's possession or under his control, relating to that bank account.[1] The payments in question are:–

(*a*) any money which has resulted from or been used in the financing of any loans, quasi-loans, credit-transactions, etc, particulars of which, in breach of ss 41 & 43 of the 1990 Act, have not been disclosed in a note to the company's accounts; or

(*b*) any money which has been in any way connected with any act or omission, or series of acts or omissions, which on the part of that director constituted misconduct (whether fraudulent or not) towards his company or its members.

In conducting the investigation an inspector may examine on oath any officer or agent of the company or of any related company under investigation and he may similarly examine any other person whom he considers to be or might be in possession of any information concerning that company's affairs. The examination may be oral or by written interrogatories. If oral, the answers may be reduced to writing and the person being examined may be required to sign them.[2] The answers given by him or given pursuant to O 74 of the Rules of Court, as well as any statement of affairs made by him or with which he concurs, may subsequently be used in evidence against him.[3]

Any failure to produce to the inspectors books and documents relating to the affairs of any company under investigation, any refusal to attend before the inspector when so required and any refusal to answer questions put by the inspector relating to that company's affairs, will be treated as a contempt of court and will be punishable accordingly.[4]

At the hearing for contempt the court may also make any other order or direction it thinks fit, including a direction to the person concerned to attend or re-attend before the inspector or produce particular books or documents or answer particular questions put to him by the inspector, or a direction that the person concerned need not produce a particular book or document or answer a particular question put to him by the inspector (for example on the basis of a successful plea of the prvilege against self incrimination[5] or on a plea of legal professional privilege is expressly protected by s 24).

1 S 10(3).
2 S 10(4).
3 S 10.
4 S 10(5).
5 This is because the court must decide whether the refusal to answer was wrongful: *McCelland, Pope & Langley Ltd v Howard* [1968] 1 All ER 569.

[18.04] While the inspector has a wide discretion regarding the manner in which he conducts the investigation, he must follow the basic rules of natural justice.

Re Pergammon Press Ltd [1970] 3 All ER 589 (Court of Appeal)

[18.05] Pergamom Press Ltd was being investigated under the UK equivalent of s 8 of the 1990 Act. The directors, Maxwell, Clark and Street,

543

refused to answer the inspectors' questions unless they were given assurances that in effect the investigation and examination were conducted as if it were a court hearing.

[18.06]   Lord Denning MR: Counsel for Mr Maxwell claimed that they had a right to see the transcripts of the evidence of the witnesses adverse to them. Counsel for Mr Clark claimed a right to cross-examine the witness. Counsel for Mr Street claimed that they ought to see any proposed finding against them before it was included finally in the report. In short the directors claimed that the inspectors should conduct the inquiry much as if it were a judicial inquiry in a court of law in which Mr Maxwell and his colleagues were being charged with an offence.

It seems to me that this claim on their part went too far. This inquiry was not a court of law. It was an investigation in the public interest, in which all should surely co-operate as they promised to do. But if the directors went too far on their side, I am afraid that counsel for the inspector went too far on the other. He did it very tactfully, but he did suggest that in point of law, the inspectors were not bound by the rules of natural justice. He said that in all the cases where natural justice had been applied hitherto, the tribunal was under a duty to come to a determination or decision but only an investigation or inquiry, the rules of natural justice did not apply . . . I cannot accept counsel for the inspector's submission. It is true, of course, that the inspectors are not a court of law. Their proceedings are not judicial proceedings: see *Re Grosvenor and West End Railway Terminus Hotel Co Ltd* (1897) 76 LT 337. They are not even quasi-judicial for they decide nothing; they determine nothing. They only investigate and report. They sit in private and are not entitled to admit the public to their meetings: see *Hearts of Oak Assurance Co Ltd v AG* [1932] AC 392. They do not even decide whether there is a prima facie case . . .

But this should not lead us to minimise the significance of their task. They have to make out a report which may have wide repercussions. They may, if they think fit, make findings of fact which are very damaging to those whom they name. They may accuse some; they may condemn others; they may ruin reputations or careers. Their report may lead to judicial proceedings. It may expose persons to criminal prosecutions or to civil actions. It may bring about the winding up of the company and be used itself as material for the winding up: see *Re SRA Properties Ltd* [1967] 2 All ER 615 . . . When they do make their report the board are bound to send a copy of it to the company and the board may, in their discretion publish it, if they think fit, to the public at large. Seeing that their work and their report may lead to such consequences I am clearly of opinion that the insepctors must act fairly. This is a duty which rests on them, as on many other bodies, although they are not judicial nor quasi-judicial, but only administrative . . . The inspectors can obtain information in any way which they think best, but before them condemn or criticise a man they must give him a fair opportunity for correcting or contradicting what is said against him. They need not quote chapter and verse. An outline of the charge will usually suffice.

That is what the inspectors here propose to do, but the directors want more. They want to see the transcripts of the witnesses who speak adversely to them and to see any documents which may be used against them. They, or some of them, even claim to cross-examine the witnesses. In all this the directors go too far. This investigation is ordered in the public interest. It should not be impeded by measures of this kind. Witnesses should be encouraged to come forward and not hold back. Remember, this not being a judicial proceeding the witnesses are not protected by an absolute privilege, but only by a qualified privilege . . . It is easy to imagine a situation in which if the name of witness were disclosed he might have an action brought against him and this might deter him from telling all that he knew. No one likes to have an action brought against him, however unfounded. Every witness must, therefore be protected. He must be encouraged to be frank. This is done by giving every witness an assurance that his evidence will be regarded as confidential and will not be used except for the purpose of the report. This assurance must be honoured. It does not mean that his name and his evidence will never be disclosed to anyone. It will often have to be used for the purpose of the report, not only in the report itself, but also be putting it in general terms to other witnesses for their comments. But it does mean that the inspectors will exercise a wise discretion in the use of it so as to safeguard the witness himself and any other affected by it. His evidence may sometimes although rarely, be so confidential that it cannot be put to those affected by it, even in general terms. If so, it should be ignored so far as they are concerned. For I take it to be axiomatic that the inspectors must not use the evidence of a witness so as to make it the basis of an adverse finding unless they give the party affected sufficient information to enable him to deal with it.

It was suggested before us that whenever the inspectors thought of deciding a conflict of evidence or of making adverse criticism of someone, they should draft the proposed passage of their report and put it before the party for his comments before including it. But I think that this also is going too far. This sort of thing should be left to the discretion of the inspectors. They must be masters of their own procedure. They should be subject to no rules save this: they must be fair. This being done, they should make their report with courage and frankness keeping nothing back. The public interest demands it. They need have no fear because their report so far as I can judge is protected by an absolute privilege . . .

Sachs and Buckley LJJ delivered concurring judgments.

Maxwell v Department of Trade and Industry [1974] QB 523 (Court of Appeal)

[The facts appear from the judgment]

[18.07] **Lord Denning MR:** The Pergamon Press affair still goes on. Three and a half years ago, we laid down some guidelines for the inspectors to follow. See *Re Pergamon Press Ltd* (para **18.05**). The inspectors have since then held their investigation. They have made two interim reports and a final report. Their reports are very critical of the plaintiff, Mr Robert Maxwell. He is very upset by these criticisms. So much so that he has launched attacks against all of the reports and against the inspectors themselves. Today we are concerned with his attack on the first interim report. Mr Maxwell said that many of the criticisms were made in disregard of the rules of natural justice. He asks us to declare accordingly . . .

I will try to state the considerations which are to be borne in mind in respect of an inquiry under the Companies Act 1948. First and foremost when a matter is referred to an inspector for investigation and report it is a very special kind of inquiry. It must not be confused with other inquiries which we have had to consider. Remember what it is not. It is not a trial of anyone, nor anything like it. There is no accused person. There is no prosecutor. There is no charge. It is not like a disciplinary proceeding before a professional body. Nor is it like an application to expel a man from a trade union or a club or anything of that kind. It is not even like a committee which considers whether there is a prima facie case against a person. It is simply an investigation without anyone being accused.

Second there is no one to present a case to the inspector. There is no counsel for the commission. The inspector has to do it all himself. He has himself to seek out the relevant documents and to gather the witnesses. He has himself to study the documents to examine the witnesses and to have their evidence recorded. He has himself to direct the witnesses to the relevant matters. He has himself to cross-examine them to test their accuracy or their veracity. No one else is there to cross-examine them. Even if a witness says things prejudicial to someone else that other does not hear it and is not there to cross-examine him.

Third, the investigation is private. This is necessary because witnesses may say something defamatory of someone else and it would be quite wrong for it to be published without the party affected being able to challenge it. The only persons present are the inspectors and their staff, the shorthand writer, the witness and his lawyers, if he desires them.

Fourth, the inspectors have to make their report. They should state their findings on the evidence and their opinions on the matters referred to them. If their report is to be of value they should make it with courage and frankness, keeping nothing back. The public interest demands it. It may on occasion be necessary for them to condemn or criticise a man. Before doing so they must act fairly by him. But what does fairness demand? That is the question.

Forbes J [the trial judge] thought that in order to do what was fair, after hearing the evidence and studying the documents, the inspectors ought to come to a conclusion (which was necessarily tentative) and put the substance of that conclusion to the witness . . . I do not think that is right. Just think what it means if after hearing all the evidence the inspectors have to sit down and come to tentative conclusions. If these are such as to be critical of any of the witnesses they have to re-open the inquiry, recall those witnesses and put

546

to them the criticisms which they are disposed to make. What will be the response of those witnesses? They will at once want to refute the tentative conclusions by calling other witnesses or by asking for further investigations. In short the inquiry will develop into a series of minor trials in which a witness will be accused of misconduct and seek to answer it. That would hold up the inquiry indefinitely. I do not think it is necessary. It is sufficient for the inspectors to put the points to the witnesses as and when they come in the first place. After hearing the evidence the inspectors have to come to their conclusions. These need not be tentative in the least. They can be final and definite, ready for their report.

Counsel for Mr Maxwell realised that we might not accept the view of Forbes J. So he put a lesser alternative. He submitted that, in order to do what was fair to a witness, the inspectors ought to take all the relevant statements made by other witnesses – or contained in documents – which were prejudicial to the man and put them to him so as to give him an opportunity of answering them. If the inspectors failed to do this on matters of substance, they failed to observe the rules of natural justice and the court should declare accordingly . . . I think this line of attack is entirely misconceived. It must be remembered that the inspectors are doing a public duty in the public interest. They must do what is fair to the best of their ability. They will, of course put to a witness the point of substance which occur to them – so as to give him the chance to explain or correct any relevant statement which is prejudicial to him. They may even recall him to do so. But they are not to be criticised because they may on occasion overlook something or other. Even the most skilled advocate, expert in cross-examination forgets now and again to put this or that point to a witness. And we all excuse him, knowing how difficult it is to remember everything. This inspector is entitled to at least as much consideration as the advocate. To borrow from Shakespeare, he is not to have 'All his faults observed, Set in a note-book, learned and conn'd by rote', to make a lawyer's holiday. His task is burdensome and thankless enough as it is. It would be intolerable if he were liable to be pilloried afterwards for doing it. No one of standing would ever be found to undertake it. The public interest demands that so long as he acts honestly and does what is fair to the best of his ability, his report is not to be impugned in the courts of law.

This disposes also of counsel for Mr Maxwell's other complaint . . .

Orr and Lawton LJJ delivered concurring judgments.

Notes

See also *Keane* at para **37.03**; *Norwest Holst Ltd v Secretary of State for Trade* [1978] 3 All ER 280; *R v Secretary of State for Trade, ex p Perestrello* [1908] 3 All ER 28.

[18.08] An investigation into the 'affairs' of the company may include an investigation into the conduct of the receiver appointed by a creditor of the company pursuant to the terms of a standard form debenture.

R v Board of Trade ex p St Martins Preserving Co Ltd [1965] 1 QB 603

[18.09] A receiver and manager had been appointed pursuant to the terms of a floating charge over the entire assets and undertaking of the applicant company. Amongst its various assets the applicant held 98% of the issued share capital of TG Tickler Ltd. The receiver dismissed the entire board of Tickler and appointed new directors, including himself. He then caused Tickler to sell its shares in a subsidiary Atholl Houses Ltd at an undervalue, cancelling a loan of over £600,000 made to Atholl by the applicant. However, he preserved the applicant's guarantee of a £600,000 loan by the bank to Atholl. The board of the applicant sought information from the receiver regarding the transaction. This was refused so at an EGM of the applicant a special resolution was passed to the effect that the affairs of the company ought to be investigated by an inspector.

[18.10] **Phillimore J:** Mr Walton moves on behalf of St Martins Preserving Co Ltd for an order of mandamus directed to the Board of Trade to require them to investigate the affairs of the applicant company pursuant to the provisions of s 165(*a*)(*i*) of the Companies Act 1948 . . . He submits that the actions of a receiver as agent for the company in disposing of its assets are actions dealing with 'its affairs'.

Mr Wheeler, on behalf of the Board of Trade has been at pains to make it clear that the board in refusing an investigation has not been actuated in any way by tenderness towards the bank or its receiver, but by the belief that the actions of a receiver and manager for a debenture holder are not the affairs of the company so that the board has no power to investigate them . . .

What are 'its affairs' when the company is in full control? They must surely include its goodwill, its profits or losses, its contracts and assets including its shareholding in and ability to control the affairs of a subsidiary, or perhaps in the latter regard a sub-subsidiary such as Atholl Houses Ltd. In ordinary parlance the affairs of the applicant company must surely have included its shareholding in TG Tickler Ltd and its power in virtue of that shareholding to control the board of that subsidiary and the disposition of Atholl Houses Ltd, the wholly owned sub-subsidiary. How were 'its affairs' changed on the appointment of a receiver and manager of the property of the applicant company by the debenture holders. Did its affairs cease to be its affairs and become solely the affairs of the receiver and manager or of the debenture holders? I think not. Could the debenture holder and/or its receiver and manager play 'ducks and drakes' with 'its affairs' without regard to any interests of the shareholders of the applicant company? Mr Wheeler himself concedes that on proof of fraud on the part of the receiver and manager the applicant company could or might have rights. Why, if not because 'its affairs' had been dealt with fraudulently . . .

In short what the receiver and manager does may in a narrow sense be his affair, but it is also the affair of the company in the broad and natural meaning of the phrase 'its affairs'. He acts in the name of the company –

what he does may ruin its shareholders or leave them with some prospect of future recovery. Under clause (2) of the debenture it is the undertaking of the company which is confided to him and under clause 13(2) it is its business that he is managing whilst under sub-clause (5) of clause 13 he is its agent and is made responsible for his acts or defaults . . . The fact that an action of the receiver and manager may be primarily designed to serve the interests of the debenture holder and to that extent be his affair does not in my judgment prevent it being an affair of the company, whose future may depend upon such action carried out in its name. If he is the agent as provided for in the debenture, why should he not be answerable for his conduct of 'its affairs'?

On a more narrow view of what has happened in the present case, it seems to me that the receiver having constituted himself as director with two nominees as co-directors of TG Tickler Ltd and thereafter disposed of Atholl Houses Ltd has dealt with the affair of the applicant company otherwise than in his capacity as receiver and this transaction by the reconstituted board justifies the special resolution of the applicant company and the present motion. True, what was done was primarily an affair of TG Tickler Ltd but it was also as I think an affair of the applicant company . . .

In my judgment the order of mandamus should issue.

Winn J delivered a concurring judgment. Lord Parker CJ concurred.

Report by the inspectors

[18.11]   The inspector must make a final report to the court at the end of the investigation.[1] They may, and if so directed by the court must, also make interim reports.[2] An inspector may, at any time in the course of his investigation, without the necessity of making a final report, inform the court of matters coming to his knowledge as a result of the investigation tending to show that an offence has been committed.[3]

The court must furnish a copy of every report of the inspectors to the Minister and may, if it thinks fit:

'(*a*) forward a copy of any report made by the inspectors to the company's registered office,
(*b*) furnish a copy on request and payment of the prescribed fee to–
  (*i*) any member of the company or other body corporate which is the subject of the report;
  (*ii*) any person whose conduct is referred to in the report;
  (*iii*) the auditors of that company or body corporate;
  (*iv*) the applicants for the investigation:
  (*v*) any other person (including an employee) whose financial interests appear to the court to be affected by the matters dealt with in the report whether as a creditor of the company or body corporate or otherwise;
  (*vi*) the Central Bank, in any case in which the report of the inspectors relates, wholly or partly to the affairs of the holder of a licence under section 9 of the Central Bank Act 1971; and
(*c*) cause any such report to be printed and published.'[4]

If the court so thinks proper it may direct that a particular part of the report be omitted from a copy forwarded or furnished to any of the above persons, or from the report as printed and published.[5]

1 See *Keane* at para **37.06**.
2 S 11(1).
3 S 11(2).
4 S 11(3)(*a*), (*b*), (*c*).
5 S 11(4).

Proceedings on foot of the inspector's report

[18.12]   Once the court has considered the report it may make such order as it deems fit in relation to matters arising therefrom including–

(*a*) an order of its own motion for the winding up of a body corporate, or
(*b*) an order for the purpose of remedying any disability suffered by any person whose interests were adversely affected by the conduct of the affairs of the company, provided that in making any such order, the court must have regard to the interests of any other person who may be adversely affected by the order.[1]

The Minister is also empowered to present a petition for the winding up of such body corporate (unless it is already being wound up by the court) where it appears just and equitable to do so from the inspectors report, or from an inspectors report into the ownership of shares or from information or documents obtained by the Minister under part II of the 1990 Act (discussed at paras **18.19–18.20**).

1 See *Keane* at paras **37.11–37.17**.

[18.13]   Under s 22 of the 1990 Act, the inspectors' report is admissible in any legal proceedings as evidence of the facts set out therein without further proof unless the contrary is shown, and is also evidence of the opinion of the inspectors in relation to any matter contained in the report.

Re Armvent Ltd [1975] 3 All ER 441 (Chancery Division)

[18.14]   The Secretary of State for Trade had previously appointed inspectors to investigate the affairs of the company. On the basis of their report he presented a petition to have the company wound up on the just and equitable ground. The company's controllers objected to the report, stating that they did not accept its findings. They contended that the court should not have regard to the report on the basis, inter alia, that it was hearsay. The controllers did not adduce any evidence to challenge the inspectors' findings.

[18.15]   Templeman J: Counsel for the opponents relied strongly on authority. He referred me first of all to the decision of Buckley J in *Re ABC*

Coupler and Engineering Co Ltd (No 2) [1962] 3 All ER 68, where the learned judge decided that where grave charges were levelled against individuals the court would not in the exercise of its discretionary jurisdiction be satisfied with prima facie evidence but require the petitioner to substantiate his case more fully; that in such cases it would require where practicable the evidence of witnesses with direct knowledge of the matters to which they were testifying and on which they could be cross-examined and which conformed to the ordinary rules of admissibility. On an affidavit similar to that which is put forward in support of the petition here he dismissed the petition.

Where the conclusions of a report are challenged, when someone comes along and gives evidence to say that the inspectors have got it all wrong, then I can quite understand why a court would be reluctant to rely on the exercise of its discretion on a report without further investigation and further evidence. But in this case a detailed report makes the most detailed findings against this company and no one who had anything to do with the company at the time has come along to deny the allegations. In my judgment I am entitled in those circumstances to rely on the report as a prima facie indication that there is fraud and a prima facie indication of the validity of the matters mentioned in the petition.

I am supported in that view by the decision of Pennycuick J in *Re Travel & Holiday Clubs Ltd* [1967] 2 All ER 606 in which he held that an inspectors' report made by persons acting in a statutory fact-finding capacity and being unchallenged was admissible as material on which the court was entitled to act and on the basis of that report and in the absence of any further evidence it was just and equitable that the company should be wound up. In that case the company did not appear and nobody argued. In the subsequent case of *Re Allied Produce Co Ltd* [1967] 3 All ER 399 Megarry J borrowing as he said the language of Pennycuick J in *Re SBA Properties Ltd* [1967] 2 All ER at 621 said that the report has a special status, not as evidence in the ordinary sense but as material on which if it is not challenged the court can proceed to make a winding up order on the ground that it is just and equitable. Counsel for the opponents says that in the present case the material is challenged. It is challenged because the opponents say they do not accept it and do not believe it. In my judgment that is not the sort of challenge which means anything. Challenge is this sense means challenge by somebody with knowledge of the facts coming along and saying the inspectors' report is wrong and being willing to put forward an affidavit and to be cross-examined and to be judged in the witness box on the evidence which he puts forward in contradiction of the inspectors' report. I do not mean that everything the inspectors say is deemed to be true and that the person who comes along must challenge and give evidence on oath effectively destroying everything; but he must challenge the material parts of the report. For myself I would go wider than that. It seems to me even if the report of the inspectors is challenged nevertheless it ought to be treated as prima facie evidence and that it ought to be left to a judge in any case having read the report and having seen the witnesses to make up his own mind whether it is just and equitable to

551

wind up the company. The whole machinery of the inspectors' report was evolved in order to enable the Secretary of State to present a winding up petition where the Secretary of State considers the public interest. It would be unfortunate if once the Secretary of State has reached that conclusion on proper grounds based on the inspectors' detailed report that the court should be right back to square one and start again as though the inspectors had never come on the scene at all. A great deal may depend on the contents of the report and the evidence set out in the report; but I would hope that a report of this nature would be accepted by the court as being prima facie evidence of the main conclusions drawn by the inspectors. Once evidence is sworn to the contrary then if the Secretary of State fails to support the report by direct evidence which removes any doubt cast on the validity of the inspectors' conclusions the court would not be slow to dismiss the petition. In the present instance I am fully satisfied that the allegations in the petition have been made out and I am even more satisfied having read the petition and the report that it is just and equitable to wind up this company and that the earlier the official receiver gets in to sort matters out the better. I make the usual compulsory order.

Notes

See also *Re St Piran Ltd* [1981] 1 WLR 1300 where it was held that the inspectors' report was also prima facie evidence of the matters stated therein, for the purposes of a petition to have the company wound up on the just and equitable ground, which is presented by a member rather than by the Minister.

Expenses of investigation

[**18.16**]   The Minister is primarily liable for the expenses of the investigation but the court may direct that any body corporate dealt with in the report, or the applicant or applicants for the investigation are to be liable, to such extent as the court may direct, to repay the Minister provided that the liability of the applicant or applicants is not to exceed in the aggregate £100,000.[1] The inspector in his report can include a recommendation as to the directions if any, that the court should make in this regard. In addition any person who is –

(*a*) convicted of an offence or a prosecution instituted as a result of the investigation;

(*b*) ordered to pay damages or restore any property in proceedings brought as a result of the investigation; or

(*c*) awarded damages or to whom property is restored in proceedings brought as a result of an investigation;

may in the same proceedings be ordered to repay all or part of the expenses of the investigation to the Minister or to any body corporate or applicant for the investigation or who has already been ordered to meet such expenses. A payment out of damages awarded or property restored may exceed 10% of the value of such damages or property, as the case may be, and may not be executed until the person concerned has received his damages or the property has been restored, as the case may be.

1 S 13.

Investigation of ownership of company

[18.17] The 1990 Act introduces new provisions for the investigation of ownership of companies. Under s 14 the Minister may appoint one or more inspectors 'to investigate and report on the membership of any company and otherwise with respect to the company for the purpose of determining the true persons who are or have been financially interested in the success or failure (real or apparent) of the company or able to control or materially to influence the policy of the company'. The Minister can make the appointment provided he is satisfied that there are circumstances suggesting that such an investigation is necessary–

'(*a*) for the effective administration of the law relating to companies;
(*b*) for the effective discharge by the Minister of his functions under any enactment; or
(*c*) in the public interest.'

The investigation may be into ownership of the company generally or may be limited to particular shares or debentures. Subject to the terms of his appointment the inspector's powers extend to the investigation of any circumstances suggesting the existence of an arrangement or understanding which, though not legally binding, is or was observed or likely to be observed in practice and which is relevant to the purposes of his investigation.

The inspector has broadly similar powers of investigation to those conferred on an inspector appointed by the court, for the purposes of preparing his report. He makes his final and any interim reports to the Minister and must inform the Minister of any matters coming into his knowledge tending to show the commission of a criminal offence.

The Minister has the same powers to furnish, forward, print or publish copies of the report as are vested in the court, where an inspector has been appointed by the court.

If the Minister is of opinion that there is good reason for not divulging any part of the report he may disclose the report with the omission of that part. He may also keep a copy of the report with the registrar and if necessary, may omit from the copy with the registrar any part which ought not to be divulged.

Under s 15 if the Minister thinks it necessary to investigate the ownership of shares in or debentures of a company but thinks it unnecessary to appoint an inspector for the purpose, he may instead 'require any person who he has reasonable cause to believe to have or to be able to obtain any information as to the present and past interests in those shares or debentures and the names and addresses of the persons interested and of any persons who act or have acted on their behalf in relation to the shares. Failure to provide such information to the Minister is an offence. Similarly, if in giving the information the person makes a statement which he knows to be false in a material particular or recklessly makes any statement which is false in a material particular he is guilty of an offence'.

A person is deemed to have an interest in a share or debenture if he has any right to acquire or dispose of the share or debenture or any interest therein or to vote in respect thereof or if his consent is necessary for the exercise of any of the rights of others persons interested therein or if the other persons interested therein can be required or are accustomed to exercise their rights in accordance with his instructions.

[18.18] Where in connection with an investigation or enquiry into the ownership of shares it appears to the Minister that there is difficulty in finding out the relevant facts about any shares (whether issued or to be issued) he may by notice in writing under s 16 direct that the shares shall until further notice be subject to the following restrictions:–

'(a) any transfer of those shares or in the case of unissued shares any transfer of the right to be issued therewith and any issue thereof shall be void;

(b) no voting rights shall be exercisable in respect of those shares;

(c) no further shares shall be issued in right of those shares or in pursuance of any offer made to the holder thereof; and

(d) except in a liquidation, no payment shall be made of any sums due from the company on those shares, whether in respect of capital or otherwise.'

The Minister must as soon as may be after the direction is given, cause notice of it to be sent to the company concerned at its registered office and to be delivered to the registrar of companies and to be published in *Iris Oifigiuil* and in at least two daily newspapers.

Any agreement in breach of these restrictions (eg. for the transfer of the shares) will be void unless approved by the court or the Minister. It is also an offence to contravene the restrictions.

Where the Minister imposes such restrictions on the shares or refuses to lift the restrictions, any aggrieved person can apply to the court for relief. Neither the court nor the Minister can lift the restrictions unless satisfied that the relevant facts about the shares have been disclosed to the company and no unfair advantage has accrued to any person as a result of the failure to make that disclosure. Even if the restrictions are lifted for the purposes of a sale by the owner or a sale by the court (discussed below) restrictions (c) and (d) may be continued in whole or in part so far as they relate to any right acquired or offer made before the transfer.

Where shares are subject to these restrictions the court may on the application of the Minister or the company order them to be sold subject to the approval of the court as to the sale and may also direct that the shares shall cease to be subject to these restrictions. Once this has been made the Minister, the company, the person appointed to sell the shares or any person interested in them may apply to the court for any further order relating to the sale or transfer of shares. The proceeds of sale of the shares less the costs of the sale are to be paid into court for the benefit of the persons who were beneficially interested in the shares. Any such person may apply to the court for the whole amount of these proceeds to be paid to him. The court will order the payment out to the applicant of that proportion of the proceeds of sale to which he is beneficially entitled. However, the court may order that the costs of the application by the Minister or company for the sale, be met out of the proceeds of sale before any sums are paid out to the beneficial owners of the shares.

Production of books and papers

[18.19] S 19 of the 1990 Act confers on the Minister the power to give directions requiring a company, at such time and place as may be specified in the directions, to produce such books or documents as may be so specified. He may also at any time, if he thinks there is good reason to do so, authorise any officer of his, on producing (if required to do so) evidence of his authority, to require any such company to produce to him forthwith any books or documents which the officer may specify. The section applies to any body corporate, whether or not it is registered in this jurisdiction and which is carrying on or has at any time carried on business in Ireland. It may be used where there are circumstances suggesting that–

(*a*) it is necessary to examine the books and documents of the company with a view to determining whether an inspector should be appointed to investigate the affairs of the company; or

(*b*) that the affairs of the company are being or have been conducted with intent to defraud its members, creditors or the creditors of any other person, or for any fraudulent or unlawful purpose, or was formed for any other fraudulent or unlawful purpose; or

(*c*) that its affairs are being or have been conducted in a manner which is unfairly prejudicial to some part of its members[1] or that may actual or proposed act or omission or series of acts or omissions of the company or on behalf of the company are or would be unfairly prejudicial to some part of its members; or

(*d*) that any actual or proposed act or omission or series of acts or omissions of the company or on behalf of the company are or are likely to be unlawful; or

(*e*) that the company was formed for any fraudulent or unlawful purpose.

Production of such books or papers can be required of any other person who appears to be in possession of them, but without prejudice to any lien they may have thereon.[2] The Minister cannot, however, require or authorise an officer of his to require, the production by a banker of a document relating to the affairs of a customer of his unless either it appears to the Minister that it is necessary to do so for the purposes of investigating the affairs of the banker or the customer has already been required to produce books or documents under this section.[3] Once the books or documents are produced copies or extracts may be taken from them and past and present officers and employees of the company may be asked to explain their contents.[4] If they are not produced, the person required to produce them must state to the best of his knowledge and belief where they are located.[5] Non-compliance with this section is an offence punishable by a fine. Statements made by a person in complying with the requirements of this section may be used in evidence against him.[6]

1 See fn 5.
2 S 19(3).
3 S 23(2).
4 S 19(4).
5 Ibid.
6 S 19(6).

[18.20]   S 20 provides that a District Justice may issue a warrant for the Gardai and other named persons to enter and search a premises where he has reasonable grounds for suspecting that books or documents required to be produced pursuant to s 19 and which have not been produced, are on said premises. Any relevant documents appearing to be such books or documents may be seized and any other steps taken to preserve them or prevent interference with them. They may be retained for three months after seizure or, if certain criminal proceeding are commenced within this period for which the books or documents are relevant, until the end of those proceedings. It is an offence to obstruct the exercise of a right of entry and search conferred by the warrant.

No information, book or document relating to a company which has been obtained under s 19 or 20 shall, without the previous written consent of that company, be published or disclosed, except to a competent authority,[1] unless the publication or disclosure is required for certain criminal proceedings (including proceedings under the Companies Acts and other proceedings in relation to the management of the company's affairs or the misapplication or wrongful retention of its property), for proceedings by the Minister for the winding up of the company, for the making by an inspector of his report, or for the purposes of an application for a search warrant under s 20.[2] Unauthorised publication or disclosure is an offence.

1 S 21(3). For the purposes of the section 'competent authority includes (*a*) the Minister; (*b*) an officer authorised by the Minister; (*c*) an inspector appointed under this Act; (*d*) the Minister for Finance; (*e*) an officer authorised by the Minister for Finance; (*f*) any court of competent jurisdiction; (*g*) a supervisory authority within the meaning of regulations relating to insurance made under the European Communities Act 1972 and (*h*) the Central Bank'.
2 S 21.

Chapter 19

WINDING UP: PART I

WINDING UP

[19.01]   Winding up is the process whereby the affairs of the company are formally terminated, its assets are realised and the proceeds applied in discharge of its liabilities.[1] After creditors have been paid, the balance, if any, is distributed amongst the members in the prescribed order and amount. After the company has been wound up it may be dissolved, ie, the process whereby it ceases to exist as a separate legal entity. There are two types of winding up. The first is known variously as winding up by the court, compulsory winding up, or official liquidation. The second type of winding up is known as voluntary winding up and is subdivided into members and creditors voluntary winding up.

1 See generally *Keane* chapters 38, 39, 40.

Voluntary winding up

[19.02]   Under s 251 of the Principal Act a company may be wound up voluntarily

'(*a*) when the period, if any, fixed for the duration of the company by the articles, expires or the event, if any, occurs, on the occurrence of which the articles provide that the company is to be dissolved and the company in general meeting has passed a resolution that the company be wound up voluntarily;[1]
(*b*) if the company resolves by special resolution that the company be wound up voluntarily;
(*c*) if the company in general meeting resolves that it cannot by reason of its liabilities continue in business and that it be wound up voluntarily.'

Within 14 days of passing the resolution, the company must publish notice of it in *Iris Oifigiuil*.[2] The date of the passing of the resolution is the date of commencement of the winding up.[3] After this date the company ceases to carry on business except so far as is required for the beneficial winding up

557

thereof[4] and any transfer of shares without the sanction of the liquidator and any alteration in the status of members is void.[5]

1 See generally *Keane* chapter 40.
2 S 252 of the Principal Act. See *Keane* para **40.03**.
3 Ibid s 253.
4 Ibid s 254.
5 Ibid s 255.

[19.03] S 256 of the Principal Act, as substituted by s 128 of the 1990 Act provides that a members voluntary winding up may only take place if preceded by a statutory declaration made by two or more of the company's directors to the effect that they have made a full inquiry into the affairs of the company, and that having done so, they have formed the opinion that the company will be able to pay its debts in full within such period not exceeding 12 months from the commencement of the winding up as may be specified in the declaration. The declaration must be made not more than 28 days before the passing of the winding up resolution and must be delivered to the registrar not later than the date for delivery to him of the winding up resolution. It must include a statement of the company's assets and liabilities as at the latest practicable date and not more than three months before the making of the declaration. A copy of a report made by an independent person who is qualified to act as the company's auditor must be attached and must embody a statement by that independent person that he has given and not withdrawn his consent to the issue of the declaration with his report attached. A copy of the declaration must be attached to the notice convening the meeting to pass the winding up resolution.

The independent person's report must state whether in his opinion and to the best of his information and according to the explanations given to him, the opinion of the directors as to the company's solvency and the statement of assets and liabilities are reasonable.

Within 28 days of the advertisements of the resolution the court may on the application of a creditor who, together with any creditors supporting represents one fifth in number or value of the creditors, make an order that the company be wound up as if in creditors voluntary winding up. Such an order can only be made if, despite the statutory declaration, the court is of opinion that it is unlikely that the company will be able to pay its debts in full within 12 months of the commencement of the winding up.

Where a statutory declaration has been made and it is subsequently proved to the satisfaction of the court that the company is unable to pay its debts, the court on the application of the liquidator or any creditor or contributory of the company may, if it thinks proper to do so, declare that any director who was a party to the declaration without having reasonable grounds for the opinion that the company would be able to pay its debts in full within the period specified in the declaration shall be personally responsible, without any limitation of liability, for all or any of the debts or other liabilities of the company as the court may direct. The court may make such further directions as it thinks proper to give effect to the declaration of personal liability. Where a company's debts are not paid or provided for in full within the period stated in the declaration of solvency, it shall be presumed until the contrary is shown, that the director did not have reasonable grounds for his opinion.

[19.04] In a creditors voluntary winding up the company must summon a creditors' meeting for the same day as or the day after the day on which the general meeting is to be held at which the resolution is to be passed to place the company in liquidation. The creditors must be given 10 days notice of the meeting, notice of which must be advertised in the prescribed manner.[1] The directors must place a statement of the company's affairs before the creditors' meeting.

1 Ibid s 266 as amended by s 130 of the 1990 Act.

[19.05] Where a company which is able to pay its debts in full has purported to go into members voluntary winding up but has failed to file the requisite statutory declaration of solvency, the appropriate course is to apply to the court to have the company wound up.

Re Oakthorpe Holdings Ltd; Walsh v Registrar of Companies [1988] ILRM 62

[The facts appear from the judgment]

[19.06] **Carroll J:** In this case the shareholders intended to have a members' voluntary winding up. However the directors failed to make and deliver a statutory declaration of solvency as required by s 256. As a result the winding up by virtue of s 256(11) became a creditors' voluntary winding up.

But no creditors' meeting was called as required by s 266 and therefore there was no appointment of a liquidator in a creditors' winding up under s 267. This provides for nomination of a liquidator at both the company's meeting and the creditors' meeting, the creditors' nominee taking precedence.

The company therefore finds it impossible to proceed. It is not a members' voluntary winding up and neither is it an effective creditors' voluntary winding up. The application before the court is made under s 280 either to annul the resolution to wind up or extend the time to call a creditors' meeting . . . S 280 provides that the liquidator or any contributory or creditor may apply to the court (*a*) to determine any question arising in the winding up or (*b*) to exercise all or any of the powers which the court might exercise if the company were being wound up by the court.

Among the general powers of the court in the case of a winding up by the court, s 234 allows the court to annul an order for winding up or make an order staying proceedings on being satisfied that it should be done. There is no express power conferred on the court in a winding up by the court to annul a resolution to wind up. But s 234(3) must be given a meaning. Therefore the reference in sub-section (3) to an order annulling the resolution to wind must mean that by analogy with the power of the court in a court winding up to annul a winding up order the court can in a voluntary winding up annul the resolution to wind up in an appropriate case, just as it can stay proceedings.

Therefore, I am satisfied that the court does have power to annul the resolution to wind up in an appropriate case. In the circumstances of this case where the company was not a trading company and had no creditors I am satisfied that the resolution should be annulled. If it had been a trading company with creditors it might well have been necessary to require that a petition to wind up should be presented which would also remedy the impasse.

As to the alternative relief sought, namely the time to call a creditors' meeting, I am not satisfied that the court has any power to extend the time. A time limit was provided by statute and no discretion was given to the court to extend it. There does not appear to be any analagous power given to the court in a winding up by the court.

There is one further matter which arises under s 280. It is the liquidator or any contributor or creditor who may apply to the court. In this case the liquidator has not been validly appointed as liquidator in a creditors' winding up. Therefore the appropriate person to apply is a contributory and I will adjourn the matter to enable a contributory to be substituted as applicant.

Winding up by the court[1]

[19.07] Compulsory winding up is initiated by the presentation of a petition[2] in the Central Office of the High Court which is then served on the company at its registered office and advertised, at least seven days before the hearing, once in *Iris Oifigiuil* and once in at least two Dublin daily newspapers.[3] The petition is accompanied by a verifying affidavit.[4] Any person intending to appear at the hearing must serve notice of intention to appear on the petitioner or his solicitor and a list of such persons must be handed by the petitioner to the registrar before the hearing.[5] Affidavits in opposition must be filed within seven days of the last prescribed advertisement and notice of such filing must be given to the petitioner or his solicitor.[6] At the hearing of the petition the court may dismiss or adjourn it or make a winding up order. It may have regard to the wishes of creditors and contributories and may direct meetings to be summoned to ascertain such wishes.[7] If a winding up order is made, the liquidation is deemed to commence at the date of the presentation of the petition.[8]

1 See *Keane* chapter 40.
2 As to the form of which see *Keane* at para **38.15**.
3 See *Keane* at para **38.22** et seq.
4 As to which see *Keane* at para **38.24**.
5 See *Keane* at para **38.25**.
6 Ibid at para **38.26**. On withdrawal of the petition, see *Keane* at para **38.27**.
7 Ibid at paras **38.28** & **38.29**.
8 S 230 of the Principal Act.

When a company may be wound up by the court

[19.08] The relevant statutory provisions regarding when and by whom a petition may be presented are ss 213 and 215 of the Principal Act as amended by sch 1 of the 1983 Act.[1]

1 See *Keane* at paras **38.09–38.12**.

[19.09] A company which is unable to pay its debts may be wound up under s 213(e), unless the company can show that there is a bona fide dispute as to the existence of the petition debt.

Re Pageboy Couriers Ltd [1983] ILRM 510 (High Court)

[The facts appear from the judgment]

[19.10] **O'Hanlon J:** Stephen Rabette, as petitioning creditor seeks an order in these proceedings for the compulsory winding up of Pageboy Couriers Ltd. He claims that the company is indebted to him in the sum of £5,000 for director's fees which it has failed to pay after demand duly made, and that it is unable to pay its debts.

The application is hotly contested by the company which disputes the entitlement of the petitioner to the amount claimed by him or to any amount in respect of director's fees and further denies the allegation that it is unable to pay its debts.

Proceedings were commenced by Mr Rabette by summary summons in the month of June 1982 claiming payment of the amount he alleged was due to him by the company, and an appearance was entered to the proceedings at the beginning of July 1982. A letter seeking particulars of the claim was sent on 20 July 1982 in which the plaintiff was asked to state when and by whom it was agreed that he should receive director's fees at the rate of £2,500 per annum. A reply was not received to that request for particulars until the present month, when by letter dated 8 April 1983 the petitioner's solicitor stated that their client's claim arose on foot of an oral agreement 'made between our client and the managing director of Contactaphone Ltd, Donough O'Connor in or about June 1980. This was later confirmed by the said Mr O'Connor our client, and Mr Timothy Childs in or about January 1981.' (The company, Contactaphone Ltd to which reference was made is a company holding a controlling interest in Pageboy Couriers Ltd).

The company say that no agreement to pay such fees or any director's fees to the petitioner was made at any general meeting of the company or by any person having authority to bind the company in this respect. It further contends that on the petitioner's own statement of the terms of agreement he was only to receive such fees if and when the company was making substantial profits and that this situation has not arisen.

The petitioner allowed the civil proceedings instituted by him in June 1982 to lie dormant after receiving the said notice for particulars of his claim and has not prosecuted them at any time since. Instead, he has brought the present petition to wind up the company in reliance upon the same claim which has at all times been disputed by the company on the grounds already mentioned.

Mr Cooke for the company, argued that proceedings to wind up a company should not be brought where the person claiming as petitioning creditor is well aware that the company has a substantial and reasonable defence to the claim which it wishes to plead, and on which it proposes to rely to defeat the entire claim brought against it. He relied inter alia, on the decision of the English Court of Appeal in *Stonegate Securities Ltd v Gregory* [1980] 1 All ER 241 where Buckley LJ said (at p 243 of the report):

'If the company in good faith and on substantial grounds disputes any liability in respect of the alleged debt, the petition will be dismissed or if the matter is brought before a court before the petition is issued, its presentation will in normal circumstances be restrained. That is because a winding up petition is not a legitimate means of seeking to enforce payment of a debt which is bona fide disputed. Ungood-Thomas J, put the matter thus in *Mann v Goldstein* [1968] 2 All ER 679 at 775; "For my part I would prefer to rest the jurisdiction directly on the comparatively simple proposition that 'a creditor's petition can only be presented by a creditor, that the winding up jurisdiction is not for the purpose of deciding a disputed debt (that is, disputed on substantial and not insubstantial grounds) since, until a creditor is established as a creditor he is not entitled to present the petition and has no locus standi in the companies' court; and that therefore, to invoke the winding up jurisdiction when the debt is disputed (that is, on substantial grounds) or after it has become clear that it is so disputed is an abuse of the process of the court."'

Having adopted that passage in its entirety Buckley LJ, concluded:–

'In my opinion a petition founded upon a debt which is disputed in good faith and on substantial grounds is demurrable for the reason that the petitioner is not a creditor of the company within the meaning of s 224 sub-s 1 at all and the question whether he is or is not a creditor of the company is not appropriate for adjudication in winding up proceedings.'

I accept the principles there enunciated as being applicable also when considering the propriety of proceeding by way of petition for the winding up of a company under the provisions of our own Companies Acts and when these principles are applied to the facts of the present case I am of opinion that Mr Cooke's submission against the petition is well-founded. The petitioner's claim for director's fees has at all times been disputed by the company since he first started proceedings for recovery of same almost a year ago and without in any way attempting to prejudge the outcome of these proceedings it can be fairly stated that the claim appears to have been disputed in good faith and on substantial grounds.

In these circumstances I propose to dismiss the present petition for the winding-up of the company.

Notes

The presentation of a petition on foot of a bona fide disputed debt may also be struck out as an abuse of the process of the court: *Re Dubend Exports Ltd* (High Court, Costello J, 9 May 1986). Pending the hearing of the motion to dismiss, the court may restrain advertisement of the petition even if the company is insolvent: *Re a Company* [1894] 2 Ch 349. Under s 214 as amended by s 123 of the 1990 Act, a company is deemed to be unable to pay its debts if:–

(*a*) it has failed to pay, secure or compound a debt of £1,000 or more within three weeks of a written demand having been served on its registered office by the creditor;

(*b*) a judgment has been returned unsatisfied; or

(*c*) it has otherwise proved to the satisfaction of the court that the company is unable to pay its debts.

A petition may be presented on the ground of inability to pay debts by a creditor, contributory or by the company itself. For restrictions on presentation of petitions generally by contributories, see s 215(*a*) of the Principal Act and *Keane* at para **38.19** and **38.20**.

A creditor who has proved that the company is unable to pay his debt is normally entitled *es debito justitiae* to a winding up order. But the court also has regard to the wishes of the majority in value of the creditors, and if such creditors show some good reason for opposing the petition the court may in its discretion refuse the order: *Re P & J Macrae* [1961] 1 All ER 302.

[19.11] Under s 282 of the Principal Act the court may on the petition of a contributory or creditor order that the company be compulsorily wound up, despite the fact that it is already in voluntary liquidation. If the petitioner is a contributory a winding up order can only be made if the court is satisfied that the rights of the contributories will be prejudiced by a continuance of the voluntary winding. If the petitioner is a creditor the court normally has regard to the wishes of the majority in value of the creditors. However, once there is evidence that a continuance of the voluntary winding up will prejudice the rights of creditors the court will as a matter of course make a winding up order.

Re George Downs & Co Ltd [1943] IR 420 (High Court)

[19.12] The company had gone into a creditors voluntary liquidation for the purpose of reconstruction. Not all creditors had received notice of the creditors' meeting to appoint a liquidator. Prior to the winding up the company had purchased a business from its controllers for a price stated to be profits of the company up to the date when the transfer of the business to the company was completed. No date for completion was stated in the agreement. The controller in his capacity as managing director drew an exorbitant salary and was according to the company's books owed other unexplained amounts. In the case of other liabilities there was no entry in the company's books. The petitioners who were creditors of the company had voted against the voluntary liquidation and claimed that they would be gravely prejudiced unless a winding up order was made.

[19.13]   Overend J: If the petitioner proves he will be prejudiced by a continuance of the voluntary winding up then he is entitled to a compulsory order, ex debito justitiae, and the court cannot refuse it. If, on the other hand, he fails to establish prejudice by the continuance of the voluntary winding up, the court still has power to make the order if the court forms the opinion that the rights of creditors will be prejudiced by a voluntary winding up . . In this case the winding up resolution was undoubtedly with a view to re-construction and that purpose has failed; the control was vested entirely in one family, but apart from these considerations there are many matters which, in my opinion, are properly matters for enquiry and investigation. All may possibly be satisfactorily explained. I have formed no final opinion and I refrain from forming any view as to the ultimate result; but I see that some explanation is called for, some investigation is necessary, and if not had, I have no doubt that creditors will be prejudiced. Such investigations can only be ensured in court.

Then it is suggested that the court is bound by the wishes of creditors. I entirely dissent from that view. The statute says 'may have regard to the wishes of creditors as proved to it by any sufficient evidence'. (ss 145 and 201). This cannot mean that the court must act on the wishes of a majority of some of the creditors present at a meeting which had only some of the facts before it, a meeting to which all the creditors had no notice. The list of creditors prepared by the Liquidator as of the 18th January 1943 comprised 116 creditors, only 35 were present at the meeting, some creditors had notice, some had not. Of those who had notice some had notice that the meeting was only with a view to reconstruction and may have stayed away. I cannot accept a resolution of such a meeting as truly or fairly representative of the views of the general body of creditors. If I could I am still in the position of knowing that I am in possession of most material facts never before them. I have given their wishes very great weight. I have even assumed that prima facie, they were right, and yet I have felt driven to overrule their resolution because I know things they did not know, things they never appreciated.

In the result I am clearly of opinion that the rights of creditors would be prejudiced by allowing the voluntary liquidation to continue, a liquidation which the voluntary liquidator says is a job he 'is not looking for' because 'it is a most troublesome one'. I am satisfied that he was right in saying that he would, as voluntary liquidator, have to come to the court again and again and in the end this would mean additional delay and expense whch would prejudice creditors and accordingly I hold the view that it is my duty to make a compulsory order, which I now do, with the addition that the liquidator be at liberty to accept any proceedings in the voluntary liquidation which seem satisfactory to him.

Notes

See also *Re Belfast Tailor's Co-Partnership Ltd* [1909] 1 IR 49 where Meredith MR in refusing to make a winding up order in respect of a company already in voluntary liquidation stated as follows:–

'Now, if ever there was an exceptional case, I have it here, in the smallness of the assets, in the independence and integrity of the liquidator and in the absence of any difficulty in the winding up. I have it also in the fact that not a single person connected with the company is accused of anything else than carrying on the business at a loss in the bona fide hope of a revival of trade.'

Notably the majority in value of the creditors were in favour of continuing the voluntary winding up. See also *Re Wicklow Textiles Ltd* (1953) 87 ILTR 72.

[19.14]   Under s 213(*f*) a company may be wound up by the court if it is just and equitable to do so.

Irish Tourist Promotions Ltd (High Court, 22 April 1974)

[The facts appear from the judgment.]

[19.15]   **Kenny J:** Irish Tourist Promotions Limited ('the company') was incorporated on 23rd of April 1970 with a nominal capital of £500 the entire of which has been issued and is fully paid. 218 of the shares are held by Mr James P Doherty ('the petitioner'), 219 by Mr Desmond Mullin and 63 by Mr Brendan Smith who has agreed to sell his shares to the petitioner but the transfer of them has not been completed.

In July 1973 the petitioner brought proceedings to have the company wound up by the court on the grounds that it was insolvent and that the petitioner and Mr Mullin, who are directors, were on such bad terms that a complete deadlock in the management of the company existed . . .

The company was formed by the petitioner and Mr Smith each of whom had fifty per cent of the issued shares. A company called The Swift Marketing Company became interested in the company and acquired a majority shareholding. The petitioner continued to manage the company. The Swift Marketing Company subsequently decided to sell their shares and the petitioner and Mr Mullin, who was introduced into the company by the petitioner bought them . . . The main business of the company has been in advertising, it arranges to get space for advertisements from commercial concerns and from race courses and hotels and then lets the space to those who want to advertise. They have also obtained the agency for an advertising device called the Rota sign which is illuminated and gives a continuous electrial show of advertisements. The company owns 66 illuminated notice boards and 65 light boxes. The light boxes are at Leopardstown Race Course. It owns a number of other machines many of which are installed in hotels, and those who wish to advertise can rent space in these.

The relationship between the petitioner and Mr Mullin began before the company was formed. Mr Mullin owned a garage where he traded under the name of the Trident Motor Co. The petitioner advanced £3,500 to him for use in the garage business which did not prosper. The petitioner says an arrangement was made that he would be repaid the loan by getting some of the second-hand cars which were part of the stock in trade of the Trident Motor Co. When the petitioner took some of the cars Mr Mullin disputed the existence of such an arrangement and began proceedings for their recovery.

Relations between Mr Mullin and the petitioner became so bad that the business of the company had almost ceased in May 1973. The petitioner had come to the conclusion that the business of the company could not be carried on and a Mr O'Byrne and he formed another advertising company called the Rota Signs International Ltd and represented that the new company were carrying on the business of the company. An injunction to restrain them making these representations was granted by this court. Mr Mullin has also commenced proceedings under s 205 of the Companies Act 1963 alleging oppression by the petitioner. These proceedings have not yet been heard.

At a meeting of the directors of the company, held on the 22nd August 1973 of which the petitioner was given notice and which was attended by Mr Mullin and by Mr Smith, the petitioner was removed from the office of chairman of the company and of joint managing director but remained a director of the company.

It has not been seriously contested by counsel for Mr Mullin and for the company that it is now insolvent. The liabilities of the company on the 15th January were £19,912 and its assets if sold will realise about £3,450. At least 30% of the liabilities are owing to Mr Mullin and in addition he has guaranteed other liabilities amounting to £4,200. The debate has been whether the company should be wound up because Mr Mullin says that though the company is insolvent, it has a reasonable prospect of making substantial profits in the future and he has submitted an estimate of these which shown that the company could have a gross income of £25,730 before payment of salaries and tax during the first twelve months of its trading if all its assets were fully utilised and if this petition were dismissed.

The result of the dispute between the petitioner and Mr Mullin about the motor cars was that the parties have not spoken to each other since May 1973 and Mr Mullin has refused to allow the petitioner to take any part in the running of the business which has not been carried on since that date. There has been a removal of some of the books and records of the company from the registered office and having regard to what has happened between the parties it is impossible that they could ever work together again. As the company is insolvent, the petitioner cannot hope to get anything out of a liquidation: indeed he admits that he will not. His motives in bringing the proceedings are that liquidation will make it possible for the new company which he has formed to get the contract for advertising from Leopardstown. There is also in his mind this hope that Mr Mullin will become liable on his guarantee for the company.

The majority of the creditors do not wish the company to be wound up. Rota Sign Ltd, the English company, to whom £2,077 is due wish the company to continue trading and objected strongly to the petitioner forming a company called Rota Signs International Ltd.

Substantial sums for wages are due to employees. Mr Mullin is now employed whole-time by another company and had made it clear that he intends to retain this position. Nobody is now employed on a whole-time basis by the company.

Mr Smith has said that he thinks that if the company could be brought back to the stage and position it was in before the dispute between the petitioner and Mr Mullin began, it could be successful.

I think that the estimate of what the company could earn, if it were to continue to trade is based upon hope and not on reasonable anticipation and that it is entirely false. Mr Mullin has made it clear that he does not intend to give up his position with Murphy & Gunn and he is determined that he will not allow the petitioner to run the business. The petitioner is still a director so no business will be transacted at any meeting at which the two of them are present. I find it impossible to believe that a company could have a turnover of £46,000 (the figure in Mr Mullin's estimate) without one whole-time employee particularly when the directors cannot meet without the risk of unruly scenes.

The company is insolvent: it cannot pay its debts. There is no prospect that it will ever trade profitably in the present circumstances and I think that it should be wound up by the court.

Before reaching this conclusion I have given consideration to the wishes of the creditors. They believe that they have a better chance of being paid if the company is not wound up as the stock-in-trade will realise little if it is sold on the open market. Despite this, I think that the company should be wound up by the court though the prospects of anyone being paid anything are remote.

Notes

For another example of a company being wound up due to deadlock between the sole shareholders/directors, see *Re Vehicle Buildings and Insulations Ltd* [1986] ILRM 239. See also *Re Murph's Restaurant Ltd* (para **14.36**). In *Re Newbridge Sanitary Steam Laundry Ltd* [1917] 1 IR 67 the managing director Llewelyn had entered into contracts with the War Office in his own name but on behalf of the company to do laundry work for the Curragh army barracks. He received £3,268 under these contracts, of which he accounted to the company for £1,038 only. In previous proceedings[1] it was suggested by the court that the balance of £32,230 was paid with the consent of his co-directors as bribes to War Office officials for securing the contracts. The court ordered him to account for this sum to the company, but he failed to do so. The majority of the shares in the company were controlled by Llewelyn and a co-director Beck. They passed a resolution in general meeting approving Llewelyn's conduct. The plaintiffs' who were minority shareholders in the company successfully petitioned to have the company wound up on the ground that it would be unjust and inequitable to allow a company which condoned and supported criminal conduct to continue in business.

A petition on the just and equitable ground can be presented by a creditor, contributory or by the company itself.

In *Re Dublin and Eastern Regional Tourism Organisation Ltd* [1990] 1 IR 579 the company had been formed to assist a statutory company, Bord Failte. When the company refused to co-operate with Bord Failte in the performance of the Board's statutory duties the court held that it was just and equitable that the company be wound up.

Closely related to s 213(*f*) is s 213(*g*) which allows any contributory to petition to have the company wound up on the grounds of oppression or disregard of members' interests.

1 *Cockburn v Newbridge Steam Laundry Ltd* [1915] 1 IR 237.

[19.16] Under s 213(*f*) the company may be wound up by the court where it has passed a special resolution to that effect in general meeting. If the directors propose to present a petition in the name of the company to have itself wound up on any other ground, they may only do so if expressly authorised by the company in general meeting.

Re Galway and Salthill Tramways Co [1918] 1 IR 62

[19.17] The directors had presented a petition in the name of the company seeking to have it wound up on the ground of inability to pay its debts. Some of the shareholders resisted the petition on the ground that it had been presented without the sanction of the general meeting.

[19.18] O'Connor MR: But the question is, had the directors power to present the petition? . . . Counsel in support of the petition maintain that they have, and they say that the authority is conferred by s 90 of the Companies Clauses Act 1845 [ie art 80 table A]. That section enacts that the directors shall have the management and superintendence of the affairs of the company and they may lawfully exercise all the powers of the company, except as to all such matters as are directed by that or the special Act to be transacted by a general meeting of the company. Counsel contend that all the powers of the company are thereby vested in the directors, except such as are specially excepted and that the power of presenting a petition for winding up is not within the exceptions. But in my opinion that part of the section which gives the directors all the powers of the company subject to the exception must be read along with the opening words giving powers of management and is merely in aid of the proper and effective exercise of such powers. If I am right in this, the powers of the directors are only powers of managing, and if the argument relied on is sound, a winding up of the company must come within the scope of its management. But the object of management is the working of the company's undertaking, while the object of a winding up is its stoppage. On this ground alone I would hold that the directors had no power to present the petition in the present case . . .

It was forcibly pointed out by Mr Dickie that by s 91 there are certain powers which can only be exercised at a general meeting. These are the choice and removal of directors, the choice of auditors, the remuneration of directors, auditors, treasurer and secretary, the determination as to the amount to be borrowed. These are important powers specially reserved to the company in general meeting and it would be a strange thing if the still more important power of putting an end to the company's business was left to the directors.

It may be that when the matter of winding up is brought before a general meeting of the company the shareholders may feel obliged to recognise that it is no longer possible to carry on the undertaking and that a winding up is inevitable. That may be so; but the possibility or even the probability of such an event does not legalize the unauthorised act of the directors.

I am, for these reasons of opinion that I ought not to make an order at present for the winding up of the company, and that the proper course to adopt is to adjourn this hearing so as to enable the directors duly to summon a meeting of the shareholders, with the object of getting authority from them to proceed on the petition. I have been asked to dismiss the petition on the ground that, as it was presented without authority an ultra vires, it cannot not legally be ratified. That is not my view. If the petition were ultra vires the company, of course, it could not be ratified; but it was quite within the powers of the company to authorize the filing of a petition on its own behalf for a winding up. That being so, it has now power to ratify the petition already filed without authority.

Notes
See also *Re Cannock Ltd* (High Court, Murphy J, 8 September 1984) noted by *McHugh* (1985) 3 ILT (ns) 93.

Effect of winding up order[1]

[19.19]   After the presentation of the petition and before the making of the winding up order, application may be made by the company or any creditor or contributory to stay or restrain proceedings against the company.[2] After the appointment of a provisional liquidator or after the winding up order has been made no action may be proceeded with or commenced against the company except with the leave of the court.[3] Any execution put in force against the company after the making of the winding up order is void.[4] A copy of the order must be delivered to the registrar forthwith[5] and within 21 days of the order.[6] The liquidator must subsequently send a copy of the statement of affairs and his comments thereon to each creditor and to the contributories.

Under s 220 of the Principal Act, the date of commencement of the winding up order is the date of the presentation of the petition, unless the company is already in voluntary liquidation, in which case it dates from the passing of the winding up resolution.

1 See *Keane* at paras **38.30–38.44**.
2 S 216 of the Principal Act.
3 Ibid s 222.
4 Ibid s 219. On execution creditors see also s 291.
5 Ibid s 221.
6 Ibid s 224. See *Keane* at paras **38.39–38.44**. For advertisement of and proceedings under the order, see *Keane* at para **38.44**.

[19.20]   Under s 218 any disposition of property of the company after the date of commencement of the winding up is void unless validated by the court. A validating order will not normally be made unless the transaction benefits the general body of creditor, or where the effect of validation would be to prefer one pre-petition creditor over another.

Re Ashmark Ltd (No 2) (High Court, 8 December 1989)

[The facts appear from the judgment]

[19.21]   **Blayney J:** This is a motion by the official liquidator of Ashmark Ltd (the company) and a cross motion by Nitra Ltd (Nitra). The liquidator seeks an order declaring void pursuant to s 218 . . . a payment of £11,898.70 made by the company to Nitra by cheque dated 7 July 1988. In its cross motion Nitra seeks an order validating the payment.

The facts giving rise to the motions are unusual. On 8 July 1988 Zanussi Ltd presented a petition for the winding up of the company. The company had for many years been the distributor of Zanussi electrical appliances and at the date of the presentation of the petition was indebted to Zanussi to the 'extent of at least two and a half million pounds. The sole shareholders in the company were John Lyons and his wife Caroline. Prior to the presentation of the petition, the company had instituted proceedings seeking to restrain Zanussi from presenting it. These proceedings were compromised on 4 July 1988 by an agreement between Zanussi, the company and the Lyons, the principal terms of which were:

(1) that Zanussi should be entitled to present forthwith a petition for the winding up of the company but would not advertise the hearing of the petition for a period of three months,
(2) the company and John Lyons undertook that the company would not trade from 4 July 1988, and
(3) the company and John and Caroline Lyons agreed to consent to the winding up of the company on the hearing of the petition.

The petition was presented on 8 July 1988 and an order winding up the company and appointing Mr Ray Jackson as official liquidator was made by Carroll J on 27 October 1988.

Nitra carried out the servicing agreement of the appliances distributed by the company. Its managing director, Noel Lambe was also a director of the company. At the beginning of July 1988 the company owed Nitra the sum of £82,873.22.

Mr Lambe had been pressing Mr Lyons for payment and on 7 July 1988 Mr Lyons gave him a cheque for £11,989.70 drawn on the company's account with Allied Irish Banks. Mr Lambe lodged the cheque on the same day to the account of Nitra in the Bank of Ireland and the records of the bank show that the cheque was credited to the account of Nitra on the same day, 7 July 1988. The cheque was paid by Allied Irish Banks on 11 July 1988. Two issues arise on the motion – first – whether the £11,898.70 was paid to Nitra prior to the commencement of the winding up; and secondly, if it were not, whether the court in the exercise of its discretion under s 218 of the Companies Act 1963 should validate the payment . . .

It was common case that, by virtue of s 220(2) of the Companies Act 1963, the winding up commenced on 8 July 1988, the date of the presentation of the petition.

On the first issue, Mr O'Donnell submitted that the drawing of the cheque by the company in favour of Nitra was a disposition. He relied strongly on the fact that the amount of the cheque had been credited to Nitra on 7 July 1988, the day before the petition was presented.

Mr Cooke in reply referred me to s 53 of the Bills of Exchange Act 1982 which provides that 'A bill, of itself, does not operate as an assignment of funds in the hands of the drawee available for the payment thereof, . . .' He submitted that, as a cheque is 'a bill of exchange drawn on a banker payable on demand' (s 73 of the Bills of Exchange Act 1882) the cheque did not itself operate as a disposition of the funds in the account of the company, so that there was no disposition until the cheque was paid by Allied Irish Banks on 11 July 1988.

In my opinion this submission is correct. It is supported by a further definition in the Bills of Exchange Act 1882, the definition in s 3(1) of a bill of exchange.

> 'A bill of exchange is an unconditional order in writing, addressed by one person to another, signed by the person giving it, requiring the person to whom it is addressed to pay on demand or at a fixed or determinable future time a sum certain in money to or to the order of a specified person or to bearer.'

The cheque was no more than an unconditional order by the company to its bankers to pay Nitra the sum named in it. Until Allied Irish Banks made the payment in accordance with the order there was no disposition. I am satisfied accordingly that the payment to Nitra was not made before the commencement of the winding up and so it is void unless I otherwise order.

The principles governing the exercise of the court's discretion were stated with great thoroughness by Buckley LJ in his judgment in the Court of Appeal in England in *In re Gray's Inn Construction Company Ltd* [1980] 1

WLR 711, a case cited with approval by Costello J in *In re Pat Ruth Ltd* [1981] ILRM 51 and by O'Hanlon J in an unreported judgment delivered on 9 June 1989 deciding another issue under s 218 in this winding up. Section 227 of the English Companies Act 1948 to which Buckley LJ refers is in exactly the same terms as s 218 of the Companies Act 1963. The passage I propose to cite is a lengthy one but it seems to me that it would be a mistake not to cite it in full as it is in the light of all the principles referred to in it that my discretion must be exercised. The passage begins at page 717D:–

'It is a basic concept of our law governing the liquidation of insolvent assets, whether in bankruptcy or under the Companies Acts, that the free assets of the insolvent at the commencement of the liquidation shall be distributed rateably amongst the insolvent's unsecured creditors as at that date. In bankruptcy this is achieved by the relation of the trustee's title to the bankrupt's assets back to the commencement of the bankruptcy. In a company's compulsory winding up it is achieved by s 227. There may be occasions however, when it would be beneficial, not only for the company but also for its unsecured creditors, that the company should be enabled to dispose of some of its property during the period after the petition has been presented but before a wind up order has been made. An obvious example is if the company has an opportunity by acting speedily to dispose of some piece of property at an exceptionally good price. Many applications for validation under the section relate to specific transactions of this kind or analogous kinds. It may sometimes be beneficial to the company and its creditors that the company should be enabled to complete a particular contract or project or to continue to carry on its business generally in its ordinary course with a view to a sale of the business as a going concern. In any such case the court has power under s 227 of the Companies Act 1948 to validate the particular contract or project or the continuance of the company's business in its ordinary course as the case may be. In considering whether to make a validating order the court must always in my opinion, do its best to ensure that the interests of the unsecured creditors will not be prejudiced. Where the application relates to a specific transaction this may be susceptible of positive proof. In a case of completion of a contract or project the proof may perhaps be less positive but nevertheless be cogent enough to satisfy the court that in the interests of the creditors the company should be enabled to proceed, or at any rate that proceeding in the manner proposed would not prejudice them in any respect. The desirability of the company being enabled to carry on its business generally is likely to be more speculative and will be likely to depend on whether a sale of the business as a going concern will probably be more beneficial than a break-up realisation of the company's assets. In each case, I think the court must necessarily carry out a balancing exercise of the kind envisaged by Templeman J in his judgment. Each case must depend on its own particular facts. Since the policy of the law is to procure so far as practicable rateable payments of the unsecured creditors' claims, it is, in my opinion, clear that the court should not vali-date any transaction or series of transactions which might result in one or more pre-liquidation creditors being paid in full at the expense of other crediors, who will only receive a dividend, in the absence of special cir-cumstances making such a course desirable in the interests of the unse-cured creditors as a body. If, for example, it were in the interests of the creditors generally that the company's business should be carried on and this could only be achieved by paying for goods already supplied to the company when the petition is presented but not yet paid for, the court might think fit in the exercise of its discretion to validate payment for those goods . . . A disposition carried out in good faith in the ordinary course of business at a time when the parties are unaware that a petition has been presented may, it seems, normally be validated by the court . . . unless there is any ground for thinking that the transaction may involve an attempt to prefer the disponee, in which case the transaction would prob-ably not be validated. In a number of cases reference has been made to the relevance of the policy of ensuring rateable distribution of the assets: *In re Civil Service and General Store Ltd* (1888) 58 LT 220; *In re Liverpool Civil Service Association* (1874) LR 5 Ch App 511 and *In re Leslie Engineers Co Ltd* [1976] 1 WLR 292. In the last mentioned case Oliver J said:–

"I think that in exercising discretion the court must keep in view the evi-dent purpose of the section which as Chitty J said in *Re Civil Service and General Store Ltd* (1888) 58 LT 220, 221, is to ensure that the creditors are paid pari passu.'

When these principles are applied to the facts of the present case I can see no grounds for validating the payment to Nitra. It was a payment of a pre-liquidation debt. Admittedly it was a payment of part of that debt only, but it seems to me that that is immaterial. The payment results in Nitra getting priority over the other creditors in respect of that part of its debt, so the rule that all the unsecured creditors be paid pari passu is broken.

Buckley LJ refers to a number of different types of transactions which may be validated such as an advantageous sale of some asset of the company, the completion of a particular contract or project or the continuation of the company's business so that it may be sold as a going concern. The payment here does not come within any of these categories. Mr O'Donnell submitted that it was a disposition carried out in good faith in the ordinary course of business at a time when the parties were unaware that a petition had been presented. In my opinion it was not. It was not carried out in the ordinary course of business because the company had agreed to cease trading as and from a date three days before the cheque was handed over; it is extremely doubtful if it was carried out in good faith since Mr Lyons had agreed three days before that Zanussi could present a petition forthwith for the winding up of the company and because of this also it could not be said that the parties were unaware that a petition had been presented since Mr Lyons must have known that if it had not already been presented it was about to be.

Mr O'Donnell submitted also that I should validate the payment on the ground that it had been beneficial to the company and he said that the averment to this effect in Mr Lambe's affidavit had not been contested by the liquidator. The averment was that Mr Lambe had been informed by Mr Desmond Peelo who had been the liquidator of the company for about six weeks from 20 September 1988, that the servicing carried out by Nitra of the appliances sold by the company was responsible for the collection of much of the company's debts. However, it is not clear that there was a definite connection between the payment and the continued servicing by Nitra. Mr Lambe merely said the Nitra 'would have seriously considered terminating at least temporarily' any further servicing if the payment had not been made. He did not say that Nitra would have terminated the servicing, and it appears that even if they had it would have been temporary only. So it seems likely that even without payment the servicing would have continued. In these circumstances it is difficult to conclude that it was the payment that was of benefit to the company. What was of benefit, if anything, was the servicing, and it is doubtful if its continuance was induced by the payment.

There can be no doubt that the interests of the unsecured creditors were prejudiced by the payment, and in my opinion the fact that it may possibly have had some beneficial effect in facilitating the collection of the company's debts is not sufficient to outweigh this and give grounds for validating the payment.

For the reasons I have given I am satisfied that the payment to Nitra should not be validated and accordingly I will make the order sought by the official liquidator and dismiss Nitra's motion.

Notes

See also *Re Ashmark Ltd (No 1)* [1990] ILRM 330; *In re Pat Ruth Ltd* [1981] ILRM 51 Costello J following Buckley LJ in *Re Gray's Inn Construction Co Ltd* [1980] 1 All ER 814, held that payments into the company's overdrawn account after the date of presentation of the petition, were dispositions within the meaning of s 218 and were therefore void. On s 218 generally see *MacCann* (1990) ILT (ns) 6, 111.

Independence of liquidator

[19.22] Under s 300A as inserted by s 146 of the 1990 Act none of the following persons are qualified for appointment as liquidator of a company:–

(*a*) a person who is, or has within 12 months of the commencement of the winding up been, an officer or servant of the company;

(*b*) except with the leave of the court, a parent, spouse, brother, sister or child of an officer of the company;

(*c*) a person who is a partner or in the employment of an officer or servant of the company;

(*d*) a person who is not qualified by virtue of this section for appointment as liquidator of another company which is the company's subsidiary or holding company or a subsidiary of that company's holding company.

References to officer or servants of the company include the company's auditor.

If a person becomes disqualified by virtue of s 300A he must thereupon vacate his office and within 14 days give notice in writing that he has vacated it by reason of such disqualification to–

(*a*) the court in a winding up;
(*b*) the company in a members' voluntary winding up;
(*c*) the company and the creditors in a creditors' voluntary winding up.

Acting as liquidator while disqualified under s 300A is an offence for which the liquidator may be fined.

[19.23] Furthermore, under s 301A as inserted by s 147 of the 1990 Act where at a meeting of creditors a resolution is passed for the appointment of a liquidator, any person who, being a creditor or representative of a creditor at the meeting, has a connection with the proposed liquidator (ie. a parent, spouse, brother, sister, child, employee or partner of the proposed liquidator) must, before the resolution is put, make the connection known to the chairman of the meeting who in turn must disclose it to the meeting. If the chairman of the meeting has any such connection he must disclose that fact together with details thereof to the meeting.

Non-compliance with this section renders the defaulter liable to a fine and the non-compliance is a factor which the court may take into account in determining whether to exercise its jurisdiction to appoint or remove a liquidator.

The official liquidator[1]

[19.24] The court having made a winding up order, then appoints a liquidator[2] known as 'the official liquidator' who is obliged within 21 days to publish notice of his appointment in *Iris Oifigiuil* and to deliver a copy of the court order appointing him to the registrar[3]. The court will also require him to give security for his appointment. Pending the hearing of the winding up petition the court may, upon application, appoint a provisional liquidator with such powers as the court determines.[4] A provisional liquidator will normally only be appointed where the company's assets are in danger and it is desired to preserve the status quo pending the hearing of the petition. Under s 228 the court fixes the official liquidator's salary, to be paid out of the company's assets; it may remove him on cause shown and fill any vacancy in his office.[5]

1 See generally *Keane* at paras **38.45–38.87**.
2 Or liquidators. See s 225 of the Principal Act.
3 S 227 of the Principal Act.
4 Ibid s 226.
5 See *Keane* at paras **38.49** & **38.50**.

[19.25]   The liquidator is an agent of the company. Although he is not a trustee, he does stand in a fiduciary position towards the company.

Re Belfast Empire Theatre of Varieties Ltd [1963] IR 41 (High Court)

[19.26]   Kenny J: While a liquidator may be a trustee for the company of which he is liquidator, he is not, in my opinion, a trustee in any sense of the word for its members or creditors. I do not think that the solution of the problem of the liquidator's position is aided by stating that he is not a trustee 'in the strict sense' for members or creditors or that he has duties corresponding to those of a trustee. The true position in my opinion, is that he is an agent with fiduciary obligations arising from his office and with statutory duties imposed on him by s 186 of the Act of 1908; if the company has not been dissolved he may be ordered to pay damages or compensation under s 215 and if the company has been dissolved he may be sued for breach of those statutory duties.

Duties of the official liquidator

[19.27]   The official liquidator is under a duty to get in and realise all the property of the company, settle a list of creditors, distribute the proceeds of sale among the creditors in the proper order of priority and distribute any surplus among the members in accordance with the terms of the s 25 contract.[1] Under s 299(1) of the Principal Act as amended by s 141 of the 1990 Act the court may require the official liquidator to report any criminal conduct in relation to the company to the DPP, to give him access to and right to inspect and take copies of all relevant documents which the DPP may reasonably require. The liquidator must also give the DPP all reasonable assistance in connection with any ensuing prosecution.[2]

1 See *Keane* at para **38.52–38.53**. See also *Re Whiterock Quarries Ltd* [1933] IR 363, 366.
2 A similar duty applies to voluntary liquidations.

[19.28]   The official liquidator is under a duty when realising the property of the company to obtain the best possible price.

Van Hool McArdle Ltd v Rohan Industrial Estates Ltd [1980] IR 237 (Supreme Court)

[The facts appear from the judgment.]

[19.29]   Kenny J: Van Hool McArdle Ltd (the company) was incorporated in the State. By order made on the 10th April 1978 it was ordered to be wound up by the court and Mr John Donnelly was appointed to be the official liquidator. The company is insolvent, it owes large sums of money which are secured by mortgages and charges and it is unlikely that its unsecured creditors will be paid anything. One of its principal assets is 20 acres of land at Irishtown . . . In July 1979 the liquidator offered these lands for sale by tender but was advised not to accept any of the offers received; he subsequently entered into negotiations with Rohan Industrial Estates Ltd and with Van Hool NV (a company incorporated outside the State) for the sale of the lands. On the 4th September 1979 Van Hool offered £750,000 to the liquidator for the lands subject to getting exchange control permission and [Land Commission] consent under s 45 of the Land Act of 1965. The liquidator thought tht Van Hool were unlikely to get both permissions and he decided to sell the lands to Rohan for £730,000 subject to court consent. This offer was open for acceptance for one day only. On the 7th September a written contract between the liquidator and Rohan for the sale of the lands was made.

Clause c of the special conditions provided:– 'The sale to the purchaser shall be subject to and conditional upon the consent of the High Court thereto being obtained and if such consent shall not have been obtained on or before 31st October 1979, either party hereto may by notice in writing to the other determine this contract . . . the liquidator shall use his best endeavours to obtain the consent of the court to this sale.'

On the 10th September the liquidator received from Van Hool an offer of £835,000 plus a contribution of £15,000 to his costs. On the 12th September the liquidator applied to the High Court for its consent to the sale to Rohan and the judge adjourned the matter to the 28th September. On the 25th September the liquidator received from Van Hool's solicitors copies of the exchange control permission and of the consent under s 45 of the Act of 1965. When the matter came before the judge on 28th September he was told of Van Hool's offer of £835,000 but he decided to authorise the liquidator to accept Rohan's offer. The judge did so on the ground that what he had to consider was whether the contract of the 7th September 1979 was a proper one for the liquidator to have made; the judge considered that, if it was, he should give his consent to the sale of the lands to Rohan.

I wish to state as emphatically as I can that this is not the principle to be applied when an application is made for consent to a sale or approval of a sale in a court liquidation. The cases which are relied on to support the contention which found favour with the judge are *In re Bartlett, Newman v Hook; Munster Bank v Munster Motor Co* [1922] 1 IR 15; *In re Hibernian Transport Cos Ltd* [1972] IR 190. Those cases deal with an entirely different matter and are not authorities for the proposition advanced. Each of them relates to an application to discharge a court order, which had approved a sale, because a higher bid was received after the court's sanction had been given. In all three of them the court, having approved the sale had to keep faith with the purchaser. In the instant case the High Court had not given its consent to the sale when Van Hool's offer of £850,000 was received.

The primary duty of the court and of the liquidator in a court winding up is to get the maximum price for the assets. A system under which a bid of £730,000 is accepted when one of £850,000 has been made would bring the court into well-deserved ridicule.

Counsel for the liquidator said that the court was concerned only with the good faith of his client and that, if he had made the contract honestly, it should be approved. I dissent from this argument. I have no doubt that the liquidator acted with the utmost good faith. However, on the critical date (the 28th September 1979) the High Court could not give its consent to the sale to Rohan when a much higher offer had been made. In my opinion, the order of the High Court should be set aside and this court should refuse to give its consent to the Rohan contract of the 7th September 1979. I think that the best course to adopt is to give liberty to Rohan and to Van Hool to make tenders to the court for the lands within one week from this date.

O'Higgins CJ delivered a concurring judgment. Parke J concurred.

Notes

See also *Re Brook Cottage* [1976] NI 78 where a shareholder and director of a company successfully applied for an order restraining the liquidator from signing a contract for the sale of company property below the best possible price. In *Re Irish Commercial Society Ltd* (High Court, 10 September 1986) O'Hanlon J refused to sanction the compromise of an action against six defendants, the terms of which compromise would have precluded the liquidator from pursuing the present or any other action against all or any of the defendants. According to O'Hanlon J there was prima facie evidence to support a second action against the first defendant on separate grounds. The compromise therefore, was refused as not being made on the best possible terms for the company.

Powers of the official liquidator

[19.30]   The main powers of the liquidator are set out in s 231 of the Principal Act[1] and are divided into powers which may be used without sanction and powers the exercise of which require the sanction either of the court or the committee of inspection (if any). The committee of inspection, if formed, is made up of creditors and contributories.[2] Notably, however, s 231(3) provides that regardless of whether the powers are exercisable with or without sanction, the liquidator is subject to the control of the court in exercising the powers. Any creditor or contributory can apply to the court in relation to the official liquidator's exercise of these powers.

1 Ibid at paras **38.52** and **38.53**.
2 Ibid at para **38.55**.

[19.31]   The appointment of a provisional liquidator who has been given liberty by the court to carry on business of the company does not operate to determine the contracts of employment of the company's employees. A winding up order, however, is presumed to act as an automatic dismissal.

Donnelly v Gleeson (High Court, 11 July 1978)

[The facts appear from the judgment.]

[19.32]   Hamilton J: The respondents in this case are constituent members of the Employment Appeals Tribunal (hereinafter referred to as 'the tribunal') which sat on the 23rd day of November 1977 to hear appeals brought by employees and ex-employees of Britain Manufacturing Limited (hereinafter called 'the company') a company in liquidation and of which the appellant was appointed official liquidator by the court on the 20th day of June 1977, against the decision of the appellant to refuse such employees and ex-employees payment pursuant to the provisions of the Redundancy Payments Act 1967–1971 and the Minimum Terms of Notice and Employment Act 1973.

By order of the court dated the 26th day of May 1977 the appellant herein had been appointed provisional liquidator of the company and had been given liberty by the court:

(*a*) to continue existing negotiations for the sale of certain assets of the company;

(*b*) to carry on the business of the company so far as might be necessary for the beneficial winding up of thereof;

(*c*) to appoint a solicitor to assist him in the performance of his duties; and

(*d*) to convene meetings of members and creditors of the company.

The order that the company be wound up pursuant to the provisions of the Companies Act 1963 was made on the 20th day of June 1977.

The tribunal found as a matter of law that the appointment of the appellant as provisional liquidator of the company did not automatically determine the contracts of employment with the company of the aforesaid employees and ex-employees . . . The tribunal then went onto to 'find that these employees who continued in employment for varying periods after the 26th day of May 1977 and who were subsequently dismissed are entitled to compensation under the Minimum Notice and Terms of Employment Act 1973 based on continuous service from their respective dates of commencement to the date their employment finally terminated at their agreed out going wages. They may also be entitled to further payments under the Redundancy Payments Act in respect of their period in continuous service' . . .

It is quite clear that the primary matter for determination by me is whether the appointment by the court of the appellant as provisional liquidator of the company automatically determined the contracts of all employees of the company.

In support of his submission that it did Mr Barron on behalf of the appellant relied on *Chapman's* case LR 1 Eq Rep 346 and *In re Oriental Bank Corporation MacDowell's* case 32 Ch 366 and referred to in *Ex parte Harding* LR Eq 341 . . .

It seems to me from a consideration of these three cases . . . that their effect is:–

(*a*) a court order for the winding up of a company is in the ordinary case deemed to be a discharge of the company's servants;
(*b*) a servant can however be kept on in the same terms as his original contract by being specifically requested to do so; and
(*c*) the effect of a winding up order as a notice of discharge can be waived.

These cases also appear to me to require that there be an actual order for the winding up of the company and that this order is the discharge of the company's servants.

It is true that s 220(2) of the Companies Act 1963 provided that 'the winding up of a company by the court shall be deemed to commence at the time of the presentation of the petition for the winding up.'

The petition for the winding up of the company was presented on the 28th day of May 1977 and the appellant was on that day given inter alia, liberty to carry on the business of the company so far as may be necessary for the beneficial winding up thereof and to continue existing negotiations for the sale of certain assets of the company.In my opinion the appointment of a provisional liquidator who has whatever the purpose and who does in fact carry on the business of the company cannot and does not operate to determine the contracts of employment of the employees of the company.

It is different from an order for the winding up of a company. An order for the winding up of a company is notice of discharge to all persons in the employment of the company.

An order for the appointment of a provisional liquidator who has been given liberty to carry on business cannot amount to notice of discharge to all the persons in the employment of the company.

Such an order and its effect on the contracts of employment of the servants of the company must be and is completely different to an order for the winding up of the company.

Consequently I am satisfied that the appointment of a provisional liquidator who has been given such liberty does not automatically determine the contracts of all employees of the company.

Notes
See *Re Evanhenry Ltd* (High Court Murphy J, 15 May 1986) where it was held that the liquidator had, in respect of two employees, waived the effect of a winding up order as a notice of discharge.

In *Re Forster & Co Ltd, ex p Schamam* (1887–88) 19 LR Ir 240 it was held that a resolution to wind up a company acted as an automatic dismissal of its employees. Chatterton VC stated that 'the resolution or order for winding up operates in law as notice of discharge to the company's servants. The liquidator is in the same position as any other employer of labour, who is bound to give notice of dismissal or compensation in lieu of such notice. The resolution operates as notice and takes effect from the expiration of the

period corresponding with the length of notice to which the person is entitled
. . . and I concur in the observations of Sir W Page Wood VC in *Ex Parte
Harding* LR 3 Eq 341 on this point, that circumstances may exist which
would amount to a waiver of the notice of discharge worked by the resolution or order or which would be evidence of a new agreement; and if such a
new agreement could be implied the terms of the old employment would be
imported into it.'

As regards the effect of the appointment of the liquidator on the powers of
the directors, see *Re Union Accident Insurance Co Ltd* [1972] 1 All ER
1105, 1113 where Plowman J stated as follows:–

> 'It is of course well settled that on a winding up the board of directors of a
> company become *functus officio* and its powers are assumed by the liqui-
> dator and my attention was drawn to *Re Mawcon Ltd* [1969] 1 All ER
> 118, 192 where Pennycuick J stated in effect that the appointment of a
> provisional liquidator had the same result. No doubt that is so, but it is
> common ground that notwithstanding the appointment of the provisional
> liquidator the board has some residuary powers, for example it can
> unquestionably instruct solicitors and counsel to oppose the current
> petition and if a winding up order is made, to appeal against that order.'

The voluntary liquidator

[19.33] In a members voluntary winding up the liquidator is appointed by
the company in general meeting which also fixes his remuneration. Upon
appointment the powers of the directors cease, except so far as sanctioned
by the company in general meeting or by the liquidator[1]. Any vacancies in
the office of liquidator are also filled by the company in general meeting.[2] If
the liquidator forms the opinion that the company will not be able to pay its
debts within the period specified in the statutory declaration of solvency he
must immediately summon in the prescribed manner a creditors' meeting
and lay before it a statement of the company's assets and liabilities.[3]

In a creditors voluntary winding up the members and the creditors may at
their respective meetings each nominate persons to act as liquidator. Where
different persons are nominated, the creditors nominee is appointed.[4] The
creditors may also at their first or any subsequent meeting appoint up to five
of their number to act as a 'committee of inspection' with supervisionary
powers regarding the conduct of the liquidation.[5] It is the committee of
inspection of (if there is no such committee) the creditors in general meeting
who fix the liquidator's remuneration in a creditors voluntary winding up.[6]

Under s 276A as inserted by s 133 of the 1990 Act the appointment of a
voluntary liquidator is of no effect unless the person nominated has prior to
his appointment, signified his written consent to the appointment. Furthermore the chairman of the meeting at which the liquidator is appointed must
notify him of his appointment unless he or his representative was present at
the meeting. If a vacancy occurs in the office of liquidator in a creditors'

voluntary winding up, it may be filled by the creditors, unless the liquidator had previously been appointed by or at the direction of the court.[7] Under s 277 the voluntary liquidator may be removed for cause shown and appoint a replacement.

1 S 258 of the Principal Act.
2 Ibid s 259. A contributory or surviving joint liquidator may convene the meeting.
3 S 261 of the Principal Act as substituted by s 129 of the 1990 Act. S 264 also provides that the creditors voluntary winding up provisions relates to annual and final meetings.
4 S 267. However, within 14 days of the creditors' nomination any director, member or creditor can apply for an order that the company's nominee be appointed instead.
5 Ibid s 268. See also *Keane* at para **38.55**.
6 Ibid s 269. See also *Keane* at para **38.49**.
7 Ibid s 270.

[**19.34**]   Under s 276 the voluntary liquidator may exercise a wider range of powers without sanction than the official liquidator. He may exercise all the powers set out in s 231(1) and (2) and only the power to pay any class of creditors in full or make compromises require sanction. In a members voluntary winding up sanction is by special resolution of the company in general meeting. In a creditors voluntary winding up sanction comes from the court or the committee of inspection or (if there is no committee) a meeting of the creditors. He may also exercise the power of the court to settle lists of contributories, make calls and summon general meetings of the company.[1]

S 131 of the 1990 Act provides where a liquidator has been nominated by the company in a creditors' voluntary winding up he cannot exercise the powers conferred on him by s 276, except with sanction of the court, during the interim period before the holding of the creditors' meeting. However, he may during this interim period:

(*a*) take into his custody or under his control all the property to which the company is or appears to be entitled;
(*b*) dispose of perishable goods and other goods the value of which is likely to diminish if they are not immediately disposed of;
(*c*) do such other things as may be necessary for the protection of the company's assets.

He must attend the creditors' meeting and report on any exercise by him of his powers. If the company fails to convene the creditors' meeting in the prescribed manner or at all, or if the directors fail to lay a statement of affairs before or to have a member of the board preside at the meeting, the liquidator must, within seven days of his nomination by the company or of becoming aware of the default (whichever is later), apply to the court for directions as to how the default is to be remedied.

The liquidator is obliged to summon general meetings of the company annually during the course of the liquidation[2] and in the case of a creditors voluntary winding up he must also summon annual creditors' meetings.[3]

1 Ibid s 276. See *Keane* at para **38.56–38.58**.
2 Ibid s 262.
3 Ibid s 272.

Powers of court in a compulsory winding up

[19.35]   Ss 234 to 249 of the Principal Act set out various powers exercisable by the court in a compulsory winding up. Many such powers will be exercised only upon application by the official liquidator. Among the courts' powers are the following:–

(*a*) Power to annul or stay the winding up order.[1]

(*b*) Power to settle a list of contributories.[2]

(*c*) Power to order any contributory, trustee, receiver, banker, agent or officer of the company to deliver up to the liquidator 'any money, property or books and papers . . . to which the company is prima facie entitled'.[3]

(*d*) Power to make calls.[4]

(*e*) Power to exclude creditors from any distribution in the liquidation if they fail to prove their debts within a time fixed by the court.[5]

(*f*) Power to 'adjust the rights of contributories among themselves and distribute any surplus among the persons entitled thereto'.[6]

(*g*) Power to order such inspection as it thinks just of the company's books and papers by creditors and contributories.[7]

(*h*) Power to order the arrest of absconding contributories.[8]

(*i*) Power, when the liquidation has been completed, to order the dissolution of the company.[9]

1 S 234 of the Principal Act.
2 Ibid s 235.
3 Ibid s 236.
4 Ibid s 239.
5 Ibid s 241.
6 Ibid s 242.
7 Ibid s 243.
8 Ibid s 247.
9 Ibid s 249.

Section 245 examination

[19.36]   Under s 245 as substituted by s 126 of the 1990 Act the court may summon before it for examination on oath 'any officer of the company or person known or suspected to have in his possession any property of the company or supposed to be indebted to the company, or any person whom the court deems capable of giving information relating to the promotion, formation, trade, dealings, affairs of property of the company'. The person's answers may be reduced to writing and he may be required to sign them. He may be required to produce in court any books and papers in his custody relating to the company. The court may, before the examination takes place, require the person to place before it a statement of any transactions between him and the company of a type or class which the court may specify. If, in the opinion of the court, it is just and equitable to do so, it court may direct that the costs of the examination be paid by the person examined.

Under s 245A as inserted by s 127 of the 1990 Act if in the course of the examination it appears that the person is indebted to the company or has in his possession or control any money, property or books and papers of the company, the court may order him to pay to the liquidator all or part of the debt or to hand over to the liquidator all or any of the money, property, books and papers.'

Furthermore, under s 244A as inserted by s 125 of the 1990 Act, where a provisional liquidator has been appointed or the company is in compulsory winding up or creditors voluntary winding up, no person may claim a lien on books, documents, deeds, instruments, etc of the company, although the production of such books, etc to the liquidator whether pursuant to s 245 or otherwise, is without prejudice to any charge or mortgage or pledge created by the deposit of any documents or papers with the person.

[19.37]   In an examination under s 245 it is provided that the person being examined is not entitled to refuse to answer any question put to him on the ground that his answer might incriminate himself. However, none of his answers are admissible against him in any civil or criminal proceedings other than the winding up proceedings, except in the case of criminal proceedings for perjury in respect of such answers. Proceedings in the course of the winding up are not 'other proceedings'.

Re Aluminium Fabricators Ltd [1984] ILRM 399 (High Court)

[The facts appear from the judgment]

[19.38]   **O'Hanlon J:** The liquidator in the course of the proceedings to wind up the company, Aluminium Fabricators Ltd has brought an application under ss 297 and 298 of the Companies Act 1963 seeking to impose personal responsibility on former directors of the company, without limitation of liability, for debts and liabilities of the company and to compel payment by them of moneys or restoration of property of the company, as the court thinks just.

In the present application under the said sections of the Act, the liquidator claims to be entitled to use in evidence against the said persons the transcript of evidence on oath taken from them in the course of their examination pursuant to an order made by the court in these winding up proceedings, under the provisions of s 245 of the Companies Act 1963.

Counsel for the directors have contended that the transcript of such evidence is not admissible in evidence in relation to the application brought under the provisions of ss 297 and 298 of the Act and they rely in particular, on the provisions of [s 245(6)] of the Act, which reads as follows:–

(6) A person who is examined under this section shall not be entitled to refuse to answer any question put to him on the ground that his answer might incriminate him but none of the answers of such person shall be admissible in evidence against him in any other proceedings civil or criminal, except in the case of any criminal proceedings for perjury in respect of any such answer.

It is submitted on behalf of the directors that the words 'in any other proceedings' include such proceedings as have now been brought by the liquidator under the provisions of ss 297 and 298 of the Act.

The provisions of [s 245(6)] . . . preclude the use of the transcript of evidence taken under s 245 of the Act 'in any other proceedings' and thereby inferentially appear to me to recognise that it is legitimate and permissible to use it in some proceedings. What are these proceedings in which it is permissible to admit the answers of the person who has been examined under s 245 of the Act in evidence against him? The entire of part VI (ii) of the Act, including s 245 applies to winding up by the court and many of the remaining provisions of part VI including ss 297 and 298 apply equally to winding up by the court and to voluntary winding up.

I am of opinion that the proceedings in which it is permissible to admit in evidence the answers given by persons examined under s 245 of the Act are the proceedings for the winding up of the company by the court, in the course of which the liquidator has successfully applied to the court for the exercise of the powers vested in it under s 245 of the Act.

I do not regard the provisions of s 245 as creating a new and separate set of proceedings for the purpose of which the answers of the person examined are to be admissible against him in evidence. The section does not state for what purpose the answers may be used or provide that anything is to happen in consequence of the examination, whether the answers given by him have been satisfactory or unsatisfactory, and whether or not they disclose a pattern of fraud or other irregularities in relation to the promotion, formation, trade, dealings, affairs or property of the company.

In my opinion the examination under s 245 merely forms part of the winding up proceedings and the answers given in the course of such examination may be used for the purposes of any application to the court in the course of such proceedings but not in any other proceedings, civil or criminal save in the case of criminal proceedings for perjury . . . In the preliminary matter which has arisen for determination in relation to the present application to the court under ss 297 and 298 of the act I hold that the liquidator is entitled to have admitted in evidence against the two directors concerned, the answers given by them in the course of their examination under the provisions of s 245 of the Act.

Notes

In *Irish Commercial Society Ltd v Plunkett* [1986] ILRM 624 Costello J held that even though answers given by a person under s 245 may not be admissible in evidence against him outside of liquidation proceedings, they could be used in evidence against other parties.

Under O 39 r 4 the s 245 examination may be heard before a judge or any officer of the court. Normally it is held before the Master of the High Court. The court may if it thinks fit, order all or part of an examination under s 245 to be held in camera: *Re Redbreast Preserving Co Ltd* (1957) 91 ILTR 12; cf *Re R Ltd* [1989] ILRM 757. Failure, without reasonable excuse, to attend the examination is punishable as contempt of court. If the person to be examined has absconded or is about to abscond he may be arrested and his books documents and movable property may be seized pending the examination.

Powers of court in a voluntary winding up

[19.39]   Under s 280 the liquidator or any creditor or contributory may apply to the court to determine any question arising in the winding up or to exercise any of the powers available to it in a compulsory winding up.[1] Such powers may be exercised if the court considers it just and beneficial to do so. See for example *Re Oakthorpe Holdings Ltd* [1988] ILRM 62.

1 See *Keane* at paras **38.16–38.18**.

Power to order contribution from related company

[19.40]   Under s 138 of the 1990 Act it is provided that 'On the application of the liquidator or any creditor or contributory of any company that is being wound up, the court, if it is satisfied that it is just and equitable to do so, may order that any company that is or has been related to the company being wound up shall pay to the liquidator of that company an amount equivalent to the whole or part of all or any of the debts provable in that winding up. Any order under this section may be made on such terms and conditions as the court thinks fit.'

Where the application is by a creditor or creditors, they must be owed individually or in aggregate, at least £10,000. This is presumably to prevent frivolous applications by creditors with small debts.

[19.41]   In deciding whether it is just and equitable to make an order the court is to have regard to the extent to which the related company took part in the management of the company being wound up and the conduct of the related company towards creditors of the company being wound up. It will also have to have regard to the effect such order would be likely to have on the creditors of the related company. Notably, however, no order to contribute can be made unless the court is satisfied that the circumstances that gave rise to the winding up of the company are attributable to the acts or omissions of the related company.

It shall not be just and equitable to make an order to contribute if the only ground for making it is that the companies are related or that the creditors of the company being wound up have relied on the fact that another company is or has been related to that company.

[19.42]   For the purposes of the Companies Acts one company is related to another if–

(*a*) that other company is its holding company or subsidiary; or

(*b*) more than half in nominal value of its equity share capital is held by the other company and companies related to that other company (whether directly or indirectly, but other than in a fiduciary capacity); or

(*c*) more than half in nominal value of the equity share capital of each of them is held be members of the other (whether directly or indirectly, but other than in a fiduciary capacity); or

(*d*) that other company or a company or companies related to that other company or that other company together with a company or companies related to it are entitled to exercise or control the exercise of more than one half of the voting power at any general meeting of the company; or

(*e*) the businesses of the companies have been so carried on that the separate businesses of each company, or a substantial part thereof, is not readily identifiable; or

(*f*) there is another company to which both companies are related.

Pooling of assets of related companies

[19.43]   Under s 141 of the 1990 Act where two or more related companies are being wound up the court may, on the application of the liquidator of any of the companies, order that they are to be partially or completely wound up together as if they were one company, provided it is satisfied that it is just and equitable to do so. The court may make the order subject to such terms and conditions as it thinks fit. In deciding the terms and conditions the court is to have particular regard to the interests of those persons who are members of some, but not all, of the companies.

The application may be made at the same time as or at any time subsequent to the presentation of a winding up petition in respect of any of the companies. Nonetheless, the section would also seem to apply to related companies which are in voluntary liquidation instead.

In deciding whether it is just and equitable to make the order, the court is to have regard

(*a*) to the extent to which any of the companies took part in the management of any of the other companies;

(*b*) the conduct of any of the companies towards the creditors of any of the other companies;

(*c*) the extent to which the circumstances that gave rise to the winding up of any of the companies are attributable to the actions or omissions of any of the other companies;

(*d*) the extent to which the businesses of the companies have been intermingled.

However, it is not just and equitable to make the order if the only ground for so doing is that the companies are related or that the creditors of the company being wound up have relied on the fact that the companies are or have been related.

In making an order that the companies be wound up together the court may make consequential orders, including orders for the removal or appointment of liquidators in relation to one or more of the companies.

The order does not affect the rights of secured creditors. Unless the court orders otherwise, the claims of all unsecured creditors of the companies rank equally among themselves. Furthermore, preferential creditors of one company to the extent that their claims have not been met, may prove in the liquidation of the related company, after the claims of the holders of any floating charges but before the ordinary unsecured creditors.

Chapter 20

WINDING UP: PART II

Administration of assets

[20.01]   Before the proceeds of sale of the company's assets may be distributed amongst its creditors by the liquidator, it is necessary first to pay the costs and expenses of the winding up. In a winding up by the court such costs and expenses are listed in order of priority in O 74 r 128 of the Rules of the Superior Courts, although s 244 of the Principal Act also provides that the court may 'in the event of the assets being insufficient to satisfy the liabilities, make an order as to the payment out of the assets of the costs, charges and expenses incurred in the winding up in such order of priority as the court thinks just.'

S 281 provides that in a voluntary winding up all 'costs, charges and expenses properly incurred . . ., including the remuneration of the liquidator shall be payable out of the assets of the company in priority to all other claims.' In practice although it is not obligatory to do so, the order of priority of costs and expenses for a compulsory winding up will be used as a guide to the priority of costs and expenses for the voluntary winding up.

Rules of the Superior Courts, O 74 r 128

[20.02]   (1) The assets of a company in a winding up by the court remaining after payment of the fees and expenses properly incurred in preserving, realising or getting in the assets, including where the company has previously commenced to be wound up voluntarily such remuneration, costs and expenses as the court may allow to a liquidator appointed in such voluntary winding up, shall, subject to any order of the court be liable to the following payments which shall be made in the following order of priority, namely:

First – The costs of the petition, including the costs of any person appearing on the petition whose costs are allowed by the court.

Next – The costs and expenses of any person who makes or concurs in making the company's statement of affairs.

Next – The necessary disbursements of the official liquidator other than expenses properly incurred in preserving, realising or getting in the assets hereinbefore provided for.

Next – The costs payable to the solicitor for the official liquidator.
Next – The remuneration of the official liquidator.
Next – The out of pocket expenses necessarily incurred by the committee of inspection (if any).

(2) No payments in respect of bills of costs, charges or expenses of solicitors, accountants, auctioneers, brokers or other persons, other than payments for costs, charges or expenses fixed or allowed by the court shall be allowed out of the assets of the company unless they have been duly fixed and allowed by the examiner or the taxing master as the case may be.

[20.03] At common law corporation tax on a capital gain incurred as a result of the disposal of an asset of the company by the official liquidator is neither an expense 'properly incurred in preserving, realising or getting in the assets' or a 'necessary disbursement of the official liquidator' within the meaning of O 74 r 128.

Re Van Hool McArdle Ltd; Revenue Commissioners v Donnelly [1983]
ILRM 329 (Supreme Court)

[The facts appear from the judgment].

[20.04] **O'Higgins CJ:** The respondent in this appeal is the official liquidator of Van Hool McArdle Ltd. In the course of the liquidation he sold certain properties which were subject to incumbrances. A liability was thereby incurred for corporation tax on chargeable gains accrued on that sale under the Capital Gains Tax Act 1975. The respondent thereupon brought a motion in the High Court before Carroll J seeking certain directions which included the following:

(1) Whether or not capital gains tax payable in relation to the sale is an 'expense' incurred in the realisation of an asset within the meaning of r 129 of O 77 of the Rules of the Superior Courts which relate to winding up.
(2) If it is, can it be deducted from the proceeds of sale payable to the mortgagees?
(3) Is the tax 'a necessary disbursement' of the liquidator under the third heading listed in r 129
[His Lordship then quoted r 129 which is the predecessor of O 74 r 128 of RSC (1986)]

The first question asked whether the tax could be regarded as covered by expenses properly incurred in preserving, realising or getting in the assets', which are contained in the opening paragraph of the rule. Carroll J answered this question in the negative. No appeal has been taken against this decision not do I think that any such appeal could succeed. By reason of this answer the second question did not arise.

The third question asked whether the tax was a necessary disbursement of the official liquidator within the meaning of the third paragraph. Carroll J answered this question in the negative. She did so because she was of the opinion that corporation tax was entitled to priority payment only in accordance with its given priority as an 'assessed tax' under s 285(2)(ii) of the Companies Act 1963 (being a priority it was given under the Capital Gains Tax Act). This priority is given however, only in relation to assessed taxes which are 'assessed on the company up to the 5th April next before' the winding up.

As this tax was not so assessed but arose after the winding up, it did not qualify for priority payment under s 285(2)(ii). Accordingly, in Carroll J's view, to give it priority under r 129 would be to make the rule dominate the section. Carroll J may well be correct in this view but I do not think it necessary to base my judgment on this reasoning.

In my view, r 129 as its heading indicates, is intended to deal with costs and expenses, and not with the liabilities of the company. Each of the paragraphs deals with either costs or expenses incurred by persons involved in the liquidation. The third paragraph must have the same meaning since the 'necessary disbursements' there referred to are expressed to be 'other than expenses properly incurred for preserving, realising or getting in the assets hereinbefore provided for'. Such must, therefore be expenses of some other kind. I would imagine that what was intended were expenses such as necessary maintenance of buildings or wages for caretaking or for other purposes. In my view, such could not include a liability of the company for corporation tax. I agree, therefore that the third question should be answered in the negative as it was so answered by Carroll J but for the reasons I have indicated, I would dismiss this appeal.

Henchy and Hederman JJ concurred.

Notes

This decision should now be read in the light of s 56 of the Finance Act 1983 which makes corporation tax on chargeable gains in the liquidation a 'necessary disbursement' of the liquidation.

[20.05] Corporation tax on income arising to the company after the commencement of the compulsory winding up is neither a 'necessary disbursement' of the official liquidator nor is it a provable debt in the liquidation.

Re Hibernian Transport Companies Ltd, Palgrave Murphy Ltd and Palgrave Murphy (Carrier) Ltd [1984] ILRM 583 (High Court)

[20.06] Three companies had gone into liquidation 13 years previously. The liquidator sought directions from the court of 4 questions:

(1) Whether income tax, corporation profits tax and corporation tax were chargeable on deposit interest earned after the commencement of the winding up; and if so

(2) was such tax a necessary disbursement of the official liquidator under O 74 r 128;

(3) was it a preferential claim under s 285 of the Principal Act; or

(4) was it an unsecured debt in the winding up.

[20.07] **Costello J:** The court is asked firstly whether deposit interest earned from time to time by the money in the hands of the official liquidator is liable to (*a*) income tax, (*b*) corporation profit tax and (*c*) corporation tax. Mr Hamill who appeared for the liquidator agrees that this question must be answered in the affirmative . . . The real problem posed by the motion is companies' admitted liability is to be discharged. Question (2) asks whether the tax payable in respect of the deposit interest is a 'necessary disbursement' of the official liquidator under the third heading of rule 129(1) of the 1966 Winding Up Rules (SI No 28 of 1966). The liquidator says that it is not, and that the Supreme Court has so decided. Mr Cooke on the Revenue Commissioners' behalf, asks me to hold that it should be so regarded. He accepts that he must fail in this court if I were to hold that the decision of the Supreme Court covers the point . . .

The *Van Hool McArdle* case was concerned with a liability for corporation tax on chargeable gains accruing on the sale of certain properties which arose by virtue of the Capital Gains Tax Act 1976. The Supreme Court held that rule 129 was intended to deal with costs and expenses and not with the liabilities of the company and that the third heading of the rule refers to 'expenses of some kind' and 'did not include a liability of the company for corporation tax'. In the present case the liability of the three companies with which I am concerned did not arise from the sale of an asset, but from interest earned on deposits. But this cannot affect the situation. It is immaterial whether the liability of the company is for income tax, corporation profits tax, corporation tax – in the light of the Supreme Court decision I cannot hold that such liability can properly be regarded as 'necessary disbursements' within the meaning of rule 129.

Mr Cooke's submission was based on the operation of the provision of the Corporation Tax Act 1976 which he said had the effect of placing a legal obligation on the company to make the payment. This section can be taken in conjunction with s 244 of the Companies Act 1963 under which the court may make an order for payment out of the assets of an insolvent company of the 'costs, charges and expenses' incurred in the winding up in such priority as it thinks just. The effect of the two sections he urges is to permit rule 129 to be interpreted in the way he suggests, but in the light of the very specific interpretation of the Supreme Court I cannot hold that the liability of the companies in this case falls to be paid in the priority given by rule 129. I must answer question (2) therefore in the negative.

I should add that it was not argued that I should amend the motion and raise a question as to whether apart from rule 129 the court could make an order for the payment of the tax under s 244 of the Act (on the basis that the liability could be regarded as a 'charge' within the meaning of the section) and the court could independently of the rules order its payment in the winding up. The revenue's case was based fairly and squarely on the rules.

The third question arises if I answer question (1) in the affirmative and question (2) in the negative, as I have done. It asks whether in such an event the tax payable ranks as a preferential payment under s 285 of the Companies Act 1963. Clearly it does not and Mr Cooke has not sought to argue otherwise. The section gives priority to taxes due before the winding up and as these taxes arose from interest accrued since the winding up it is clearly of no avail to the revenue. This question must, therefore, be answered in the negative.

The fourth and last question is this: 'If the answer to question 1 is in the affirmative and the answers to questions 2 and 3 are each in the negative' (as has in fact been the result) 'does any tax payable on such deposit interest rank as an unsecured debt in the winding up of the company?' The answer to this question (startling and all as it may seem) must be 'no'. The liquidator's duty is very clear . . . He must, having made the payments authorised by rule 129 pay off the creditors in the order and in the manner provided for in the Act and distribute any surplus assets (an academic point in this case) amongst the contributories. There is no provision for the payment of a debt due to the revenue for liability to tax incurred in the post liquidation period. The situation (an unsatisfactory one from the revenue's point of view) has been remedied by s 56 of the Finance Act 1983, but the section has no retroactive effect and does not avail the revenue in the present case.

The result must be that if the revenue cannot recover the tax due under rule 129 although there is a statutory obligation on the company to pay the tax there are no assets out of which it can be paid because they will have been used as required by the provisions of the Companies Act to pay other creditors (when a company is insolvent) and other creditors and the contributories (when the company is solvent).

Notes

Cf *Re National Building and Land Co* (1885–86) 15 LR Ir 47, 49 where Chatterton VC stated that there is a distinction between 'debts and liabilities of the company existing at the commencement of the winding up which must be proved for and paid pari passu, and must abate rateably in case the assets of the company prove insufficient, and debts and liabilities which arise only in the course of the liquidation and as incidental to it, which must be paid before any distribution of the assets.

[20.08] Corporation tax on income arising to the company after the commencement of a voluntary winding up is a cost charge or expense properly incurred in the liquidation within the meaning of s 281 of the Principal Act.

Re A Noyek & Sons Ltd; Burns v Hearne [1989] ILRM 155 (Supreme Court)

[20.09] The company, which was in a members voluntary winding up was assessed to corporation tax on deposit interest accruing after the commencement of the liquidation. The liquidator conceded that the interest was liable to as assessment to corporation tax but applied for a determination as to whether such tax was 'a cost charge or expense properly incurred in the winding up' within the meaning of s 281 of the Principal Act. The Supreme Court (affirming the decision of Carroll J) held that the tax was such a 'cost, charge or expense'.

[20.10] **Griffin J:** In *Re Van Hool McArdle Ltd* (para **20.04**) the official liquidator in the course of the winding up sold certain properties of the company and liability was thereby incurred for corporation tax under the Corporation Tax Act 1976. The question for decision was whether that tax was 'a necessary disbursement' of the official liquidator. O'Higgins CJ delivering the judgment of this court held that rule 129 as the heading indicates is intended to deal with costs and expenses and not with the liabilities of the company and could not therefore include a liability of the company for corporation tax. That rule applies only to a winding up by the court and therefore does not apply to a voluntary liquidation. It is to be noted that rule 129(1) refers only to costs and expenses and does not refer to 'charges'. Rule 129(2) however, does provide that:

> 'no payments in respect of bills of costs, charges or expense of solicitors, accountants, auctioneers, brokers or other persons other than payments for costs, charges or expenses fixed or allowed by the court shall be allowed out of the assets of the company, unless they have been duly fixed and allowed by the Examiner or the Taxing Master as the case may be.'

The 'charges or expenses' therein referred to are expressly and specifically set out. The words 'costs and expenses' and 'costs, charges or expenses' in that rule are much narrower and more limited than 'all costs, charges and expenses incurred in the winding up' in s 281. The decision of this court in the *Van Hool McArdle* case is confined solely to the interpretation of that rule . . .

In my view, in the phrase 'all costs, charges and expenses', 'charges' is patently distinguishable from 'costs' and must have a meaning which is not synonymous with 'expenses' otherwise the expression used would have been 'costs and expenses'. The word 'charge' is sufficiently wide to encompass any imposition such as tax or whatever constitutes a burden or duty, on land or property and income tax and corporation tax are, in my opinion, clearly 'charges'. The Corporation Tax Act 1976 is in its long title to be 'an Act to charge and impose on certain profits a duty of inland revenue to be known as corporation tax' . . . By s 1(1) of that Act corporation tax is described as being a tax charged on profits of companies.

I can see no reason for restricting or limiting the words 'charges properly incurred in the winding up' to such charges by way of fees or the like as might have been made by those engaged by the liquidator in the course of the winding up, as was submitted on behalf of the liquidator. Rule 129(2) expressly limited the payments therein referred to in respect of costs, charges and expenses to the categories mentioned . . . If the Oireachtas had chosen to limit in the same way the costs, charges and expenses referred to in s 281 it could have done so but did not . . .

Finlay CJ and Henchy J concurred.

Notes

See also *City of Dublin Steam Packet Co v Revenue Commissioners (No 2)* [1930] IR 217 and *Spa Estates Ltd v O hArgain* (Inspector of Taxes) (High Court, Kenny J, 30 June 1975).

[20.11] While the liquidator retains a company's leasehold property for the benefit of the winding up any rent accruing constitutes an expense of the liquidation and is payable accordingly.

Re GWT Ltd (High Court, 16 November 1987)

[20.12] GWT Ltd rented premises from Erris Investments Ltd ('Erris'). On 29 January 1986 a petition was presented for the winding up of GWT Ltd. A provisional liquidator was appointed and on 10 February 1986 a winding up order was made. On 31 January 1986 the provisional liquidator vacated that part of the premises of which the company had been in actual occupation. Thereafter that part remained vacant. By order of the court dated 23 July 1986 the liquidator was given leave to disclaim the lease. The amount of the rent which would have accrued from the commencement of the liquidation to the date of the disclaimer was £15,013.00. Part of the premises had been sublet by GWT Ltd in 1980. The sum of £3,999.96 was received by GWT Ltd from the sublessee for the period from the commencement of the winding up to the date of disclaimer. Erris claimed that the £15,013.00 should be treated as an expense of the winding up.

[20.13] **Murphy J:** The official liquidator contends that he did not at any time retain any part of the premises demised by the headlease for the benefit of the liquidation and on behalf of Erris it is contended that having regard to the receipt of the rent payable under the sublease the official liquidator has had the use and benefit not merely of the premises comprised in the under lease but all of the premises demised by the headlease.

In a line of authorities stretching from the decision of the Court of Appeal in England in *Oak Pits Colliery Co* (1882) 21 Ch D 322 to the decision of Keane J in *Tempany v Royal Liver Trustees Ltd* (para **20.32**) it has been established that where a liquidator takes possession or remains in possession of leasehold property for the purpose of the winding up, the rent of the

595

premises ought to be regarded as a debt contracted for the purpose of winding up the company and ought therefore to be paid in full like any other debt or expense properly incurred by the liquidator for the same purpose. This principle was discussed at some length by Plowman J in *ABC Coupler v Engineering Company Ltd* [1970] All ER 650 and Pennycuick VC in *Re Downer Enterprises Ltd* [1974] 1 WLR 1460. The principle was clearly applied though without reference to any decided cases, *In Re M Power and Sons Ltd; Grant v Aston* 103 ILTR 39 where the late Mr Justice Kenny made an order directing a liquidator to pay rent from the commencement of a liquidation to the date on which the property was disclaimed by him . . .

Both Plowman J and Pennycuick VC cited with approval a passage from James LJ in *Re Lundy Granite Co* (1871) 6 Ch App 462 at 466 in the following terms:–

> 'But in some cases between the landlord and the company, if the company for its own purposes, and with a view to the realisation of the property to better advantage, remains in possession of the estate, which the lessor is therefore not able to obtain possession of, common sense and ordinary justice require the court to see that the landlord receives the full value of the property'.

Apart from the application of principles of common sense and ordinary justice it is easy to see that commercial realities will frequently necessitate the continued payment of rent after the commencement of a liquidation. If the premises are held at something less than a rack-rent it is probable that they will have some realisable value. Clearly if a liquidator is to complete a sale he must discharge all of the arrears of rent. Even if the leasehold premises have no saleable value but the liquidator is coerced into retaining occupation thereof for the purpose of carrying on a trade or otherwise for the advantageous winding up of the company, he would be faced with an application by a competently advised lessor with the threat of proceedings either for ejectment for non-payment of rent or perhaps distraint. It is difficult to see how a court could refuse liberty to the lessor to exercise such rights if the leasehold premises were being withheld by the official liquidator without paying any rent or fee for the occupation thereof. Indeed it appears that the duty to pay rent or a fee equivalent to the accruing rent was originally seen as the necessary corollary of a prohibition on the right of distress. On the other hand it was clearly held in the *Oak Pits Colliery* case that the right of the landlord to recover was not limited to the amount which could have been realised by a distress but should indeed extend to the full amount of the rent which accrued during the period over which the premises were retained by the liquidator for the purposes of the winding up of the company.

On the other hand, it is equally clear that the official liquidator as such is not liable to pay rent. He could not be sued on foot of any covenant or agreement in that behalf. The liability to pay rent remains that of the corporate body and what the courts have done is to operate, as has already been pointed out, a principle based upon common sense and ordinary justice under which the lessor may be compensated for being kept out of his premises during the period whilst they are retained by the liquidator for some benefit which he anticipates will accrue to the liquidor as a result of the retention thereof.

What the applicants contend in the present case is that the liquidator in fact retained possession of the premises the subject matter of the underlease in the only way in which he could enjoy possession thereof, that is to say, by the receipt of the rent payable by the underlessee. The argument then goes on to claim that the receipt of the rent could only be justified or explained by a claim to the interest of the lessee under the headlease so that it followed that the official liquidator Mr Grace, was, notwithstanding his statement to the contrary, maintaining a claim to the entire of the premises for the benefit of the liquidation. The effect of this argument would be to compel the official liquidator to pay in full a sum in excess of £17,000.00 for the reason and only for the reason that he had received a sum just under £4,000.00. Such a consequence would not accord with the principles of commonsense and ordinary justice invoked by James LJ.

I am satisfied that Mr Grace vacated as he said he did, all of the demised premises which had physically been in the occupation of the company within some weeks of his appointment as provisional liquidator. I accept that he made no positive efforts to collect the rent payable on foot of the underlease and I believe that he did not at any time anticipate that he could dispose of the leasehold interest with the benefit of the underlease on terms which would be advantageous to the creditors of the company. If Erris had applied to the court for liberty to institute proceedings for recovery of the premises for non-payment of rent or otherwise I anticipate that it would have been granted by the court with the acquiescence of the liquidator. I can see nothing in the actions or inactions of the official liquidator which would justify me in permitting him to make any payment to Erris in respect of the rent which accrued due on foot of the headlease subsequent to the commencement of the liquidation. On the other hand I do accept that the retention by the official liquidator of the rent of nearly £4,000.00 received by him from the underlessee would represent an injustice and that I should properly order the payment of that sum by the official liquidator to Erris.

The decision of the court falls to be determined not by the particular provisions of any legislation but in accordance with the dictates of justice and commonsense as James LJ pointed out or what Templeman J (as he then was) describes as what was 'fair and reasonable' or what was 'equitable' as between the lessor and the creditors whom the liquidator represents (see *Re HH Realisations Ltd* 31 P & CR 249).

Applying these principles it seems to me that the appropriate order is to direct the official liquidator to pay to the applicants all of the rent payable under the sublease which was received by him from the date of the commencement of the liquidation to the date on which the headlease was disclaimed.

[20.14]   The proper costs incurred by a liquidator in litigation instituted on behalf of the company (including the costs of a litigant who has successfully defended an action brought against him by the liquidator) rank as an expense of the winding up.

Comhlucht Paipear Riomhaireachta Teo v Udaras na Gaeltachta and Others (Supreme Court, 23 November 1989)

[20.15]   The liquidator of the plaintiff company had instituted proceedings against the defendants to set aside certain transactions under s 286 of the Principal Act as fraudulent preferences. The defendants, contending that the plaintiff would be unable to pay their costs if successful in their defence, applied for security for costs under s 390 of the Principal Act. The Supreme Court refused to make an order for security for costs on the ground that if the defendants were successful their costs would rank as an expense of the liquidation.

[20.16]   McCarthy J: During the hearing of this appeal the court raised the question, not apparently adverted to in the High Court, as to whether or not the costs of a successful defendant in an action brought by the liquidator of an insolvent company are deemed to be within the terms of s 281 and/or s 285. If they fall within either category, then these applications fall *in limine* since the company will not be unable to pay the costs of a successful defendant, there being sufficient funds to meet the requirements specified in s 281. [His lordship then referred to several authorities and concluded as follows:]

The overwhelming line of authority establishes that in the cases such as the present, where an action is brought after liquidation, the costs of a successful litigant against the company appear to rank in priority to all other claims. As a simple proposition it would seem supported in principle; it would be a great injustice if a company were free after liquidation, to maintain an action for the benefit of the general body of creditors and if unsuccessful, successfully contend that the costs of the successful litigant against the company should only rank pari passu with the claims of the creditors.

Notes

See also *Re National Building & Land Co* (1885–86) 15 LR Ir 47 where the costs awarded to the plaintiff in an action brought after the commencement of the winding up, were an expense of the liquidation. In *Irish Commercial Society Ltd v Plunkett* (High Court, 6 June 1984) Carroll J indicated obiter that damages payable under a liquidator's undertaking as to damages, given on behalf of the company in injunction proceedings would also rank as an expense of the winding up.

The costs of legal costs of accountants employed to tax the costs of the liquidator's solicitors are not costs properly incurred by the liquidator in a winding up: *Re Castle Brand Ltd* [1990] ILRM 97. See generally *Mac Cann* (1990) 8 ILT (ns) 245.

Application of the rules of bankruptcy

[20.17] It is provided by s 284 of the Principal Act that in the winding up of an insolvent company the same rules shall prevail regarding 'the respective rights of secured and unsecured creditors and to debts provable and to the valuation of annuities and future and contingent liabilities'[1] as apply in the law of bankruptcy. It is only the bankruptcy rules on these matters that are incorporated into liquidations.[2] These rules are to be found in the Bankruptcy Act 1988. See *Keane* at paras **38.68–38.70**.

On the procedure for ascertaining the creditors and proving their claims, see *Keane* at para **38.66–38.67**.

In applying the rules of bankruptcy to liquidations it has been held that where there are mutual debts between the company in liquidation and a creditor, the debts must be set off against one another: *Re Tailteann Freight Services Ltd; Freaney v Bank of Ireland* [1975] IR 376; *Re McCairns (PMPA) plc* [1989] ILRM 501. A right of set-off can only apply to monies actually owing to and by the company at the date of the liquidation. Monies paid into the company's account by mistake are akin to lost property and in the absence of a defence of equitable estoppel, may be traced by the payer and may not be subjected to a set-off: *Re Irish Shipping Ltd* [1986] ILRM 518.

In the winding up of an insolvent company neither secured nor unsecured creditors are entitled to claim interest on their debts in respect of any period after the commencement of the winding up: *Re McCairns (PMPA) plc*.

1 See *Keane* at paras **38.68–38.70**.
2 *Re Irish Attested Sales Ltd* [1962] IR 20 which held that the now abolished doctrine of reputed ownership had no application on liquidations.

Preferential debts

[20.18] After the costs and expenses of the liquidation have been paid, certain classes of unsecured creditors, known as 'preferential creditors' are entitled to payment of their claims in priority to other unsecured creditors of the company. To the extent that uncharged assets are insufficient to meet the claims of preferential creditors, they have priority over the claims of holders of debentures under any floating charge.[1] Under s 134 of the 1990 Act debts lose their preferential status unless within the period of six months after advertisement by the liquidator for claims in at least two daily newspapers circulating in the district where the company's registered office is situated, the debt has either been notified to him or has become known to him.

[20.19] Unpaid PRSI deductions (often referred to as 'super-preferential debts') are payable in advance of all other preferential claims.[2] This category of claim is confined to liquidations and does not arise at all in receiverships. After the super-preferential debts, all other preferential claims rank equally and abate rateably in the event of an insufficiency of assets.[3] The various categories of preferential debts are set out primarily in s 285 of the Principal Act as amended by s 10 of the 1982 Act. This section applies principally to certain categories of unpaid taxes and to employees' claims for arrears of pay and holiday pay. Also preferential are certain claims under the Minimum Notice and Terms of Employment Act 1973, the Redundancy Payments Acts, the Unfair Dismissals Act 1977, the Capital Gains Tax Act 1975, the Corporation Tax Act and the Value Added Tax Acts.

Under the Protection of Employees (Employers Insolvency) Act 1984 the Minister for Labour may pay certain debts owing to employees, out of the redundancy fund, where the company becomes insolvent (including going into liquidation). The Minister is then subrogated to the rights of the employees including, where appropriate, any preferential claim in a winding up.

1 S 285(7) of the Principal Act.
2 See Social Welfare (Consolidation) Act 1981.
3 S 285(7) of the Principal Act.

[20.20] An employer's contribution in respect of prsi or arrears of preferential wages and holiday pay does not constitute a preferential debt in the winding up of a company.

Re Castle Mahon Poultry Products Ltd [1987] ILRM 222 (Supreme Court)

[20.21] Under s 285(2)(e) of the Principal Act PRSI contributories 'payable' by the company as employer during the 12 months prior to the winding up order or resolution, constitute a preferential claim. Under s 10(10(*b*) of the Social Welfare Act such contributions were 'payable' where payment of wages was made to the employee. The company having gone into liquidation the employees had preferential claims for arrears of wages and holiday pay. The liquidator having paid these arrears, the Revenue Commissioners claimed that employer's PRSI contributions in respect of these payments were also preferential debts.

[20.22] **McCarthy J:** Clearly, the arrears of wages and holiday pay within the four month limitation and the employee's contribution to the Social Insurance Fund were all preferential payments; the liquidator recognised this and discharged them as such. The question raised is whether or not the employer's contributions comprise 'amounts due in respect of contributions payable during the twelve months next before the relevant date'. The liquidator says that in order that they may be 'amounts due' they must necessarily have been payable during the twelve months before the relevant date. The learned trial judge posed the question for determination as whether the employer's contributions which were not paid before the liquidator's appointment can properly be regarded as payable in the period referred to in the subsection. Counsel for the liquidator submitted that this was posing the wrong question, that the question should have been whether or not the amount was due at the relevant date. In whatever manner one approaches the true construction of s 285(2)(*e*) in dealing with the employer's contribution, the learned trial judge correctly identified the effect of s 10(1)(*b*) in stating that a liability to pay the employment contribution only arises when a payment is made to an employed contributor in respect of reckonable earnings . . . That no legal liability to pay the employment contributions which are in contention in this case arose prior to his (the liquidator's) appointment because the reckonable earnings to which they relate, although due, had not been paid.

The overriding canon of construction is that words should be given their ordinary meaning; despite the persuasive analogies cited by the learned trial judge in his judgment, the wording of s 10(1)(*b*) admits of no other meaning than that the pre-condition of payment in respect of reckonable earnings being in any contribution year in order to create a liability to pay the employment contribution is clear and unambiguous. It may well be that the result is a situation which the legislature did not envisage – that the preferential status of the debt due to the State depended on whether the company had or had not paid the wages to which the arrears of contributions related, but I am concerned only with the true construction of the relevant statutes in their ordinary meaning. It is common case that an employer had to adjust the payments made during a contribution year in respect of the employer's contribution – a balancing figure is struck after the contribution year has ended; in the circumstances, ordinarily the continuing employment would remedy any shortfall in respect of employer's contribution.

I would allow the appeal and declare that the employer's contribution in respect of pay related social insurance on arrears of preferential wages and holiday pay does not constitute a preferential debt in the winding up by virtue of s 285(2)(*e*) of the Companies Act 1963.

Notes

See also *Re Palgrave Murphy Ltd* (High Court, Hamilton J, 20 February 1979)

[20.23] Under s 285(6) where payment of wages or holiday pay of employees of the company has been made out of money advanced for that purpose, the person who made that advance has a preferential claim in the winding up to the extent that what would otherwise have been a preferential claim of the employee, has been reduced.

Station Motors Ltd v Allied Irish Banks Ltd [1985] IR 756 (High Court)

[20.24] On 15 September 1980 the directors of Station Motors Ltd resolved that by virtue of its insolvency the company should be placed in creditors voluntary winding up. On 30 October 1980 the company went into liquidation. A wages account was opened with the respondent bank on

17 September 1980. On 30 September 1980, £32,519.11 was debited from the wages account, credited to the company's overdrawn current account and used to pay wages. Between 17 September 1980 and 3 October 1980 a further £4,348.72 was debited to the wages account. On 15 September 1980 £23,278.13 was lodged to the current account from a different source. This, the court held to be a fraudulent preference. The respondent bank claimed that it had a preferential claim under s 285(6) for £47,027.66 (being money paid by the company for wages for four months prior to the liquidation). The liquidator sought directions from the court regarding the extent, if any, of the validity of the respondents preferential claim.

[20.25]   Carroll J: Mr O'Sullivan contends that the wages cheque paid out of the overdraft were not paid out of money advanced by the bank for that purpose; that the bank had not addressed its mind to the payment of wages and this was proved by the fact that a separate wages account was not opened until 17th September 1980. Therefore, there was no awareness by the lender at the time of making the loan.

Mr Blayney on behalf of the bank argued that ultimately it is a question of fact whether the monies were advanced by the bank for the purpose of paying wages and that it must necessarily follow that where cheques are drawn in favour of employees in discharge of wages and cashed week after week that the money was advanced for that purpose.

One of the cases cited was *Re Rampgill Mill Ltd* [1967] 1 All ER 56. This was an action between a bank and a liquidator and it was common ground that within the limit of £500 per week, there was no restriction on the purpose for which cheques could be drawn on the bank. It was also common ground that the arrangement was made with wages in mind. In that case, as in this, the bank did not insist on a wages account being opened and operated in such a way as to allow the bank to get maximum priority. In that case Plowman J said at page 60:–

'In my judgment counsel for the liquidator seeks to apply too rigid a test. The object of s 319(4) (the equivalent of s 285(6) of the Companies Act 1963) as I see it, was to establish a principle of subrogation in favour of banks (although its operation is not, of course, confined to banks) and the subsection should therefore, in my judgment, be given a benevolent construction rather than one which narrows the limits of its operation . . . In the present case the bank clearly had a purpose in advancing money to the company – namely the purpose of enabling it to meet its commitments. I then ask myself 'what commitments?', and my answer, so far as the money provided under the Alston arrangement is concerned, is wages, which were the whole raison d'etre of that arrangement.'

He therefore held the money was advanced for the purpose of paying wages.

It is not possible to be quite as clear cut in this case. The money was undoubtedly in this case to meet the commitments of the company. It also seems clear to me that part of those commitments included wages and this must have been known to the bank. Individual weekly wages cheques were drawn for each employee and were honoured by the bank each week. I agree with Plowman J that the section should be given a benevolent construction. The bank in fact advanced money knowing part of it would be used for wages. Therefore in my opinion, insofar as that part is concerned, they are entitled to the benefit of subrogation provided in s 285(6).

The last issue is whether the rule in *Clayton's* case (1816) 1 Mer 572, applies. This is expressed as follows at p 608 of the report:

'In such a case, (ie. a banking account where all the sums paid in from one blended fund the parts of which have no longer any distinct existence), there is no room for any other appropriation than that which arises from the order in which the receipts and payments take place, and are carried into the account. Presumably, it is the sum first paid in, that is first drawn out. It is the first item on the debit side of the account, that is discharged, or reduced by the first item on the credit side.'

There were substantial lodgements made by the company during the period from the 3rd June to the 3rd October 1980 . . .

The rule was applied in *Re Primrose Builders Limited* [1950] Ch 561 where advances were made for the payment of wages. In each case the bank insisted on being satisfied before honouring the cheques (some being made out to wages and some to cash) that lodgments substantially equal to or exceeding the amount would be paid in. Wynn Parry J held not only that there was no sufficient evidence but that there was no evidence at all on which a court could come to the conclusion that the rule was to any extent by agreement between the parties not to apply in any particular instance. So too in this case. There was no separate wages account until the 17th September. All lodgments went to reduce the general overdraft and the money advanced for wages formed part of that general overdraft. Insofar as the earlier wages cheques were cleared by subsequent lodgments, they cannot be the subject of a claim by way of subrogation.

[20.26] The parties to a scheme of arrangement under ss 201 to 203 of the Principal Act, may be bound by a term thereof conferring on an ordinary unsecured claim the status of preferential debt in the winding up of the company.

Re MFN Construction Co Ltd (Supreme Court, 12 May 1988)

[20.27] On 17 June 1980 a scheme of arrangement was approved by the High Court the terms of which provided that the Collector General was to be paid £210,250 in arrears of taxes as if he were a preferential creditor in a liquidation and that the remaining unsecured creditors were to be paid 40p in the £1. It was further provided that the company should be placed in voluntary liquidation on 31st March 1982. The special resolution to wind up the company was passed on 6th July 1982, by which date the Collector General had not yet been paid the £210,250. It was agreed that arrears of taxes owing in respect of the period after June 1981 constituted a preferential debt. The Collector General also sought to prove, however, as a preferential creditor for the £210,250, even though this sum would not constitute a preferential debt under statute. The unsecured creditors argued that the court should disregard the scheme of arrangement and adhere to the statutory order of priorities.

[20.28]   McCarthy J: The unsecured creditors say that the court must disregard the scheme and adhere to s 285 as the statutory direction to the liquidator on priority of payments. They say that the Collector General benefitted from the scheme in that he continued to collect the statutory sum where, otherwise, these might have not been received. Whether or not that is a benefit to the Collector General and consequently to the revenue, if the work was going to be carried out to complete the contracts, as no doubt, it must have been, then those statutory sums would have been paid to the revenue in any event by somebody. It is also said that a winding up at the time in June 1981, would have left the Collector General short of payment; be it so, but the present argument would also leave him short of payment, in respect of the debt then, in June 1981 due. The effect of yielding to the Collector General's claim, it is argued, would mean over-riding the statute.

The Collector General relies upon the enforcability of the scheme of arrangement which involved the Collector General in staying his hand until at least the 31 March 1982, and that this scheme is binding on the company, and consequently on the liquidator. Reliance was placed upon s 201(3) of the Act as support for the view that the liquidator is statutorily bound by such an arrangement; in my view there is no statutory support for such a proposition, since subsection 3 in that regard, is related to an arrangement etc. made by a company in the course of being wound up, whereby the liquidator would be bound. In my view, a more fundamental equitable principle is involved. The unsecured creditors cannot be permitted to approbate and reprobate; they secured the advantage of the company continuing to trade in the completion of the contracts, thereby greatly increasing the amount available for distribution. But they now seek to deny another part of the self same agreement; they cannot be permitted to do so. As long as all interested parties are protected, I see no reason why those immediately concerned may not make a valid and enforceable agreement to waive or amend the order or priority of payment. If other parties not involved in the scheme were to be concerned in the winding up, different consideration would apply. Here, however, the court has before it effectively the two parties to the scheme who have vital interests in the winding up; the liquidator provides the machinery. It is beyond question that the parties intended that the preferential claim of the Collector General should stand in the event of a winding up as of the 31 March 1982 (which date was unilaterally extended until the 6 June 1982). To order that the parties adhere to the terms of that scheme of arrangement and to give the Collector General the priority claimed seems to me to be 'in accordance with law'.

Finlay CJ, Henchy J, Griffin and Hederman JJ concurred.

Notes

Similarly, under s 132 of the 1990 Act it is expressly permitted in a voluntary liquidation, for one ordinary unsecured creditor to subordinate his claim to the claim of any other creditor. This is a statutory exception to the rule (which cannot otherwise be contracted out of) that there should be a pari passu distribution of uncharged assets among the general body of unsecured creditors: *Glow Heating Ltd v EHB* (High Court, 4 March 1988).

Execution creditors

[20.29]   It has already been noted supra that under s 219 of the Principal Act 'any attachment, sequestration, distress or execution put in force against the property of the company' after the commencement of a compulsory winding up is 'void to all intents'. It was decided in *Re Leinster Contract Corporation Ltd*[1] that a judgment creditor does not rank as a secured creditor merely through having obtained a judgment against the company.

If the judgment creditor has registered his judgment against property of the company as a judgment mortgage, he then becomes a secured creditor to the extent of that mortgage. Notably, however, under s 284(2) of the Principal Act (which incorporated s 331 of the Irish Bankrupt and Insolvent Act 1857, into Irish Company law) any judgment registered against property of the company within three months before the commencement of the winding up shall be void. See *Re Irish Attested Sales Ltd.*[2]

As regards other forms of execution, s 291 of the Principal Act states that 'where a creditor has issued execution against the goods or lands of a company or has attached any debt due to the company, and the company is subsequently wound up, he shall not be entitled to retain the benefit of the execution or attachment' unless it has been completed before the commencement of the winding up.

For the circumstances in which an execution or attachment is regarded as completed, see s 291(5). See also s 292 of the Principal Act on the duty of the sherriff to hand over goods in his possession to the liquidator.

1 [1903] 1 IR 517.
2 [1962] IR 70.

Disclaimer[1]

[20.30]   Under s 290 the liquidator may within 12 months[2] of the commencement of the winding up and with the leave of the court, disclaim by writing any property of the company which consists of 'land of any tenure burdened with onerous covenants, of shares or stock in companies, of unprofitable contracts, or of any other property which is unsaleable or not readily saleable by reason of its binding the possessor thereof to the performance of any onerous act or to the payment of any sum of money.' He is not barred from disclaiming property merely because he has tried to sell it, has taken possession of it or exercised any act of ownership in relation to it.

If a person interested in the property serves notice on the liquidator requiring him to decide whether to disclaim it and he fails to notify the applicant within 28 days (or such longer period as the court may allow) that he intends to disclaim it, he is then barred from any future disclaimer of that property.

1 See *Keane* at para **38.58**.
2 Subject to extension by the court. However, if the property does not come to the knowledge of the liquidator within one month of the commencement of the winding up, time only starts to run from the date when he became aware of the property.

[20.31]   Under s 290(3) the disclaimer operates 'to determine, as from the date of disclaimer, the rights, interests and liabilities of the company and the property of the company, in or in respect of the property disclaimed, but shall not, except in so far as is necessary for the purpose of releasing the company and the property of the company from liability, affect the rights or liabilities of any other person'.

Tempany v Royal Liver Trustees Ltd [1984] ILRM 273 (High Court)

[20.32]   In April 1976 Royal Liver Trustees Ltd ('the lessors') granted a lease to Farm Machinery Distributors Ltd ('the lessee') the terms of which incorporated a guarantee by an associate of the lessee, Massey-Ferguson Holdings Ltd ('the surety') to make good and pay to the lessor all losses, costs and expenses sustained by the lessor should the lessee fail to comply with its obligations under the lease. In 1979 TMG Group Ltd acquired the share capital of the lessee and unsuccessfully tried to obtain a release of the surety from its guarantee. In 1983 the lessee went into liquidation and the liquidator applied for leave to disclaim the lease. Two questions were put to the court: (1) whether the court in exercising its discretion to grant leave to disclaim should consider the effect of any disclaimer on the rights and liabilities inter se of the lessor, the surety and TMG Group Ltd, and (2) the effect, if any, of a disclaimer on the continuing liability of the surety under the guarantee.

[20.33]   **Keane J:** What is not immediately clear is the effect which any disclaimer might have on the rights and liabilities inter se of the lessors and the surety and the rights and liabilities inter se of the surety and the TMG Group Ltd. Moreover, while it is clear, and again was not seriously disputed by the parties that the court, in considering whether to exercise its

606

discretion, is bound to take into account the extent to which the interest of the creditors will be protected or otherwise by a disclaimer, it is not immediately clear to what extent, if any, the court may take into account the effect of any permitted disclaimer on the rights and liabilities inter se of the lessors, the surety and the TMG Group Ltd. In relation to both of these matters, it is necessary to bear in mind the concluding words of sub-s (3) which makes it clear that the disclaimer is not to affect the rights or liabilities of any other person except so far as is necessary for the purpose of releasing the company and the property of the company from liability.

In relation to the first of these matters, two possibilities must be considered. In the first place, the effect of the disclaimer may be to put an end to the liability of the surety and as a consequence the liability of the TMG Group Ltd. This was the view taken by the Court of Appeal in England in *Stacey v Hill* [1901] 1 KB 660 . . . and it is based on the proposition that the liabilities of a surety are in law dependent upon those of the principal debtor and that, where the liabilities of the latter are determined, the former must inevitably be also determined. The alternative possibility is that the liability of the surety remains, notwithstanding the termination of the lessees' liability, because under the express language of s 290(3) the disclaimer is not to affect the rights or liabilities of any other person. In considering these alternative possibilities, it must be borne in mind that, if the liability of the surety continues notwithstanding the disclaimer, the surety will then be entitled to be indemnified by the lessees and accordingly, to prove in the liquidation for the appropriate amount.

The question as to which of these two possible views of the effect of a disclaimer is correct only arises if the court is entitled to take into account on an application such as this the effect of the disclaimer on the rights and liabilities inter se of the lessors, the surety and the TMG Group Ltd. [After an exhaustive review of caselaw his lordship made the following conclusions:]

(1). The exclusive concern of the court in an application for leave to disclaim must be the interests of all persons interested in the liquidation. I think it is clear that this was the overriding intention of the legislature in both the bankruptcy and companies code and should be given effect to by the courts. The principle was established in law beyond doubt by *Hill v East and West India Dock Co* 22 Ch D 14 and has not been significantly dislodged since then.

(2). In considering the extent, if any, to which the interests of those interested in the liquidation will be affected by the operation of a disclaimer it is necessary to consider whether the release of third parties such as (in the case of leasehold property) original lessees and sureties, is necessary 'for the purpose of releasing the company and the property of the company from liability.'

(3). In the case of leasehold property which has been assigned by the original lessee to a company in liquidation, the release of the original lessee is not necessary for the purpose of releasing the company and the property of the company from liability. The position of a surety for the payment of the rent

607

and performance of the covenants by a company holding property under a lease which goes into liquidation is no different; the release of the surety is not necessary for the purpose of releasing the company and the property of the company from liability.

(4). The release of the surety, the case mentioned in the preceding paragraph, not being necessary for the purpose of releasing the company and the property of the company from liability, the liability of the surety is not affected by the disclaimer by the liquidator of the interest of the company in the property. This is consistent with the principles enunciated in *Harding v Preece* (1882) 9 QBD 281 and *Hill v East and West India Dock Co* and avoids what James LJ called 'the most grievous injustice and the most revolting absurdity' of permitting the lessor's rights against third parties to be adversely affected by the operation of a disclaimer which he has done nothing to bring about . . .

It remains to consider the application of these principles to the present case. There is not the smallest doubt and the contrary was not seriously urged, that the giving of leave to the liquidator to disclaim could only be in the interests of those interested in the liquidation, although the financial benefit accruing to the unsecured creditors may be marginal in the extreme, having regard to the huge deficiency. The disclaimer will, however, facilitate the liquidator in bringing the liquidation to a speedy close and this can only be in the interests of all those interested in the liquidation. The rights and liabilities of the lessor, the surety and the TMG Group inter se having regard to the terms of the guarantee and the letter of offer dated 26 March will not be affected by the disclaimer.

There remains the question of the date at which the disclaimer should become operative. In *Peter Henry Grant v Aston Ltd* (1969) 103 ILTR 30) the only reported Irish case on s 290 Kenny J made an order that the liquidator should pay the rent under the lease from the date of the commencement of the liquidation until the date of the order of the court. The reported judgment is rather terse and accordingly, the decision does not afford me such assistance in determining what are the principles which are applicable in determining the date at which the disclaimer should be treated as operative. There is, however, an English decision of *Re HH Realisations Ltd* (1975) 31 P & CR 249) in which Templeman J considered in detail the principles which should be applied. He came to the conclusion that the only period during which it was equitable for the landlords to claim rent in full was the period during which the property was actually being retained by the liquidators for the benefit of the creditors in general. I am satisfied that I should apply the same principle in the present case and it would follow that the lessors are entitled to the apportionment rent in full from the date of the appointment of the liquidator, 4 January 1983, to the date on which they were given notice of the liquidator's intention to disclaim, 4 February 1983. Accordingly, the order will provide that the disclaimer takes effect as and from 4 February 1983 . . . It appears to me that, having regard to the conclusions I have reached, I should make a form of speaking order which should recite that the court is of the opinion that the release of the surety and the TMG Group from their respective liabilities under the lease and the acquisition agreement, the terms of which are set out in the letter dated 26 March 1979, is not necessary for the purpose of releasing the company and the property of the company from liability and that accordingly the rights and liabilities inter se of the lessors, the surety and the TMG Group will not be effected by the disclaimer of the lease by the applicant.

The question as to whether an order should be made under sub-s (9) vesting the disclaimed property in one of the parties was canvassed during the original hearing. No application has been made to me for such an order at this stage; but, as the parties may wish to consider the position in the light of this judgment, the order will reserve liberty for each of the parties to apply.

Notes

Cf *Re Madeley Homecare Ltd* [1983] NI 1.

On the power of the court to make any consequential vesting orders when granting leave to disclaim, see s 290(7), (8) and *East and West India Dock Co v Hill* (1882) 22 Ch D 14. In the absence of vesting order, the company's former interest in the disclaimed property is left in a limbo. For example, in *Tempany v Royal Liver Trusteees Ltd* (para **20.32**) the lease did not cease to exist after disclaimer and liabilities of the guarantor in respect of rent continued.

[20.34] Under s 290(9) any person who suffers loss as a result of the disclaimer is deemed to be a creditor of the company and may prove for the amount of that loss as a debt in the winding up.

Re Ranks (Ireland) Ltd [1988] ILRM 751 (High Court)

[20.35] By three agreements made between Irish Telephone Rentals Ltd ('Rentals') and Ranks (Ireland) Ltd ('Ranks') between 1976 and 1979 Rentals agreed to install and let on hire to Ranks certain telephone equipment. Each of the agreements was to continue for a period of 14 years with rent to be paid quarterly in advance. Rentals also entered into four agreements with Ranks providing for the maintenance of the hired equipment. All of the hiring contracts contained the following clause:

'If the subscriber shall repudiate this contract and the company (Rentals) shall accept such repudiation so as to terminate this contract the company may thereupon remove the installation and the subscriber shall pay to the company all payments then accrued due and also a sum equal to the present value on a 3% basis of the remaining rentals that would have been payable under this contract if not so terminated less an allowance of 25% to cover the estimated cost of the maintenance and value of recovered material. The sum shall be payable as liquidated damages it being an agreed estimate of the terms the company would suffer.'

On 22 November 1983 a petition was presented for the winding up of Ranks. On 5 December 1983 the winding up order was made. Upon application under s 290 and by order dated 18 February 1983 Barr J gave the liquidator liberty to disclaim the hire contracts and also gave the liquidator liberty to pay to Rentals the sum of £11,272.03 being the amount of rental due on foot of the hire contract from 22 November 1983. No further order was made in relation to the right, if any, of Rentals to prove for any other claim which they might have in the winding up by virtue of the hire contracts. The liquidator then applied for directions regarding the interpretation and effect of s 290.

[20.36] **Murphy J:** There was some dispute between the parties as to the extent of the argument addressed to Barr J and as to his express or implied intentions in making the order aforesaid. It does not seem to me that this is a dispute which I could enter upon. I propose to take the order of 18 February 1985 as I find it. I have every confidence that it represents the decision of the court. If the position were otherwise it would have been appropriate for the parties to apply to the judge by whom the order was made in accordance with the slip rule to have the same rectified.

It seems to me that Barr J was concerned with two distinct if closely associated issues. First the exercise of a discretion of the court in granting the official liquidator liberty to disclaim onerous contracts and secondly ascertaining expenses incurred in the course of the liquidation and directing payment thereof.

If I may reverse the order in which Barr J dealt with the matter and take the question of expense first. It seems to me that the learned judge in giving liberty to the official liquidator to discharge the rent of the telephones which accrued during the period of occupation of the premises by the official liquidator in which the equipment was installed was applying a clearly established line of authority from *Oak Pits Colliery In re* (1882) 21 Ch D 322 to *HH Realisations Ltd, In re* (1975) 31 P and CR 249 in which it has been laid down that where property is retained by a liquidator for the benefit of the creditors of the company that the proportion of the rent due by the company and relating to the period of the liquidator's occupation should be discharged as an expense of the liquidation. That principle was applied in *Peter Henry Grant v Aston Ltd* [1969] 103 ILTR 30 and subsequently by Keane J in *Tempany v Royal Liver* (para **20.32**). In the two Irish cases the payment of the expense was dealt with in conjunction with an application to disclaim onerous leasehold property but the principle is clearly of equal application whether or not a liquidator disclaims or is given liberty to do so.

It seems to me that the essence of s 290 is to be found in three of the subsections thereof, namely subs(1) which creates the statutory power to disclaim onerous property, subs(3) which defines the effect of a disclaimer, namely, that it should operate to determine 'the rights, interests and liabilities of the company and the property of the company, in or in respect of the property disclaimed' and subs(9) which is expressed in the following terms:

'Any person damaged by the operation of a disclaimer under this section shall be deemed to be a creditor of the company to the amount of the damages and may accordingly prove the amount as a debt in the winding up.'

It seems to me that the clear effect of these subsections is to achieve the position that the company is relieved of the continuing onerous obligations (and any further benefit in the property) but only on the terms that the other party to the contract (who would see it as beneficial to him as it was detrimental to the company) had the right to prove for the injury sustained by him as a result of the termination of his valuable contractual rights. Not only is that, in my view, the proper interpretation of the section but if the matter were to be otherwise it might well be of doubtful constitutionality.

Again, in my view, it is proper that subs(9) should relate not solely to persons who are at the date of the commencement of the winding up of the company creditors theref, but to all persons who have entered into contracts which are beneficial to them and onerous to the company whose rights are subsequently affected by a disclaimer permitted by the court.

The question which then remains is the manner in which the injury to the claimant should be measured. The answer may be stated by quoting one sentence from Keane J's book on *Company Law* at page 321 as follows:

'The measure of such damage is the difference between the rent which would have been paid by the company under the lease and the rent which the lessor is likely to obtain during the unexpired residue.'

In my view this represents a clear and correct statement of the law . . . In this case it was contended before me – as I understand it was contended before Barr J – that the appropriate measure of damages would be that provided for under cl 11 of the hire agreements. In my view that submission is not well founded. That method of computing loss or damages is appropriate only where the hirer has repudiated the contract. A disclaimer is not the same as repudiation nor could it be described properly as a form of 'statutory repudiation'. Repudiation by one party to a contract does not operate as a discharge thereof, unless and until the repudiation is accepted by the other party. Indeed that principle was clearly recognised by the draftsmen of cl 11 who provided that the clause should operate 'if the subscriber shall repudiate this contract and *the company shall accept such repudiation'*. In the case of a disclaimer authorized by s 290 the action is effective without the acceptance, indeed in spite of the opposition of the other party to the contract . . . It seems to me that the loss would properly be calculated as of the commencement of the liquidation and accordingly it follows that from the amount as so calculated Rentals would be required to give credit for the amount received by them for the use of the hired equipment by the liquidator.

Invalidity of floating charges

[20.37]   See ss 288 and 289 of the Principal Act, discussed in chapter 15 and in *Keane* at paras **38.80–38.83**.

Misfeasance summons

[20.38] Under s 298 of the Principal Act as substituted by s 140 of the 1990 Act, if in the course of winding up a company it appears that any person who has taken part in the formation of promotion of the company or any past or present director manager, liquidator or receiver, or any officer of the company has misapplied or retained or become liable or accountable for any money or property of the company, or been guilty of any misfeasance or breach of trust in relation to the company the court may, on the application of the liquidator or any creditor or contributory, examine into the conduct of that person and compel him to repay or restore all or part of the money or property or to contribute such sum to the assets of the company by way of compensation in respect of the misapplication, retainer, misfeasance or other breach of duty or trust as the court thinks just.[1]

The s 298 remedy, known as the misfeasance summons, does not create any new cause of action. It is merely procedural, providing a more expeditious remedy than would otherwise be available.[2]

The scope of misfeasance prodeedings is extended by s 146 of the 1990 Act which provides that where a subsidiary company is being wound up and is unable to pay its debts, summary proceedings may be taken by the liquidator or any creditor or contributory of the subsidiary, against any director of the holding company has been guilty of misfeasance in relation to the subsidiary.

1 See *Keane* at paras **38.88–38.89**.
2 *Re Irish Provident Assurance Co* [1913] 1 IR 352.

[20.39] Relief under s 298 is limited to cases where there has been a breach of duty by an individual in his capacity as officer of the company.

Re SM Barker Ltd [1950] IR 123 (High Court)

[20.40] Shortly before the presentation of a petition for the winding up of the company the sole directors and shareholders of the company (the Latchmans) caused the company to voluntarily release a number of debts owing by them to the company. An order was subsequently made to wind up the company. The liquidator, finding himself with a heavy deficiency of assets issued misfeasance proceedings against the Latchmans for an order declaring them liable to contribute to the assets of the company a sum by way of restitution or as damages for misfeasance, equal to the value of the debts released.

[20.41] **Gavan Duffy J:** The three Latchmans at the material times were the directors of the company; naturally, because they were the owners of the entire share capital; and because they were the owners, they were the complete masters of the company's situation; it is as such that they were in a position to profit and did profit and not as directors or trustees for the shareholders.

They had from time to time incurred simple contract debts to the company individually for their own purposes; and the company, instead of exacting payment of those debts, saw fit to annul, as if it were a single liability, that valuable indebtedness or most of it, casually describing it in the ill-advised resolution as indebtedness of the directors. That annulment, whether valid in law or void or voidable was the act of the company in general meeting; and the comparatively small amendment of the amount forgiven effected by the owners of the undertaking was endorsed by another general meeting. There was, moreover, on the evidence, no concealment by the Latchmans, no trickery and no fraud. In that state of the case, it would in my judgment be a distortion of the law to allow the liquidator to recover against the Latchmans in their capacity of directors under s 298.

I cannot express the principle to be applied more tersely than in the words of Mr Justice Maugham, as he then was in *In re Etic* [1928] 1 Ch 861 at p 875: 'The conclusion at which I have arrived is that s 215 is . . . limited to cases where there has been something in the nature of a breach of duty by an officer of the company as such which has caused pecuniary loss to the company.'

I must refuse the liquidator's application, since any damage occasioned to the company by the release of the Latchmans' debt was not the result of any breach of duty committed by them in their role of officers of the company, while the pecuniary gain to themselves from the same release was not acquired by them as directors nor because they were directors, nor in breach of their duty to the members of the company, who, whether or not the profit be justifiable in law, were the real gainers in their personal capacity from the company's largesse.

Notes

Would the result of this decision be the same today in the light of cases such as *West Mercia Safety-Wear Ltd v Dodd* [1988] BCLC 250. In that case the impugned transaction was effected by the directors who were also the sole shareholders, but because the company was insolvent at that time, the directors were held to be guilty of misfeasance and breach of duty.

[20.42]   Relief under s 298 is not available in respect of mere negligence or carelessness on the part of an officer of the company. However, where that officer has so conducted the affairs of the company as to create the impression that there is a prima facie case of misfeasance, he may be liable for the costs of proceedings brought under s 298 even if successfully defended by him.

Re Mont Clare Hotels Ltd; Jackson v Mortell (High Court, 2 December 1986)

[20.43]   The liquidator of Mont Clare Hotels Ltd brought proceedings against the company's three directors, Brian Mortell and his mother Pauline Mortell and Anthony Hussey (who was also the company's solicitor) claiming damages for misfeasance. It was alleged that they were guilty of misfeasance in causing Mont Clare Hotels Ltd to make an unsecured loan of £20,000 with interest at 10% to an associated company, Cluney Construction Ltd in 1973. It was alleged that they had also been guilty of misfeasance in failing to institute proceedings on behalf of Mont Clare Hotels Ltd for the recovery of the loan once Cluney Construction Ltd ran into financial difficulties.

[20.44]   Costello J: Cluney Construction Ltd was established and run by Mr Mortell, one of the directors of Mont Clare Hotels Ltd, in association with a Mr Power. Mr Mortell had the power of signing cheques for the company but the company was mainly run by Mr Power who had some expertise in the construction industry, but not a great deal of expertise, Mr Mortell having none.

Cluney Construction Ltd started developing in Newbridge and later in Bray but the company did not prosper. The company met very great difficulties in respect of its activities in Newbridge and its bankers insisted on obtaining the funds generated on the sale of its houses. The result of this was that the company was unable to repay the loan given to it by Mont Clare Hotels Ltd . . .

The evidence established that on 13th September 1977 Mr Mortell informed his co-directors that £6,000 would be paid back off the loan. This was not done. I am satisfied there was no fraud in connection with that statement. I am satisfied that Mr Mortell may well have been guilty of errors of judgment in relation to this whole transaction but that he was not guilty of any fraud in relation to it, and it has not been shown that he did not believe that what he said would come to pass. Unfortunately it did not come to pass.

On 27th February the minutes again record that Mr Mortell expressed the view that the loan was secured. Again, I am of the view that it has not been shown that this was said recklessly or fraudulently. It may well have been that Mr Mortell was being over-optimistic and it may well be an error of judgment on his part, but I do not think his statement in itself amount to misfeasance.

On 14th February 1980 Mr Mortell expressed in writing to the bank, who were then lending money to Mont Clare Hotels Ltd, that the loan was good and that it would be repaid in four instalments, as stated in the letter. Again, in my view, it has not been shown that Mr Mortell acted fraudulently in signing this letter. Again, it may well be a case of misplaced optimism on his part.

The relevance of the evidence is this: It is said that there was misfeasance on the part of the directors of Mont Clare Hotels Ltd in failing to enforce the obligation of Cluney Construction Ltd to repay the loan.

In relation to Mr Hussey, I am quite satisfied that during this period Mont Clare Hotels Ltd was apparently financially all right. There was no reason to doubt what he was being told by Mr Mortell and there was no reason to insist that proceedings be instituted against Cluney Construction Ltd I can exculpate him of any misfeasance for failing to urge as a director of Mont Clare Hotels Ltd, that proceedings be instituted against Cluney Construction Ltd.

The same considerations apply to Mrs Mortell. There is no evidence to suggest other than that she was merely acquiescing in what her son was informing her and accepting his assurances on their face value. In these circumstances there is no case of misfeasance on her part.

The question arises, however, as to whether or not Mr Brian Mortell was guilty of misfeasance in the way he dealt with this outstanding loan. This is not an easy question to decide but I have come to the conclusion on the authorities quoted by Mr Foley and Mr Fennelly that a case of misfeasance has not been made against him. It is not every error of judgment that amounts to misfeasance in law and it is not every act of negligence that amount to misfeasance in law. It seems to me that something more than mere carelessness is required, some act that, perhaps may amount to gross negligence in failing to carry out a duty owed by a director to his company. During this period I think Mr Mortell was genuinely hopeful that the difficulties of the construction company would be overcome.

Mr Mortell was not at this period – in 1977, 1979 and 1980 – in a position where his other company Mont Clare Hotels Limited, was in serious financial difficulty. These difficulties arose later at a time when Cluney Construction Limited was unable to repay the money and when, in fact, he had to mortgage his own dwellinghouse in order to infuse some finance into Mont Clare Hotels Limited.

So it does not seem to me that it has been possible to establish that as a matter of law Mr Brian Mortell was guilty of misfeasance as alleged, during the time that Cluney Construction Limited owed the money to Mont Clare Hotels Limited and no proceedings to recover the money were instituted or authorised by the directors.

It seems to me that it was proper for the liquidator to institute these proceedings and he is entitled to his costs out of the assets. Mr Hussey is also entitled to his costs out of the assets and I will so order.

A question arises as to whether the first and second named respondents are entitled to their costs . . . It seems to me that Mr Mortell was himself to blame to a considerable extent for the fact that these proceedings were instituted; that the various actions which he took and the statements which he made, particularly as late as the statement made to the creditors, indicated to the liquidator that there was a situation which justified him in bringing these proceedings. It is only now, when the matter has been considered on the oral evidence given by Mr Mortell, that it has been possible to determine that he was not guilty of misfeasance. In those circumstances he contributed in my view, to the fact that these proceedings were instituted. I think it would be fair not to require him to pay the costs as he was succeeded technically so I will refuse the application that his costs be paid out of the assets.

Notes

On the question of costs, see also *Re David Ireland & Co* [1905] 1 IR 133 where the liquidator had issued a misfeasance summons against the controlling director and shareholder for the recovery of monies allegedly improperly drawn by him for his personal use out of the company's account. The action was successfully defended on the ground that, although the respondent had been guilty of the alleged misconduct, he had lodged to the credit of the company's account more money than he had personally withdrawn. Nonetheless, he was ordered to pay the costs of the action. As Fitzgibbon LJ stated 'If misconduct was proved, and if, but for that misconduct, the proceedings would not have been necessary, the causa causans of the proceedings was the misconduct of the directors; and if the proceedings were prima facie proper, and even necessary for the liquidation, the fact that the misconduct did not result in ultimate loss does not oust the jurisdiction to make the parties who caused the litigation bear the cost of it.'

Fraudulent preferences

[20.45] S 286 of the Principal Act as substituted by s 133 of the 1990 Act provides that 'any conveyance, mortgage, delivery of goods, payment, execution or other act relating to property made or done by or against a company which is unable to pay its debts as they become due in favour of any creditor, or any person on trust for any creditor with a view to giving such a creditor, or any surety or guarantor for the debt due to such creditor, a preference over the other creditors, shall, if a winding up of the company commences within 6 months of the making or doing the same and the company is at the time of the commencement of the winding up unable to pay its debts (taking into account the contingent and prospective liabilities), be deemed a fraudulent preference of its creditors and be invalid accordingly.'[1]

Where the transaction is in favour of a connected person (ie a director or shadow director of the company, or a person connected with either of them, a related company, or a trustee of or surety or guarantor for a debt due to any of the aforementioned) the 6 month period is extended to two years and there is a rebuttable presumption that the transaction to have been made with a view to giving such person a preference over the other creditors and to be a fraudulent preference.

S 286 does not, however, affect the rights of any person made in good faith and for valuable consideration through or under such a creditor.

However, the section provides that any conveyance or assignment by a company of all its property to trustees for the benefit of all its creditors shall be void to all intents.

1 Ibid at paras **38.80–38.85**.

[20.46] A transaction with an unconnected person will not be caught by s 286 unless the liquidator can prove that its effect was to give a preference to the creditor, surety, guarantor as the case may be, over the other creditors.

Re Welding Plant Ltd; Cooney v Dargan (High Court, 27 June 1984)

[The facts appear from the judgment]

[20.47]   McWilliam J: Welding Plant Limited (hereinafter called the Company) was incorporated on 8th April 1976, and carried on business at premises at Green Lane, Carlow until September 1981, when it ceased to trade. John and Patrick Dargan and Seamus Doorley were the directors but Seamus Doorley seems to have taken no part in the running of the company and is not concerned with these proceedings. In September 1981, the company was indebted to Allied Irish Banks Limited (hereinafter called the bank) in the sum of £23,000.

As security for the money due by the company, the bank held an instrument of guarantee limited to the sum of £30,000 executed by John and Patrick Dargan on 22nd September 1980, and undertakings by two letters from a solicitor for the company dated 14th July 1977, and 21st November 1977 to lodge documents of title to the premises at Green Lane when the registration of the title to the premises should have been completed. These undertakings were not registered as a charge or charges in the Companies Office and no documents of title have been lodged with the bank. The first letter related to a leasehold interest in the property and the second related to the fee simple.

In September 1980, the company had an overdraft of £30,000 and it may be assumed that this was the reason why the guarantee by the Dargans was given for that sum. At the same time the permitted overdraft of the company was reduced to £10,000 and the balance of £20,000 was altered to a term loan for five years. It appears that the company's auditor was pressing the directors for accounts from August 1979, until August 1981 but that these accounts were not presented although, in or about August 1981 the directors asked for a statement of affairs to be prepared by the auditor. The auditor commenced to prepare such a statement and soon realised that the situation of the company was very serious, but he was unable to prepare more than a preliminary draft owing to the failure of the directors to provide the necessary information. The last audited accounts had been presented in August 1979 and these showed that the company was then financially sound but that problems were arising, such as a high number of debtors and considerable liabilities, including arrears of value added tax.

The bank was at this time, writing regularly for audited accounts, and for the documents of title to the Green Lane premises. Although the manager of the Carlow branch of the bank stated that he had no reason to believe, at the end of November 1981, that the company was going down, the sequence of events suggests that he must have been getting worried at this stage, particularly having regard to the absence of any title deeds. Whatever about the appreciation of the situation by the bank, there can be no doubt but that the cessation of trading, the requests for information from the auditor and the draft statement of affairs could have left the Dargans under no illusion as to the insolvency of the company. Subsequently the company went into liquidation and on the 31st March 1982, Hugh Cooney (hereinafter called the liquidator) was appointed liquidator.

The transaction which is challenged in these proceedings was entered into on or about 30th November 1981 at a meeting between the Dargans and the Carlow Manager of the Bank. This consisted of an arrangement whereby the bank advanced sums of £10,500 to each of the Dargans personally to enable the Dargans to purchase the Green Lane premises from the company. The total sum of £21,000 was then lodged by the bank to the credit of the company's account in discharge of part of the indebtedness of the company to the bank. I am satisfied that the Dargans assumed that this transaction enabled them to take the Green Lane property free from the undertakings to lodge the title deeds which the manager considered created a lien over the premises in favour of the bank.

The issues which have been set down for this hearing are:–

(*a*) whether the payment of £21,000 was a fraudulent preference in favour of either the Dargans or the Bank, and

(*b*) if so, whether they are liable to pay the sum of £21,000 to the liquidator . . .

On behalf of the liquidator it is accepted that the onus is on him to show that the payment to the bank was made in order to prefer either the Dargans or the bank but it is submitted that this has been established by the evidence and that the proper order for the court to make is to direct the bank to repay the sum of £21,000 to the liquidator with interest from the date of the liquidation...On behalf of both the bank and the Dargans it was argued that the liquidator must establish a dominant intention to prefer and that this had not been done . . .

I have come to the conclusion that an agreement was reached whereby the Dargans would take loans in their own names from the bank and with the money lent pay off the major part of the debt owed by the company to the bank, the Dargans would buy the premises at Green Lane from the company for the amount of the loan given to them by the bank and would then mortgage these premises to the bank as security for their loans. I am satisfied that the Dargans believed that the letters of undertaking on behalf of the company would then be released by the bank so that they would hold the property free from any liabilities by the company to the bank although subject to the mortgage by them to secure the loans made to them by the bank.

Whatever agreement was reached, the only steps taken on foot of it were that the bank lent the Dargans £21,000 which was appropriated to the discharge of the greater part of the debt due by the company to the bank and the Dargans got their solicitor to draft an agreement for the sale of the premises by the company to them. This draft agreement is dated 2nd December 1981, with the closing date given as the same day and the purchase price expressed to be £21,000. John Dargan stated in evidence that this agreement was not executed and the photocopy exhibited in the affidavit of the liquidator is of an unexecuted agreement. I conclude that it was not executed either by the company or by the Dargans and that the Dargans have no agreement in writing to purchase the property from the company. The bank retained the letters of undertaking given by the solicitor for the company in 1977 and by letter of 6th May 1982 to the liquidator stated that the bank would hold the letters of undertaking until a similar undertaking was given by the solicitor for the Dargans although the solicitor for the company had, by letter dated 16th April 1982 informed the solicitors for the liquidator that 'on the 2nd December 1981 the company disposed of its interest in the property to John and Patrick Dargan for £21,000 and my undertaking was discharged.'

The result seems to be that the company still owns the premises at Green Lane although the Dargans have been using them for their own businesses and may be liable for an occupation rent. The Dargans as guarantors have paid the company's debt to the bank to the extent of £21,000 having been advanced money by the bank for that purpose. It has not been suggested that the Dargans, as guarantors were not liable to pay the amount due to the bank by the company. Nor has it been suggested that the liquidator and the creditors of the company, other than the bank could have any claim against the Dargans as guarantors of the debt due to the bank. The question of any possible right of the liquidator to require the bank to rely on the guarantee given by the Dargans before claiming in the liquidation does not arise on this proceeding.

In my opinion, this transaction was entered into by the Dargans at a time when the company was insolvent and as John Dargan stated in evidence, they had been thinking of putting the company into liquidation and it was entered into by them with a view to obtaining the property at Green Lane to the prejudice of the creditors of the company. Had a conveyance of the property to them been executed and a mortgage of it given by them to the bank there would have been grounds for seeking to have the transactions set aside. That is not the position. The company still owns the property and has paid nothing to the bank or anybody else. The bank still claim some sort of a lien over the property for any money due to the bank. The bank has reduced the amount of the debt due to it by the company by means of a loan to the Dargans who now owe £21,000 to the bank and it is a matter between the Dargans and the bank as to the validity of the loan to them for the discharge of the company's debt.

Under these circumstances the transaction does not appear to have accomplished any preference of the bank or the Dargans over the creditors, either fraudulent or otherwise whatever the intention of the Dargans may have been.

[20.48] In order to prove that a transaction is a fraudulent preference, however, it is not sufficient to prove that the effect of the transaction was to give a preference. The liquidator must also establish a dominant intention to prefer.

Corran Construction Co Ltd v Bank of Ireland Finance [1976–7] ILRM 175

[20.49]   In 1973 the company (then known as Coakley & O'Neill Ltd) obtained a loan from the defendant bank in order to buy a licensed premises. The sole shareholders of the company were Coakley and O'Neill, although only the latter was involved in the management of its affairs. The bank had obtained a charge over the premises as security for the loan, but had failed to register it under s 99 of the Principal Act. In early 1975 the bank was informed that the company was insolvent and in September 1975 threatened to wind up the company if the loan was not repaid. On 9 October 1975 representatives from the bank called round to O'Neill who was ill, in bed and requested that a fresh charge be executed. O'Neill was anxious to continue the business of the company, so he duly executed and registered the charge on 16 October 1975. Less than one month later the company went into liquidation and the liquidator subsequently applied to have the new charge set aside as a fraudulent preference.

[20.50]   McWilliam J: It is accepted on behalf of the liquidator that the onus of proof is on him to establish an intention to prefer the defendant but it is argued that the evidence is open to no other construction, particularly in view of the statement by Mr O'Neill in his evidence that he signed for security for the money they had borrowed in case they would not be able to pay it back . . . On behalf of the defendant it is argued that a dominant intention to prefer must be established by the liquidator and that the evidence does not establish this . . .

I accept the proposition that the liquidator has to establish that the dominant intention of the company was to prefer the defendant. I am satisfied that Mr Coakley took no considered part in the affairs of the company with regard to this transaction and, when he was found, probably had no intention of any sort except to retire again, as quietly as possible. This being so, I am bound to consider the matter on the basis of the intentions of the members of the company who was at that time in sole control of the affairs of the company. I am satisfied that Mr O'Neill was anxious to keep the company going notwithstanding the advice of the accountant and his knowledge of the unfortunate state of the company's affairs. He still had houses to complete and dispose of and he was hoping that the licensed premises would be purchased by his brother through the bank, however unlikely it might appear to a more acute business mind that such a transaction could be effected. Although the defendant was not using pressure in the ordinary sense, I got the impression from the evidence that Mr O'Neill was trying to avoid their representatives because they had been continually trying to get back the money due to the defendant and that, when they finally caught up with him when he was ill in bed, it was something of a relief to find that they would be satisfied if he would remedy some defect in the mortgage. Although he undoubtedly appreciated that this would give the defendant security in case the company would not be able to pay the money back and should have appreciated that there was no real likelihood of the company being able to pay it back, this falls a long way short of making the deposit with the dominant intention of preferring the defendant over the other creditors.

Accordingly, I will refuse the plaintiff's claim.

Notes

Compare this decision with *Re FP & CH Matthews Ltd* [1982] 2 WLR 495; where the Court of Appeal held that a bona fide belief that the company will be able to pay its debts in full at some future date, does not negative an intention to prefer in circumstances where, at the time of the payment the company was aware of its own insolvency.

It seems from *Corran Construction Co Ltd v Bank of Ireland Finance Ltd* that if the creditor puts sufficient pressure on the company to pay the debt, the transaction may not be regarded as a fraudulent preference. The payment will be regarded as having been made, not with a view to preferring the creditor, but rather with a view to removing the pressure under which the company or its controller had been placed. Therefore, the more weakwilled the company and the more oppressive the creditor, the less likely that the payment will be caught by s 286. This result has been criticised. See *Bankruptcy Law Committee Report* (1972) Prl 2714 and *Report of the Review Committee on Insolvency Law and Practice* (Cmnd 8558).

The notion that pressure may remove an intention to prefer is well established in the law of bankruptcy. See *Re Boyd* (1885) 15 LR Ir 521; *Taylor (Assignees of) v Thompson* (1869–70) IRCL 129; *Taylor (Assignees of) v Killeleagh Flax Spinning Co* (1869–70) IRCL 120. In *Daly & Co Ltd* (1887–88) 19 LR Ir 83, 93 Porter MR stated as follows:–

'Where pressure exists so as to overbear the volition of the debtor a payment is not made with a view to prefer the creditor exerting it, but because the debtor cannot help it. The view to prefer is absent; or at least is not the real view, or motive or reason, actuating the debtor . . .'

[20.51] In the absence of direct evidence of an intention to prefer, the court may be entitled to infer such an intention from the surrounding circumstances.

Station Motors Ltd v Allied Irish Banks Ltd [1985] IR 756 (High Court)

[20.52] Station Motors Ltd ('the company') was effectively controlled by William Murphy and his wife Marie Murphy. By 16 June 1980 the company's overdraft with the respondent bank was £78,116.08. On that date the bank obtained a joint and several guarantee from the Murphy's in respect of the overdraft, up to £75,000 with interest. On 15 September 1980 the directors of the company (including the Murphy's) passed a resolution that by virtue of the insolvency of the company an EGM and creditors' meeting should be held on 30 October 1980 to put the company into creditors voluntary winding up. Between 15 September and 3 October lodgments of £23,278.13 were made to the overdrawn account. The company went into liquidation on 3 October and the liquidator subsequently sought a determination from the court as to whether the lodgments of £23,278.13 constituted a fraudulent preference.

[20.53] **Carroll J:** It is common case that the onus is on the liquidator to establish a dominant intention to prefer one creditor over another . . . Since this is a company managed and run by Mr Murphy it is Mr Murphy's intention which falls to be considered. There is no direct evidence here by Mr Murphy as to what his intention was. Nevertheless the court is not precluded from drawing an inference of an intent to prefer: *Re M Kushler Ltd* [1943] 2 All ER 22 deals with the following points:–

(1). The phrase 'with a view to giving such creditor a preference' means that the intention to prefer must be the dominant intention which actuated the payment (per Lord Greene MR at page 24).

(2). It is not enough to prove that there was actual preferment from which an intention to prefer can, with hindsight be inferred. The liquidator must prove an intention to prefer at the time the payment is made (per Goddard LJ at page 28).

(3). Where there is no direct evidence of intention there is no rule of law which precludes a court from drawing an inference of an intention to prefer, in a case where some other possible explanation is open (per Lord Greene MR at page 26).

Also in relation to the absence of direct evidence as to intention, Lord Greene MR says at p 27:–

'. . . it does not seem to me that he (ie. Lord Tomlin in *Peat v Gresham Trust Ltd* [1934] AC 252) could have meant that in every case where there is no direct evidence you are bound to say the onus is not discharged on the grounds that there may have been another explanation. Of course, there may have been other explanations. One can scarcely imagine a case of circumstantial evidence where it would not be possible to say that there might be another explanation where it would not be possible to say that there might be another explanation of the fact.'

(4). The method of ascertaining the state of mind of the payer is the ordinary method of evidence and inference, to be dealt with on the same principles which are commonly employed in drawing inferences of fact (per Lord Greene MR at page 26). He goes on to say that the inference to be drawn in a case of fraudulent preference is an inference of something which has about it, at the very least, the taint of dishonesty and that being so, the court, on ordinary principles is not in the habit of drawing inferences which involve dishonesty or something approaching dishonesty unless there are solid grounds for drawing them.

As to the question of whether the taint of dishonesty is necessarily involved in a case of fraudulent preference Maugham J in *Re Patrick and Lyon Ltd* [1933] 1 Ch 786 at p 790 expressed the view that a fraudulent preference within the meaning of the Companies Act 1929 or the bankruptcy act 1914 whether in the case of a company or of an individual possibly may not involve moral blame at all.

However, also in the *Kushler* case [1943] 2 All ER 22 the same point was dealt with by Goddard LJ at p 28:– '. . . the matter stands as it does in any matter relating to a state of mind where any criminal or civil court, if the person upon whom the onus lies proves no more than a state of facts which is equally consistent with guilt or innocence (using the expression 'guilt' for convenience because in bankruptcy, there is no question of crime or criminal intent.) In such a case the court is not entitled to draw the one unfavourable inference and find the payment was a guilty rather than an innocent preference and if any court is left in doubt as to the inference, then the trustee has not proved his case.'

Having considered the established facts in this case, I am satisfied that the overwhelming inference to be drawn from those facts is that the lodgments made after the 15th September 1980, were made with a composite intention to prefer (*a*) the bank as the direct creditor and (*b*) the Murphys themselves as guarantors of the company's overdraft. The facts which support this view are:–

(1). This is a guarantee case. The attitude of Lord Greene MR in *Re M Kushler Ltd* to such cases is expressed as follows at page 26:– 'At the other end of the scale there comes the type of case which is extremely familiar nowadays, where the person (such as a director) who makes the payment on behalf of the debtor is himself going to obtain by means of it a direct and immediate personal benefit. These cases of guarantees of overdrafts and securities deposited to cover overdrafts are very common indeed and where for example, you have directors who have given guarantees, the circumstances of that strong element of private advantage may justify the court in attaching to the other facts much greater weight than would have been attached to precisely similar facts in a case where that element did not exist.' In this case a guarantee of £30,000 in January 1980, was increased to £70,000 in June 1980.

(2). Because at the directors' meeting of the 15th September 1980 it was resolved that an extraordinary general meeting and creditors' meeting be called for the purposes of a creditors' voluntary winding up, one must draw an inference that on and from the 15th September the directors knew that the company was insolvent and it was only a question of time until it went into liquidation and that the payment of any trade debtors on or after the 15th would have the effect of preferring them . . .

(3). Only six cheques were paid out of the company's account on and after the 15th September and then only as a result of special representations made by Mr Murphy. Instead of inferring, as put forward in the bank's affidavit, that the account was being operated normally in the ordinary course of business because of the payment of these six cheques. I find exactly the opposite. It seems to me that the necessity to make a special case for these cheques infers that the account was not being operated normally. Also there were four other cheques presented but not honoured during that period and this does not represent ordinary trading.

(4). The fact that one of those cheques was drawn after the 16th September by Mr Murphy for himself does not weaken the inference of an intention to prefer the bank. As I have said the intention to prefer the bank was coupled with an intention to prefer the guarantors. The payment of a cheque for £2,730 to Mr Murphy was a direct preferment of himself rather than an indirect one by reducing the amount payable on foot of the guarantee.

(5). The payment of the five other cheques during this period, does not in my opinion, negative an intention to prefer the bank directly and the guarantors indirectly. For whatever reason, Mr Murphy decided those creditors should be paid even though as guarantor he would ultimately be responsible. In proportion to the lodgments totalling £23,278.13 the amounts involved in four of the cheques were very small.

(6). Once the directors had decided on the 15th September to hold meetings for a creditors' voluntary winding up, there could not be normal trading as the company at that stage must have been unable to pay its debts. The opening of the wages account on the 17th September was an indicator that the end was nigh.

I find the inference overwhelming that the lodgments after the 15th September were made to prefer the bank directly and the guarantors indirectly, and that this was the dominant purpose of the lodgments.

Notes

For another recent case with remarkably similar facts see *Re Industrial Design and Manufacture* Ltd (High Court of Northern Ireland, Carswell J, 25 June 1984). See also *Kelleher v Continental Irish Meats Ltd* (High Court, Costello J, 9 May 1978); *Re Northside Motor Co Ltd; Eddison v Allied Irish Banks Ltd* (High Court 24, July 1985).

A disposition of property of a company will not constitute a fraudulent preference unless the party preferred is a creditor, surety or guarantor of that company. S 286 has no application if the beneficiary of the disposition is only a creditor surety or guarantor of some other company, albeit an associate of the disponor company: *Re John C Parkes & Sons Ltd; John C Parkes & Sons Ltd v The Hong Kong and Shanghai Banking Corporation* [1990] ILRM 341, noted by MacCann *Winding Up: Setting Aside Antecedent Transactions.* (1990) 8 ILT (ns) 111.

Fraudulent trading

[20.54] Prior to the 1990 Act s 297 of the Principal Act imposed both civil and criminal liability on persons who were party to the carrying on of the company's business in a fraudulent manner. Criminal and civil liability has now been split.[1]

S 297(1) as amended by s 137 of the 1990 Act provides as follows:–

'If any person is knowingly a party to the carrying on of the business of a company with intent to defraud creditors of the company or creditors of any other person or for any fraudulent purpose, that person shall be guilty of an offence.'

Previously a prosecution could only take place where the company was in liquidation. This is no longer the case. Any person who is convicted of fraudulent trading is liable on summary conviction to imprisonment for a term not exceeding 12 months or to a fine not exceeding £1,000 or to both. On indictment he is liable to imprisonment for a term not exceeding 7 years or to a fine not exceeding £50,000 or to both.

1 Ibid at para **38.85**. See also Ussher *Fraudulent trading* (1964) 6 DULJ (ns) 58.

[20.55] Under s 297A as inserted by s 138 of the 1990 Act provides that: If in the course of the insolvent winding up of a company it appears that:

(*a*) any person was, while an officer of the company, knowingly a party to the carrying on of any business of the company in a reckless manner; or
(*b*) any person was knowingly a party to the carrying on of any business of the company with intent to defraud creditors of the company, or creditors of any other person or for any fraudulent purpose;

the court on the application of the receiver, liquidator or any creditor or contributory of the company, may, if it thinks it proper to do so, declare that any persons who were knowingly parties to the carrying on of the business in the manner aforesaid shall be personally responsible, without any limitation of liability, for all or any of the debts or other liabilities of the company as the court may direct.

An application can only be made by or on behalf of a creditor or contributory, if he suffered loss or damage as a result of the fraudulent trading.

[20.56] The concept of reckless trading is new and introduces an objective standard for directors. S 297(2) provides that a person is deemed to have been knowingly a party to the carrying on of any business of the company in a reckless manner if –

(*a*) he was a party to the carrying on of such business and, having regard to the general knowledge, skill and experience that may reasonably be expected of a person in his position, he ought to have known that his actions or those of the company would cause loss to the creditors of the company, or any of them, or
(*b*) he was a party to the contracting of a debt by the company and did not honestly believe on reasonable grounds that the company would be able to pay the debt when it fell due for payment as well as all its other debts (taking into account the contingent and prospective liabilities).

625

In deciding whether it is proper to make a person personally liable for reckless trading the court must have regard to whether the creditor in question was, at the time the debt was incurred, aware of the company's financial state of affairs and, notwithstanding such awareness, nevertheless assented to the incurring of the debt.

If the officer is made personally liable for reckless trading the court may having regard to all the circumstances, relieve him in whole or in part from such personal liability, provided it appears that he had acted honestly and reasonably.

Under s 297A(7) the court may charge any personal liability for fraudulent or reckless trading on the assets of the defendant. It may also determine to whom the proceeds of any successful application are to be paid.

[20.57] Fraudulent trading typically involves a pattern of continuous conduct in deliberate fraud of the company's creditors.

Re Kelly's Carpetdrome Ltd (High Court, 1 July 1983)

[20.58] Kelly's Supermarket ('supermarket') was wholly owned by the respondents Matthew and Eamon Kelly, both of whom were directors. Supermarket ceased trading in September or October 1976 and its stock was taken over by Kelly's Carpetdrome Ltd ('Carpetdrome'). Eamon Kelly was a director of Carpetdrome. Matthew Kelly though not registered as such, was the de facto controller of Carpetdrome and beneficial owner of its entire share capital. Carpetdrome took possession of supermarket stock which it sold and used to pay all of Supermarket's creditors in full with the exception of the Revenue Commissioners. Subsequently, in 1977 Supermarket went into liquidation owing substantial sums to the revenue. During the course of its trading life large sums of money were syphoned out of Carpetdrome by the respondent and placed in the account of Monck Properties Ltd, a company in which Matthew Kelly held 99 shares, the remaining share being held by Eamon Kelly. Monck Properties Ltd used these monies to buy various properties. In late 1980 when it became clear that the revenue was about to take action to recover large sums owing by Carpetdrome, the respondents transferred all of Carpetdrome's stock to Kelly' Carpet Drive-In Ltd ('Drive-In') another company beneficially owned by Matthew Kelly. Drive-In sold the stock and paid off all the Carpetdrome's creditors with the exception of the revenue. Carpetdrome went into liquidation in June 1981 owing large sums to the revenue. The liquidator commenced the present proceedings against the respndents under s 297 for an order making them personally liable for Carpetdrome's debts. Prior to the present proceedings however, a consent order had been made aggregating the assets of Carpetdrome and Monck Properties Ltd and ordering that the two companies should be treated as one.

[20.59] Costello J: It is clear from the evidence what happened was this, that from the time that the Carpetdrome Company started to trade in the

Autumn of 1976, it used the stock of the Supermarket Company for its purposes. It paid cheques to the Supermarket Company from the proceeds of the sale of the stocks as it had no other capital and the Supermarket Company used the money which it had obtained to pay its creditors, ie. all its trade creditors other than the revenue, and eventually the company went into liquidation owing a not insubstantial sum to the revenue . . . I think that it has been established beyond any doubt on the evidence that the business of Carpetdrome was being carried on in a fraudulent manner for a number of years. Very considerable debts were incurred to the revenue for corporation profits tax, VAT, PAYE and PRSI. No adequate records were kept and I am satisfied the absence of proper records was part of the scheme to avoid liability for tax. I am further satisfied that important records of the company were deliberately destroyed for the same purpose. I am further satisfied that the company permitted funds from which its liability to the revenue could be discharged to be transferred to Monck Properties and no record of these transactions were kept. The object was to avoid liability to the revenue. The cash received was not recorded for the same purpose, and it was used by Mr Matthew Kelly for his own purpose, and not for the purposes of the company. I am further satisfied when it became apparent round about the latter part of 1980 that the revenue were about to take action to recover very substantial sums due to it, the company transferred all its stock to another company, and that the purpose of this was to avoid liability to the revenue, liability which it was known existed, and that the purpose was a fraudulent one. There was no commercial justification for this transfer and the company, Drive-In acted in the way which I have described in paying off the creditors other than the revenue. I have indicated that Mr Matthew Kelly was the beneficial owner of the shares in Carpetdrome. I am satisfied that he decided to allow his brothers to run Drive-In but I am equally satisfied that he had maintained the beneficial ownership in the shares in the company. It is not possible for me to know the extent of this beneficial ownership, nor is it necessary for me to do so. While he allowed his brother and brother in law to run the company, I am quite satisfied he did not give over a business with a turnover of £2 million by way of gift, and that he retained a beneficial interest in the equity of the company.

So the liquidator has established that the fraud was carried on in this way and also in the ways to which I have referred in relation to the concealment of the books and the falsification of the records. Finally I am satisfied Mr Matthew Kelly was a party to this fraudulent trading and Mr Eamon Kelly was a party to this fraudulent trading.

I will discuss with counsel the form of the draft order but it seems to me I should make a declaration in accordance with the terms of the section that the business of Kelly's Carpetdrome Limited was carried on from approximately the month of October 1976 until the end of February 1981 with intent to defraud the creditors of the company and for other fraudulent companies. I think I should make a declaration the respondents, Matthew Kelly and Eamon Kelly were knowingly parties to the carrying on of the business in the manner I have said. I think I should declare the respondents to be jointly and severally and personally responsible without limitation for all the debts of the company.

I will also order they are jointly and severally responsible for any further interest that may be due on the capital sums. In addition, I think I should order that for the purposes of giving effect to the declaration, that if Mr Matthew Kelly is owed any sum by Monck Properties Limited, that his liability under this order should constitute a charge on any such debt.

I will also order that Mr Matthew Kelly and Mr Eamon Kelly pay the costs of these proceedings.

Notes

See also *Re Aluminium Fabricators Ltd* (High Court, 13 May 1983). The facts were that on 6 May 1981 a petition was presented to wind up Aluminium Fabricators Ltd and a winding up order was made on 25 May 1981. The liquidator on reaching the company's premises, discovered that in the time between the presentation of the petition and the date of the winding up order all stock, materials and furniture in the company's premises had disappeared. An examination of the books and records indicated accounting irregularities and large sums of money were unaccounted for. After a s 245 examination of the directors, Phelan and Barrett it was discovered that the directors had kept two sets of books and records. In one set of accounts, the income of the company was deliberately understated for the purposes of tax evasion. The evidence also indicated that Phelan and Barrett had syphoned off large amounts of the company's money to bank accounts in their own names in the Isle of Man. The disappearance of assets after the presentation of the petition was also the work of the directors. It was further established that for several months, at least, prior to the winding up the directors had caused the company to continue trading when they knew it could not pay its debts as they fell due. Finally they had used the company's monies to buy an aeroplane for Phelan and to buy motor cars for themselves and had used materials supplied by the company without paying therefor in carrying out works on their own houses. In the circumstances the court declared Phelan and Barrett personally liable for all the debts of the company. O'Hanlon J commented that 'The privilege of limitation of liability which is afforded by the Companies Act in relation to companies incorporated under the Act with limited liability, cannot be afforded to those who use a limited company as a cloak shield beneath which they seek to operate a fraudulent system of carrying on business for their own personal enrichment and advantage.'

[20.60] One single fraudulent transaction may also constitute 'fraudulent trading'.

Re Hunting Lodges Ltd [1985] ILRM 75 (High Court)

[20.61] In January 1983 Hunting Lodges Ltd ('the company') received a valuation of £750,000 for its principal asset, a public house known as 'Durty

Nelly's'. The company was, at this time hopelessly insolvent and the Revenue Commissioners had issued summonses against it for arrears of taxes. The company had an issued share capital of £12,000, of which £9,000 was held by Mr Porrit, the balance being held by his wife. The Porrits were the sole directors, Mr Porrit also being the secretary. In March 1983 Mr Porrit began negotiations with Mr O'Connor for the sale of 'Durty Nelly's'. In May 1983 the Revenue Commissioners having been informed of the company's insolvency threatened to wind it up. In June 1983 'Durty Nelly's' was purchased by Mr O'Connor through a 'shelf' company acquired for that purpose, known as Plage Services Ltd. The purchase price was £640,000, of which only £480,000 was officially recorded. The balance of £160,000 was paid to Mr Porrit in cash and by way of drafts made out to fictitious payees. Mr and Mrs Porrit then proceeded to open various bank accounts in false names, into which the £160,000 was placed. Two days later the Revenue Commissioners who were owed £756,395.84 petitioned for the winding up of the company, a provisional liquidator was immediately appointed and a winding up order was subsequently made. The company's records for 1976 to 1980 had been destroyed in a fire in 1980 but reconstructed records showed that drawings by the Porrits during this four year period amounted to £113,889 of which £100,000 was allocated to remuneration. No formal resolutions were ever passed authorising such remuneration. In the period shortly before liquidation Mr Porrit doubled his drawings. By way of a s 245 examination the liquidator subsequently discovered the existence of the £160,000 payment and also discovered the false accounts. He recovered a total of £148,000 from these accounts and then proceeded to apply for an order rendering the Porrits, Mr O'Connor and Plage Services Ltd personally liable for all the debts of the company on the ground that they were guilty of fraudulent trading.

[20.62]   Carroll J: The following issues are raised: (1) Can a single transaction be described as carrying on business within the meaning of s 297? (2) Was any business carried on with intent to defraud creditors of the company or creditors of any other person or for any fraudulent purpose? (3) Was each one of the persons sought to be made liable, 'knowingly' a party to the carrying on of such business with such fraudulent intent?

I am satisfied that carrying on business is not synonymous with trading: see *In re Sarflax Ltd* [1979] Ch 592. In my opinion it is not necessary that all the company's business should be carried on with fraudulent intent nor is it necessary that there should be a course of dealing or series of transactions before the section can be called into operation. The section refers to 'any business'. In the course of the conduct of its affairs a company will have many different aspects of its business. One single transaction can properly be described as 'business of the company' and so also can constituent parts of a transaction. One single act committed with the fraudulent intent specified by the section can, in my opinion, suffice to ground a declaration which involves the sale of the entire assets of the company does not alter the position in any way . . . In this case, while the sale of the premises with a payment on the side can be viewed as one transaction, it also breaks into different elements. There are the negotiations culminating in the signing of the contract, the closing of the sale and the disposition of the purchase money. Each of these elements can be designated together or separately as 'business of the company'. In particular I include the disposition of the purchase money as part of the business of the company. Unlikely though it was, Mr Porrit could have deposited the £160,000 to the credit of the company, which would have negatived an intent on his part to defraud creditors in respect of that money. Instead he concealed the money under false names in the building society accounts, thus completing the transaction which was part of the business of the company.

Having decided that any business of the company includes a single transaction or part thereof I intend to refer the 'business' in this case as the sale or a constituent part thereof. This is the common denominator between Mr and Mrs Porrit and Mr O'Connor and Plage Services Ltd.

I am satisfied that all four parties were 'parties' to the sale within the meaning of the section. The phrase in the corresponding section to the English Act (s 322 of the Companies Act 1948) has been defined in *In re Maidstone Buildings Provisions Ltd* [1971] 1 WLR 1085 st p 1092 as indicating no more than 'participating in'; 'takes part in' or 'concurs in'. Pennycuick VC added that it seemed to him that involved some positive steps of some nature.

There is no problem in proving positive steps in this case as each of the parties participated in the sale. Mr Porrit participated from start to finish. He was involved in all the negotiations; he required the payment on the side; he produced at closing the resolution of the directors authorising the sale at £480,000; he countersigned the affixing of the seal to the conveyance; he took the additional £160,000 and he opened the accounts with the building society under false names. Mrs Porrit participated in part of the sale. While she denied any knowledge of the resolution of the directors, she attended the closing of the sale and countersigned the affixing of the seal to the conveyance without objection. She signed a false name to the signature cards in respect of the building society accounts. Therefore she took an active part in the closing of the sale and the disposition of part of the purchase money.

Mr Humphrey O'Connor participated in the sale up to and including the closing. He negotiated directly with Mr Porrit and agreed to provide the money on the side. He co-operated by providing the three bank drafts in false names together with cash and the endorsed bank draft for the deposit and handed them over secretly to Mr Porrit without the knowledge of their solicitors or the company's auditor.

Plage Services Ltd is the actual vehicle which Mr O'Connor used to take the conveyance. It was therefore a party to the sale at closing. The next issue is whether the sale or individual elements of it were tainted with an intent to defraud creditors (whether of the company or of any other person) or any fraudulent purpose and if so, did each of the parties knowingly participate.

In my opinion, in order for the section to apply it is not necessary that there should be a common agreed fraudulent intent. If each of the participants acts for a fraudulent purpose then each may be liable. In this case I am satisfied that Mr Porrit intended to defraud the creditors of the company by abstracting money secretly from the company. Insofar as Mr O'Connor is concerned, he was a willing partner in completing the sale by paying part of the purchase money on the side in such a way that it could be concealed. It is irrelevant in my opinion whether he knew or did not know that the company was insolvent. He made the payment on the side in circumstances which could have had no purpose other than a fraudulent one. Either the creditors were going to be defrauded, if the company was insolvent, or the Revenue Commissioners were if the company were solvent. The false names of the bank drafts were indicative of Mr O'Connor's guilty participation in Mr Porrit's scheme.

In addition both Mr Porrit and Mr O'Connor had the further fraudulent purpose of defrauding the revenue of stamp duty on the full consideration. While it appears to me that the evidence of stamp duty was not their primary concern, it was nevertheless the necessary consequence of the secret payment. Since every person is deemed to intend the natural and probable consequences of his acts, so Mr Porrit and Mr O'Connor must be deemed to have intended the avoidance of stamp duty and thus added an additional fraudulent intent to their actions.

Plage Services Ltd has the knowledge of Mr O'Connor as a director imputed to it. It therefore, participated in the closing of the sale with the same guilty knowledge of Mr O'Connor.

As far as Mrs Porrit is concerned I am satisfied that she did not know of the payment of money on the side as part of the agreement with Mr O'Connor but that does not absolve her from liability under the section. She knew about the sale itself and she countersigned the affixing of the company's seal to the conveyance to the purchaser without demur. When her husband brought home the signature cards from the IPBS she signed a false name. On her own evidence she assumed the money was part of the purchase money (which it was). It therefore belonged to the company. She assisted in the concealment of that money by signing the false name. That could have had no purpose other than a fraudulent purpose. It is therefore immaterial as far as she is concerned that she did not know of the payment of money on the side. She was prepared to conceal and did assist in concealing the company's money arising from the sale of the property.

I am satisfied therefore, that it is proper to make a declaration under s 297 of the Companies Act 1963 that Charles Roger Porrit, Joan Porrit, Humphrey O'Connor and Plage Services Ltd to be personally responsible for the debts of the company.

The last remaining question is the extent to which each of them shall be liable. In this regard it is important to look to the entire circumstances. In *In re Cyona Distributors Ltd* [1967] Ch 889 Lord Denning MR said at p 902: 'In my judgment that section [referring to the corresponding section in the

English Act] is deliberately framed in wide terms so as to enable the court to bring fraudulent persons to book. If a man has carried on the business of a company fraudulently, the court can make an order against him for the payment of a fixed sum . . . The sum may be compensatory or it may be punitive.'

In *Re William C Leitch Bros Ltd* [1932] 2 Ch 71 at p 79 Maugham J said: 'I am inclined to the view that s 275 is in the nature of a punitive provision, and that where the court makes such a declaration in relation to any of the debts or other liabilities of the company, it is in the discretion of the court to make an order without limiting the order to the amount of the debts of those creditors proved to have been defrauded by the acts of the director in question, though no doubt the order would in general be so limited.'

In the case of Charles Roger Porrit I am satisfied that at the time he entered into negotiations with Mr O'Connor the company was insolvent and that all his efforts were directed to getting as much money out of the company as he could before the revenue moved against it. His personal drawings doubled; his personal overdraft at Allied Irish Banks was discharged out of the company's monies. He deliberately deceived the revenue officials about going to England in order to avoid a meeting, when in fact he did not go. In my opinion it is entirely proper that Mr Porrit should be personally responsible without any limitation of liability for all the debts of the company. The benefit of limited liability should, in my opinion, be totally withdrawn and he should be put in the same position as if he were a trader carrying on business personally.

In relation to Mrs Porrit the case has been made on her behalf that she played no part in the running of the company. The day has long since passed since married women were classifed with infants and persons of unsound mind as suffering from a disability so far as responsibility for their acts was concerned, or since a married woman could escape criminal responsibilty on the grounds that she acted under the influence of her husband. Mrs Porrit cannot evade liability by claiming that she was only concerned with minding her house and looking after her children. If that was the limit of the responsibilities she wanted, she should not have become a director of the company, or having become one she should have resigned.

Any person who becomes a director takes on responsibilities and duties particularly where there are only two. The balance sheet and profit and loss account and directors' report for each year should have been signed by her. A director who continues as director but abdicates all responsibility is not lightly to be excused. If she had reasonably endeavoured to keep abreast of company affairs and had been deceived (and there is not such evidence) it might be possible to excuse her.

Mrs Porrit was concerned with the concealment of £148,000 all of which has been recovered, therefore no loss arises. In deciding whether to make Mrs Porrit liable for debts where nothing was lost through her actions, it is necessary that there should be 'real moral blame' attaching to her. In my opinion this does arise because Mrs Porrit took all of the advantages and none of the responsibilities connected with the company. I consider that she should be personally liable without limitation of liability of all the debts of the company not exceeding the amount or value of any advancement from her husband since 1 December 1976. I have chosen that date as it is the start of the four year period when the accounts had to be reconstructed. I direct that Mrs Porrit make discovery on oath of any such advancement. She is already liable to the company on foot of the directors' loan account.

So far, as Mr O'Connor and Plage Services Ltd are concerned, I have decided that their liability should be limited to the sum of £12,000.

This was the cash sum given to Mr Porrit which has disappeared and has not been accounted for. Mr O'Connor and Plage Services Ltd and jointly and severally liable for this amount. I make this liability a charge on any debt or obligation due from the company to either of them. Mr O'Connor is already liable to the company in respect of the balance of monies due for the stock-in-trade.

Notes

See Collins (1984) 6 DULJ (ns) 138.

[20.63] 'Fraudulent trading' connotes actual dishonesty, involving according to current notions of fair trading among commercial men, real moral blame. If a company incurs a debt in circumstances where the directors know or have reasonable grounds to believe that it will not be able to repay that debt upon the due date for payment then, unless the creditor expressly or impliedly consented to late payment when the debt was first incurred, the proper inference to be drawn is that the company' business has been carried on with intent to defraud.

Re EB Tractors Ltd; Lombard and Ulster Ltd v Edgar and Bradley
(High Court of Justice in Northern Ireland, Chancery division, Murray J, 21 March 1986)

[20.64] The sole directors of EB Tractors Ltd ('the company') were Edgar and Bradley. The company which was involved in the retail sale of tractors had an overdraft facility of £12,000 with Ulster Bank Ltd. This overdraft was secured by a floating charge over the companies assets and was personally guaranteed by each of the directors. In March 1979 the company entered into a 'stocking agreement' with Lombard and Ulster Bank Ltd ('Lombard') the terms of which provided that whenever the company was supplied with a tractor by a firm called Saville Tractors (Belfast) Ltd, the invoice was to be made out to Lombard which would itself pay Saville Tractors (Belfast) Ltd. Lombard, in turn was to be paid the purchase price with interest by the company once it had sold the tractor. Four transactions took place pursuant to the stocking agreement. In the first, a tractor was sold by the company in June 1979 but Lombard was only paid in October 1979. Nonetheless, in September 1979 a second tractor was invoiced to Lombard who duly paid for it. The tractor was sold by the company on 10 October 1979. Three weeks later further tractors were invoiced to Lombard and these were sold on 31 May and 3 September 1980. Lombard was never paid for the last three tractors. The proceeds of sale were applied by the company instead, in reduction of its overdraft. On 4 February by reason of its insolvency the company was placed in liquidation. Lombard subsequently applied to have Edgar and Bradley made personally liable for the debts of the company, claiming that they had been parties to the carrying on of the business of the company with intent to defraud creditors.

[20.65]   Murray J: I propose to begin by considering the effect of s 298 in the light of the decided cases (of which there are several) on the section (or its statutory predecessor) and I start with *Re William C Leitch Bros* [1932] 2 Ch 71 . . . On the meaning of the expression carrying on business 'with intent to defraud creditors' Maugham J said this:

> 'In my opinion I must hold that if a company continues to carry on business and to incur debts at a time when there is to the knowledge of the directors *no reasonable prospect* of the creditors *ever* receiving payment of those debts, it is, in general a proper inference that the company is carrying on business with intent to defraud and as I have intimated I am satisfied that the respondent knew what the position was as from March 1 1930: and I hold further that the respondent deliberately went on trading in the name of the company in order, as he hoped to safeguard his own position and without any regard to the interests of creditors'. . .

In *Patrick & Lyon Ltd* [1933] Ch 786 Maugham J again had to consider s 275 of the 1929 Act, the fraudulent trading section. The precise facts of the case are difficult to glean from the report and I propose only to refer to certain passages in the judgment. In the course of his judgment Maugham J made the following very firm pronouncement about the section: '. . . I will express the opinion that the words "defraud" and "fraudulent purpose" when they appear in the section are words which connote actual dishonesty involving, according to current notions of fair trading among commercial men, real moral blame' . . .

R v Grantham [1984] 2 WLR 815 is a recent case which was much canvassed at the hearing before me. As its name indicates, this was a criminal prosecution for fraudulent trading, not a civil application by a liquidator or creditor . . . The prosecution arose out of the import into England of a large quantity of potatoes from a French exporter called Jacob at a total price of £88,000. There were several defendants, including Grantham (the appellant) and they each played a different part in the purchasing, importing and distribution of the potatoes, but the net result of all their efforts was that the potatoes were sold for £68,000 ie. at a loss of £20,000 and Mr Jacob received only £19,668 of his total entitlement of £88,000. Moreover, each of the defendants helped himself liberally out of the proceeds of sale for his own costs and expenses in the various operations involved in the transactions. The trading in question continued over a very short period indeed, viz. 29 May – 25 June and the cause of the trouble was that within a day or two of the purchase of the first lot of potatoes the bottom dropped out of the potato market in England. However, as Lord Lane CJ (giving judgment of the Court of Appeal) said: 'This [collapse of the market] did not deter those who were running the company from continuing to pursue their course of purchases unabated.' The learned Lord Chief Justice then continued:

'There was, in short ample evidence that the company was being operated dishonestly. Indeed had there been a charge of conspiracy laid against the appellant, it would, questions of jurisdiction apart, probably have succeeded. From the outset, no or no sufficient capital was available. No overdraft facilities were sought. There was some suggestion in the later stages that the situation might be retrieved by trading in other commodities, or by raising a loan from a merchant bank or by introducing fresh backers, but nothing came of these suggestions.'

The jury convicted the appellant of fraudulent trading and the appeal was based mainly on the trial judge's address to the jury on the meaning of 'intent to defraud'. What he said was this:–

'A man intends to defraud a creditor either if he intends that the creditors shall *never* be paid or alternatively if he intends to obtain credit or carry on obtaining credit when the rights and interests of the creditor are being prejudiced *in a way which the defendant himself has generally regarded as dishonest. . .* Some fraudulent traders intend from the outset never to pay or never to pay more than a fraction of the debt. If this is true in your view in this case then the intent to defraud if he obtains credit when there is a substantial risk of the creditor not getting his money or not getting the whole of his money, and the defendant knows that this is the position and *knows that he is stepping beyond the bounds of what ordinary decent people engaged in business would regard as honest.*'

There then follows this passage in the trial judge's charge against which the main thrust in the appellant's argument was directed:

'Members of the jury, if a man honestly believes when he obtains credit that although funds are not immediately available he will be able to pay them when the debt becomes due or *within a short time thereafter* no doubt you would say that is not dishonest and there is no intent to defraud but if he obtains or helps to obtain credit or further credit when he knows there is no good reason for thinking funds will become available to pay the debt *?when it becomes due or shortly thereafter then*, though it is entirely a matter for you this question of dishonesty, you might well think that is dishonest and there is an intent to defraud.'

I here interpose the comment that the passage appears to be markedly different from Maugham's statement of the law. Lord Lane referred to the Chancery Division cases I have cited above, viz *Leitch* and *Patrick & Lyon*

Ltd on which the appellant's counsel relied as authority for the proposition
that the learned trial judge was wrong to tell the jury they could find an
intent to defraud if the appellant had – 'no good reason for thinking funds
[would] become available to pay the debt when it [became] due or shortly
thereafter.' But pointed out however, that Maugham J in the Chancery cases
had expressly disavowed any intention of defining 'fraud' and the court went
on to say this:–

> 'What the judge in the present case was doing was to direct the jury in the
> first passage as to the general meaning of the section and then, in the later
> passage as to which complaint is made, directing the jury that it is possible
> for them, if they thought fair to come to a conclusion that the appellant
> was acting dishonestly and fraudulently if he realised at the time when the
> debts were incurred that there was no reason for thinking that funds would
> become available to pay the debt when it became due or shortly there-
> after. We do not think the judge was in error in this direction.'

I shall cite two further passages from the Court of Appeal's judgment in
Grantham and then make some comments on its relevance to this case:–

> 'In the present case it was open to the jury to find, it not inevitable that
> they would find, that whoever was running this business was intending to
> deceive or was actually deceiving Jacob into believing that he would be
> paid in 28 days or shortly thereafter, when they knew perfectly well that
> there was no hope of that coming about. He was plainly induced thereby
> to deliver further potatoes on credit. The potential or inevitable detriment
> to him is obvious.'
>
> 'In the present case . . . there was a great deal more than the bare fact of
> preferring one creditor to another as was the case of Sarflax [1979] Ch 592.
> Here Jacob was allowed or induced to continue to supply potatoes with no
> real prospect of being paid at the due date.'

It seems to me to emerge from *Grantham* that mere proof that when he
incurred the relevant debt the debtor had no prospect of paying the debt on
the due date or shortly thereafter is not sufficient to establish an intention to
defraud. Many a person who has been leniently treated by his creditor in the
past and has been allowed to postpone payment of debts till long after the
due date, incurs a further debt with little or no hope of paying on the due
date or near it. But such a person is not guilty of fraud. An essential
additional element which must proved and I stress this, is 'deliberate dishonesty'. In *Grantham* the Court of Appeal cited with approval the following direction to the jury in *R v Sinclair* [1968] 1 WLR 1246:

> 'It is fraud if it is proved that there was the taking of a risk which there was
> no right to take which would cause detriment or prejudice to another . . .
> You have to be sure that it was deliberate dishonesty.'

Again in the charge by the trial judge in the *Grantham* case he instances
the situation where the defendant–

636

'intends to obtain credit or carry on obtaining credit when the rights and interests of the creditor are being prejudiced in a way which the defendant *himself has generally regarded as dishonest.*'

and finally he refers to the situation in which

'the defendant knows he is stepping beyond the bounds of what ordinary decent people engaged in business would regard as honest,'

My second comment on *Grantham* is that unlike the present case, it was a brief dealing between strangers and as soon as the original purchase of potatoes had been agreed the defendants were fully aware that the market had gone and that the purchase price they were contracting to pay could not be recovered. Notwithstanding this, they went on ordering large amounts of potatoes at a completely uneconomical price. The facts of this case are completely different. Here there was a considerable amount of successful trading between the parties in tractors over a couple of years before the trouble over the last four tractors arose. Again, in the *Leitch* case, there was the clearest possible dishonesty in the director who ordered goods for which his company had no means to pay and did so, no doubt to bring the goods into the company's ownership so that the receiver could seize them under the director's own debenture. It seems to me that in each of these cases the conduct of the defendant(s) went well 'beyond the bounds of what ordinary people engaged in business would regard as honest.' I must say, with respect that I prefer this test of dishonesty to the alternative test based on the defendant's own view of whether his conduct was dishonest – as posed in *Grantham* and some other cases.

Two other recent authorities are helpful on what constitutes 'trading' in the context of 'fraudulent trading' – *Re Sarflax* [1979] Ch 592 and *Re Gerald Cooper Chemicals* [1978] Ch 262 and *Sarflax* also shows that to pay one lawful debt rather than another is not fraudulent trading though it may be a fraudulent preference . . .

I shall now summarise my reasons for rejecting Lombard's claim against the defendants but before I do so I record my view that in deciding this case I was in effect in the position of a jury asking myself whether 'ordinary decent people engaged in business' would regard what either of the defendants did as 'stepping beyond the bounds' of honesty, or alternatively whether either of the defendants acted in a way which he or she 'generally regarded as dishonest'. Furthermore in answering either of these questions I had to remember that the onus on Lombard to bring me to answer 'Yes' was, in view of the allegations against the defendants, a heavy one.

Now for my reasons:

(1) With one possible exception (to which I shall refer below) the 'badges' of fraud were missing from the defendants' conduct: the books were meticulously kept and were up to date as the liquidator freely acknowledged in the witness box. There was nothing even approaching the blatant self-serving manoeuvres which were denounced as fraudulent trading in the

Leitch and *Grantham* cases: the overall impression I received was to two people with fairly modest business acumen and resources who, after two years of quite successful trading, ran into a collapsing market and despite their efforts to survive it, went under. It may well be that their hopes of survival were unrealistic, but I did not see them as dishonest.

(2) Both defendants denied dishonesty or improper motive and I accept the denials as genuine. I am clearly of the view that Mr Edgar was in effect the financial director of the business and Mrs Bradley (an obviously timid lady) the financial mechanic (if I may so describe her, without offence) who kept the books and who, when the financial situation became difficult sought and obeyed Mr Edgar's directions as to what was to be done.

(3) There is no doubt that in the summer of 1980 Mr Edgar and on his instructions Mrs Bradley impeded the attempts of Lombard to find out what had happened to the three tractors then unpaid for, but I accept their evidence that their reason for so doing was to avoid the embarrassment to their customers of a call (if made) by Lombard on them, not to cover a criminal disposal of the tractors. For reasons which I have already explained, I do not think there was in law any question of Lombard's being able to upset any of the sales to third parties.

(4) It seems to me to be wrong to say (as Mr Thompson appeared to be saying) that failure of the company to repay Lombard for tractor 1 for about four months after receipt on 15 June 1979 of the proceeds of sale of the tractor to Robb Bros was dishonest or evidence of an intention to defraud Lombard. Unpunctual payment by a debtor of his debt (without more) is certainly not fraud. Again complete failure by a debtor to pay his debt is not (without more) fraud. Moreover, the validity of this proposition in the present case is strengthened by the fact that so long as the debts were not paid a high rate of interest was running in favour of the creditor. There is the further point that Mr Thompson's argument proceeded as if the four tractor sales were the only transaction which took place between the parties and this gave an unreal picture of the debtor's performance. From the 'coalesced' account which appears on p 16 et seq., of the agreed bundle of documents, and which is an account covering advances, capital repayments and interest payments under both the stocking agreements of 7 March 1979 (No 3) and 2 November 1979 (No 4) it emerges that between 15 June 1979 (the date of receipt of the Robb money) and 11 October 1979 (the date of payment to Lombard for the Robb tractor) the company made no less than four large repayments to Lombard of the following amounts:

15 June 1979	£ 7,556.13
20 June 1979	£ 5,934.60
8 August 1979	£ 7,273.63
20 August 1979	£ 7,371.04
	£28,135.40

In addition the company was over this period making regular interest payments as required by the agreement. It is also interesting to note that despite the company's delay over the repayment for the Robb tractor, Lombard saw fit to advance a further £8,327.84 on 28 October 1979 which was repaid in full on 7 January 1980. They also saw fit to advance the further sum for tractor 2 on 2 October 1979 and on 8 November 1979 two further sums totally £16,364.34 for tractors 3 and 4. Finally it advanced yet one further sum of £9,477.36 on 11 January 1980. As regards interest, the last payment of this seems to have been as late as 19 December 1980 when £390.88 was paid. I summarise all that by saying that the overall picture emerging from the coalesced account seems to me to be that of struggling debtors but not fraudulent ones . . .

As regards the non-payment of Lombard it seems to me that there are two answers, one factual and one legal to Mr Thompson's contention that this was fraudulent as regards Lombard. The crucial question is the mental state of the defendants at the relevant times: the evidence is that in July 1980 after tractors 2 and 3 had been sold Mrs Bradley consulted the company's accountant, Mr Michal O'Donnell, and received a reasonably reassuring reply about the company's position viz., that the last available accounts, the accounts to 31 October 1979 showed a reasonable profit, and that both years 1 and 2 had shown growth of sales and profitabiity and there was not a serious problem. As Mr O'Donnell put it. 'No need to rush for the panic button' though he did advise a reduction of stock level. Mr Edgar agreed that agricultural sales had collapsed in the spring of 1980 but this (he said) had happened before and he expected them to rise again. Mrs Bradley next saw Mr O'Donnell in mid-September – by which time tractor 4 had been disposed of – and the main problem raised was the company's inability to work within the overdraft. Mr O'Donnell advised her, inter alia, to look more closely at the expenses and as he put it, to 'turn the light off when not in use.' However it was not till January 1981 that Mr O'Donnell said that insolvency was present and advised a liquidation. No doubt Mr Ross in March 1980 detected round figure payments to creditors and outgoings being matched with receipts but I firmly reject a submission that in the period during which tractors 2, 3 and 4 were being sold, there was knowledge in the defendants or either of them (*a*) that the company was insolvent or (*b*) that Lombard would never be paid. I would accept that there was knowledge that Lombard would not be paid on or about the due dates, as had been possible in the better days but, and this is the vital point, I reject the presence of an additional mental element of dishonesty or of fraudulently taking the view that this did not matter to the defendants. On the contrary I believe that both defendants hoped – perhaps optimistically but not dishonestly – that sales, including sales of trade-ins would pick up and Lombard would be paid.

Mr Stitt attempted to make much of the overdraft difficulties arising from the £12,000 limit; the plain fact is the limit was frequently exceeded with the bank's co-operation . . . There is no doubt that the bank was more than adequately secured with, inter alia, real security in the form of the land certificate of Mr Edgar's property supporting his letter of guarantee and I am far from accepting that if a real crisis had hit the company in the summer of 1980 the bank would not have come to the rescue. The legal answer to the point about non-payment of Lombard seems to be provided by *Re Sarflax* (supra) which shows that merely to pay one lawful debt rather than another is not fraudulent trading but can be a fraudulent preference.

Notes

The definition of fraudulent trading put forward by Murray J is remarkably close to the definition of reckless trading in s 297A. On the requirement of 'actual dishonesty' for proof of fraud see *R v Cox and Hodges* [1983]; *R v Lockwood* (1986) 2 BCLC 99; *Hardie v Hanson* (1960) 105 CLR 451; *Peake v Hall Ltd* [1985] BCLC 87.

[20.66] An order can only be made under s 297A(1)(b) against persons who were 'knowingly parties to the fraudulent trading. Mere knowledge of the fraud, without active participation is not enough to incur liability.

Re Kelly's Carpetdrome Ltd; Kelly's Carpetdrome Ltd and Monck Properties Ltd v Gaynor and Tuffy (High Court, 13 July 1984)

[20.67] The liquidator having brought successful proceedings under s 297 against Matthew and Eamon Kelly, he then issued the present proceedings against Gaynor and Tuffy of Gaynor & Tuffy & Co, the company's accountants, claiming that they had also been parties to the fraudulent trading. The evidence before the court established that while Gaynor and Tuffy were made aware of the fraud, they had not actively participated in it.

[20.68] **O'Hanlon J:** In these proceedings the liquidator of Kelly's Carpet-drome Limited invoke the provisions of s 297 of the Companies Act 1963, for the purpose of asking the court to make an order which would have the effect of imposing personal liability on the members of a firm of accountants – Messrs Gaynor, Tuffy and Company – in respect of the debts or other liabilities of the company. This claim in turn is based on the contention that the two partners in the firm – Fergal Gaynor and Patrick Tuffy – were knowingly parties to the carrying on of the business of Kelly's Carpetdrome Limited with intent to defraud creditors of the company or creditors of some other person or for some fraudulent purpose.

There are, accordingly, two essential features involved in the claim. In the first place, it must be established to the satisfaction of the court that the business of the company, was in fact, carried on in such a manner and with such intent as to achieve one or more of the fraudulent purposes referred to in section 297 and secondly, it must also be established to the satisfaction of the court that the respondents were knowingly parties to the carrying on of the business in the manner aforesaid.

The liquidator has succeeded in bringing home the charge of fraud against the company in these proceedings, just as he had already done in earlier proceedings before Mr Justice Costello, in the course of which an order has already been made under the provisions of section 297 of the Act imposing personal liability on two other persons – Matthew Kelly and Eamon Kelly. [His Lordship then reviewed the evidence and concluded:]

While I am satisfied that they [the defendants] were employed in an important consultative capacity from time to time not only by Matthew Kelly but also by the company, and while they have laid themselves open to a good deal of criticism, for their failure to adopt a much tougher line with clients who gave many indications of sailing windward of the law, I have come to the conclusion that the evidence in the case stops well short of satisfying me that they were, or either of them was, knowingly party to the carrying on of the business of Carpetdrome with intent to defraud the creditors of that company or creditors of any other person or for any fraudulent purpose . . . I must therefore refuse the liquidator the relief sought by him in the present proceedings under s 297 of the Companies Act 1963.

Notes

See also *Re Maidstone Building Provisions Ltd* [1971] 3 All ER 363. From *Re Kelly's Carpetdrome Ltd* (para **20.67**) and *Re Hunting Lodges Ltd* it can be seen persons other than just directors and shareholders can be knowingly parties to fraudulent trading for the purposes of s 297A. In *Re Gerald Cooper Chemicals Ltd* [1978] 2 WLR 867 it was held that a creditor of the company could be made personally liable for the debts of the company where it received payment of monies which it knew had been fraudulently procured by the company from their creditors.

In *Re Augustus Barnett & Son Ltd* (1986) BCC 98 Hoffman J held that it is a necessary condition of the court's power to make an order under s 297A in respect of fraudulent trading, that someone has done an act which can be described as carrying on some business of the company and that in so doing he had intent to defraud or some other fraudulent purpose. Once this condition has been satisfied, the court may impose personal liability on any persons who were knowingly 'party' to the carrying on of the business in a fraudulent manner. The section applies not only to directors and shareholders, but also to outsiders who could not be said to have carried on or even assisted in the carrying on of the company's business, but who nevertheless in some way participated in the fraudulent acts. But the requirements of s 297A could not be satisfied if no fraudulent intent is alleged against any person who actually carried on the business. In such a case there would have been no fraudulent acts to which the outsider could have been party and his own state of mind will be irrelevant for the purposes of s 297A. He may, however, be liable in deceit or some other cause of action.

Return of improperly transferred assets

[20.69] S 139 of the 1990 Act provides what is in effect an updated remedy in respect of fraudulent conveyances. It provides that where, on the application of a liquidator, creditor or contributory of a company which is being wound up, it can be shown to the satisfaction of the court that–

(*a*) any property of the company of any kind whatsoever was disposed of either by way of conveyance, transfer, mortgage, security, loan, or in any way whatsoever whether by act or omission, direct or indirect, and
(*b*) the effect of such disposal was to perpetrate a fraud on the company, its creditors or members,

the court may, if it deems it just and equitable to do so, order any person who appears to have the use, control or possession of such property or the proceeds of the sale or development thereof to deliver it or pay a sum in respect of it to the liquidator on such terms or conditions as the court thinks fit.

In deciding whether it is just and equitable to make an order under s 137 the court is to have regard to the rights of persons who have *bona fide* and for value acquired an interest in the property in question. S 137 is also expressed not to apply to transactions which are fraudulent preferences.

Application of provisions to other companies

[20.70] Under s 251 of the 1990 Act where execution has been returned unsatisfied against a company or it is proved to the satisfaction of the court that the company is unable to pay its debts, and it appears to the court that the reason for its not being wound up is the insufficiency of its assets, a number of winding up remedies can then be used in respect of the company.

These include the misfeasance summons, the provisions relating to fraudulent and reckless trading, the power to order the return assets which have been improperly transferred in defraud of creditors, the provisions relating to s 245 examinations, and the power of the court to order related companies to contribute to the debts of an insolvent member of the group.

Presumably it will, in practice, be creditors, who avail of these remedies. They will, hopefully, prevent dishonest or reckless directors and officers of the company in some cases at least, from going unpunished merely because of the fact that the company is so hopelessly insolvent that nobody will accept appointment as liquidator.

Termination of the winding up and dissolution[1]

[20.71] When a compulsory winding up has been completed the official liquidator reports to the court which makes any final order regarding the application of any balance in the liquidation and orders the dissolution of the company.[2] Application may be brought within two years to have the dissolution declared void.[3]

When a voluntary winding up has been completed the liquidator convenes meetings of the members (and in the case of a creditors' voluntary winding up) of creditors, presents his final report and sends his accounts to the registrar for registration.[4] Three months after registration of the accounts the company is deemed to be dissolved, unless upon application the court defers the date of dissolution.

As with a compulsory winding up, upon application within two years, the court may annul the dissolution.[5]

1 See *Keane* at paras **40.32** and **40.33**.
2 S 249 of the Principal Act.
3 Ibid s 310.
4 Ibid ss 263 and 273.
5 See fn (3) *supra*.

Chapter 21

COMPANIES UNDER PROTECTION OF THE COURT

[21.01] The Companies (Amendment) Act 1990 introduces a new procedure for the rescue of ailing companies whereby an official, known as an examiner, is appointed to report on whether it is possible to prepare a scheme of arrangement or the rescue of the company, and if so to implement such a scheme. The procdure is loosely based on chapter XI of the US Bankruptcy Code. All references in this chapter are to the 1990 Amendment Act except where otherwise stated.

Petition

[21.02] S 2 as amended by s 181 of the 1990 Act provides that where a company is or is likely to be unable to pay its debts, and no resolution subsists for the winding up of the company and no winding up order has been made in relation to it, the court may on application either by the company or any director, creditor or any member holding at least one tenth of the voting share capital, appoint an examiner to the company for the purpose of examining the state of the company's affairs and performing such duties in relation to the company as may be imposed by or under the Act. In particular such an order may be made if the court thinks it likely to facilitate the survival of the company, and the whole or any part of its undertaking as a going concern. It should be noted that the proposal for a reconstruction is the key issue.

[21.03] Under s 3 the petition should nominate a person to be appointed as examiner, and be supported by such evidence as the court may require for the purpose of showing that the petitioner has a good reason for requiring the appointment of the examiner. When it is presented by the company, it should include a statement of its assets and liabilities. The petition should be accompanied by a consent signed by the person nominated to be examiner, and by proposals for a compromise or scheme of arrangement, if any have been prepared at this stage.

The court may not give a hearing to a petition presented by a contingent or prospective creditor until such security for costs has been given as the court thinks reasonable, and until a *prima facie* case for the protection of the court has been established to the satisfaction of the court.

Neither may the court give a hearing to a petition if a receiver stands appointed to the company and has stood so appointed for a continuous period of at least three days prior to the presentation of the petition.

[21.04] The court on hearing the petition can dismiss it, or adjourn the hearing conditionally or unconditionally or make any interim order, or any other order it thinks fit. An interim order may restrict the powers of the directors. If the liabilities do not exceed £250,000 the court can remit the matter to the Circuit Court. There is also provision for extending the order to related companies under s 4.

Appointment

[21.05] Section 5 provides that where an examiner is appointed, the company will be deemed to be under the protection of the court for a period of three months from the date of the presentation of the petition, or until the date of the withdrawal or refusal of the petition, whichever is earlier.

The examiner must advertise in the manner prescribed by s 12 the date of his appointment and the date, if any, set for hearing the matters arising out of his subsequent report to court. All documentation emanating from the company bearing the company's name must include the words 'under the protection of the court'

S 28 provides that a person will be disqualified from acting as examiner if he would be disqualified from acting as liquidator of the company.

Under s 13 he may resign or on cause shown be removed by the court. The court has power on application by any committee of creditors or the company or any creditor or member of the company, to fill any vacancy in the office of examiner.

His acts are deemed valid even if afterwards it is discovered that there were defects in his apppintment or qualification.

His position is akin to that of a receiver, in that he is personally liable under s 13(6) on any contracts entered into by him in the performance of his functions (whether the contract is in his own or the company's name) unless he expressly excludes personal liability. He is entitled to an indemnity out of the company's assets in respect of such liability.

Under s 29 the remuneration, costs and expenses of the examiner are to be paid out of the company's revenue and, subject to the sanction of the court, will be paid in full before any secured or unsecured other claim under any compromise or scheme of arrangement or in any receivership or winding up of the company. He may also employ persons to assist him in his functions but he is required, as far as possible, to use the existing staff and facilities of the company concerned.

S 10 as amended by s 181 of the 1990 Act provides that any liabilities incurred by the company during the protection period shall be treated as expenses properly incurred if they are certified by the examiner to have been incurred in circumstances where, in his opinion, the survival of the company as a going concern during the protection period would otherwise be seriously prejudiced.

Effect of court protection

[21.06] It is provided by s 5 as amended by s 180 of the 1990 Act that while a company is under court protection no proceedings may be commenced or resolution passed for the company to be wound up. The appointment of a receiver is prohibited. Under s 6 any existing receiver is prohibited to act except to the extent permitted by the court, and the court can also order that he vacate office, hand over all books, papers and property relating to the company to the examiner and give the examiner full particulars of all his dealings with the property or undertaking of the company. No attachment, sequestration, distress or execution may be put in force against the property or effects of the company. Likewise, no action may be taken to realise any security over all or part of the company's property. The moratorium applies with equal effect in respect of enforcement against any person who has guaranteed the company's debts.

No other proceedings may be commenced against the company without the leave of the court, and no order for relief may be made under s 205 of the Principal Act against the company in respect of complaints as to the conduct of the affairs of the company or the exercise of the powers of the directors prior to the presentation of the petition.

S 5(4) provides that an order for relief under s 205 of the Companies Act 1963 can only be made in respect of events occurring before the petition for the appointment of the examiner. However, since there is a moratorium on proceedings against the company, the presentation of the petition would have to be delayed until after the expiration of the protection order, if it is intended to join the company as a party.

Finally s 5(2)(*h*) as inserted by s 181 of the 1990 Act provides that no set-off of bank accounts is permissible, except with the consent of the examiner.

[21.07] Under s 6(2) where a petition is presented for the appointment of an examiner and a provisional liquidator already stands appointed, the court can order that he be appointed examiner, or that he is to cease to act as provisional liquidator, and appoint some other person as examiner. The provisional liquidator can be directed to deliver all books of the company to the examiner and to give him full particulars of all his dealings with the property or undertaking of the company.

Where a petition is presented for the appointment of an examiner after the presentation of a petition to wind up the company, the court must hear both of them together and presumably has a choice regarding which order to make.

Powers of the examiner

[21.08] Under s 7 the examiner has the powers of a company inspector or auditor as regards access to information, which is supplemented by s 8 as amended by s 180 of the 1990 Act. S 180 of the 1990 Act also provides that s 244A of the Principal Act which applies to liquidators (regarding the enforceability of liens) applies equally to examiners.

The examiner may convene, set the agenda for and preside at meetings of the board of directors and general meetings of the company and may propose resolutions and give reports to such meetings. He is entitled to reasonable notice of such meetings and to notice of the nature of the business to be transacted therein. He also has power to prevent or take remedial steps in respect of any acts or omissions, which, in his opinion, are or are likely to be to the detriment of the company or of any interested party. This power could, for example, be used to close down loss making aspects of the company's business. However, it will not affect the rights of third parties acquiring an interest in good faith and for value.

[21.09] Where it appears to the court, on the application of the examiner that it is just and equitable to do so, it may make an order under s 9 that all or any of the functions or powers which are vested in or exercisable by the directors (whether by virtue of the memorandum or articles or by law or otherwise) are to be exercisable only by the examiner. This would seem to include provision for the transfer of managment of the company to the examiner.

It may also confer on the examiner the powers of an official liquidator, in which case the court also has the powers which would be conferred on it by the Principal Act in relation to a compusory winding up. In deciding whether it is just and equitable to make the order, the court is to have regard to the following matters:–

(*a*) that the affairs of the company are being conducted, or are likely to be conducted, in a manner which is calculated or likely to prejudice the interests of the company or of its employees or of its creditors as a whole, or
(*b*) that it is expedient for the purpose of preserving the assets of the company or of safeguarding the interests of the company or of its employees or of its creditors as a whole, that the carrying on of the business of the company by, or the exercise of the powers of, its directors or management should be curtailed or regulated in any particular respect, or
(*c*) that the company or its directors, have resolved that such an order should be sought, or
(*d*) any other matter in relation to the company the court thinks relevant.

Power to deal with charged property

[21.10] Under s 11(1) where, on an application by the examiner, the court is satisfied that the disposal (with or without other assets) of any property of the company which is subject to a security which, as created, was a floating charge or the exercise by the examiner of his powers in relation to such property would be likely to facilitate the survival of the whole or any part of the company as a going concern, the court may by order authorise the examiner to dispose of the property or exercise his powers in relation to it, as the case may be, as if it were not subject to the security.

S 11(2) applies to assets subject to any other type of security, hire purchase agreement, conditional sale agreement, retention of title agreement or agreement for the bailment of goods which is capable of subsisting for more than three months. The court can only make an order under s 11(2) if it is satisfied that the disposal (with or without other assets) of the property subject to the security or the goods the subject of the agreement, would be likely to facilitate the survival of the whole or any part of the company as a going concern. If so satisfied the court may authorise the examiner to dispose of the property as it were not subject to the security or to dispose of the goods as if all rights of the owner under the agreement were vested in the company.

It is a condition of any such order that–

(*a*) the net proceeds of the disposal, and
(*b*) where those proceeds are less than such amount as may be determined by the court to be the net amount which would be realised on a sale of the property or goods in the open market, by a willing vendor, such sums as may be required to make good the deficiency,

are applied towards discharging the sums secured by the security or payable under the agreement.

[21.11]   Where there are two or more securities over the property, the proceeds or market price, as the case may be, must be applied in discharging the securities in their proper order of priority. If more is realised on the sale than is needed to discharge the sums in question, the balance will go into the general funds held by the examiner. If less, the shortfall will rank as an unsecured debt, unless the sale was below market value.

Power to apply for directions

[21.12]   Under s 7(6) the examiner, the company and any member, creditor, contributory or director of the company may apply to the court for the determination of any question arising out of the performance or otherwise by the examiner of his functions.

Duties of the examiner

[21.13]   Under s 15 the examiner must conduct an examination of the affairs of the company and report to the court within 21 days of his appointment or such longer period as the court may allow. To assist him s 14 requires the directors to submit a statement of affairs to him within 7 days of his appointment. The court has power to impose further duties on him if it deems it appropriate. The examiner must also deliver copies of the report to the registrar of companies, the company and to any member or creditor of the company who applies in writing. The court can direct that parts of the report be excluded from the copies supplied to any member or creditor, if it considers that the inclusion of such information would be likely to prejudice the survival of the company, or the whole or any part of its undertaking.

[21.14] The report is to include details of the officers and shadow directors of the company, together with the names of any other bodies corporate of which the director of the company are also directors. A detailed statement of affairs and a list of creditors should also be included, segregated according to class. He should state in the report whether in his opinion any deficiency between the assets and liabilities of the company has been satisfactorily accounted for or, if not, whether there is evidence of a substantial disappearance of property that is not adequately accounted for.

[21.15] The report should contain the examiner's opinion as to whether the whole or any part of the undertaking of the company would be capable of survival as a going concern and a statement of the conditions which he feels are essential to ensure such survival. He should also express his opinion as to whether a compromise or scheme of arrangement would facilitate such survival. The report should state whether an attempt to continue the whole or part of the undertaking of the company would be likely to be more advantageous to the members as a whole, and the creditors as a whole, than a winding up of the company. If warranted, draft proposals for a compromise or scheme of arrangement should be included, as well as a recommendation as to the course he thinks should be taken in relation to the company.

He should express his opinion in the report as to whether further inquiries are warranted into possible fraudulent or reckless trading.

[21.16] A formal court hearing will be held at this stage if the examiner sees no prospects for saving all or part of the company or there has been serious irregularities in the conduct of the company's business. The examiner, the company and members and creditors may be heard by the court, which has the power to make any order it thinks fit. It may discharge the protection order or continue it on such terms as it sees fit. It can order that the company be wound up or order the sale of the whole or part of the undertaking and may order the distribution of the proceeds of sale. If necessary, for this purpose, a receiver may be appointed. The examiner could instead be directed to formulate proposals for a compromise or scheme of arrangement and to convene meetings of creditors and members to consider the proposals. Such a course would be most exceptional if it had been rejected by the examiner in his report.

[21.17] S 18 provides, however, that where the examiner in his report, is of the opinion that the whole or part of the undertaking of the company would be capable of survival as a going concern and an attempt to do so would be likely to be more advantageous to the members as a whole or to the creditors as a whole, than a winding up of the company *and* a compromise or arrangement would facilitate such survival, he must formulate proposals therefor. Meetings of the various classes of creditors and members must be convened to consider these proposals and he must report to the court on the results of these meetings within 42 days of his appointment. He must file a copy of the report with the registrar of companies and is to provide a copy free of charge to the company and to any member or creditor who applies in writing for one.

[21.18] Where proposals for a compromise or arrangement are to be formulated the company, and not the examiner, may under s 20, subject to the approval of the court, affirm or repudiate any contract under which some element of performance other than payment remains to be rendered by the company and the other party. However, the other party will rank as an unsecured creditor for the amount of any loss or damages. Such amount may be quantified by the court in order to facilitate the processing of the compromise or scheme. Notice must be served on the examiner before the company applies to repudiate the contract.

Content of proposals

[21.19] S 22 requires the proposals to separate claimants into various classes, in the same manner as a s 201 scheme. They should specify which classes will be impaired and which will be left unimpaired. There should be equal treatment for all members of a particular class unless the holder of a particular claim or interest in that class agrees to less favourable treatment. The proposals should contain details of the method for their implementation and, if it is deemed necessary for adequate supervision of their implementation, specify whatever changes whether in relation to the management and direction of the company or otherwise may be required in the memorandum and articles of association.

[21.20] A statement of the assets and liabilities of the company as at the date of the proposals is to be attached to each copy of the proposals laid before the various class meetings. In order to assist the various classes in deciding whether they should accept the proposals, an estimate of the dividend they would receive in a winding up should be laid before the meeting as well.

The definition of impairment in s 22 provides that a creditor's claim is impaired unless he receives the full amount that was due to him at the date of the presentation of the petition for the appointment of the examiner. A shareholder's interest is impaired if the nominal value of his shareholding is reduced, or any fixed dividend to which he is entitled is reduced, or he is deprived of all rights accruing to him by virtue of his shareholding, or his percentage interest in the total issued share capital is reduced, or he is deprived of his shareholding. His claim will also be deemed to be impaired where, although he is to be paid in full, payment is to be in instalments

Re Jetmara Teo (High Court, Unreported, 10 May 1991)

[The facts appear from the judgment]

[21.21]   Costello J: This is an application under the Companies (Amendment) Act 1990, s 24, for the consideration by the court of the examiner's report relating to the affairs of Jetmara Teoranta.

The first issue to be considered is the standing of the Bank of Nova Scotia, the only secured creditor of the company, to appear and be heard on this application. According to s 24(2) of the Act, only creditors whose claim or interest would be impaired if the proposals were implemented can be heard.

It is urged on behalf of the examiner that the Bank of Nova Scotia has no standing because by virtue of s 22(5) of the Act a creditor's claim is impaired if he receives less in payment of his claim than the full amount due in respect of the claim at the date of presentation of the petition for the appointment of the examiner. That is not the case in relation to the claim by the bank, it is said.

It is said that the bank's claim against the company would not be impaired within this definition because it would be paid in full the amount due to it at the date of the petition. This is true, but the bank was to be paid the sum due to it by instalments and it would be deprived of access to immediate repayment and would receive less in interest than the interest to which it is contractually entitled.

It seems to me therefore that the bank has a contractual interest which will be impaired and that this gives it a standing under section 24(2) to be heard on this application . . .

Consideration of proposals

[21.22]   Under s 23 the notice summoning the meetings should contain a statement explaining the effect of the compromise or arrangement. A majority in number and value of a class of creditors voting in person or by proxy is required for approval of the proposals by that class. As regards members, a majority of votes cast is required for approval by a particular class. The proposals may only be modified with the consent of the examiner.

Confirmation

[21.23]   Under s 24, after the meetings have considered the proposals the examiner's report is laid down for consideration by the court. The court may confirm, modify or reject the proposals. If confirmed, they bind all members and creditors who are affected by them, as well as any other persons (eg. guarantors) who may be liable for all or any of the debts of the company.

The court cannot confirm the proposals unless at least one impaired class has confirmed them. The court must be satisfied that they are fair and equitable in relation to any class that has not accepted them and whose interests would be impaired by implementation and that they are not unfairly prejudicial to the interests of any interested party.

At the hearing any member or creditor whose interest or claim will be impaired may object to the decisions of the meetings under s 25, on the following grounds:

(*a*) that there was some material irregularity in relation to the meeting,
(*b*) the acceptance of the proposals by the meeting was obtained by improper means,
(*c*) that the proposals were put forward for an improper purpose,
(*d*) that the proposals unfairly prejudice the interests of the objector.

[21.24]   If he has voted to accept the proposals he can only object to their confirmation on the grounds that his acceptance was obtained by improper means or that after voting to accept, he became aware that the proposals were put forward for an improper purpose.

If the court refuses to confirm the proposals or the examiner's report concludes that following the meetings of creditor and members, it has not been possible to reach agreement on a compromise or scheme of arrangement, the court may, if it considers it just and equitable, make an order for the winding up of the company.

The company will cease to be under the protection of the court on the commencement of the compromise or arrangement or such earlier date as the court directs, at which date the examiner ceases to hold office.

[21.25]   Under s 27 within 180 days of confirmation of the compromise or arrangement any interested party may apply to the court for the revocation of the confirmation on the ground that it was procured by fraud. Revocation must be made with regard to the protection of third parties who acquired interests or property in good faith and for value. This is a particularly long period within which the proposals can be set aside and could create uncertainty for the examiner. He may be reluctant to implement the scheme until he can be certain of the finality of the court's confirmation. This sort of delay would undoubtedly be to the detriment of the creditors. The 180 day period should therefore be shortened.

Where the examiner has been appointed to a group of companies, his rescue proposals may be formulated by reference to the group as a whole, rather than preparing separate proposals for each member of the group. Where modifications are proposed at the hearing for confirmation of the proposals, these may be approved by the court without the need to call further meetings of creditors and members, unless the effect of the modifications is to fundamentally alter the original proposals.

In the Matter of Goodman International and related Companies
(High Court, Unreported, 28 January 1991)

[The facts appear from the judgment]

[21.27] Hamilton P: On the 29th day of August 1990 Peter J Fitzpatrick was appointed as examiner to Goodman International in accordance with the provision of section 2 of the Act.

On the 31st day of August he was appointed as examiner to the companies listed in appendix 1 to the judgment, the said companies being related companies of Goodman International and herinafter referred to as 'the companies'.

On the 28th day of September 1990, he was appointed examiner to a further 30 related companies in Goodman International, which are set forth in appendix 2 to this judgment and are hereinafter referred to as 'the Cork companies'.

On the 30th day of October 1990 the examiner delivered to the court his report in respect of 'the companies', 'the Cork companies' and Goodman Holdings in accordance with the provisions of section 15 of the Act, the time for delivery thereof having been extended by the court.

A report was delivered in respect of each individual company.

In his report he expressed the opinion that the whole of the undertaking with the exception of certain non-essential subsidiaries was capable of surviving as a going concern, the three companies AIBP Nenagh Exports, Nenagh Chilled Meats Limited and AIBP Southern where a minority representing 25% voted against.

With regard to the creditors, the requisite majority of banking creditors was obtained save in respect of 5 companies *viz*. Irish Agricultural Development Company, AIBP Carlow Exports, Anglo Irish Meats, Ven Air and Munster Proteins. The first three of these companies are non-trading and the other two are solvent and no order is required in respect of same.

Certain modification to the examiner's proposals were made and accepted by the examiner as appear in his affidavit.

The report of the examiner pursuant to the provisions of section 18 of the Act was presented to the court on the 11th day of December the time for presentation thereof having been extended by the court and was set down for consideration by the court on the 29th day of December 1990.

The persons entitled to appear and be heard at such hearing were 'the company' the examiner and any creditor or member whose claim or interest would be impaired if the proposals were implemented.

All such parties were notified of the date fixed for consideration by the court of the proposals.

At the hearing the following parties appeared:–

The Examiner,
Goodman International,
Lloyds Bank,
Banck Bilbao,
Credit Agricole,
Banque National de Paris,
West Deutche Landesbank,
Monaghan Nominees Limited,
Midland Bank,
Barclays Bank.

The matter was heard by me on the 29th, 20th, 21st and 28th of December 1990. It is not necessary for me to set forth in detail what transpired during the course of these hearings as a transcript of the proceedings is available.

Certain modifications to the proposals were suggested by counsel on behalf of Banque National de Paris, West Deutche Landesbank, Goodman International, Lloyds Bank and Barclays Bank and were accepted by the Examiner as not being contrary to the spirit and terms of his proposals.

I also am prepared to accept the said modifications. The only serious question which arose in connection with these modifications was whether it was necessary to convene a further meeting of the members and creditors of 'the companies' to consider and approve of the proposals as modified.

Section 24, sub-section 3 of the Act provides that:–

'At the hearing under sub-section 1, the court may, as it thinks proper subject to the provisions of this section and section 25, confirm, confirm subject to modifications, or refuse to confirm the proposals'.

This section appears to me to give absolute discretion to the court in this regard. It is of course a discretion that must be exercised judicially and if the modifications suggested were to fundamentally alter the proposals which considered by the members and creditors of 'the companies' than a court would be slow to modify the scheme in a fundamental manner without having the modifications considered by the members and creditors. I am however, satisfied that the modifications to the scheme do not fundamentally alter the proposals.

Mr Fitzsimons on behalf of Banco Bilbao opposed the confirmation of the proposals on the following grounds:–

(4) The proposals as made by the Examiner and sought to be confirmed relate to a group of companies and that there should be separate proposals in respect of each company.

The examiner has prepared and submitted to the court a report in respect of each of 'the companies' to which he has been appointed examiner.

Each of 'the companies' is "a related company" to Goodman International and by virtue of the terms of section 4 of "the Act", the court is empowered at the same or any time after the appointment of an examiner to a company to appoint him to be an examiner for the purposes of the Act to a related company'.

I have already set forth in the course of this judgment what I consider to be the purposes of the Act which I consider would be nullified if the examiner were not entitled to take into account the position with regard to each and everyone of the related companies and to formulate a scheme of arrangement which would deal with the overall picture and I am satisfied that this ground of objection must fail.

Having considered the report of the examiner presented on the 11th day of December 1990 and his earlier reports I am satisfied that the undertaking of the companies would be capable of survival as a going concern, that the proposed scheme with the modifications agreed at the meeting of creditors held on the 10th day of December 1990 and the modifications accepted by the examiner during the course of the hearing would facilitate such survival and that the attempt to continue the undertakings of the companies referred to in the said reports is likely to be more advantageous to the members as a whole and the creditors as a whole than a winding up of the companies.

Consequently, I will make an order confirming subject to the modifications to which I have referred the proposals for the scheme of arrangement presented by the examiner and I direct that the said proposals shall come into effect on the 18th day of February 1991 which is 21 days from this date and that 'the companies' other than Irish Agricultural Development, AIBP Carlow Exports, Anglo Irish Meats, Ven Air and Munster Proteins, 'the Cork Companies' and Goodman International remain under the protection of the court until that date . . .

Index